# Books in the Security Series

*Computer Security Fundamentals*
ISBN: 0-13-171129-6

*Information Security: Principles and Practices*
ISBN: 0-13-154729-1

*Firewalls and VPNs: Principles and Practices*
ISBN: 0-13-154731-3

*Security Policies and Procedures: Principles and Practices*
ISBN: 0-13-186691-5

*Network Defense and Countermeasures: Principles and Practices*
ISBN: 0-13-171126-1

*Disaster Recovery: Principles and Practices*
ISBN: 0-13-171127-X

*Computer Forensics: Principles and Practices*
ISBN: 0-13-154727-5

*To Ron—thank you for your patience and support.*
*—Jana*

*To Michael, Annie, and Sarah for making me smile when the coffee wore off.*
*—Rey*

# Computer Forensics

## *Principles and Practices*

**Linda Volonino, CISSP**

**Reynaldo Anzaldua, CISSP**

**Jana Godwin, CISSP**

**Contributing author: Gary C. Kessler**

Upper Saddle River, New Jersey 07458

**Library of Congress Cataloging-in-Publication Data**

Volonino, Linda.
Computer forensics : principles and practices / Linda Volonino, Reynaldo Anzaldua, Jana Godwin; contributing author, Gary C. Kessler.—1st ed.
p. cm.
Includes bibliographical references and index.
ISBN 0-13-154727-5 (alk. paper)
1. Computer security. 2. Computer crimes. I. Godwin, Jana. II. Anzaldua, Reynaldo. III. Title.
QA76.9.A25V59145 2006
005.8—dc22 2006021780

**Vice President and Publisher:** Natalie E. Anderson
**Associate VP/Executive Acquisitions Editor, Print:** Stephanie Wall
**Executive Acquisitions Editor, Media:** Richard Keaveny
**Executive Acquisitions Editor:** Chris Katsaropoulos
**Product Development Manager:** Eileen Bien Calabro
**Editorial Supervisor:** Brian Hoehl
**Editorial Assistants:** Rebecca Knauer, Kaitlin O'Shaughnessy
**Executive Producer:** Lisa Strite
**Content Development Manager:** Cathi Profitko
**Senior Media Project Manager:** Steve Gagliostro
**Project Manager, Media:** Alana Meyers
**Director of Marketing:** Margaret Waples
**Senior Marketing Manager:** Jason Sakos
**Marketing Assistant:** Ann Baranov
**Senior Sales Associate:** Joseph Pascale
**Managing Editor:** Lynda J. Castillo
**Production Project Manager:** Lynne Breitfeller
**Manufacturing Buyer:** Chip Poakeart
**Production/Editorial Assistant:** Sandra K. Bernales
**Design Manager:** Maria Lange
**Art Director/Interior Design/Cover Design:** Blair Brown
**Cover Illustration/Photo:** Gettyimages/Photodisc Blue
**Composition:** Integra
**Project Management:** BookMasters, Inc.
**Cover Printer:** RR Donnelley/Harrisonburg
**Printer/Binder:** RR Donnelley/Harrisonburg

Credits and acknowledgments borrowed from other sources and reproduced, with permission, in this textbook appear on appropriate page within text.



Pearson Education LTD.
Pearson Education Singapore, Pte. Ltd
Pearson Education, Canada, Ltd
Pearson Education–Japan
Pearson Education Australia PTY, Limited
Pearson Education North Asia Ltd
Pearson Educación de Mexico, S.A. de C.V.
Pearson Education Malaysia, Pte. Ltd

10 9 8 7 6 5 4 3 2
ISBN 0-13-154727-5

# Contents in Brief

# Contents

# Security Series Walk-Through

The Prentice Hall Security Series prepares students for careers in IT security by providing practical advice and hands-on training from industry experts. All of the books in this series are filled with real-world examples to help readers apply what they learn to the workplace. This walk-through highlights the key elements in this book created to help students along the way.

**Chapter Objectives.** These short-term, attainable goals outline what will be covered in the chapter text.

**Chapter Introduction.** Each chapter begins with an explanation of why these topics are important and how the chapter fits into the overall organization of the book.

## Chapter Objectives

**After reading this chapter and completing the exercises, you will be able to do the following:**

- Explain the reasons for policies and procedures.
- Formulate policies and procedures.
- Identify the steps in a forensic examination.
- Conduct an investigation.
- Report the results of an investigation.

### Introduction

Computer forensics is such a new field that legal and even academic models for computer forensics science are in a constant state of revision. Furthermore, with the ever-expanding role of e-evidence in civil, criminal, and employment cases, it is not possible to specify guidelines for each type of case. However, it is possible to specify comprehensive policies and procedures that, if followed, will produce admissible e-evidence. It is necessary for computer forensics organizations and investigative agencies (which will be referred to as organizations) to have comprehensive policies and procedures. But, if investigators are unaware of them, they are of little value.

**IN PRACTICE:** Searching for Evidence

Do not use the suspect system itself to carry out a search for evidence. The investigation will be compromised. As an example, using the integrated Windows facilities to search and open files on the computer being investigated will change the respective metadata associated with those files. This could cause all evidence uncovered on the machine to be disallowed for presentation in court. In addition to only using the forensically sound image of the suspect system for searches, the original

**In Practice.** Takes concepts from the book and shows how they are applied in the workplace.

**FYI.** Additional information on topics that go beyond the scope of the book.

**FYI** *Elements of a Crime*

Virtually all crimes require a physical act, and most require mental intent. The wrongful act is called the *actus reus*. The wrongful intent, or state of mind, is the *mens rea*. Intent is a state of mind whereby the person knows and purposes either the act or the act and its consequences.

that the intended target was
-year-old South African girl.
y remarks about Americans
y logged on to the chat ses-
ight on September 20, 2001.
over Bokkie's IP address and
service program (Computer-
n attack against Bokkie or if
against the Port of Houston

concluded that Caffrey was
the Port, which indicates that
t of a large-scale debilitating

**Caution**

**Remain Objective**

It is tough not to jump to conclusions about who is telling the truth and who is lying. Stay objective, or you put the entire investigation at risk.

**Caution.** Critical, not to be forgotten information that is directly relevant to the surrounding text.

# Test Your Skills

Each chapter ends with exercises designed to reinforce the chapter objectives. Four types of evaluation follow each chapter:

**Multiple Choice Questions.** Tests the reader's understanding of the text.

**MULTIPLE CHOICE QUESTIONS**

1. What type of software is used to actually send and receive e-mail across the Internet?
   A. Electronic message conveyance program.
   B. E-mail server.
   C. E-mail client.
   D. Instant Mail program.
2. Which of the following programs stores e-mail files on the PC itself?
   A. Outlook.
   B. Yahoo! Mail.
   C. Gmail.
   D. Hotmail.

**Exercises.** Brief, guided projects designed around individual concepts found in the chapter.

**EXERCISES**

**Exercise 8.1: Identifying E-Mail Clients and Servers**

If you have ever sent an e-mail, you have used an e-mail client. Perhaps you use different e-mail accounts for different purposes, as many people do, such as one for your general public contacts, one for private e-mail, one for business electronic correspondence, and so on.

1. Make a list of the e-mail programs you use and classify them as either resident or webmail.

**Projects.** Longer, guided projects that combine lessons from the chapter.

**PROJECTS**

**Project 7.1 Alternate Data Streams**

A lot of information can be hidden using the alternate data stream (ADS) feature of NTFS. To understand how this data is seen by the operating system, you will hide a picture as an alternate data stream. Then, you will use a free tool, LADS, to reveal its presence. This project requires a Windows system that uses NTFS.

1. Create the folder **4ensics** on your system's C: drive.
2. Open Notepad and type **This is simply a small test file used for an alternate data stream project** in the text input area.

**Case Study.** A real-world scenario to resolve using lessons learned in the chapter.

**Case Study**

You are a senior forensics investigator in a corporate firm that handles large financial transactions for a variety of customers. The head of internal auditing has called to request that you perform a forensic analysis of an employee's computer. The auditor has found evidence of financial discrepancies but needs you to confirm how the financial transactions were done on the computer. The employee is very knowledgeable in both the financial and computer areas and has been with the company for many years.

1. Determine what steps you will follow to begin the investigation and what questions you might ask the internal auditor.

This icon appears in the margin wherever additional information or links to downloads can be found at the series' Companion Website, **www.prenhall.com/security.**

# Preface

Crime has a new frontier—the vast digital world of wired and wireless communications and devices that record activities with precision. Since the development of the World Wide Web in 1991, we have witnessed astonishing growth in the personal, professional, and criminal use of networked computers, the Internet, e-mail and voice-mail systems, and wireless devices. Computers and communication devices create and store huge amounts of "digital details" in their memory, data files, and logs. In addition, as files and messages are saved or sent, software automatically generates detailed records of them.

Far more information is retained on a computer or handheld device than most people realize. This creates breeding grounds for electronic evidence (e-evidence). Rarely are users aware that their activities have left *multiple* trails of evidence. Users make insufficient or no attempt to purge those trails regardless of how incriminating they may be. Even techno-savvy users who want to go undetected may not be able to completely delete or disguise all trails of their activities or artifacts. In some cases, deleting evidence may not be possible. The following four cases illustrate the key role of computer forensics:

- The FBI learned that a former defense contractor was trying to sell secrets to foreign governments about the B-2 stealth bomber, one of the most powerful weapons in the U.S. defense arsenal. They analyzed deleted documents from the suspect's computer, including electronic correspondence with people the suspect had contacted. On October 26, 2005, Noshir S. Gowadia, who had worked for a defense contractor for 18 years, was arrested and indicted on three counts of illegally transmitting national defense information and three counts of violating the Arms Export Control Act.
- The creator of the Melissa virus, David L. Smith, who was the first person convicted for spreading a computer virus, was tracked down by a combination of e-evidence. A few of those trails included the following: the unique hardware identification number in Office 97 files that made it traceable to the PC on which it was created; the AOL return-address used in the virus's original post and AOL's log files showing the phone line that had been used to send the virus; online bulletin board postings used by Smith indicating his interest in learning about viruses; and a destroyed and disposed-of PC used to create and launch the Melissa virus in the trash bin at David L. Smith's apartment complex.
- Turkish and Moroccan hackers had devised a moneymaking scheme: release an Internet worm to covertly steal credit card numbers and other financial information from infected computers around the world. But instead of digitally hijacking masses of credit card numbers, the Zotob malicious code they released in August 2005 crashed innumerable computer systems worldwide. Authorities gathered data, including IP addresses, e-mail addresses, names linked to those addresses, hacker nicknames, and other clues uncovered in the computer code. Less than eight days after the malicious code hit the Internet, two suspected Zotob perpetrators were arrested. The FBI's CAT (Cyber Action Team) computer forensic experts verified that the code found on seized computers matched what was released into cyberspace.

- An event data recorder, or "black box," installed in most new cars stores facts about the driver's speed and handling. In November 2004, Danny Hopkins was convicted of second-degree manslaughter in the death of Lindsay Kyle in a car accident. Hopkins's vehicle's event data recorder showed that his speed was 106 mph four seconds before he crashed into the back of Lindsay's car, which was stopped at a red light. Had the car not been equipped with the new event data recorder, a forensic investigation of skid marks and crash damage could have been used to estimate the speed of the car. In this case, the recorder evidence improved both the precision and degree of confidence that the driver's speed was 106 mph and the precise time of the impact.

Hacking. Bots. Phishing. Spoofing. Malware. Electronic espionage. Cyberterrorism. Identify theft. Child exploitation. Internet scams and spam. Computer sabotage. Employment discrimination. All of these crimes require a new set of technological and investigative skills and tools. They even require new vocabulary. To illustrate: In January 2006, in the first prosecution of its kind in the United States, bot herder Jeanson James Ancheta, a 20-year-old member of the botmaster underground, pled guilty to fraudulent adware installs and selling zombies to hackers and spammers.

These cases and crimes indicate with near certainty that computer forensics will be needed in most types of investigations. While we use the term "computer forensics," it's being used in a generic sense. In addition to standard computer forensics, the term also refers to e-mail and IM forensics, cellular phone and digital camera forensics, PDA and iPOD forensics, GPS and Internet forensics—and the list is growing.

By 2003, 92 percent of new information was created and stored on electronic media. Paper and hardcopy no longer carry all of the necessary information. Electronic records can be used not only to prove straightforward charges such as illegal possession of pirated software or child pornography, but also to imply motive or intent by forming a "digital profile or dossier" of an individual or the circumstances surrounding a lawsuit or case.

- Prosecutors trying Alejandro Avila for the rape and murder of 6-year-old Samantha Runnion in California introduced e-evidence of child pornography allegedly found on his computer hard drive.
- In Scott Peterson's double-murder trial, prosecutors introduced GPS data from Peterson's car, cell phone records, and Internet history files from his personal and business computers to provide jurors with enough circumstantial evidence to imply a motive.

Civil litigations can readily make use of personal and business records found on computer systems that bear on fraud, divorce, discrimination, and harassment cases. Insurance companies may be able to mitigate costs by using e-evidence of possible fraud in accident, arson, and worker's compensation cases.

According to the *2004 Workplace E-Mail and Instant Messaging Survey* of 840 U.S. companies from American Management Association and The ePolicy Institute, over one in five employers (21 percent) have had employee e-mail and IM subpoenaed in the course of a lawsuit or regulatory investigation—up from 9 percent in 2001 and 14 percent in 2003 **(www.epolicyinstitute.com).** Another 13 percent have battled workplace lawsuits triggered by employee e-mail.

## Audience

Imagine not being able to investigate crimes or bring criminals to justice; or not knowing of an attack on a critical infrastructure or database of confidential information; or how to identify those causing harm to security and privacy. This book was written for students who want to learn about electronic evidence—including what types exist and where it may be found—and the computer forensics methods to investigate it. It is intended for those with basic knowledge of computers and networks. It is appropriate for students interested in a career in information security, criminal justice, accounting, law enforcement, and federal investigations—as well as computer forensics.

## Overview of the Book

Quite simply, we undertook the writing of this book to share our expertise and experience in computer forensics with those who need or want to learn—and hopefully to spark greater interest. The demand for computer forensics experts greatly exceeds the supply.

The book is designed in five parts covering legal, technical, investigative, intrusive attacks, and ethical issues.

**Part One** lays the legal foundation for understanding traditional and electronic evidence and evidence-handling procedures. These topics are absolutely critical to ensure that your forensic methods, techniques, and tools comply with Federal Rules of Evidence and Procedure, the Fourth Amendment, and other laws regarding search warrants and civil rights. If the legal matters concerning evidence gathering and handling are violated, the e-evidence will be found inadmissible and no technology can undo that decision.

**Parts Two and Three** focus on technical knowledge and detail the forensic examination of computers and electronic media. Sound computer forensic procedures are vital to successful investigations involving electronic evidence. Using the right investigative tools and methods maximizes the effectiveness of forensics work and ensures that e-evidence is kept in pristine condition so that it is admissible in a legal action. Recognizing what constitutes evidence and knowing where to find it is both science and art. Using a best-practices approach and recognized tools facilitates the investigative process and eliminates much of the guesswork.

**Part Four** provides a framework for understanding and investigating large-scale attacks that typically require the collaborative effort of national or international agencies. It also discusses fraud at several levels—individual, organizational, national, and global. Identity theft, botnet attacks, fraud, phishing, extortion, malware infections, threats to critical infrastructures, Internet-based hostilities, and cyberterrorism all generate network traffic. The complexity of computing environments has made network perimeters essentially borderless meshes of connectivity to customers, criminals, and those with the intent to do harm on a large scale.

**Part Five** focuses on federal rules of evidence and procedures that govern the admissibility of e-evidence and the testimony of expert witnesses. It covers laws governing privacy protection, national security, and privacy versus security challenges. It discusses how laws are changing in response to new crimes, global terrorism, and threats to critical infrastructures. This part explains how to prepare and give expert testimony in court and the challenges experts face in court. Ethics is discussed because the integrity of the investigator—and the legal system itself—depends on uncompromising ethical conduct.

---

## Conventions Used in This Book

To help you get the most from the text, we've used a few conventions throughout the book.

Snippets and blocks of code are boxed and numbered, and can be downloaded from the Companion Website (**www.prenhall.com/security**).

New key terms appear in ***bold italics.***

This icon appears in the margin wherever more information can be found at the series Companion Website, **www.prenhall.com/security.**

**IN PRACTICE: About In Practice**

These show readers how to take concepts from the book and apply them in the workplace.

**FYI** *About FYIs*

These boxes offer additional information on topics that go beyond the scope of the book.

**Caution**

**About Cautions**

Cautions appear in the margins of the text. They flag critical, not-to-be forgotten information that is directly relevant to the surrounding text.

# Instructor and Student Resources

## Instructor's Resource Center

The Instructor's Resource Center is distributed to instructors only via our Companion Website and is an interactive library of assets and links. It includes:

- Instructor's Manual. Provides instructional tips, an introduction to each chapter, teaching objectives, teaching suggestions, and answers to end-of-chapter questions and problems.
- PowerPoint Slide Presentations. Provides a chapter-by-chapter review of the book content for use in the classroom.
- Test Bank. This TestGen-compatible test bank file can be used with Prentice Hall's TestGen software (available as a free download at **www.prenhall.com/testgen**). TestGen is a test generator that lets you view and easily edit test bank questions, transfer them to tests, and print in a variety of formats suitable to your teaching situation. The program also offers many options for organizing and displaying test banks and tests. A built-in random number and text generator makes it ideal for creating multiple versions of tests that involve calculations and provides more possible test items than test bank questions. Powerful search and sort functions let you easily locate questions and arrange them in the order you prefer.

# Companion Website

The Companion Website (**www.prenhall.com/security**) is a Pearson learning tool that provides students and instructors with online support. Here you will find:

- Interactive Study Guide. A Web-based interactive quiz designed to provide students with a convenient online mechanism for self-testing their comprehension of the book material.
- Additional Web projects and resources to put into practice the concepts taught in each chapter.

# About the Authors

**Linda Volonino, Ph.D., CISSP, ACFE** is a Professor of Information Systems at the Richard J. Wehle School of Business, Canisius College. She is a member of and speaker for the FBI's InfraGard, ISSA (Information Systems Security Association), ISACA (Information Systems Audit and Control Association), and AIS (Association for Information Systems). She is also a member of FEI (Financial Executives Institute) and the ACM (Association of Computing Machinery). Her computer forensics training includes Foundstone's Ultimate Hacking courses, the SANS Institute training, CERIAS at Purdue University, and ISACA symposiums. Linda is a frequent speaker on computer forensics and security, Sarbanes-Oxley compliance, and antifraud management for the business and legal communities. She has authored articles in academic and practitioner journals, including the *Communications of the AIS, Rutgers Computer and Technology Law Journal,* Erie County Bar *Bulletin, Ohio Trial,* and two textbooks. Since 1998, Linda has been lecturing on computer forensics and electronic evidence and has been a computer forensics investigator and expert witness in both civil and criminal cases.

**Reynaldo Anzaldua, CISSP, EnCE** is an Instructor of Information Technology at South Texas College. He is a member of the International Information Systems Security Certification Consortium ($ISC^2$) and the Institute of Computer Forensic Professionals (ICFP). His computer experience began as a computer technician and continued to IT director. He has worked on and supported platforms such as Microsoft, Novell, AS/400, and Unix/Linux. His computer training includes Guidance Software computer forensic courses, SANS Institute training, and TechNow. He is also the owner and founder of Computer Security International **(www.csi-worldwide.com),** an international computer security/forensics solutions provider. He has performed security assessments for organizations ranging from penetration testing to policy/procedures audits and has done forensic examinations from local to federal levels in addition to private organizations. His expertise also includes expert witness and pretrial consulting for both civil and criminal cases. He is a regular speaker on topics such as computer security, identity theft, and computer forensics for civic organizations, radio, television, and print media.

**Jana L. Godwin, CISSP, SSCP, SCNP** is the Department Chairperson of the Computer Networking Administration/Information Systems Security program at Louisville Technical Institute. She is a member of the Information Systems Security Association (ISSA), the High Tech Crimes Network (HTCN), and InfraGard, and sits on the Alumni Board of the University of Louisville J.B. Speed Engineering School. Her experience in the IT industry has spanned from network technician to Global Security Manager of a Fortune 500 company. She founded Godwin Consulting Group, LLC, in 2002 to provide consulting in computer forensics and IT security, where she has worked with several law firms. Her training includes graduate security, ethics classes, and computer forensics courses with Guidance Software. She has given presentations at security conferences and at InfraGard and provides quarterly community service programs on home computer security. Jana holds a B.S. and M. Eng. in Computer Engineering from the University of Louisville.

# Acknowledgments

Accomplishing this book depended on *momentum* from Chris Katsaropoulos and *magic* from Cat Skintik—our developmental editor extraordinaire who helped us express our ideas as brilliantly as possible. Thanks to our talented reviewers, Eric Salveggio, Tom Martin, and Ruth Watson, whose insights and expertise improved the value of each chapter. We are grateful to Steve Elliot, who triggered this collaborative effort and the many others at Prentice-Hall who contributed to this effort.

We also thank our research associates, Jennifer and Rick, and creative designer, Rose, for responding skillfully to our intense requirements.

***Research Associates***
Jennifer C. Keem, Legal and Expert Testimony Research
Richard P. Volonino, Forensic Accounting and Fraud Research

***Creative Graphic Design***
Rose Twardowski

# Quality Assurance

We would like to extend our thanks to the Quality Assurance team for their attention to detail and their efforts to make sure that we got it right.

### Technical Editor

**Eric Salveggio, MSIA, CHS-III**
IT Program Director, CSO
Virginia College Online
Birmingham, Alabama

### Reviewers

**Thomas B. Martin, Ph.D.**
Chair, MIS Department
School of Business Administration
Holy Family University
Philadelphia, Pennsylvania

**Ruth A. Watson, Ph.D.**
Associate Professor
Computer Technology
Kent State University
Kent, Ohio

# Part One

## Admissibility of Electronic Evidence

As society and businesses move steadily in the direction of electronic communication, computer files, and data storage, the "smoking guns" and evidence trails are in electronic format. Computers and Internet activities record what has been said and done. Laptop computers, PDAs, iPods, DVDs, digital cameras, and cell phones leave cybertrails of evidence.

In Part One, you will learn about crimes, principles of forensics evidence, and laws guiding crime investigations. You will apply that knowledge to the admissibility of evidence and the proper handling of computer forensics investigations.

By the end of Part One, you will understand the legal foundations for recovering and examining computer forensics evidence. You will have learned the principles of evidence, criminal investigations, and evidence collection and handling procedures that must be followed to ensure that the e-evidence you retrieve is admissible in court or legal action. You will realize the challenges facing computer forensics investigators throughout the lifecycle of a crime or legal case.

# Admissibility of Electronic Evidence

# Chapter 1

# Forensic Evidence and Crime Investigation

## Chapter Objectives

**After reading this chapter and completing the exercises, you will be able to do the following:**

- Understand what constitutes a crime and identify categories of crime.
- Understand law enforcement's authority to investigate information warfare and terrorist threats to national security.
- Explain the different types of evidence.
- Identify what affects the admissibility of evidence.
- Identify how electronic evidence differs from physical evidence.
- Identify what computer forensics tools and techniques can reveal and recover.
- Explain the process of discovery and electronic discovery.

## Introduction

Crime investigations are searches for evidence to figure out, or reconstruct, what happened. For crime reconstruction, crime scene investigators may have to analyze and interpret ballistic or bloodstain patterns, gunpowder residue, tire tracks, fingerprints, or evidence left by electronic (digital) devices. In the 21st century, evidence about what did or did not happen or about when, where, or by whom a crime was committed often exists as electronic evidence (e-evidence). What is common to all crime scene investigations is that they first raise questions—not answers. For example, what type of weapon could have caused a specific fatal injury? What type of person is responsible for a kidnapping? What was the motive for the sniper attack? How fast was the car traveling when it struck and killed the pedestrians? Each forensic investigation requires that the investigators use their expertise, objectivity, and problem-solving skills to first ask and then answer questions.

The expanding wave of Internet connectivity and digital technologies offers tremendous opportunities for crime—and criminals are taking full advantage of every opportunity. That makes the Internet the crime scene in countless numbers of cases. It also makes the Internet and everything connected to it the source of e-evidence, or digital evidence as it is also called. Computers, digital technologies, and Internet activities record what has been said or done, leaving trails that can be investigated later. E-mail and instant messages (IM), word processing documents, file transfers, and Web site visits leave traces. E-evidence can exist on a laptop or tablet PC, server, digital camera, PDA (personal digital assistant), fax machine, iPod, or smart phone; or in a cookie, log of downloaded files, or IRCs (Internet relay chats). In effect, e-evidence is the digital equivalent of fingerprint, smoking gun, ballistics, or DNA evidence—and central to every computer forensics investigation.

Crime investigation involves the legal system, and evidence searches must follow federal and state laws. Therefore, this first chapter helps you understand the legal foundations for recovering and examining computer forensics evidence. It introduces you to the concept of crime and principles of evidence and the admissibility of evidence. Proper evidence collection and handling procedures must be followed to ensure that the e-evidence you retrieve is admissible evidence. You begin with a close look at crimes and the evidence that they may leave and the laws that they involve. The search for e-evidence for crime reconstruction is a key step in many computer forensics investigations.

You will understand the reasons for the increasing demand for computer forensic investigators, particularly in criminal investigations. We discuss skills forensic investigators need in order to recover and examine e-evidence. Then we discuss the use of computer forensics and electronic discovery in ***white collar crimes.*** White collar crimes are nonviolent crimes, such as fraud and extortion.

---

## Basics of Crimes

The first Internet-based destructive computer worm on record was called the *Morris worm.* Worms are independent programs that replicate from machine to machine across network connections, often clogging networks and information systems as they spread. The Morris worm was unleashed on the Internet by Robert Tappan Morris, Jr., on November 2, 1988. It infected and crashed over 6,200 servers, which was a large percentage—over 10 percent—of the Internet at that time. At the time of the attack, there were approximately 56,000 hosts connected to the Internet. As the Morris worm swept through the Internet, it repeatedly replicated itself on infected machines. Each additional copy (replication) of the worm slowed down the server by consuming additional CPU resources. By slowing so many servers, the Morris worm effectively caused the world's first Internet denial of service (DoS) attack.

Investigators were able to track down Robert T. Morris, Jr., in part because he had chatted about his worm for months before he actually released it on the Internet. The U.S. General Accounting Office (GAO) estimated that Morris caused between $10 million and $100 million in damages. Others estimated that his worm caused $186 million in damages plus recovery costs.

**FYI** *Analysis of Morris Worm*

A comprehensive analysis of the Morris worm was written by Eugene H. Spafford of the Department of Computer Sciences at Purdue University. You can find his report at **http://protovision.textfiles.com/100/tr823.txt.**

Consider the implications of this destructive act. What would have happened to Robert T. Morris, Jr., if he had physically damaged all those computers? Would he have been convicted of a federal crime and spent time in jail? Most likely, Morris would still be in a federal prison today. But he caused multimillion dollars of damage that was invisible except when examined forensically from a byte or digital perspective. Morris's Internet-mediated crime was ahead of the system of laws that made it illegal. There were no laws against destructive computer programs under which Morris could be charged with a crime.

Federal prosecutors instead charged Morris with violation of the ***Computer Fraud and Abuse Act (CFAA),*** which makes unauthorized access to a federal computer a crime. He became the first person prosecuted and convicted under the 1986 CFAA. This CFAA law could be applied because at least one of the infected computers was a federal computer protected by law. Morris's sentence was three years probation, 400 hours of community service, and a $10,500 fine (*United States v. Morris,* 1991). Many of the Morris worm victims, as well as law enforcement professionals, were angered by his light sentence.

Arrested in another case was Onel De Guzman, author of the Lovebug virus that caused $7 billion in damage in 2000. But De Guzman was released because at the time his native Philippines had no law making what he had done a crime.

As the Morris worm and Lovebug virus cases illustrate, an act (or action) must violate an existing law for it to be a crime. In practice, many times crimes committed with or against a computer are prosecuted using traditional laws defining physical crimes with tangible evidence.

Your first step in learning about recovering and examining evidence is to understand the types of crimes and their characteristics.

**Caution**

**Criminal Statutes**

All criminal statutes define crimes in terms of required acts and a required state of mind, usually described as the person's "intent." These requirements are known as the "elements" of the offense. A prosecutor must convince a judge or jury that the person charged with the crime (the defendant) did the acts and had the intent described in the statute.

## Definition of Crime

A ***crime*** is an offensive act against society that violates a law and is punishable by the government. There are two important principles in this legal definition of crime. First, in order for an act to be a crime, the act must violate at least one ***criminal law.*** Criminal laws protect the public, human life, or private property. Criminal laws are defined in rules that are called ***statutes.*** Second, it is the government that seeks to punish the violator who committed the offensive act. Take, for example, a case where a person steals a car. Stealing a car is a violation of a criminal law against taking someone's private property. That violation is prosecuted by the government and not by the owner of the car.

## Crime Categories and Sentencing Guidelines

Crimes are divided into two broad categories: felonies and misdemeanors. Felonies are more serious crimes and carry stiffer sentences. Felonies, such as murder and kidnapping, are crimes that are punishable by a fine and more than one year in prison. A felony may even be punishable by death. Misdemeanors, such as careless driving, are lesser crimes that are punishable by a fine and less than one year in prison.

Crime sentencing guidelines give federal judges clear directions for sentencing ***defendants,*** the persons or parties being charged, in their courts. The guidelines take into account the seriousness of the criminal behavior and the defendant's criminal record. See the United States Sentencing Commission at **http://www. ussc.gov/.** The U.S. Sentencing Commission wrote new, tougher punishments for certain types of computer crimes that came into use as of November 1, 2003. In cases where a virus sender intends to cause death, perhaps by tying up 911 emergency telephone lines, the virus sender could face a life sentence.

## Cybercrimes

The terms *computer crime, cybercrime, information crime*, and *high-tech crime* are used interchangeably by most people, the courts, and the legal system. These terms refer to two categories of offenses that involve computers.

- **Computer as target.** A computer or its data is the target of a crime. Crimes against a computer include attacks on networks that cause them to crash, such as the attacks by the Morris worm, and unauthorized access to, or tampering with, information systems, programs, or data. Other common examples include viruses, worms, industrial espionage, software piracy, and hacking. If you have a continuous Internet connection, such as cable or DSL, you should know that it is almost embarrassingly easy for a hacker to break into your computer or transmit a virus to infect it.
- **Computer as instrument.** A computer is used to commit the crime. Many crimes committed with a computer are traditional crimes, such

as theft, fraud, forgery, stalking, or distribution of child pornography. The difference is that these traditional crimes are committed using a computer, computer network, or communications technology. Newer types of crimes that fall into this category are threatening e-mail, identity theft, spam, and ***phishing.*** Phishing is sending an e-mail to a user falsely claiming to be a legitimate enterprise in an attempt to scam the user.

As you would expect, a cybercrime can fall into both of these categories. An example would be someone using a computer to break into a medical database to change a patient's medication or lab results or to cover up a medical mistake that could trigger a malpractice lawsuit.

The Department of Justice (DOJ) broadly defines cybercrimes as "any violations of criminal law that involve a knowledge of computer technology for their perpetration, investigation, or prosecution." When computer crime involves money, it is referred to as ***computer fraud*** or ***electronic fraud (e-fraud).*** There are also specific laws against securities fraud, tax fraud, antitrust violations, bankruptcy fraud, and health care fraud. To protect the public as well as computers, there are laws against spam. On December 16, 2003, President George W. Bush signed the Controlling the Assault of Non-Solicited Pornography and Marketing Act, or CAN-SPAM Act, into law. CAN-SPAM went into effect on January 1, 2004. The law makes it a crime to send commercial e-mail messages with false or misleading message headers or misleading subject lines. Major laws related to computers and crime are covered in Chapter 12.

**Caution**

**CAN-SPAM Act**

The text of the CAN-SPAM bill can be found at **http://www.spamlaws.com/federal/can-spam.shtml.**

## Statutes Amended to Keep Pace with Cybercrimes

As new electronic devices and technologies emerge, so will crimes that take advantage of their strengths and weaknesses. Criminal laws and sentences for violating them continue to be passed or amended as new types of crimes or ways to commit crimes emerge. No matter how many new cybercrime statutes are passed to help prosecutors deter or prosecute cybercriminals, catching the criminals remains difficult.

Major changes in the statutes were passed in the 1980s. Prior to the early 1980s, very few laws defined crimes committed with a computer or against a computer. Until laws clearly defined cybercrimes, or computer crimes, U.S. government prosecutors had to rely on more traditional criminal statutes. The Morris case illustrated this situation. Since the mid-1980s, the U.S. Congress has been actively passing new and amended cybercrime statutes to deal with new types of computer crimes.

The major cybercrime law, the Computer Fraud and Abuse Act, was passed in 1984 and has been amended several times. Initially, the CFAA was intended to protect government computers and financial industry computers from criminal theft by outsiders. In 1986, the CFAA was amended to include stiffer penalties for violations, but it still protected only computers used by the federal government or financial institutions. Then, as the Internet expanded in scope, so did the CFAA. In 1994, a significant revision of CFAA added a civil law component and civil charges to this criminal law. Compared to criminal law, civil law deals with noncriminal injuries. Civil law gives an injured party the opportunity to bring a lawsuit (civil charge) against a violator in order to obtain compensation for the injury or harm.

## Civil vs. Criminal Charges

Civil charges are those brought by a person or company. Criminal charges can be brought only by the government. An offensive act or omission, such as failing to take reasonable care to prevent injury to another party, may violate both criminal law and civil law.

While there are many similarities between criminal law and civil law, there are also several important differences. Those differences are outlined in Table 1.1.

As Table 1.1 shows, a criminal case is brought by law enforcement. These criminal cases bring the broad powers of law enforcement to bear in the investigation and prosecution. For example, law enforcement's ability to gather evidence is more immediate than in civil cases (Conry-Murray, 2002). Generally the FBI has the power to seize information and bank accounts, issue subpoenas or search warrants, or even break down doors. Civil cases do not include that type of authority. In civil cases, parties need to show proof that they are entitled to evidence. Meanwhile, relevant evidence can be destroyed, lost, or deleted.

**TABLE 1.1** Comparison of criminal and civil laws.

| Characteristics | Criminal Law | Civil Law |
|---|---|---|
| **Objective** | To protect society's interests by defining offenses against the public | To provide an injured private party the opportunity to bring a lawsuit for the injury |
| **Purpose** | To deter crime and punish criminals | To deter injuries and compensate the injured party |
| **Wrongful act** | Violates a statute | Causes harm to an individual, group of people, or legal entity |
| **Who brings charges against an offender** | A local, state, or federal government body | A private party, which may be a person, company, or group of people as in a class-action lawsuit |

CONTINUED ON NEXT PAGE

CONTINUED

| Characteristics | Criminal Law | Civil Law |
|---|---|---|
| **Deals with** | Criminal violations | Noncriminal injuries |
| **Authority to search for and seize evidence** | More immediate; law agencies have power to seize information and issue subpoenas or search warrants | Parties need to show proof that they are entitled to evidence |
| **Burden of proof** | Beyond a reasonable doubt | Preponderance of the evidence |
| **Principal types of penalties or punishment** | Capital punishment, fines, or imprisonment | Monetary damages paid to victims or some equitable relief |

## IN PRACTICE: Distinction Between Criminal and Civil Cases

The distinction between criminal and civil cases may not always be clear. Consider the following civil case. In *Werner v. Lewis* (Civil Court of N.Y. 1992), Donald Lewis was hired by Werner Corp. to update its computer system and insurance claim software. Lewis updated the system as he was hired to do, but he went beyond his authorized job. Lewis also inserted a ***time bomb,*** or malicious computer program, that would disable Werner's computer system when the claim number 56789 was reached (Raysman and Brown, 1999). Lewis called the company every month asking how the system was working and what claim number had been reached. His devious plan was to have Werner hire him to fix the problem. When the system crashed, however, Werner hired a consultant rather than Lewis to investigate and fix the problem. After the investigation revealed what had happened, Werner sued Lewis for breach of contract. The consultant testified that Lewis had entered a "conditional statement" in the program that caused the system to stop running when a certain claim number was entered. The court awarded the company compensation for the damages, which Lewis had to pay.

## Information Warfare, Electronic Attack, and Terrorism

Deliberate and devastating attacks against data confidentiality, integrity and authenticity, and availability of data that control critical infrastructures are national priorities. To detect evidence of information warfare and other terrorist acts, e-mail and other online activities are being monitored. Next-generation war-fighting capabilities will incorporate even greater electronic surveillance.

In this section, you learn about the risks of information warfare and terrorism—and laws to defend against them. Tracking terrorists, including cyber-terrorists, involves investigating their electronic trails to try to learn of their plans, as shown in Figure 1.1.

### Information Warfare

Information warfare can harm individuals, corporations and private organizations, government departments and agencies, and nations. Information warfare may be considered as the extension of war into and through cyberspace. Military planners have recognized this extension and included computer forensics in their defenses, referring to them as C4I, which stands for Command, Control, Communications, Computers, and Intelligence.

Several legislative acts, or laws, have expanded the authority of law enforcement to investigate suspected or potential threats to national security. The most far-reaching law is the ***USA PATRIOT Act of 2002*** that gave law enforcement agencies greater authorization to obtain ***electronic evidence.*** Electronic evidence, or e-evidence, is information stored electronically on any type of computer or electronic device that can be used as evidence in a legal action. You will learn more about e-evidence throughout this chapter.

The USA PATRIOT Act expanded the list of records that law enforcement authorities may obtain with a subpoena. Subsection 2703(c)(2) of the act states that

**FIGURE 1.1** Computer evidence examiners review the contents of a computer hard drive.

authorities can gain access to "records of session times and durations" and "any temporarily assigned network address." Despite criticism by privacy advocates, law enforcement can require that an Internet service provider (ISP), such as AOL or Yahoo!, reveal the ***Internet Protocol (IP) address*** assigned to the user for a specific online session and the remote IP address from which a user connected to the ISP. With these records as e-evidence, the process of identifying cybercriminals or cyberterrorists and tracing their Internet communications is faster and easier. Catching and convicting cybercriminals remains difficult, however. Cyberspace is one of the most versatile and insidious tools of terrorists in the 21st century and is one of law enforcement's greatest challenges.

## Terrorism and Cyberterrorism

The technological revolution in communications and information exchange has made the United States, European nations, and many other countries substantially more dependent on information processing and management than on manufacturing. Countries that depend on information systems are highly vulnerable to information warfare and the disruptions such warfare can cause.

Intelligence experts fear terrorists could use the Internet or other computer technology to attack the United States. The Department of Homeland Security (DHS) is concerned that al Qaeda or another radical group could launch cyber and physical attacks simultaneously, attempting to disable safety systems at nuclear plants, air traffic control systems, or other critical infrastructures. Those critical infrastructures include financial, telecommunications, energy, water, and transportation systems.

Protecting national security means preventing attacks. Since 1984, the FBI Laboratory and other law enforcement agencies have been examining computer evidence to track terrorist activity. In 2003, Tom Ridge, while director of the DHS, said that his team was monitoring the Internet continuously for "state-sponsored information warfare" (Rowan, 2003).

## FBI's Computer Forensics Advisory Board

In April 2004, the FBI announced the launch of the National Steering Committee (NSC), an intergovernmental advisory board that provides advice and recommendations to the FBI leadership on a range of issues surrounding the ***Regional Computer Forensic Laboratory (RCFL)*** program. The program was launched because computer forensics was one of the fastest growing disciplines within law enforcement. Since September 11, 2001, the RCFL program has provided technical support for over 200 cases involving terrorism. RCFLs provide computer forensic expertise to any law enforcement agency in their specific service area in support of federal, state, and local criminal investigations and prosecutions. Kerry E. Haynes, Assistant Director, Investigative Technologies Division, said, "Computer forensics is one of the most specialized sciences available to law enforcement, making the RCFL Program one of the most dynamic tools we have to fight crime and terrorism."

Because of the explosive growth of computer forensics within law enforcement, the FBI recognized that an advisory board composed of a cross section of stakeholders could benefit the national program overall. Tony Whitledge, director of the Internal Revenue Service's Electronic Crimes Program, said "This is a very exciting development for RCFLs and the science of computer forensics. Because the NSC has brought together experts in computer science and security, forensic science, prosecutors and law enforcement, the NSC is positioned to make an immediate and meaningful contribution to the RCFL program."

**FYI** *Computer Crime*

For more information on computer crime, see the DOJ's Computer Crime Section at **http://www.cybercrime.gov.**

## Computer Forensics Evidence and Investigations

As you have learned, computer forensics is multidisciplinary. Your effectiveness as a computer forensics investigator depends on the set of skills diagrammed in Figure 1.2. Without an understanding of these three areas—computer technology, recognized investigative techniques, and legal issues—mistakes will be made.

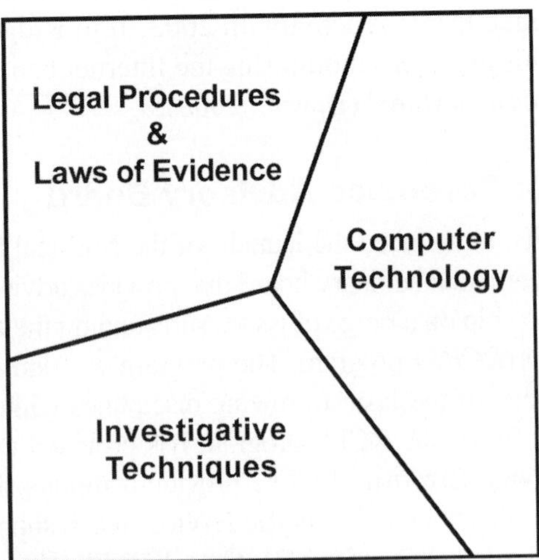


**FIGURE 1.2** Areas of expertise needed by computer forensics investigators.

Important e-evidence may be overlooked, or potentially good evidence may not be admissible. An investigator who jumps to conclusions, does not remain objective, or makes unfounded generalizations puts the evidence at risk. Failure to stick to proper investigative procedures could lead to the evidence's being regarded as tampered with or tainted. In summary, the value of recovered evidence depends on these three areas of expertise, as does your value as a computer forensics investigator.



## Evidence: The Starting Point for Understanding What Happened

***Evidence*** is the starting point for understanding all types of forensics investigations. *Evidence* is one of those words that has many different meanings depending on the context.

In general, evidence is proof of a fact about what did or did not happen. This simple definition is deceptive, as you will soon realize. Consider what is needed to *prove a fact* about a crime when there is no eyewitness. From actual cases that you have watched on TV or read in the media, you know that proving a fact about what has happened can be very complex.

When presented to a judge or jury at a trial, evidence is used to support or refute the allegations of a crime or civil wrong. During a trial, evidence is presented to persuade belief in a claim or to refute it (Gleim and Ray, 1992). All evidence must be reliable and relevant to the case to be legally admissible. Admissible evidence is evidence that can legally and properly be used in court. It may be testimony that is allowed to be given in court because it conforms to the rules of evidence. Juries can use only admissible evidence to make their decision.

Three primary types of evidence can be used to persuade someone to believe a claim or assertion.

- Testimony of a witness
- Physical evidence
- Electronic evidence

Testimony of an eyewitness can be based on what the person experienced through any of the five senses. The two senses most commonly relied on are sight and hearing. Physical evidence is anything tangible, such as a bullet, knife, wound, footprint, DNA, piece of clothing, traces of poison, or evidence learned through an autopsy of a body. Electronic evidence is in digital format, such as an IP address, computer virus, e-mail, voice-mail, cookie, log file, instant message, digital image, or electronic fund transfer (EFT). It has been referred to as nonflammable evidence. E-evidence can be gathered through a computer or IT autopsy. The type and volume of electronic evidence is increasing at a

**Caution**

**Testimony**

Comments and arguments by attorneys, statements by a judge, and witnesses' answers to questions are not evidence. Maps, models, and other materials used to demonstrate or explain matters are also not evidence. Each of these is testimony that may be allowed as evidence.

staggering rate. Every use of a computer or digital device creates potential e-evidence. Virtually everything we do is recorded by at least one digital device or leaves a digital footprint that documents our preferences, buying power, health, and hobbies.

## Evidence Investigative Skills

The easiest part of dealing with evidence is identifying facts, such as which Web sites someone visited or what was "said" in a chat room. It is much more difficult to analyze the facts and interpret what they mean. Analysis of facts or clues that can help reveal why someone visited particular Web sites requires more critical thinking and hypothesis (or theory) testing.

Problem-solving skills are also needed to determine how to use the facts to help the investigation. An investigation is a process that develops and tests hypotheses to answer questions about events that occurred. An event is a crime or incident that violates a policy or law. Specifically, a computer forensics investigation uses science and technology to examine digital data and objects, developing and testing theories that can be entered into a court of law to answer questions about events that occurred. E-evidence contains reliable information that supports or refutes a hypothesis about an incident or crime.

Based on preliminary evidence obtained at the start of an investigation, the investigator may form a theory about what happened. That theory is then tested as new evidence is recovered or examined. Once evidence is found to refute the theory, the process begins again. For example, in the widely publicized double-murder trial of Scott Peterson, prosecutors' underlying theory was that Peterson killed his wife and dumped her weighted body into San Francisco Bay to escape his marriage and the impending pressure of fatherhood. It would seem that evidence refuting that theory was not discovered, given the jury's verdict of guilty.

## Cybertrails of Evidence

Digital crime investigations are not limited to cybercrimes or cyber terrorist activities. Traditional or physical crimes or misconduct may involve e-evidence and, as a result, leave ***cybertrails*** of those activities.

Cybertrails left by Internet and e-mail usage and digital devices may be the only way to collect enough evidence to solve a crime. In the high-profile 2001 investigation into the disappearance of Chandra Levy, Washington, D.C., police investigated the cybertrail of e-mail and history of visited Web sites left on her laptop. This trail of e-evidence was used to identify people she generally kept in contact with and to gain insight into her frame of mind. It provided guidance in creating a profile of Chandra and a theory for how to go about reconstructing what crime might have occurred.

1

## IN PRACTICE: Forensics Saves a Life

In 2004, it was neither a fingerprint nor physical evidence that led authorities to the woman suspected of strangling a mother-to-be and kidnapping her fetus by cutting it from the womb. Rather, the key piece of evidence was an 11-digit computer code. Within hours of the killing of Bobbie Jo Stinnett at her Skidmore, Missouri, home, investigators realized that information on her computer could help in finding her killer. Using the Kansas City RCFL, police investigating the murder and kidnapping zeroed in on Lisa Montgomery by searching computer records, examining online message boards, and most important, by tracing an IP address to a computer at her Melvern, Kansas, home. An IP address is the unique number given to every Internet-connected computer. The IP address in and of itself led the FBI to Montgomery's home. Investigators said that just before the slaying, Montgomery had corresponded over the Internet with the victim about buying a dog from her. By analyzing the e-evidence on the victim's PC, authorities were able to crack the case in a matter of hours and rescue the premature baby.

## FYI Forensics

In Latin, *forensics* means "belonging to the forum." Currently, it means "pertaining to the courts." For example, *forensic testimony* means testimony that is used to assist the court, or testimony to help attorneys in a trial or legal matter.

### Artifact, Inculpatory, and Exculpatory Evidence

As the Levy and Stinnett cases indicate, crime reconstruction is the determination of the actions or events surrounding the commission of a crime. It depends on the evidence recovered from a crime scene, a suspect, or a victim—or collected for analysis as part of an investigation. The quality of that evidence and the evidence collection method play crucial roles in crime reconstruction.

One risk that investigators need to be alert to is ***artifact evidence.*** Artifact evidence is any change in crime scene evidence or addition to crime scene evidence that could potentially cause an investigator to infer incorrectly that the "evidence" is related to the crime. Because computers are often the crime scenes and e-evidence can be altered, computer forensics investigators must consider the possibility of artifact evidence.

Computer evidence is not always the "smoking gun." Usually computer evidence either provides leads to other evidence or corroborates other evidence. As such, it is ***inculpatory evidence.*** Inculpatory evidence is evidence that supports or helps confirm a given theory. In contrast, ***exculpatory evidence*** contradicts a given theory.

**Stages in Crime Scene Investigations**

The main stages in crime scene investigations include crime scene preservation and documentation, evidence search and documentation, and event reconstruction and documentation. You will read more about these stages of investigation in Chapter 4.

## Admissible Evidence

The ultimate goal of a forensic investigation is to gather evidence to reconstruct what happened. For the evidence to be useful in court or a legal action, the forensic investigator must ensure that it is gathered in such a way that it is ***admissible evidence.*** Admissible evidence is any type of proof legally presented at trial and allowed by the judge. Conversely, ***inadmissible evidence*** is evidence that is not allowed. While these definitions are simple, the determination of what is and is not admissible evidence is complicated by the fact that determination is subject to judgment and interpretation. In general, if established methods for evidence collection are not followed, the evidence will be considered inadmissible and cannot be used. At a minimum, all evidence must be reliable and relevant to the case to be legally admissible.

For any item of evidence to be admissible, it must first be ***authenticated.*** In order for an item of evidence to be authenticated, there must be sufficient proof that it is what it claims to be. When dealing with e-evidence, it is more difficult to provide sufficient proof for several reasons. One reason is that e-evidence is easily altered, either deliberately or accidentally. This characteristic of e-evidence can make it unreliable. Another reason is that the judge or jury may not have the technology background to understand e-evidence without a lot of explanation.

The main reason why evidence is ruled inadmissible is its lack of reliability. An expert's opinion that is not based on generally accepted principles in the field would be unreliable testimony. Evidence will also be declared inadmissible if presenting it would take too long relative to its value or if it was illegally gathered.

Evidence obtained from an illegal search or seizure is referred to as ***tainted evidence*** and is inadmissible in court. To avoid being tainted, evidence must be searched for and seized according to legal procedure. Search and seizure typically require a ***search warrant.*** A search warrant is a written order issued by a judge allowing law enforcement to conduct a search of specified premises for specified things or persons and to seize those items or people.

### IN PRACTICE: Search Warrant for Admissible Evidence

A search warrant is issued only after law enforcement provides a judge or magistrate with sufficient proof that there is ***probable cause*** that a crime has been committed. Probable cause is a legal standard that states there must be proof beyond just the possibility that a crime has been committed.

To get a search warrant, the law officer must specify what premises, things, or persons will be searched. If the search warrant is issued, the law officer is limited to searching only what has been identified. Any things or persons on the premises not identified in the search warrant cannot be searched, with few exceptions, such as to frisk, or superficially search, someone for a weapon. Evidence that is discovered during the search can be seized. Evidence collected from an illegal search and seizure is inadmissible.

Obviously, without sufficient evidence, there is no way to reconstruct with reliability what has happened. However, no matter how reliable the evidence an investigator obtains, without proper care and control of evidence, what seems like the reliable reconstruction of the events could be misleading or wrong. To guard against reaching wrong conclusions, there are very strict legal standards or rules for collecting, preserving, and interpreting evidence. ***Rules of evidence*** are the rules by which a court determines what evidence is admissible at trial. At the federal level in the United States, those rules are called the ***Federal Rules of Evidence*** and are abbreviated as Fed. R. Evid. State rules of evidence generally apply to state courts. In establishing what evidence is admissible, many rules of evidence concentrate first on the relevancy of the offered evidence.

## Federal Rules of Evidence

Before any physical or e-evidence is searched and seized, investigators must have at least a basic understanding of both the legal and technical issues pertaining to e-evidence under the Federal Rules of Evidence.

A critical rule is Fed. R. Evid. 1002, which is the ***"best evidence rule."*** The best evidence rule of the Fed. R. Evid. states that to "prove the content of a writing, recording, or photograph, the original writing, recording, or photograph is required, except as otherwise provided in these rules or by Act of Congress."

**Caution**

**Incriminating Evidence**

To incriminate is to make a statement admitting to committing a crime. Under the Fifth Amendment to the U.S. Constitution, a person cannot be forced to answer any question or give any information that could be incriminating to himself or herself.

Terms or words used in rules, such as "original writing" in Fed. R. Evid. 1002, are sometimes explained in some other rule. To explain what is legally considered to be an "original" writing or recording, Fed. R. Evid. 1001 states that "[i]f data are stored in a computer or similar device, any printout or other output readable by sight, shown to reflect the data accurately, is an 'original.'"

When combined, Fed. R. Evid. 1001 and 1002 mean that paper printouts of electronic materials qualify as originals as long as they are accurate. These rules are important to computer forensics investigators because they mean that there is no need to drag computer equipment into a courtroom simply to admit an electronic document or e-mail message into evidence (Federal Guidelines for Searching and Seizing Computers, July 1994).

## Circumstantial Evidence

Recall that the best evidence is direct testimony by an eyewitness. When such direct evidence is not available, ***documentary evidence*** tends to be the next most compelling form of evidence in criminal and civil cases. Physical evidence and electronic evidence are documentary evidence. Unlike testimony of a witness, which is direct evidence, documentary evidence is ***circumstantial evidence.***

Circumstantial evidence is not a direct statement from an eyewitness or participant but rather shows surrounding circumstances that logically lead to a conclusion of fact. This type of evidence may be necessary if there are no eyewitnesses. Circumstantial evidence can be so strong that there is almost no doubt as to a vital fact. This is referred to as "beyond a reasonable doubt" in criminal cases or by "a preponderance of the evidence" in civil cases. E-evidence, such as threats e-mailed to a victim, or physical evidence, such as fingerprints found at the crime scene, are both examples of circumstantial evidence.

In these cases, the prosecution will attempt to provide evidence of the circumstances from which the jury can logically deduce, or reasonably infer, a fact that cannot be proven directly. The prosecutor believes the fact can be proved by the evidence of the circumstances, or circumstantial evidence.

In other words, in these cases it is up to the prosecutors to show through a set of circumstances that their theory of what took place is the only logical deduction, that the circumstances can be explained by no other theory.

Conversely, in circumstantial evidence cases, it is the job of the defense to show that the same circumstances could be explained by an alternative theory. In order to avoid a conviction, all a defense attorney has to do is put enough doubt into one juror's mind that the prosecution's explanation of the circumstances is flawed.

## Hearsay Evidence and Expert Testimony

Another significant rule about the admissibility of evidence is the ***hearsay rule.*** The hearsay rule states that testimony which quotes a person who is not in court is inadmissible because the reliability of the evidence cannot be confirmed.

***Hearsay evidence,*** or simply *hearsay,* is secondhand evidence. That is, the witness does not tell what he heard, saw, or knew personally, or firsthand, but only what others have said to him secondhand. Because the person who knows the facts firsthand is not present, neither that person's credibility nor recollection of facts can be judged.

It may seem that because e-evidence falls into the category of hearsay evidence, it is not admissible. Fortunately, e-evidence is one of the exceptions to the hearsay rule. It is considered reliable provided that it is handled properly.

Typically, a person's opinion cannot be used at trial. Expert testimony is one of the exceptions to the rule against giving an opinion in trial. As the term implies, an ***expert witness*** is a person who is a qualified specialist in a subject. ***Expert testimony*** refers to the opinions of an expert witness that are stated during a trial or ***deposition,*** which is testimony under oath before trial. Expert witnesses are allowed to give their expert opinion even though they were not eyewitnesses to events relating to the lawsuit or case. In summary, admissible evidence can be oral testimony of witnesses, documents, public records, objects, photographs, and depositions.

**Caution**

**Demonstrative Evidence**

***Demonstrative evidence,*** such as pictures, models, videos, or other visual aids, can be used to clarify facts for a judge or jury. These items are not actual evidence. They are only demonstration aids to help people better understand what happened or how or to explain the consequences of a criminal act, such as an attack by a hacker or virus.

### Material Evidence

Evidence that is relevant and significant to a case or lawsuit is referred to as ***material evidence.*** Conversely, evidence that is not relevant or significant is referred to as ***immaterial.*** Relevant evidence has some reasonable and important connection with the facts of a case or issue. Precisely what is relevant to a case is subject to interpretation.

The concept of relevant evidence is important early in the investigation during ***discovery.*** Discovery is the process of gathering information in preparation for trial, legal investigation, or administrative action. All material or information, including electronically stored information, that is considered relevant to a case must be made available for discovery. Discovery and relevant evidence are critical topics discussed in detail later in this chapter.

## Electronic Evidence: Technology and Legal Issues

You will recall that e-evidence is electronically stored information on any type of computer device that can be used as evidence in a legal action. Legal actions include civil disputes, criminal cases, class action lawsuits, employment grievances, and government or DHS investigations. In a legal action, opposing parties may submit a ***discovery request*** to each other. A discovery request is an official request for access to information that may be considered as evidence.

The party receiving the discovery request is required by law to retrieve and produce that evidence.

Consider the complex evidentiary issues surrounding electronic documents. Electronic documents are ***volatile*** by their intangible nature. This means that electronic information can be intentionally or unintentionally altered, deleted, lost, corrupted, or overwritten. In fact, by just opening or viewing an electronic file, you can alter its ***metadata.*** Metadata is data describing the file or its properties, such as creation date, author, or last access date. Another perspective on metadata is that it is invisible information that programs such as Microsoft Word, Excel, and Outlook attach to each file or e-mail. For example, Outlook metadata might include who was bcc'd (blind copied) on an e-mail and when and to whom an e-mail was forwarded. This can be very important in figuring out *who knew what and when.*

## Deleted, But Not Gone

Even though e-evidence is quite easy to alter, ironically, it is difficult to remove completely. An advantage of e-evidence is that it is more difficult to destroy than physical evidence and in some cases may be impossible to destroy. Electronic documents that are deleted are almost never really gone. Electronic files can be deleted or partially overwritten, but a computer system never actually deletes electronic files.

When a file is created or saved onto a hard disk, three things happen:

1. An entry is made into the file allocation table (FAT) to indicate where the actual file data is stored in the data area.
2. A directory entry is made to indicate file name, size, the link to the FAT, and other information.
3. The file data is written to the data area wherein the file is saved.

When a file is deleted, only two things happen:

1. The FAT entry for the file is zeroed out so it shows that that area is available for use by a new file.
2. The first character of the directory entry file name is changed to a special character.

Note that nothing is done to the data area, so the file remains intact. Only two steps are required to restore data that has been deleted:

1. The FAT entry for the file must be linked to the particular location in the data area where the file data is stored.
2. The first character of the directory entry file name has to be changed to a legal character, which restores access to the file.

Again, nothing is done to the data area.

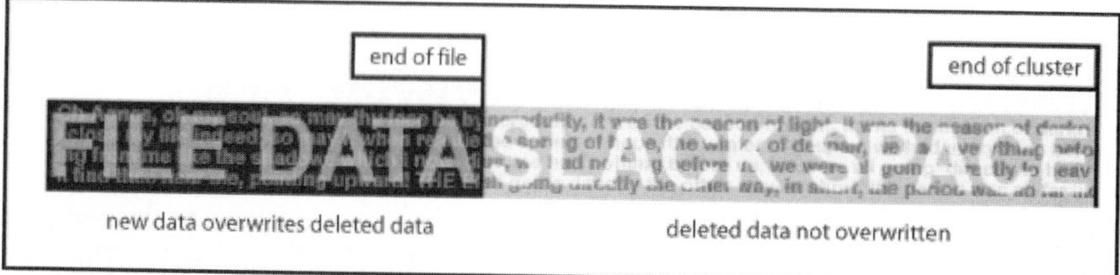

**FIGURE 1.3** Recoverable deleted data.

As shown in Figure 1.3, as long as the actual file data in the data area does not get overwritten by a new file, deleted data in the slack space can be recovered and subsequently used as e-evidence. Even when a hard disk drive or disk is formatted, the data area is left untouched. Both the FAT and directory entry are zeroed out, so more steps are required to recover data from a disk that has been formatted. However, normally most of the original data can be recovered from formatted media.

## E-Mail Evidence

E-mail systems have become breeding grounds for e-evidence in investigations, litigation, and audits of financial statements. As of 2000, e-mail had become the most common type of e-evidence. In 2003, e-mail evidence had become so prevalent it became known as ***evidence-mail.*** According to Garry Mathiason, whose law firm defends major corporations in employment cases, almost every case they handle has a "smoking e-mail" component (Varchaver, 2003). In legal actions where evidence-mail or other e-evidence is used, it is as powerful as a smoking gun or DNA evidence and just as hard to deny or refute.

Any communication or file storage device is subject to computer forensic searches to identify, examine, and preserve potential e-evidence. According to a survey of 1,100 U.S. companies conducted by the American Management Association and the ePolicy Institute, 14 percent of respondents said they had been ordered by a court or regulator to preserve and produce employee e-mail in 2002, which was up from 9 percent in 2001 (Zaslow, 2003).

### FYI *E-Mail Evidence*

In April 1994, Matthew Thomas sent an e-mail message to President Bill Clinton with the warning that he was going to "come to Washington and blow your little head off." The threat itself was a crime even though there was no statute specifying that a threat sent via e-mail was a crime. In June 1994, Thomas pled guilty to a felony.

## Computer Forensics: A Growing Field and Practice Area

Computers, cell phones, PDAs, and other electronic devices are replacing paper as the primary means of storing information. The Internet is replacing the postal system as the primary means of transmitting information. Where once people typed memoranda on paper and sent them by mail, now they generate word processor files on their computers and send them by e-mail.

In our digital world where paper increasingly is replaced by electronic media, common terms such as *document* and *evidence* refer to electronic documents and electronic evidence. The new types of evidence and crimes depend on computer forensics for investigation, crime reconstruction, and prosecution.

Many types of criminal investigations, civil proceedings, and legal actions rely on evidence revealed by computer forensics investigations.

- Criminal prosecutors use computer and e-mail evidence in a variety of crimes where incriminating documents or communications can be found, such as homicides, financial fraud, drug and embezzlement record-keeping, and child pornography.
- Civil litigations can readily make use of personal and business records found on computer systems that bear on fraud, divorce, discrimination, and harassment cases.
- Insurance companies may be able to mitigate costs by using discovered computer evidence of possible fraud in accident, arson, and workers' compensation cases.
- Corporations often hire computer forensics specialists to ascertain evidence relating to sexual harassment, embezzlement, theft or misappropriation of trade secrets, and other internal/confidential information.
- Law enforcement officials frequently require assistance in pre–search warrant preparations and postseizure handling of the computer equipment.
- Individuals sometimes hire computer forensics specialists in support of claims related to work, such as wrongful termination, sexual harassment, or age discrimination, or in divorce or custody cases.

Computer forensics is a fast-growing field of study and practice that brings together many areas of expertise. As you have read, it encompasses investigations of computer crimes, cyberterrorism, network intrusions, and e-fraud, as well as traditional crimes. Computer forensics also plays a role in disaster recovery. Computer forensics is an area of practice in public law enforcement at the federal and state levels that deals with cybercrime, cybervandalism, cyberpredators, and cyberterrorism.

Computer forensics has been widely recognized as an academic field of study by many certifying agencies and institutes. The most important ones are CERT, NSA, and the SANS Institute. Computer forensics is a domain of knowledge that is required in A+ and CISSP (certified information systems security professional) certifications.

1

### FYI Locard's Exchange Principle

In 1920, Dr. Edmund Locard set up the first forensic lab in Lyons, France. Locard was studying how to use trace, or contact, evidence to solve crimes. He believed that during a crime, there was an exchange of physical information between the criminal and the crime scene. Locard proposed a theory called the ***exchange principle,*** which states that whenever a criminal comes into contact with a victim, an object, or a crime scene, she leaves behind some evidence of her presence and also takes away some evidence. For example, burglars will leave traces (e.g., fingerprints) of their presence at the scene and take traces (e.g., carpet fibers) away with them. Crimes committed with or against a computer also leave trace evidence.

Computer forensics is used for important purposes other than finding and recovering e-evidence to reconstruct the crime. It is used to prevent, detect, and respond to cyberattacks or to counteract hacker attacks. Computer forensics can be used in almost any type of criminal investigation even if computers are not involved. A high-profile example is the probe into alleged White House leaks of a covert CIA agent's identity. As part of the investigation, White House employees received e-mail stating: "You must preserve all materials that might in any way be related to the department's investigation." E-mail, telephone logs, and other electronic documents were specifically mentioned.

Table 1.2 lists what can be revealed and recovered using computer forensics tools and techniques.

### IN PRACTICE: Largest Computer Forensics Case in History—Enron

Most investigations of suspected corporate crime involve computer forensics investigations. The outcomes of the U.S. government's investigations into Enron Corporation and Enron-related cases were determined by

CONTINUED ON NEXT PAGE

▶▶ CONTINUED

forensics e-evidence. The enormous scope of the Enron financial fraud case made it the largest computer forensics investigation in history. Government investigators searched through more than 400 computers and handheld devices, plus over 10,000 computer backup tapes. Eric Thompson, chairman of Access Data, Inc., which provided forensic software for the Enron investigation, said even encrypted or password-protected e-mail and documents that had been erased were recovered (Harrington, 2002).

The House Energy and Commerce Committee asked Arthur Andersen, Enron's accounting firm, to turn over hundreds of documents from the firm's audits of Enron. The Senate's Permanent Subcommittee on Investigations went beyond simply asking for documents and issued 51 subpoenas to Enron and Andersen demanding the documents. Within the mountain of records that investigators looked at were *hot documents*—spreadsheets, invoices, contracts, memos—that showed a pattern of illegal wrongdoing and massive fraud (Iwata, 2002).

In the billion-dollar insurance investigation into J. P. Morgan Chase & Co.'s financing of Enron (*J. P. Morgan Chase Bank v. Liberty Mutual Insurance Co.*), the determining factor was Judge Jed S. Rakoff's ruling to allow "explosive" e-mail into evidence. Eleven insurance companies were suing Chase claiming that the bank knew that Enron's futures contracts for oil and gas were really loans. On December 23, 2002, the judge ruled that internal bank e-mails written over nine months be admitted as evidence (Eoannou, 2003b). In one of the e-mails, a senior Chase official allegedly called the transaction a "disguised loan." J. P. Morgan tried to refute the evidence-mail unsuccessfully by claiming that the e-mails did not refer to the Enron transactions in question. Other internal e-mails suggest J. P. Morgan Chase officials were shocked to learn in October 2001 just how much Enron had outstanding. "$5B in prepays!!!!!!!!!" wrote one employee. The e-mailed response that also became e-evidence was "shutup and delete this e-mail" (Reason, 2002).

**Caution**

**Rights Protected by the Fourth Amendment**

The Fourth Amendment protects individuals and corporations from unreasonable searches and seizures. The amendment provides for protection of privacy of the person, home, workplace, and automobile. Authorities generally may not arrest people or search their persons, homes, or possessions without some objective reason to believe that a crime has been or will be committed.

Several other cases that involved e-evidence to a significant degree are described in Appendix D.

The Enron and Andersen cases clearly have drawn a lot of attention to e-evidence and computer forensics. Before the Enron cases, there was not much concern about the risk of electronic records and communications turning into e-evidence.

**TABLE 1.2** What computer forensics can reveal or recover.

| What Can Be Revealed |
|---|
| ■ Theft of intellectual property, trade secrets, confidential data |
| ■ Defamatory or revealing statements in chat rooms, usenet groups, or IM |
| ■ Sending of harassing, hateful, or other objectionable e-mail |
| ■ Downloading of criminally pornographic material |
| ■ Downloading or installation of unlicensed software |
| ■ Online gambling, insider trading, solicitation, drug trafficking |
| ■ Files accessed, altered, or saved |
| **What Can Be Recovered** |
| ■ Lost client records that were deleted by an employee who had been stealing funds from the company |
| ■ Proof that an ex-employee stole company trade secrets for use at a competitor |
| ■ Proof of violations of noncompete agreements |
| ■ Proof that a supplier's information security negligence caused costly mistakes |
| ■ Proof of a safer design of a defective item in a product liability suit |
| ■ Earlier drafts of sensitive documents or altered spreadsheets to prove intent in a fraud claim |

## Discovery

In preparation for trial or other legal action, each party has the right to learn about, or discover, as much as possible about the opponent's case. This pretrial process is called discovery. Discovery is the disclosure of facts by the parties who have some knowledge considered relevant to the investigation. The purpose of discovery is to help the parties determine what the evidence may consist of, who the potential witnesses are, and what specific issues may be relevant. Discovery is necessary to make sure that relevant evidence is preserved. Discovery is mandatory and not optional. When a party receives a discovery request, that party is required by law to disclose information. Discovery can take days, weeks, months, or years to complete.

A discovery request is an official request for access to any type of information that may be considered evidence (Arent et al., 2002). Information is discoverable (i.e., subject to discovery) if it is relevant to the facts that led to the lawsuit or litigation, often regardless of whether or not it was personal or private (Gleim and Ray, 1992).

There are several discovery processes. The most common methods of discovery are listed below.

- **Interrogatories** are written answers made under oath to written questions.
- **Requests for admissions** are intended to ascertain the authenticity of a document or the truth of an assertion (e.g., a request to admit ownership of certain real property).
- **Requests for production** involve the inspection of documents and property.
- **Depositions** consist of out-of-court testimony made under oath by the opposing party or other witnesses.

The courts and statutes have put computer records and other electronically stored data clearly within the scope of discovery. The expanding wave of Internet connectivity has increased the proportion of information subject to discovery under the ***Federal Rules of Civil Procedure*** (Fed. R. Civ. P.).

## Federal Rules of Civil Procedure

In 1970, ***Rule 34*** of the Federal Rules of Civil Procedure was amended to address changing technology and communication. Amended Rule 34 made electronically stored information subject to subpoena and discovery for use in legal proceedings. This is the rule that made e-records and communications breeding grounds for evidence of company activities and conduct. And every computer-based activity—whether it is sending e-mail, invoices, viruses, or hack attacks—leaves an electronic trace.

The Notes to the 1970 Amendment to Rule 34 include the following explanation:

> *The inclusive description of "documents" is revised to accord with changing technology. It makes clear that Rule 34 applies to electronic data compilations from which information can be obtained only with the use of detection devices, and that when that data can as a practical matter be made usable by the discovering party only through respondent's devices, respondent may be required to use [its] devices to translate the data into usable form.*

Stated simply, Rule 34(b) allows a party to inspect the documents or log files of another party if there is a legitimate reason to do so. There are no special rules governing discovery of electronic information; rather, it proceeds under the same framework as discovery of any other information under Rule 34.

## Federal Rules of Discovery

According to ***Rule 26*** of the ***Federal Rules of Discovery*** (Fed. R. D.), each company has the duty to preserve documents that may be relevant in a case (Scheindlin and Rabkin, 2002b). This duty to preserve is fundamental to, and inseparable from, the duty of disclosure. When involved in a legal action, companies are bound by the duty of disclosure to turn over requested e-records in readable format by a specified date.

Fed. R. D. categorize e-records as follows:

- **Computer-stored records.** This category includes active data, replicant data, residual data, backup data, and legacy data.
- **Computer-generated records.** This category includes cache files, cookies, Web logs, and embedded data or metadata.

The company must be able to produce all e-records that may be relevant in the case as requested in the subpoena, court order, or discovery motion. Furthermore, the Fed. R. D. specifically require that electronic documents be produced, regardless of whether or not paper versions are produced.

---

# Electronic Discovery (E-Discovery)

E-discovery refers to the discovery of electronic documents and data. Electronic documents include e-mail, Web pages, word processing files, computer databases, and virtually anything else that is stored on a computer. Technically, documents and data are electronic if they exist in a medium that can only be read through the use of computers. Such media include cache memory, magnetic disks (such as computer hard drives or floppy disks), optical disks (such as DVDs or CDs), and magnetic tapes. E-discovery is often distinguished from "paper discovery," which refers to the discovery of writings on paper that can be read without the aid of some device.

Just as with traditional discovery of tangible evidence, if an opposing party submits a discovery request for a company's e-mails or other e-records, the company is required by law to retrieve and produce them in readable format. Generally, courts view the failure to respond to e-discovery or disclose information as an attempt to hide guilt and obstruct justice. For example, a court fined Prudential Insurance Co. $1 million for not turning over electronic data because failure to disclose that data harmed a plaintiff's ability to establish legal claims against the company (Sleek, 2000).

The legal duty to preserve e-evidence is further complicated by the requirement that organizations that might be involved in legal action must take steps to preserve e-evidence even before being ordered to do so. Destruction of evidence is called ***spoliation***. Spoliation is considered an obstruction of justice, which is a very serious crime.

## Discovery of E-Evidence

Computer users are generally aware that word processors, spreadsheets, e-mail, and other digital devices generate information that is either stored in files they created or in audit logs the devices created automatically. It is also commonly understood that images and music files stored or sent via the Internet leave traces. However, all of these devices and activities generate far more information than most users realize. For example, most word processing programs automatically store prior drafts or versions of documents, as well as the time and dates of past edits and the name of the person who made those edits. Hidden, unexpected, and unknown electronic data are all discoverable e-evidence.

Networked computer systems require users to log on to the system by entering a user ID and password. This information records who signed onto the system, when, from where, and for how long. Computer systems that monitor employees can track and store information about which users accessed specific programs or Web pages, for how long, and what they did with those programs or pages. These details may be relevant in a lawsuit and, therefore, are discoverable.

E-mails have replaced other forms of communication besides just paper-based communication. Many informal messages that were previously relayed by telephone or at the water cooler are now sent via e-mail. Additionally, computers have the ability to capture several copies (or drafts) of the same e-mail, thus multiplying the volume of documents. All of these e-mails must be scanned for both relevance and privilege. Also, unlike most paper-based discovery, archived e-mails typically lack a coherent filing system. Moreover, dated archival systems commonly store information on magnetic tapes that have become obsolete. Thus, parties incur additional costs in translating the data from the tapes into useable form.

## Landmark Case Involving E-Discovery

In the landmark case of *Zubulake v. USB Warburg* (2003), issues related to e-discovery were outlined by U.S. District Judge Shira A. Scheindlin, who stated:

> *As individuals and corporations increasingly do business electronically—using computers to create and store documents, make deals, and exchange e-mails—the universe of discoverable material has expanded exponentially. The more information there is to discover, the more expensive it is to discover all the relevant information until, in the end, "discovery is not just about uncovering the truth, but also about how much of the truth the parties can afford to disinter."*

In August 2003, Judge Scheindlin issued a revised test for determining how e-discovery costs should be allocated to the parties involved in the legal case.

When addressing the burden and expense issues associated with e-discovery, the courts recognized five categories of stored data.

1. **Active, online data.** This data is in an "active" stage in its life and is available for access as it is created and processed. Storage examples include hard drives or active network servers.
2. **Near-line data.** This data is typically housed on removable media, with multiple read/write devices used to store and retrieve records. Storage examples include optical disks or magnetic tape.
3. **Offline storage/archives.** This represents data on removable media that have been placed in storage. Offline storage of electronic records is traditionally used for disaster recovery or for records considered "archival" in that their likelihood of retrieval is minimal.
4. **Backup tapes.** Data stored on backup tapes is not organized for retrieval of individual documents or files because the organization of the data mirrors the computer's structure, not the human records management structure. Data stored on backup tapes is also typically compressed, allowing storage of greater volumes of data but also making restoration more time-consuming and expensive.
5. **Erased, fragmented, or damaged data.** This is data that has been tagged for deletion by a computer user but may still exist somewhere on the free space of the computer until it is overwritten by new data. Significant efforts are required to access this data.

For data in an accessible format, the usual rules of discovery apply, which means that the responding party is required to pay for production. When inaccessible data is at issue, the judge can consider shifting costs to the requesting party.

## Increased Demand for E-Discovery

The types of electronic data typically sought in discovery are internally produced e-records and internal and external communications, primarily e-mail. Discovery of e-mail occurs in nearly 100 percent of federal civil and criminal litigation cases and major employment disputes.

Since the 1990s, the amount of electronic material that is discoverable for use as e-evidence has increased enormously. The number of cases that involve the discovery of electronic material has also increased. By 2000, it was standard practice for lawyers who were engaged in discovery to request electronic information that had been created, stored, transmitted, discarded, or deleted. There are several reasons for this increase in the use of e-evidence in legal actions.

1. Most business operations and transactions are done on computers and stored on digital devices. Over 85 percent of this information never

> **Caution**
>
> **Exclusionary Rule**
>
> There is an ***exclusionary rule*** to protect civil liberties. The exclusionary rule stipulates that any evidence obtained by law enforcement using a method that violates a person's constitutional rights is inadmissible in a criminal prosecution against that person. A private person who works with a law enforcement official becomes an agent of that official, so his actions are also subject to the exclusionary rule. But any relevant evidence obtained by private parties is admissible in court.

existed in paper format. Magnetic tapes used for backup can retain enormous amounts of data. For example, one 8 mm backup tape can hold as much information as 1,500 boxes of paper.

2. The most common means of communication are electronic—e-mail, IM, and fax. Companies could not survive in the modern business world without relying heavily on electronic methods of information storage and communication.
3. People are candid in their e-mail and instant messages.
4. E-evidence is very difficult to destroy.

## IN PRACTICE: E-Discovery in Boeing Case

E-discovery can get at evidence that does not exist in any other format. Even more important, e-discovery can get at the truth that exists or persists in e-evidence. Consider the effectiveness of e-discovery in the Boeing case—and whether the results would have been the same without e-discovery.

In October 1997, Boeing announced a $1.6 billion write-off because of production problems earlier that year. When this news was released to the public, the value of the company's shares dropped so sharply that a class-action lawsuit for securities fraud was filed against Boeing (Melnitzer, 2003).

During the pretrial investigation, the attorney for the plaintiffs (the party that is suing) learned that Boeing had 14,000 e-mail backup tapes stored in a warehouse in Washington, D.C. The attorney filed a discovery request for all Boeing's e-mail related to their production problems. Company officials had to produce those computer tapes for use as evidence. Boeing faced serious problems because the IS staff could not figure out whose e-mails were on which tapes without restoring and searching all 14,000 of them.

Tapes are rarely configured so that they can be easily searched. They are designed primarily for disaster recovery wherein the entire tape is reloaded. Regardless of how difficult or expensive it is to retrieve files from backup tapes, companies must comply with discovery requests and produce the e-mails or records that are requested (Varchaver, 2003). Boeing had no choice but to restore all tapes, which took thousands of hours of employee time. In addition to the huge cost of responding to the discovery request, the e-mails that Boeing produced for the plaintiffs' attorney contained so much damaging evidence that the company paid $92.5 million to settle the class-action case.

1

## Summary

You have learned that e-evidence plays an important role in crime reconstruction. Those crimes are not limited to cybercrimes because many traditional crimes leave cybertrails. To ensure that the evidence is admissible, the investigators must perform an objective examination of the evidence and objectively interpret the evidence.

Different types of evidence vary in their ability to prove a fact about what has happened, when, how, and by whom.

Without evidence of an act or activity that violated a statute, in effect, there is no crime. To guard against wrongfully finding a person guilty of a crime, the processes involved in gathering, searching, seizing, and admitting evidence must follow rules of evidence and other official procedures.

Electronic discovery, or e-discovery, refers to the discovery of electronic documents, data, e-mail messages, or other potential e-evidence. Technically, data or files are electronic if they exist in a medium that can be read only through the use of computers. E-discovery can be more complex than traditional paper discovery, which refers to the discovery of writings on paper that can be read without the aid of some devices, because e-evidence is more volatile and easily altered without obvious detection.

Many of the processes and tools used to discover and recover e-evidence can also be applied to recover data lost due to a disaster or sabotage. Like most electronic files and e-mail messages, they are rarely ever gone because they leave traces or backups.

## Test Your Skills

### MULTIPLE CHOICE QUESTIONS

1. What is a crime?
   A. An offensive act that causes financial damage.
   B. An offensive act against society that violates a law and is punishable by the government.
   C. An offensive act that causes intentional injury to one or more individuals.
   D. An offensive act against a person or organization that violates a federal law and is punishable with jail time.

2. Which of the following is not a criminal law?
   A. Law to protect the public.
   B. Law to protect private property.
   C. Law to protect human life.
   D. Law to protect contracts.

3. Criminal laws are defined in rules that are called
   A. statutes.
   B. common laws.
   C. felonies.
   D. misdemeanors.

4. What is the purpose of civil law?
   A. To punish the violator.
   B. To deter civil crimes with fines and prison.
   C. To compensate the injured party.
   D. To settle disputes between a civilian and the government.

5. Examples of crimes in which the computer is used as an instrument to commit the crime but in which computers are not the target of the crime are often
   A. traditional crimes, such as theft, fraud, forgery, stalking, or distribution of child pornography.
   B. computer viruses and worms.
   C. political or ideological malice, such as defaced Web sites.
   D. criticisms of a political party or government official.

6. When a file is deleted
   A. the file remains intact.
   B. the FAT entry for the file is zeroed out so it shows that that area is available for use by a new file.
   C. the first character of the directory entry file name is changed to a special character.
   D. all of the above.

7. Why might e-mail be a good source of e-evidence?
   A. E-mail is used by almost everyone for most of their communication.
   B. Users are careless or candid in their e-mail messages.
   C. E-mail cannot be deleted.
   D. E-mail does not require a search warrant.

8. Which of the following is not one of the three main methods to persuade someone to believe a claim or assertion?
   A. Direct testimony.
   B. Physical evidence.
   C. Circumstantial evidence.
   D. Electronic evidence.

9. Determination of the actions surrounding the commission of a crime is referred to as
   A. physical evidence.
   B. material evidence.
   C. electronic discovery.
   D. crime reconstruction.

10. Of the many responsibilities of forensic investigators, which of the following is not one of the most important?
    A. Reconstruction of what happened.
    B. Reconstruction of the circumstances.
    C. Reconstruction of the physical and electronic evidence.
    D. Reconstruction of the behaviors involved in the crime or matter under investigation.

11. In establishing what evidence is admissible, many rules of evidence concentrate first on the ______ of the offered evidence.
    A. relevancy
    B. admissibility
    C. material
    D. search and seizure

12. What is secondhand evidence?
    A. Irrelevant evidence.
    B. Hearsay.
    C. Artifact evidence.
    D. Exculpatory evidence.

13. Which of the following is not a purpose of computer forensics?
    A. To counteract hacker attacks by logging malicious activity.
    B. To find and recover e-evidence.
    C. To collect hearsay evidence.
    D. To help prevent, detect, and respond to cyberattacks.

14. An official request for access to information that may be considered as evidence is known as a(n)
    A. discovery request.
    B. search warrant.
    C. invasion of privacy.
    D. Federal Rule of Evidence.

15. The most common methods of discovery include all of the following except
    A. civil procedure.
    B. interrogatories.
    C. depositions.
    D. production requests.

16. Destruction of e-evidence is considered an obstruction of justice. This serious crime is called
    A. deposition.
    B. spoliation.
    C. incrimination.
    D. inadmissible.

## EXERCISES

### Exercise 1.1: Worldwide Cybercrime Laws

Nations around the world are very concerned about cybercrime. This concern is shared by many international organizations, including the United Nations.

1. Search the Internet to find an example of a cybercrime law in a European country or an international organization.
2. Name one act or activity that is criminalized by that law.
3. Identify the penalty for violators.

### Exercise 1.2: Key Terms Defined in the Computer Fraud and Abuse Act

1. Use the Internet to search for a copy of the Computer Fraud and Abuse Act of 1986 (18 U.S.C. §1030).
2. Find three key terms defined in the Computer Fraud and Abuse Act.
3. Explain why those key terms need to be so precisely defined.

### Exercise 1.3: Characteristics of E-Mail

Several researchers have observed that people tend to express their thoughts and make statements using e-mail that they would not otherwise say or put down in writing.

1. Review five of your e-mail messages from close friends.
2. Review five e-mail messages that you have sent to close friends.
3. Calculate what percentage of those ten e-mail messages contain thoughts or statements that were said in the "heat of the moment" and probably would not have been spoken or sent in a letter.

### Exercise 1.4: Metadata

1. Open a document file that you have created with Microsoft Word and stored on your hard drive or disk.
2. Click **Properties** on the File menu.
3. Look at the properties of that file.
4. List five examples of metadata and what they reveal about your document.

### Exercise 1.5: Traces of E-Evidence Left by Computer Attackers

1. Go to the Computer Security Institute's Web site at **http://www.gocsi.com.**
2. Search for the results of the most recent *CSI/FBI Computer Crime and Security Survey.*
3. Find the top three sources of desktop attacks.
4. Identify the type of e-evidence that could have been left by each of these sources.

## PROJECTS

### Project 1.1: Top Ten Viruses Reported to Sophos

1. Visit Sophos's Web site at **http://www.sophos.com/virusinfo/topten/.**
2. Review the top ten viruses.
3. Write a list of three possible crimes committed by the virus creators.

### Project 1.2: Understanding Forensics

Using an online search engine, find a legal dictionary or glossary.

1. Search for a definition of the word *forensic*.
2. Explain the origin of the word *forensic*.
3. Explore five other words or terms that are suggested to you by the dictionary. Write a list of those terms and briefly define them.
4. Keep a record of all the types of e-evidence you leave in one half day that could be discovered by a forensics investigator.
5. Identify the devices or locations where that e-evidence could be found.

### Project 1.3: CBS Forensics Timeline

1. Go to **http://www.cbsnews.com/htdocs/forensics/timeline.html.**
2. Find out when forensics methods were first used in court.
3. Explain the case and whether the approach was appropriate.
4. Write how the outcome of the case might have been different if forensics had not been used.

### Project 1.4: Cases Involving Admissibility of E-Evidence

Admissibility of electronic evidence over authenticity objections and hearsay objections has been addressed multiple times in various cases. Those cases include *United States v. Tank* (9th Circuit 2000), *United States v. Siddiqui* (11th Circuit 2000), and *Kearley v. State* (Mississippi. Ct. App. 2002).

1. Using an online database, such as Lexis-Nexis© or a law school's Web site, search for information about one of these cases.
2. Write a report on the e-evidence admissibility issues in the case.
3. In your report, describe the response to the hearsay objections or the authenticity objections. Explain whether they may have had an impact on the outcome of the case.

### Project 1.5: The Freedom Cyber Force Militia Hijacks Al-Jazeera's Web Sites

On March 27, 2003, hackers calling themselves the *Freedom Cyber Force Militia* sabotaged the Web sites of the Arab television network Al-Jazeera. Internet traffic directed toward Al-Jazeera's Web site in English was hijacked and diverted to a Web site located on servers operated by an ISP in Salt Lake City. On that Web site was a Stars-and-Stripes U.S. logo with messages, "Let freedom ring" and "God bless our troops," and signed "Patriot." When someone clicked onto Al-Jazeera's Web site in Arabic, a pornography Web site displayed instead. Both the Arabic and English language sites were down for almost two days. The hackers had used free Web sites (Bridis, 2003). Hackers impersonating an Al-Jazeera employee had tricked a Web addressing company into making technical changes that gave them temporary control of the English and Arabic Al-Jazeera Web sites (*Newsday,* 2003).

1. Write a list of three evidentiary problems that you would be facing as a computer forensics investigator who was investigating this hijacking.
2. List three types of e-evidence that could be included in a discovery request.

## Case Study

From watching police investigation shows or reading detective stories, you are aware of the specially trained forensics experts who search crime scenes looking for clues. In real life, computer forensics specialists use the same skills to look for e-evidence on hard drives and digital devices.

Search online news-media Web sites, such as CNN.com or MSNBC.com, and advisory resources, such as ISS.net or Foundstone.com, for information about how the creators of the Netsky worm, Sasser worm, and Goner were tracked down. Write a report that explains how the creators of these pests were identified using e-evidence. Identify the similarities and differences in the capture and conviction of the suspects.

For this case study you might also consult any of the following resources to find information:

How Goner suspects were tracked down:

**http://www.theregister.co.uk/content/56/23292.html**
**http://newsbot.msnbc.msn.com**
**http://www.cnn.com**
**http://iss.net**
**http://foundstone.com**

# Chapter 2

# Computer Forensics and Digital Detective Work

## Chapter Objectives

**After reading this chapter and completing the exercises, you will be able to do the following:**

- Recognize the role e-evidence plays in physical, or violent, and computer crimes.
- Describe the basic steps in a computer forensics investigation.
- Identify the legal and ethical issues affecting evidence search and seizure.
- Identify the types of challenges to the admissibility of e-evidence.
- Understand how criminals' motives can help in crime detection and investigation.
- Explain chain of custody.
- Explain why acceptable methods for computer forensics investigations and e-discovery are still emerging.

## Introduction

In Chapter 1, you learned about forensic evidence and crime investigation procedures. In this chapter, you will learn that computer forensics investigators are "detectives of the digital world" who need to understand both legal and technical procedures to find admissible evidence. The chapter begins by examining why almost every crime at some point touches a computer or digital device. You will look at examples of how e-evidence has helped investigations of both nonviolent crimes, such as Internet fraud and extortion, and violent crimes, such as murder and kidnapping.

Often the story of what really happened is hidden in various places or devices—and must be found and used to reconstruct what happened. It's likely that the e-evidence was created over a span of time and involved at least two entities, such as an identity thief and a victim or a hacker and a corporation. Like a detective, you need to know where and how to look for clues, or forensic evidence. These clues may be in e-mail, logs of chat rooms or visited Web sites, and computer memory. In 2005, an estimated 105 million e-mail users in the United States sent more than 1.5 billion e-mails daily, or approximately 547.5 billion e-mails per year. Another complication is that the evidence may be stored with a lot of other digital data so the investigator needs to filter out the evidentiary content from the nonevidentiary content. Methods for doing the latter will be explained in detail in later chapters.



Much more e-evidence is retained on a computer than most people realize. As the case examples in this chapter illustrate, users rarely purge records of their activities regardless of how incriminating they might be. Not all users are aware that their activities have left a trail of evidence. Hackers, intruders, and other criminals may not be able to delete or disguise all trails of their activities because it is extremely time consuming to remove information completely.

This chapter introduces you to generally accepted computer forensics methods. These methods are illustrated with real-world examples. You will become familiar with the architecture of computers, the Internet, and digital devices and the types of evidence trails they leave behind. You will understand why protecting e-evidence is as important as protecting fingerprints, footprints, and body fluid evidence at a murder scene.

---

## The Role of E-Evidence in Solving Physical and Computer Crimes

In December 2003, *Chief Security Officer Magazine* predicted that "cybercrime will only get worse" (**www.csoonline.com/**). The following month, in January 2004, the Federal Trade Commission (FTC) reported over half a million identity theft complaints in 2003, up 40 percent from 2002 (FTC, 2004). The FTC's recommended remedies to this problem are effective investigation and prosecution. In an investigation of potentially illegal tax shelters, eight accountants at KPMG were indicted for tax fraud. The case depended not on how flimsy the shelters were but on some incriminating e-mails in which the accountants snickered about misleading the IRS.

### E-Evidence Trails

As you learned in Chapter 1, e-evidence has proved to be critical in solving all types of crimes. Recovering evidence from computers seized in criminal investigations is now common practice by law enforcement agencies throughout the world. The reason is simple. Computers are routinely used to plan and coordinate almost every type of crime.

You will not be surprised to learn that ***file-wiping software*** is available to delete and overwrite data. One such program is the Privacy Suite from CyberScrub **(www.cyberscrub.com).** This software claims to remove all evidence of online activity, erase deleted files, and securely destroy e-mail. There are legitimate uses for these capabilities, such as eliminating financial or health records from your computer before you sell it. Criminals use the software to cover their tracks, but the process is time-consuming and requires precision. It can take four or five hours to remove everything, and the file-wiping software has to know exactly where to wipe. If the software doesn't know where to wipe, traces of e-evidence will be left.

## Finding Hidden Files on a Computer

Whether at home or work, your computer logs all Internet activities and stores them in your browser or other hidden files on your computer. Log files of Internet activities are often hidden on the hard drive, so users may not know to delete their tracks. To understand what information is available to investigators and how to recover hidden files, perform the two searches of your PC detailed below.

- Click on START and then click Search.
- Select "All files and folders."
- For the Search criteria, enter "cookie" as part of the file name; then click Search.

Notice how many files and folders appear in the results window.

- Adjust your search by clicking on "Include hidden and system files," as shown in Figure 2.1.
- Notice how many files and folders appear when hidden files are also searched. Also notice what is revealed about a user's Internet activities.

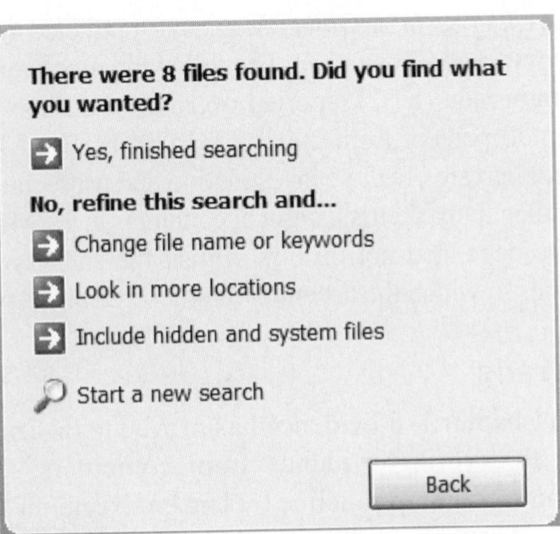


**FIGURE 2.1** Use this menu to search for hidden and system files.

You can also configure the operating system to display all files by default. Use the following steps to display hidden and system files in Windows XP and Windows 2000.

1. From the desktop, double-click the My Computer icon (or click My Computer on the Start menu).
2. Select the Tools menu and click Folder Options.
3. Select the View tab.
4. If you are using Windows XP, put a checkmark in the checkbox labeled *Display the contents of system folders*.
5. Under the Hidden files and folders section, select the option button labeled *Show hidden files and folders*.
6. Remove the checkmark from the checkbox *Hide file extensions for known file types*.
7. Remove the checkmark from the checkbox *Hide protected operating system files*.
8. Click the Apply button and the OK button, and then close the My Computer window.

After performing this procedure, the computer is configured to show all hidden files.

## Knowing What to Look For

As shown in the next example, investigators' technical knowledge of how data and metadata are captured and stored affects what e-evidence they find. Another factor is the plan formulated by investigators based on characteristics of the case to guide their work. The skills of computer forensics investigators must also constantly evolve to keep pace with new devices that can store data.

Consider the importance of technical knowledge in finding evidence in the following three cases—one involving Dr. Harold Shipman, a medical doctor who was one of the most prolific serial killers in the world; the second an e-commerce retailer whose employees were stealing customers' credit card numbers; and the third illustrating the use of Internet trails to find evidence to aid in the investigation of violent crimes.

- Dr. Harold Shipman was a serial killer responsible for at least 236 murders (possibly as many as 459) from 1975 to 1998. The doctor had modified evidence on his computer and was caught by the date stamp on the medical records. The computer analyst team discovered that Shipman's MicroDoc records were lies, as exposed by the system's shadow chronicling the real date of input. Shipman was convicted in January 2000 and sentenced to life in prison.

- An e-commerce retailer suspected that some employees were using customers' credit card numbers to make online purchases for themselves. Using information from their computers, management first identified which credit card numbers were stolen and from which Web sites purchases were being made. Then, forensic copies of each hard drive were made and searched for those credit card numbers and Web sites. The pattern of activity on the hard drives indicated that employees had emptied the Web cache and deleted temporary files after completing an order. Fortunately, after deleting traces of an order, they revisited the Web site to confirm the order. At the revisit, the credit card number along with the name and address of the person who placed the order were saved again in hidden HTML code that was not visible in the Web browser.
- Police examined Neil Entwistle's laptop computer for financial documents, to-do lists, and e-mails that might have set off the slayings of his wife and child in their home near Boston in January 2006. They also searched through the cache and hidden files, which revealed that during the week of the killings Entwistle had surfed the Internet for Web sites that described how to kill people. E-evidence indicated that he was leading a secret life online, visiting Web sites for escort services and swingers. Entwistle, who fled to England after the murders, was arrested in London and charged with fatally shooting his wife, Rachel, and baby daughter, Lillian.

Increasingly, Internet and e-mail evidence are used to learn about love affairs, secret financial assets, or debts. E-mail evidence of affairs caused the breakups of famous actors and artists, such as Heather Locklear, Richie Sambora, Denise Richards, and Charlie Sheen.

## Answering the 5 Ws Helps in Criminal Investigations

The preceding cases show how computer forensics examinations can be the key to cracking a case by finding facts about the five *W*s: who, what, where, when, and why.

Anything that helps law enforcement or investigators better understand what happened or what suspects were doing before a crime was committed is enormously useful. Three days after the terrorist attack in London on July 7, 2005, Scotland Yard announced that examination of e-evidence confirmed that three of the four rush-hour bombs had exploded within 50 seconds of one another. This evidence refuted initial reports that the bombs had detonated half an hour apart and alerted officials to the fact that there had been a high degree of coordination in the bombings.

Often the only way to find out what happened is e-evidence. For instance, corporate/international spies or identity thieves can download confidential documents to handheld devices and walk off with them without anyone's noticing.

That's how former FBI agent Robert P. Hanssen was caught. Hanssen used his Palm III PDA to keep track of when to pass information to his Russian contacts. Apparently believing that he would not get caught, he had even asked the FBI for an upgrade to a Palm VII for its wireless capabilities. He was sentenced to life in prison in May 2002 for selling secrets to Moscow.

2

**IN PRACTICE: PDA Forensics**

PDA forensics is increasingly being used in homicide investigations and white-collar crimes. With wireless capabilities, handhelds can be used to track a person's movements, which might then be used in civil and criminal investigations.

In the investigation of the murder of 7-year-old Danielle van Dam in California in February 2002, police examined the contents of four computer hard drives and a Palm Pilot PDA belonging to the man who was convicted in the case, David A. Westerfield.

Federal investigators from the Department of Health and Human Services used schedules found on doctors' own PDAs to catch them for falsely billing for Medicaid and Medicare patients they had never seen. What is unique to this type of investigation is that investigators do not need a search warrant because doctors must agree to make records available as a condition of their participation in these health-care programs.

**Caution**

**Preserving Evidence**

The methods used to recover data must be legally defensible to ensure that nothing in the original evidence was altered and that no data was added to or deleted from the original. To ensure the integrity of the findings, scientific methods must be used.

Although the cases presented in this chapter have been criminal, computer forensics investigations are used in almost 100 percent of civil cases to find evidence that supports or refutes wrongful dismissals, breaches of contract, or discrimination violations.

## Computer Forensics Science

In the United States, courts at many levels and in many jurisdictions have recognized computer forensics as a bona fide scientific method of discovering and proving facts that can be used to solve and prosecute crimes. Recently, the forensic discipline of acquiring, preserving, retrieving, and presenting electronic data has been called ***computer forensics science.*** The new emphasis on this field as a science is important because it shows that computer forensics is a discipline based on generally accepted scientific methods. This recognition helps reinforce the credibility and stature of computer forensics investigators.

Consistent with other scientific research, a computer forensics investigation is a process. The process consists of five stages.

1. **Intelligence:** The process begins with an analysis of the situation to gain a basic understanding of the issues surrounding the incident, crime, or crime scene.
2. **Hypothesis or Theory Formulation:** Based on what is learned during Intelligence, the investigator formulates a hypothesis or theory of the case. The theory is important in interpreting the evidence to come up with answers to the five *W*s.
3. **Evidence Collection:** Evidence is gathered that will be used to test the hypothesis. It is critical that the search for evidence is not limited only to supporting evidence.
4. **Testing:** The e-evidence is examined to identify what could or could not have happened. It may be necessary to collect more evidence or to start over from the Intelligence phase.
5. **Conclusion:** Based on the e-evidence available at the time, a conclusion is reached that the evidence either supports the hypothesis or fails to support the hypothesis.

Even though the scientific method is stable, because computer forensics is a new science, you can expect to see changes and improvements in investigative tools and techniques, which you will learn about throughout the book.

## Admissibility of Evidence

The typical goal of an investigation is to collect evidence using generally acceptable methods so that the evidence is accepted in the courtroom and admitted as evidence in the trial. A judge's acceptance of evidence in a trial is referred to as ***admission of evidence.*** If evidence is not accepted and admitted, a lot of time and effort has probably been wasted.

At a minimum, evidence admissibility requires a legal search and seizure—usually with a search warrant or court order—and a ***chain of custody.*** Chain of custody refers to the process by which computer forensics specialists or other investigators preserve the crime scene. The chain of custody is, in effect, documentation that the evidence was handled and preserved properly and that it was never at risk of being compromised. The documentation must include:

- Where the evidence was stored
- Who had access to the evidence
- What was done to the evidence

Each step in the process must be carefully documented so that, if the case gets to court, prosecutors can show that the electronic records were not altered as the investigation progressed. Without a documented chain of custody, it is impossible to prove after the fact that evidence has not been altered.

2

## Tradeoffs to Be Considered

Successful prosecution of the criminal is not always the most crucial outcome. In some situations, you may not be able to follow proper procedure. In some cases, the primary objective is to protect the network or business operations rather than to obtain admissible evidence. In these circumstances, quick response to contain the situation outweighs prosecuting the violator. An example of such a tradeoff occurred at CD Universe.

### IN PRACTICE: CD Universe Prosecution Failure

An extortion attempt involving credit card numbers stolen from the computers of Internet retailer CD Universe occurred in January 2000. Someone calling himself "Maxim" said that he had copied 300,000 credit card numbers from their database in December 1999. Maxim threatened to post that confidential data on the Internet unless he was paid \$100,000. The chairman of eUniverse, the company that operated the Web site, confirmed that Maxim did have their data. eUniverse refused to give in to the cyber shakedown. As he had threatened, Maxim posted 25,000 card numbers to a Web site. Several thousand people downloaded the file before it was yanked.

Six months after Maxim had broken into CD Universe, U.S. authorities were unable to find him. But even if law enforcement had found him, they probably would not have been able to prosecute the case because e-evidence collected from the company's computers had not been properly protected. The chain of custody had not been properly established.

Although it was not clear exactly how the CD Universe evidence was compromised, it seemed that in the initial rush to learn how Maxim got into the company's network so that it could be hardened (secured), FBI agents and employees from three computer security firms accessed original files instead of working from a forensic copy of the network files. Working on the only copy changed the last-access dates, which were important pieces of data needed to authenticate evidence.

As the Maxim case illustrates, to meet the minimum requirements for computer forensics investigations, you need to understand the technical nature of computers, file systems, and Internet transmissions; the investigative process and established forensics/discovery practices; and tools and procedures to ensure the integrity of collected evidence. Investigations may well end up in criminal court—so the importance of using appropriate methodologies based on established procedures cannot be overemphasized. For these reasons, the biggest legal issue of these fact-finding investigations is admissibility of evidence. Unless investigators remain objective, or free from bias, and follow strict forensic and discovery processes, e-evidence cannot stand up in court or legal cases.

## Digital Signatures and Profiling

Computer data leaves a trail in the machines it touches that can be used in the investigation of violent crimes. A knowledgeable investigator with the right tools can reconstruct information that the user thought had been deleted.

### Digital Signature Left by Serial Killer

In 1974, a serial killer who called himself "BTK," the abbreviation for the killer's *modus operandi* of "bind, torture, kill," strangled to death four members of a Wichita, Kansas, family. For 16 years afterward, BTK killed many others. After each crime, BTK sent letters and even possessions of his victims to the media, but there was not enough evidence to identify the killer until February 2005. Dennis L. Rader was arrested February 25, 2005, and charged on March 1, 2005, with ten BTK slayings—seven women, one man, and two children from 1974 to 1991.

Experts believe that Rader would not have been caught had he not decided to resume contact with the media 30 years after his first crime. His first renewed contact in March 2004 was a letter to the *Wichita Eagle* containing a photocopy of the driver's license of Vicki Wegerle, who was strangled in her bed by BTK in 1986. The letter also contained photographs of the body that only the killer could have taken. Rader sent more packages and letters to Wichita's TV stations containing dolls with bags over their heads, cryptic word and number puzzles, and official documents belonging to victims. But there was not enough evidence to determine BTK's identity. His eleventh package in February 2005 to KSAS-TV contained a computer floppy disk that finally gave police the break they had needed for 30 years. The computer disk provided evidence that reportedly tied Rader to the murders. Sources said the disk was handed over to FBI analysts, who were able to recover data from it even though it had been reformatted. Unknown to Rader, the disk contained a hidden electronic code that led police to a computer at the Christ Lutheran Church in nearby Park City. Rader, who had recently been elected president of his congregation, was one of just ten people who had access to the computer.

There are at least two ways a disk might reveal where it has been and provide a digital signature. Old files that seem to be erased might actually still be accessible on the disk, or the disk might preserve an Internet protocol address particular to an individual computer that is attached to the Internet.

In the BTK investigation, detectives apparently used data reconstruction to track the disk sent to KSAS. What likely happened was that the disk was erased and reused for the message sent to the TV station. The station passed the disk directly to police. Technicians probably recovered deleted data referring to

Christ Lutheran Church from the disk and then checked the hard drive on the church computer to verify that the disk had once been used there. The FBI was able to authenticate several of the 2005 communications sent by BTK.

Once DNA was obtained surreptitiously from Rader's daughter and compared with DNA found at three of the crime scenes, police had all the evidence they needed. Police reported that Rader confessed his crimes during questioning.

Computer forensics technology of the type employed to link an alleged message from the BTK killer to a computer at suspect Dennis Rader's church is used by investigators every day. It has been a crucial factor in everything from high-profile murder cases to obscure investigations over intellectual property rights. Another high-profile prosecution where the technology was used was the Beltway Sniper case. Lee Boyd Malvo and John Allen Muhammad were convicted of murder in an October 2002 killing spree in and around Washington, D.C., that left ten people dead and three wounded. In that case, technicians reconstructed deleted conversations from a digital recording device found in the suspects' vehicle. Several violent criminals, their crimes, and the e-evidence linking them to their crimes are listed in Table 2.1.



**TABLE 2.1** Computer forensic investigations of violent crimes.

| Criminal | Type of Crime | Type of E-Evidence |
|---|---|---|
| Dennis Rader | Serial killer | Deleted files on a floppy disk used by the criminal at his church's computer |
| Lee Boyd Malvo<br>John Allen Muhammad | Snipers | Digital recordings on a device in suspects' car |
| Lisa Montgomery | Murder and fetus-kidnapping | E-mail communication between the victim and criminal—tracing an IP address to a computer at criminal's home |
| David A. Westerfield. | Murder | Files on four computer hard drives and a Palm Pilot PDA |
| Scott Peterson | Double murder | GPS data from his car and cell phone; Internet history files from his personal and business computers |
| Alejandro Avila | Rape and murder | E-evidence of child pornography on his computer |
| Zacarias Moussaoui | Terrorism | E-mail, files from his computers |

### Digital Profiling of Crime Suspects

Information stored on or created by computer hard drives, e-mail systems, cellular devices, or even TiVo accounts can tell a lot about a person. Of course, the validity and reliability of that information may be more difficult to prove. But the e-evidence can be used to deduce or infer what has happened.

There is a growing trend toward relying on e-evidence, not only to prove straightforward charges, such as illegal possession of pirated software or child pornography, but also to imply motive or intent by generating a "digital profile" of a crime suspect. For example, prosecutors trying Alejandro Avila for the rape and murder of 6-year-old Samantha Runnion in California introduced e-evidence of child pornography allegedly found on his computer hard drive.

In Scott Peterson's double-murder trial, prosecutors searched GPS data from Peterson's car and cell phone, wiretaps of phone conversations with his mistress, and Internet history files from his personal and business computers to determine a motive for the crimes.

---

## Computer Forensics and the E-Evidence Collection Process

As you have learned, computer forensics investigation methods must be robust to ensure that all probative information is recovered. Methods used by investigators must achieve, to the fullest extent possible, the following set of objectives:

- To protect the computer system, devices, files, and logs during the forensic examination from any possible alteration, damage, data corruption, or virus introduction.
- To discover all files, including existing files, deleted files that still remain, hidden files, password-protected files, and encrypted files.
- To recover deleted files, or as much of them as still remains.
- To reveal the contents of hidden files as well as temporary or swap files used by application programs or the operating system.
- To access the contents of protected or encrypted files.
- To use steganalysis methods to determine the existence of and potential locations of steganography, which is hidden information. Steganography generally involves hiding a message in an image. Steganography hides the message, but not the fact that two parties are communicating with each other.
- To analyze potentially material data found in hard-to-access areas of a disk. This includes *unallocated space* on a disk, which is space that is

not currently used to store an active (not deleted) file, but previously may have stored a file; and ***slack space,*** which is the remnant area at the end of a file. These are discussed in detail in the next section.

- To print out an overall analysis of the computer and devices and create a list of all potentially relevant files and discovered file data.
- To provide an opinion of the system layout; the file structures discovered; discovered data and author information; attempts to hide, delete, protect, encrypt information; and anything else that has been discovered that appears to be material to the investigation.
- To provide expert consultation or testimony.



### IN PRACTICE: The Role of a Computer Forensics Expert Witness

Computer forensics experts preserve the chain of custody of e-evidence according to legal rules. Expert witnesses present the evidence in court in a professional and easy-to-understand format. They often need to explain, in simple terms, the complicated processes of how a computer works and how the evidence was obtained and preserved.

The hard drive or media need to be replicated (duplicated) exactly on a sector-by-sector basis ensuring that the integrity of the media and evidence are preserved. How to preserve data by creating duplicate copies is covered in detail later in this book. Sectors are explained in the next section. Work should be done only on the replicated copy so that there is no contamination of the original data. A preliminary examination should provide a report detailing the file structures, integrity, and recoverability of deleted files. This report may be used to determine if the files are relevant to the investigation. This report allows others to make informed decisions as to how to proceed.

## Unallocated Space and File Slack

File slack is created at the time a file is saved to disk if the file does not take up the entire ***sector.*** A sector is the smallest unit that can be accessed on a disk, as shown in Figure 2.2. All Microsoft operating systems read and write in blocks of data called *clusters*. A ***cluster*** is a fixed block of data that consists of an even number of sectors, such as 1024 bytes or 4096 bytes. The operating system (OS) assigns a unique number to each cluster and then keeps track of files according to which clusters they use. When a file is deleted under DOS, Windows, Windows 95, Windows 98, or Windows NT/2000/XP, the data remains in the cluster.

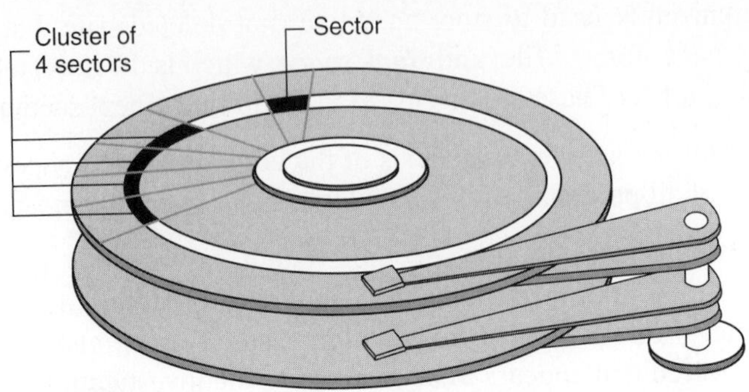


**FIGURE 2.2** Clusters and sectors on a computer hard drive.

The number of sectors needed for a cluster depends on the type of storage device, the OS, and the size of the logical storage device. The clusters that make up a deleted file are released by the OS, which means that they remain on the disk as unallocated space until that space is overwritten with data from a new saved file.

File slack can involve several hundred megabytes of data. It is important that you understand file slack because it could hold data dumped randomly from the computer's memory. It could contain network logon names, passwords, or other confidential data. File slack might also reveal prior uses of the computer, or ***legacy data.*** Fragments of prior e-mail messages, documents, or desktop faxes may be found in file slack. File slack potentially exists on floppy disks, hard disks, zipped disks, and other computer storage devices.

### FYI Fourth Amendment to the U.S. Constitution

The Fourth Amendment to the U.S. Constitution, adopted in 1791, reads:

> *The right of the people to be secure in their persons, houses, papers and effects against unreasonable searches and seizures shall not be violated, and no Warrants shall issue, but upon probable cause, supported by Oath or affirmation, and particularly describing the place to be searched, and the persons or things to be seized.*

## Example of Standard Forensics Investigative Procedure

Table 2.2 outlines the computer forensics investigative procedures conducted by the New York State (NYS) Police. The table also includes a discussion of what occurs during each of the eight stages and the electronic tools used to support the investigation.

**TABLE 2.2** Computer forensics investigative procedures of the New York State Police.

| Stage of Investigation | Electronic Tools | Discussion |
|---|---|---|
| Seizing the computer | None | Currently, the computer and technology are seized by the NYS Police under the rules, evidence, and the warrant that they hold. The evidence is then transported to the NYS Forensic Investigation Center (FIC) typically by the officers who collected the evidence. Once brought to the FIC, the evidence is checked into the vault and secured. |
| Backup | Safeback, Expert Witness, Snapback | The first step in the actual investigation process is to perform a bit-stream backup of the device. They currently use one of the tools listed to perform the operation. There may be problems associated with the backup process as follows:<br>■ Backup tools won't perform the backup due to technical difficulties with the age of the systems, format of the drive (double-spaced or compressed can cause great difficulty), operating systems (especially have problems with Macintosh devices), and new high-capacity devices (9GB drive).<br>■ Drive compatibility with both hardware and software setups that they place. In some cases, it may take up to two weeks to successfully create a backup.<br>Once the drive is successfully backed up, they attempt to get the drive information on write optical disks and create a case file in order to begin the next phase. |
| Evidence extraction | Expert Witness | The newest tool in the FIC arsenal is Expert Witness. They are working toward moving as much of the investigative process to the Expert Witness tool as possible. The tool has advantages that allow them to deal with the raw extraction |

CONTINUED ON NEXT PAGE

2

▶▶ CONTINUED

| Stage of Investigation | Electronic Tools | Discussion |
|---|---|---|
| | | and the organization of the evidence. Searching for evidence is done currently using regular expression searches. The investigator simply enters the searches manually. The evidence is viewed through built-in content viewers within Expert Witness or external views that the user adds. |
| Case creation | Expert Witness | The case creation process allows the extracted information to be placed in a case file, on a floppy disk, hard disk, or removable media. |
| Case analysis | None | During this process, the investigators use their experience and training to search the computer evidence for documents, deleted files, images, e-mail, slack space, and unallocated disk space. They look for any information that will provide them with evidence. |
| Correlation of computer events | None | During this process, the investigator attempts to piece together the different computer evidence in order to establish a timeline, order of events, related activities, and contradictory evidence. |
| Correlation of noncomputer events | None | During this process, the investigator pieces together noncomputer events, such as telephone records, credit card receipts, eyewitness testimony, physical forensic evidence, and crime scene reports. The process here can be simple or quite difficult depending upon the evidence. The investigator manually attempts to sort out and correlate the information. |
| Case presentation | Standard office software | Finally, the information that has been extracted, analyzed, and correlated is put together in a form ready for presentation to a judge or jury. |

## Suppression, Probable Cause, and Search Warrants

Technology and telecom developments have given people greater freedom and more ways to do as they choose. This freedom extends to law-abiding citizens and criminals, citizens and noncitizens, nonterrorists and terrorists. The flip side of freedom is that these same techno-devices leave digital footprints or records for investigators to follow. Tracing footprints can easily lead to invasions of privacy because they may detail what events occurred; when, why, and where they occurred; and who was involved.

To protect our civil right to privacy, both the Fed. R. Evid. and Fed. R. Civ. P. define allowable fact-finding procedures. Federal rules regulate the fact-finding process to ensure that the evidence obtained by that process did not taint or alter it in any way—or violate a person's civil rights. If these rules of evidence are followed, there is virtually no doubt that the evidence accurately and truthfully reflects the facts about the case; therefore, it can withstand challenges to admissibility. These rules serve another important purpose—to protect a person's right to privacy and to prevent someone from being charged with a crime she did not commit.

Numerous cases point out the importance of knowing and following federal rules. However, not much has been written about the legal requirements for admissibility of computer forensics evidence or about the ethical and regulatory issues related to this new field (Wegman, 2004). Because these laws struggle to keep up with new technologies, they tend to be reactive. In fact, some rules of evidence date back to the eighteenth century. In contrast, the field of computer forensics is only about 15 years old. With new types of crimes and ways to commit them, investigative and legal norms are still emerging. To the extent possible, investigators rely on existing laws until new or updated laws are passed.

### Withstanding Challenges to Evidence

Criminal trials are often preceded by a ***suppression hearing,*** at which the admissibility or suppression of evidence is determined. At this hearing, the judge determines whether the Fourth Amendment has been followed correctly by the police in the search and seizure of evidence. This hearing can often be the determining factor in criminal cases.

If proper discovery procedure is not followed, defendants can challenge the admissibility of the evidence and the methods used by law enforcement to obtain the evidence. A defendant is the person or party being charged with a crime or being sued in a civil dispute.

In one ironic case, two Russian hackers tried to convince the court to suppress evidence the FBI had gained by hacking their computers. However, a judge found that the evidence had been properly gathered.

## IN PRACTICE: Hacker's Lawyer Attempts to Suppress Evidence

Alexey Ivanov and Vasily Gorshkov used the Internet to gain illegal access to at least 38 companies' computers by exploiting a vulnerability in Windows NT. According to prosecutors, Ivanov and Gorshkov broke into the computer systems of U.S. companies and stole information. The Russian hackers then e-mailed company officials telling them that their companies' computer networks and databases had been hacked. They used a variety of e-mail accounts to execute their attacks, including Hotmail and e-mail accounts from companies they had hacked into.

The two hackers had, in fact, accessed financial records and customer data and provided proof that they had done so. They then sent extortion demands via e-mail demanding payment in exchange for not distributing or destroying sensitive financial or customer data. Most executives, afraid of bad publicity and data loss, paid the extortion demands.

One victimized company, Lightrealm Communications, an ISP, gave in to the separate demand to hire Ivanov as a security consultant after he broke into the ISP's computers. Ivanov then used a Lightrealm account to hack into other companies' computers.

The break in the investigation came when Ivanov identified himself in an e-mail while attempting to extort money from another victimized company. Armed with that information, the FBI agents then found Ivanov's résumé online.

To catch these hackers, the FBI set up a bogus security company named Invita and invited the hackers to its headquarters in Seattle, Washington, for a job interview. After Ivanov arrived in Seattle, accompanied by Gorshkov, agents posing as Invita officials asked the men to demonstrate their talent on a computer. Unknown to the hackers, **sniffer software** was installed on that computer to record every keystroke. A sniffer program recorded the hackers' keystrokes—logging Internet addresses and passwords needed to access the suspects' PCs in Russia.

After arresting the two men, agents used the account numbers and passwords obtained by the sniffer program to gain access to the data stored in the hackers' computers in Russia. These actions were a "search" that took place without a search warrant. There are exceptions to the search warrant requirement if and only if the search is for a legitimate purpose and the person has already been arrested lawfully.

▶▶ CONTINUED ON NEXT PAGE

CONTINUED

U.S. District Judge John C. Coughenour of Seattle, Washington, rejected several motions filed on behalf of Vasily Gorshkov seeking to suppress the evidence obtained from the computers.

In one motion, Gorshkov's lawyer argued that the FBI agents had violated Gorshkov's Fourth Amendment right against unreasonable search and seizure. He alleged that agents had violated his right by secretly obtaining the passwords and account numbers using a sniffer program that recorded his keystrokes when he accessed the computers in Chelyabinsk, Russia. In another motion, the defense claimed that Gorshkov and Ivanov had an expectation of privacy and that it had been violated.

In a May 23, 2001, ruling, Judge Coughenour stated that Gorshkov and his alleged co-conspirator, Alexey Ivanov, had no expectation of privacy when they sat down at computers in the offices of Invita. The judge wrote: "When (the) defendant sat down at the networked computer . . . he knew that the systems administrator could and likely would monitor his activities." The judge also rejected defense arguments that the FBI's actions "were unreasonable and illegal because they failed to comply with Russian law," on the basis that Russian law does not apply to the actions of FBI agents.

The tests of admissibility of the e-evidence were in favor of law enforcement because they had followed proper search and forensic evidence procedures. The judge upheld the rights of law enforcement to cross national borders in pursuit of cyberspace criminals. Specifically, the judge ruled that FBI agents did not act improperly (or illegally) when they tricked the suspected hackers out of their passwords and account numbers. Nor did the agents act improperly when they downloaded forensic evidence from the hackers' computers in Russia.

Judge Coughenour also ruled that the Fourth Amendment did not apply to the computers "because they are the property of a non-resident and located outside the United States." Nor did the Fourth Amendment apply to the data as long as it resided outside the United States. However, once that data was transmitted to the United States, it became subject to all U.S. laws and required a search warrant for the search.

In his rulings on May 23, 2001, Judge Coughenour noted that investigators obtained a search warrant before viewing the data in the United States. There were over 250 gigabytes of data. He rejected the argument that the warrant should have been obtained *before* the data was downloaded. The judge's basis for this ruling was that "the agents had good reason to fear that if they did not copy the data, (the) defendant's co-conspirators would destroy the evidence or make it unavailable."

A key lesson to remember is that the success of any forensic investigation depends on proper and ethical investigative procedures, qualified investigators, and authenticated evidence gathered according to accepted forensic investigation tools and techniques.

## Probable Cause and Search Warrants

For the most part, investigators need a search warrant to search and seize evidence. To get a search warrant, an officer must prepare an affidavit that describes the basis for probable cause. A probable cause is a reasonable belief that a person has committed a crime. The affidavit must define the area to be searched and the evidence being sought. The search warrant gives the officer only a limited right to violate a citizen's privacy. For example, if there is probable cause of e-evidence on a CD, this would not justify seizing every computer on the premises (Brenner, 2001/2002). If police want to seize a computer and analyze it later, the probable cause statement should demonstrate the impracticality or danger of examining the computer on the premises and the need to confiscate and analyze it off-site.

If the officer exceeds that limited right or scope, or if a warrant is required but the police have not first obtained one, then any evidence seized must be suppressed (U.S. Department of Justice, **www.usdoj.gov**). Suppressed evidence may not be used in court. The criminal charges may be dismissed, even if the defendant's guilt is clear. The benefit of such strict rules is that admissible evidence can convict a defendant on the strength of that evidence (Dershowitz, 2002). A few exceptions to these search warrant requirements will be discussed later in this chapter.

## Proper Procedure and Limitations Built into the Law

In addition to the requirements needed to get a search warrant or court order, courts ensure that law enforcement agents act within the limits of their power by suppressing, or excluding, illegally collected evidence. This rule is referred to as the exclusionary rule. The exclusionary rule, which was established in *Boyd v. United States*, states that evidence collected in violation of the Fourth Amendment must be excluded in a trial against the suspect. This requirement not only protects the suspect, but it also discourages inappropriate searches because agents know that if they do not follow the correct procedures the criminals might go free (Etzioni, 2002).

There are only two legitimate purposes for which a law enforcement officer may search a person or his property without a search warrant when there has been a lawful arrest.

- The officer may search for and remove any weapons that the arrested person may use to escape or resist arrest.
- The officer may seize evidence in order to prevent its destruction or concealment (Gleim and Ray, 1992).

**Caution**

**Definition of Terrorism**

U.S.C. § 2656f(d) defines terrorism as premeditated, politically motivated violence perpetrated against noncombatant targets by subnational groups or clandestine agents, usually intended to influence an audience.

See Appendix B for government online references and links to the Federal Guidelines for Searching and Seizing Computers, U.S. DOJ, Fed. R. Civ. P., and Fed. R Evid.

## IN PRACTICE: A Terrorist's Trial: Federal Investigation of Zacarias Moussaoui

Zacarias Moussaoui has been referred to as the twentieth hijacker in the September 11, 2001, terrorist attacks against the United States. He was the only individual charged in connection with those attacks. He faced terrorism and hijacking conspiracy charges that could bring him the death penalty. The investigative process and e-evidence collected about him revealed that Moussaoui had e-mailed several flight schools and used a computer at Kinko's to log on to the Internet (Jackman, 2002).

FBI agents were worried about why Moussaoui was taking flight training. They tried to get permission to search his laptop computer to discover what his plans were. The agents' request was turned down because they lacked sufficient probable cause for the search. As you recall from Chapter 1, probable cause is a standard that states there must be proof beyond just the possibility that a crime has been committed or is being planned.

The terrorist attacks on September 11, 2001, provided the evidence the FBI needed to get a search warrant for Moussaoui's computer and other belongings. The agency learned of Moussaoui's xdesertman@hotmail.com account when he disclosed that information in a motion filed with the court in July 2002. Microsoft Network Hotmail erases users' account information after 30 days of inactivity. It is not able to retrieve records of user activity 90 days after an account is dormant. Because more than 90 days had elapsed since he had used the account, it was too late to find Moussaoui's xdesertman@hotmail.com account. E-mails from this account might have been available for seizure if the FBI had been able to search it when they first recognized him as a possible threat.

Moussaoui also used the alias Zuluman Tangotango to register pilotz123@hotmail.com, another Hotmail e-mail account. The FBI confirmed Moussaoui used that account to contact the two flight schools, according to a floppy disk seized along with Moussaoui's laptop. The e-mail from that diskette was examined and used at trial.

Agents also checked e-mail service providers such as Yahoo!, America Online, and Earthlink, but found no records that Moussaoui had used them.

CONTINUED ON NEXT PAGE

▸▸ CONTINUED

On December 11, 2001, a federal grand jury indicted Moussaoui for conspiring with Osama bin Laden and other al Qaeda members "to murder thousands of innocent people in New York, Virginia and Pennsylvania." An ***indictment*** is a grand jury charge that the defendant should stand trial.

According to prosecutors, evidence in the case *United States v. Zacarias Moussaoui* (Crim. No. 01–455-A) included 140 computer hard drives. Investigators discovered that Moussaoui had used four of the 140 computers (CNN, 2002).

As in all criminal and civil cases, a crucial evidentiary issue is authentication of the e-evidence. Authentication meant ensuring that each duplicate of the 140 computer hard drives provided an exact copy of that which the FBI had acquired originally.

In 2003, Moussaoui (the defendant) tried to refute the authentication of the e-evidence discovered by the FBI. One of his claims was that the U.S. government had failed to provide him with information that was retrieved from the various computers the defendant had used. In response to Moussaoui's challenge against the evidence, the federal court held (ruled) that the government had provided the defendant with sufficient information, including:

- Information about the authentication of the computer hard drives
- Confirmation that the electronic discovery and computer forensics computer evidence had not been contaminated
- The timing of the forensic examinations
- The software used to restore a hard drive image

The court further stated that the defense (Moussaoui) possessed the computer hard drives at issue and had sufficient expert resources and subpoena power to conduct any further investigation it deemed necessary (Nimsger and Brill, 2002).

This case demonstrates that the U.S. legal system guards against violations of the Constitution even for the worst of suspected criminals. It further demonstrates that forensic evidence must be authenticated. Authentication is even more challenging when e-evidence of criminal activities exists in many locations and covers extended periods of time—or has been deleted, overwritten, encrypted, or stored on large or multiple servers or databases.

**FYI** *The Chinese Cyber Sledgehammer*

The importance of rigorous protections of civil rights was reinforced when it was made public that Chinese secret police were reviewing e-mails of Chinese citizens. Congressman Christopher Smith, the Global Human Rights Subcommittee chairman, remarked on these violations in an opening statement at a February 15, 2006, hearing on "The Internet in China: A Tool for Freedom or Suppression?" According to Smith, the Chinese government had detained 49 "cyberdissidents" and 32 journalists for posting on the Internet information critical of the regime. Smith voiced concerns over U.S. technology companies' collaborating with China to "decapitate the voice of dissidents." He was referring to Yahoo!'s cooperation in 2005 with Chinese secret police that led to the imprisonment of the cyberdissident Shi Tao. Yahoo! also handed over data to Chinese authorities on another of its users, Li Zhi. Li Zhi was sentenced on December 10, 2003, to eight years in prison for "inciting subversion." His "crime" was to criticize in online discussion groups and articles the well-known corruption of local officials. "Women and men are going to the gulag and being tortured as a direct result of information handed over to Chinese officials," Smith said.

*Source:* "China Uses Internet as Tool of Repression, Says Congressman Smith; Human rights panel chair says China's crackdown benefits from U.S. technology." From State Department Documents and Publications, Feb. 15, 2006.

## Conclusions and Lessons

The lessons these cases teach you are that the outcomes of investigations depend on an understanding of the laws, use of proper investigative procedures, qualified investigators, and authenticated evidence. As you will learn in greater detail throughout this book, the authentication and admissibility of evidence depends on accepted forensic investigation tools and techniques and forensic rules.

Before discussing proper legal procedure and forensic rules, the next section focuses on technical issues. Not surprisingly, the primary technical factors are the increasing uses of personal computers, electronic devices, networks, and the Internet. Technology alone is not responsible. There were also economic, social, and international changes. Among them are unemployment, the rise of hacker societies, poverty, the breakup of the U.S.S.R., the reunification of Germany, and anti-American sentiments.

**FYI** *The Patriot Hacker and the Wardriving Hacker*

In 2004, Benjamin Stark, 22, known as the Patriot Hacker, pleaded guilty to charges that he hacked into eleven networks belonging to nine U.S. government departments. Stark hacked in to post warnings on government Web sites about security holes that exposed the country to terrorists. Regardless of his intentions, under mandatory federal sentencing guidelines, the Patriot Hacker faces a prison term of 24 to 36 months. (See *Security Focus*, 5/19/2004, **www.securityfocus.com**).

In another case, Brian Salcedo pleaded guilty to hacking into a Lowe's homeware store's unsecured wireless network. He hacked into a network in Southfield, Michigan, to steal credit card numbers from the company's data center in North Carolina. Salcedo and his accomplice discovered the wireless network through ***wardriving.*** Wardriving is driving around with laptop computers and antennae looking for unprotected wireless Internet connections (See *Security Focus*, 6/4/2004, **www.securityfocus.com**).

## Types of Motives and Cybercrimes

You learned in Chapter 1 that cybercrimes fall into two general categories: crimes in which a computer is the target of the crime and crimes in which a computer is the instrument of the crime. This section expands on that discussion. Here you will learn about the motives that lead to various types of computer and computer-mediated crimes. In practice, there is a lot of overlap in the classifications, in part because multiple crimes can be occurring at the same time.

### Finding the Motive—The "Why" of the Crime

In addition to technical and legal knowledge, understanding the reasons why certain types of crimes are committed and the motivations of criminals helps in the initial stages of the computer forensics investigative process. In the following example, physical evidence provided the intelligence to support the other four stages of the investigation.

When police found 72-year-old Shirley Noe stabbed and beaten to death in her home in July 1999, they had enough DNA and physical evidence to connect her financial consultant, Walter Elze, Jr., to the crime. But they didn't know the reason, or motive, for the killing. That motive was discovered from Elze's computer files. The 31-year-old consultant had embezzled over $200,000 from Noe. To protect himself, he killed her when she caught on to what he had done. You will read more about motives later in this chapter.

Crimes are committed for a purpose, at least in the minds of those who commit them. Motives may be ideological, such as those of the Patriot Hacker, or financial, as with the wardriving hackers. The crimes may seem totally irrational or even self-destructive. By being aware of cybercrime motives, forensic investigators may be better able to understand the digital clues that criminals leave.

Some cybercriminals, particularly those who steal identities, confidential documents, or trade secrets, do not want to get caught and do not reveal their activities in chat rooms or Web sites. In contrast, criminals whose purpose is *trophy hunting* need to brag about their exploits. Trophy hunters are motivated by their desire for fame or notoriety in a counterculture. Security companies such as Symantec and McAfee are targeted by intruders because of the inherent value in breaking into their Web sites. Symantec estimates that 3,000 or 4,000 people each day try to break into its Web site, many of these attacks being trophy hunting by the intruder.

Table 2.3 lists common motives and characteristics of cybercrimes. You will notice that the probability of detection of the crime or intrusion and identification of the intruder are related closely to the motive. Although several motives are possible, one motive may predominate.

## Computer Is the Crime Target

Information is the currency of modern life. Profit-motivated crimes in which the computer is the target typically involve the search for information. Hackers are comparable to bank robbers—they go after valuable content. These offenses might be theft of intellectual property, customer credit card numbers, customer lists, pricing data, or other marketing information. More visible cybercrimes are blackmail based on information gained from computerized files, such as medical information, personal history, or sexual preference. Another motive for targeting computers is extortion, as in the case of Ivanov and Gorshkov.

These types of crimes also could be motivated by the desire for revenge or sabotage. Disgruntled employees or stockholders devastated by corporate fraud may exact revenge by sabotaging computer systems or ***spoofing*** Web sites to create chaos in a business's operations. Spoof means to trick, disguise, or deceive. A spoofed Web site is a phony site that replaces a legitimate Web site address.

Unlawful access to criminal justice and other government records is another crime that targets the computer directly. This crime covers changing a criminal history; modifying want and warrant information; creating a driver's license, passport, or another document for identification purposes; changing tax records; or gaining access to intelligence files.

***Techno-vandalism*** occurs when unauthorized access to a computer damages files or programs for the challenge or sport rather than for profit. Damage or loss may be intentional or accidental. Sophisticated hackers are

**TABLE 2.3** Taxonomy of computer crimes, motives, and discoverability.

| **Cybercrime Motives** | |
|---|---|
| ■ For financial gain, including extortion and blackmail | |
| ■ To cover up a crime, mistake, or potentially incriminating act | |
| ■ To remove incriminating information or correspondence | |
| ■ To steal goods or services without having to pay for them | |
| ■ For competitive advantage or industrial espionage | |
| ■ For political or military objectives | |
| ■ For retaliation or vengeance | |
| ■ For ideological purposes | |
| ■ For curiosity or the thrill of vandalism | |
| ■ For fame or notoriety | |
| **Type or Source of the Crime/Intrusion** | |
| **External** | Malware (viruses, worms, Trojan horses), hackers, script kiddies, former employees, spies, adversaries, terrorists |
| **Internal (insiders)** | Management, employees, staff, consultants, contract workers, maintenance crew, temporary staff |
| **Blended** | An external attack that occurs because of inadvertent or deliberate help by insiders |
| **Type of Crime/Intrusion** | |
| **Directed or focused at a particular company or person** | ■ Industrial espionage<br>■ Theft of marketing or customer data<br>■ Trojan horses<br>■ Hacker attacks<br>■ Trophy hunting<br>■ Web site spoofing or defacing<br>■ Extortion, blackmail<br>■ Time bombs or other deliberate deletion of files or software |
| **Random or autonomous** | ■ E-mail viruses<br>■ Hoaxes<br>■ Worms or Trojans<br>■ Stealth Web sites<br>■ Bogus Web sites enticing users to register<br>■ Internet scams or other confidence tricks |

CONTINUED ON NEXT PAGE

| Probability of Detection | |
|---|---|
| **Low**<br>Stealth attack (human or malware) | Intruder wants to avoid detection.<br>■ Information retrieval or theft<br>■ Espionage<br>■ Redirection of funds<br>■ Cover-up of criminal activity<br>■ Cover-up of negligence by altering data or records |
| **High**<br>Visible or blatant intrusion (human or malware) | Intruder wants the attack to be noticed or detected. Many of these intrusions arise from the technology explosion (e.g., hacker tools).<br>■ Web site defacement<br>■ Posting of damaging news or information<br>■ False postings in online bulletin boards or Usenet groups<br>■ Denial of service (DoS) attack<br>■ Data corruption |
| **Postintrusion** | |
| **No escalation beyond the initial state** | Intruder gains some minimum access to the target system but does not attempt further penetration. Popular among juveniles, disgruntled employees, or professional hackers who want to show off their skills. These offenders are motivated mostly by mischief, malice, or desire for fame rather than financial gain. |
| **Escalate to higher penetration state, possibly to root (total) access** | Intruder gains administrative "root" access to a network or application and then escalates the intrusion. Criminals in this category tend to be well-funded and invest heavily in avoiding detection. |

professional criminals, making it harder to find forensic evidence because they are smart enough to enter without being detected and to erase logs that could reveal their presence. Amateur script kiddies are more likely to get caught.

Another crime in this category is *techno-trespass*, the technological equivalent of criminal trespass. In these crimes, the intruder uses the computer to steal information or damage/disrupt computer operations. If the trespasser is able to gain *super user* status, in effect gaining *root access* or the same privileges as the system's administrator, the intruder has full access to the computer system. A super user can commit cybercrimes against, and with, the full power of the computer network. Root access will be discussed in later chapters.

Economic and foreign espionage also fall into this category. On June 17, 2004, several top Internet sites were attacked with a DoS attack. A DoS attack on a network or Web site server causes a network to receive more hits (requests for service) than it can respond to—resulting in denied service. DoS happens when a server or network is deliberately overwhelmed, usually by a hacker. The companies targeted by the DoS attack included Yahoo!, Google, Microsoft, Symantec, FedEx, Apple, AltaVista, and Lycos. The targeted companies lost about 20 percent of their availability for two hours, but there seemed to be no financial gain to the hackers. All of these companies use network services provided by Akamai. It was not clear whether the attack was against Akamai or its high-tech customers.

**FYI** *Elements of a Crime*

Virtually all crimes require a physical act, and most require mental intent. The wrongful act is called the *actus reus*. The wrongful intent, or state of mind, is the *mens rea*. Intent is a state of mind whereby the person knows and purposes either the act or the act and its consequences.

## Computer Is the Crime Instrument

These cybercrimes tend to be profit-motivated, financial frauds. Forensic investigations of these crimes may require not only knowledge of how the computer system is supposed to function but also an understanding of auditing or ***forensic accounting.*** Forensic accounting is the integration of accounting, auditing, and investigative skills. Most of the crimes targeting computers, as you have just read, fall into this category, but the motives may differ.

A criminal might insert malicious code to control the computer's processes. A variation is to use legitimate computer processes for illegitimate purposes. Common examples of this type of crime are fraudulent use of ATMs (automated teller machines), illegal electronic funds transfer (EFT), credit card fraud, fraud from computer billings, and telecommunications fraud.

In companies with computer networks, which would be almost every company, employees' activities can be monitored as a way to deter or detect crimes. From the time an employee logs on, IT departments can track all computer actions, such as the keys that were pressed; Web sites visited; and e-mails sent, received, and forwarded. Monitoring makes it possible to know if employees are using their access to steal data, transmit trade secrets, or the like.

Qualities of the Internet may motivate a criminal to use it instead of traditional means for several reasons. The Internet offers excellent communication facilities and the possibility of hiding one's identity. The risk of being caught or subjected to criminal investigation, in any nation, is relatively low.

The laws of most countries do not clearly prohibit cybercrimes. Existing "terrestrial" laws against physical acts of trespass, or breaking and entering, often do not cover their "virtual" counterparts. E-commerce Web sites hit by DoS attacks may not be covered by outdated laws as protected forms of property. New kinds of crimes can fall between the cracks, as the Philippines learned when it attempted to prosecute the creator of the May 2000 Love Bug virus for causing huge damages worldwide (McConnell, 2000).

## Computer Is Incidental to Traditional Crimes

In this category of cybercrime, the criminal does not need a computer to commit the crime, but use of a computer facilitates the criminal act. These are traditional crimes that became easier or more widespread because of telecommunication networks and powerful PCs. Money laundering, organized crimes, illegal gambling and drugs, child pornography, and other exploitations are the most common of these crimes. What's more, a person can commit murder by changing a patient's medication data and/or dosage in a health center's computer—and then cover it up by changing the data back.

Searching for e-evidence while investigating these crimes can be particularly challenging because they tend to be high-profit crimes. Criminals invest heavily in ways to avoid or deter detection. In drug raids, money laundering seizures, and other arrests, computers and electronic storage media with incriminating information are seized. But the data may be encrypted or the system set up to erase files if they are not properly accessed. In some instances, criminals even destroy the storage media, such as disks, to eliminate e-evidence of their illegal activities. All of these situations require unique data recovery techniques in order to gain access to the evidence.

Another illustration of how criminals use technology to further their illegal activities involves child pornography. Historically, consumers of child pornography have trafficked photographs and related information through newsletters and tightly controlled exchange networks. Now, with the advancement of computer technology, child pornographers exchange this information through chat rooms and F-servers (file servers). U.S. Customs agents raided 40 locations in 15 states serviced by a Denmark-based child pornography bulletin board service (BBS). These criminals used computer networks for more efficient distribution of illegal material.

### FYI Growth in Computer Forensics

U.S. companies spent $118 million on computer forensics in 2000. In 2004, estimated expenditures doubled to $277 million, and they are expected to continue to grow at an even faster rate.

## New Crimes Generated by the Prevalence of Computers

Computers generate new versions of traditional crimes by creating new crime targets. Software piracy, Internet and auction fraud, copyright violation of computer programs, counterfeit equipment, black market computer equipment and programs, and theft of technological equipment fall into this category of computer crime. Viruses and worms can fall into this category. The Love Bug virus/worm was designed to steal passwords that, in turn, would be used fraudulently to obtain Internet services and other items of value. Counterfeit computers and peripherals (items such as modems and hard disks) are being manufactured and sold as originals, similar to knock-offs of Rolex watches and Louis Vuitton handbags.

One widespread crime in this category is the violation of copyrighted commercial software. This offense may not seem like a serious crime, but lost profits are huge. Thirty-five percent of the software installed on personal computers worldwide was pirated in 2004, a one percentage point decrease from 36 percent in 2003. Yet, losses due to piracy increased from $29 billion to $33 billion according to a study by the research company IDC (EDP, 2005). In the United States, the piracy rate was 22 percent, and that was the lowest rate among the nations surveyed. By contrast, Vietnam and China had the highest piracy rates of about 92 percent in 2003, according to the study.

Technological advances are not solely to blame for their use as crime tools. For example, the incidence of corporate fraud has risen not because technology made it easier but because fewer people are involved in the process of reviewing company matters.

The impact of greater computer power and less supervision is seen in the 2002 fraud case of John M. Rusnak. Rusnak received seven and a half years in prison as part of a plea agreement with federal prosecutors. He had been a currency trader for Allfirst Financial, Inc., a U.S. banking subsidiary of Allied Irish Banks. Rusnak pleaded guilty in Maryland federal court to bank fraud. According to court records, Rusnak entered fictitious options trades in Allfirst's computer system in the late 1990s. He hid his $691 million in trading losses by showing millions of dollars in fake profits. The computer manipulation allowed Rusnak to illegally collect an extra $850,000 in salary and bonuses. Rusnak circumvented the bank's oversight systems and covered his tracks electronically from 1997 to 2001.

The KPMG Fraud Survey 2002 estimated the average loss for an organization that was victimized by fraud was $1.4 million. More than 55 percent of the businesses surveyed had been hit by fraud at least once. Although fraud by internal managers accounted for 28 percent of frauds, it made up 67 percent of the loss by value. The most significant losses from fraud committed by internal management came from theft of information, which averaged a $2.5 million loss per incident.

## IN PRACTICE: Car Reveals Speed of Driver, Who Gets a Prison Term

Most new vehicles come equipped with an event data recorder, or "black box," that stores facts about the driver's speed and handling. These black boxes contain e-evidence that is being used in investigations. In November 2004, Danny Hopkins, 47, was convicted of second-degree manslaughter in the October 2003 death of Lindsay Kyle in a car accident. Hopkins' vehicle's event data recorder showed that he was traveling 106 miles per hour four seconds before he crashed into the back of Lindsay's car, which was stopped at a red light. As a result of the evidence provided by the data recorder, Hopkins faces 5 to15 years in prison in New York.

Had the car not been equipped with the new event data recorder, skid marks and crash damage could have been used to estimate the speed of the car. In this case, technology improved the precision and degree of confidence that the driver's speed was 106 mph.

## Forensics Rules and Evidence Issues

E-evidence must be preserved and authenticated like other types of evidence. The handling of e-evidence must follow the ***three C's of evidence:*** care, control, and chain of custody. These are legal guidelines to ensure that the evidence presented is the same as that which was seized. It requires documentation of the maintenance of evidence in its original state and preparation for civil or criminal proceedings. These guidelines are more burdensome for easily altered digital data. For instance, with e-mail evidence, an investigator might have to establish the origin of the message, the integrity of the system in which the message was transmitted, and the chain of custody of the message.

The operations used to collect, analyze, control, and present e-evidence cannot modify the original item being studied in any manner. Any alteration to the primary source of evidence could contaminate it and make it inadmissible in court. Care and control of evidence is impossible unless the investigator understands its properties. For example, the proper care of blood samples requires that they be kept at a certain temperature. You would not store such evidence in your pocket or near a heat source or in the trunk of a vehicle because it is known that the evidence could be affected. Likewise, e-evidence and computers are affected by magnetic forces, so they should not be placed in a vehicle or trunk that also contains electromagnetic equipment.

Another critical evidentiary issue is that everyone who touches evidence can contaminate it. Therefore, maintaining a chain of custody is essential for computer forensics investigators. Chain of custody is a legal guideline to ensure that the evidence presented is the same as that which was seized. Furthermore, chain of custody is an identification system that establishes a record of how evidence was handled, shows who handled it, and documents the integrity of the handling of the evidence that was collected.

Each piece of original evidence that is seized should have a ***chain of custody log*** associated with it. Computer forensics tools such as MD5 (message digest) or MD5sum create a unique value for each file. If the file is changed in any way, its MD value also changes. This tool helps ensure that the files have not been altered and can be admitted into evidence. Computer forensics tools and techniques are discussed in detail in Parts 2 and 3 of this text.

## Chain of Custody Procedures

During an investigation, the following procedures should be followed to ensure the chain of custody.

- A record or evidence log should be kept to show when all items of evidence, such as server logs, computers, hard drives, and disk, are received or seized and where they are located.
- If the items are released to auditors, authorities, or the court, those release dates should be recorded.
- Access to evidence should be restricted throughout the investigation and any subsequent proceedings.
- To preserve the chain of custody, the original hard disk should be placed in an evidence locker and appropriate notations should be made in the evidence log.
- All computer forensics should be performed on the mirror image copy, never on the original.

## Report Procedures

Reporting procedures are equally important to the success of the investigation and prosecution of a case. The investigator performing or participating in the investigation may be required to testify in court, so all procedures need to be documented. The following recommendations help ensure proper documentation.

- All reports of the investigation should be prepared with the understanding that they will be read by others. Those who might read the report include the authorities, opposing counsel, the court, the press, and the general public.
- The investigator should never comment on the guilt or innocence of a suspect or suspects or their affiliations.
- Only the facts of the investigation should be presented. Opinions should be avoided.

Chain of custody and report procedures must be free of bias and opinion, regardless of who or what is being investigated. When the federal government is investigating a state or local government, as in the following case, the procedures are no different from other forensics investigations.

### IN PRACTICE: E-Discovery at Los Angeles City Government

As part of an investigation of possible corruption in contracting in Los Angeles city government, federal prosecutors asked the city to preserve all e-mails sent to or from Mayor James K. Hahn's office since just before he was sworn in. In an April 12, 2004, letter to the city clerk, U.S. Attorney Debra W. Yang, the federal prosecutor, asked the city to preserve electronic records dating back to June 2001. Yang asked that all of the electronic communication be preserved for 90 days "pending further legal process." The letter warned that "Destruction of any documents or electronic files may impede a federal investigation." Letters such as this one intended to preserve documents are a standard law enforcement tool. The scope of Yang's request included e-mails to and from mayoral employees as well as anyone associated with Hahn's office (McGreevy et al., 2004).

Federal authorities have subpoenaed records and e-mail from several sources associated with the city. Federal prosecutors may not have known exactly what evidence was available. The purpose of their letter was to preserve e-evidence while they sought search warrants to determine whether crimes had been committed.

### FYI Copyright Infringement Case

In a copyright infringement case, defendant Burns was accused of posting copyrighted photographs on a Web site hosted by Yahoo! The advisory committee interpreted the federal rules to mean that "computerized data and other electronically-recorded information" will include but not be limited to "voice mail messages and files, backup voice mail files, email messages and files, backup email files, deleted emails,

CONTINUED ON NEXT PAGE

▶▶ CONTINUED

data files, program files, backup and archival tapes, temporary files, system history files, Web site information stored in textual, graphical or audio format, Web site log files, cache files, cookies and other electronically recorded information." The court also noted that "the disclosing party shall take reasonable steps to ensure that it discloses any backup copies of files or archival tapes that will provide information about any 'deleted' electronic data" (Burke, 2003).

---

## Computer Forensics Investigator's Responsibilities

The Federal Guidelines for Searching and Seizing Computers state that "any home PC can be connected to a network simply by adding a modem." Consequently, in any case where a modem is present, investigators should consider the possibility that the computer user has stored valuable information at some remote location.

In addition to this directive, investigators have other responsibilities to perform. Those duties include the following.

- Investigate and/or review current computer and computer-mediated crimes
- Maintain objectivity when seizing and investigating computers, suspects, and support staff
- Conduct all forensics investigations consistently with generally accepted procedures and federal rules of evidence and discovery
- Keep a log of activities undertaken to stay current in the search, seizure, and processing of e-evidence

Another legal issue in computer forensics cases is how much time the police may have to analyze a computer after seizing it. Federal Rule of Criminal Procedure 41(c)(1) gives the police ten days after issuance of the warrant to serve it. But there is nothing in the rule about how long the police may keep and analyze the computer. Procedures for seizing computers and other devices will be covered in Chapter 4.

## Summary

You have learned that the widespread use of computers and the Internet have contributed to traditional and computer crimes. Effective forensic investigation of these offenses requires evidence gathered from computers, storage media, digital devices, e-mail, chat rooms, and the Internet—and any technology that tracks what was done, who did it, and when.

Law enforcement and other investigators will produce, during the discovery process, imaged or exact copies of the digital media being investigated. These copies need to be examined by trained professionals to ensure that the media have been secured and examined in the correct manner and all evidence has been recovered.



There are numerous legal and ethical issues of evidence seizure, handling, and investigation. Updated and new federal rules and laws regulate forensic investigations and lead to challenges to the admissibility of e-evidence. The need for e-evidence has led to a new area of criminal investigation, namely computer forensics. This new field is less than 15 years old and is evolving rapidly. Computer forensics depends on an understanding of technical and legal issues. The most consequential legal issue in computer forensics is the admissibility of evidence in criminal cases. Computer forensics investigators must identify, gather, extract, protect, preserve, and document computer and other e-evidence using acceptable methods to ensure admissibility. An understanding of behavioral issues and a grasp of the ethical problems that investigators face are also valuable skills.

The law of search and seizure, as it relates to computers and electronic equipment, must be followed. Failure to follow proper legal procedure will result in evidence's being ruled inadmissible in court and a guilty criminal's going free. In addition, it is equally important to prevent innocent people from being charged with crimes they did not commit.

## Test Your Skills

### MULTIPLE CHOICE QUESTIONS

1. What is the most significant legal issue in computer forensics?
   A. Preserving evidence.
   B. Seizing evidence.
   C. Admissibility of evidence.
   D. Discovery of evidence.

2. E-discovery of documents or data
   A. is playing a larger role in both civil and criminal cases.
   B. is the same as the discovery of paper documents and data and has the same challenges.
   C. always requires a search warrant or court order.
   D. all of the above

3. Federal rules regulate the fact-finding process for all of the following reasons, *except*
   A. to ensure that the forensic process does not taint or alter the evidence in any way.
   B. to ensure that a suspect's civil rights are not violated.
   C. to prevent someone from being charged with a crime she did not commit.
   D. to ensure that the guilty person is charged with the crime and arrested.

4. Which of the following statements is true?
   A. A search warrant gives a law enforcement officer full right to violate a citizen's privacy.
   B. Evidence that has been suppressed cannot be used in court.
   C. If a search warrant was required before a search of a suspect's computer but was not obtained the e-evidence can still be used in court.
   D. To get a search warrant, an officer only has to show probable cause.

5. In order for a law enforcement officer to search a person or his property without a search warrant, certain conditions must be met. Which of the following is *not* one of those conditions?
   A. There must have been a lawful arrest.
   B. The officer may seize evidence in order to prevent its destruction or concealment.
   C. The officer may search and seize evidence if the suspect does not object.
   D. The officer may search for and remove any weapons that the arrested person may use to escape or resist arrest.

6. Which is an example of steganography?
   A. A message that is hidden in an image.
   B. A message that is in a hidden file.
   C. An image that is hidden in file slack.
   D. An image that is encrypted.

7. "The right of the people to be secure in their persons, houses, papers and effects against unreasonable searches and seizures shall not be violated . . ." is part of the
   A. First Amendment.
   B. Fourth Amendment.
   C. Fourteenth Amendment.
   D. Privacy Act.

8. Which cybercrime would be the most difficult to detect?
   A. Industrial espionage.
   B. Hacker attacks.
   C. Web site spoofing or defacing.
   D. Internet scams.



9. What is a chain of custody?
   A. A legal guideline that is less rigorous for e-evidence than physical evidence.
   B. A legal guideline for searching computers.
   C. A legal guideline to ensure that the evidence presented in the court or legal action is the same as that which was seized.
   D. All of the above.

10. Traditional crimes that became easier or more widespread because of telecommunication networks and powerful PCs include all of the following *except*
    A. money laundering.
    B. illegal gambling and drug distribution.
    C. DoS attacks.
    D. child pornography.

11. Searching for e-evidence while investigating high-profit crimes, such as drug distribution or money laundering, can be particularly challenging because criminals engaged in these crimes
    A. rarely use the Internet or computers.
    B. may destroy the storage media, such as disks, to eliminate e-evidence of their illegal activities.
    C. always encrypt their data and communications.
    D. hide their data in slack space.

12. Which of the following is (are) true about crimes?
    A. Virtually all crimes require a physical act.
    B. The wrongful act is called the *actus reus*.
    C. The wrongful intent or state of mind is the *mens rea*.
    D. All are true.

13. Computer forensics tools such as MD5 create a unique value for each file. This unique value is important because
    A. it proves that the file was not deleted.
    B. it proves that the file was recovered from a specific computer.
    C. it helps ensure that the files have not been altered and are able to be admitted into evidence.
    D. All of the above.

14. Which of the following reporting procedures helps ensure successful investigation and prosecution of a case?
    A. All reports of the investigation should be prepared with the understanding that they will be read by others.
    B. The investigator should never comment on the guilt or innocence of a suspect or suspects or their affiliations.
    C. Facts of the investigation should be presented but not opinions of the investigation.
    D. All of the above.

15. Federal Rule of Criminal Procedure 41(c)(1) gives the police ______ after issuance of the warrant to serve it.
    A. 3 days
    B. 7 days
    C. 10 days
    D. 14 days

## EXERCISES

### Exercise 2.1: Detecting E-Evidence from Web Site Visits

1. Use a search engine to locate online stores selling audio/video equipment or online travel agencies.
2. Click onto five of the links.
3. Perform a search of your hard drive to find files and folders named *cookie*.
4. Perform another search of all files created that day.
5. List what content has been placed on your computer hard drive as a result of these searches.
6. Estimate how many cookies were deposited on the hard drive as a result of those Web site visits.

### Exercise 2.2: E-Evidence of Corporate Crime

The drug Vioxx was taken off the market in 2004 because it was learned that it could have fatal side effects. Vioxx was manufactured by Merck.

1. Search the Internet to find articles that indicate Merck's executives knew of the dangerous side effects.
2. List the type of e-evidence that was discovered.
3. Explain whether the e-evidence was sufficient to prove that the company or any of its managers or employees knew the drug has potential health risks.
4. List the reasons why Merck's executives might have thought their e-records would never be revealed.

### Exercise 2.3: Understanding the Meaning of Probable Cause

1. Using an online search engine, find a legal dictionary or glossary.
2. Search for one explanation of the term *probable cause*, which is referenced in the Fourth Amendment. According to the Fourth Amendment, there can be no unreasonable search and seizures and no warrants without probable cause.
3. Write one of the definitions of probable cause. Note how complex the concept of probable cause is.

### Exercise 2.4: Fourth Amendment

1. Use the Internet to search for a Web site pertaining to privacy and Fourth Amendment issues.
2. Find a case or story about a violation of a person's privacy.
3. Explain the circumstances of the situation.
4. Report on whether or not you agree that the person had a legitimate right to privacy.

### Exercise 2.5: How to Minimize Metadata in Microsoft Word Documents

1. Go to **support.microsoft.com/support/kb/articles/Q223/7/90.ASP.**
2. Find out what metadata is available in Microsoft Word documents.
3. Explain the various methods that you can use to minimize the amount of metadata contained within your Word documents.

## PROJECTS

### Project 2.1: Searching and Seizing Computers

1. Review Federal Guidelines for Searching and Seizing Computers, U.S. DOJ at **www.usdoj.gov/criminal/cybercrime/searching.html.**
2. Write a list of three challenges that you would face when performing a search and seizure.
3. What forensic tools and equipment would help you deal with those challenges?

### Project 2.2: What Motivates Hackers?

Sarah Gordon has done extensive research into the psychology and motivations of virus writers and hackers. She commented on her research for PBS's *Frontline*: "Hackers: Who Are Hackers? Studying Their Psychology." Read her remarks at **www.pbs.org/wgbh/pages/frontline/shows/hackers/whoare/psycho.html.**

1. Review the top reasons why hackers hack.
2. Research other Web sites that discuss the motivations of hackers.
3. Report what you learned about the e-evidence trails these hackers might leave.

### Project 2.3: Global Software Piracy

Consider the IDC study on global software privacy that found 35 percent of the software installed on personal computers worldwide was pirated in 2004, a 1 percentage point decrease from 36 percent in 2003. Despite the decrease in piracy rates, losses due to piracy actually increased by $1 billion to $33 billion.

1. Using the taxonomy in this chapter, classify the criminals who commit this type of crime.
2. Write a report outlining how you would go about investigating this type of crime at a university.

## Case Study

The sheer scale and pervasiveness of technology throughout the world is truly staggering. Most of us are oblivious to the evidence our activities leave on our computers, phones, and handheld devices—or how we can be profiled using credit card and toll debit cards.

1. Using an online database or an Internet search engine, search for a situation in which an electronic device or recorder implicated someone of a crime or wrongdoing.
2. Write a report on the e-evidence admissibility issues in the case.
3. In your report, describe how that evidence was discovered and retrieved by law officers or computer forensics experts.

For this case study you might also consult any of the following resources to find information:

**www.cybercrime.gov**
**www.cnet.com**
**www.e-evidence.info/ccunits.html**

# Part Two

## E-Evidence Collection and Preservation

Part One provided you with the legal foundation to understand the significance of using approved tools, procedures, and technology to acquire relevant e-evidence and ensure its admissibility. In Part Two, we begin with an explanation of defensible and effective search methods, documentation, forensics toolkits, and certifications. We apply legal and technology knowledge to the role of procedures and standards in the handling of e-evidence. We examine technology of storage devices, PDAs, and cell phones and explore methods to acquire and analyze their data. By the end of Part Two, you will understand how to collect and preserve e-evidence from a number of different devices.

# Chapter 3

# Tools, Environments, Equipment, and Certifications

## Chapter Objectives

**After reading this chapter and completing the exercises, you will be able to do the following:**

- Explain how to manage e-evidence throughout the life-cycle of a case.
- Identify the requirements for acquiring and authenticating evidence.
- Describe acceptable methods for searching and analyzing evidence.
- Explain investigative environments and analysis modes.
- Explain the functions and features of forensics tools and toolkits.
- Describe the types of equipment a forensics lab should have available.
- Describe types of certification programs and credentials available for a computer forensics investigator.

## Introduction

In Chapters 1 and 2, you learned that a computer forensics investigator's job involves finding, analyzing, and preserving the relevant digital files or data for use as e-evidence. That evidence may be the difference between making a case and losing it. The case may require that several hard drives or other devices be searched, and those devices may hold gigabytes of data. Adding to the challenge: Some of the digital contents may be private, confidential, encrypted, or privileged information that cannot be searched. To control the amount of data and avoid invasions of privacy or disclosure of confidential or privileged information, the investigator has to filter out irrelevant and unusable information. Performing these tasks correctly and efficiently requires using forensics tools, equipment, and environments. The complexity of tools or software may require specialized training or certification.

This chapter describes how to manage a case, authenticate evidence, and search and analyze data. You learn about computer forensics tools and toolkits, equipment, and specially-designed environments needed to avoid damaging or contaminating electronic data when it is being handled or transported. Following a standard methodology is crucial to successful and effective computer forensics. At the end of the chapter, you learn about training and certification that may be necessary to use a tool or defend one's investigation results.

---

## Managing the Life-Cycle of a Case

Each computer forensic case has a life-cycle that starts with the transport of devices to a computer forensics lab, with the on-site collection of evidence, or with a combination of both. Admissible evidence requires that the chain of custody be preserved right from the start because a flawed chain of custody cannot be undone.

### Maintaining a Defensible Approach

Maintaining the integrity of e-evidence requires a standardized ***defensible approach*** to data handling and preservation throughout the case life-cycle. A defensible approach is an objective and unbiased approach that is

- Performed in accordance with forensic science principles.
- Based on standard or current best practices.
- Conducted with verified tools to identify, collect, filter, tag and bag, store, and preserve e-evidence.
- Conducted by individuals who are certified in the use of verified tools, if such certification exists.
- Documented thoroughly.

**Caution**

**No Shortcuts**

Results of every step of the investigative process have to verify the chain of custody. Shortcuts must be avoided at all costs.

Evidence verification depends on the use of the proper software and hardware tools, equipment, and environment, which are covered in this chapter. Preserving e-evidence and good documentation of the steps taken during the evidence processing are essential for success in computer crime cases. At a minimum, preserving the chain of custody for e-evidence requires proving that

- No information has been added, deleted, or altered in the copying process or during analysis.

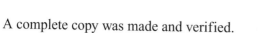

- A complete copy was made and verified.
- A reliable copying process was used.
- All media were secured.
- All data that should have been copied has been copied.

Recall that a chain of custody is the process of validating how the e-evidence had been collected, tracked, and protected. Tools and techniques for copying, verifying, and securing the digital contents will be explained in this chapter.

3

Forensic investigators should expect that they will have to defend their findings. Their e-evidence processing methods, tools, or techniques might be challenged rigorously by the opposing side. Documentation is important so that investigators can refresh their memories about the steps taken and duplicate the results of processing if necessary. Examples of chain of custody forms for hard drives and image files are in Appendix C. (For an example of a chain of custody form provided by Navigant, see the CSO Online Web site at **www.csoonline.com/read/120105/sample_chain_custody.pdf**). Critical evidence may be subject to reasonable doubt if an investigator is unable to reconstruct accurately what steps have been taken in the process of investigation.

## Selecting the Right Tools for a Case

There is no single methodology or set of tools for preserving the chain of custody while conducting a computer forensics investigation. From the many cases that you have read about, you can understand that the many different situations and variables cannot be resolved by a single type of solution. Some of the many factors affecting the choice of tool or tools are

- Type of device.
- Operating system.
- Software applications.
- Hardware platforms.
- State of the data.
- Domestic and international laws.
- Concerns about bad publicity or liability.

These and other factors will be discussed in this chapter and throughout Chapters 4 through 9.

## IN PRACTICE: Easy Access to Criminal Tools

Criminals use a number of software tools and devices to hide evidence of cybercrimes. Many of these tools are available for free download on the Internet:

- **Nuker:** Software used by intruders to destroy system log trails.
- **Anonymous remailers:** Tools used by intruders to mask their identities. These devices are configured to receive and resend Internet traffic by replacing the original (actual) source address of the sender with the address of the anonymous remailer machines.
- **Password cracker:** Software used to break encrypted password files, often stolen from a victim's network server.
- **Scanner:** Software used to identify services that are running on a network so that those services can be exploited to gain unauthorized access to the network.
- **Spoofer:** Software used to impersonate someone else to hide the identity of the actual sender of the e-mail.
- **Steganography:** Steganography is the science of hiding messages in messages. The point of it is to hide data or the existence of the message; that is, to hide the fact that the parties are communicating anything other than innocuous graphics or audio files. Steganography has been used by terrorists or intruders to spy, steal, or communicate information via electronic "dead drops," typically Web pages.
- **Trojan horse:** Malicious software disguised as a legitimate computer file or program. Trojan horses are used to create backdoors into networks to gain unauthorized access to the network.

These crime-supporting tools make it more difficult to recover e-evidence. With the proper investigative tools and methods, that evidence may still be recoverable.

The next section describes the features and functions of computer forensics tools for acquiring and authenticating e-evidence and how they can support the investigator and investigation.

3

## Acquiring and Authenticating the E-Evidence

Table 3.1 shows the objectives of an investigation and the corresponding chain-of-custody practices for acquiring and authenticating e-evidence. Ensuring the admissibility of the evidence must guide all activities.

These practices and the challenges they create are explained in the following sections. Keep in mind that there are no hard and fast rules to guide every activity (or task) of a forensics investigator. Those activities are documentation, collection, authentication, analysis, and preservation of the evidence—followed by the production and reporting of the findings to the client or the court in an organized and concise format. There are a variety of tools to support one or more of those activities.

**TABLE 3.1** E-evidence acquisition and authentication objectives and practices.

| Investigation Objectives | Chain of Custody Practices |
|---|---|
| Document the scene, evidence, activities, and findings | Document everything that is done. Keep detailed records and photographs. All activity relating to the seizure, access, storage, or transfer of digital evidence must be fully documented, preserved, and available for review. |
| Acquire the evidence | Collect and preserve the original data by creating a copy without altering or destroying the original. |
| Authenticate the copy | Verify that the copy is identical to the original or source. |
| Analyze and filter the evidence | Perform the technical analysis while retaining its integrity. Evaluate what could have happened and what could not have happened. Extensive time is spent filtering out irrelevant data. |
| Be objective and unbiased | Ensure that the evaluation is fair and impartial to the person or people being investigated. |
| Present the evidence and an evaluation of the findings in an understandable and legally acceptable manner | Interpret and report the results correctly. Conclusions must be accurate, complete, and usable. It can be difficult to explain the findings of computer evidence in a court, especially to nontechnical persons. The value of the evidence will ultimately depend on the way it is presented and defended in court. |

### Document and Collect the Data

The first step in analyzing data is to collect it. Collecting data can be a very long or tedious process because everything must be documented. Before removing or seizing a PC, document all the connections, devices, and cables attached to or in the vicinity of the PC. The documentation can consist of written or voice-recorded notes, high-resolution photographs, or video. Some combination of these is advisable. This documentation should also identify other devices such as PDAs or digital cameras that could contain evidence. If the PC is running, document it by photographing the open screens and programs that are running.

The documentation needs to be precise and organized. Checklists and forms help keep the documentation organized. Document each of the following:

- Location, date, time, witnesses
- System information, including manufacturer, serial number, model, and components
- Status of the computer, such as whether it was running and what was connected to it
- Physical evidence collected

### Power Down or Unplug?

When a PC is running, and after photographs have been taken to document it, the decision has to be made as to how to power down the PC. Using the operating system to power down the PC can be risky because the operating system might delete temporary files and change some of the date/time stamps. These operating system changes are discussed in detail in Chapter 7. The current best approach is to unplug the PC from the power source because this action preserves the data environment as it was at the time power was cut off.

**Caution**

**Exceptions to the "Copy Rule"**

Searching the original data is unavoidable under certain circumstances. During a network intrusion or other crime in progress, the primary goal may be containing the attack or stopping the crime—not preserving evidence. Also, it is not always possible to copy entire systems.

**IN PRACTICE: Write Blocking and Protection**

Never turn on the PC without having ***write-blocking*** devices or software in place. Write-blocking devices prevent any writes to the drives attached and offer very fast acquisition speeds. The simple act of turning on the PC can possibly alter critical data. While booting up, Windows-based operating systems alter many date/time stamps in the system and the date/time stamps of documents.

CONTINUED ON NEXT PAGE

▶▶ CONTINUED

To protect from adding to or changing the data on the mirror image, the image should be write-protected. All copies and originals should be labeled by time, date, and source and stored in a secure place. When restoring the image for search and examination, it is a best practice to check for viruses on any software and media to be used with up-to-date virus checking utilities. Use a hardware write-blocking device, such as the NoWrite Hardware Write Blocker, on all forensics analysis workstations to prohibit the operating system from writing to the disk.



### Create a Drive Image or Bit-Stream Image

Physical evidence at a crime scene has to be put into an evidence bag to protect and preserve it from alteration. The scene of a cybercrime needs to be secured just like the scene of any other crime. E-evidence must be put into a "digital container" so that it cannot be tampered with. That digital container is an exact duplicate, or image, of the computer or device. Investigators then work off the image while the original hard drive remains locked up securely.

Given that e-evidence is fragile by nature, the original data must be protected against any type of alteration, including alterations that happen when a file is opened. To protect the original evidence from any alteration, a copy of a hard drive or data storage medium is created. A forensic review can be done only on a verifiable copy of the original. Since you cannot work from the original data, you must make a ***forensic copy*** of the hard drive or device.

**FYI** *What Is a Forensic Copy (Duplicate)?*

*Forensic copy* is the technical term for the end-product of a forensics acquisition of a computer's hard drive or other storage device. That end-product is a bit-stream copy (duplicate), which is a bit-for-bit digital copy of a digital original document, file, partition, graphic image, entire disk, or similar object.

Making several forensic copies is recommended so if something happens to one copy, another backup is readily available. A drive can be imaged (duplicated) without anyone viewing its contents so privacy or confidentiality issues are not at risk.

There are several ways to make a forensic copy, but all require specialized software. Using normal operating system utilities to make a copy would be a mistake because the hidden areas and deleted file spaces would not be copied.

***Drive imaging*** is a means of evidence preservation because it captures a "snapshot" of everything on the drive. One method of capturing or copying all data on a drive is to make a noninvasive ***mirror image*** of the drive. A more advanced and preferred capability provided by some forensic software is the ability to produce a ***sector-by-sector image*** or ***bit-stream image*** (also called a bit-stream copy) by starting at the very beginning of the drive and making a copy of every bit (0 or 1) to the end of the drive without in any way deleting or modifying the contents or characteristics of the evidence. A bit-stream image is more precise and thorough than a mirror image of a hard drive. The bit-stream copy involves copying every bit of data on an evidence hard drive, including the file slack and unallocated file space that often contain deleted files and e-mail messages. These imaging processes capture all data, including ***residual data,*** on the drive surface. Residual data is data that has been deleted but not erased.

Residual data may be found in unallocated storage or file slack space. File slack space, also referred to as *slack*, is the extra space from the end of the file to the end of the cluster. It exists when the size of the file is less than the size of the cluster. All Microsoft operating systems store data in fixed length blocks of bytes called clusters. Clusters consist of sectors. A sector is 512 bytes, never more or less. Computer hard drives can only "grab" data in sector-size chunks. A sector is the smallest individually addressable physical unit of information used by a computer.

When the data file does not fill the last sector in the cluster, the operating system fills the "slack space" with data from the memory buffers.

File slack consists of

- ***RAM slack.*** This is the area from the end of the file to the end of a sector, except for the last sector.
- ***Drive slack.*** If additional sectors are needed to fill a cluster, a different type of slack is created called *drive slack*. It is stored in the ending sectors needed by the operating system to fill the last cluster assigned to the file. Drive slack can consist of data that was actually created a long time ago.

The following example illustrates RAM and drive slack. Assume that the cluster consists of only two sectors. If a file is saved that consists solely of the word "Investigation," then the data that gets stored to disk and written in file slack can be represented as

```
Investigation++++++++++(EOS)########################(EOC)
```

The + signs indicate the RAM slack that extends from the end of the file to the end of the sector (EOS). The # signs indicate the drive slack that extends from the end of the first sector to the end of the second sector, which in this example is also the end of the cluster (EOC).

File slack is created at the time a file is saved to disk. When a file is deleted under DOS or Windows, the data associated with RAM slack and drive slack remains in the cluster that was previously assigned to the end of the deleted file. The clusters that made up the deleted file are released by the operating system and remain on the disk as unallocated storage space until the space is overwritten with data from a new file.

3

### FYI Why File Slack is Important

It is important to understand the significance of file slack. Because file slack potentially contains data dumped randomly from the computer's memory, it is possible to identify network logon names, passwords, and other sensitive information associated with computer usage. File slack can also be analyzed to identify prior uses of the computer. On large disk drives, file slack can involve several hundred megabytes of data. Fragments of prior e-mail messages and word processing documents can be found in file slack. Slack potentially exists on floppy disks, hard disks, zipped disks, and other computer storage devices. If a computer has been left on for several days, the file slack may contain a lot of information.

When a copy is made, the contents of a hard drive are stored as a series of compressed image files and not as bootable hardware that can be attached to a computer and examined. The advantage of compressed images is that it is easier to access, store, and authenticate the copy—making it less likely to be altered by the operating system or during the examination.

Specialized software enables the investigator to assemble the image files as a single virtual hard drive, identical in every way to the original. If a physical duplicate is needed, the investigator reconstitutes those image files to a forensically clean hard drive and uses cryptographic algorithms such as MD5 or SHA-1 to demonstrate that the restored drive is a faithful duplicate of the original. You will learn about MD5 later in this chapter.

**Caution**

**Avoid Using Hacker-Type Tools**

Do not use hacker-type tools to acquire data or passwords from a computer. You do not want to have to explain in court that your data acquisition tool was written by someone named Evil-Hacker.

**IN PRACTICE: Be Precise about Terminology**

It is important to use the correct terminology in reference to evidence originating from a computer or other digital device and in the proper context. As an example, suppose the term *mirror image* is used in court to describe a forensically acquired copy of a hard drive rather than the more accurate term *bit-stream copy*. In computer forensics terminology, a mirror image retrieves only a fraction of the important content that can be acquired with a bit-stream copy. Those who understand the terminology would realize that a thorough investigation could not have been done on a mirror image of a hard drive. Even more hazardous to the outcome of a case is the fact that analysis of anything less than a bit-stream copy of a hard drive when presenting recovered deleted files as evidence is unlikely to be admissible in court.

When e-evidence is involved, accuracy is extremely important, and the making of a bit-stream backup is sometimes described as the preservation of the "electronic crime scene." The courts have continually upheld the use of copies of a computer hard drive or other electronic media as admissible evidence, provided that the image is an exact replica of the original drive. While getting a copy of the suspect media sounds as simple as cut and paste, not all products available in the market create an "evidence grade" bit-stream copy of a disk.

**Caution**

**Imaging**

The creation of a true forensic hard drive image is a highly detailed process.

## Use a Forensically Clean Hard Drive for Copying

Before an image of the suspect drive is written to a hard drive, that acquisition hard drive has to have been ***forensically wiped*** clean of all prior data. Forensically wiping a hard drive means that all areas of the disk are written with a single character, usually 0, thus overwriting every file ever stored on the drive. Under no circumstances should you attempt to create a forensically clean hard drive by simply formatting the drive. As you learned in Chapter 1, formatting may not completely erase all prior data. The formatting process simply erases the master file table and, if a full format is performed, checks for and repairs bad sectors on the hard drive. The DoD has an approved method for forensically wiping a drive, but there are also some good third-party applications available for this.

If a drive has not been forensically wiped before an image is written to it, that image can be tainted by data left over on the drive. This tainting not only will affect the ***hash*** value but also will call into question the validity of the data. A hash can be thought of as a file's fingerprint. In theory, no two hashes are alike except for identical files.

**Caution**

**Don't Just Format**

Formatting a drive does not create a forensically clean drive. Formatting does not write over every bit of data, and therefore, files or file fragments from before the new formatting remain on the hard drive in unallocated space.

## Verify the Accuracy of the Copy

Making a bit-stream image is simple in theory, but the accuracy of the backup must meet evidence standards. Accuracy is essential, and to guarantee accuracy, bit-stream imaging programs rely upon mathematical ***cyclic redundancy check*** (CRC) computations to validate that the copy is exactly the same as the original. CRC validation processes compare the bit-stream of the original source data with the bit-stream of the acquired data.

A drive image is "fingerprinted" using an encryption technique called *hashing*. This is also referred to as ***cryptographic hash verification.*** Hashing ensures the integrity of the file because any modification of the data can be detected. Hashing generates a unique digital signature for the data, called the ***message digest (MD).*** The currently used MD is MD5 (Message Digest algorithm 5), which was developed in 1991 to replace and eliminate the flaws in MD4.

If the bit-streams of the data files have not been altered, the resulting hash values will be exactly the same. The slightest change to the data will result in a different MD5 when it is hashed again. If even one bit of data has been altered, such as a 0 changed to 1, the resulting hash value will differ greatly from the hash value of the original drive.

The MD5 is one-way, which means that it cannot be reverse-engineered to reveal anything about the data except that it has changed. If the data signature, or MD5, of the duplicate drive is given to the court or requesting party, anyone can be custodian of the duplicate because an undetected alteration would be impossible.

### IN PRACTICE: Computer Forensics—A Legal Duty

In *Gates Rubber Co. v. Bando Chemical Industries,* the court defined a mandatory legal duty to perform proper computer forensics investigations. The court criticized one of the party's forensics experts for not making an image copy. The court stated that when collecting evidence for judicial purposes, a party has "a duty to utilize the method which would yield the most complete and accurate results."

---

## Searching and Analyzing the Data

Once the forensic copies have been made, the data is then searched and analyzed. Searching for case relevant information can be a monumental task given the vast amounts of data that might have been recovered.

**FYI** *Prepare for Your Day in Court*

Computer forensics investigators may be called as witnesses to testify for either the defense or prosecution. Once a witness testifies, he is subject to rigorous cross-examination by either side. To withstand a harsh cross-examination, witnesses must be confident enough to testify in court as to the validity of their decisions and actions. Witnesses need documentation of their work.

### Effective Data Searches

The key to effective data searches is to prepare and plan carefully. Poor preparation in the early stages of an investigation can lead to failures in prosecution because information can be ignored, destroyed, or compromised. Take time to understand and carefully plan what is critical to the investigation or case. The following tasks need to be performed to maximize search results.

- Interview members of the IT staff to learn how and where data has been stored, if applicable.
- Confirm or define the objective of the investigation.
- Identify relevant time periods and the scope of the data to be searched.
- Identify the relevant types of data.
- Identify search terms for data filtering, particularly words, names, or unique phrases to help locate relevant data and filter out what is irrelevant. Metadata can be invaluable to the filtering process.
- Find out usernames and passwords for network and e-mail accounts, to the extent possible.
- Check for other computers or devices that might contain relevant evidence.

**IN PRACTICE: Search Strategies**

Experienced computer forensics examiners are skilled in formulating search strategies that are likely to find revealing data. That process is much better if the examiner has a sense of what she is seeking before the search begins.

CONTINUED ON NEXT PAGE

CONTINUED

Questions such as these can help to guide the scope and nature of the investigation:

- If the focus is on documents, are there names, key words, or parts of words that are likely to be found within those documents?
- If the issue is trade secrets, are there search terms uniquely associated with the proprietary data?
- If the focus is pornography, are there Web site addresses (URLs) uniquely associated with prohibited content?



## Identify Data Types

Because e-evidence exists in many forms and locations, finding useful information requires an understanding of the types of information available and where that information might exist.

**Active Data** ***Active data*** is the information readily available and accessible to users. This data can easily be viewed through file manager programs. Active data includes spreadsheets, databases, word processing files, business application files, e-mail, electronic calendars, and address books.

**Deleted Files** In the ordinary course of business, files may be deleted. Or individuals may try to destroy documents by deleting them. But what happens when a file is deleted? As you learned in Chapter 1, in most operating systems *deleted* does not mean destroyed. When a file or e-mail is deleted with a computer operating system, the data itself is not removed. Rather, the process of deleting simply indicates to the computer operating system that the physical space belonging to the deleted file is available for additional data to be stored. As a result, the file remains on the hard drive until it is overwritten by new data or wiped through the use of utility software. Unlike active data, deleted data cannot be viewed with file manager programs.

Deleted files can often be restored. If deleted files are overwritten by new data or if new software is loaded, then only pieces of the file may be recoverable. Partially recovered files should not be ignored. Partial files can help to identify possible motive or intent, passwords, addresses, assets, or other information that may shed valuable light on the investigation.

**Hidden, Encrypted, and Password-Protected Files** Relevant data may be hidden, encrypted, or password protected in attempts to thwart anyone who is trying to retrieve sensitive or incriminating information. Information can be hidden by renaming files to a common name that appears to be part of the operating system, such as files containing the file extension .com or .sys. While on the surface they may appear to be legitimate files, a computer forensics specialist can examine the ***file header*** to reveal the true identity of the file.

Encrypted and password-protected files may require more effort and analysis than files that are hidden in a simple manner. A variety of tools can be used in an attempt to gain access to files protected in this manner. Some tools work by "brute force" attack; other tools work by dissecting the encryption key. A brute force attack can result in quick access to a file. A tool that dissects the encryption key is required with complex encryption, which takes more time. However, use of the tools does not guarantee that the file will be accessed and that the information will be retrieved.

**Automatically Stored Data** Computers store a great deal of data automatically. Many software manufacturers build in automatic backup features that create and periodically save copies of the file while they are being worked on. These files are created and saved to help users recover data lost due to a computer malfunction. Typically, these automatic file copies are not stored in the same directory as the active file, so users don't know of their existence. Additionally, on most networked systems, file copies are saved to the user's hard drive rather than to the network file server. As a result, a document (or some version of it) that was purged from the file server may still exist as a file copy on the user's hard drive.

Other examples of automatically stored data that may be relevant to a case include cache files and history files revealing visited Internet sites, temporary files, swap files, and enhanced metafiles. As with partially recovered files, automatically stored data can provide information valuable to the investigation. Even if the user deleted this data, it may still exist in unallocated space as with deleted files discussed previously.

**E-Mail and Instant Messages** Because of its informal nature, users treat e-mail and IM more like casual conversation and less like formal correspondence. Users also tend to believe that their electronic messages will remain confidential. Not only do e-mail and IM create a more permanent record than most users realize, the computer tracks when the messages were sent and opened in multiple locations.

One e-mail can be saved on numerous servers and be forwarded to a person unknown to the original author. These characteristics make e-mail an excellent potential source of evidence. As with all evidence, the messages must be authenticated.

**Background Information** An electronic trail is left every time a user logs on to the network. Computer logs track network usage, typically containing information about who was logged on and when, where, and how long the user was on the system. Information may also reside about who modified a file last and when the modification was made. Additionally, the computer log may indicate when and by whom files were downloaded to a particular location, copied, printed, or deleted.

Employers in increasing numbers are installing software designed to monitor employees' use of company computers. This software records information such as programs used, files accessed, e-mail sent and received, and Internet sites visited.

You have learned about many locations where e-evidence might be located. Next, you learn about the two basic types of environments where investigations are conducted. Then you learn about tools, toolkits, and equipment used by computer forensics investigators during various stages of the case life-cycle.



### IN PRACTICE: IM Evidence Provides Just Cause for Dismissal

*Smoot v. Comcast Cablevision,* decided by the Delaware Superior Court on November 16, 2004, was a case involving an employment dispute. In the case, the plaintiff had engaged in a four-hour IM conversation with two of her co-workers on her company laptop.

The conversation included numerous sexual references as well as racially derogatory remarks and profanity. The IM transcript served as more than sufficient evidence to find that the company had ***just cause*** for discharging the employee.

---

## Investigative Environments and Analysis Modes

There are two types of environments in which an investigation can take place: trusted environments and untrusted environments. Analysis of the e-evidence is done either in dead mode or live mode.

### Trusted Environments

The integrity of a tool may depend on where it is used. Some tools for examining hardware need to be used in a ***trusted environment*** (or trusted computing environment), typically in a lab. Trusted environments have dedicated systems set up for the sole purpose of conducting computer forensics investigations. In these labs, there is no threat of malicious programs or security risks to the data. The government's trusted environments are the FBI's Regional Computer Forensics Labs. There are also trusted environments owned and operated by commercial companies.

A ***dead analysis*** refers to an examination of a suspect's computer or device performed on a dedicated computer forensics analysis system, or workstation. The term *dead analysis* is used because the suspect computer is not running when the analysis is done in the lab. This type of analysis is also referred to as a ***postmortem analysis*** because the crime or incident has already happened. Only ***nonvolatile data*** can be acquired from a dead analysis. Nonvolatile data is data that still exists after the computer is turned off or the power is removed. Another term for nonvolatile data is ***persistent data.***

### Untrusted Environments

If volatile data must be acquired, a ***live analysis*** is needed. Volatile data is data that will be lost when the power is turned off. A live analysis occurs when the suspect system is analyzed in its own environment while it is running. In cases such as a network intrusion or other crimes in progress, it is vital for a forensic investigator to do a live analysis as quickly as possible. These on-site locations are ***untrusted environments.*** A live analysis would be needed during a hacker attack or other intrusion to confirm the ***compromise*** while it was occurring. A compromise is an intrusion or malicious access of a computer or network.

---

## Forensic Tools and Toolkits

At the outset of a case, investigators may know very little about the types or locations of e-evidence—and not know how that evidence will be used. These are challenging situations. Despite the need for speed or the uncertainty of the case, the safest approach is for investigators to follow standard procedures and use the right tools to ensure the recovery of the maximum amount of admissible e-evidence.

The type of analysis and environment are factors that determine, or limit, the type of tools and equipment that are needed for the analysis. Note that the investigation, as a norm, may require several tools provided by different vendors.

Finding digital data that can be used as evidence to incriminate or clear a suspect accused of a wrongdoing is not easy to do, especially if there is a lot of data and a short amount of time. Tools and equipment are needed. Tools available range from those intended to be used only by properly trained computer forensics specialists to ones that anyone can load on machines and begin working with after only minimal instruction. This section focuses on tools for dead analyses (the computer has been turned off since the incident occurred) that are considered industry standards. Tools for live analyses (before the computer has been turned off) and that require the investigator to type commands are covered in later chapters. For example, the Coroner's Toolkit (TCT) and Sleuth Kit (**www.sleuthkit.org/sleuthkit/**) have a tool called ils that can show files which have been deleted but are still open. The command to see those files is shown below to illustrate why training is necessary to use such a tool.

```
/cdrom/ils -o /dev/hda1 | /cdrom/nc -w 3 10.0.0.1 9000
```



**FYI** *Computer Forensics Tool Testing Programs*

Test results of various imaging and forensics tools are available at the National Institute of Standards and Technology Web site (**www.cftt.nist.gov/disk_imaging.htm**) and the National Institute of Justice Web site (**www.ojp.usdoj.gov/nij/topics/ecrime/cftt.htm**).

Tools support the investigator by helping to

- Recreate a specific chain of events or sequence of user activities, including Internet activity, e-mail communication, and file deletions.
- Search for key words and dates and determine which of the data is relevant.
- Search for copies of previous document drafts.
- Search for potentially privileged information.
- Search for the existence of certain programs, such as file-wiping programs.
- Authenticate data files and their date and time stamps.

As a forensics expert, you cannot rely solely on tools. While the tools are essential to your work, both as a time saver and as a point of accountability, the tools find only what they are programmed to find. For example, on more than one occasion, programs have reported the existence of only one graphics file where there were actually two. Plus, forensics tools do not generally provide support for bypassing password-protected files or detecting the use of steganography. It is recommended that you become familiar with a wide range of tools across multiple platforms.

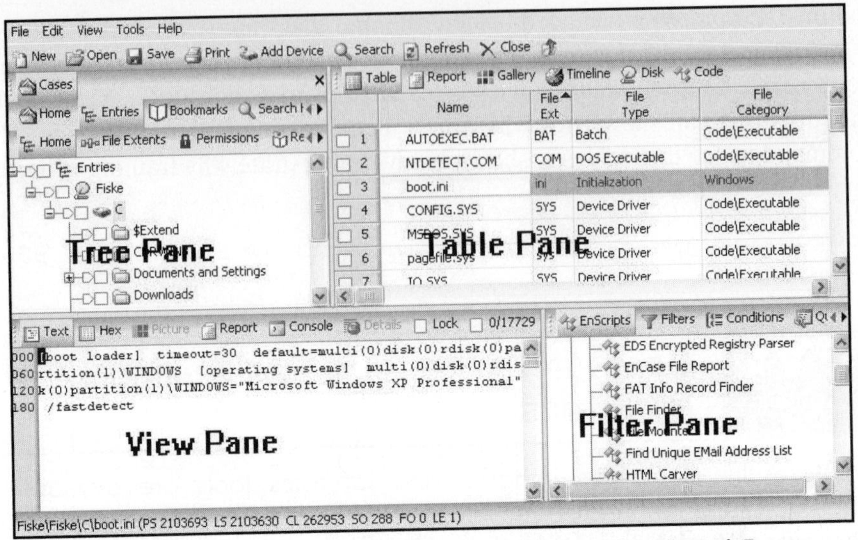


*Source:* Guidance Software, **www.guidancesoftware.com/products/v5_screenshots.asp.**

**FIGURE 3.1** The four panes in the EnCase® software's examiner window.

In the next section, you will first learn about the most widely used tools and then about a variety of specialized tools, such as a tool for PDA forensics.

## EnCase Forensic Version 5

EnCase® Forensic V5 from Guidance Software (**www.guidancesoftware.com**) consists of computer forensics products for the private sector and law enforcement. EnCase software is a tool for gathering and evaluating electronic information and one of the DoD approved tools. The graphical user interface (GUI) of the EnCase software's examiner window is a series of panes, as shown in Figure 3.1, that makes it very easy to use the software.

In addition, EnCase software can be used in e-mail investigations because it supports the file types of the following e-mail systems:

- MSN Hotmail®
- Microsoft Outlook and Outlook Express
- Yahoo!®
- AOL® 6, 7, 8, and 9
- Netscape®
- mBox (Unix)

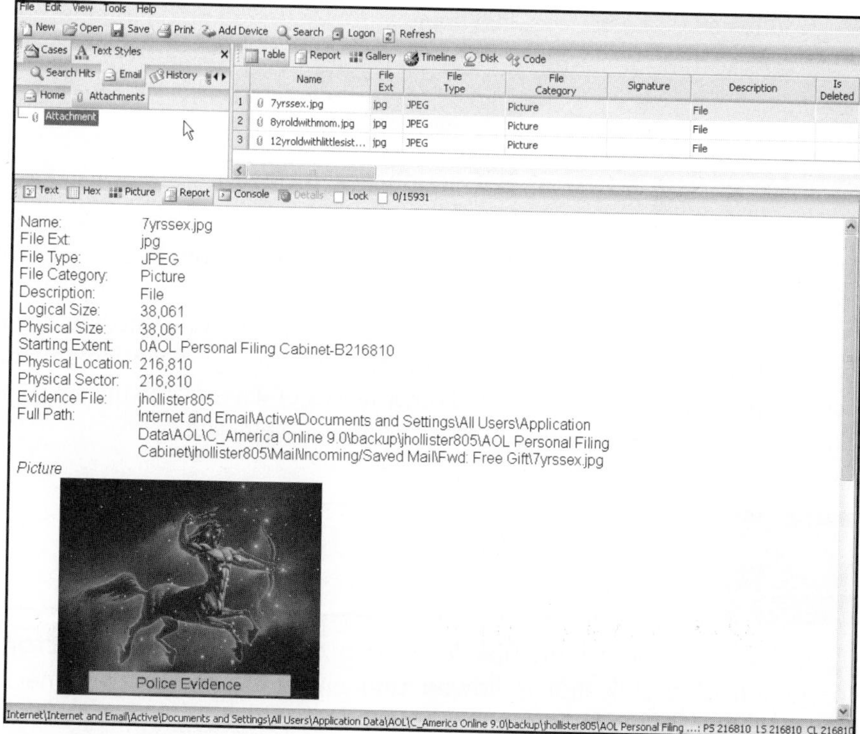


**FIGURE 3.2** Example of e-mail data acquired by EnCase V5 software, including a view of an attached file and its location.

Figure 3.2 shows information revealed with EnCase V5 software, including e-mail attachments.

**EnCase Software Installation Steps** The basic steps involved in operating the EnCase software are:

1. Load the software onto the computer that will be used to collect and examine the e-evidence, which will be referred to as the "examining machine."
2. Slide the USB ***security key*** (also called a ***dongle***) provided by Guidance into a USB slot, attach the appropriate cables, and you are ready to start. Security keys for accessing data through parallel ports also are available. A security key is shown in Figure 3.3.
3. Connect the examining machine to the target device and select the medium you want to investigate, such as a hard drive, USB drive, CD, or floppy disk.
4. Following a preestablished procedure, create an exact duplicate, bit-by-bit image of the medium.
5. The software creates hash values that can be used for chain-of-custody or verification purposes.

**FIGURE 3.3** Security key (dongle).

**Preview Mode** EnCase software can be used in preview mode to take a look at the contents of the medium before making a copy. In preview mode, you can browse through the contents as you would browse through the medium using Windows Explorer. Preview mode is important because you can look at free space, swap space, file fragments, and other pieces of data, search the data, and open files without risk of changing the files or their metadata.

### *Potential Hash Differences from the Same Hard Drive*

It's not unusual for a hard disk to have a damaged or ***bad sector*** (a portion of a disk that is flawed and unusable). If two examiners acquire the same hard drive with different tools and those tools treat bad sectors in a different way, their MD5 hashes will be different. Because the hashes were not identical, someone could conclude that the data on the drive had been altered, when the difference was really due to the way each tool handles bad sectors. This situation reinforces why examiners need to document their acquisition process in detail in case their evidence is challenged on the witness stand.

**Case Management** After the medium (drive) has been copied, that copy can be added to the case. A single case may require copies of multiple hard drives, floppy disks, and whatever other media have been duplicated.

Several investigation tools are available for filtering, key word searches, making hash analyses, and looking at file signatures. Because the software logs the activities, steps taken throughout the case life-cycle can be retraced. EnCase software does not index the files before searching them, so be prepared for the possibility that some queries will take a substantial amount of time.

## EnCase Cybercrime Arsenal

The EnCase Cybercrime Arsenal software bundle (**www.cybercrimearsenal.com/**) was designed with law enforcement in mind. The customizable package of software, hardware, and training make it possible for agencies to rapidly acquire all the resources they need to conduct computer forensics investigations in-house.

"With the explosion of crimes leaving trails of digital evidence, there is a growing need to increase the forensic capabilities at law enforcement agencies around the nation," said Sergeant Darin Meadows of the Houston County, Georgia, Sheriff's Office. "Whether the crime involves drugs, violence, fraud, child pornography or even acts of terrorism, following the electronic trail is a critical component of putting the pieces of the puzzle together" (source of Sergeant Meadows' remarks: **www.guidancesoftware.com/corporate/press/20050728.asp**).

The software bundle is available in three packaged solutions, including Arsenal Forensic Edition, Arsenal FIM (Field Intelligence Model), and Arsenal FIM with Snapshot, a unique feature that allows capture of volatile data running in computer memory.

3

The EnCase application offers four views of the collected data.

- Table view displays files in a spreadsheet-style format.
- Gallery view provides a view of all images—JPGs, GIFs, TIFs, and so on—in an evidence file.
- Timeline view provides a calendar-style picture of file activity.
- Report view helps create tailored reports.

Like most tools, EnCase software requires training. Guidance offers extensive training on the correct use of its tools.

## Forensic Toolkit and Ultimate Toolkit

Forensic Toolkit® (FTK)™ from AccessData (**www.accessdata.com**) is designed for finding and examining computer evidence. FTK version 1.61 was released in December 2005 and is the version discussed in this section. FTK has full-text indexing, deleted file recovery, and data-carving. It contains tools for searching, filtering, and analyzing e-mail and zipped files. FTK includes FTK Imager, the Hash Library-KFF, and Registry Viewer. FTK can be used to acquire images; to read images acquired using other systems, such as the EnCase system and to view numerous file formats. It includes the tool dtSearch for full-text indexing and searching.

Ultimate Toolkit™ (UTK) is primarily for computer crime investigators. It contains all AccessData's recovery modules, which are the FTK, Password Recovery Toolkit, Registry Viewer, 100-client Distributed Network Attack, WipeDrive Professional, Microsoft NT Utility, and Novell Utility. UTK contains components for recovering lost or forgotten passwords, analyzing and decrypting registry data, and wiping hard drives. A dongle is required to use the product.

Like Guidance, AccessData offers training for its products and demo versions that can be downloaded from the company's Web site.

## WinHex

WinHex (**www.x-ways.net/winhex/index-m.html**) is a universal hexadecimal editor, used for computer forensics, data recovery, low-level data processing, and

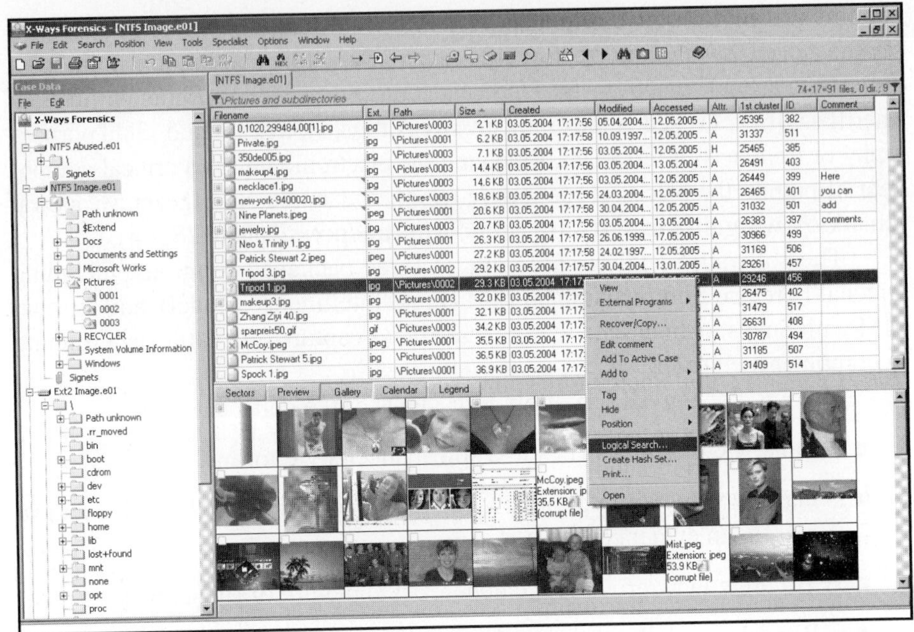


Source: **www.x-ways.net/winhex/screenshot.html.**

**FIGURE 3.4** WinHex screenshot listing the contents of the suspect computer.

IT security. It is an advanced tool used to inspect and edit all types of files. It can recover deleted files or lost data from hard drives with corrupt file systems, or from digital camera cards. WinHex capabilities include drive imaging, file analysis, and forensic disk cleaning. Figure 3.4 is a screenshot from WinHex showing the DiskTools available to clone a disk or do a file recovery by filename or type. WinHex can be used to inspect and edit all kinds of files, recover deleted files, or retrieve lost data from hard drives with corrupt file systems.

## Autopsy, Sleuth Kit, and dtSearch

For those who prefer Linux, there are several products available such as the Autopsy Forensic Browser (**www.sleuthkit.org/autopsy**). It is a graphical interface to the command-line analysis tools in the Sleuth Kit. With these tools, you can investigate the file system and volumes of a computer. These tools can also be used to analyze Windows and UNIX disks and file systems.

The Sleuth Kit and Autopsy are both open source and run on UNIX platforms. Autopsy is HTML-based so it can be connected to the Autopsy server from any platform using an HTML browser. Autopsy provides a file manager–like interface and shows details about deleted data and file system structures.

For combing through large amounts of data, dtSearch leads the market with support for over 250 file types. Huge collections of files can be searched quickly once a document index has been created. An index is a database that stores the location of every word in a collection of documents, and each word's corresponding location throughout. Results are listed and highlighted with their exact locations. Results also can be exported to a format recognized by Microsoft Excel for reporting.

## Macintosh Forensic Software: BlackBag and MacQuisition

BlackBag (**www.blackbagtech.com/**) is a set of 19 tools that provide forensic examiners with a flexible, open environment within which to perform their analyses. The suite works within Mac Classic environments 8.1–9.2 and OS X. The applications are designed to efficiently carve and copy the most pertinent sectors of a target hard drive. Three of the applications contained within the suite are:

- **Directory Scan:** Creates a directory listing of a volume or specific folder (see Figure 3.5). This scan retrieves all active file information (including invisible files) from a mounted volume.
- **FileSpy:** Obtains a quick preview of any file by displaying the ASCII text for that file (Figure 3.6). A user can move the file sector by sector, jump to the start or end of a sector, or jump to any specific sector within the file.

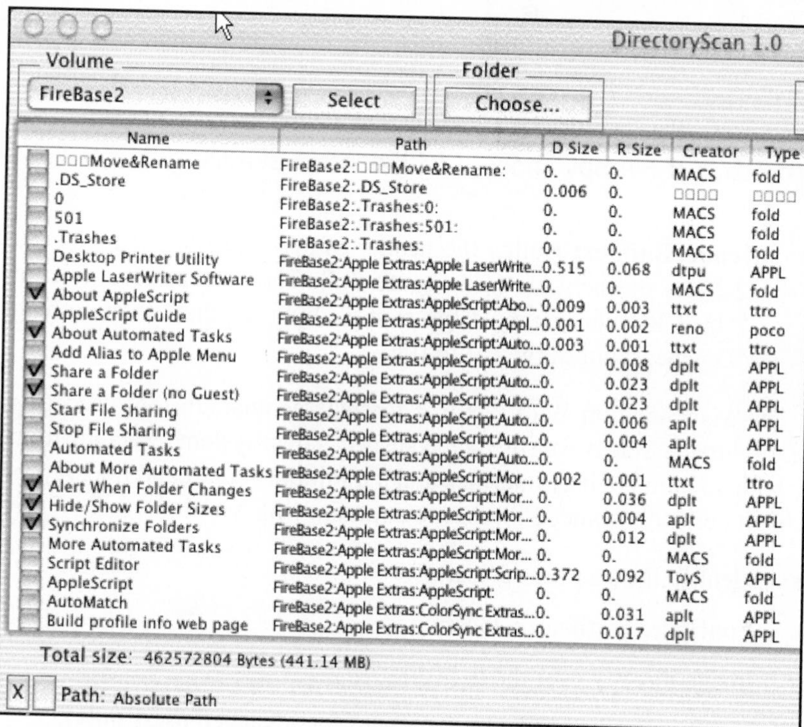


*Source:* **www.blackbagtech.com/software_mfs.html.**

**FIGURE 3.5** Screenshot of Directory Scan 1.0, which enables you to create a directory listing of a volume or specific folder.

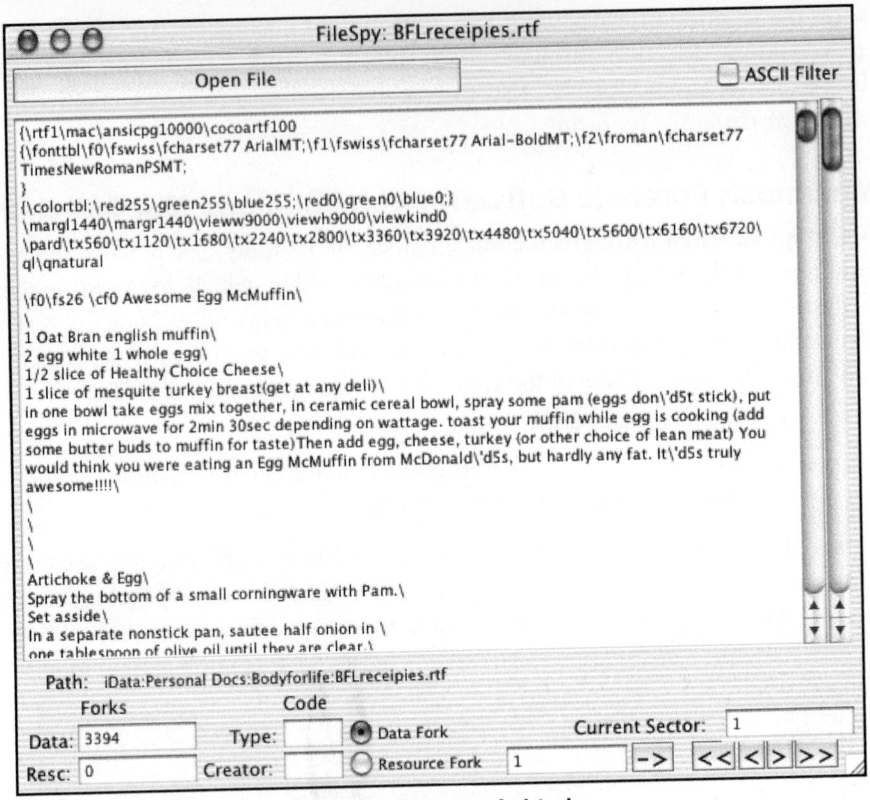

*Source:* **www.blackbagtech.com/software_mfs.html.**

**FIGURE 3.6** FileSpy shows ASCII content of a file.

- **HeaderBuilder:** Builds the header of specific files. It reads the first 32 bytes of each file (see Figure 3.7). The header CRC calculates a 32-bit CRC checksum of the first 32 bytes of the file and creates an MD5 checksum of the entire file.

The MacQuisition Boot CD is a forensic acquisition tool used to safely and easily image Mac drives using the suspect's own system. MacQuisition provides both an intuitive user interface and a traditional command line. It provides both beginner and advanced forensic examiners with a tool to

- Identify the suspect device(s).
- Configure destination location.
- Image directly over the network.
- Use the command line (recommend for advanced users only).
- Log case, exhibit, and evidence tracking numbers and notes.
- Generate MD5 hashes automatically.

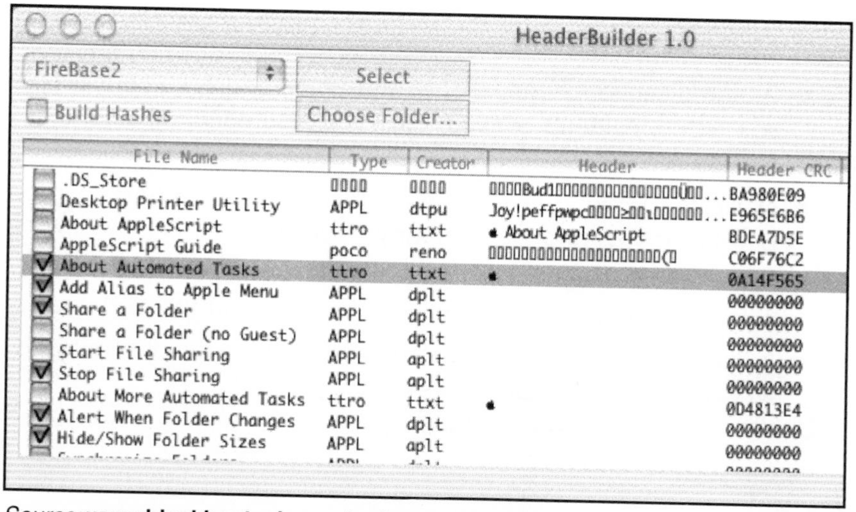

HeaderBuilder 1.0

FireBase2 | Select

Build Hashes | Choose Folder...

| | File Name | Type | Creator | Header | Header CRC |
|---|---|---|---|---|---|
| | .DS_Store | 0000 | 0000 | 0000Bud100000000000000000... | BA980E09 |
| | Desktop Printer Utility | APPL | dtpu | Joy!peffpwpc0000≥00ı000000... | E965E6B6 |
| | About AppleScript | ttro | ttxt | About AppleScript | BDEA7D5E |
| | AppleScript Guide | poco | reno | 0000000000000000000000(0 | C06F76C2 |
| ✓ | About Automated Tasks | ttro | ttxt | | 0A14F565 |
| ✓ | Add Alias to Apple Menu | APPL | dplt | | 00000000 |
| ✓ | Share a Folder | APPL | dplt | | 00000000 |
| | Share a Folder (no Guest) | APPL | dplt | | 00000000 |
| | Start File Sharing | APPL | aplt | | 00000000 |
| ✓ | Stop File Sharing | APPL | aplt | | 00000000 |
| | About More Automated Tasks | ttro | ttxt | | 0D4813E4 |
| ✓ | Alert When Folder Changes | APPL | dplt | | 00000000 |
| ✓ | Hide/Show Folder Sizes | APPL | aplt | | 00000000 |

*Source:* **www.blackbagtech.com/software_mfs.html.**

**FIGURE 3.7** HeaderBuilder 1.0 displays headers of selected files.

## IN PRACTICE: Do Nothing Without Competence

Too often, the reason for failing to secure a prosecution stems from inexperienced people getting to the scene of the crime first and inadvertently compromising evidence by not following correct procedures. A common error is rebooting computers before an image file has been taken. Rebooting changes the dates recorded on the machine showing when systems or files were last accessed.

One problem is that many companies do not have proper incident response teams (IRT) and procedures in place. When something goes wrong, staff may perform some tasks out of panic because they do not know to whom to report incidents or even what to report.

Responding to incidents requires critical thinking and tough decisions. One decision is whether or not to shut down systems when an attack is suspected. Shutting down a system could destroy valuable evidence relating to the processes running at the time. It might also alert the attacker. The cost of downtime must be considered.

Companies should develop policies that guide decisions about reporting incidents and shutting down PCs and networks. To avoid compromising e-evidence, companies should prepare by doing the following:

- Make sure the chain of command is clear and members of the IRT include the information security, legal, and human resources departments.

CONTINUED ON NEXT PAGE

▸▸ CONTINUED

- Assign a central phone number and e-mail address where people can report incidents or suspicions. Make sure that all calls to this number are logged, followed up, and any patterns identified.
- Make the IRT and contact information visible by posting it on bulletin boards and the company intranet.
- Arrange for a computer forensics investigation team, either external or internal, to be on call for when an incident occurs.
- Include incident response procedures in training for all employees, including all contractors.

### PDA Seizure

PDA Seizure, from Paraben Forensics (**www.paraben-forensics.com**), is a comprehensive forensic tool for investigating the contents of Palm, Pocket PCs that run on Windows CE (or WinCE, an operating system for handheld devices), and BlackBerry devices. Use this tool to acquire, view, and report on PDA data, including Palm data that has been backed up and stored on a PC.

PDA Seizure's features include the ability to produce a forensic image of Palm and Pocket PC devices, to perform examiner-defined searches on data contained within acquired files, and to generate a report of the findings. PDA Seizure also provides bookmarking capabilities to organize information, along with a graphics library that automatically assembles found images under a single facility, based on the graphics file extension of acquired files.

PDA Seizure can crack passwords for the Palm OS prior to version 4.0. Due to a weak, reversible password-encoding scheme, it is possible to obtain an encoded form of the password, determine the actual password, and access a user's private data.

Because PDAs store all data in memory, slight changes to data occur in the acquisition process. However, the changes that occur are so minor that they do not affect the integrity of the data.

When the acquisition is complete, the program shows a summary of the acquired files as shown in Figure 3.8.

**Caution**

**PDA Data Affected by Battery Life**

PDAs use memory, not hard drives, to store user data. If a PDA loses power, such as when its battery dies, all data will be lost.

## Forensics Equipment

The type of investigation and data to be analyzed in the computer forensics lab determines hardware requirements. In addition to workstations and software, all labs should have a wide assortment of power cables, USB 2.0 and FireWire cables,

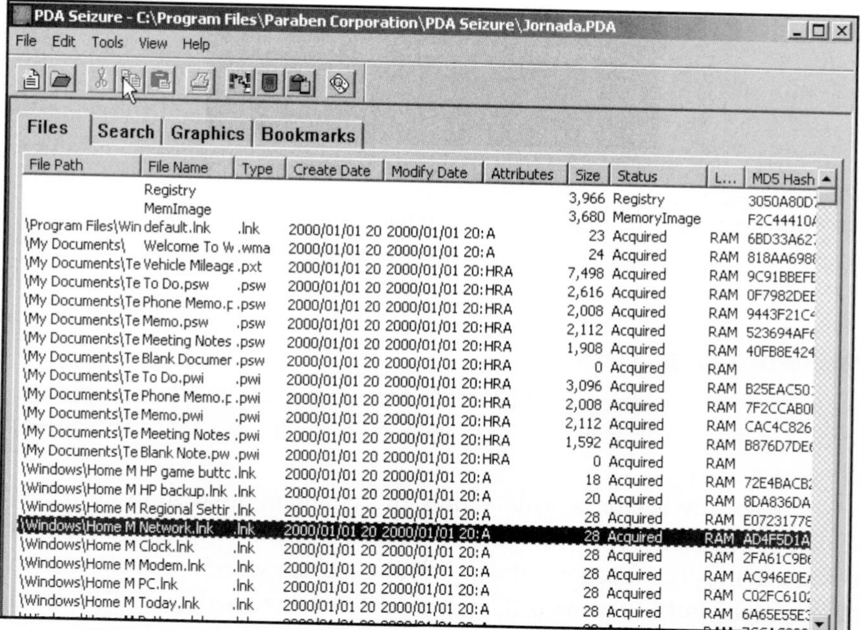

*Source:* Paraben's PDA Seizure Software, Paraben Corporation, **www.paraben-forensics.com/.**

**FIGURE 3.8** PDA Seizure displays a summary of acquired files.

power supplies, electrostatic mats on which to place hard disks, and spare expansion slot cards.

Since acquired e-evidence is generally copied to hard disks as part of the imaging process, hard disks are necessary equipment. E-evidence files should be archived to DVDs as the next step. The archive should be made immediately after acquisition because a hard disk could fail. At the conclusion of the case, the hard disk can be forensically wiped and reused. The DVDs need to be stored securely.

Disaster recovery plans should be in place. A disaster recovery plan specifies how to rebuild an investigation workstation after it has been severely contaminated by a virus.

Software requirements include all operating systems on the market.

- Microsoft operating systems Windows XP, 2000, NT 4.0, NT 3.5, 98, 3.11, and DOS 6.22.
- Apple Macintosh operating systems OS X 10.x, Tiger, and older.
- Linux operating systems, including Fedora, Caldera Open Linux, Slackware, and Debian.

Although most high-end computer forensics tools can open or display data files created with popular programs, they do not support all software

**Caution**

**Valid Software Licenses**

Investigators need to have a valid software license for each copy of software they use. Any "borrowed" copy is considered piracy and, if discovered, damages the evidence and the expert's credibility.

programs. So the software inventory should include Microsoft Office products (Office XP, 2003, 2000, 97, and 95 versions); Intuit's Quicken; programming languages such as Visual Basic and Visual C++; specialized viewers such as Quick View, ACDSee, ThumbsPlus, and IrfanView; the Corel Office Suite, and StarOffice/OpenOffice; and Peachtree's accounting software.

Table 3.2 lists some popular forensics software and hardware equipment. Each type of equipment is discussed further following the table.

## Password Crackers

Password-cracking tools might be needed to recover files with encrypted passwords. Graphical password crackers such as Passware and John the Ripper are easy to use.

Passware works on a wide variety of commonly used software products, including Microsoft Office files, mail files, and QuickBooks files. It is graphical and easy to use. The functions of this software include several different password-cracking techniques all combined into one tool. It is designed to handle more than one application at a time.

**TABLE 3.2** Forensics equipment and Web sites.

| Type | Tool or Toolkit | Free Demo | Web Site |
|---|---|---|---|
| Password cracker | Passware Kit and Passware Kit Enterprise | Yes | **www.lostpassword.com/kit.htm** |
| Password cracker | John the Ripper | Yes | **www.openwall.com/john** |
| Portable hard disk duplicator | Disk Jockey | | **www.diskology.com** |
| Portable hard drive and media duplicator | Logicube | | **www.logicube.com/** |
| Forensic intrusion detection, and scanning tools | Foundstone | Yes | **www.foundstone.com/resources/forensics.htm** |

John the Ripper is a fast password cracker, currently available for many versions of UNIX (11 are officially supported), DOS, Win32, BeOS, and OpenVMS. Its primary purpose is to detect weak UNIX passwords.

## Portable Hard Disk Duplicators

Disk Jockey is a portable hard disk duplicator. The tool includes a write-blocking feature essential for computer forensic examinations. Disk Jockey is available as part of a forensic kit that also includes a serial-ATA (SATA) adapter and longer cables (ranging from 2.5 inches to 12 inches) for connecting to hard-to-reach drives mounted inside a computer.

Disk Jockey is considered a Swiss-Army-Knife type of product because of its versatility. It can be used on a Microsoft Windows or Apple Macintosh computer connected via the high-speed FireWire or USB 2.0 ports or as a stand-alone device. It can be used to mirror, span, copy, compare, and test hard disk drives.

Logicube is a leader in hard drive duplication, backup, data recovery, and computer forensics systems. Logicube's products are used in many Fortune 500 companies and by most government and law enforcement agencies. Their hard drive duplicators offer hardware solutions for copying hard drives, data recovery, and disaster recovery.

Foundstone, a division of McAfee, offers numerous free forensic tools on its Web site. One example is the Forensic ToolKit (FTK), which contains several Windows command-line tools for examining the files on a disk for unauthorized activity.

### IN PRACTICE: Forensic Sterilization Required

Clearing your donated, sold, or discarded hard drives of sensitive information isn't just good practice. It's now also required by law. Effective June 1, 2005, the Federal Trade Commission's Disposal Rule (16 CFR Part 682) requires businesses, including medical offices and law firms, to take reasonable measures to dispose of sensitive information derived from credit reports and background checks so that the information cannot practicably be read or reconstructed.

The FTC rule, which applies to both paper and digital media, requires implementing and monitoring compliance with disposal policies and procedures for this information. Comments to the rule suggest using disk-wiping utilities but also suggest that electronic media may be economically disposed of by "simply smashing the material with a hammer."

**FYI** *E-Evidence in All Shapes and Sizes*

When U.S. government agencies investigating a crime or a cybercrime have digital evidence that's too difficult to analyze, they send it to the DoD computer forensics lab. E-evidence comes in all shapes and sizes: pallets full of computers, a hard drive with an AK-47 bullet hole in it, audio tapes fished out of the ocean, mangled floppies, and garbled 911 calls, among other examples.

## Certification and Training Programs

Computer crime represents one of the fastest growing crime rates, and the need for computer forensics is growing. If you are interested in becoming a cybercrime investigator, you may want to consider becoming certified in one or more areas. Computer forensics certifications range in topic from computer crimes against children to file system recovery.

Some manufacturers offer certification and training programs for proficiency in the use of their forensic products, even though no single tool can provide the solution to every situation. Some of the most useful certifications and training programs are listed below.

**IN PRACTICE:** CompTIA A+ Training and Certification

Requiring that an established IT professional pursue A+ training and certification will be a tough sell, since this is a basic IT certification. However, it is a requirement for examiners at the FBI's Regional Computer Forensics Labs, and it ensures that the forensics examiner has a good understanding of hardware.

- **EnCE®:** EnCE (EnCase Certified Examiner) certification is offered by Guidance Software. The certification requires 18 months of investigative experience, extensive classroom training, and successful completion of computer-based and practical tests.
- **Global Information Assurance Certification (GIAC) Certified Forensics Analyst:** GIAC certified forensics analysts (GCFAs) handle and investigate incidents. GCFAs have the knowledge, skills, and abilities to conduct incident investigations and carry out forensic investigation

of networks and hosts. GIAC was founded by the SANS Institute (**www.sans.org**), which offers the training and certification. See **www.giac.org/certifications/security/gcfa.php.**

- **Computer Hacking Forensic Investigator (CHFI):** A CHFI has the skills necessary to identify an intruder's footprints and gather evidence necessary to prosecute in a court of law. See **www.securityuniversity.net/classes_CHFI.php.**
- **Computer Forensic External Certification (CCE):** Designed for law enforcement by the International Association of Computer Investigative Specialists (IACIS) to certify forensic examiners in the recovery of evidence from computer systems. See **www.iacis.info/iacisv2/pages/ training.php.**
- **TruSecure ICSA Certified Security Associate:** This is a security certification that includes essential forensics procedures.
- **Computer Forensic Training Center Online:** This is an online training and CCE certification offered through Kennesaw State University.
- **Certified International Information Systems Forensics Investigator (CIFI):** The International Information Systems Forensics Association (IISFA) is a nonprofit organization that provides information forensics education for the certified international information systems forensics investigator (CIFI).

## Summary

You have learned that the quality of e-evidence depends on skilled investigators following standard procedures and using trusted technology throughout the lifecycle of a case or investigation. Maintaining the integrity of e-evidence requires a defensible approach to data handling and preservation. There can be no weak links in the investigative process. With widespread use of computers to plan, facilitate, or carry out violent and nonviolent crimes, it is vital for a forensics investigator to be able to extract and analyze data quickly and present the evidence in an understandable format.

Frequently, investigators have to defend their findings, processing methods, tools, and techniques against challenges raised by the opposing side. Therefore, e-evidence processing must be done correctly and documented thoroughly or else any resulting court case may be thrown out. A key principle is that the technologies and methodologies used must be well documented and repeatable.

Documentation, collection, authentication, analysis, preservation, and production and reporting of the findings require the use of specialized software and hardware tools and equipment. Because of the complexity of many of the tools, training in their use and certification is necessary. There are also general training and certifications available for computer forensics investigators.

## Test Your Skills

### MULTIPLE CHOICE QUESTIONS

1. Characteristics of a defensible approach include all of the following *except:*
   A. It is performed in accordance with forensics science principles.
   B. It includes opinions and assumptions of the investigator.
   C. It is documented completely.
   D. It is conducted by individuals who are certified in the use of verified tools, if such certification exits.

2. The successful outcome of an investigation of a computer crime depends on
   A. preserving the evidence.
   B. documenting some steps in the processing of the evidence.
   C. interviewing all of the suspect(s).
   D. reporting the findings in technical terms.

3. Preserving the chain of custody for e-evidence requires proving all of the following *except* that
   A. a complete copy was made and verified.
   B. a reliable copying process was used.
   C. photographs were taken before removing computers or other devices.
   D. all media were secured.

4. A nuker is a tool used by criminals to
   A. intercept network traffic.
   B. destroy system log trails.
   C. create undocumented backdoors into networks.
   D. impersonate someone else to hide their real identities.

5. _________ is the science of hiding messages in messages.
   A. Scanning
   B. Steganography
   C. Spoofing
   D. Encryption

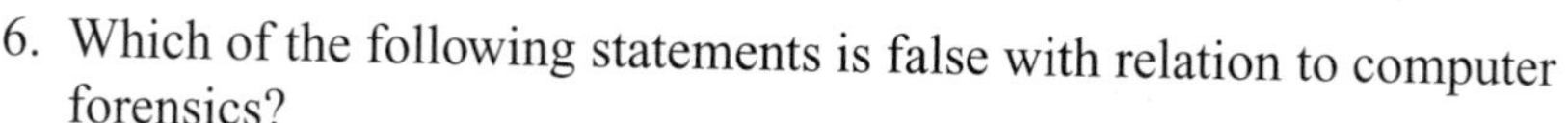

6. Which of the following statements is false with relation to computer forensics?
   A. The value of the evidence depends on the way it is presented and defended in court.
   B. Each activity relating to the seizure, access, storage, or transfer of e-evidence must be fully documented, preserved, and available for review.
   C. The suspect needs to be interviewed and evaluated fairly and impartially.
   D. All of the above statements are true.



7. Which of the following statements about documentation is true?
   A. Checklists and forms are important because they help keep documentation organized.
   B. Documentation must include opinions of the investigators.
   C. Only written reports are usable as documentation.
   D. The responsibility for documentation must be assigned to only one person.

8. When an investigator encounters a computer that is running, the investigator should
   A. not use the operating system to power down the computer until the screens and area have been photographed.
   B. immediately use the operating system to power down the computer to preserve the status of the machine.
   C. not use the operating system to power down the computer until a copy of the hard drive has been made.
   D. not use the operating system to power down the computer because the operating system might delete temporary files and change some of the date/time stamps.

9. __________ devices prevent altering data on drives attached to the suspect computer and also offer very fast acquisition speeds.
   A. Encryption
   B. Imaging
   C. Write blocking
   D. Hashing

10. Drive imaging is a means of
    A. evidence preservation.
    B. evidence verification.
    C. evidence presentation.
    D. evidence analysis.
11. It is important to understand the significance of file slack because
    A. it may contain useful information such as network logon names, passwords, and other sensitive information associated with computer usage.
    B. it may be analyzed to identify prior uses of the computer.
    C. it may contain fragments of prior documents or e-mail messages.
    D. all of the above.
12. Which duplication method produces an exact replica of the original drive?
    B. Image copy.
    B. Mirror copy.
    C. Bit-stream copy.
    D. Drive image.
13. What is residual data?
    A. Data that has been created automatically when a file is saved.
    B. Data found in allocated file space.
    C. Data that has been erased.
    D. Data that has been deleted, but not erased.
14. When a forensic copy is made, in what format are the contents of the hard drive stored?
    A. As compressed images.
    B. As bootable files.
    C. As executable files.
    D. As operating system files.
15. Before creating an image of a suspect's drive to an acquisition drive, that acquisition drive must be
    A. formatted to remove all prior data.
    B. forensically wiped clean.
    C. erased of all data.
    D. any of the above.

16. Which of the following statements about hashes is false?
    A. A hash is a file's "fingerprint."
    B. No two hash values can be the same unless the files are identical.
    C. Hashes are used to verify the preservation of the copy.
    D. Hashes are used to verify or validate the integrity of the copy.

17. __________ can be valuable when attempting to filter out irrelevant data.
    A. Algorithms
    B. Password crackers
    C. Metadata
    D. Hashes



18. Information that is readily available and accessible is called:
    A. active data.
    B. live data.
    C. metadata.
    D. header data.

19. Which of the following statements is false?
    A. Dead analysis refers to an examination that is done on a dedicated computer forensics workstation.
    B. Live analysis is an examination done on volatile data on a computer that has not yet been turned off.
    C. Computer forensics labs are trusted environments.
    D. All of the above are true.

20. Which of the following statements is true?
    A. EnCase software, Forensic Toolkit, WinHex, and BlackBag are forensics toolkits that can be used without any training.
    B. PDA forensics can only be performed on a PDA after its battery has died or been removed.
    C. Equipment needed by labs includes a variety of power cables, power supplies, electrostatic mats, and expansion slot cards.
    D. A limitation of portable hard disk duplicators is their lack of write-blocking features, which are essential for computer forensics exams.

## EXERCISES

### Exercise 3.1: Maintaining the Integrity of E-Evidence

Maintaining the integrity of e-evidence requires a defensible approach to the handling and preservation of the data from the outset of the investigation.

1. Make a list of four data-handling or data-preservation procedures that are important to a defensible approach. State whether each procedure applies to data handling, data preservation, or both.
2. Explain potential risks to the outcome of the case if these required procedures are not followed.

### Exercise 3.2: Tools or Techniques for Hiding Evidence of a Crime

A criminal can use readily downloadable tools and techniques to try to hide the crime or disguise his identity.

1. Make a list of three tools or techniques that can be used to hide or disguise evidence of a crime. Search an online computer technology dictionary, such as Wikipedia **(en.wikipedia.org)**, Webopedia **(www.webopedia.com)**, or Techdictionary **(www.techdictionary.com)** for detailed descriptions of how these tools work.
2. Explain how each of these tools or techniques can make it more difficult for an investigator to recover admissible e-evidence.

### Exercise 3.3: Documenting the Seizure of E-Evidence

Assume that you are a member of an investigation team who will be going to a location where you expect to find computers connected to the Internet and other media for storing digital files. It is your responsibility to document the computer and media before they are removed and transported to a forensics lab.

1. Identify the types of equipment that would produce high-quality or reliable documentation.
2. Prepare a checklist of items that should be documented.

### Exercise 3.4: Forensics Tools and Credentials

When a computer is identified as possibly containing electronic evidence, it is imperative to follow a strict set of procedures to ensure admissible seizure of evidence. The first thing to remember is the "golden rule of electronic evidence"—never, in any way, modify the original media, if at all possible.

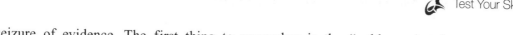

1. Identify three widely-used software tools from three different vendors that can be used during the acquisition, authentication, or analysis of the data. Explain the purpose of each tool and the operating system it works on.
2. Identify the credentials or training needed to properly use each software tool. If no training is needed, explain why.



### Exercise 3.5: National Institute of Justice Tool Testing Program

1. Visit the National Institute of Justice (NIJ) Web site that reports the test results of various imaging tools at **www.ojp.usdoj.gov/nij/topics/ecrime/cftt.htm.**
2. Create a chart that lists the NIJ's top-level requirements for hard-disk-imaging tools and hard-disk-write-block tools.

## PROJECTS

### Project 3.1: Documenting and Acquiring Evidence from Employees

Consider cases of employee misconduct that may call for computer forensics work. The offense may be improper use of the company's e-mail or Internet access for online gambling, or illegal theft of confidential customer, product, or marketing information.

1. You have been tasked with developing a checklist of the devices that are to be acquired or collected if such an investigation were conducted, and to outline how to document the scene, procedures, personnel, and potential e-evidence. Write a draft of a checklist.
2. You have also been tasked with developing a plan for documenting the scene, procedures, personnel, and potential e-evidence. Write a draft of a documentation plan.
3. List the locations that should be searched for devices that could contain e-evidence.

## Project 3.2: Handheld Device Forensics Tools

You have been tasked with developing a list of forensics tools for handhelds. Search the Internet for forensics tools for handheld devices, such as cell phones, smart phones, PDAs, or BlackBerrys.

1. Select four specific tools designed to collect evidence from any of these devices.
2. Explain the characteristics, capabilities, and requirements for each tool.
3. List the steps that would show that the chain of custody was preserved.

## Project 3.3: Using a Password Cracker

Try your hand at using a password cracker by following these instructions:

1. From the Companion Website at **www.prenhall.com/security,** download the file **03_pass.xls** to a known location on your hard drive. The file is password protected.
2. Go to the Passware Kit for Excel Web site at **www.lostpassword.com/excel.htm** and download the Excel key (**xlkeyd.exe**) to a known location on your hard drive. (You can also go to this site using the link on the Companion Website.)
3. Double-click the **xlkeyd.exe** icon to install the demo program, Excel Key Demo; and then launch the program. (Note: This demo version is limited to recovering passwords no longer than two characters.)
4. In the Excel Key window, click the **Settings** button on the toolbar. The Settings window opens.
5. Click the Dictionary tab and change the "Run for passwords from" setting to **2** to **4.**
6. Click the Xieve optimization and Brute-force tabs and make the same change to set password length to **2** to **4.** Then click **OK** to close the Settings window.
7. In the Excel Key window, click the **Recover** button on the toolbar. In the Select file to recover window, navigate to the location where you stored the **03_pass.xls** file. Select the file and click **Open.**
8. After the password has been recovered, list the password for the file and the type of attack that cracked the password.
9. Close the Excel Key window.

3

## Case Study

Several recent cases have included e-evidence. Three examples are:

- Juju Jiang was sentenced to 27 months in prison after being convicted for installing keystroke loggers on computers at Kinko's throughout Manhattan. He illegally collected confidential information that gave him access to individuals' confidential bank account data. (February 2005)
- Allan Eric Carlson was convicted of 79 counts of computer and identity fraud and sentenced to 48 months in jail. Because he was unhappy with the poor performance of the Philadelphia Phillies, he sent spoofed e-mails complaining about the team. His spoofed e-mails indicated that they were from newspaper writers at Fox Sports, ESPN, and other media outlets. (July 2005)
- Scott Levine was found guilty of 120 counts of unauthorized access of a protected computer, two counts of access device fraud, and one count of obstruction of justice. He and several co-workers at Snipermail, an e-mail distributor, stole more than a billion records containing personal data from Acxiom, a business partner firm. (August 2005)

*Source:* Adapted from Harris, Shon, "To Catch a Thief." *Information Security.* December, 2005.

1. In each of these situations, consider the potential types and locations where e-evidence might have been left by these computer crimes. Create a list of those potential types and locations.
2. How might the criminals have attempted to cover up the trails of e-evidence of their crimes?
3. Draft a plan for finding and collecting the e-evidence of each crime.

# Chapter 4

# Policies and Procedures

## Chapter Objectives

**After reading this chapter and completing the exercises, you will be able to do the following:**

- Explain the reasons for policies and procedures.
- Formulate policies and procedures.
- Identify the steps in a forensic examination.
- Conduct an investigation.
- Report the results of an investigation.

## Introduction

Computer forensics is such a new field that legal and even academic models for computer forensics science are in a constant state of revision. Furthermore, with the ever-expanding role of e-evidence in civil, criminal, and employment cases, it is not possible to specify guidelines for each type of case. However, it is possible to specify comprehensive policies and procedures that, if followed, will produce admissible e-evidence. It is necessary for computer forensics organizations and investigative agencies (which will be referred to as organizations) to have comprehensive policies and procedures. But, if investigators are unaware of them, they are of little value.

In this chapter, you are introduced to best practices and generally accepted guidelines and procedures used by computer forensics practitioners. These guidelines and procedures need to be customized to meet the requirements of each case and may require that the investigator "think outside of the box." In all cases, you must document every aspect of the case to the fullest extent. You will learn that there is no such thing as overdocumenting a computer forensics case.

# Reasons for Policies and Procedures

From a management perspective, policies and procedures are valuable because they simplify operations by providing established rules and methodology. From practical and legal perspectives, forensic investigators establish generally accepted policies and procedures to ensure that:

- A baseline or benchmark is set for all cases as needed for external audits or other reference.
- Processes throughout the case lifecycle from *first contact to release of evidence* are understood.
- Technical procedures are well-documented.
- Integrity is automatically built into the handling of the case.
- Different forensic investigators can work or collaborate on the same case without significant disruption.
- The final report has a standard format.



## Personnel Hiring Issues

When creating policies and procedures, you are basically setting up the rules and regulations for how your computer forensics investigation department is going to work. One of the first and most important considerations for a computer forensics unit is personnel issues. From a policy standpoint, it is necessary to establish a set of basic qualifications the members of the unit must have. The importance of qualifications dealing with education, training, and experience are obvious. Equally important, but less evident, is having members who have certifications, integrity, team-player attitudes, and inquisitive personalities.

Fundamental personnel questions for selecting members of a forensic unit include:

- **Experience:** Does this person have experience in computer forensics? Does he have law enforcement or security experience?
- **Education:** Does this person have a formal college education? Does she have computer forensics training?
- **Certifications:** Does this person have any certifications in computer forensics tools or techniques; networking; or information security? Are the certifications valid?
- **Integrity:** Does this person have the integrity and judgment to work in a computer forensics department?
- **Team player:** Does this person seem like a team player or a lone wolf?

- **Ability to adapt:** Does this person have the ability to learn and adapt to new things? This single trait often makes or breaks a good computer forensics investigator.
- **Pressure:** Can this person work under intense pressure whether it be in the field or in a court of law?

Once the minimum qualifications are determined, those qualifications need to be written into a job description. Doing so saves the Human Relations (HR) department future headaches if someone gets hired who is not capable of meeting the qualifications.

## Personnel Training

Training of the personnel is a must to keep up with current technology. In an ideal situation, a scheduled rotation would specify who is going to training and when they can go. Certain areas of the military are extremely good at scheduled rotations—always sending members off to training whether they like it or not. The training should not be limited to forensic science but may include areas needed to round out the abilities of the staff. Some training areas include:

- **Computer forensics:** Data imaging of common computer types, such as PCs, servers, and laptops
- **Network forensics:** Data imaging of live networks and their different nodes
- **PDA forensics:** Data imaging of PDA devices
- **Cellular phone forensics:** Data imaging of cellular phone devices
- **Legal issues:** Training on the legal aspects and responsibilities of computer forensics
- **Industry-specific issues:** Training in specific areas or industries; for example, Sarbanes-Oxley or Health Information Portability and Accountability Act (HIPAA) compliance requirements
- **Management training:** Training in management skills or objectives. Remember, you are building a team with depth and expertise in mind
- **Investigative techniques:** Training in nonforensic investigative techniques to help develop sharp observation skills, consider a broad range of possibilities, and even think outside of the box

Once personnel duties are laid out, the next step is to outline the structure of the forensics unit.

## Structure of a Forensics Unit

As with most organizations, a forensics unit is structured as a hierarchy of jobs and lines of responsibility. This structure defines the roles and function of the forensics team.

A forensics unit is like a football team. Players have different responsibilities on the team and specific jobs to do, all of which contribute toward achieving one goal—to win. In the case of a forensics team, the team is structured so it can conduct a forensically sound investigation that has the ability to withstand scrutiny in a court of law.

**IN PRACTICE:** Administrative Issues

A forensics unit has administrative issues like those in any other organization. Personnel issues need to be addressed, budgets need to be prepared, and the art of office politics must be mastered. It is also critical to square away all software, hardware, and licensing issues. You do not want opposing counsel to point out that you used pirated software in the investigation.

Because you are going to be dealing with issues of licenses and computer hardware, a budget process is mandatory. Having sufficient resources both in terms of money and personnel tends to be an ongoing organizational battle. Having senior management's commitment and understanding of what needs to be done and why facilitates the budgeting process. Avoiding budget cuts will depend on how you maneuver your organization's politics in order to make sure they understand how important your work is to the organization.

With the team members and structure in place, next the processes used throughout the case lifecycle must be specified.

**Caution**

**Accepting a Case**

You must consider the team's ability to ensure that the e-evidence is unchanged, unspoiled, and unassailable when considering whether to accept a case.

## Pre-Case Preparations

As you have read, this chapter teaches you about generally accepted policies and procedures to be used as investigative guidelines. These policies are detailed sufficiently for processing standard cases but also have sufficient flexibility to allow for changes when a case warrants it. It is up to you as the investigator to interpret and apply those policies to each individual case in a legally-defensible way. This section deals with the preliminary steps required before you begin your case, such as securing the basic forms and tools you are going to need.

**Caution**

**Evidence Value Is Time Sensitive**

Environmental conditions can affect evidence as time passes.

**Caution**

**Links to Digital Information Can Degrade**

Links to Web sites visited, documents on servers, and temporary IP addresses may disappear over time.

## Deciding to Take a Case

The first thing to consider when presented with a case is whether or not to accept it. Many factors influence and ultimately determine whether you accept, or take in, a case. Forensics is a very labor-intensive and tedious task. There are no quick or magic investigations. You may need to turn down a case if it does not meet certain criteria. Common criteria for taking a case include:

- Whether it is a criminal or civil case
- The impact on the investigating organization
- Whether the evidence is volatile or nonvolatile
- Legal considerations, such as the types of data that might be exposed
- The nature of the crime
- Potential victims, such as children in child pornography cases
- Liability issues for the organization
- The age of the case
- Amount of time before the court date

**FYI** *Types of Data That Might Be Exposed in an Investigation*

Information that can be exposed in an investigation that is not within the scope of your investigation includes:

- Personal financial data
- Personal e-mail
- E-mail or documents containing company secrets
- Instant messaging logs
- Privileged communications
- Proprietary information (corporate)

### General Case Intake Form

A ***general case intake form*** needs to be completed when reviewing a potential case and determining whether to accept it. Among other issues, the form requests information to check for any conflict of interest between the forensics company, investigators, and other concerned parties. The completion of this form is often overlooked when developing standard operating procedures.

This form confirms the understanding and agreement among the parties involved and sets the stage for everything else about the case, such as chain of custody and basic evidence documentation. Intake forms differ depending on whether the case is being accepted by a law enforcement agency or a private company.

For an example of an intake form used by law enforcement, see the DOJ's National Institute of Justice Special Report at **www.ncjrs.gov/pdffiles1/nij/199408.pdf,** pages 58–61. A sample case intake form is also included in Appendix C.

The intake form summarizes the case and indicates the items to be analyzed and the legal basis for conducting the search that is being requested. The names of the plaintiff and defendant lawyers and their firms are needed to check for any conflict of interest. Members of the same computer forensics firm cannot represent opposing interests in a case. Before accepting a case, you must have a signed written agreement. No relationship is formed without such an agreement.

If the case is accepted, an agreement or contract is signed detailing as much as possible the scope of the investigation, names of the investigators, deadlines, and costs.

Once you have established the starting point for your process, the next set of procedures to focus on is documenting, receiving, handling, and disposing of e-evidence.

4

### IN PRACTICE: Triple Constraint of an Honest Estimate–"Pick Two"

Investigations can be done

1. Right.
2. Fast.
3. Inexpensively.

You can deliver any two of these factors, but never all three. If the client wants the investigation done correctly and fast, then it can't be inexpensive. If the client wants the investigation done inexpensively and correctly, then it won't be fast. For example, if there are a large number of target systems, the size of the case may not allow time for an effective investigation.

## Documenting the First Steps in the Case

The process of documenting the e-evidence actually begins when you receive the first call about the case. It cannot be emphasized enough how important it is to take the time to fully document every aspect of a case.

Even before you travel to the site where the target PCs or other devices are located, you should do a preliminary assessment by asking basic questions. The first question you need answered is why you are being called upon to do an investigation. What circumstances surrounding this case require a computer forensics expert? Your second question should be, What types of hardware and software are involved? You save time and mistakes by knowing what equipment to take to the onsite location.

## Equipment in a Basic Forensics Kit

As a matter of policy and procedure, a basic computer forensics kit should always be used. Every investigation will have some unique characteristics, but the basic equipment required by a forensic expert remains the same. The following list is a guideline for what should be included in a forensics kit:

- **Cellular phone:** There will always come a time when you need to find additional information or call for help of some kind.
- **Basic hardware toolkit:** Items such as standard screwdrivers, pliers, scissors, duct tape, and so on should always be part of your forensics kit.
- **Watertight/static-resistant plastic bags:** Make sure you have Ziploc®-type bags of various sizes to store collected evidence.
- **Labels:** Include in your kit various types of labels to tag items such as cables, connections, and evidence bags.
- **Bootable media:** You will need to have handy a variety of bootable media such as DOS startup disks, bootable CDs, and even bootable USB drives. Depending on the type of forensic software you are going to use, your choice of bootable media will vary.
- **Cables (USB, printer, FireWire):** Depending on what type of forensic software you plan to use, your choice of cables will vary. Always carry at least a CAT 5 crossover cable, straight–through cable, and rollover cable. A spare power cable always comes in handy.
- **Writing implements:** You always want to have a soft, permanent marker to write on labels, floppies, or CDs. A Sharpie®-type marker is always preferable because these markers are felt tipped and will not damage CD labels.
- **Laptop:** A laptop is always a good tool to have even if it is not your forensic examination platform. A laptop allows you to carry a veritable library of forensic tools, gives you access to the Internet, lets you keep updated manuals/schematics on hand, allows you to store information immediately if need be (volatile information such as that

stored in PDAs), and gives you flexibility to adjust to different investigative situations.

- **PDA:** This is a relatively new piece of equipment, but depending on the capacity and your use of a PDA it could be extremely valuable. One investigator may use it for keeping notes whereas another may use it to photograph the crime scene and upload the files to a central server in the office.
- **High-resolution camera:** In order to document everything properly, you should take a series of photographs before you start working. Photographs taken during and after are always recommended, but you must photograph the initial scene. A camera that labels the date/time on the photo is always a good idea.
- **Hardware write blocker:** You never know when you will need to take a hard drive out and do a hard drive transfer, so a hardware write blocker such as FastBloc or DriveLock is a small device that you should carry just in case.
- **Luggage cart:** A simple luggage carrier will save your back and several trips back and forth if you must transport equipment.
- **Flashlight:** You never know when you are going to need a strong light to read or see something either behind or inside the computer.
- **Power strip:** You can always count on never having enough power outlets around when you need them.
- **Log book:** Make a habit of carrying a log book to record investigators' actions.
- **Gloves:** As a forensic examiner, you always need to keep in mind that there are other forms of evidence such as fingerprints to keep intact. Additionally, a good set of gloves used when handling evidence shows your attention to even the smallest details of evidence preservation.
- **External USB hard drive:** Such a drive gives you a relatively quick and easy way to transfer large amounts of data or images in the field.
- **Forensic examiner platform:** Platforms vary from laptops to fully equipped desktop units. The next generation of mobile forensic platforms should make the acquisition of data in the field or in untrusted environments more convenient with faster connection speeds via wired transfers, wireless acquisitions, and smaller forensic platform units.

Now that you have a signed intake form, you are ready to take the next steps in the forensic examination.

4

## Steps in the Forensic Examination

Assume that you get your first call on a case and head out to do the initial assessment of the scene. Verify that you have the necessary tools, equipment, and forms. It's absolutely necessary that you have a chain of custody form. This document will become the heart of your documentation and will be referred to by all parties in their attempts to either prove or disprove the e-evidence. You can find samples of a generic chain of custody form and a chain of custody form for images in Appendix C.

### Verify Legal Authority

The issue of legal authority to do a search depends on whether you are doing a civil or criminal case. If you are involved in a criminal case, the legal authority to conduct a search is up to the local jurisdiction. Within the legal framework of a criminal investigation, you need a search warrant that specifies the scope of your search, as you learned in Chapter 1. Keep in mind the guarantees provided by the Fourth Amendment to the U.S. Constitution, detailed in Chapter 2.

**IN PRACTICE:** Key to a Good Search Warrant

The key to a good search warrant is to be as precise as possible about what you are going to search. This does not mean you have to get down to the serial number of a computer, but it does mean you should word the search warrant in such a way that it specifies you are going to seize a computer.

There are going to be times in a criminal case when the search warrant does not cover some aspect of the search. You may even find evidence of a different or unrelated crime. In these situations, you need to use sound judgment (and perhaps the cell phone). You may need to amend, expand, or get a new search warrant. Law enforcement can use what is commonly referred to as the ***plain view doctrine.*** When police are lawfully engaged in a search of one thing and find another that is of evidentiary value or forensic importance, they are entitled to seize it. The plain view doctrine is limited, however, by the probable cause requirement: Officers must have probable cause to believe that items in plain view are contraband before they may search or seize them.

In a civil case when you are dealing with corporate-owned computers and equipment, you have greater latitude to search and seize. The legal framework in the United States has consistently ruled on the side of the corporation and made it clear that employees using the computer equipment do not have any expectation of privacy or ownership of the data on the computer.

This judicial view is not shared around the world. In fact, the opposite view is held in Great Britain. The judicial system in Great Britain has sided with the employee as to the right of privacy and ownership of the data. It is a best practice to check with local legal authority to make sure you are not setting up the investigation to fail.

## Collect Preliminary Data

Once you have ascertained the legal authority and scope of your investigation, the next steps are to fully document the scene by taking pictures and then gather initial information. There will usually be a lead investigator who is generally your best source of initial information.

Before you begin collecting, you should be prepared to ask a number of questions. Questions to be asked and related considerations are listed in Table 4.1.



**TABLE 4.1** Preliminary questions and considerations.

| Questions | Considerations |
|---|---|
| What types of e-evidence am I looking for? | Are you being tasked to look for photographs, documents, databases, spreadsheets, financial records, or e-mail? |
| What is the skill level of the user in question? | The more sophisticated the user, the more likely that he has the capability to alter or destroy evidence. |
| What kind of hardware is involved? | Is it an IBM-compatible computer or a Macintosh computer? This consideration determines to a certain degree how you extract the data. |
| What kind of software is involved? | To a large degree, the type of software you are working with determines how you extract and eventually read the information. For example, if you are looking for spreadsheet information, you are not going to be searching for Microsoft Access or FoxPro data files. |
| Do I need to preserve other types of evidence? | Will you need to worry about fingerprints, DNA, or trace evidence? |
| What is the computer environment like? | Are you dealing with a network? If so, what is the physical/logical topology? Is there an ISP? What usernames and passwords are being used? What is the operating system? |

## Determining the Environment for the Investigation

After acquiring initial information, the next step is to determine whether to do the forensic work onsite or transfer the equipment to a trusted lab environment. As always, there are various considerations to take into account. However, the primary consideration is always the integrity of the evidence. The best practice as a computer forensics investigator is to always do your examination in a trusted environment, such as a forensics lab.

Factors to consider when deciding where to conduct the examination include:

- **Integrity of the evidence collection process:** This is the chief consideration for any investigation. By doing my examination onsite, do I degrade the integrity of my evidence collection? Is the evidence volatile enough that by waiting or transporting the evidence back to the lab I am going to risk losing it?
- **Estimation of the time required to do an examination:** A short examination is usually worth doing onsite, especially when you are doing a preview or cursory search to confirm initial information from the lead investigator or search warrant. If the investigation is extremely critical or appears that it may take some time, the best practice is to do this type of exam in the lab.
- **Impact on the target organization:** Taking into consideration the impact your examination will have on the organization is an important consideration for two reasons. One, the legal liability of bringing an organization to a standstill and potentially shutting the organization down is something done only in extreme cases. Two, from a financial standpoint, if the examination takes an important part of the organization out for some time, the financial aspect of the investigation may start to outweigh the actual cost of whichever policy or even law was broken. More than one investigation or examination has been suspended because its cost outweighed the perceived transgression. If the investigation is turned over for criminal actions, this consideration will be taken out of the investigating team's hands and control will be effectively handed over to law enforcement.
- **Equipment resources:** Will the equipment you bring onsite be enough to handle the job of doing an examination thoroughly and professionally? Can you bring the equipment from the lab or will that be impractical?
- **Personnel considerations:** The impact an onsite examination will have on investigative personnel correlates directly to how long it will take. A lengthy examination will obviously take more resources than, say, a quick preview. To have an examiner onsite doing one job when the same examiner can have several simultaneous investigations going on in the lab is a strong factor in determining whether to do an onsite exam.

The environment decision determines what you do next. If the investigation is to be done in the forensics lab, the processes of evidence collection, documentation, and transportation come into play. If the examination is onsite, the process of examining and extracting evidence begins.

In the following section, you learn the proper techniques to collect, document, and transport the evidence back to the forensics lab.

## Securing and Transporting Evidence

Once you have the initial information from the lead investigator and you are set to begin moving the evidence offsite, the sequence of common steps is as follows: Document the evidence, tag it, bag it, and transport it to the forensics lab.

4

**Document the Evidence** There is no such thing as overdocumenting a case. When you begin your initial documentation, you should do the following:

- Locate all evidence to be seized.
- Record a general description of the room, including:
  - Type of media found
  - All peripheral devices attached to the computer(s)
  - Make, model, and serial numbers of all devices (computers or otherwise) to be seized
  - What types of media devices are located in, near, or on the computer
- Note all wireless devices.
- Make use of chain of custody forms.

In addition to writing down this information, the best way to preserve this type of documentation is to take photographs of the scene. Besides photographing the computer systems, you should also photograph the layout of the room and, if it is a fairly large area, anything within 20 feet of the computers.

**Tag the Evidence** The next step is to begin tagging everything that is going to be transported back to the forensics lab. Types of tags will differ depending on what you are going to transport. Tags also vary by organization, but common tags can be as simple as colored dots or as detailed as full-sized paper sheets. Because you are photographing everything, the tags serve as backup documentation and show a physical documentation audit trail. On these tags, you should note the time, date, location, and general condition of the evidence. Some items will be small enough that tagging may be difficult. The best way to tag this type of evidence is to use an antistatic bag and tag the bag.

The items you should tag include:

- **All removable media:** Tag all floppy, USB, CD, DVD, Flash, and tape drive media. Additionally, you should tag any memory cards, external hard drives, and mobile phone SIMs.
- **All computer equipment:** The tag information follows the chain of custody forms closely with regard to the computer equipment. The tags used on the computer equipment should have the make, model, serial number, location, and general condition when seized. Do not disconnect anything from the computer yet; at this point you are only tagging the equipment for documentation purposes.
- **Books/magazines:** Because you will be analyzing a computer and related media for evidence used by an individual, getting to know how this person thinks is vitally important. The technical aspects of computer forensics science are well known and understood by most forensic technicians. What separates the good forensic investigators from the great forensic investigators is understanding how people think and, in so doing, how they use the computer. By taking note of books and magazines in the area and generally looking at the environment, an investigator can ascertain a general impression of this person. Often, an investigator can mirror a suspect's actions and way of thinking by studying what he reads or what interests him.
- **Trash contents:** Nothing tells an investigator who a person is like his garbage. Hackers use dumpster diving to glean information from their intended targets this way, and as an investigator you can virtually pull gems out of a trash can. Suspects have been known to toss CDs and even written evidence when they suspect an investigation is under way.
- **Peripherals:** Equipment such as cameras, scanners, printers, keyboards, mice, biometric devices, monitors, plotters, UPS power supplies, and wireless devices should all be tagged and collected.
- **Cables:** This is often the most overlooked aspect of tagging evidence, but it is just as important as the others. You always want to tag all cables attached to the suspect computer. There will be times when you try to reassemble a suspect computer in the lab and cannot figure out which cable was attached to which plug. Tagging the cable and associated socket or plug eliminates this headache and further improves the integrity of your case should it go to trial. Remember, the more you document and show attention to details, the better your case will stand up in court.
- **Notes/miscellaneous paper:** The number of times a suspect has written a password on a sticky note and pasted it to her monitor is so common

a cliché that most investigators check for this automatically. Anything at all that is attached to the computer or within the general area should be photographed and tagged. Additionally, any journals, printouts, and photographs should also be tagged as evidence.

**Bag the Evidence** After you have finished tagging all evidence items, it is time to start the process of putting the evidence into containers for transport back to the computer forensics lab. The types of containers you use will vary by the type and size of the evidence you are going to transport. Small media, sticky notes, and USB drives can be put into antistatic bags that are quite small. Larger items such as external hard drives or even computers can be transported via antistatic boxes. There are several reasons for bagging evidence:

- **Protection of the evidence:** First and foremost, you must take every precaution to protect potential sources of evidence. Using an antistatic bag is the single most important method of protecting sensitive magnetic material such as floppy disks. In the case of cellular phones, you should usually opt for a ***Faraday bag*** to keep unwanted radio frequency (RF) signals out. It is critically important to control RF signals when you have a device such as a BlackBerry that is constantly checking for e-mail and trying to download new e-mail. Because you do not want any changes to your device after a certain point, it is best to block the RF signals.
- **Organization of the evidence:** Since you probably have multiple cases going on at the same time, organization of evidence is critical to completing a case successfully. Store evidence in containers whenever possible to make organization easier. It is much easier to store a container of floppies than a loose pile of disks, just as it is much easier to organize paperwork in a file cabinet in folders than to strew it loose in the file drawer.
- **Preservation of other potential evidence:** When you keep evidence in a sterile environment such as a bag or other container, the potential to obtain other trace evidence from the object is much better than if you just have the evidence lying around where many people might be able to handle it.

**Transport the Evidence** Now that you have everything ready to go, you need to start looking at how to transport the evidence back to your lab. The tools and equipment you need for transport depend on the amount and types of evidence to be transported. Aside from the containers you are using already, when transporting evidence the following list of equipment and supplies can make your life easier:

- Luggage cart
- Hand cart
- Bungee cords with hooks or clamps

- Duct tape
- Small cargo net
- Leather gloves
- Twist ties
- Plastic cable ties/PlastiCuffs

When transporting evidence, take the following considerations into account. You must realize you are dealing with magnetic material that is sensitive to certain environmental factors. Most investigators realize speed is of the essence, so going straight from the scene to the forensics lab is usually a straightforward process. The problems usually arise when there are delays and the evidence is exposed to environmental factors that could destroy or degrade the evidence. Factors such as electromagnetic fields, high humidity, high heat, excessive vibration, high G forces (experienced during a car crash, for instance), and direct exposure to sunlight all have detrimental effects on the evidence. The safest vehicle (for evidence purposes) to transport the majority of evidence types is an air-conditioned vehicle with cargo tie-downs on antistatic mats. You normally do not want to have the evidence in a hot car, sliding around and generating a static charge on the carpet.

### IN PRACTICE: Timeline and Photo-Documentation

Photo-document how you transported the evidence to the forensics lab. Create a timeline that notes the date and precise time you left the scene and when the evidence arrived at the forensics lab. An exact timeline reinforces the integrity of chain of custody for the evidence. Additionally, taking pictures will show the efforts you put forth to preserve the evidence and what precautions were taken to keep the evidence from degrading.

Once you arrive at the forensics lab, document the time and date and complete the chain of custody forms. Store the evidence in a secure area where access is limited and controlled. Ideally, you should have a locked vault with labeled shelves or drawers to store and organize your evidence.

## Acquisition of Evidence Procedures

The acquisition aspect of an investigation can take place either in the field or in the forensics lab. In both cases, steps must be taken to ensure the integrity of the evidence. The preferred method is in the trusted environment whenever the circumstances permit.

The acquisition of e-evidence is arguably the most crucial part of a forensic investigation simply because this is the point at which original evidence may most easily be altered. It is vitally important to follow standard procedures and document all actions in order to prove beyond a shadow of a doubt the integrity of the evidence.

The first thing you must do when beginning the acquisition process is to document the computer hardware and software that will be used to conduct the acquisition and analysis.

- **Hardware:** Document the make, model, and serial numbers of your computer in addition to the amount of RAM and hard drive space your computer has.
- **Software:** Document the forensic software you are using and any tools you plan to use after acquisition to analyze the evidence extracted. Include version numbers and any major updates.
- **Media:** The hard drive you will use to store or examine the evidence must be sanitized or wiped prior to starting your case. (Don't confuse this drive with the one used for the examiner's operating system.) Document the wiping process and generate a report showing the successful completion of the process.



**Disassembly** Once you have completed this documentation, the next step is to disassemble the suspect's computer. The main purpose for disassembly is to gain access to the storage device(s) on the suspect computer. There are several reasons for wanting access to the storage device. First and foremost, you need to get all the data off the label of the storage device. Additionally, you want to identify all storage devices both internal and external. Storage device labels document drive geometry (cylinders, heads, and sectors); this information can be compared with information from the computer to make sure a savvy user has not customized the drive to create storage space only he knows about. You should also document the location of jumpers and the general condition of the drive.

Because you are already inside the computer system, it would be a good idea to document other aspects of the computer system also. A camera becomes invaluable at this point, but you should also document items such as MAC numbers on network interface cards (NICs), types of cards installed (sound or video), number of memory modules, specialized equipment installed, and number of storage devices. (You learn more about MAC addresses and NICs in Chapter 6.)

After you have documented items inside the computer, the next big step is to disconnect the power to the internal and external storage devices. Disconnecting the power ensures that no changes are made to the data on this storage device when you boot up the suspect's computer.

Once you have the storage devices disconnected, you are ready to turn on the suspect computer.

**Acquiring the Hard Drive** The computer can provide you with additional information to help build as solid a case as possible given time and cost constraints. You can acquire the following types of information after you boot the computer:

- **BIOS (basic input/output system) information:** ***BIOS*** is built-in software that determines what a computer can do without accessing programs from a disk. The system BIOS starts the computer running when it is turned on. The type of information you are looking for here is hard drive geometry settings, removable media settings, memory information, CPU information, and any serial numbers assigned to the computer. Screen shots with a camera are usually the preferred method to capture this information.
- **Boot sequence:** The ***boot sequence*** determines which of the computer's media is used to start the computer. Normally, a computer boots to the operating system on the main hard drive. You need to document the original boot sequence for case purposes. If you choose to use the suspect computer for evidence acquisition, you also need to change the boot sequence so the computer will boot off your removable media rather than its own media.
- **Time and date:** You should determine how the time and date shown by this computer relate to a known benchmark, such as GMT (Greenwich Mean Time). A screen shot with a camera showing both the BIOS time and GMT baseline time is best.

During the initial boot process, you usually see a screen with information on how to enter the Setup area of the suspect's computer. Some computers, however, do not show anything except a company logo, such as Compaq. In these cases, the Internet is the best source of information on the key sequence to use to enter the Setup or BIOS area.

You may encounter an obstacle at this point if the system requires a password. You have three options for overcoming this obstacle:

1. You can ask the suspect for the password.
2. You can acquire and use a password cracker (the Internet is a good source of such programs).
3. You can wipe the BIOS password out via jumpers.

Of these three options, the third is the worst-case scenario simply because it may wipe out BIOS information that you could have used to bolster the case.

Depending on the BIOS type, you may have one or more pages of information to navigate to find the relevant information you are looking for. Once you have documented the information you need from the BIOS, you are ready to decide how to acquire the hard drive image. You have two options:

1. You can use the suspect's machine as the platform from which to acquire the evidence. That is, you will work directly on the suspect's hard drive using the suspect's computer. This usually entails your hooking up the forensic examiner's computer platform in some fashion to the suspect's machine, using a USB, Ethernet, or wireless connection.
2. You can plug the suspect's drive directly into the examiner's machine and then use the examiner's computer as the forensic platform from which to acquire the hard drive image. This method is by far the preferred method simply because the examiner has more control and knows the forensics computer much more intimately than the suspect's computer system.



If you plan to use the suspect's machine as the forensic platform, you must make sure the boot sequence does *not* include the storage device you are trying to acquire. Test the boot sequence *before* you plug in the storage device. Make sure the computer will boot first from the floppy or CD. After you have tested the boot sequence, turn off the computer and reconnect all power and data cables to the suspect hard drive. Turn on the power and observe that the computer is actually booting off the floppy or CD. Once you have the computer system booted from either the floppy or CD, conduct the acquisition using whichever method you normally use, making sure to document every step.

As noted above, the preferred method for image acquisition is to use the forensic examiner's computer platform. Just remember to use whichever write protection method you normally use, whether software- or hardware-based. Because there are always new forensic software suites being released, this book can offer only general rules. The following items are basic guidelines when you are doing an acquisition:

- Wipe all media you plan to use and use a standard character during that wipe. Writing a standard character over the whole surface of the disk makes it easy to delineate the extent of the forensic data you will transfer to the disk.
- Activate the write protection.
- Perform a hash of the original drive and of the forensic copy to make sure you have a bit-for-bit copy.
- Do a physical acquisition to capture space not accessible by the operating system.

**Making a Working or Backup Copy** Now that you have a forensic copy of the original evidence, it is time to power down the system and remove the original evidence from the computer. Document when the image was made and where the original evidence is stored. From this point forward, you should not need to use the original evidence.

With the original evidence safely stored, you need to make a working copy of the forensic image. Duplicate the forensic image and then store the first copy of the evidence. You should use this working copy for your analysis. If for some reason it is destroyed, damaged, or becomes corrupted, you have the original copy to fall back on. If you need to access your original copy, you should immediately make another working copy. Again, you must perform a hash analysis to document the integrity of the working copy and store the original copy in a safe place.

## Examining the Evidence

This is the point in the computer forensics field where the *science* of computer forensics starts to take a back seat to the *art* of computer forensics. Because of the wide variety of computer forensics cases, it would be pointless to lay out specific rules for examination; they would very quickly become obsolete.

That being said, there are, of course, basic rules and areas where a computer forensics examiner should begin an investigation. However, expert forensic examiners develop an understanding of how a particular computer user thinks and works, and they adjust their examination methods accordingly. For example, if your suspect is a novice user, then your examination usually covers only the basics. In contrast, examining the machine of an expert user who can hide or manipulate data forces the examiner to become creative when searching for evidence.

At this point, you should have your forensic examiner computer ready to go with clean or wiped media and a basic file structure in place to organize evidence you find. Usually you work with an image of the suspect's drive and use a separate hard drive to do the work of saving evidence and tools for the case.

### IN PRACTICE: How to Stay Organized

Use the forensic examiner's hard drive as little as possible. Always strive to keep your case work on a separate drive and organized in a way that seems logical to you or your department. You always use the data drive that was wiped to work on cases. Never use the forensic platform boot drive. In other words, try to have your forensic station separate from your normal everyday work station.

There are two ways of doing the examination or extraction: physical and logical. A logical examination/extraction sees only what the operating system can see. If the operating system can see only 38GB of hard drive space on a 40GB hard drive, 2GB of space on that hard drive may be used to store data the operating system cannot see.

## Physical Extraction or Examination

A physical examination of the hard drive involves doing searches in areas the operating system does not recognize as areas normally used for file access or storage. Depending on the forensic software used, this may be as simple as running a script or using a GUI to select options, or as complicated as entering a command-line string. You are looking for evidence in areas such as the space between partition tables, host protected areas, unused hard drive space, and damaged sectors. A typical search of this type consists of key words, file header analysis, and binary data strings in areas not normally used by an operating system or user.



## Logical Extraction or Examination

A logical examination is where most of the work is done in the computer forensics field. Logical examination involves searching a computer based on the type of operating system it has installed and the type of file structure installed by the operating system. The main reason for this is quite simple. The majority of users do not have the tools or training necessary to really hide information outside the normal boundaries of operating systems. You may run across the occasional computer-savvy individual who can do so, but the normal user will not go to extreme lengths to hide information in, say, a damaged area of the hard drive. Most users employ software designed to hide information or come up with creative ways to hide information on their own. This is why it is so important to understand the individual from whose computer you are extracting evidence. Computer forensics tools are fairly easy to master; it is the human mind that truly great forensic examiners understand.

There are several general steps involved in doing a logical examination and a few key areas that any computer forensics examiner must cover. Think of a logical examination as a pyramid. As the examiner, you first do the basic examinations that are essentially the foundation of your case. If you find the evidence you need at this level, then your case is fairly simple and you can complete it and move on to the next case. If your basic search fails to turn up the evidence, then you move up to the next level and explore a little further. As you move up the pyramid, the searches become more complex and exacting; for example, techniques such as steganography and encryption are at the higher levels of the pyramid. If you reach the final level of the pyramid and all your searches have come back negative for evidence, the issue then becomes whether the evidence was there to begin with or whether the suspect was successful in

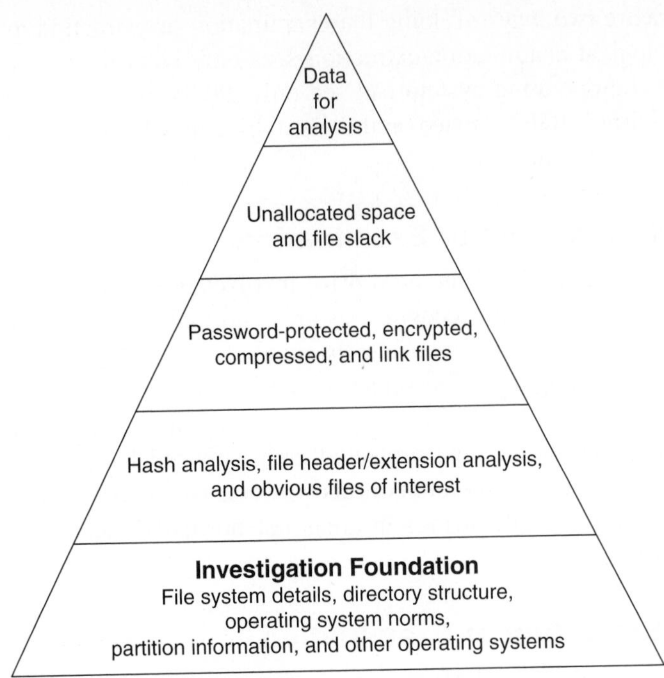


**FIGURE 4.1** Logical examination pyramid.

masking or destroying the evidence. As you go higher up the extraction pyramid, you will end up with evidence or data of interest that you will then analyze. At this point, you are still just extracting the data you need in a systematic fashion, much like a checklist. Figure 4.1 shows a typical pyramid scheme of what steps to conduct in a logical exam.

## Bottom-Layer Examinations

The bottom layer of this extraction model is primarily concerned with developing a picture of how the computer system is set up. You need to determine what is considered normal for this operating system because most evidence you are looking for will stand out once you have eliminated the common or normal aspects of a computer system.

**File System Details** At this level, look for information such as which operating system is being used on the computer, the version of the operating system on the computer, known issues with this operating system, and workstation/server configuration.

**Directory/File System Structure** Look at the type of directory or file structure for information such as FAT versus MFT, file attribute types used by this system, time/date stamp formats, cluster size allocations, and typical file locations associated with this directory structure. (You learn more about file systems in Chapter 6.)

**Operating System Norms** How does this operating system operate on a normal basis? Which directory does it normally spool printer files in? Which directory will documents and data files default to? Where are temporary files kept?

**Other Partition Information** In addition to the active partition, other partitions may be installed on this storage device. Some partitions will be obvious in that they will be easy to spot, such as a hard drive D. Other partitions such as LINUX or OS2 may be a bit tougher to spot because you have to know what markers delineate that type of partition. One of the easiest methods for spotting an additional partition is to look for large amounts of space on the storage device the active operating system does not recognize. This is usually a sign you have a partition, or possibly a deleted partition.

**Other Operating Systems (Dual/Multiboot System)** Somewhat related to multiple partitions, a dual boot system replaces the master boot record with a boot manager so the user can select the operating system to boot from. Detecting such a system tells you quite a bit about the sophistication of the user. Additionally, this information also gives you a better picture of how the storage device is set up with regard to boot sectors, partition information, and allocation tables.



## Second-Layer Examinations

With this layer, you start working with the files on the suspect drive. This layer is generally where you begin to sort and catalog files of interest.

**Exclusion of Known Files Using Hash Analysis** The most efficient method to eliminate common files is to do a hash comparison between known file hashes of common operating system files and the ones on your suspect storage device. If the hashes match, you can eliminate these files as potential evidence because they have not been modified by the user.

**File Header and Extension** This extraction method is used to ferret out changes to either a file extension or a file header. Most users are familiar with file extensions and the basic purpose they serve. For example, if you change the extension of a Word document file from .doc to .xyz, the operating system will not recognize it as a Word document; this constitutes a minor form of data hiding. However, Microsoft Word will still be able to open the file because the file header is still the same. What you are doing in essence is comparing the file header to the file extension to see if they match. If they do not, then you may have a file that warrants further review.

**Obvious Files of Interest** There will be times when you find the file you are looking for in plain sight. You may be working a child pornography case and the files are located in the My Pictures folder on the suspect drive. Remember, this is only the extraction phase; the analysis of the evidence and how it arrived on this machine is still several steps away.

## Third-Layer Examinations

In this layer, you are beginning to look for files that are protected or locked in some way. The purpose here is to dig out files that for whatever reason the user deemed important enough to hide or attempt to conceal.

**Extraction of Password-Protected Files** Password-protected files should always be extracted. The data may be innocuous, but with a password to protect it you do not know at this point. Extract the file and note the type of software used to place the password on it for use when analyzing the file later. For example, if a Word file has a password, chances are that Word was used to apply the password. This information will help you to find the right tools to crack the password. For a password-protected Word file, for example, you can use a Word password cracker to open the file.

**Extraction of Encrypted Files** Like a password-protected file, an encrypted file may be benign, but you will not know this until you decrypt the file. There are various forms of encryption, and your best bet is to find the software used to encrypt the file and go after the keys used to encrypt the file. Brute-force decryption takes time, and going after the keys used to encrypt the file is usually a quicker way to analyze the file.

**Extraction of Compressed Files (Outlook PST or AOL BAG)** You will find that most compressed files are compressed by software makers not to make them less accessible but to save space on the storage device. Most forensic tools can decompress the files for you and save you the headache of doing it manually, so extracting them for further analysis is fairly easy.

**Extraction of Deleted Files** Files are deleted on computer systems for a variety of reasons that may not have anything to do with the investigation you are working on. That being said, the safe assumption is to extract any deleted files for further analysis just to make sure they have no evidentiary value.

**Link Analysis** With removable storage devices around, you can be sure there will be link files on the suspect computer. A link file basically records where a file has been saved recently and usually includes the path, date, and time. If the suspect has a removable drive, chances are you will find links to it.

### Fourth-Layer Examinations

At this layer, you are looking in areas the computer uses as "scratch pad" areas. These areas of the storage device usually contain large amounts of data that can be "carved" out, such as Web pages or e-mails.

**Extraction of Unallocated Space Files of Interest** At this point, you are looking for files, images, and data that have been written to the disk at one point and then erased. This can occur with cache, temporary files, and intentionally deleted files. For example, when you are viewing your Yahoo! e-mail, the system is actually saving that screen shot to the hard drive in a cache or page file. Once you log off, your computer system deletes this temporary file from the logical file structure; however, the file is actually still on the disk.



**Extraction of File Slack Space Files of Interest** When a file is written to a hard drive or storage device, the file is written into areas called clusters. Clusters are basically electronic storage bins. Let's say a file is 15KB in size and the cluster is 32KB in size. This file will fit into this one cluster with 17KB of space left over. The space from the end of the file to the end of the cluster is called *file slack space*. Previous fragments of data can be culled from this area because files vary in size and previous data written to these clusters is not always overwritten.

### Fifth-Layer Examinations

By the time you have reached this point at the top of the pyramid, you will have several files and areas of the disk to analyze. The previous steps were basically a checklist to make sure you systematically examine the hard drive in an orderly fashion. At this point, your documentation should reflect how the evidence was extracted and where it has been extracted for further analysis.

---

## The Art of Forensics: Analyzing the Data

To a large degree, data extraction is based on the science or technology of how and where data is stored on a computer system. Most forensic tools extract data easily because the technology used to store the data in the first place is well known and understood. The analysis of the extracted data is where the art of forensics takes center stage. This is where you begin to think like the user of the computer to emulate how he would or could save, hide, or destroy evidence.

Let's take a simple example to illustrate this point. You have extracted a word processing document that was deleted hours before the computer was seized. The file is 80KB in length and was created and modified within a week before it was deleted. After extracting this file, you proceed to open it and view the contents. The first thing you notice is a big blank screen. At first glance, it appears that there is absolutely nothing typed in this document. Because you have learned a little about the user, you know this person is a very able secretary with years of experience in word processing. As the forensic examiner, you think to yourself, "How could I hide a document in plain view?" The easiest way, of course, is to make the text in the document invisible. A careless examiner might assume the document is a blank, but you don't. With a little more digging, you notice the font color is the same as the background color, thus making the document appear empty when in reality it has 80KB of evidence. The forensic software knew there was a deleted file, registered the date and time attribute, and even detected how big it was. What the software didn't know was how the user hid the information.

## File Analysis

When doing a file analysis, you must keep a couple of factors always in mind. First and foremost, you should never discount or take anything for granted. This may seem like a cliché, but as a forensic professional you must always remember that you have been called in for a reason, and the reason is that you understand how data can be stored, manipulated, hidden, and deleted in a computer system.

The other guidelines you usually follow are necessarily generic because each case will be different, and the tools you use will also be quite different. The following guidelines are just that, guidelines. Do not infer that these are the absolute set of rules written in stone.

**File Content** As with the example above, you should first examine obvious files for evidentiary content. If you are working a financial fraud case, for example, files dealing with finance or spreadsheets would be an obvious choice to open to check file content.

**Metadata** As you've learned, metadata is information embedded within files, such as when the file was last edited or last printed. This information is often useful, but it really is used to corroborate the information you find with the user and solidify the connection between the data and who actually created it.

**Application Files** Whenever you are looking at files on a computer system, you are bound to find a file that has no apparent application associated with it. Sometimes the reverse will also be true—you have an application on the computer that shows it has been used recently, but there are no data files to be found on this storage device. Because you have already done a file signature/header analysis, you know the headers and extensions match. This scenario usually indicates there is an offsite method of storage or another storage device being used that contains the data files or application software.

**Operating System File Types** Operating system file systems and the operating systems themselves are programmed to work in specific ways. That is to say, a Microsoft operating system has file formats different from those of a Macintosh operating system. If you are doing an analysis of files and you find a file with an extension such as .tar on a Microsoft operating system, you know automatically there is another operating system available to this user on this computer or via a network because this extension is commonly used on UNIX/Linux systems.

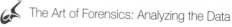

**Directory/Folder Structure** Operating systems and application software always have a standard folder or directory in which to store files. Part of your job as the forensic examiner is to indirectly or directly prove intent. When a suspect changes or creates another folder for files that are involved in the investigation, you prove two things. One, you prove the suspect has the technological prowess to accomplish this, and, two, you show the suspect intentionally saved those files in folders or directories other than standard folders or directories to prove intent. Creating another directory or folder and moving files into this new structure takes a small amount of work, and most people will not go to this trouble unless it is important to them.



**Patterns** For the most part, humans fall into habits or patterns that you can identify if you look hard enough. As the forensic investigator, you must try to find patterns particular to the suspect. The way files are named or saved may indicate a pattern, as will time and date patterns. Let's say you see a pattern of files saved at 2:00 a.m. every Thursday. This may indicate the suspect has access to the computer at this time or simply that he has insomnia every Thursday. The point is that you will need to dig a little further once you see a pattern, and it may lead to further evidence or correlation of evidence.

**User Configurations** User configurations are part of file analysis in the sense that you are looking to see what the user has customized on this computer system that leads you to find evidence. As an example, a user can set the standard Microsoft Windows backup utility to back up certain files at a certain time and to a certain storage device. This type of information can lead you to further investigate other areas of interest. Do the user passwords expire, is there a remote login feature enabled, what kind of network settings are in place, what printers are on the system, and is that printer physically near this computer? These are typical configuration questions you should ask yourself to put together a picture of the evidence and to possibly locate more evidence.

## Data Hiding Analysis

Once you get past the initial file analysis and start looking at downright data hiding, the computer forensics world gets to be very interesting. You saw in the section above a mild version of data hiding by changing the file extension to hide the file. This form of data hiding is easily foiled because most good forensic software packages will do an analysis of file headers and compare them to established file extensions. Passwords on files usually yield clues in and of themselves in the fact that some passwords are very personal in nature and connect the user to this password and file. The other reason a password is evidentiary in nature is quite simply that it proves the user or suspect intended to keep the contents of this file from anyone else. The following list of ways data is hidden are much more sophisticated and point to a user with both expertise and intent.

**Password-Protected Files** In the extraction phase, you extracted password-protected files for further analysis. Now that you have reached the part in the investigation where you begin to analyze a password-protected file, you are going to need some information. The most obvious thing you will need is the password. If you have a user or suspect that is willing to give you the password, then your work is nearly done. The problem arises when the user or suspect either will not give you the password or does not remember it.

You have several options for cracking passwords:

- Check the Internet for password cracking software for this data file type.
- Check with the software developer of the application to see if they can crack their own passwords.
- Contact a firm that specializes in cracking passwords for this type of data file.

The ability to crack a password is usually in direct correlation to the sophistication of the user. If the user uses a standard password and password algorithm such as those supplied in Excel or Word, you stand a greater chance of cracking the password than if your user created a 128-bit encrypted password.

**Compressed Files** File compression has been around for decades and is fairly easy to do. The main reason for file compression is to save space either on the storage device or in transmission across networks. In the computer forensics world, file compression can also be used to hide information. Files can be compressed not only to save space but also to make them unreadable by anything other than the compression utility. Compression utilities can also add passwords to a compressed file to make it one step more difficult to analyze the data.

Because compression has been around for some time, the utilities that compress files are usually well known also. Most common compression software applications have an extension that tips you off to which compression utility is being used. Depending on the compression software, you simply let the software reverse the compression process and specify where the uncompressed version is saved.

**Encrypted Files** Like compressed files, encrypted files are changed to the point that they are unreadable until the software used to compress or encrypt is used to reverse the process. Unlike compression, encryption is used for one purpose only: to hide data. Because encryption's purpose is to hide data, the algorithms used for this purpose are much more sophisticated and the cracking of encrypted data is exponentially more difficult. In truth, the cracking of encrypted files is usually an exercise in futility because the permutations of most modern encryption methods far exceed the capabilities of modern computers to crack them. For example, messages coded by the Nazi code machine Enigma in World War II have still not been cracked, and modern encryption far exceeds anything the Nazi war machine had. The method that holds the key to success in cracking encrypted files is quite literally the key. A key is the initial input into the encryption algorithm that generates the unique encryption for that file. If you crack the key, you don't have to crack the encrypted file. Encryption programs such as PGP (Pretty Good Privacy) have been cracked in this fashion because the encryption of the file itself is so strong it would literally take decades to decipher.



**Steganography** This type of data hiding comes from the school of "hide in plain sight." Steganography is quite simply the ability to hide data within another file such as a picture or music file. The technology behind this varies, but the basic premise is to substitute or replace a small portion of the existing file with the embedded or hidden file. This can be done simply because most picture or audio software has a built-in level of error with which it can work, and thus a small error rate is acceptable. Software used to do this varies in quality, and some applications are better than others. If you suspect "stego," it is going to be very hard to find a file that has it unless you have a before-and-after type of situation: Some users will keep the original file on the storage device and embed data on the second copy. If you have both versions of the same file, you can compare them bit for bit and figure out rather quickly if one of them is different. The next step is to find out which program was used, and that is usually a problem because only the software used to create the stego can realistically reverse the process. You will learn more about steganography in Chapter 7, "Investigating Windows, Linux, and Graphics Files."

## Time Frame Analysis

When doing a file analysis, one of the aspects you must address is the issue of time frame. It is not enough to say the evidence is on the storage device and proclaim the suspect is guilty. As the forensic examiner, you must be able to link the suspect and the data via time frame analysis.

The files you analyze will have associated file attributes, such as:

- Creation date/time
- Modified date/time
- Accessed date/time

These dates and times give information as to when the file was used, but by themselves they will not tell you who was using them. Most operating systems now require username and password to log in, and this is where you might be able to correlate a user with a file. The word *might* is used simply because different operating systems log users differently, if at all. If you can identify a log that spells out who logged in at what time, then you have the basis to begin correlating a user with a file. You are closer to being able to prove a link if that user was logged in to that system when the file was used. The second issue involved with this is proving the username and password used to access the computer are known only to the suspect. You can log in as the president of the United States, but that does not mean the president actually logged in. It only means you used his username and password.

---

## Reporting on the Investigation

The last step in a forensic examination is to finish documenting your investigation and put your report together. Up until this point, you should be documenting all the procedures, findings, and conclusions as part of the forensic process. At this step, you are compiling and essentially finalizing your documentation into a report. Your case will have a core reason for doing this investigation, for example child pornography or embezzlement. The evidence you cite in the report is used to correlate or support this allegation. The opposite can also be true when you find evidence that exonerates an individual. Your job as a forensic investigator is to extract evidence in an impartial manner to either prove or disprove an allegation. Your report should remain neutral in tone and report only facts that can be proved via forensic science.

Most organizations have a standard set of forms that are used to help the forensic examiner document the case while at the same time giving her a guideline to follow. The following sections detail the basic information reports should include. However, your organization will have specific requirements and may have additional requirements above and beyond the basic set we are putting forth.

### Ongoing Documentation

Your documentation process should have started from the point of being contacted by a lead investigator, and it should end once your final report has been drafted and accepted by the legal authority you are working for, whether that authority is law enforcement or a corporate attorney. The idea behind this level of documentation is to be able to recreate your investigation or investigative actions via your notes if need be. Your final documentation should include these basic items:

- Notes taken during your initial contact with the lead investigator and any notes taken during subsequent meetings with other investigators, attorneys, or management
- Any forms used to start the investigation such as intake or chain of custody forms

- A copy of the search warrant or legal authority to conduct your search
- Documentation of the scene where the computer was located including photographs and notes
- Documentation of computer components such as storage devices, peripheral devices, or other noteworthy items
- Documentation of any networks, physical/logical topology, off-site storage, or wireless links
- Any passwords, pass phrases, encryption, or data hiding software you have identified
- Any changes to the scene or computer equipment authorized by authorities and why they were authorized
- The names of those at the scene and anyone involved in handling the evidence
- Procedures used to acquire, extract, and analyze the evidence
- Any irregular or noteworthy items usually outside the scope of a computer forensics investigation

The above list is the basic level of documentation needed to generate a basic report. Computer forensics software packages available today often generate reports automatically and in great detail as to what evidence is found, how it was found, and data such as time/date attributes. The EnCase® application from Guidance Software can be run to generate such a report; however, it is up to the forensic examiner to enter the field notes into software of this type for inclusion in the final report. With that being said, an examiner should have the basic knowledge of what a report requires and how to formulate a report.

## Creating a Detailed Report

Every case is unique and every report will be unique to that case; however, there are basic guidelines to follow in terms of what a detailed final report should include. At a minimum, your report should include:

- The case investigator information such as name and contact details
- The organization requesting the investigation
- The suspect user information
- Computer equipment and peripheral details such as serial numbers
- Computer software, both operating and application, on the suspect computer

4

- Case numbers or identifiers used by your department to organize and catalog investigations
- Location of examination
- Forensic tools used during the examination
- Type of information you have been requested to find

Your report should be organized into several sections, the most important of which are listed below.

- Brief summary of how you processed the evidence, including acquisition, extraction, and analysis
- The body of the report, containing a detailed explanation or summary of your findings
- A conclusion section
- Supplementary sections such as a glossary and an appendix

**The Report Summary** Your report summary should include:

- Files found with evidentiary value
- Supporting files such as deleted or hidden files that support the allegations
- Ownership analysis of files
- Analysis of data within suspect files
- Search types including text strings, keywords, and signature analysis
- Any attempts at data hiding such as passwords, encryption, and steganography

When you write a summary of your findings, you are essentially writing an abstract of your complete report. Most people are not going to read all 200 pages of your complete report, but they will read your summary or abstract. The key to a good summary is to cover all the relevant points without going into references and microscopic detail such as is contained in the body of your report.

**Body of the Report** The main part of your report explains or summarizes your findings in a very detailed fashion. The body of the report contains as much detail and documentation as you can clearly and cohesively include. You should detail everything from the beginning when you were first contacted all the way to the final analysis, but you must organize this information in a way that logically flows from one point to the other. Much like planning a trip from California to New York, you need to go step by step and lead the reader of your report in a logical fashion so as not to lose him. Your report should be easy to read and organized in a way that even the most nontechnical person can follow the evidence trail. The basic idea for the body of the report is to explain in great detail your investigation as to what you were looking for, how you went about finding the evidence, and what that evidence means.

**Conclusion** The conclusion is usually a relatively short summary of your findings and what those findings lead you to conclude. Your conclusion should be based on the evidence found and will use the evidence as the foundation of your conclusion. There will be times when your opinion will be based more on your experience than on the actual evidence found. As an expert witness, you can give an opinion based on the evidence and try to infer what might have happened, but a sharp attorney can and will turn this around on you if you are not careful. Always base your conclusion on the facts of the case and not on assumptions or inferences.



**Supplementary Materials** Computer forensics by its very nature has a vocabulary all its own. For the benefit of nontechnical individuals, it is always a good idea to include at least a basic glossary of terms used in your report. Try not to interchange different terms for the same item because this may tend to confuse the reader and may lead to questions from others down the road.

You may also want to include one or more appendices to the report to present technical references, any graphs you may have used, references to law, and any other material you will need to support your conclusions in the report.

## Summary

In this chapter, you have seen that the key to a consistent and methodical investigation is a good set of policies and procedures that serve as guidelines or baselines for any investigation. These policies and procedures are designed not only to delineate the process of an investigation but also to aid in the management of a computer forensics lab. This is not to say you cannot be flexible; to the contrary, your policies and procedures should be designed to be flexible and adjust as necessary for each case.

This chapter also took you step by step through the actual process of conducting a forensic examination from the first phone call you receive to the time when you turn over the final report. The four main steps of any computer forensics investigation are planning, acquisition, analysis, and reporting. Forensic investigation is not an exact science, and steps will vary depending on the case, so the processes outlined for each step provide broad guidelines; however, these steps are generally accepted by most computer forensics professionals and can be adapted to your needs.

The science behind the technology is fairly well understood, and the tools used by computer forensic analysts are becoming much easier to use. The field of computer forensics science will gradually give way to the field of computer forensic art. The science of computer forensics will always strive to keep up with the technology of the day, but it is the computer forensic analyst, who understands how people use this technology, who will be able to solve the difficult cases. In essence, the scientist must also be a psychologist with the ability to use high-technology tools.

## Test Your Skills

### MULTIPLE CHOICE QUESTIONS

1. One of the first forms you will use to begin a case is the
   A. intake form.
   B. inventory form.
   C. software form.
   D. chain of custody form.

2. You should begin documenting a case when
   A. you reach the suspect computer.
   B. you are ready to analyze the data.
   C. you receive the first call about the case.
   D. you are ready to finalize the report.

3. Aside from written field notes, the best way to document in the field is to use a
   A. camera.
   B. witness.
   C. laptop.
   D. microrecorder.

4. Search warrants need to be
   A. general in nature.
   B. precise.
   C. long.
   D. double-spaced.

5. The best source of initial information about a case comes from the
   A. suspect.
   B. computer.
   C. lead investigator.
   D. victim.

6. The computer boot-up sequence is located in the
   A. BIOS.
   B. RAM.
   C. NVRAM.
   D. FAT.

7. To verify the original drive with the forensic copy, you use
   A. a hash analysis.
   B. a password.
   C. disk-to-disk verification.
   D. none of the above.

8. The part of the investigation when you extract data is called the
   A. analysis phase.
   B. extraction phase.
   C. acquisition phase.
   D. documentation phase.

9. A computer with multiple operating systems is often called a
   A. multiuser computer.
   B. dual-boot system.
   C. multiboot system.
   D. either B or C.

10. A hash comparison is often used to eliminate
    A. unknown files.
    B. known files.
    C. user profiles.
    D. evidence.

11. Information embedded within a file such as a Word document is
    A. encryption.
    B. metadata.
    C. hidden data.
    D. nonstandard data.

12. Files that have been changed so as not to be easily read are
    A. encrypted.
    B. compressed.
    C. password protected.
    D. hidden.

13. The ability to hide data in another file is called
    A. encryption.
    B. steganography.
    C. data parsing.
    D. A and B.

14. Time frame analysis ties the data with the
    A. user.
    B. investigator.
    C. organization.
    D. court system.

15. Ongoing documentation should include all of the following *except*
    A. notes taken during initial contact with the lead investigator.
    B. passwords or data-hiding software you have identified.
    C. the basis for the investigation.
    D. procedures used to extract the evidence.

## EXERCISES

### Exercise 4.1: Policies and Procedures

1. Research and find a computer forensics lab near your location and ask for policies and procedures used in their investigations.
2. Write a two-page report on what you find.

### Exercise 4.2: Hide Word Data

1. Using data-hiding techniques, attempt to hide data using Microsoft Word.
2. Write a one-page report on how you accomplished this.

### Exercise 4.3: Search and Seizure

1. Research the Fourth Amendment to the Constitution of the United States to determine how it affects the legality of search and seizure.
2. Write a one-page report on your findings.

### Exercise 4.4: Search Warrants

1. Research and locate a legal authority in your area such as a district attorney or U.S. attorney to gather information on how they formulate search warrants.
2. Write a two-page report on your findings.



### Exercise 4.5: Computer Forensics Platforms

1. Search the Internet for computer forensics platforms that can be taken on site or on location.
2. Compare the different products in terms of price, features, and ease of use and write a two-page report on your findings.

## PROJECTS

### Project 4.1: Pre-Case Planning

1. You receive a call from the corporate attorney requesting your help in an investigation.
2. Detail what steps you will complete *before* agreeing to take the investigation.

### Project 4.2: Know the Computer User

While speaking with the lead investigator on a case, you survey the room in which the computer equipment is located. On one side of the room there is a large bookshelf with up-to-date books on computer topics; a nearby table has current computer magazines; a new scanner is attached to the computer; and the computer is a new model with state-of-the-art equipment.

1. With this information, what can you deduce about the user?
2. How will this affect your investigation?

### Project 4.3: Transporting Evidence

You are wrapping up the onsite investigation and are preparing to transport the evidence back to the lab.

1. Detail the steps you will take to prepare the equipment for transport.
2. Describe how you will transport the equipment.

### Project 4.4: Asking the Right Questions

You are preparing for a meeting with the local district attorney regarding a criminal check fraud case.

1. What questions should you prepare in anticipation of this meeting and why?
2. Create a checklist of your questions.

### Project 4.5: The Final Report

You are finalizing the report for a computer forensic examination and are going over the details of what needs to be included in the report.

1. Based on this chapter, what needs to be included in your report and why?
2. Create an outline of the basic parts you need to include in your report.

## Case Study

You are a senior forensics investigator in a corporate firm that handles large financial transactions for a variety of customers. The head of internal auditing has called to request that you perform a forensic analysis of an employee's computer. The auditor has found evidence of financial discrepancies but needs you to confirm how the financial transactions were done on the computer. The employee is very knowledgeable in both the financial and computer areas and has been with the company for many years.

1. Determine what steps you will follow to begin the investigation and what questions you might ask the internal auditor.
2. Considering the expertise of this user, explain how you believe the user may have hidden or masked her actions. Describe what actions you might take to investigate the user's methods.
3. Assuming you find evidence, describe the steps you would then take to formulate a report and what specific items need to be included in this report.

# Chapter 5

# Data, PDA, and Cell Phone Forensics

## Chapter Objectives

**After reading this chapter and completing the exercises, you will be able to do the following:**

- Recognize and identify types of drives and media storage devices.
- Describe PDA and cellular phone technologies.
- Explain techniques for acquiring and analyzing data from hard drives and other storage media.
- Describe techniques for acquiring and analyzing data from PDAs and cellular phones.
- List and describe tools that can be used to analyze disk images, PDA data, and cellular phone data.

## Introduction

This chapter brings together the various aspects of how to acquire evidence properly from a suspect media device. The media devices you will cover in this chapter include hard drives, removable media, PDAs, and cellular phones. As part of this coverage, the technology and standards used in the industry are covered to give you an understanding of how these devices work. After you have a firm grasp of the technology, you will study some of the more common tools used by forensic technicians when dealing with various types of media and how they are used to extract images and analyze data from the various media types.

Some of this material you will have seen before in one form or another, but this chapter will go deeper into the technology behind the various media types. A forensics examiner must be able to prove beyond a shadow of a doubt that the evidence collected was not altered or tainted in any way, and knowing how the technology works will help the forensic examiner understand how data can be saved or altered.

---

## Basic Hard Drive Technology

Most computer users are familiar with the idea of computer hard drives and how they are used to store computer programs and data. For most users, this is enough information, but a forensic technician must understand the hardware components and how they work to save data.

Looking at a hard drive externally, you will notice that most standard hard drives are no larger than a small book, yet they can store encyclopedic amounts of data. If you look at the top of a hard drive, you will usually see a nice shiny cover with a label affixed that supplies information on the hard drive's parameters. If you turn the hard drive over, you will see a circuit board (otherwise known as the hard drive controller) that controls how the information is stored, transferred, and buffered.

> **Caution**
>
> **Handle with Care**
>
> Keep in mind that by opening a hard drive, you destroy it, unless you are a certified technician.

When you open a hard drive, you see shiny circular disks with read and write arms attached to a motor. No matter how closely you look, however, you will never see the 0s and 1s stored on those shiny platters because they are magnetically written and read. To understand how the hardware works, you must understand the ***geometry*** of how drives store all those 0s and 1s.

### Platters

The ***platters*** of a hard drive—the shiny disks mentioned above—can be made of aluminum, ceramic, or even glass and are designed to spin at very high speeds. The platters are coated with a magnetic material of some type such as iron oxide that can be charged either negative or positive, which is how the 0s and 1s are "written" to the platters. A typical hard drive usually has more than one platter, and data can be written to both the top and bottom of each platter.

### Heads

The ***read/write heads*** of a hard drive are the devices that can read or alter the magnetic signature on a hard drive. Every platter has two heads to be able to read/write both the top and bottom of the platter (see Figure 5.1).

### Cylinders

To understand ***cylinders,*** you must look at the tracks on a hard drive. To visualize what a track looks like, think about how track athletes run in circles around an oval track in certain lanes. These lanes are the same concept as tracks on a hard drive. A hard drive platter has literally thousands of these concentric circular tracks.

**FIGURE 5.1** Heads write to both the top and bottom of the platter.

Imagine looking at a hard drive with four different platters stacked one on top of the other from a side view, as shown in Figure 5.2. A cylinder is basically grouping the same tracks vertically through the stack of platters.



### Sectors

The last part of what is called drive geometry is something called a *sector*. The easiest way to understand sectors is to think of a round cake. The way a cake is sliced in triangular pieces is the same way drives are divided into sectors. The common size for a sector is 512 bytes; however, never take that size for granted.

### Locating Hard Drive Geometry Information

Remember that label affixed to the top of the hard drive? The information on this label contains the drive geometry required to install the hard drive in a computer. Additionally, the label will also have the pin assignments for any jumpers on the hard drive along with serial and model numbers. If this hard

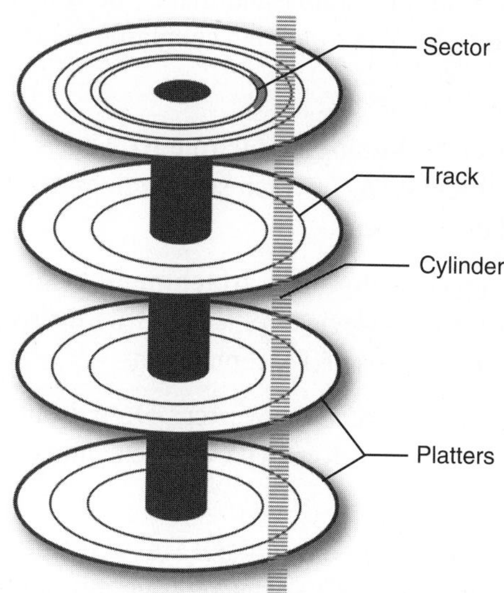


**FIGURE 5.2** A cylinder is a vertical grouping of tracks.

drive does not have a label, you may have to resort to the Internet to find its exact specifications. The thing to remember about drive geometry is that new computers will automatically read the hard drive controller BIOS and insert the information into the computer BIOS. Also remember, a user can change the drive geometry settings and essentially create a custom-sized drive for which only that user knows the exact geometry settings. The three components that determine the size of the hard drive are cylinders, heads, and sectors, and as mentioned before, these can be modified by technically adept users.

## Hard Drive Standards

Now that you have looked at basic drive geometry, you will look at the different technologies used to connect the hard drive to your computer. As a forensic analyst, you will need to know how these technologies work and, more important, how they affect the way in which you access the data on a hard drive.

The two most popular hard drive technologies in use today are enhanced integrated drive electronics (EIDE) and small computer systems interface (SCSI). Of the two, EIDE is the most widely used with a rate over 90 percent usage in the market today. The best way to identify the drive technology when looking at the hard drive (apart from reading the label) is to look at the ribbon connector on the back of the hard drive. The standard EIDE connector is 40 pins, whereas the SCSI connector is a 50- or even 68-pin type.

The hard drive industry has created various standards that at best can be confusing and are often misunderstood. You may be wondering why if all these standards exist and work you should know them. The simple answer is that as a forensic examiner, you need to understand the basic technology you use to help you work your cases more efficiently and make you a more credible expert in the computer forensic field. The following standards are the ones you will most likely encounter:

- **ATA (advanced technology attachment).** This is the umbrella standard for ATA-1 through ATA-7, which standardizes everything from connections to hard drive speeds.
- **ATAPI (advanced technology attachment programmable interface).** This standard allows devices other than hard drives such as compact disk or tape drives to use ATA connections.
- **EIDE** (the name invented by Western Digital but in reality the ATA-2 standard)**.** Allows up to four ATA devices and is now used to describe ATA standards 2 through 5.
- **IDE (integrated drive electronics).** This is the original ATA-1 standard and is no longer used. This standard supports only two drives, unlike ATA-2 that supports up to four.

- **PIO (programmable input/output).** Used in ATA-1 for transferring data between hard drive and RAM.
- **UDMA (ultra direct memory access).** Currently used to transfer data between hard drive and RAM for ATA-2 through ATA-5.
- **ATA speed rating.** This term refers to the speed at which a hard drive is capable of transferring data to the computer. Common references to these speeds are listed as ATA33, ATA66, ATA100, and ATA133.
- **SATA (serial advanced technology attachment).** This new standard uses a more efficient serial hard drive controller interface to achieve speeds of up to 150MBps. The cables are not the flat ribbon type, and every drive is considered a master drive. Additionally, some SATA drives are hot pluggable, which means you can connect and disconnect these devices with the computer on.



### Master and Slave Configurations

Because the ATA standards allow for more than one hard drive or device per cable, there has to be a way for both devices to communicate via this one cable. The solution hard drive makers came up with is the master/slave configuration. The controller on board the hard drive designated as the master controls both devices. The device designated as the slave device is set to allow the master device to assume control.

Most hard drives have a set of jumpers used to designate a hard drive as master or slave (or "carrier select"). Remember that label on the hard drive cover? On that label, you will find the settings on how the pins are "shorted" to make the hard drive a master or slave. If for some reason there is no documentation, the Internet and the manufacturer's site are your best sources of information.

---

## Other Storage Technologies

Although you will probably focus most of your efforts as a forensic examiner on suspect hard drives, you may also be required to examine a variety of other storage devices, from floppy disks to USB flash drives. Each type of storage media has its own technology you must be familiar with to acquire data safely from it.

### Floppy Disks

A floppy disk works on the same principle as a magnetic hard drive. Floppy disks are now going the way of the dinosaur thanks to CDs, DVDs, and USB drives, but many computers still have floppy disk drives and you may be dealing with floppy disks for several more years to come.

From a physical standpoint, a floppy disk is a film of Mylar with a magnetic coating. The reason floppy disks are called *floppy* is because the early 12-inch floppy disks were literally floppy. The Mylar disk was encased in a plastic cover, and you could actually flop it back and forth. You are unlikely to deal with many 12-inch disks; these disks have been replaced over the years and through a series of modifications by high-density 3.5-inch disks that are enclosed in a hard plastic cover. Bear in mind that floppy disks are relatively unreliable in comparison to hard drives and CDs, so you may find yourself unable to read a floppy disk.

**FYI** *Incredible Shrinking Floppies*

The large floppy disks mentioned above were used to store data for early mainframes such as those manufactured by IBM. As the computer revolution gained speed and technology improved, floppies shrank from 12 inches to 10 inches, to 8 inches, and finally to the last truly "floppy" size of 5.25 inches. Despite their size, original disks had very little storage capacity and were read only. The first commercially available 8-inch floppies could store less than 100KB.

## Tape Drive Technologies

As a forensic analyst, you will at some point run across tape backups that you need to examine. Tape media is the oldest form of magnetic technology and is still widely used simply because it can store huge amounts of data cheaply and reliably.

The problem with tape media is that there are three distinct groups and each group requires a specific tape drive. The following are the different types in current use:

- **QIC (quarter-inch cartridge).** This is one of the older standards and has a useful size of 2GB. Because modern drives exceed this size by a wide margin, you more than likely will not see this tape group very often.
- **DAT (digital audio tape).** Unlike QIC, which uses an analog encoding scheme, DAT uses a digital encoding scheme. The typical size of a DAT tape cartridge is 24GB; this type of tape system is being replaced more and more by DLT.
- **DLT (digital linear tape).** DLT has a larger capacity of storage, in the 200GB range, and is incredibly fast and reliable.

## ZIP and Other High-Capacity Drives

Before the introduction of USB thumb drives, users were clamoring for larger capacity removable media. The 3.5-inch floppy disks could hold only 1.44MB, and user files were exceeding this size. Iomega® introduced a removable media device called the ZIP® drive. Essentially, Iomega introduced a floppy disk with much more capacity and reliability. The first ZIP drive held 100MB of data compared to the paltry 1.44MB of a typical floppy. The most recent ZIP drives can work with disks that hold up to 750MB; these drives can read previous 250MB and 100MB ZIP disks, but they cannot write to a 100MB disk.

Other technologies such as JAZZ drives and SuperDisk follow the same basic principles of ZIP drives. The main thing to remember is that you need to have the right drive to handle the removable media type. In other words, a JAZZ drive will not read a ZIP disk.



## Optical Media Structures

Unlike the magnetic devices covered in the previous section, optical media use light from laser or LED sources to determine the 0s and 1s. Philips and Sony developed the compact disk (CD) technology in the late 1970s and released it to the general public in the early 1980s. Early CD technology was designed for audio and in fact was intended to replace vinyl records. Audio CD technology and data CD technology use the same basic techniques for storing data such as pits and lands; however, the formats are completely different in logical structure.

The basic physical structure of a CD is a spiral groove much like that of an old-fashioned vinyl record. CDs use a combination of chemical reactions and heat to create pits and lands depending on what type of CD you are using: CD-ROM disks use a different technology than CD-RWs. Pits and lands are used to differentiate or create 0s and 1s on a CD platter. A laser will either reflect or not reflect off the surface of the media depending on whether it focuses on a pit or land, and it will be interpreted as either a 0 or 1. In addition to different physical properties, different CD types—CD, compact disk recordable (CDR), and compact disk rewritable (CD-RW)—use different logical formats.

For the most part, CD manufacturers have tried to standardize formats so that most drives and operating systems can read different formats without much trouble. As the forensic examiner, you will eventually run across a CD written in a nonstandard file format or with a mixture of different formats, and you will have to ascertain what type of CD format you are dealing with and what type of CD drive will read that CD. In some cases, too, you may need RW software on your computer to read a CD that hasn't been closed.

**Single Session vs. Multisession CDs** Originally, all CD formats were single session in nature. Basically, a single table of contents was used per CD because the CD was read only and could not be appended to or altered.

When technology improved to make it possible to write and rewrite CDs, multisession CDs were introduced. A multisession CD has more than one table of contents written onto its file system, and as a forensic examiner you must understand that not all CD drives will read multisession disks.

**FYI** *Destroying CD Data*

As a practical matter for forensic recovery, some suspects believe that by scratching a CD, they can make the disk unreadable. With a good polishing, almost any CD can be made readable again and data extracted from it. The only truly reliable way to destroy CD data is to destroy the CD itself.

**DVDs** With the introduction of high-capacity storage and the availability of writable media, DVDs will become more commonplace to answer the need for larger capacity removable media. Physically, CD and DVD disks look exactly the same; however, the internal file structures are considerably different. DVDs can be written on both sides, whereas the common CD writes to only one side. With up to 8GB of storage space available, DVDs have ample storage capacity. The new Blue DVDs have storage capacities in the 20GB range and above, so you may see storage capabilities in the DVD storage arena that rival hard drive capacities.

As with CDs, the software drivers and DVD drive handle access to the file system and allow the forensic examiner to examine the contents of the DVD just like a regular disk drive.

### USB Flash Drives

As memory chip prices have dropped, USB drives have become inexpensive and commonplace among many in the computer field. A standard USB drive is literally the size of a person's thumb and can store gigabytes of information in NAND (Not AND)-type flash memory (or small, square-shaped optical discs with a USB connector). USB drives are also impervious to scratches that plague floppy- and CD-type media in addition to being able to store larger amounts of data. Additionally, the USB system has become universal among computers, and you would be hard pressed to find any new computer without at least one USB port.

The file system used by USB drives varies, but the file allocation table (FAT) is typically used because most operating file systems can read this file system type. On larger USB drives, NTFS has replaced FAT as the preferred file system, but HFS and others are not uncommon. Because these file systems are common for hard drives, the operating system views them as regular hard drives, and by default your forensic software will see them as regular hard drives also. You will read more about file systems such as FAT and NTFS in Chapter 6.

# Personal Digital Assistant Devices (PDAs)

Personal digital assistants (PDAs) have rapidly become commonplace in both personal and business arenas. The typical PDA can be used to keep up with appointments, send and receive e-mail, and even surf the Web.

The modern PDA comes with a microprocessor, ROM, RAM, and a way to input data either via QWERTY keypad or touch screen. (The term *QWERTY* derives from the first six letters in the top letter row of standard input hardware such as a typewriter or keyboard.) A small device such as a PDA or mobile phone has a miniaturized keypad that allows the user to literally type a letter or e-mail almost as if using a normal sized keyboard (see Figure 5.3). Obviously this is not a perfect solution, because most QWERTY keypads have keys only a 5-year-old can use easily, but they do work once you get the hang of them. Most ROMs found in PDAs are the flash type and thus can be rewritten multiple times. User data is kept in the RAM section of the device and is kept active by the use of batteries. This data is thus vulnerable to erasure if power is disconnected for any length of time. The newest generation of PDAs comes equipped with wireless capabilities such as WiFi, IR, and Bluetooth.

Depending on the manufacturer of the PDA, up to 128MB of RAM can be accessed and up to 64MB of ROM can be used for the operating system. As of this date, there are five major PDA operating systems:

- BlackBerry
- Open Embedded (Linux)
- PalmSource (Palm OS)
- Symbian (Psion)
- Windows Mobile (Pocket PC)

**FIGURE 5.3** A QWERTY keypad.

All PDA devices come with ***personal information management (PIM)*** software, which provides basic functionality with address book, appointments, mailbox, and memorandum capabilities. The data used in the PIM modules resides in the PDA; however, because most PDA devices are synchronized with a computer, the PIM data can also be extracted from the computer after synchronization occurs.

The last thing to consider with PDA devices is that they also can include external storage devices such as Compact Flash. When collecting evidence, make sure to thoroughly examine the area surrounding the computer for any external storage devices, no matter how small.

---

## Cellular Phones

The line between PDAs and cellular telephones has become somewhat blurry these days, and the newest cellular phone products in the market actually have their lineage based on PDA architectures.

The new cellular phones are basically low-end portable computers. The capabilities of modern cell phones include:

- PDA functionality (PIM scheduling and e-mail)
- Text messaging via
    - Short message service (SMS): Used to send simple text messages between cellular phones and even land lines.
    - Extended message service (EMS): Used to send formatted text messages, pictures, and even animation.
    - Multimedia message service (MMS): In addition to text, the service allows video and audio clips to be sent between cellular phones.
    - Instant messaging (IM): Used for real-time text conversation ability between mobile devices.
- Single photo and/or movie video capable
- Phonebook
- Call logs
- Subscriber identity module (SIM)
- Global positioning systems (GPS)
- Video streaming
- Audio players

The latest cell phones have up to 64MB of RAM and up to 64MB of ROM, so these mobile devices have plenty of room; with 300 megahertz processors, they also have plenty of processing power for the use they are designed to handle.

The forensic community as a whole has focused on the computer and network forensic field and is just now beginning to see the type of data that can be retrieved from the latest cell phones. As an example, al Qaeda's number-three man was caught in Pakistan simply because the cell phones al Qaeda was using were being tracked by the information assigned to the cell phone via the ***subscriber identity module (SIM).***

**FYI** *More Feature-Rich Cell Phones*

New phones were displayed at the CTIA Wireless 2006 trade show in Las Vegas that ranged from simple handsets for making voice calls to fancy phone-shaped computers that receive television signals.

For example, Sony Ericsson's new camera phone, K790 Cyber-shot phone, offers relatively fast Web browsing and e-mail on the GSM network. When flipped over, it becomes a 3.2-megapixel Cyber-shot digital camera with autofocus, a Xenon flash, and a feature called BestPic, which takes a series of nine rapid-fire shots by pressing the shutter button. According to reviewers, the flash is handy because a lot of camera-phone photos are taken in bars. "The pictures can then be blackmailed, er, e-mailed to your personal blog, or transferred to a printer via Bluetooth or USB" (Lewis, 2006).

## Drive and Media Analysis

In the previous sections, you have studied the basics of the hardware you are likely to encounter. Now you will begin look at the forensic analysis of each of these technologies. Chapter 4 discussed the general procedures an investigator must follow to prepare for forensic examination. The list below reviews and summarizes those procedures.

- Wipe all media you plan to use and use a standard character during that wipe. Using a standard, unique character makes it easy to demarcate the extent of any data you copy to your media.
- Assemble all needed computer components such as floppies, hard drives, and so on that you will need for this investigation.

- Document, photograph, and otherwise inventory the computer equipment and surrounding environment on which you are performing the forensic analysis.
- Document the process of how you acquired the forensic image from the suspect computer via bit-stream or disk-to-disk image.
- Document the chain of custody.
- Document your methods and reasons for conducting the investigation.

## Acquiring Data from Hard Drives

After you have prepared the target media and assembled all the forensic tools you need for this investigation, you are ready to make an image or exact copy of the suspect drive. As a forensic investigator, your job is to make an exact copy of a suspect's system and to be able to prove you have not made any changes to the computer system in the process. At face value, this may seem easy; but remember that any time you move the mouse or disconnect a cable you are making changes to the computer system.

The next consideration is whether to do a disk-to-disk drive image or do a disk to bit-stream image. Each method has pros and cons, but the bit-stream images generated from disk-to-image transfers are the easiest to work with.

**Bit-Stream Transfer** As discussed in Chapters 3 and 4, you first have to decide onsite whether to disconnect the computer from its power source or perform a system shutdown before you start the disk duplication process. The simple rule is that you disconnect or pull the power plug on everything but servers. The main reason you power down servers is simply because a server will usually have open files or data that can be damaged if the power is suddenly disconnected. A workstation, by contrast, will usually have minimal files open and will not be affected as severely as a server where you may have dozens or even hundreds of users accessing at the same time. The trade-off with servers is that you will alter some data when you shut down in this fashion. As with all things forensic, you must make the judgment call whether you will chance damaging data or risk changing possible evidence.

After you have shut down the computer, you must prevent the hard drive from booting when you restart it to make the data transfer. As you learned in Chapter 4, you do this by unplugging the computer, opening the case, and physically disconnecting the hard drive.

You can then restart the computer, enter the BIOS setup, and change the boot order so that the computer boots to a floppy or CD. If possible, remove the hard drive from the boot sequence and save the changes you have made. By doing this and documenting your work, you have essentially proven that it would have been difficult for the hard drive to boot after it was powered down.

Remember, you must document as much as possible. When you are in the BIOS system, make sure to document the following:

- Time and date as shown in the BIOS
- The boot order as shown in the BIOS

As further insurance against inadvertently writing to the suspect computer system, use a software write blocker or hardware drive blocker. EnCase® software and FTK™ use software write blockers, but you can also use hardware write blockers such as FastBloc. Just make sure you use one.

A write blocker works in a simple fashion. Whenever a system call is sent to the controller to write to the hard drive, the write blocker (either software or hardware) intercepts this call and reports back to the operating system that the write was successful. The operating system reports the write was successful, but the data is *never* written to the hard drive. If you use a write blocker that is built in to the application such as the EnCase software, you essentially just let the software handle the write blocking. It is basically automatic. If you use a hardware-based system, it is also handled automatically except that you will be plugging hard drives into the device and must have a basic knowledge of hardware such as SCSI and EIDE connections.

5

At this point, you should have a bootable floppy or CD ready for whichever forensic tool you will be using—EnCase software, FTK, or any other tool. Boot the suspect computer with the bootable media and proceed to do a bit-stream image transfer. Most forensic software has the ability to generate a one-way hash of the suspect drive and of your bit-stream image. The two hash results should be identical and thus prove the suspect drive and your image are mathematically identical. Keep in mind that if your hash values do not match, a court of law can and more than likely will disallow that evidence from being presented because the copy is not an exact duplicate of the original.

Once you have your bit-stream copy and have hashed it, you need to make *another* copy of the duplicate, as detailed in Chapter 4. This second copy is the working copy you should use for your analyses. Store your original in a safe place, and as a general rule try never to touch the actual suspect drive more than once.

Now that you have a working bit-stream image, you have several options available to you as a forensic examiner. You can choose to work on the image itself using the built-in tools of applications such as Ilook, EnCase, or FTK software. Bear in mind that tools such as Ilook are used by law enforcement only, whereas EnCase and FTK software are used both by law enforcement and private interests. Because these tools have been around for some time, they include automated searches for information such as e-mail, chat, and file evidence. You can also restore this logical image file to a hard drive and work on the hard drive as if it were in the suspect's machine. If you restore an image to another hard drive, you must wipe that drive to ensure a clean drive is used. To ensure that you have wiped or cleaned the drive properly and to demarcate where the image restore ends, write a unique character across the entire hard drive.

**Disk-to-Disk Imaging** The second method used to acquire a disk image is to do a disk-to-disk acquisition. In concept, you are literally copying one hard drive to another. In a nonforensic situation, you would just do a regular disk copy of the entire drive, and any changes made during the transfer would be inconsequential. Because you are doing a forensic copy, however, *all* data transferred must be identical in both the source and target hard drive or storage device. The term *bit-level copy* is used to explain that you are literally copying every single bit on the original drive from the first sector to the last sector on the storage device. To this end, special precautions must be used to ensure that no writes are made to the original suspect storage device.

Equipment such as Logicube's Talon system is a hardware-based forensic acquisition device. The device has a multitude of capabilities, but its core function is to transfer data from one storage device to another and to authenticate that the data has not changed. In addition to this, because it is a hardware device and does the transfer directly, the transfer speeds are somewhat higher than software-based forensic tools.

Make one copy of the original evidence and then make a *second* copy from the first copy to use for the actual analysis. Once you have the second copy imaged, the process of analysis is carried out in the same fashion as other investigations.

## Acquiring Data from Removable Media

Removable media such as floppies, CDs, and tape are handled in much the same way as hard drive media with a couple of added precautions. By their very nature, removable media are not as stable or robust as a standard hard drive. Floppies and tape are especially notorious for losing data when you need it the most.

As noted before, you should document all aspects of any forensic investigation, including taking pictures of the subject computer and its surrounding environment. A good rule of thumb is to document everything within reach of the person using that computer. This includes all peripherals, books, and removable media within a 20-foot radius. Investigators can deduce many things by simply looking around a suspect's work area. If you notice a ZIP drive on the system, then by deduction you should also look for any ZIP disks. The following checklist is useful for handling removable media:

- Document the scene.
- Place all removable media in a static-proof container.
- Label the container with the type of media, where the media were found, and the type of reader required.

- Transport directly to lab.
- *Do not* leave any media in a hot vehicle or environment.
- Store media in a secure and organized area.

Once you have control of the media in your lab, the next step is to make a forensic duplicate and a working copy of the media. The process depends on the type of forensic software used, but the same principles used to make a forensic copy of hard drives apply to removable media. At this point, you should make sure you have the correct hardware to read the type of media you are going to work with. For example, a floppy disk will require a floppy drive. For common media such as floppies, ZIP drives, or memory cards, you should have these types of devices in your lab. If necessary, you can use the suspect's equipment to read the media if you run across a unique situation, but this is generally not the preferred method. (If you need to use the suspect's equipment, you can remove the device from the suspect computer and use it on the forensic platform.)

The first step is to make sure the media is write-protected. Floppy disks have a write protect notch you can use to make sure no writes are done to the floppy. You generally do not have to worry about writing to CDs because they are usually read only unless you use a burner. Remember that for CD media, there are different drive types, and that may affect how you are able to get an image off that CD. Certain drives, for example, will not read CD-RW media because the material used in the CD does not have a sharp enough contrast for that particular drive laser to differentiate the pits and lands. For tape backups, the best solution is to use the write protect tabs available on all tape backup media. Keep in mind that many tape backup systems may appear to use the same type of tape simply because physically they look the same. If you look closely, however, you will notice that density and tape capacities are radically different for different systems.

Once you have made sure the media is write-protected, the next step is to acquire a forensic image of the media. The most important thing to do when making this image is to make a hash to document both the hash value of the original and the hash value of the image. They should match exactly to prove you have not changed anything on your image copy. Most forensic software will view external media such as tape drives as just another drive, so acquiring the image will be the same as if you were acquiring a hard drive. Using whichever forensic tool you prefer, make an image of the removable media or even a set of removable media. Once you have the image done, make a duplicate working copy of the image and put away the original image in case you need to access it. After this is all done, store the original media in a secure and organized place.

### Acquiring Data from USB Flash Drives

USB drives may seem a little different to forensic examiners at first, but they logically appear to most operating systems as a regular hard drive using a FAT file system. As with all other examinations, you must first set a write protect

5

method in place to keep from writing to the USB drive. Most USB drives come with a physical switch of some type to prevent writes to the drive. If you do not find any physical switches on the device, the manufacturer may provide software that accomplishes the write protection. The only problem with that solution is that there is a chance of a write occurring on the examiner's computer before the software has a chance to lock down the USB drive. In addition to this, remember that USB drives also configure themselves automatically when plugged into a PC and thus may make some changes without the examiner's intending to. Bear in mind that this is a rare occurrence, but it can happen when you are dealing with a device that requires device drivers to work.

Internally, a USB drive uses flash memory (memory registers) to store information. The information is literally stored as a series of on and off sequences in the memory registers of the USB drive. Most operating systems will view the USB drives as a regular FAT hard drive and query the USB controller chip just as if it is querying a hard drive controller. Because the operating system treats the USB drive as a regular drive, your forensic software will interact with the USB drive just like a regular hard drive.

## IN PRACTICE: PDA-Configured iPod Reveals Employee Theft

For 15 years, Joe was a diligent bookkeeper. After he retired, the new bookkeeper noticed that the company had paid a small bank fee with every transaction during Joe's tenure, but the bank records showed no such deposits. A review of the fees revealed that they were deposits made into Joe's account that totaled hundreds of thousands of dollars. The police were called in to investigate further.

Once Joe's prior actions became suspect, the owner remembered that Joe had kept an iPod on his desk and brought a laptop to the office so that he could take work home.

After the investigating officer obtained a search warrant for Joe's residence, the police and a team of forensic investigators went there and seized several computer systems, a series of external hard drives, and an iPod. In the lab, forensic investigators found no evidence against Joe on any of his computers.

Next, the iPod was analyzed. The investigator treated the iPod like any other external hard drive by imaging the iPod's hard drive first and using the copy for analysis. The investigator knew that iPods have features that PC hard drives do not. For example, the iPod

CONTINUED ON NEXT PAGE

▶▶ CONTINUED

creates a separate partition that will contain firmware settings for the device (that is, the actual iPod operating system) and application information for iPod applications, including the calendar, contacts, and notes.

After imaging the drive, the investigator noticed that Joe's 40GB iPod was configured with two data partitions: one 20GB partition to hold music and another 20GB partition to store data files, like a PDA. iPods can also function as a PDA, with documents, spreadsheets, a calendar, notes, and address book.

The investigator ran a directory listing, which showed all the files on the drive that held the data files. This directory listing revealed Excel and Word documents, which contained data critical to the investigation. The Excel spreadsheets contained detailed reports of each transaction Joe made, including time and date of deposit, as well as a record of each account number the bookkeeper used over the years. This evidence showed that Joe had been updating his records each time he embezzled money from the company; he had then saved the file to his iPod, which appeared to his employer to be nothing more than a portable jukebox.

The evidence taken from the iPod helped convict the bookkeeper.



## PDA Analysis

The area of PDA forensic analysis is a more specialized area than personal computer forensic analysis. The amount and types of forensic tools available for the examiner are few and not as sophisticated as their counterparts in the PC world. The majority of PDA forensic tools available are tailored for the two most popular PDA platforms, Palm OS and Pocket PC. You will learn later in this chapter about tools used to forensically examine a PDA and how each tool works.

Unlike most PC examinations, PDA examinations deal with a device that has a very volatile memory configuration. The paramount consideration when dealing with a PDA device is to make sure power to the device is not interrupted. If the battery dies or the power adapter is unplugged, you will lose all user data. The Association of Police Chief Officers (APCO) offers these guidelines (which can be located at **www.acpo.police.uk/policies.asp**) for seizing PDAs.

- On seizure, the PDA should not be switched on, if already off.
- The PDA should be placed in an envelope and the envelope should then be sealed before being put into an evidence bag, to restrict physical access while it is still sealed in the evidence bag.

- Where the PDA is fitted with only a single rechargeable battery, the appropriate power adapter should be connected to the device with the cable passing through the evidence bag so that it can be kept on charge.
- If the PDA is switched on when found, the device should be kept in an active running mode (e.g., by tapping on a blank section of the screen) and supplied with power until an expert can examine it, to avoid the consequences of activating security mechanisms such as user authentication and content encryption. If sufficient power cannot be supplied, consideration should be given to switching off the PDA to preserve battery life, documenting the current device state, and noting the time and date of the shutdown.
- A search should be conducted for associated flash memory devices, such as Secure Digital (SD), MultiMedia Card (MMC), or CompactFlash (CF) semiconductor cards, microdrives, and USB tokens.
- Any power leads, cables, or cradles relating to the PDA should also be seized, as well as manuals.
- Anyone handling PDAs before their examination should treat them in such a manner that gives the best opportunity for any recovered data to be admissible as evidence in any later proceedings.

**FYI** *PDA Chain of Custody*

According to the NIST's Special Publication 800–72, "Guidelines on PDA Forensics" (2004), documentation of the chain of custody throughout the lifecycle of a case involving a PDA should answer the following questions:

- Who collected the device, media, and associated peripherals?
- How and where? That is, how was the e-evidence collected and where was it located?
- Who took possession of it?
- How was it stored and protected while in storage?
- Who took it out of storage and why?

After the power issue, wireless connectivity is the second issue that must be considered when seizing a PDA. Newer PDA devices come equipped with wireless capabilities and may transmit/receive signals that will alter the evidence. To avoid this situation, you can either turn off the device or transport it via an isolation bag (a Faraday bag) used to keep out radio frequency (RF) signals.

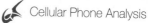

As mentioned before, a forensic examination normally must be done on a device that does not have any security or authentication mechanisms enabled. If you encounter a device that has a password or security device enabled, you have very few options for dealing with it. The following list should serve as a guideline when you encounter this situation:

- Ask the suspect what the password is.
- Contact the manufacturer for backdoors or other useful information.
- Search the Internet for known exploits for either a password crack or an exploit that goes around the password.
- Call in PDA professionals who specialize in data recovery.

Just as for a storage medium, a PDA can be examined either physically or logically. The physical acquisition method is the acquisition of a bit-by-bit copy of the physical parts of a PDA such as the RAM, ROM, or disk drive. This has the advantage of copying every physical bit, which in turn means you are copying potentially hidden or deleted information. A logical acquisition copies only what the operating system can see, such as files and directories, but leaves out areas considered to be empty or nonexistent. The best method to use for a PDA forensic examination is *both*. Using physical and logical acquisition techniques ensures that you capture all the data, have it in a logical format, and have the ability to compare images for obvious differences.

To get to the point of being able to connect the forensic examiner's software to the suspect's PDA requires a physical connection of some type. The best solution is to use the cradle the PDA comes with and use the USB port to transfer the data across. EnCase software will work best in this fashion. Other forensic tools can use the protocols built in to the PDA such as HotSync or ActiveSync and use cables specially designed for PC to PDA acquisitions, as is the case with Paraben®.

---

## Cellular Phone Analysis

As mentioned earlier, today's cellular phones have much in common with the PDA devices in the market. Modern cellular phones have RAM, ROM, memory cards, and something PDA devices do not have: a SIM card.

When you have to do a forensic examination of a modern cellular phone, you have to break the investigation down into two very distinct components. The first component is the acquisition of the physical memory associated with the PIM aspects of the cellular phone. The second part of the investigation focuses on the SIM card and all the information found there.

The primary function of a SIM card is to identify the subscriber and authenticate the subscriber to the cellular phone network. In addition to this, a SIM card usually contains the phonebook, text messages, call information, and network configuration information for the user and not necessarily the phone. Physically, a SIM card has between 16 and 64KB of memory, a processor, and an operating system. SIM cards can be removed from the cellular phone and placed into a special SIM card reader and the information extracted rather quickly, unless a personal identification number (PIN) has been assigned as a security precaution.

A consideration you must also be aware of when dealing with cellular phone SIM cards is the phase of the standard they can support, which basically means the SIM card with the latest generation phase has more capabilities than earlier generations. Currently, the phase generations in the field are phase 1, phase 2, phase 2.5, and phase 3. The tools used to display or extract this information must be up to date to work with the newest generation of SIM cards, and even then you may have to use more than one tool to extract every piece of information.

A serious consideration you must anticipate is that the user may have some form of authentication enabled on the cellular phone. Much like the PDA device scenario, the software used to extract the information from the cellular phone must have complete access to extract an image correctly. In other words, you must be able to get past the authentication before you can begin your examination. To further complicate matters, there may be multiple forms of authentication because you are dealing with a PIM and a SIM. We have covered the basics of personal information manager (PIM) authentication in the PDA section, so we will now look at SIM methods of authentication.

A SIM is usually protected by a PIN or card holder verification (CHV) number and can have more than one number set. If you are lucky, the PIN will not be set by the user, and you have unfettered access to the SIM. If the user has enabled one or both PIN authentication features, you have to disable or work around the PIN authentication. You have two main options for disabling the PIN: ask the user, or ask the service provider for a PIN unblocking key (PUK). The PUK will reset the PIN and allow you past the authentication. A very important thing to remember is that most SIM cards allow only three attempts to get past the PIN before you are locked out. On the off chance that you use the PUK and still cannot get in, do not attempt to brute force the PUK. After a predetermined amount of tries, if the PUK fails, you will be permanently blocked from access to the SIM.

As with all forensic examinations, you can do a physical or a logical acquisition of the device. Because we are dealing with cellular phones, you will have to do this with both the PIM and SIM devices. The physical aspects of connecting to the cellular phone vary depending on the type of cellular phone and the type of forensic software you are going to use. Most modern PIM/SIM cellular phones come with a cradle that is designed to synchronize with the user's computer. These cradles usually come with a USB connection but sometimes will be connected via a serial cable. Whichever method is used by the manufacturer, you must use forensic software that can access via this method. Because you are dealing with a wireless device, you have other options when trying to acquire these devices. Most modern cellular phones now come equipped with a WiFi, Bluetooth, or IR interface, and if your forensic software can support that type of interface, you can acquire via this method.

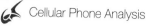

The guidelines and steps used in a cellular phone forensic analysis are the same basic steps you use in any other forensic analysis and will look very familiar to any forensic examiner. As with other examinations, you have to adjust to your particular investigation and bear in mind you are dealing with a relatively new field in forensics that changes very rapidly. You are strongly urged to follow the guidelines previously listed for PDA seizures because most modern cellular phones have PDA qualities to them. Some additional guidelines for working with cellular phones are listed below.



- In the laboratory environment, determine which forensic software package will work with the suspect cellular phone. Different software packages are used for different cellular phones.
- Ascertain the connection method you will use. If the cellular phone has a cradle, you will normally use the USB interface. If the cellular phone has the capability to use Bluetooth or IR, you can use this method, assuming your forensic software can also interface using these wireless methods.
- Some devices need to have certain protocols in place before you start your acquisition. Common protocols used are Microsoft ActiveSync, Palm HotSync, and BlackBerry Desktop Manager. These protocols are primarily used to generate a guest account on the suspect device for the simple reason that the PDA does not allow any synchronization between the forensic computer and the PDA device *before* acquisition.
- Once you have ascertained which connection method and forensic software is most appropriate for this particular investigation, you physically connect the cellular phone and forensic workstation via whichever interface you intend to use.
- Before you go any further, make sure you have all the equipment and basic data in place to start. A checklist would include a battery backup or charger for the device, any passwords on the device, cables/cradles needed, external SIM readers, and manuals for all devices.
- Most software packages are GUI based and will walk you through a wizard. The wizard will normally ask the following questions:
  - Manufacturer or global system for mobile communication (GSM) SIM card?
  - Cellular phone model?

- Connection type (USB, Bluetooth, or IR)?
- Type of data you want to acquire?

- Once you have the forensic software connected to the device, you follow the regular procedures to obtain a bit-stream copy of the device and generate hash values to prove the integrity of the data.
- Depending on the forensic software capabilities, you can now do searches for evidence and generate reports detailing your findings.

**IN PRACTICE: Cell Phone Forensics Identifies Suspect**

A child molester was caught with cell phone forensics. The suspect entered a home that had two young girls inside. The suspect ran away after the girls started screaming, and he dropped his cell phone in the process. The SIM card was examined and text messages were extracted. In some of the messages, the suspect was referred to by name, which helped detectives locate his residence.

## Disk Image Forensic Tools

The tools used to create a forensic image of hard drives and other storage devices have been around for some time. At this point, new tools come on the market very frequently purporting to do forensic images and reports, but only a few products on the market today can extract a forensic image and generate a detailed report and have been accepted in a court of law. The software discussed below is by no means the extent of the tools available in the market today but is a small list of the software that has been vetted by many in the field.

### Guidance Software

Guidance Software™ forensic tools are considered by many to be the gold standard in computer forensics investigations. The software has been accepted by courts around the world and is used by most major law enforcement organizations around the world as well. The biggest plus for Guidance software is the fact that the GUI interface makes this software very intuitive. The other plus is the fact the search features and functionality of the software make the job of a forensic investigator much easier in the sense that many of the common searches are now automated.

### Paraben Software

Paraben® takes a divide-and-conquer approach to computer forensics in that they have developed specialized tools for different types of searches. Paraben has tools ranging from e-mail forensic work to password recovery. In addition to the software tools, Paraben also has hardware forensic tools such as Faraday bags and SIM USB readers.

The software tools offered by Paraben are GUI based and fairly easy to work with once you get the hang of them. Paraben offers the same functionality of the EnCase software with a slightly less intuitive feel.

### FTK

FTK by AccessData is a highly regarded GUI forensic tool. As with Paraben, the initial feel of FTK is not intuitive; however, once you learn the software completely it is one of the most useful forensic tools available commercially. The search functionality is impressive, and FTK's ability to generate detailed reports is also quite good.

### Logicube

Logicube uses a hardware-based philosophy to acquire data images and has partnered with AccessData to round out their computer forensics offerings. Logicube has developed some of the most reliable and quickest hardware-based tools to extract images from hardware devices. With the introduction of Access-Data software, Logicube has essentially taken the best of both hardware and software forensic tools and combined them into very impressive computer forensic kits.

5

**IN PRACTICE:** Using an iPod as a Forensic Tool

An iPod can be configured to be a forensic tool by performing the following steps.

1. Configure the iPod as an external hard disk by using a built-in configuration tool. Choose a check box to select "Use as Hard Disk." The iPod itself is used as the investigative tool. Retrieved data is stored on a separate external hard drive.
2. Load the latest version of the Macintosh operating system, OS X. Get the latest version by running a software update utility that automatically checks the version installed and displays all available upgrades.

CONTINUED ON NEXT PAGE

▶▶ CONTINUED

3. Turn off "disk arbitration." This feature of OS X provides plug-and-play functionality so that when another device is plugged in, it can automatically be seen and recognized. Because this process can alter potential evidence, this function needs to be disabled through a set of commands.
4. Configure the iPod as a forensically sound system so that when it is connected to a suspect computer it does not write to the drive and contaminate any potential evidence.
5. Equip the iPod with software tools used to examine and analyze systems for potential evidence. Even some deleted data can be found using these software programs. The investigator uses the forensic software to quickly preview or image Mac systems using only the iPod and a small external hard drive on which to store the image.

## PDA/Cellular Phone Forensic Software

The newest field in the computer forensic world is the PDA/cellular phone field. The tools used for this type of forensic work are only just beginning to mature simply because PDA/cellular phone devices have only recently become essentially low-powered computers. Some of the GUI tools are fairly easy to use, while some of the command-line tools require some expertise in command-line gymnastics. Because the line between PDA and cellular phone is not always clear, some of the tools in the next section will work with one device but not another, so you may have to use more than one software tool to get all the information you require from one device.

### Tools for Examining PDAs

There are a limited number of tools used for PDA investigations, and those tools tend to be specialized. Some forensic examiners prefer to use their own tools or tools that have not been vetted in a court of law. These home-grown tools may be the only way to transfer or examine data from a PDA, but they should be tested extensively and by third parties to make sure the data does not change. The following sections cover some of the most commonly used PDA examination tools.

**EnCase and Palm OS Software** In addition to standard personal computer acquisitions, EnCase software has the ability to examine Palm OS devices. At present, EnCase software does not support Pocket PC, Linux, or BlackBerry devices. EnCase software can do a bit-stream copy of the entire physical area of a Palm OS device and perform constant cyclic redundancy check (CRC) calculations to ensure data integrity. The CRC checks are mathematical algorithms that check to make sure the data transmitted from the original computer is the exact same data that was received on the target computer. The EnCase application creates what it calls an evidence file (a file with an extension .e01) and mounts it virtually on the examiner's PC. Because EnCase software uses a software write-blocking technique and can hash the data, issues of data corruption or modification are eliminated. Bear in mind that a PDA stores the majority of the user data in RAM and that the date and time functions change on a continual basis, thus affecting any hash value done. In other words, hashing an image will yield different results from one second to the next simply because the time stamp has changed.

EnCase software has the added ability to generate extensive reports, has great search functions, and can save (bookmark) important data for the examiner. Another advantage to using this program is its excellent reputation and frequent use in numerous court cases.

**PDA Seizure** Unlike the EnCase software, Paraben's PDA Seizure can do forensic examinations on Palm OS, Pocket PC, and BlackBerry devices. PDA Seizure also has the incredibly nice feature of being able to crack Palm passwords and eliminate that barrier to doing a forensic examination on a Palm OS.

PDA Seizure is extremely easy to use and very graphical in nature. Once you have the hardware hooked up using USB or PDA specific cables (Paraben sells cables just for PDA forensic acquisitions), PDA Seizure guides you through the acquisition process; the software ensures there are no writes to the PDA and also ensures the data integrity of the image being transferred.

Because PDA Seizure can analyze various PDA devices, you as the forensic examiner will have to have a good supply of device drivers for the various models of PDA devices. For example, you will have to install the BlackBerry device drivers for the forensic software to open the USB port to do an acquisition; otherwise, it will be looking for a serial port.

Once the image has been transferred, PDA Seizure has a complete set of tools to work on the image that include:

- Multilanguage support
- Search functions

- Bookmark functions
- HTML reporting
- Ability to view images internally
- Report generation

**Palm dd (pdd)** Palm dd (pdd) is a command-line tool used within a Windows environment to acquire the physical image of a Palm OS device. Pdd does not have any graphical user capabilities at this time and in fact is no longer supported, so the possibility of pdd's becoming a GUI tool is fairly remote.

Because you are working with only Palm OS devices, the hardware required for this type of acquisition is the Palm device cradle and a USB cable. Once you have the physical hardware installed, you run the command **pdd** and acquire the physical bit image. A shortcoming of pdd is that it does not have the capability to generate a hash of the Palm OS device or the image file. In fact, pdd generates two files for the forensic examiner to work with. The first file contains data on the size of RAM/ROM, processor type, and OS version. The second file contains the bit image and is in binary form.

Once you have the binary file loaded on the examiner's computer, you can use a hex editor to parse the file or import the file into another tool such as EnCase software to complete the examination.

**POSE (Palm OS Emulator)** POSE is a software program that emulates the Palm OS device on a personal computer when the ROM from a physical Palm device is loaded into memory. The POSE software comes with a tool to extract the image from the Palm device; however, you can also use Palm dd (referenced above) or even regular dd to extract an image. The original use of the dd command comes from the UNIX operating system. The dd utility is primarily used to do low-level bit-level copying of storage media and has been adapted for use with PDA devices.

Once the ROM image is in place, POSE completely emulates a real Palm device down to the buttons and I/O functions. Keep in mind that this software is primarily used to test ROM images without having to use a real Palm device and only works with Palm OS version 4.x and below.

Once you have the emulator working, you can explore all the PIM functions in the PDA such as the address book and task list; however, the more useful aspect of using this software is the fact that you can generate screen shots of the Palm device desktop for either report appendices or court of law proceedings.

**PDA Memory Cards** Unlike personal computers, PDA memory storage devices normally do not include USB type devices. Aside from the inconvenience of having a relatively large piece of plastic and integrated circuit sticking out of the side of the device, the power requirements of USB drives tend to make them impractical for PDA devices. What a PDA usually comes with are memory cards. These cards vary in size from a single postage stamp to a book of stamps and usually have an external card reader for use on a regular personal computer. These memory cards do not lose data when the power is disconnected and can be a great source of information for a forensic investigator. Most cards on the market use a form of flash memory similar to USB drive technology but on a much smaller scale with storage capacity ranges from 8MB to over 2GB. The following is a list of common flash memory cards:

- Compact Flash Cards (CF)
- Extended Memory Cards (EM)
- Memory Sticks (MS)
- MicroDrives (MD)
- MultiMedia Cards (MMC)
- Secure Digital Cards (SD)

To do an examination of these memory cards, you need an external card reader of some type. To most forensic software applications, the memory card will look like an ordinary hard drive; in fact, the most prevalent file system used on these memory cards is the FAT system. Most high-end laptops and desktop computers now come equipped with these card readers, so if you shop carefully, the hardware you need may already be built into your forensic workstation.

## Tools for Examining Cellular Phones

The tools used to acquire information from cellular phones vary widely simply because at this time there are effectively two devices contained in a cellular phone: PIM and SIM. As of this date, only a few software companies have come out with a forensic software package that can work with both aspects of the cellular phone forensic analysis. Table 5.1 breaks down the tools by PIM/SIM.

## Tools for Examining Both PDAs and Cellular Phones

Paraben's Device Seizure and Logicube's CellDek have the most comprehensive sets of tools for both PDA and cellular phone analysis. Because this part

**TABLE 5.1** Forensics tools that can be used on cellular phones.

| Name | Capabilities | Interface Type |
|---|---|---|
| | **Cell Phone Capable** | |
| Bit PM | CDMA phones | Cable |
| GSM.XRY | GSM phones | Cable, Bluetooth, and IR |
| Cell Seizure | Supports GSM, TDMA, and CDMA phones | Cable |
| MOBILedit! Forensic | GSM phones | Cable and IR |
| Oxygen PM | GSM Phones | Cable |
| PDA Seizure | Palm OS, Pocket PC, and BlackBerry phones | Cable |
| Pilot-link | Palm OS phones | Cable |
| TULP 2G | GSM and CDMA phones | Cable, Bluetooth, and IR |
| | **SIM Capable** | |
| Cell Seizure | Internal SIM acquisition | Cable |
| Forensic SIM | External SIM acquisition | External Card Reader |
| Forensic Card Reader | External SIM acquisition | External Card Reader |
| GSM.XRY | Internal SIM acquisition | Cable, Bluetooth, and IR |
| MOBILedit! Forensic | Internal SIM acquisition | Cable and IR |
| SIMCon | External SIM acquisition | External Card Reader |
| SIMIS | External SIM acquisition | External Card Reader |
| TULP 2G | Internal SIM acquisition | Cable, Bluetooth, and IR |

of the forensic field is still evolving rapidly, you can get tools specifically for certain devices and essentially cherry pick which tools you will use for certain devices. As this part of the forensic field matures, companies such as Paraben and Logicube are beginning to offer comprehensive tools and, more important, updates for new devices as they come out that will work with their tools.

**Paraben Software** Paraben's Device Seizure is one of the few tools that combines both cellular phone and PDA forensic acquisition capabilities. The software is GUI based and resembles the rest of Paraben's stable of forensic tools. The investigator will normally have to use all the cradles and cables the PDA or cellular phone has and fit them to whatever forensic platform he is using. Several drivers are included in the Paraben installation, but the operating system of the computer forensics platform will also need specific drivers such as ActiveSync or HotSync to function.

The extraction of the forensic image is done much the same as with any other forensic examination with the exception that you are usually dealing with volatile data and must keep power flowing to the device or risk losing the data.

Once you are into the analysis part of your investigation, Device Seizure has the ability to do text and hex searches of the forensic image. Figure 5.4 shows a typical search using Device Seizure.



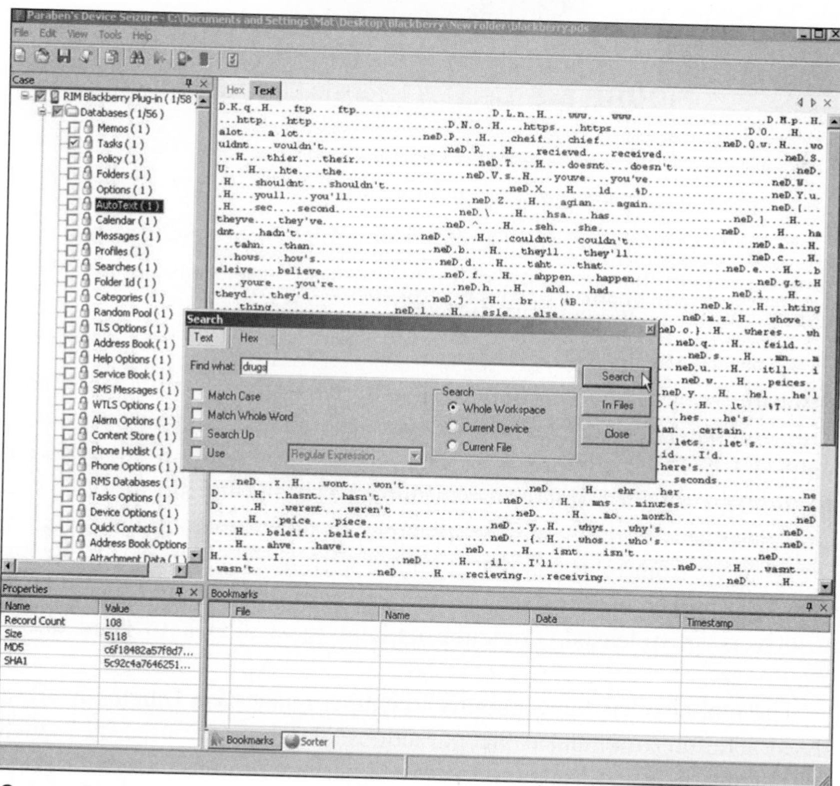


*Source:* Paraben's Device Seizure Software, Paraben Corporation, www.paraben-forensics.com.

**FIGURE 5.4** Carrying out a search using Device Seizure.

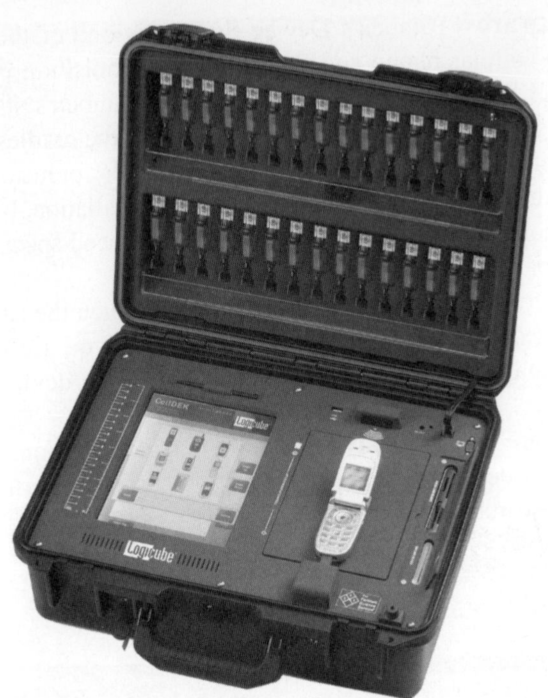


**FIGURE 5.5** CellDek forensic computer.

As with most other computer forensic tools, Device Seizure has report-generating capabilities to help the forensic investigator organize the evidence found into a logical and cohesive format.

**Logicube** Logicube has applied their hardware-based philosophy to the mobile computer forensic field. Logicube has introduced a hardware device it calls the CellDek (Figure 5.5). This device is actually a small forensic computer (the size of a small piece of luggage) with forensic software specifically designed for PDA and cellular phone image extractions. What sets this tool apart from others is that it comes with most adapters used by PDA and cellular phone manufacturers. The support for the CellDek is such that as new drivers are released, Logicube updates the CellDek to keep up with those drivers.

The tool also has the capability to extract images via Bluetooth, IR, and WiFi in addition to regular cable extractions. The software used by Logicube has the standard searches and report capabilities other forensic tools have and is completely GUI based for ease of use. The touch screen shown in Figure 5.6 eliminates the need for a mouse.

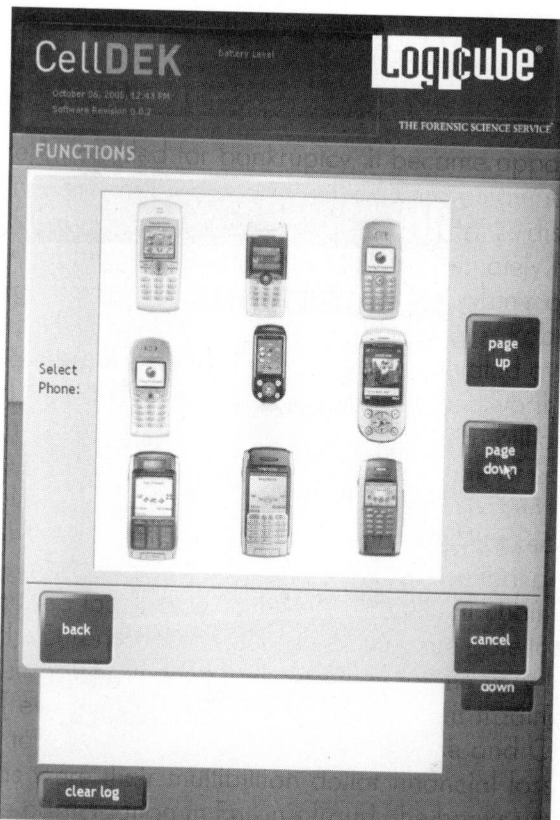


**FIGURE 5.6** CellDek GUI touch screen.



## Summary

In this chapter you covered the basic media types and devices that you will encounter when doing a forensic examination. You are most likely to encounter magnetic media devices such as hard drives and optical media devices such as CDs, but electronic devices such as USB drives are becoming more prevalent. Your job as a forensic investigator may also require you to know about data from PDAs and cellular phones.

After learning how data is stored in these various types of devices, you learned specific methods for acquiring data from each category. Some guidelines for data acquisition are the same for any device, such as the importance of making at least two copies of the data so that you can work on one copy while safeguarding the original copy and the suspect's device. Other guidelines are specific to a device, such as the importance of maintaining power to a PDA to avoid data loss.

A number of suppliers such as Guidance, Paraben, AccessData, and Logicube have developed tools for capturing and analyzing data. Some of these tools are designed to work with a specific type of data, such as that acquired from PDAs, while others can be used for several different types of data.

## Test Your Skills

### MULTIPLE CHOICE QUESTIONS

1. The main parts to the geometry of a hard drive are
   A. platters, heads, and cylinders.
   B. heads, cylinders, and sectors.
   C. cylinders, sectors, and platters.
   D. none of the above.

2. The two most popular hard drive technologies in use today are
   A. IDE and EIDE.
   B. IDE and SCSI.
   C. SCSI and EIDE.
   D. SCSI and PIO.

3. When two hard drives are on the same data cable, both drives must have which two settings for them to work?
   A. One and two.
   B. Master and slave.
   C. Primary and secondary.
   D. First and second.

4. Which of the following is not a tape drive technology?
   A. QIC.
   B. SLT.
   C. DAT.
   D. DLT.

5. Most hard drive technologies use magnetic technology to designate 0s and 1s, whereas CDs and DVDs use _____ technology.
   A. optical
   B. magnetic
   C. linear
   D. chemical

6. The original CD format was
   A. single session.
   B. multisession.
   C. writable.
   D. rewritable.

7. USB drives use
   A. RAM memory.
   B. flash memory.
   C. cache memory.
   D. none of the above.

8. Most USB drives use the _____ file system:
   A. FAT
   B. NTFS
   C. ATA
   D. HFS

9. All PDA devices come with a
   A. SIM.
   B. TIM.
   C. PIM.
   D. DIM.

10. Which of the following is not a messaging service available on cellular phones?
    A. MMS.
    B. EMS.
    C. SMS.
    D. XMS.

11. Two items to document in the BIOS are
    A. time/date and boot order.
    B. time and date.
    C. number of hard drives and boot order.
    D. RAM and boot order.

12. On seizure, a PDA that is switched off should be
    A. turned on.
    B. left off.
    C. disconnected.
    D. opened.

13. Which of the following is a phase generation standard for cellular phones?
    A. 802.11.
    B. WiFi.
    C. Phase 3.
    D. Bluetooth.

14. To identify and authenticate the phone subscriber, cellular phones use a
    A. PIM.
    B. TIM.
    C. CIM.
    D. SIM.

15. PDAs have all of the following except
    A. ROM.
    B. RAM.
    C. microprocessors.
    D. SIM.

## EXERCISES

### Exercise 5.1: Third-Generation Cellular Phone Networks

The new generation of cellular phone networks has the capability to transfer various types of data across their networks.

1. Search the Internet for details on third-generation cellular phone systems.
2. Look for future trends or directions this technology may take.
3. Write a summary of what you have learned.

### Exercise 5.2: Compact Disk Standards

1. Using your computer lab PC, find out what type of session your CD drive supports and which CD standards are applicable to your PC.
2. Research the various standards used by compact disk manufacturers.
3. Compare compact disk standards with the newer DVD standards.
4. Create a table to summarize your information.

### Exercise 5.3: Tape Backup Systems

In large organizational environments, tape backup systems are the standard used for large data backups. The chance of a forensic examiner encountering these systems is almost guaranteed.

1. Research the current DLT systems on the market today.
2. Write a report that discusses how these standards will affect your job as a forensic technician.

### Exercise 5.4: PDA Devices

With PDA devices increasingly being used by criminals, the computer forensic industry is creating more sophisticated forensic image tools for these devices.

1. Research the latest PDA devices available on the market today.
2. Compare the capabilities of these devices with regular desktop computers.
3. Research the tools used by law enforcement to extract forensic images from PDAs.
4. Write a report that discusses whether the tools currently used will be able to keep up with new advances in PDA technology.

### Exercise 5.5: Hard Drive Technology

The hard drive technology used today is fairly well understood by computer forensic technicians the world over. Even with the technology being fairly stable, there are new innovations on the horizon for hard drive storage solutions.

1. Research the new trends or innovations in the hard drive field.
2. Write a summary of how these innovations will affect the computer forensic field.

## PROJECTS

### Project 5.1: Unlocking Mobile Phone SIMs on the Internet

With the ability of the Internet to disseminate information of any type, computer forensic examiners can find answers to almost any question. In particular, the area of unlocking or bypassing the password in a mobile phone can be invaluable for the modern computer forensic technician.

1. Visit eBay and find a popular mobile phone that is being auctioned.
2. Research how to unlock this mobile phone and bypass the SIM password.
3. Explore the reliability of this information on the Internet.

### Project 5.2: Messaging Services

The advent of high-speed wireless devices has led to the development of video messaging and video streaming on PDA and mobile phone devices.

1. Research the requirements of the mobile devices to handle the larger bandwidth requirements.
2. Visit the Web sites of companies such as Sprint or T-Mobile to gather information on the new systems they use to provide video messaging service.
3. Research countries such as Japan and Spain to see how the infrastructure is set up to handle the new mobile phone technology.

### Project 5.3: Flash Memory

The term *flash memory* is used to cover a wide variety of chip-based memory storage devices. Most flash memory devices are based on NAND-type technology manufactured overseas.

1. Research which companies are at the forefront of flash memory research and development such as Motorola or Texas Instruments.
2. Examine the technology of how NAND memory works from the electronic point of view and how this compares to RAM memory.
3. Use Google to find information on the miniaturization of flash memory and the current research in this field.

## Case Study

You work for a regional computer forensic lab and have been tasked with recovering all data from a suspect's cellular phone, which is also a PDA. The case revolves around cyberstalking, and evidence is needed to prove these allegations. Use the Internet to research the different ways in which a person can be stalked in cyberspace. Discuss in detail your steps in recovering any and all information from the device and how cyberstalking can be proved via this evidence.

# Part Three

## Forensic Examination of Computers and Digital Media

Part Three focuses on technology and the hands-on forensic examination of computers, networks, and other electronic devices. It begins with an exploration of operating systems and data transmission involved in investigating cybertrails related to crimes involving networks. You learn where and how to search for content in data and graphic files, e-mail messages, and Internet logs. You will also learn methods commonly used to hide or disguise content—and how to identify and retrieve it.

This section is not limited to technology. Recognizing what constitutes evidence and knowing where to find it is both science and art. You gain an understanding of computer forensic equipment and procedures that are crucial to successful investigations involving e-evidence. Using the right investigative tools and methods maximizes the effectiveness of forensics work and ensures that e-evidence is kept in pristine condition so that it is admissible in a legal action.

- **Chapter 6:** Operating Systems and Data Transmission Basics for Digital Investigations
- **Chapter 7:** Investigating Windows, Linux, and Graphics Files
- **Chapter 8:** E-Mail and Webmail Forensics

# Chapter 6

# Operating Systems and Data Transmission Basics for Digital Investigations

## Chapter Objectives

**After reading this chapter and completing the exercises, you will be able to do the following:**

- Define and recognize an operating system.
- Identify the different types of operating system interfaces.
- Identify the different components of an operating system.
- Understand and identify the different file systems.
- Understand the OSI and TCP models.
- Understand the basics of how data is transmitted on networks.

## Introduction

The operating system of a computer is often overlooked by users and forensic examiners for the simple reason that most users take for granted the software that operates all the bells and whistles of their computers. Most users assume the computer is a one-piece unit when, in reality, the hardware and software are two separate components that work in tandem to run the computer. The importance of being able to recognize what operating system the forensic examiner is dealing with plays a major role in how he will extract evidence. Additionally, knowing how the particular operating system works also plays a vital role in understanding where evidence may be found.

This chapter introduces and gives a broad overview of what an operating system is and the components that are generic to operating systems. The next section helps you identify the different types of operating systems encountered out in the field. Building on that, you learn how different operating systems use different file systems to achieve the same goal of organizing data on a storage device. Next, you study the two predominant models used to understand and break down data communications. Finally, you are introduced to fundamental concepts of how data is transmitted and received by hosts on a network and how the network keeps data flowing in an organized and systematic way.

---

## What Is an Operating System?

John walks into his office on Monday morning after having a great weekend with the family and finds a brand new computer in his office with all the assorted gadgets a new computer comes with. After panicking for a split second, John realizes his files are stored on the office server and boots up his new computer. Other than the screen looking more colorful and the icons looking different, John does not really notice any major differences from his old computer. The word processor looks identical in function, and his spreadsheet program seems to be the same. After getting used to the new color scheme and new icons, John is busy working as if this new computer had been in his office for years.

What John fails to realize is that his operating system has changed completely. What John sees is that his application programs function the same, and thus, he sees no real changes. In reality, the computer that sits on his desk is a far cry from the one that is now sitting on the auction block.

For forensic examiners to do their job correctly, they must understand which operating system they are working with. One operating system may use FAT and the other may use NTFS. Don't worry if you don't know what those mean yet; but it is imperative that by the end of this chapter you understand there are differences between operating systems.

An ***operating system*** is a program that controls how a computer functions. For example, the operating system controls how data is accessed, saved, and organized on a storage device. The operating system also acts as the intermediary between the hardware and application software of a computer. The main part, or core, of the operating system is called the ***kernel.*** The kernel remains in active memory controlling the different aspects of the computer while the user is busy using application software. In the next section, we look at the various components common to all operating systems.

# Major Components of an Operating System

The following section introduces you to the basic functions an operating system handles. The way a user interacts with the operating system will be covered as well as the methods used by operating systems to keep data moving and organized within a computer system. Keep in mind during this section that all operating systems have the same basic role of managing data and hardware within a computer; it is just how they perform those chores that varies from operating system to operating system.

## Types of Interfaces

A user interface is simply the way a user communicates with her computer. The two types of interfaces generally accepted are command-line interface (CLI) and graphical user interface (GUI). On more sophisticated and powerful operating systems, the user interface is also known as a ***shell.*** Let's look more closely at our two types of operating system interfaces.

A command-line interface is composed of a character-driven command line. In other words, you type the command to make the computer do something. The most common command-line interface is the MS-DOS CLI. It consists of white letters against a blue or black background with a blinking cursor at the location where the command is to be typed. Figure 6.1 shows the original MS-DOS prompt.

There are advantages and disadvantages to the CLI. One major advantage is that computer resources being used are minimal. All the operating system has to worry about is a little blinking dash and executing whatever command is entered. The major disadvantage is that you must also memorize commands and all their switches to make this operating system work. For most people, memorizing the daily lunch menu is tiresome enough, much less having to memorize

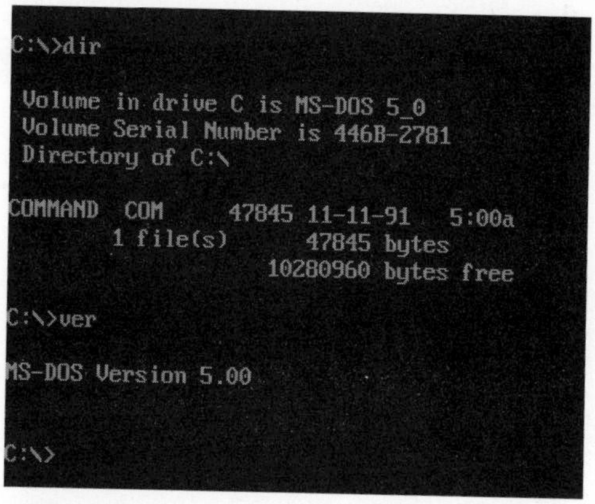

```
C:\>dir

 Volume in drive C is MS-DOS 5_0
 Volume Serial Number is 446B-2781
 Directory of C:\

COMMAND  COM     47845 11-11-91   5:00a
        1 file(s)       47845 bytes
                     10280960 bytes free

C:\>ver

MS-DOS Version 5.00

C:\>
```

**FIGURE 6.1** The original MS-DOS prompt.

very precise commands and syntax, and only people such as forensic examiners or hard core computer professionals take the time to really use CLI systems to their full potential.

Graphical user interfaces, in contrast, use graphics to allow a user to interface with the operating system. The basic idea behind this approach is to allow the user to interact with a graphic that has been preprogrammed to carry out a task once it has been selected. To understand this concept, imagine a bunch of dots on your screen grouped together to form a picture. These dots are called *pixels* and are the basic blocks used to make graphics on a GUI system. The graphics used to interface with the operating system can vary from icons to drop-down menus. For example, most of us have used Internet Explorer to access the Internet by clicking on the big blue *E* and having the browser come right up. Most users think that they are clicking on the program, but in reality they are clicking what is called a shortcut. The technical term used by those in the industry is *objects*. Most people find the GUI interface much more intuitive and less cumbersome than command-line interfaces, and thus they are more popular. Figure 6.2 shows an early Windows GUI interface.

## Single-User and Multiple-User Systems

Operating systems usually fall into two broad categories of use. Single-user systems, as the name implies, are designed to be used by a single person. That is

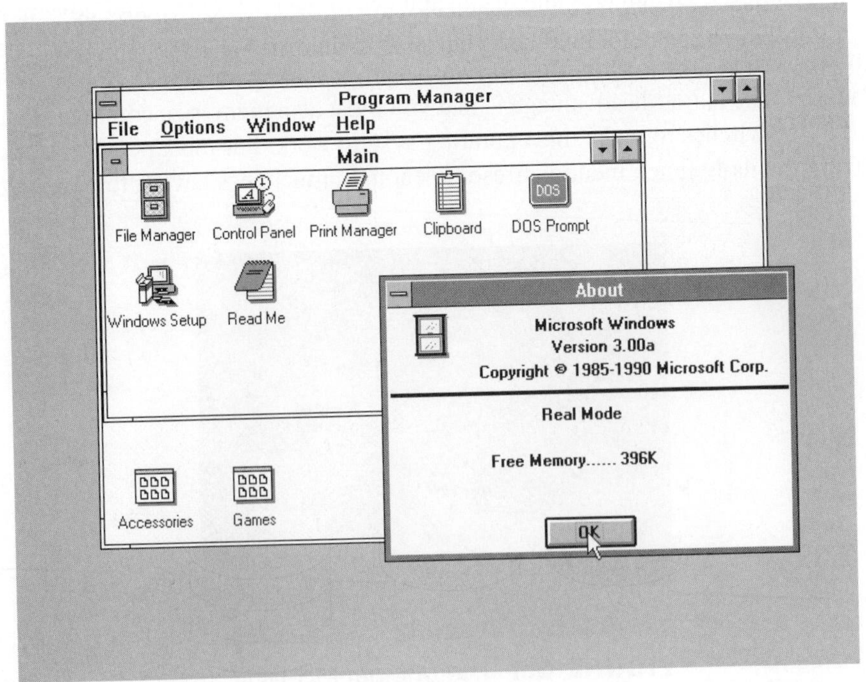


**FIGURE 6.2** An early Microsoft Windows graphic user interface.

not to say a single user cannot multitask, but that a single-user system cannot have more than one user running the same application at the same time. Multiple-user systems, on the other hand, are by definition able to allow multiple persons to use a single application at the same time.

DOS is the operating system that comes to mind as an example of a single-user system. In fact, DOS is a single-user and single-tasking operating system. Most desktop systems with Windows or Macintosh operating systems are designed as single-user multitasking systems. One user can run multiple programs at the same time; however, multiple users cannot run the same application on the same computer. This is not to say it has not been done, but the operating system is actually switching between tasks instead of running them simultaneously.

A multiple-user system such as the Windows Server family or UNIX/Linux can allow multiple users access to the same application program. These operating systems have been designed from the beginning with multiple users in mind.



## File Management

File management is an operating system function that controls the reading, accessing, writing, and modification of data. The basic unit used in file management is called a ***file.*** The next step up in the hierarchical structure is called a ***directory*** or ***folder.*** The best analogy for explaining the concept of file management is that of the office file cabinet. In a real file cabinet, folders are used to keep items organized by function or type. In the context of the computer, the storage device takes the function of the file cabinet, and files or programs that are similar in use or function are kept together in folders or directories.

## Memory Management

An operating system controls where applications and data are stored in memory, and the operating system keeps track of what is being used and what is available. You should not confuse data storage with memory management. Storage deals with the saving or archiving of data, while memory management deals with the temporary storage or use of applications and data. Different operating systems have different ways of handling memory; however, the general concepts are basically the same over all operating systems.

More advanced operating systems such as Windows use memory managers to utilize memory more efficiently and with more flexibility. One way Windows does this is by using a *virtual memory manager*. Virtual memory is created by using a part of the hard drive as if it were RAM memory. This gives the operating system more room to work; however, it can slow the computer down because hard drive access times are measured in milliseconds (thousandths of a second) while RAM module access speeds are measured in nanoseconds (billionths of a second).

## Job Management

The function of job management within an operating system is the same as a traffic light regulating the flow of traffic at an intersection. For all their power, computers can execute only one instruction at a time per processor or CPU. Imagine two programs vying for control of the CPU at the same time. If the operating system does not set up the order in which the programs will execute, then the computer will more than likely lock up and nothing will be processed. There are several ways this can be accomplished; however, for this discussion it is important to understand that the operating system will schedule which set of instructions will be processed and when.

Certain operating systems use job management to a greater degree than others. Server platforms use job management on a much higher level than a desktop computer simply because there are more users accessing the computer at one time.

Two terms you may hear related to job management are *batch* and *interactive*. In the days of mainframes and limited user interaction with computers, the tasks computers were asked to do were submitted in batches. Essentially the jobs were put into a holding area and executed one at a time by the computer without any real control from users. Interactive job control is more in line with what we have today. The user interacts with the computer and the computer processes data as the user requests.

## Device Management

Most operating systems in place today act as intermediaries between application software and the physical hardware. To interface properly between various applications and a seemingly endless array of hardware devices, the operating system must be able to manage devices with ***device drivers.*** A device driver is simply a piece of code that tells the operating system and the hardware device how to communicate with each other. Some operating systems have device drivers built into their system kernels, whereas other operating systems rely on hardware manufacturers to supply specific device drivers for the hardware device. The basic role of the device driver is to act as an interpreter between the operating system and the hardware device.

## Security

The role of security in operating systems has taken on new meaning and importance in recent years. With the exception of operating systems such as UNIX, most operating systems did not take security very seriously until just recently. The primary method of security is to have the user authenticate his credentials when he logs in. This is a fancy way of saying the user must prove who he is to the operating system to be allowed access. The operating system assumes that if your username and password match, it must be you because you are the only one with that information.

Additionally, newer operating systems are implementing rights and permissions to files and folders to increase the security of the operating system. Rights and permissions can help to eliminate unauthorized usage in this day of the Internet, hackers, and internal sabotage.

### IN PRACTICE: Iraqi Computer Disks and Hard Drives Recovered

Photographs and documents about Iraqi training camps during Saddam Hussein's regime were part of a collection of 2 million items that were captured from Iraq and Afghanistan (Hayes, 2006). The items include handwritten notes, typed documents, audiotapes, videotapes, compact discs, floppy disks, and computer hard drives. Data retrieved from the digital devices together with photographs and other items could give U.S. intelligence officials an inside look at the activities of Hussein's regime in the months and years before the Iraq war.

The secret training took place primarily at three camps—in Samarra, Ramadi, and Salman Pak—and was directed by elite Iraqi military units. Interviews by U.S. government interrogators with Iraqi regime officials and military leaders corroborate the documentary evidence. Two thousand terrorists were trained at these Iraqi camps each year from 1999 to 2002. Intelligence officials believe that some of these terrorists returned to Iraq and are responsible for attacks against Americans and Iraqis. Computer forensics investigators are searching for valuable intelligence from data files recovered in Afghanistan and Iraq over the past four years.

The discovery of this information on jihadist training camps in Iraq exposes flawed assumptions of the experts that a secularist like Saddam Hussein would never work with Islamic radicals and that jihadists would never work with an infidel like the Iraqi dictator.

6

## Common Operating Systems

The operating systems we see today are a far cry from the operating systems on the first computers. In fact, the first computers did not have operating systems. They did not need one. The application software handled all the functions required to access memory, storage, and general management of the computer. Early computers generally performed one function or used one application and thus did not need a separate operating system to coordinate different application software. Most computers in the 1950s, 1960s, and 1970s were fairly simple by today's standards.

As computers became multipurpose machines, the need for software that could coordinate and control different applications, hardware, job management, and users became necessary. The early operating systems were quite simple in many regards. The first computers had little in the way of peripheral variety, and RAM was generally 16KB. Operating systems were generally used only on large computers in mammoth organizations.

The personal computer changed this. With the introduction of the personal computer, the operating system was pushed into the mainstream of computing. For the first time, a computer that could fit on your desktop had the capability to solve business or statistical problems at the touch of a key. Take for example the user who before had to have the IT department run a series of calculations on her budget. The user had to take the data for processing and wait a couple of days for the results to come back. With a desktop personal computer, the calculations could be entered and run in a matter of moments.

To accomplish their job functions, most users relied on various software packages, a wide range of hardware options, and infinite combinations of peripherals. The new computers were going to need an operating system that could handle all this. IBM decided on a new operating system called DOS manufactured by a small company called Microsoft.

## DOS

Disk Operating System (DOS), originally available for the IBM personal computer, is considered one of the first personal computer operating systems. It is a command-line character-based user interface with several advantages and disadvantages. In today's computing world, DOS is not seen as often, but investigators should still be familiar with DOS for two reasons: There are still applications that use DOS, and DOS can be used to troubleshoot computers when the GUI fails.

The primary advantage of DOS is its small footprint. There is very little overhead to DOS because it uses no graphics. Additionally, the files needed to boot DOS fit on a floppy disk. You can literally run the operating system from a floppy drive.

DOS has several disadvantages when compared to newer operating systems. The primary disadvantage with DOS is the 640KB barrier. Programs and data can use only 640KB or less to run applications or temporarily store data. Imagine using a modern application such as Microsoft Word and only being able to use 640KB! If by some miracle you could make the program run under DOS, you could start the application up and go out for coffee and maybe it would have loaded by the time you returned. Another disadvantage to DOS is that you can run only one application at a time. Multitasking is beyond the capabilities of DOS.

Because DOS is a command-line system, users have to memorize the commands that run the program. The set of rules that govern how commands are entered into DOS is called *syntax*. Without the proper syntax, DOS will execute the command wrong or give an error message and sometimes do both. See Figure 6.3 for an example of a syntax error.

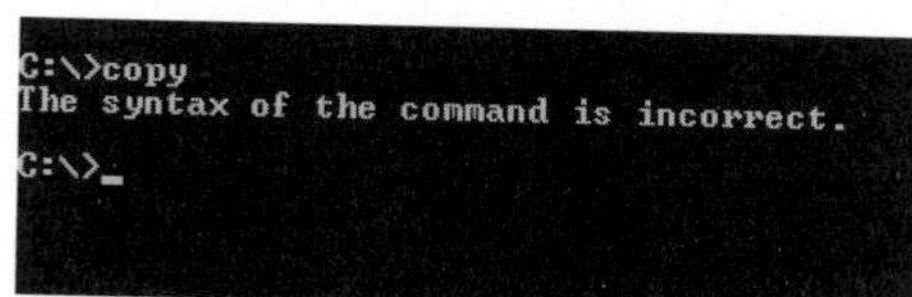


**FIGURE 6.3** DOS syntax error message.

## Windows

The graphical user interface we know as Windows has its roots at Xerox. In the 1970s, Xerox was a pioneer in the field of computer research at their Palo Alto Research Center. It was there the mouse, graphical user interface, and laser printer were first researched and developed. Early pioneers such as Steve Jobs visited this facility and from those visits came operating systems such as the Apple Macintosh and Microsoft Windows operating systems.

## Windows 3.X

Windows 3.1 was not the first GUI introduced by Microsoft, but it was the first stable one. Previous versions of Windows were notorious for being unstable. Unlike DOS, which was a true operating system, Windows 3.1 was not a true operating system. It was literally an application on top of DOS. Figure 6.4 shows the classic 3.1 desktop.

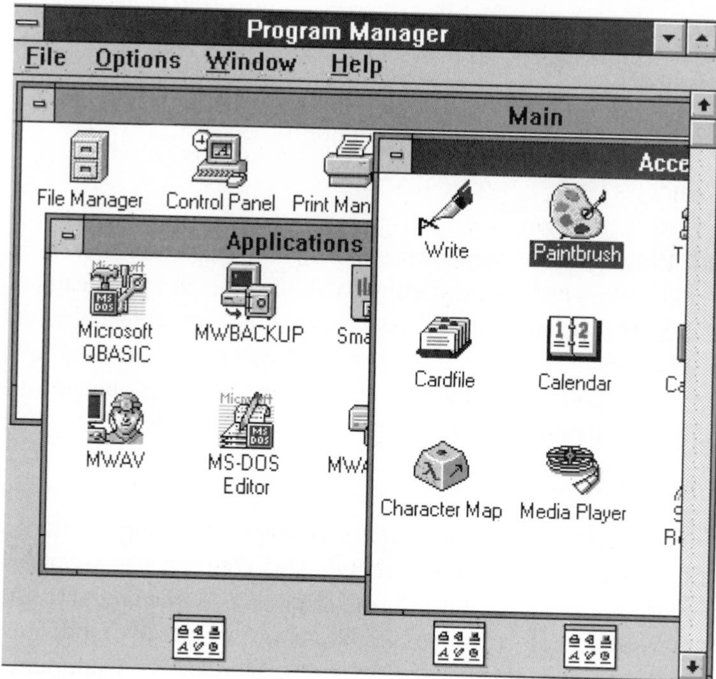


**FIGURE 6.4** Windows 3.1 desktop.

Windows 3.11 was introduced to address the lack of networking capability of the Windows 3.1 system. The Windows 3.11 system added the ability to network with other computers on the same segment, or LAN, that were also running Windows 3.11. By adding the capability to share drives and create workgroups, Microsoft took its first steps into creating a true network operating system. The type of network Microsoft had created with Windows 3.11 is considered a peer-to-peer network rather than a client/server network. To delve a little further into this distinction, a peer-to-peer network is one in which the computers have no central server or computer to rely on for files or print jobs. Essentially all the computers are "equal." In a client/server network, multiple computers called clients access one computer, the server, for files, Web pages, or printer functions.

## Windows 95

With the introduction of Windows 95, Microsoft jumped into the realm of 32-bit computing. The desktop was radically different from the Windows 3.11 desktop, and the new system had much more power and many more features. Figure 6.5 illustrates the Windows 95 desktop. With these new features and power also came the overhead to support them. At this point, CPU power via the Pentium processors and advances in 32-bit architecture enabled Windows 95 to work relatively well. The innovations Microsoft introduced in Windows 95 and that have become standard include

- Plug and play
- The registry
- Built-in network and Internet capability
- Windows GUI

**Plug and Play** Before Windows 95, installing hardware was usually done manually and often with some difficulty. With the plug and play feature built into Windows 95, the installation of new hardware was essentially automated. Windows 95 automatically detects the new hardware and determines settings such as the IRQ, DMA, and device drivers. The hardware being installed must also have some plug and play capability; not all new hardware installed at the time had this capability.

**Registry** Windows 95 introduced the concept of a single database where all operating system information is stored. This concept was simply called the registry. Before Windows 95, this information was scattered randomly throughout the operating system. Information regarding hardware settings, software settings, and general system parameters are all stored in the registry. A sampling of items found in the registry include

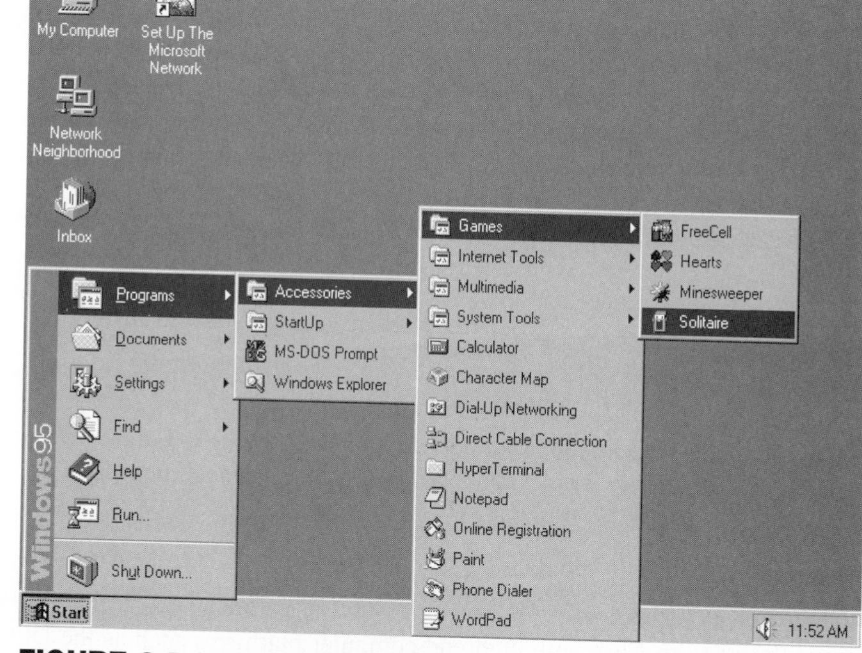

**FIGURE 6.5** Windows 95 desktop.

- Hardware configuration
- Software configuration
- Desktop configuration
- Device driver information and configuration

**Network and Internet Capability** The original version of Windows 95 did not have a Web browser integrated into the operating system, but in 1997 Microsoft fully integrated a Web browser called Internet Explorer into the Windows 95 operating system. With the growing popularity of the Internet, this integration of Web browser and operating system added a new dimension to the communication and network abilities of Windows 95.

The network drivers, protocols, and services were built into the Windows 95 operating system, unlike previous versions such as Windows 3.11 or Windows 3.1. Additionally, Windows 95 had the capability to work with non-Windows networks such as Novell with few or no configuration headaches.

6

## Windows 98

Windows 98 had the same basic functionality of Windows 95 with some enhancements dealing with multimedia and network capabilities. Universal serial bus (USB) support was added to take advantage of the new USB devices being developed at the time to replace the older serial and parallel ports. Microsoft had intended Windows 98 to be a home-user operating system, but nobody told Corporate America this, and thus you will find Windows 98 operating systems in many corporate and government settings. Many computing environments where security is highly important still use Windows 98 even though it was not originally designed with security in mind.

Other enhancements included

- Power management features (mostly for laptops)
- Upgrade capability via the Internet
- Automated registry checks and repairs
- Upgraded plug and play support

## Windows NT

Windows (New Technology) NT was developed in parallel with Windows 95 but was designed to work with high-end computer platforms such as the DEC Alpha. The look and feel of Windows NT is much the same as Windows 95 and Windows 98 because the GUIs have much in common. The similarity is only superficial, however.

Under the hood, the code for Windows NT is designed from the ground up as a 32-bit operating system. Another significant improvement is the way the Windows NT kernel, or operating system core, works in a protected method called *privileged mode*. The Windows NT operating system working in privileged mode acts as the intermediary between the different applications and its interactions with physical memory and hardware. Working in this fashion, Windows NT can isolate the different applications to such a degree that if one application hangs or becomes unstable, it can be shut down without affecting the rest of the computer system. UNIX and other large operating systems already had this capability from the beginning; but this was Microsoft's first successful foray into high-performance operating systems that could work in this fashion.

In addition to having privileged mode capability, Windows NT could support multiple CPU processors depending on whether the system kernel was optimized for client use or server use. The client version of Microsoft NT was named Microsoft NT workstation and could support two CPUs. The server version of Microsoft NT was named Microsoft NT Server and could support four CPUs. Another major difference in both kernels was their ability to handle radically different numbers of users. Windows NT workstation has been throttled back to 10 concurrent users while Windows NT Server can handle up to 15,000 concurrent users.

One of the major differences between the Windows NT line and the Windows 9.x line is security. Windows 9.x has little security built into the operating system, to the point that clicking on the Cancel button on the login screen still allows you in. In contrast, Windows NT requires a user name and password to access the desktop. The security functions of Windows NT are multilayered in their approach to security. Besides the initial login security screen, the following layers of security are used:

- File and folder access protection via permissions
- Network share protection
- Auditing capabilities
- Use of domain controllers

**FYI** *NTBugtraq*

NTBugtraq (**www.ntbugtraq.com**) is a mailing list for the discussion of security exploits and security bugs in Windows NT, Windows 2000, and Windows XP plus related applications.



### Windows 2000

Based on the Windows NT code, Windows 2000 improves on the original code in several significant ways. The GUI retains much of the same feel of its predecessors with several improvements in the area of security and networking. Figure 6.6 shows the Windows 2000 desktop.

Windows 2000 introduced several improvements that are listed below:

- Group policies
- Secure authentication
- File encryption

The introduction of group policies is the most significant improvement in the ability to manage security for a large network. Setting group policies for literally hundreds of users with a single click versus customizing each and every user account is a real time saver. Group policies can be set through what is called active directory. Active directory is an enhanced version of the Windows NT domain idea. A central Windows 2000 server acts as the database repository for information on user accounts, computers, and printers within its domain.

The enhancements in the security of Windows 2000 begin with the introduction of the Internet protocol security (IPSec) protocol. With the introduction

**FIGURE 6.6** Windows 2000 desktop.

of the IPSec protocol, Microsoft addressed the issue of securing data across a network connection. Using IPSec in conjunction with the new technology of ***virtual private networks (VPNs),*** users could create a secure tunnel through the Internet (or even inside a LAN) and be reasonably sure no third parties could intercept and decode the data stream. Additionally, user authentication was dramatically improved with the Kerberos protocol for use on an open network connection. Kerberos authentication is a rather interesting subject in and of itself. Developed by MIT, it uses a symmetric key methodology in the way of "secure" tickets. It is far more complex than simple tickets in that encryption and decryption algorithms are used, but the Kerberos system is fairly secure against replay attacks and network sniffing attacks.

Another feature Windows 2000 introduced was the ability to encrypt files and folders. The approach Microsoft used to encrypt these files is simple and transparent to the user once the files are encrypted. Encrypting files is as easy as opening the properties of the file or folder and checking the encryption checkbox. Once the encryption is set, the user who set the encryption notices nothing new about the file because Windows 2000 automatically decrypts and encrypts data based on the user account that encrypted the data. Windows 2000 assumes the user who encrypted the file has been authenticated via his password and has proven his identity. If a second user logs in to a separate account, she will not be able to decrypt the file even if she has permissions and rights to access the file.

### IN PRACTICE: Man Charged with Accessing USC Student Data

Federal prosecutors charged Eric McCarty, a San Diego computer expert, with breaching the security of a database server at the University of Southern California (USC) and accessing confidential student data. He exploited a flaw in USC's Web server and database system used to accept online applications from prospective students. The FBI discovered the Internet address of McCarty's home computer on USC's systems. He could face up to a maximum of 10 years in federal prison (Lemos, 2006).

## Windows XP

The next evolution in the Windows product line is Windows XP. Based on the Windows 2000 kernel, it has several improvements and a new GUI desktop. Figure 6.7 shows the Windows XP desktop. Windows XP has both a workstation version and a server version, just as Windows 2000 has. The workstation edition of Windows XP is called Windows XP, and the server edition is named Windows Server 2003.

Along with a new GUI, Windows XP has implemented a simple firewall and remote control access and increased the speed of the operating system.

**FIGURE 6.7** Windows XP desktop.

Another feature new in Windows XP is the activate feature. In order for the operating system to be activated, the user must contact Microsoft to obtain the activation code. The code is specific to the physical computer system, and if the operating system is reinstalled on another computer, a new activation code must be obtained.

Within the Windows XP family, two editions are available: Windows XP Home and Windows XP Professional. Windows XP Professional is the equivalent of Windows NT Workstation in concept. Windows XP Professional supports up to 10 concurrent users, works with up to two processors, and can be used on 64-bit Itanium platforms. Windows XP Home, in sharp contrast, works with only one 32-bit processor, supports only one user, and is considered an upgrade product from Windows Me. (Windows Me, in turn, was an upgrade path from Windows 95 and Windows 98 that provided some fixes for those systems as well as new features such as the ability to restore from a backup and protect system files.)

## IN PRACTICE: Spyware Compromises Windows Operating Systems

On November 21, 2005, Texas Attorney General Greg Abbott filed an action against Sony BMG Music Entertainment for illegal spyware. The suit alleges that Sony spyware was installed on CDs that consumers inserted into their computers and that the spyware compromised the users' operating systems.

The complaint also alleges that Sony's audio CDs that use XCP are marked Content Protected on the CD package, but the package does not disclose that anything will be installed on the user's computer. Once a user places a Sony BMG copy-protected CD in his or her computer for play, the CD triggers a pop-up multipage Sony end-user license agreement. After the user clicks "agree," Sony's media player loads, allowing the user to listen to the CD. If the consumer clicks "disagree," the CD ejects from the computer.

During the installation of its media player, Sony allegedly creates and installs components of its XCP technology in a folder named C:/Windows/System32/§ysilesystem. Unknown to the user, Sony's CDs also install a file named Aries.sys in the same folder, which conceals the XCP files and the folder in which they are installed. The owner of the computer performing a search of the file system would not be able to locate and remove the XCP technology. The Aries.sys driver masks any folder or file name on a consumer's computer that begins with the

CONTINUED ON NEXT PAGE

▶▶ CONTINUED

characters §ys$, which are the first characters of the folders, files, and registry entries associated with the XCP technology. These hidden files and folder are installed within the consumer's Microsoft Windows System32 subfolder, so a user could confuse that software with essential files needed to run the computer's operating system (*The Computer & Internet Lawyer*, 2006, pp. 31–33).

## Linux

Linux is a relatively new operating system based on the UNIX operating system. Developed in the early 1990s, it has garnered a strong following. The original incarnations of Linux were command-line driven and mostly used by hard-core Linux enthusiasts. As Linux has become more mainstream, it has developed a GUI interface that is easier to use than the cryptic command-line interface. Linux also has the advantage of being open source. You can view the source code for the operating system and customize the kernel to tailor the operating system to work with specific hardware on your computer. In effect, you can customize the operating system for a specific computer, something Microsoft Windows cannot do. Figures 6.8 and 6.9 show a CLI and GUI interface for Linux.



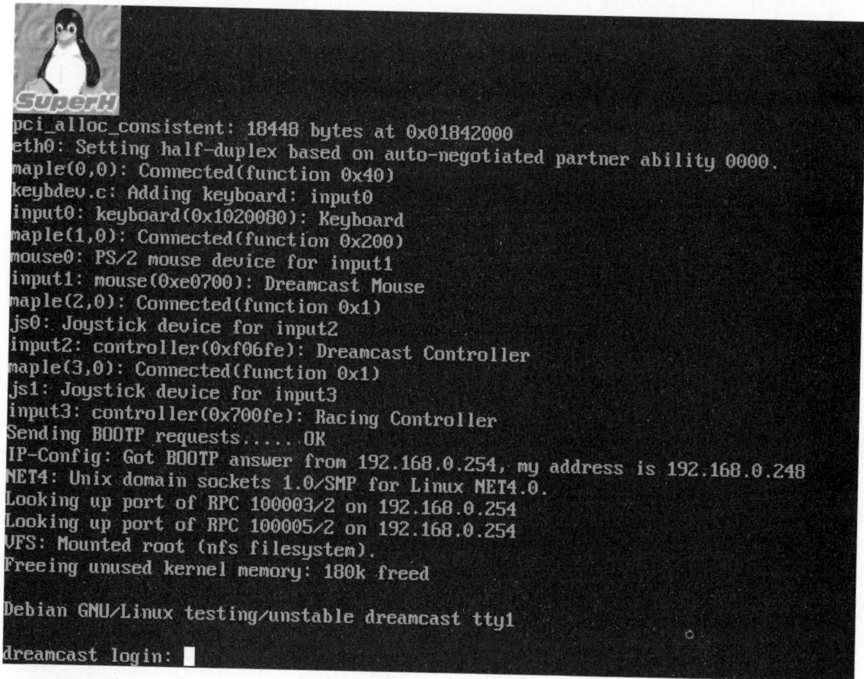


**FIGURE 6.8** Linux CLI interface.

**FIGURE 6.9** Linux GUI interface.

Several factors have made Linux the fastest growing operating system in the world:

- Linux is free or inexpensive.
- Linux can run on older equipment.
- Linux can run a multitude of hardware platforms.
- Linux is fast.
- Linux is stable.

In addition to being an open-source operating system via the GNU organization, Linux is free. (GNU is a recursive acronym for "GNU's not UNIX.") Within the GNU license agreement, Linux software cannot be sold. That is not to say customer support and documentation cannot be sold, but the actual code (kernel) itself cannot be sold. The monetary advantage of using such an operating system can be significant. Imagine a company engaging in a computer rollout of 1,000 new computers. Let's say the cost of Windows XP is $100 per computer and any future upgrades will cost roughly the same amount. Thus, the basic installation will cost $100,000 with upgrades costing another $100,000 down the road. Licensing fees may add to this sum. With a Linux installation, we are looking at zero cost for the actual operating system. On the disadvantage side, Linux has a limited set of software applications such as word processing and spreadsheet programs. As Linux gains in popularity, however, vendors are creating application versions for the Linux OS such as OpenOffice.

### FYI Corporations Invest in Linux

The advantage of no or little cost for an operating system that is extremely stable is gaining popularity among large corporations such as IBM and Sun Microsystems. IBM has decided Linux has a strong future and has put well over a billion dollars into research and development on Linux and its use with IBM equipment.

Linux can run on almost any hardware platform and run fairly reliably. Older Intel 386 processor computers have been brought out of the attic, so to speak, and work quite well with Linux. In fact, Linux has a feature that displays the uptime of the computer, and numerous users of Linux have gone literally months and years without a reboot of their systems. Windows cannot claim that distinction.

Because a true Linux system is basically a CLI system, overhead for the operating system is very minimal. As a result of this low overhead, the amount of processor power directly applied to processor tasks rather than pretty graphics allows the Linux system to execute code in a lean and efficient fashion.

Since Linux is modeled on the UNIX kernel, it has the stability of its larger brother. Linux code is well written and very efficient because so many people can view, modify, and critique the code. This is one advantage of the open-source philosophy. Additionally, because the code is well documented and open, any flaws found in the beta testing phase are usually corrected quickly before the final code is released as a new version. Even after final release, users regularly make changes to the operating system and share their changes on the Internet so that others may use their new and updated version.

With Linux becoming popular among nontechnical folks, GUIs are becoming more common in the Linux operating system. Linux is currently making the same kind of transition from command-line to GUI interface that Microsoft made in going from DOS to Windows. GUI front ends such as XFree and GNOME are rapidly making Linux an operating system Windows and Apple users can relate to and use fairly easily.

Linux has been making great strides in the server area of the computer world because it is such a stable platform. Servers on the Internet and high-volume networks, for example, have switched to Linux. As Linux becomes more GUI, the regular user may take notice and begin to see Linux as an alternative to Windows; this is already happening in countries such as China and South Korea.

## UNIX

The roots of most modern operating systems can be traced back to UNIX. Created by Bell Labs in the early 1970s, it was the basis for many current operating systems procedures and syntax structure. The UNIX system was initially used by universities and large organizations on large computer systems. Since its inception, UNIX has been ported to smaller and more powerful computers, and the chances of running across a UNIX system in a small to midsize company are pretty good. With its stability and security, UNIX has a strong presence within the Internet community. Practically speaking, the Internet would grind to a halt if the UNIX systems were taken down. Figure 6.10 shows a screen shot of a typical UNIX operating system.

While there are many "flavors," or versions, of UNIX in the wild, the basic concepts apply to most versions. The syntax varies from flavor to flavor, but a user can easily find documentation on the particulars of any version. There are two main camps in the UNIX world: the Berkeley Software Distribution (BSD) and the System V Release 4 (SVR4). Many different organizations have modified the system kernel of these two versions to create their own unique versions of UNIX.

UNIX is a true multiuser and multitasking operating system that is designed from the ground up with security in mind. UNIX also gives the user many options on how they wish to interact with the system kernel. The way in which UNIX accomplishes this varies depending on which shell the user chooses. In UNIX, a shell is simply the interface the user wishes to use to

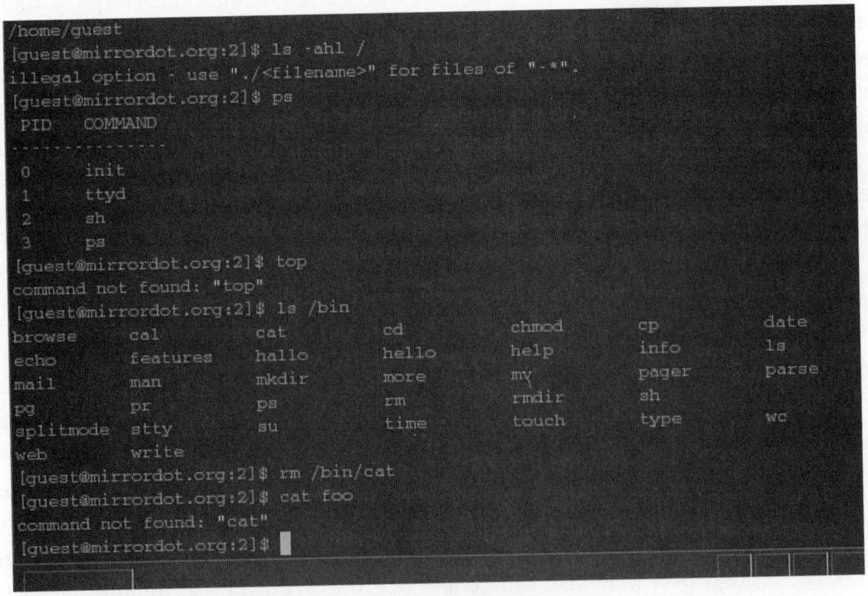

```
/home/guest
[guest@mirrordot.org:2]$ ls -ahl /
illegal option - use "./<filename>" for files of "-*".
[guest@mirrordot.org:2]$ ps
 PID  COMMAND
--------------
 0     init
 1     ttyd
 2     sh
 3     ps
[guest@mirrordot.org:2]$ top
command not found: "top"
[guest@mirrordot.org:2]$ ls /bin
browse     cal       cat      cd       chmod    cp      date
echo       features  hallo    hello    help     info    ls
mail       man       mkdir    more     mv       pager   parse
pg         pr        ps       rm       rmdir    sh
splitmode  stty      su       time     touch    type    wc
web        write
[guest@mirrordot.org:2]$ rm /bin/cat
[guest@mirrordot.org:2]$ cat foo
command not found: "cat"
[guest@mirrordot.org:2]$
```

**FIGURE 6.10** UNIX operating system.

communicate with the operating system, much as a DOS CLI shell is used to communicate with the DOS system kernel. The two most popular shells in the UNIX world are the Bourne shell (sh) and the Bourne Again shell (bash). In addition to CLI shells, certain versions of UNIX now offer a GUI-based interface such as X Windows; however, UNIX gurus still prefer the CLI for convenience and power.

## Macintosh

From the beginning when Steve Jobs and Steve Wozniak released their first Apple computer in 1976, they have taken a different approach to computing from most other vendors. One of the major differences between Apple and other computer vendors is Apple's absolute control over the hardware platform and how the software interacts with it. Basically, Apple controls the design, production, and implementation of the hardware over which the operating system will run. In effect, this allows Apple's programmers to tailor their code for one basic hardware platform. The Windows/Intel line of computers has to contend with literally endless combinations of hardware/software interfaces.



This philosophy has been tweaked a bit by Apple within the last couple of years. Most recently, Apple announced it was changing processors to the Intel line and has introduced a program called Boot Camp that allows an Apple user to install Windows XP on her machine. Essentially, Apple has allowed the Apple architecture to become a dual boot system.

Another interesting approach Apple has taken is to make multimedia a standard feature from the beginning and not an optional feature as done in the Windows/Intel world. Video, sound, and graphics capability were built into the system both on a software level and a hardware level, unlike the early IBM computers which had monochromatic monitors, no sound card, and no graphics capability.

Depending on your level of expertise, the Macintosh GUI interface was either maddening or a joy to work with. The Macintosh philosophy of letting the users control as little as possible on a system level was a joy for novice users or users who just wanted the computer to work and not worry about what was going on under the hood. Power users, on the other hand, wanted more control over the system and generally wanted to tinker under the hood.

Because Apple has controlled almost every aspect of the Macintosh computer and did not license their product in the same way as the Windows/Intel world, their market share is quite a bit smaller. For this reason, we look at the Macintosh OS with a more general view than the Windows line.

The Macintosh GUI is generally thought to be one of the most intuitive ones on the market. The first thing users notice is a startup screen with an apple or smiley-face icon but no system startup messages. In keeping with the Apple philosophy of keeping users as far from the operating system as possible, system messages are kept to a minimum. The newer Macintosh systems are based on the

*Source:* Macintosh® computer screen shot reprinted with permission from Apple Computer, Inc.

**FIGURE 6.11** Macintosh computer operating system.

UNIX operating system, so their security and stability are rock solid. Once a user passes the login screen, she will see a GUI resembling a Windows computer. Figure 6.11 shows a Macintosh operating system.

The newest Macintosh operating system, called Mac OS X, is UNIX based and has been tailored for better networkability and even more impressive graphics. Additionally, the power users are finally getting their wish and have better access to the root level area of the Macintosh operating system.

---

## Common File System Types

In the beginning of this chapter, you read that a file system is like your office file cabinet with folders organized in a logical way. Now you are ready to learn how the file system works in more detail.

The general function of a file system is to manage files and folders on a computer system. To accomplish this task, an operating system performs the following functions:

- Partitions and formats storage devices
- Creates a standard for naming files and folders
- Maintains the integrity of files and folders

- Provides for error recovery
- Provides for security of the file system

Most operating systems accomplish the tasks listed above but differ in their approach as to how they accomplish those tasks. In the following sections, we look at how different file systems accomplish the above tasks and describe the basic features of each one.

## FAT File System

The basic file system used primarily by MS-DOS and as an option on most modern file systems is the ***file allocation table (FAT)*** file system. The original MS-DOS FAT system is now known as FAT 16, and the file system introduced with Windows 95 is known as FAT 32. The FAT file system, like all other file systems, manages the files and folders on a storage device.

There are two main components to any FAT file system after the storage device has been partitioned and formatted: the file allocation table and the root directory.

6

**File Allocation Table** A phone book best describes how the FAT file system works. The file allocation table is simply a directory the operating system uses to keep track of where files are on a storage device. A cluster is the smallest unit in a FAT system. Typically, a cluster is 32,768 bytes, or 32KB, in size. The file allocation table assigns a status to each cluster on a storage device. Basically, the table details whether a given cluster is the beginning of a file, in use, the end of a file, or empty.

**Root Directory** The root directory is the top directory on any FAT file system. Every directory and file put into the computer is located within the root directory. A directory is a special type of file that lists other files and directories. The types of information directory entries list include file name, date and time of creation/modification, size, any attributes, extension, and starting cluster number.

## FAT 16

The FAT 16 file system is so named because this file system uses 16 bits in the file allocation table. When a storage device is partitioned and formatted, two file allocation tables are created. The first is the primary table, and the second is the backup copy in case the first is disabled or unusable.

FAT 16 has an upper limit of 4GB of volume space and a maximum file size of 2GB. FAT 16 supports two partitions per hard drive with the secondary partition further divided into three logical drives if need be. Considering the sizes of storage devices currently available, the FAT 16 system is very limited. Imagine having to partition a 60GB hard drive into 20 separate volumes. Another limitation of the FAT 16 system is the "8.3" file naming convention. In this file system, a file name can have up to 8 characters with a 3-character extension. In addition to this rule, certain characters are illegal or invalid to use in creating file names for a FAT 16 system. They are: / \ [ ] | < > + = ; , * ?

The FAT 16 system uses the three-character extension to help determine file type. The following list identifies common extensions and their file types:

.bat A batch file
.com An executable binary file
.doc A word processing file
.exe An executable binary file
.txt A file containing text
.xls A spreadsheet file

In addition to file types, FAT 16 can assign attributes to files and folders. These attributes are:

Read only Indicates the file may not be modified or deleted.
Archive Indicates the file has been modified since the last backup.
System Indicates a system file, such as io.sys or msdos.sys.
Hidden Attempts to hide files.
Volume label Used to give a disk a label or name.
Directory Indicates the entry is a directory and not a file.

FAT 16 was extended to include the capability for long file name (LFN) support. With this new support, FAT 16 could provide for a file name 255 characters long. The same characters not allowed in 8.3 format are still not allowed under the LFN format, however.

## FAT 32

The FAT 32 file system is designed to accommodate large hard drives and expand the capabilities of FAT 16. Cluster size is also smaller because it is set at 4KB, thus making for a more efficient use of available space. The reason 4KB clusters are more efficient than 32KB clusters is simply because less space is wasted when a cluster is not completely used. For example, if you have an 8KB file, it will fill up to two 4KB clusters while not completely using a 32KB cluster and thus wasting 24KBs of space. Windows 95 Release 2, Windows 98, Windows Me, Windows 2000, Windows XP, and Server 2003 all support FAT 32 file systems. The upper limit for hard drive partitions is 2 terabytes, but a realistic volume size is roughly 32GB. File size is 4GB, which doubles the amount of file size space FAT 16 could handle.

The system file type structures and attributes did not change from FAT 16 to FAT 32. In fact, the only real change was the extension of more bits in the file allocation table entry.

## NTFS

The native file system for Windows NT, Windows 2000, Window XP, and Server 2003 is called ***New Technology File System (NTFS).*** The NTFS concept was a complete departure from the FAT file system and introduced the following features:

- Long file name support
- Ability to handle large storage devices
- Built-in security controls
- POSIX support
- Volume striping
- File compression
- Master file table (MFT)

6

Long file name support is native to NTFS and has the ability to translate LFN FAT file names for compatibility with FAT 16 and FAT 32 systems. Though both FAT and NTFS support long file names, there is a difference in how the FAT system and NTFS system store long file names. FAT uses multiple table entries to accommodate larger file names, whereas NTFS just has more room in the MFT entry.

Because the attributes (read, archive, system, and hidden) in FAT and NTFS differ in some respects, some features will not translate well. This may not seem significant at first glance; however, imagine having security attributes set up on an NTFS file that are translated into the LFN FAT file system. One of the attributes not carried over is the security permissions. Imagine making a copy of your payroll file that has all the file permissions set on NTFS and then losing all those permissions when your file is sent to accounting for use with their FAT file system.

The security features inherent in NTFS are quite powerful. Access to files and folders can be set based on user accounts or on a file/folder individual basis. For example, a database file can have the permissions set to allow read-only permissions for certain users while allowing full access to database administrators. The security features built into NTFS are sufficient to get a C2 Top Secret level security standard from the U.S. government.

The master file table (MFT) used by NTFS is similar to the file allocation table used in a FAT system. The MFT holds much more information regarding the file than a comparable FAT system. The MFT uses *attributes* to describe the file or directory. One of these is the data attribute. This is the actual data contained in the file, and because attributes are stored within the MFT, a small enough file can literally be stored *inside* the MFT. For larger files, the MFT creates pointers as to which cluster contains the next section of the file, and you simply follow the cluster chains to read the entire file. When the MFT is created, a "buffer" of hard drive space is created to allow for expansion of the MFT. The reason for this is to keep the MFT from becoming fragmented. In essence, the MFT is itself a file. Bear in mind that once a hard drive is used up, the MFT buffer will be used as a last resort.

## UNIX/Linux

Because Linux is actually a free version of UNIX, the file systems used by both are identical. For the purpose of brevity, we are going to cover them together. In addition to UNIX/Linux being a multiplatform operating system, it can also handle different file system types. It is this flexibility that makes UNIX and Linux such powerful operating systems. A list of the popular file systems UNIX/Linux can use includes:

- Extended file system (EXT)
- High-performance file system
- Microsoft DOS
- CD9660
- Network file system
- UNIX file system (UFS)
- VFAT
- NTFS

The UNIX file system (UFS) is the most native of the UNIX file system formats. The UFS system is extremely reliable, has been tested over time, and has strong security features built into the system. Additionally, the UFS system handles large-capacity storage devices, is expandable, and is based on a hierarchical system.

The extended file system, or EXT, is a file system primarily used by Linux but which can be run on a UNIX machine. The EXT file system is modeled on the UNIX file system, but there are significant differences in reliability. The UNIX file system by default handled a feature called journaling. Journaling is the ability of the file system to track file changes so as to reconstruct files if a system crash does occur. The first version of EXT does not come with this feature. The second and third versions of EXT (EXT2 and EXT3, respectively) solved the reliability issues and implemented functions such as journaling to make the system more reliable.

Because UNIX handles a multitude of file system formats, only the two most popular formats are covered below. The UFS and EXT file system formats are the most prevalent and the most reliable of the UNIX/Linux file systems.

The first concept that is different from the desktop-based file systems is the concept of information nodes. The UNIX world refers to information nodes as *inodes*. An inode is simply a storage "clearinghouse" of information regarding a file on a UNIX system. The following is a list of items commonly found in an inode:

- Inode number
- Owner of the file
- File group
- File size
- Creation date of file
- Modification date of file
- Number of links to the inode
- Where the file is stored in relation to the physical blocks

Because inodes cannot be increased after the system is created, they are generally set at 4KB per inode so as to have more of them than needed. To access the actual file system, a superblock is created. The superblock contains information about the blocks, sectors, and cylinder groups on the file system. Without the superblock, the file system cannot be accessed simply because the superblock contains basic information such as block size and layout of the file system; effectively, the superblock is to a UNIX computer what a legend is to a map.

A directory entry is a special type of file on a UNIX system. Inside the directory file is stored the information of which files and inodes are connected to that directory. There is a special relationship called a hard link when several directories point to a single inode. What this does for the file system is to create multiple file entries in different directories that point to a single file. In effect, there is one file on the system, but it appears in several directories.

## OSI and TCP/IP Models

In the early 1980s, networks were being implemented as a way to reduce costs and improve productivity. With numerous vendors selling proprietary network architecture, the ability to connect these different networks became a serious problem. As networks continued to expand, it became apparent to these companies that a single open standard needed to be developed which allowed the different network companies' products to communicate with each other.

The International Organization for Standardization (ISO) stepped in and began research into the different network architectures of the time. As a result of this research, ISO created a network model vendors could pattern their products after. This open model standard was called the ***Open System Interconnection (OSI)*** reference model.

The OSI reference model was released in 1984 and was soon adopted as the standard companies would follow to allow their products to communicate with other network systems. The OSI model is primarily an attempt to break down the complexity of data communications into a simple layered approach. Once layers are defined, the processing, or flow, of data can be seen easily and problems are easier to resolve. Constructing network flow is in some ways like the process of building a house. A house must be constructed in a systematic fashion, and no one person can do all the work easily. A layered approach to building a house is used to ensure the process is understood by each person doing his specific task, such as the electrician or plumber. Many houses are built the same way, and everyone involved knows what to expect.

A layered approach to network data communication helps define which part of the network communication is assigned to which layer. A layered approach also shows the interaction between the layers both above and below.

The layered approach that the OSI model follows has several advantages:

- Different hardware/software vendors have a standard that allows them to design products that can communicate with each other.
- Collaboration between companies to develop network components is easier.
- Changes in one layer are not carried over into other layers.
- Network design is broken down into smaller, more manageable parts.
- Problem resolution is easier because problems are usually confined to a single layer.

In the following section we dissect the OSI reference model in detail.

## OSI Model

The OSI model is much more than simply a network model for data communication. The OSI model in fact starts with data at the application level within the computer system. This is significant in that data protocols and standards are defined from the application level of one computer to the application level of another computer. An example would be an e-mail sent from one computer to the receiving e-mail application on the receiving computer. The standards that make this possible are defined by the OSI reference model.

The OSI reference model is broken down into seven layers. Each layer has a specific network function to handle. The OSI reference model layers are:

Layer 7—Application layer
Layer 6—Presentation layer
Layer 5—Session layer
Layer 4—Transport layer
Layer 3—Network layer
Layer 2—Data link layer
Layer 1—Physical layer

**Layer 7: The Application Layer** The application layer is the top layer of the OSI reference model. This layer provides services to applications such as e-mail or Internet browsers. The functions of this layer include:

- Allowing access to network services that support applications
- Handling network access, flow control, and error recovery

**Layer 6: The Presentation Layer** The presentation layer supports the functions of the application layer by ensuring the data formats from the application layer of one computer can be read by the application layer of another computer. The functions of this layer include:

- Conversion of all formats into a common uniform format
- Protocol conversion
- Character conversion
- Encryption/decryption

**Layer 5: The Session Layer** The session layer provides services to the presentation layer by creating a communication link between the two hosts. It does this by establishing, managing, and terminating communication sessions. In addition to this primary function, the session layer also:

- Establishes identification to exclude noncommunicating hosts
- Establishes checkpoints
- Manages data transmit times and length

**Layer 4: The Transport Layer** The transport layer is where the OSI reference model switches from application level standards to data transfer standards. The primary function of this layer is to segment data and prepare these segments for transport across a network. Related to this function, this layer

6

reassembles those same segments on the receiving side to provide a reliable data stream to the session layer. This layer also:

- Regulates flow control
- Uses acknowledgements
- Enables error handling

**Layer 3: The Network Layer** The network layer is responsible for the connectivity and path selection between two hosts on a network. This layer is where network protocols such as IP and IPX are located. Other functions of this layer include:

- Logical addressing
- Translating logical addresses to physical addressing
- Packet switching
- Routing

**Layer 2: The Data Link Layer** The data link layer is primarily concerned with physical addressing across a network. To accomplish this, the data link layer provides:

- Conversion of packets into raw bits
- Error correction
- Flow control

**Layer 1: The Physical Layer** The physical layer is concerned with the physical connectivity issues in a network. Specifications for voltage, timing, and physical connections are defined at this layer. This layer also:

- Defines hardware standards
- Transmits raw data over different mediums
- Defines protocols on how to transmit raw data over different mediums

**Data Flow in the OSI Model** To see how the OSI reference model is used, we need to look at how data flows from one host to another within the context of the OSI reference model. The first thing to keep in mind is that each layer on a host communicates with the same layer on the other host. Layer 4 on Host A will communicate with Layer 4 on Host B, as an example. For this to occur, the layers must pass information from one layer to another, both up and down the OSI model. Layers communicate within the OSI reference model via protocol data units (PDUs). Each layer depends on the layer below it for services, and in turn, each layer above adds PDUs via ***encapsulation.*** To see how this is done, let's look at a typical flow of data from one host to another.

Let us assume a picture is being sent from one host to another. The application, presentation, and session layers add PDUs to establish such information as what type of graphics standard the file will use and synchronization with the receiving host. The true encapsulation of data really begins at the transport layer when the data stream is broken down into segments. The PDUs encapsulated from the layers above are put into the data "load," and a header is put on the segment for the layer to communicate with the other host layer.

The network layer receives the segment with its associated header and further encapsulates the data by adding a layer 3 header and creating a packet. The layer 3 packet header contains information regarding the logical addressing required to ensure delivery of the packet via the network.

The data link layer then receives the packet and further encapsulates the data by adding another header and creating a layer 2 PDU called a frame. The header and possibly a footer added to the data load will contain information regarding the physical aspects of addressing data through a network. Things such as a media access control (MAC) address would be included in this PDU. From here, the frame is sent down to layer 1 and transported via a medium such as copper wire or optical fiber to the receiving host.

Once the data is received on the other host side, the reverse process occurs. As the data is sent up the layers, the layers strip off the headers and send the data and remaining PDUs up the layer chain until they reach the application layer.

6

**FYI** *Criminal Probes*

Criminals use readily available automated scanners to scan entire networks for vulnerable systems and services. These scans, called *probes*, occur daily and originate from network addresses throughout the world.

## TCP/IP Model

While the OSI reference model is the standard everyone wants to follow, the ***TCP/IP model*** is the de facto standard for communications. The TCP/IP model and protocol is a direct result of the Department of Defense's (DOD) requiring a network communication protocol that could survive under any conditions up to and including nuclear war. The basic premise was that if one part of the network was disabled, the communication protocol could find a way around the problem and still communicate with other hosts on the network. The DOD envisioned a network that comprised not only copper cable but also microwave links, satellite uplinks, and fiber connections. With this mesh system in place, a protocol that could survive and keep the communication links open was needed.

**TABLE 6.1** TCP/IP model.

| OSI Model | TCP/IP Model |
|---|---|
| Application | Application |
| Presentation | |
| Session | |
| Transport | Transport |
| Network | Internet |
| Data Link | Network Interface |
| Physical | |

The TCP/IP model has only four layers compared to the seven of the OSI model. Table 6.1 compares the TCP/IP model to the OSI model.

Some of the layers have the same name, but they do not all perform the same function. The TCP/IP model layers are as follows:

- Application layer
- Transport layer
- Internet layer
- Network interface layer

**Application Layer** The application layer of the TCP/IP layer combines the application, presentation, and session layers of the OSI model. All functionality of the top three OSI layers have been combined into one efficient layer in the TCP/IP model.

**Transport Layer** The transport layers of both the TCP/IP and OSI models are similar in both function and protocols used. The TCP protocol resides at this layer in both models and provides end-to-end reliable service. In fact, this layer is often referred to as the reliability layer.

**Internet Layer** The Internet layer of the TCP/IP model also corresponds to the OSI model layer of the same name in both form and function. The primary function of this layer is the logical addressing scheme used to route packets over a network. Unlike the transport layer, where reliability is provided by the TCP protocol, the Internet layer uses an unreliable protocol called IP. The classic analogy of TCP versus IP is registered mail versus regular mail. When a person sends a registered letter, he receives an acknowledgement that the letter was received, much like TCP does in the transport layer. A person who sends a letter via regular mail hopes the letter makes it to the destination but never receives an acknowledgement, much like the IP protocol in the Internet layer.

**Network Interface Layer** The network interface layer combines the data link layer and the physical layer of the OSI model. As in the OSI model, the TCP/IP model layer is concerned with the physical aspects of the network, such as physical addressing and hardware specifications.

**FYI** *Packet Analyzer*

IPAudit (**ipaudit.sourceforge.net/index.html**) is a tool that can analyze all packets entering and leaving a network. It listens to a network device in promiscuous mode, as does an IDS sensor, and provides details on hosts, ports, and protocols. It can monitor bandwidth and connection pairs, detect compromises, discover botnets, and see who is scanning a network. IPAudit is a free network monitoring program available from GNU (**www.gnu.org**).



## How Data Is Transmitted on a Network

Now that you have a fairly good understanding of how the theory works, let's look at how data flows through a network. Data networks can best be understood by looking at other types of networks. The flow of traffic through a city or the flow of water through pipes are great examples of how data flows.

Let's take roadway traffic as an analogy on how data flows. A vehicle on the road must follow certain rules, stay on the roadway, obey traffic lights, and avoid collisions at all costs. Data on a network must also follow certain rules, uses routers like traffic lights, and avoids collisions at all costs.

You already know how data flows down the OSI model from application layer to physical layer. Once the data leaves the network interface card (NIC), the network hardware takes control of how data is transmitted and where it is transmitted. All data transmitted across a network has two addresses encapsulated: logical and physical. The logical address scheme is usually an IP address and the physical address is usually a MAC address.

The two main network devices found on modern networks are switches and routers. Switches use the MAC address to determine if a frame should be forwarded and where to forward it. Switches have multiple ports and have the ability to microsegment. What this means in practical terms is that two computers on a switch can communicate without any other computer on the switch receiving data meant for these two computers. This reduces the amount of traffic on a network and further reduces the chances of a collision. Routers, on the other hand, use the IP address to determine where a computer is on the network. IP addresses are based on a hierarchy system and thus are more efficient when using large networks. The reason an IP structure is more efficient is simply because each computer does not need to know every other computer's

MAC address to communicate. Realistically, a router does not need to know the exact address or location of a specific computer on a network, it just needs to know which router on the network might know this information and send the packet to that router. For example, if you were sending a data packet to Japan using a MAC address scheme, you would have to know the MAC address of every computer between you and the computer in Japan. Using an IP scheme, all your computer has to know is the next router "upstream"; jumping from router to router will take you all the way to Japan. A router looks at the IP address and tries to determine the best path to the destination computer and then switches the data onto this path.

Let's assume we have two computers on a network separated by two switches and a router. The first computer sends out the data that arrives at the switch. The switch receives the data and first looks at the MAC address destination to determine where the frame will be forwarded. Keep in mind that the MAC address used is not the final computer's MAC address. The MAC address at this point is the next device upstream, which in this case is the router. Once the switch determines on which port the destination MAC can be found, it forwards the frame to that port. After clearing the switch, the data reaches the router. At the router level, the packet is examined to determine the destination address. Once the router determines where the destination IP address is located, it strips the old MAC address and inserts the MAC address of the next device downstream. The router then selects the port on which the data will find its destination and sends the data down that port. In this example, the router sends the data to a switch. The switch determines that the MAC address can be found at a certain port and switches the data to this port. Directly connected to this port is the second computer, which then receives the data from the first computer. Based on this example, you can plainly see that the IP address does not change, whereas the MAC address is constantly changing from device to device on the network.

## Packet Switching and Circuit Switching

Data packets must traverse the network via one of two methods. Packet switching is the method in which data packets flow across a network via multiple paths. When these packets are sent in this way, they may not always arrive in the order they were sent or may not arrive at all because of a break in the network. In order to resolve these problems, a protocol must have the ability to reorder the data packets and ensure reliability of the data. TCP/IP resolves these problems by numbering the data packets and using acknowledgements to ensure all data packets have arrived.

Circuit switching is the method in which data packets follow a single contiguous path from sender to receiver. The most basic circuit switching network is the telephone call. You pick up the telephone, dial the number, and are connected to the receiver. Once the telephone connection is made, the connection between sender and receiver does not change.

## Summary

The operating system of a computer is the program that controls the basic functions of a computer and acts as the intermediary between the application programs and hardware of a computer. The two types of interfaces used to communicate with an operating system are command-line interface (CLI) and graphical user interface (GUI). The CLI interface consists of a text-based interface where commands are entered via a prompt. A GUI interface usually consists of a pointing device such as a mouse being used to interface with graphical objects, such as icons or menus, on a monitor.

The functions basic to an operating system are file management, memory management, job management, device management, and security management. Early computers did not need an operating system because applications handled all computer functions. Modern computers have many applications and thus require a centralized operating system to handle applications and system information. DOS, Windows, UNIX/Linux, and Macintosh OS X are all examples of operating systems used on modern computer systems.



File systems manage the basic unit of data storage called a file. Various file systems in use include FAT 16, FAT 32, NTFS, efs, UFS, and OS X.

The OSI model standardized the methods used to transmit data on a network. The OSI model consists of a seven-layer approach. While the OSI model is the theoretical model to follow, the TCP/IP model is the de facto standard of the Internet. The TCP/IP model consists of a four-layer approach.

The two address schemes used to transmit data across networks are logical addressing and physical addressing. Logical addressing usually consists of IP addressing, and physical addressing consists of media access control addressing.

## Test Your Skills

### MULTIPLE CHOICE QUESTIONS

1. Which of the following is a false statement?
   A. Job management is a function of the operating system.
   B. Memory management is a function of the operating system.
   C. File management is a function of the operating system.
   D. File name management is a function of the operating system.

2. A text-based user interface is called a
   A. GUI.
   B. TCI.
   C. CLI.
   D. KBI.

3. Virtual memory is created by using a part of the hard drive as if it were
   A. ROM memory.
   B. RAM memory.
   C. hidden memory.
   D. module memory.

4. Operating systems interface with hardware such as printers and scanners using
   A. security keys.
   B. device drivers.
   C. FAT systems.
   D. memory drivers.

5. Which of the following is not a true operating system?
   A. DOS.
   B. Windows 3.1.
   C. Windows 2000.
   D. UNIX.

6. A drawback of using DOS was that users had to
   A. install DOS each time the computer booted.
   B. put up with very slow operating speeds.
   C. memorize the commands that ran the program.
   D. use a floppy disk to boot the program.

7. The technology that allows a user to create a secure tunnel through the Internet or a LAN is a
   A. virtual memory tunnel.
   B. private network pipe.
   C. virtual pipeline.
   D. virtual private network.

8. Windows NT is a ______ operating system.
   A. 16-bit
   B. 24-bit
   C. 32-bit
   D. 64-bit

9. FAT file systems can be ________ or 32 bits.
   A. 8
   B. 16
   C. 24
   D. 64

10. UNIX uses a file system called ________ as a native system.
    A. NTFS
    B. MFT
    C. UFS
    D. EFS

11. The OSI model was developed by
    A. Microsoft.
    B. IEEE.
    C. ISO.
    D. IBM.

12. The top layer of the OSI model is the
    A. application layer.
    B. presentation layer.
    C. data link layer.
    D. physical layer.

13. The de facto protocol standard for the Internet is
    A. Netbui.
    B. TCP/IP.
    C. IPX.
    D. OSI.

14. All data transmitted across a network has two addresses encapsulated:
    A. virtual and logical.
    B. logical and applied.
    C. physical and virtual.
    D. logical and physical.

15. A switch and ______ direct data packets on a network.
   A. hub
   B. NIC
   C. router
   D. media

## EXERCISES

### Exercise 6.1: Learn to Use the DOS Shell in Windows

1. Click **Start** and then click **Run.**
2. Type **cmd** in the dialog box and click **OK.** You should see a new window with a DOS prompt.
3. Type the command **help** and press **Enter.** What do you see?
4. Use the help command to find help on several commands listed. Practice with the commands to display a list of directory entries, copy a file, and make a directory. Use the different switches available for each command to see what changes.
5. Type **exit** and press **Enter** when you are done.

### Exercise 6.2: Learn to Use the Task Manager

1. Right-click the Windows taskbar and then click **Task Manager.**
2. Click the Performance tab.
3. You will see two graphs: CPU Usage History and Page File Usage History. Describe what the graphs are doing. Does the memory usage indicate the computer is using too much memory based on the scale of the graph?
4. Click on the Processes tab.
5. You will see different processes listed. Which process has the highest CPU percentage listed? Does it change or stay the same?
6. Close the Task Manager.

### Exercise 6.3: Find the Shell for Linux

1. Open a terminal window.
2. At the prompt, type **echo $SHELL.** Linux is case sensitive, so make sure to type the command just as shown here. What do you see? If you see /bin/sh,

you are using the Bourne shell. If you see /bin/bash, you are using the Bourne Again shell.

3. If you get an error message, type **echo $shell** in lowercase. What do you see? If you see /bin/csh, then you are in the C shell.

### Exercise 6.4: Learn How to Access Windows Explorer

1. Click the **My Computer** icon on your desktop, or click **My Computer** on the Start menu.
2. Click the **Folders** button located in the toolbar.
3. What information is displayed in the right pane?
4. What information is displayed in the left pane?
5. In the left pane, click on the + sign to the left of the icon that has a C. What do you see?
6. Click a folder called **Documents and Settings** to select it. Click the **View** menu and then click **Details.** What information do you see in the right pane?
7. Click the **Close** button in the title bar to exit the My Computer window.



### Exercise 6.5: Display the Directory Structure Via a DOS Shell

1. Click **Start** and then click **Run.**
2. Type **cmd** in the dialog box and then click **OK.** You should see a new window with a DOS prompt.
3. Type the command **tree** and press **Enter.** What do you see?
4. Type **tree/?** and press **Enter** to see if any switches are available for this command. You should see that two switches are available to control the display of files in the directory tree.
5. Type **tree/f** and press **Enter.** What do you see?
6. Type **exit** and press **Enter** when you are done.

## PROJECTS

### Project 6.1: Create a Folder in Windows to Hold Copied Files

1. Click the **My Computer** icon on your desktop, or click **My Computer** on the Start menu.
2. Double-click **Local Disk.**

3. Double-click the **Documents and Settings** folder.
4. Click the **File** menu, click **New,** and then click **Folder.**
5. Type your name as the new folder name. Press **Enter** to complete the process of renaming.
6. Right-click on your new folder and then click **Properties.**
7. Record the information you find in the Type, Size, and Created lines.
8. Close the Documents and Settings window.
9. Open a DOS shell (Click **Start,** click **Run,** type **cmd,** and click **OK.**)
10. Insert a floppy or CD that contains several files into the computer.
11. From the DOS shell, copy the contents of the floppy into the new directory/folder you have just created. (You will have to use DOS commands to copy the files. To tell DOS to recognize the Documents and Settings folder, you will have to enclose the destination path in quotes, such as "C:\Documents and Settings\[your folder]".)
12. Display the contents of the directory/folder to verify you have copied successfully. Use My Computer to view the contents of the folder and compare them to the floppy.

## Project 6.2: Use a DOS Shell to Test for Connectivity between Computers

1. Click **Start** and then click **Run.**
2. Type **cmd** in the dialog box and click **OK.** You should see a new window with a DOS prompt.
3. Type the command **ping** and press **Enter.** What do you see?
4. Type **ping** again with a remote computer's IP after the command. (Ask your instructor which computer you will use as the remote machine.) What do you see?
5. What could be the reasons the **ping** command fails to get an echo? What layers of the OSI model are used?
6. Type **exit** and press **Enter** to close the DOS shell.

## Project 6.3: Use chkdsk to Check Folder and File Integrity

1. Click**Start** and then click **Run.**
2. Type **chkdsk** in the dialog box and then click **OK.**
3. What do you see? Did chkdsk find any problems?

## Project 6.4: Using Ethereal to Capture Data Packets

1. Go to **www.ethereal.com** and download a version of Ethereal for your computer with the permission of your instructor. (You can also go to this site using the link on the Companion Website, at **www.prenhall.com/security**.)
2. Install Ethereal on your workstation. A good guide for installation and use can be found at **http://wiki.ethereal.com**.
3. Capture and analyze data packets from your local machine. Use Ethereal to see what protocols are being used on the network.
4. Send an e-mail from your computer and capture the data to see what you can view and what you can't view.
5. Close Ethereal and document your findings.

## Case Study

The International Organization for Standardization (ISO) developed a model to help standardize and understand computer networks. Before this model was introduced, networks for the most part could not communicate with one another easily and became islands within organizations. The OSI model is widely used in industry as a way to ensure compatibility with other vendors' network equipment and in the education setting to teach the complex nature of computer networking in a layered approach.

1. Using the Internet, find an instance where the OSI model has been used to ensure the compatibility of network architecture.
2. Write a report based on your findings.
3. In your report, describe how the OSI model helped two separate vendors design equipment that would communicate well.

6

# Chapter 7

# Investigating Windows, Linux, and Graphics Files

## *Chapter Objectives*

**After reading this chapter and completing the exercises, you will be able to do the following:**

- Conduct efficient and effective investigations of Windows systems.
- Find user data and profiles in Windows folders.
- Locate system artifacts in Windows systems.
- Examine the contents of Linux folders.
- Identify graphic files by file extensions and file signatures.
- Identify what computer forensics graphic tools and techniques can reveal and recover.

## Introduction

In Chapter 3, you learned that when presented with a hard drive to investigate, you may have gigabytes—even terabytes—of data to search. Given this immense amount of potential evidence, you need to be able to answer several questions: Where and how do you start? How do you manage the search for efficiency? How do you ensure thoroughness? Because Windows is the predominant operating system, this chapter explains how to find evidentiary data in Windows folders and files. In addition, you learn about Linux folders and files. With Linux becoming an increasingly popular operating system, this knowledge is important.

Many computer users are content to use Windows default settings without bothering to change them. For instance, when you save a Word document, the document will be saved by default in the My Documents folder—unless you intentionally save the file to some other folder. The My Documents folder often contains other revealing content, such as images, spreadsheets, and e-mail. Starting your search in the default folders and files maximizes the return on your time.

When investigating computer-savvy suspects, expect them to disguise their files' existence and deliberately hide incriminating data in hard-to-find folders. One common hiding trick is to rename files with disguising file types or use hidden files or folders.

In this chapter, you learn how to search default and stealth locations, and you become familiar with stealth techniques wrongdoers use to obstruct discovery of their activities. You also learn about graphics tools and techniques for efficient recovery of potential evidence.

---

## Investigating Windows Systems

In this section, you learn about the locations in a Windows system where e-evidence might reside and the types of data files that investigators need to examine.

There are generally two types of data files to review: ***user/system data*** and ***artifacts.*** User/system data consists of files that are intentionally added to the system through installation or user creation. Artifacts are files that are generated by the system itself for operational purposes, such as logs, temporary files, and so on.

User data is created as a result of activities of the user. Examples of user data include:

- **User profiles:** Data that was created by a user or that specifically pertains to that user.
- **Program files:** Applications (programs) that were installed on the computer.
- **Temporary files (temp files):** Files that were created by applications to hold data temporarily. Although temp files are used for only a short time, they are not automatically deleted.
- **Special application-level files:** Files such as Internet history and e-mail.

System data and artifacts are data files generated by the operating system. The most important types of system data and artifacts are:

- **Metadata:** Data about information such as file modification, access, creation, and deletion dates, as well as revision information in desktop files such as documents.
- **Windows system registry:** A database used by a Windows operating system (Windows 9x, NT, 2000, XP) to store configuration information.
- **Event logs or log files:** Files that record and document ***events.*** An event is any significant occurrence in a system or program. For example, the event logs record application, security, and system events such

as antivirus and Windows updates, user logon/logoff events, and equipment driver malfunctions.

- **Swap files:** Computer memory files that are written to the hard drive. This is a very important area because it has traces of volatile memory that show what the operating system was most recently processing.
- **Printer spool:** A file that is sent to a printer is first loaded into a ***buffer,*** which is a storage area, a technique known as *spooling.* From the buffer, the printer "pulls off" the file for printing at its own rate. Spooling also lets you send multiple files for printing instead of waiting for each file to finish before sending the next one because those files are sent into a queue of print jobs.
- **Recycle Bin:** This is a location where deleted files are temporarily stored. On a Macintosh computer, this location is called ***Trash.*** Files in the Recycle Bin are not hidden, and they can be restored easily.

**Caution**

**Hidden Files**

Hidden files exist on a computer but do not appear by default on the screen during a search or list process. Hidden files on an active system can be unhidden by following this method in Windows Explorer: Tools > Folder Options > View > Hidden files and folders > (Select) Show hidden files and folders.

While the user has some control of user files and can delete or wipe (purge) them, the system files and artifacts remain intact—unless someone uses extraordinary attempts to alter or purge them. For each type of user or system file, the directory locations for Windows 95 and Windows 98 (collectively referenced as Windows 9x), and Windows NT, Windows 2000, and Windows XP (collectively referenced as Windows NT and above) will be presented.

## Data and User Authentication Weaknesses of FAT

As a refresher, recall that Windows 9x does not truly accommodate multiple users securely. In Windows 98, you can create userids, but they are not required. A ***userid*** is a computer account created for each person who is authorized to use the computer or a resource. When prompted to logon to a userid in Windows 98, the user can bypass the process by simply closing the logon screen. Thus, the userid is used merely to establish individual user preferences, such as customizing the desktop, and is not really a security feature. In effect, there are no true security restrictions preventing other users from updating or deleting another user's files.

Windows 9x systems use the file allocation table (FAT) system to keep track of files on a disk, so locking down a file securely without special software is not possible. With FAT, only the attributes of a file or folder, such as read-only, archive, hidden, or system, are associated with that object, and no authorization permissions are available. As a result of this open access to files, recovered data may be impossible to authenticate to a specific user.

## Data and User Authentication Improvements in NTFS

Windows NT and above systems have the option to use a more secure userid and file management structure, New Technology File System (NTFS). *Separation of duties*, or separation of rights, can be implemented for the files or folders of differing user accounts with NTFS. The utilization of a distinct userid and its associated permissions, or rights, improves the ability to correlate a file to a user account, but it does not necessarily correlate a file to a specific person because a userid can be shared.

**Separation of Duties** With Windows NT and above, unique files and folders are created for each user who logs onto the machine, whether locally or through a network. This logon feature is important because a person cannot log on and use a computer without a valid userid and password for that computer. Authentication is the process by which users provide credentials, a password in this case, to identify themselves.

By default, no one has access to another user's files unless the user specifically grants that access through the use of permissions. This means that when a file is updated or deleted, a userid is associated with this action and must have the appropriate authorization to do so.

**Anonymity of the User** Because a user of Windows 9x does not have to authenticate to logon, he can remain essentially unknown. This anonymity is eliminated by the required use of userids in NTFS except in any of the following circumstances:

- If the default guest account is used
- If only one generic userid is created and the password is provided to all users
- If a generic userid is created that does not require a password

In any of the above user account situations, it is not possible to determine the identity of the user from the logon information. This is a key point when making observations in your forensic analysis. When no true authentication takes place, be sure that you do not make claims of file activity that cannot be supported.

The most reliable authentication means is through the use of multifactor authentication, such as the implementation of a token that requires the user to physically have the token in addition to supplying a password. Biometrics typically offer more reliable security than passwords, especially those based on iris or retinal scans.

**FYI** *Refuting E-Evidence*

Finding a true smoking gun can be very difficult depending on the file structure and whether the userids and passwords can uniquely and reliably identify the real user. Until computers store the user's DNA with the data, there is no unequivocal proof from the data itself that a specific user created it. A user can claim that someone else used her PC, which may be hard to dispute.

7

### Identifying the Operating System of a Target Hard Drive

Based on what you have just learned about file systems, a crucial issue is how to identify which operating system (OS) was implemented on a harvested computer hard drive. Having a thorough understanding of the operating system under investigation is imperative before testifying. This book provides a basic overview of the differences but cannot, within the scope of forensics, go into the technical details necessary for an expert testimony. Figure 7.1 shows examples of the ***directory tree structures*** for Windows 98, Windows 2000, and Windows XP. A directory tree structure is a hierarchical listing of folders and files on the computer.

The key differences that are used to identify an operating system are:

1. Operating system folder names
2. The folder for the Recycle Bin
3. The construction of the user root folders because of the differences in the way user data is kept

**IN PRACTICE:** Partitioned Hard Drive

A physical hard drive in a computer can be divided into logically separate sections called ***partitions.*** This is similar to a house divided into rooms. If the hard drive is partitioned, different operating systems can be installed on each partition.

---

## Finding User Data and Profiles in Windows Folders

In the Windows 9x platform, users were defined as separate entities only to preserve their personal desktop preferences. Data files created by users on the PC were all stored under one common My Documents folder by default. With the advent of Windows NT, separation of user accounts and their associated personal files became the new default. Now, user profiles contain not only user preferences and data files but customized application settings as well.

### Documents and Settings Folder

The Documents and Settings folder is the primary default Windows folder in Windows 2000 and XP. It contains a subfolder, called the ***user root folder,*** for each user account created on the computer. The user root folder is the

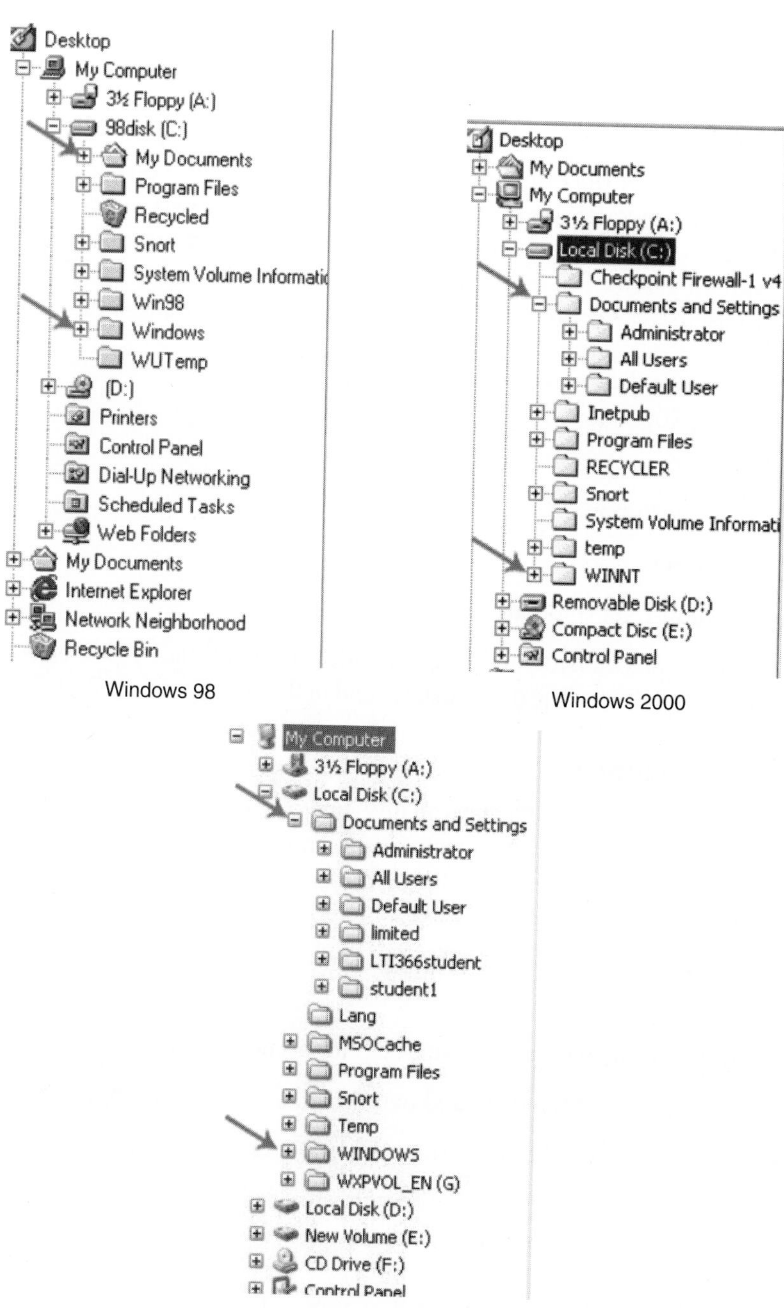


**FIGURE 7.1** Directory tree structures for Windows platforms.

cornerstone location where all folders and files that are specifically created for this particular computer account are kept. In most cases, the name of the user root folder is the same as the userid that is logged in, even if the user is accessing the computer in a domain or LAN environment.

**FYI** *User Account Names in Windows NT and Above*

Typically the user account name, or userid, is also the name of the user root folder. However, if you change the name of an existing account, a new folder is *not* created! Instead, the OS continues to use the folder for the original userid. For example, if you create an account, JSMITH, then later rename the account to JOE, the user root folder will still be JSMITH.

When a Windows NT and above system is installed initially on a computer, three user root folders are automatically created:

- Administrator
- All Users
- Default User (hidden)

There is no Documents and Settings folder in either Windows NT or Windows 9x. Instead, the user-specific data can be found in the corresponding Profiles folder.

### User Root Folder

The user root folder is the first place an investigator should look for data that is user oriented as opposed to system oriented. It is important to note that the user root folder for a userid does not get deleted automatically if the user account is deleted.

Data stored in the user root folder include:

- Desktop settings, such as wallpaper, screensavers, color schemes, and themes
- Internet customizations, such as the homepage, favorites, and history
- Application parameters and data, such as e-mail and upgrades
- Personal files and folders, such as My Documents, My Pictures, and so on

Typically, the user root folder contains the following subfolders (although differing Windows platforms may exclude some):

- Application Data (hidden)
- Cookies
- Desktop
- Favorites
- Local Settings (hidden)
- My Documents
- NetHood (hidden)
- Recent (hidden)
- SendTo (hidden)
- Start Menu
- Templates (hidden)
- Tools
- UserData
- Windows

As indicated in the list, several of the above folders are hidden and would not be shown by default on a Windows Explorer folder/file display. Because typical users would not see these folders, it is not likely that they would deliberately modify or delete them.

However, as you have learned, users can store their files anywhere. Also, an informed user would know how to easily change Windows settings to be able to view hidden files/folders. The list above simply shows the default settings of storage locations used by the Windows operating system.

**User Registry Files** The user registry file in the user root folder contains valuable information. The user registry file contains the personal preferences and computer settings for a user.

In Windows 9x, this information is contained in the USER.DAT file, while in Windows NT and above, it is found in the NTUSER.DAT file. Table 7.1 shows where the user root folder and associated user registry files are found on the different Windows platforms.

This data is not stored in a format that can be read by simply opening the file. While special software can be used to read the data, the preferences (such as desktop size, background, screensaver picture, and so on) typically do not provide significant evidence for the extra work. However, reviewing the metadata on these registry files can reveal the first time the user logged on, which is represented by the creation date, and the last time the user accessed the machine, which is represented by the last modified date.



**Application Data Folder** The Application Data folder within the user root folder is a hidden folder by default. It is used by applications to store user-customized information; examples of applications that store data here include Adobe, Ethereal, Macromedia, Real Media Player, Outlook, Outlook Express, and the most common, Microsoft Office.

**TABLE 7.1** Locations of Windows user root folders and registry files.

| Operating System (Platform) | User Root Folder | Location of User-Specific Registry Information |
|---|---|---|
| Windows 9x | *<partition>*:\WINDOWS\Profiles*userid** | USER.DAT file |
| Windows NT | <partition>:\WINNT\Profiles*userid* | NTUSER.DAT file |
| Windows 2000 and Windows XP | *<partition>*:\Documents and Settings*userid* | NTUSER.DAT file |

**Partition* is typically C:\, and *userid* is generic for the user's ID.

Confusingly, Windows 2000 and XP use two Application Data folders—one found as a user profile subdirectory and the other found under the Local Settings folder, which will be addressed later in this chapter.

When exploring the Documents and Settings*userid*\\Application Data folder using Windows 2000 or XP, you will find subfolders named for the applications that have placed data here.

In Windows 9x, however, this folder (found as WINDOWS\\Profiles*userid*\\Application Data) is significant because it contains e-mail data. Within the Identities subfolder are some odd-looking folder names. These are GUIDs, **g**lobally **u**nique **id**entifiers, developed by Windows as a unique 128-bit hexadecimal number that it assigns to each computer user account and to each e-mail account defined under Outlook or Outlook Express.

Outlook Express compound files, such as Inbox.dbx and Outbox.dbx, are contained in each of these GUID folders. Chapter 8 covers e-mail forensics relating to these compound files.

Windows 2000 and XP handle the Outlook and Outlook Express files a bit differently and store the e-mail data under the Documents and Settings*userid*\\Local Settings\\Application Data subdirectory.

Some other high-value forensic information can be found in the many subfolders under the Microsoft folder (\\Documents and Settings*userid*\\Application Data\\Microsoft). Those fertile sources of e-evidence include:

- The list of programs included on the Quick Launch bar
- The user's address book
- Pointers to the Office files (such as Word documents, Excel spreadsheets, Access databases, and so on) on which the user has worked recently

Finding those programs that have desktop or Quick Launch pointers helps identify a user's predominant tools of choice and may give you a clue as to possible file types to include in your search. This is a great place for an investigator to explore for additional leads.

**Cookies Folder** The Cookies folder is used by Internet sites to store information about the user, the user's online browsing patterns and preferences, and session information. Cookie files are usually named in the format *userid@website.txt*. If the Internet history file has been deleted, cookies may still provide information about what Web sites the user has visited.

**Desktop Folder** The Desktop folder is used differently by Windows 9x and Windows NT and above.

In Windows 9x, the Desktop folder contains shortcuts to resources (programs, folders, files) and any actual folders and files that need to be accessed directly from the Active Desktop display (the screen you see after Windows starts that has icons on it). This folder is shared among all users and is not specific to a user.

In Windows NT and above, the Desktop folder is positioned as a subfolder beneath each user root folder. The default desktop icon designations for every user's Active Desktop display on the computer are defined in the folder \Documents and Settings\All Users\Desktop.

Users can add more shortcuts or icons to their customized Active Desktop display by storing the desired shortcut or file in the \Documents and Settings\ *userid*\Desktop folder for their userid. Thus, in investigating a suspect, one could check this folder to see what shortcuts, files, and programs were of particular interest to him.

### IN PRACTICE: Determining Whether Removable Media Have Been Used

The Recent folder in the user root subfolder (Documents and Settings\ *userid*\Recent) generally has little direct evidence. However, it is a good source for determining the user's main applications, folders, and files that are helpful in prioritizing how to proceed in the investigation.

Each shortcut contains the actual path to the desired resource, so the properties of the link can be looked at to determine if removable media have been used. If the user accessed a floppy drive, the Properties would show the partition is A:, or if the user accessed a CD or DVD, the Properties would typically include F:, depending on how the hard drive has been partitioned.

**Favorites Folder** The Favorites folder (\Documents and Settings*userid*\ Favorites) contains Web links that are preferred or often accessed by the user. Windows (or Internet Explorer) provides a default list of sites provided by Microsoft, such as radio stations, weather channels, and online hosts. However, users can customize their favorites lists by adding or removing Web sites through this user-specific folder.

**Local Settings Folder** The Local Settings folder (\Documents and Settings\ *userid*\Local Settings) is, by default, a hidden folder. This folder and its subfolders are of considerable importance to investigators. As shown in Figure 7.2, this folder is composed of several subfolders that contain ***content files.*** The content files found in each of the Local Settings subfolders—Temporary Internet Files, History,

| Name | Size | Date Modified | Date Created | Date Accessed |
|---|---|---|---|---|
| Temporary Internet Files | | 1/15/2005 4:38 PM | 9/16/2004 6:57 AM | 3/2/2006 8:26 PM |
| History | | 9/16/2004 10:39 AM | 9/16/2004 6:57 AM | 3/2/2006 8:26 PM |
| Temp | | 3/2/2006 8:25 PM | 9/16/2004 6:57 AM | 3/2/2006 8:26 PM |

**FIGURE 7.2** Windows XP Local Settings folder.

**FIGURE 7.3** Contents of History subfolder in Local Settings.

and Temp—contain the details of URLs and their content that have been accessed on the Internet.

The Temporary Internet Files subfolder can be a rich source of key evidence because it contains the actual graphic, text, and HTML files used to display the visited Web site. These files can be deleted easily by the user through Internet Explorer > Tools > Internet Options > Delete Files or, of course, by accessing the files directly through Windows Explorer.

The History subfolder, as shown in Figure 7.3, lists the files that the user accessed over several time periods. In Windows NT and above, this folder also reveals Windows e-mail data.

## IN PRACTICE: Temp Internet Files Provide Valuable E-Evidence

Windows saves images and text from visited Web sites on the hard drive in the Temporary Internet Files folder. This data can be valuable supporting evidence, even if deleted. For example, in *United States v. Tucker*, 150 F.Supp.2d 1263 (D. Utah 2001), evidence of Internet viewing of child pornography in the form of deleted Internet cache files was strong enough for a conviction.

Although Tucker argued that "the images viewed on his Web browser were not child pornography under the statute because they were not 'stored' [by him] on his computer," 18 U.S.C. §2256(8) does take into account possession of child pornography as [any] data stored on computer disk that is *capable of conversion into a visual image*. Thus, Tucker's argument was found unconvincing.

As mentioned earlier, the Local Settings folder also includes another version of the Application Data folder. Within the Application Data folder, Microsoft uses the subfolder called ***Identities*** (\Documents and Settings*userid*\Local Settings\Application Data\Identities) to store information for Outlook Express. Each GUID

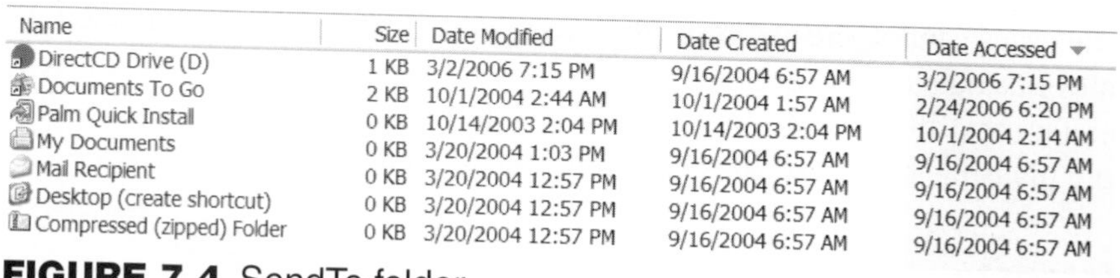

| Name | Size | Date Modified | Date Created | Date Accessed |
|---|---|---|---|---|
| DirectCD Drive (D) | 1 KB | 3/2/2006 7:15 PM | 9/16/2004 6:57 AM | 3/2/2006 7:15 PM |
| Documents To Go | 2 KB | 10/1/2004 2:44 AM | 10/1/2004 1:57 AM | 2/24/2006 6:20 PM |
| Palm Quick Install | 0 KB | 10/14/2003 2:04 PM | 10/14/2003 2:04 PM | 10/1/2004 2:14 AM |
| My Documents | 0 KB | 3/20/2004 1:03 PM | 9/16/2004 6:57 AM | 9/16/2004 6:57 AM |
| Mail Recipient | 0 KB | 3/20/2004 12:57 PM | 9/16/2004 6:57 AM | 9/16/2004 6:57 AM |
| Desktop (create shortcut) | 0 KB | 3/20/2004 12:57 PM | 9/16/2004 6:57 AM | 9/16/2004 6:57 AM |
| Compressed (zipped) Folder | 0 KB | 3/20/2004 12:57 PM | 9/16/2004 6:57 AM | 9/16/2004 6:57 AM |

**FIGURE 7.4** SendTo folder.

folder under Identities contains customizations and compound files, such as Inbox.dbx and Sent Mail.dbx, for its associated e-mail account, or identity.

**My Documents Folder** The My Documents folder is the default location for storing files created or downloaded by the user when the PC is used in a stand-alone mode. However, if the user is connected to a corporate network, that data may get backed up automatically to a file server or storage area network (SAN). Because the My Documents folder is the default location for user file storage, it contains a wealth of information about the user and the user's computer habits.

**NetHood Folder** The NetHood folder contains links to network connections that a user specifically adds to a session. The .lnk or link files found here help the investigator determine if additional systems need to be reviewed and what Web sites suspects may have linked to for data.

**SendTo Folder** The SendTo folder (C:\Documents and Settings*userid*\SendTo) may contain links to other media, prompting the investigator to review additional storage media such as floppy disks, flash drives, CDs, and DVDs. This is important because you may be able to link evidence on a removable medium to the mapped drives reflected in this folder. Figure 7.4 shows the contents of a SendTo folder, which reveals that the user accessed the D drive on 3/2/2006 at 7:15 P.M.

**Start Menu Folder** The Start Menu folder contains shortcuts, or links, to those programs the user wants to appear when selecting the Start button. Generally this folder provides information concerning the programs the user typically works with. While this is not definitive evidence, it may provide a starting point for preparing search criteria for specific file types, such as Corel or Adobe graphics, or perhaps WordPerfect documents. Typically this folder contains the last six shortcuts implemented by the user.

---

## Investigating System Artifacts

System artifacts are files methodically created by the operating system for a user during a session, such as the metadata, duplicate pointer files, link files, swap files, event logs, and temporary data/cache files. The users do not, and in some cases cannot, create these files arbitrarily. Because the system itself generates this data, information contained in these files can be valuable evidence. The fact that the files are not readily visible to the casual user also makes it more plausible that these files have not been altered.

## Metadata

Metadata is essentially data about data. While the term is widely known in relation to the hidden tags in HTML coding, in a forensics context it refers to the hidden information about files and folders. The National Information Standards Organization recognizes three main types of metadata:

1. **Descriptive metadata,** which describes a resource for purposes such as discovery and identification. It can include elements such as title, abstract, author, and keywords.
2. **Structural metadata,** which indicates how compound objects are put together; for example, how pages are ordered to form chapters
3. **Administrative metadata,** which provides information to help manage a resource, such as when it was created, last accessed, and modified; the file type and other technical information; and who can access it

Metadata has been directly supported in the courts as having evidentiary value. In the case of *Armstrong v. Executive Office of The President* 1F.3d 1274 (D.C. Cir. 1998) where e-mails and other electronic documents generated by the Reagan Administration National Security Council were being reviewed for the Iran-Contra affair, the court determined that paper copies of the documents were not sufficient. The court required that the entire electronic copy of the data had to be maintained for the case. In this way, important metadata, such as e-mail headers that contained server paths, intermediate addresses, and access dates/times, could be preserved. These details would have been lost if only paper copies of the files were used as evidence.

### IN PRACTICE: Searching for Evidence

Do not use the suspect system itself to carry out a search for evidence. The investigation will be compromised. As an example, using the integrated Windows facilities to search and open files on the computer being investigated will change the respective metadata associated with those files. This could cause all evidence uncovered on the machine to be disallowed for presentation in court. In addition to only using the forensically sound image of the suspect system for searches, the original

CONTINUED ON NEXT PAGE

▶▶ CONTINUED

medium should be preserved in an environmentally controlled facility safe from magnetic forces and unauthorized access to ensure its integrity. Any time the evidence is handled, it should be documented on the corresponding chain of evidence form. This policy should be strictly enforced.

One application of metadata used by Windows, starting with Windows NT version 3.51, is an uncommon data storage concept called ***alternate data streams (ADS).*** These data streams allow multiple forms of data to be *associated* with a file and are available only using NTFS. The data streams were essentially created to provide compatibility with the older Macintosh (prior to OS X) hierarchical file system (HFS), which used the construct of data forks and resource forks.

Because it is truly hidden information associated with a file, the data stream will not show up in any conventional Microsoft directory listing. Without using special software, the only way to display an ADS on a Windows system is to already know that it exists.

The syntax for a data stream is simply the name of the file followed by a colon and the ***stream identifier***:

```
filename:stream_identifier
```

The above syntax is entered using the command-line prompt. The "stream_identifier" portion of the syntax can be a text line—or it can be a file. A clever user can hide nefarious files in this manner because they will not show up using a DIR command, nor will they appear in Windows Explorer.

For example, an employee wants to hide information from the casual observer and corporate workstation administrator in the form of a graphics file. He first creates an innocuous text file and names it TEST.TXT, then creates his unapproved graphics file called NTRESTNG.JPG. He then uses the command shell and enters this command:

```
type ntrestng.jpg > test.txt:funpix
```

After hiding the data in this way, he deletes the original NTRESTNG.JPG file using a wiping program to cover his tracks. Note that the data stream identifier does not have to be the same name as the file being hidden. Now he can use the Run option from the Windows Start menu to view his JPG file, as shown in Figure 7.5.

## Registry

The system registry is a vital place to look for evidence. All configuration information needed by the operating system is found in the registry. It can reveal current and past applications, as well as those programs to be started automatically at system initialization (a favorite setting used by malware).

7

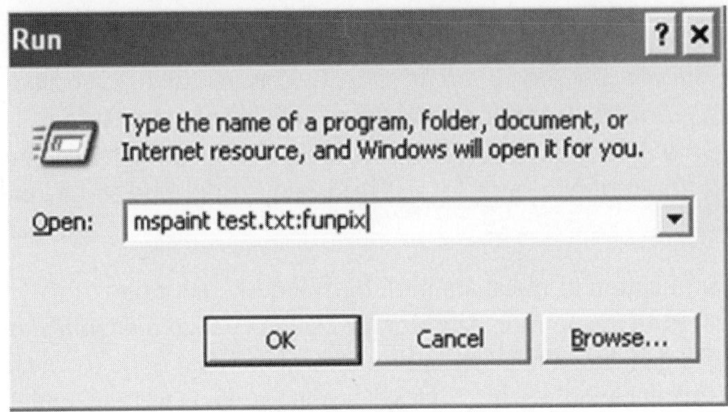


**FIGURE 7.5** Viewing a hidden graphic that is an alternate data stream.

Usually uninstalling an application leaves traces in the registry of its existence. Also, the registry logs Web site histories, Web search arguments, typed URLs, e-mail IDs used in Web sites, the service pack level of the current operating system, downloaded files/programs, and more. You may want to check for utilities, such as wiping applications, that would indicate attempts to destroy e-evidence.

In Windows 9x, the registry is the combination of USER.DAT and SYSTEM.DAT files. The advent of Windows NT changed this configuration, so the registry is a logical mixture, or a database, of several files called "hives." The location and associated registry keys for these files can be found in Table 7.2.

**TABLE 7.2** Registry keys and associated files for Windows NT and above.

| Registry Key | Hive File | Primary Location |
|---|---|---|
| HKEY_CLASSES_ROOT | Software | C:\%system root%\system32\config\Software |
| HKEY_CURRENT_USER | n/a | C:\%user root%\NTUSER.dat |
| HKEY_LOCAL_MACHINE\Hardware | n/a | Created dynamically at startup |
| HKEY_LOCAL_MACHINE\SAM | SAM | C:\%system root%\system32\config\SAM |
| HKEY_LOCAL_MACHINE\Security | Security | C:\%system root%\system32\config\Security |
| HKEY_LOCAL_MACHINE\Software | Software | C:\%system root%\system32\config\Software |
| HKEY_LOCAL_MACHINE\System | System | C:\%system root%\system32\config\System |
| HKEY_USERS\.Default | Default | C:\%system root%\system32\config\Default |
| HKEY_CURRENT_CONFIG | System | C:\%system root%\system32\config\System |

## FYI Viewing the Registry

Reviewing the registry requires using a registry editor such as regedit.exe or regedt32.exe. To get to regedit from the Windows Start menu, click Run. Type regedit in the command line; then click OK. A window appears that looks similar to Figure 7.6.

You can import the hives from the evidence file, but make sure to name the import uniquely, so it does not get confused with the live forensic tool machine. It is actually easier to build a forensic duplicate and boot from there to review the logs and the registry.

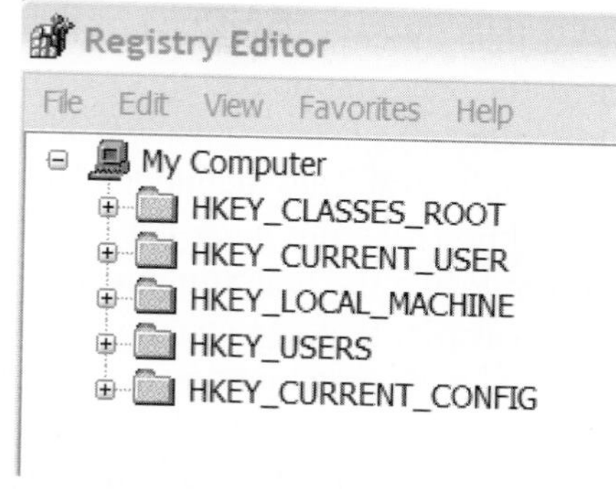


**FIGURE 7.6** Registry.

7

## Event Logs

Windows NT and above provide a way to easily log system events, such as when a user logs on, when antivirus updates occur, when drivers fail, and other types of significant occurrences. The files used for this information are databases that require the use of the Windows Log Viewer to interpret the data and display it in a readable fashion.

Windows provides three logs:

- Application log
- Security log
- System log

The application log tracks actions that particular software applications identify as events. Antivirus applications typically use this log to record when the program gets updates, and the Microsoft Security Center will write a record to this log when it starts up. This could be significant—especially the record from the Microsoft Security Center—to identify when the computer was last turned on and the operating system started up.

The security log is basically used for logon attempts. It can be configured to monitor resource activity such as creating, opening, and deleting files, but this is not the typical scenario for a workstation. The security log can be used in forensics to determine when a user logged on to the computer.

The system log is used by the operating system to track events such as driver failures or when a system component does not start up correctly.

## Swap File/Page File

The operating system expands a computer's memory capabilities through the use of swap files. When primary memory (RAM) is filled to capacity but more memory space is needed for data, the operating system exchanges (swaps) a portion of data in RAM (called a page or segment) with a portion of data from secondary memory. By default, swap files are hidden files.

The swap file, also known as the ***page file,*** is used by the operating system as virtual memory. When the operating system uses a program or a file that is bigger than the available RAM can store, it writes the overage to the swap file on the hard drive, from which location it can be retrieved later. When the operating system needs the data, it exchanges, or swaps out, a page of less-used RAM for data on the hard drive. By using this swap or page file, a computer can effectively use more memory than is physically installed.

A swap file can provide the investigator with a snapshot of the volatile memory and can assist in proving the existence of a file (not the owner or modifier of one) or the use of a program or database. In Windows 9x, the file is WIN386.SWP, and in Windows NT/2000/XP, it is PAGEFILE.SYS. Both are hidden files in the root directory and can be very large.

Consider this example of how investigating the swap file can be beneficial to investigators. Assume a suspect is working on a spreadsheet and wants to check her e-mail. She does not close the spreadsheet window but instead opens a new window to read the e-mail. In order to free up RAM, the operating system places memory being used by the inactive window (spreadsheet) in the page file and then proceeds to address the active window. If the user goes back and forth between the spreadsheet and e-mail, valuable information is stored in the page file from both the spreadsheet and the e-mail program.

As you've read, these swap files can become quite large, with a 300MB swath of data-rich swap space not uncommon. (By default, Windows allocates 1.5 times the size of RAM in the system.) In particular, it becomes a great mine of information that may not have been saved by the user to other media (hard drive, CD, flash drive, and so on) because it reflects data from volatile memory.

## Print Spool

When files are printed in Windows, they are actually sent to a system hard drive file called the print spool. In this way, the operating system creates temporary copies of the print data, enhanced metafiles (EMF), and runs the printer process in the background so the application can continue processing.

The EMF process actually creates two files associated with each page of the print job: a file that contains the actual print data for the page (denoted by the .SPL file extension) and a "shadow" file (.SPH file extension) that contains valuable information about the print job itself, such as the owner, the printer name, and the name of the file being printed.

As with the swap file, EMF files are created regardless of whether the user saved the data to media. If the printer is networked, the spool data is created on both the local machine and the server. The default location for the print spool is typically %SystemRoot%\system32\spool\PRINTERS. However, a savvy user can change this location by updating a value in the registry: HKEY_LOCAL_MACHINE\SYSTEM\CurrentControlSet\Control\Print\Printers: DefaultSpoolDirectory.

7

Once the EMF files are printed, Windows deletes them unless the print job fails, in which case the EMF files remain in the spool directory. Because these print files generally do get deleted by the operating system when the print job completes, the investigator should also look for EMF data in unallocated space.

## Recycle Bin/Recycler

There is a wealth of evidence in the Recycle Bin (stored as the Recycler folder in Windows NT/2000/XP). This is where files that have been deleted by the user are stored until the Recycle Bin is emptied. When files are deleted by a user, Windows removes the file system pointer value, moves the file to the Recycle Bin, changes the first character of the file name, and adds information about the file (such as the original path and file name, and the date/time of deletion) to a hidden system file named INFO (Windows 9x) or INFO2. The user can restore these "deleted" files until the Bin is emptied, at which time the file system pointers are completely removed from the active file system. In this case, the operating system recognizes that the storage is now available for reallocation.

In many cases, however, this data is not entirely written over, and by using tools such as EnCase® or FTK™ software, the investigator can restore the deleted files. This can be significant in an investigation because a user may feel smug about cleverly deleting an incriminating file and emptying the Recycle Bin, only to have you later find that data as evidence.

**Caution**

**"Shredding" Data**

When a user deletes a file with a third-party software, typically known as a "shredder," the data is actually overwritten by some binary pattern and is essentially irretrievable.

**FYI** *Recycle Bin and Recycler*

The major difference between the Recycle Bin (Windows 9x) and Recycler (Windows NT/2000/XP) is that the Recycler creates a subfolder for each user (actually the Windows security identifier, SID, for the account is used) and puts the files deleted by that user under the associated user subfolder.

---

## Investigating Linux Systems

Linux takes a different approach to system and data files and user accounts. While there can be many users with administrator access in Windows, in Linux there is only one administrative account. That account is called ***root***. This root account has complete control of the system. Individual user accounts are created, and then the administrative users are given access to the root account by implementing the "substitute user," or **su,** command. Logging is essential to associate the actual user to the administrative activity performed. In some installations of Linux, a command called **sudo** ("superuser do") may be configured that, in effect, gives a form of administrative access to authorized users and requires individual passwords to be used. If this is implemented, then the root account is disabled, and there is no generic root password, providing a much safer environment.

Another significant difference with Linux is that everything—devices (including monitors, removable media players/writers, and even keyboards), partitions, and folders—is seen as a unified file system. Unlike Windows, there is no easy delineation between partitions when using the Linux OS; instead, one must look in the /dev directory to determine the physical structure. However, when the hard drive is viewed using a forensic tool, such as EnCase software, the partition structure is readily apparent. A typical installation will create three partitions: the root partition, the boot partition, and the swap partition.

### File Systems

There are many operating systems running on Linux/UNIX-based kernels. Many companies utilize the commercial versions of this OS base, such as Red Hat, SUSE Linux, Solaris, HP UNIX, and IBM's AIX. However, in the field, you may see open-source operating systems such as Fedora, Mandrake, Ubuntu, MEPIS, Debian, and Knoppix, just to name a few. Obviously, there are feature differences in each, but they basically reference the file systems similarly. A ***file system*** (also referred to as ***filesystem*** in some documentation) includes the data structure as well as the processes that manage the files in the partition. Every object addressed by the OS in Linux is accessed by mounting—that is, creating a connection to—a file system; for example, each partition on a hard drive needs to be mounted, and when files on any removable media are to be read, they must first be mounted. Even accessing the monitor, keyboard, and mouse is preceded by mounting each device as a file system.

Linux can accommodate many different file systems by enabling VFS (virtual file system) within the kernel itself. VFS provides a common set of data structures to be used: superblock, inode, dentry, and data block.

- A superblock is created for every file system that is mounted. It stores information about the file system that includes a set of inodes uniquely addressed with that superblock, the total number of inodes and how many are free, the total number of data blocks and how many of those are free, and the state of the file system. Every file within a superblock is assigned an inode.
- Inodes contain the metadata for each file, which consists of the address, file type, size, owner, references to the file's data, and time stamps for the file's last access and modification.
- A dentry object links a file name to an inode number. Unlike the superblock and the inode, it contains information about the directory structure, or the hierarchy, of the file.
- A data block is a unit of allocation for the storage of the actual data contained in a file.

To view information about a file system on an active Linux machine, use the **ls –l** (long listing) command. Figure 7.7 shows a sample output of the **ls –l** command. This command will display an entry for each file within the current directory. Remember that the term *file* is used in a somewhat different context in Linux—everything in a Linux machine is associated with a file. There are seven different file types available in Linux: normal files, directories, links, named pipes, sockets, block devices, and character devices.

- **Normal files:** These are typical data files that can be text files, image files, binaries (executable files), or any other general file.
- **Directories:** A directory is a hierarchical container that allows you to organize data in a logical tiered fashion, rather than in one flat manner.
- **Links:** Similar to shortcuts in Windows, these files are actually location pointers that allow several file names access to the same file.
- **Named pipes:** Pipes are special files that allow communications between independent processes. They provide a FIFO (first in first out) mechanism to read or write to a process.

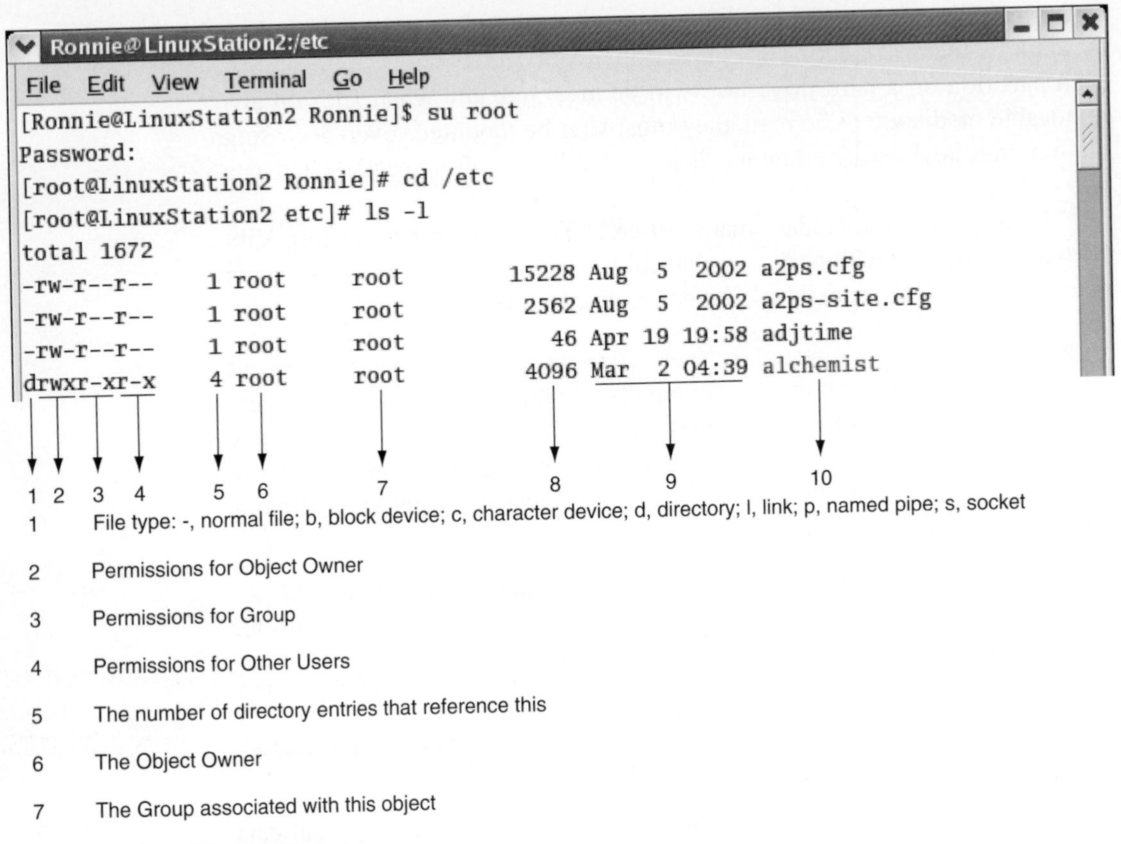


**FIGURE 7.7** Output of the long listing command.

- **Sockets:** Very similar to named pipes; however, these files are virtual connections between two processes and can be unidirectional or bidirectional.
- **Block devices:** These are buffered files used to exchange data between random-access block devices, such as hard drives and floppy drives, and the CPU.
- **Character devices:** These are unbuffered files used to exchange data between serially attached devices, such as a modem, keyboard, or serial mouse, and the CPU.

Currently, EXT2 is the de facto file management system used in most Linux implementations. In some newer Linux distributions, EXT2 has been enhanced with journaling capabilities and is known as EXT3. Also becoming popular is ReiserFS, the default of SUSE. All of these technologies utilize the VFS standard data structures to handle file allocation and management.

The component and operational details of file systems are somewhat lengthy and exceed the scope of this book. However, if you are working on a Linux/UNIX case, becoming more familiar with file systems is imperative.

## System Directories

Default Linux installations generally have the following directories to store system information that may be helpful to your case:

- /bin: (mandatory) executable binary files that are needed to boot and/or repair the system. If a hack is suspected, this may provide evidence of tampering, along with the /boot directory below.
- /boot: (mandatory) stores the operating system kernel and other files needed for system startup.
- /dev: (mandatory) Linux device description files.
- /etc: (mandatory) system configuration files (such as the password and shadow password files, xinetd configuration, welcome message, and message of the day just to name a few) for the local machine.
- /home: (optional) typically contains user account directories and files (similar to My Documents in Windows); structure is /home/*useraccountname*. This is a good place to begin looking for user-specific files.
- /lib: (mandatory) library files (similar to Windows DLL files) used by the programs and utilities in the /bin and /sbin directories.
- /lost+found: (optional) used by the file system check (fsck) utility to place files with no names (orphaned files).
- /mnt: (optional) the mount point for file systems such as hard drives and partitions, and removable media (tapes, CDs, DVDs, floppies, and so on).
- /proc: (optional) a virtual directory (one that is not actually stored on the disk) that contains special files which represent the current state of the kernel (details of the system hardware and any processes that are currently running).
- /root: (optional) the home directory of the superuser that contains configuration files for the root user account. In most distributions, however, this directory is not seen as "/root", but as just "/".
- /sbin: (mandatory) executable binary files for system/administrative utilities. These can only be used by the root (superuser).

7

- /tmp: (mandatory) temporary files are placed here and are usually cleaned out at boot or by a regularly scheduled job process; this directory has global read/write access for all users and processes. This could be a rich source of evidence if it has not been recently cleaned.
- /usr: (mandatory) the largest directory structure because it contains all user (i.e., nonsystem) programs and associated data that are to be shared across a whole site. It should be available to users with read-only access.
- /var: (mandatory) variable data such as printer spool files, administrative data, log files, and transient and temporary files. The files in this directory can prove to be a good source of evidence.

## Key Linux Files and Directories to Investigate

Just as in Windows, several files in Linux may provide significant evidence upon initial inspection. These include configuration files and system logs.

- /etc/passwd: This file contains information about every account created for this machine. In some cases it may even provide the encrypted password (typically, however, a function called "shadow passwords" is used, and the password field in this file contains an asterisk (*) not the encrypted password).

  Each entry contains the following information delimited by colons:

  - Account ID (the ID used to login)
  - Encrypted password (or *, if shadow passwords are enabled)
  - Numeric UserID (UID)
  - Numeric GroupID (GID)
  - Account information: typically the user's name (this is a free-form text field)
  - Home directory (like the counterpart to Windows' My Documents)
  - Login shell

  As mentioned previously, the Home Directory is usually /home/accountID for users, but it might have been changed, so look at this field for any users that are suspect in your case.

- /etc/shadow: This file is only found if the installation has been configured to use shadow passwords. When shadow passwords are implemented, then the encrypted password is not kept in the /etc/passwd file that can be read by everyone; instead, the encrypted password and associated user account information are kept in this /etc/shadow/ file, which is accessible only through root privileges. An asterisk symbol is used as a placeholder for the encrypted password in the /etc/passwd file. Information about each account's password management is kept here—such as last password change date.

- /etc/hosts: Contains local domain name system (DNS) entries. This may reveal often-used or redirected Web site names.
- /etc/sysconfig/: Contains many configuration files such as scripts run at boot time, keyboard configuration, and mouse configuration.
- /etc/syslog.conf: Identifies the location of log files; this can be helpful if you are unable to locate typical log files in the /var directory. Check here to see if other directory structures were used instead.

## Deleted Files

Interestingly, most versions of Linux have a Trash function similar to the Windows Recycle Bin. In like fashion, user-deleted files are placed in this receptacle and can be recovered before being permanently released to unallocated space (emptying the Trash). The Trash can is not communal—there is a separate Trash can for each login user. So look in the /home/useraccountID/.Trash folder for the files that a particular user (useraccountID) has deleted.



## Using Grep to Search File Contents

Grep is a powerful search tool typically used in the Linux/UNIX environment. EnCase software has provided this facility in their keyword search utility to reduce the amount of redundant search arguments and to employ text relationships. Using the flexible and powerful tokens, or regular expressions, in the table below, an investigator can home in efficiently on the search target. The most important thing to note is that grep is a character-based search tool. It does not look for the values of numeric terms—only the number characters they represent. Table 7.3 shows the grep tokens and their functions.

Searching files for specific data is effective for most files such as text files and e-mails; however, a user can utilize simple techniques such as compression and encryption to thwart this effort—albeit sometimes unknowingly. For instance, most Linux rollouts come with the free product OpenOffice for creating documents and spreadsheets. If a file is saved as an OpenOffice Writer document (file extension .sxw), which is the default for the Writer (comparable to Word) function of this product, the text data is compressed. When using a forensic product for discovery, you must ensure that compressed files such as those listed in Table 7.4 and these special file types, such as .sxw, are associated with the correct viewer in the forensic product. In addition, you may want to copy those files to an intermediate location and uncompress them, then perform a search against the uncompressed data.

**TABLE 7.3** Grep tokens and their associated functions.

| Grep Token | Function |
|---|---|
| char | A text character, or string of characters, can be used for a search and are, in EnCase software, not enclosed in quotes. For example, you can search for "john doe" or "evidence." In the case of "john doe," the characters have to match the exact order, (i.e., there must be a single space between john and doe—johndoe would not be a match), but the search is not case sensitive (i.e., John Doe would be a match as well as john doE) unless specified. |
| . | A period is used to match any single character. For example, a search for " **d..a**" would produce a hit for " Data," " dynamic," or " DYNApage" (note the space before each hit), but not for "ISDN adapter" or "Honduras." |
| * | An asterisk placed *after* a character is used to match any number of occurrences of that character, including zero occurrences. For example, using the search argument **jane,*doe** would produce a hit for "janedoe" (zero occurrences of the comma character), "jane,doe" (one occurrence of the comma), or "jane,,,,doe" (four occurrences). |
| + | A plus sign placed *after* a character is used to match any number of occurrences of that character *except* zero occurrences. So, unlike the *, the example from above would *not* produce a hit for "janedoe." All other hits are valid as described for the *. |
| # | A pound sign is similar to using a period to search, but it is used to match any single *numeric* character from 0 to 9. For example, using **###-###-####** would produce a hit for "502–555–1212" or "123–456–7890." |
| \xHH | A backslash followed by a lowercase x preceding two hexadecimal characters (the HH in the token) is used to match the ASCII hexadecimal representation of a single character. For example, if the search was for the file signature of a bitmap file, which would be the characters BM, the search argument would be **\x42\x4D**. The ASCII code for the character B is hexadecimal 42, and the code for M is 4D. Both hex digits must be present, even if one is an unprintable character (i.e., the ASCII representation of a carriage control line feed is \x0A and is shown in text as either a period or sometimes a zero). |
| ? | A question mark is used *after* a character or set of characters to indicate a match of *one* or *zero* occurrences |

CONTINUED ON NEXT PAGE

<table>
<tr><th>Grep Token</th><th>Function</th></tr>
<tr><td></td><td>of that search string. For example, using the search argument ##?/##?/#### would find a hit for “1/1/2000” and “12/03/1945,” but not for “1/1/00” or “123/3/1234.”</td></tr>
<tr><td>[ ]</td><td>Using brackets implements a Boolean OR type situation. Brackets enclosing several characters means to match any one of the characters identified. For example, using john[ bdc]doe would produce a hit for “john doe,” “johnbdoe,” “johnddoe,” or “johncdoe,” but not for “john b doe.”</td></tr>
<tr><td>[^]</td><td>A circumflex symbol at the start of a string in a bracket implements a NOT situation. For example, using john [^psz] doe would produce a hit for “john q doe” and “john a doe” but not for “john p doe” or “john s doe.”</td></tr>
<tr><td>[-]</td><td>A dash within the brackets denotes a range of characters. For example, [a-z] denotes the entire alphabet, while [a-h] specifies only the characters a through h, inclusive. It is important to note that numerals within the brackets are treated as characters, not as number values. In other words, using [0–255] would not look for the number 0 through the number 255 but instead would look for one of the characters 0 through 2 (i.e., 0, 1, 2) or the character 5 (see the use of the bracket symbol above).</td></tr>
<tr><td>\</td><td>A backslash before a character means that character is to be treated literally, not as a grep special search character. For example, using tom\+ harry would produce a hit for “tom+ harry” because the + is treated as a literal character.</td></tr>
<tr><td>{X,Y}</td><td>Braces after a token indicate a certain range of times to repeat: X to Y times. For example, inducte{2,4} would produce a hit for “inductee,” “pinducteeen,” and even “ginducteeeer,” but not for “inducted“ or “pinducter.”</td></tr>
<tr><td>( )</td><td>Parentheses are used in grep to group characters for a function. The token ban(an)? would mean to search for the characters “an” in that order for zero or one time. Therefore, “ban” would produce a hit as well as “banana.”</td></tr>
<tr><td>\w1234</td><td>The \w is followed by 4 integers that represent the Unicode code for a particular character.</td></tr>
<tr><td>a|b</td><td>The pipe symbol | acts like a Boolean OR for groups of characters (where the brackets are used for single characters). For example \.(com) | (net) | (biz) would search for the characters .com or .net or .biz.</td></tr>
</table>

**TABLE 7.4** Common file extensions for compressed files.

| | | | | | |
|---|---|---|---|---|---|
| .arc | .bz | .lha | .pf | .tar.gz | .uue |
| .arj | .cpt | .lzh | .rar | .tbz | .z |
| .as | .gz | .mim | .sea | .tbz2 | .zip |
| .b64 | .hqx | .mme | .sit | .tgz | .zoo |
| .btoa | .iso | .pak | .sitx | .uu | |

## Graphic File Forensics

Not long ago, digital photography was an expensive endeavor but not today. Taking pictures and editing them digitally is a common practice. There is a plethora of editing tools, both free and commercial, and each offers a multitude of ways to save the resulting graphic image.

When graphic files are found in unallocated file space or file slack, special tools must be used to ***carve*** the image from the raw data. This requires the investigator to understand the hexadecimal composition of special file types. ***File signatures,*** specific combinations of hexadecimal characters, are used to determine where the data starts and, in some cases, ends, and the type of special file.

### File Signatures

In many cases, looking at the file extension is a simple way to determine the type of file that is present. However, the file extension can be easily changed by renaming the file. For example, a picture that has been saved by a photo-editing program as a JPG (or JPEG) file—say, BADPICTURE.JPG—can easily be renamed through Windows to a different name and file extension—say, BENIGN.TXT. To an unsuspecting eye, as well as to Windows, BENIGN.TXT looks like a text file if viewed in Windows Explorer. It has the .TXT file extension, and Windows accordingly uses the icon for text files to represent it graphically on the Explorer display.

Renaming can change the file name extension, but it does not change the actual data contained *in* the file. The first (and in the case of some graphics files, the last) several bytes of a file typically contain data patterns that identify the type of file, known as the file signature. The initial hexadecimal characters in a file that reflect information about the file and are not part of the useable file data, called the ***data header,*** tell a program how to display the image.

Forensic tools usually have a mechanism to resolve file signatures and file types. The tool looks at the file signature and compares it to the file extension on the file name and generates a message to indicate whether the match was successful—that is, whether the file is truly the file type indicated by its file name extension. If the file signature or file extension is unknown or if the file signature is known but does not match the file extension, the investigator may want to inspect why the file is not named correctly. It may be that the user has intentionally renamed the file to hide or disguise the contents.

## Data Carving

When looking for images in unallocated or slack space, remember that Windows does not always store data contiguously. Files are essentially fragmented, and each piece must be recovered before a complete image can be recreated. The process of retrieving the relevant pieces of information is called ***data carving*** or ***data salvaging.***

Understanding file signatures is a key component of this process. In many cases, the data header may be partially overwritten, so the investigator may have to reconstruct the header. You should be able to use the identifiable portion of the header (or trailer) to compare with known image file signatures to determine the file type and reconstruct the header (see Table 7.5).

## Layered Graphic Files

Now that digital cameras are prevalent, many image editing programs have come on the market, both free and commercial. When editing images, a user may create a number of layers to apply desired effects, such as adding a filter or adjusting color balance. One of the benefits of using layers is that a change can quickly be reversed by simply deleting the layer, and another benefit is that the

**TABLE 7.5** Common graphics file extensions and file signatures.

| File Extension | Description | Hex Signature |
|---|---|---|
| BMP | Windows bitmap image | 42 4D |
| GIF | Graphics Interchange Format file: | 47 49 46 38 37 61 |
| | GIF87a | 47 49 46 38 39 61 |
| | GIF87b | Trailer: 00 3B |
| ICO | Windows icon file | 00 00 01 00 |
| JPEG, JPG | Compressed graphics file (usually photos) | FF D8 FF E0 xx xx 4A 46 49 46 00<br>FF D8 FF E1 xx xx 45 78 69 66 00 |
| | Digital camera JPG using EIFF | Trailer: FF D9 |
| PNG | Portable Network Graphics file | 89 50 4E 47 0D 0A 1A 0A |
| TIFF, TIF | Tagged Image File Format | 49 49 2A 00 |

layers themselves can be hidden from view. If an investigation relies on image data, the investigator should look closely at image layers for more in-depth changes. A user can, for example, place an image on a layer and then hide that layer so the image is not visible to a casual inspection.

Some images can be hidden behind these picture layers in images that preserve the layers as part of the file, such as Adobe Photoshop or CorelDraw. If the image has been saved as a JPEG, GIF, TIFF, or BMP, then the layers cannot be uncovered.

## Steganography

***Steganography*** is the science of "covered writing" and is one of the newer tools in the arsenal of the cybercriminal and cyberterrorist—or any moderately computer-astute user. It is often referred to colloquially as "stego"; for example, references to stego software are common. This tool provides the means whereby two parties can communicate in such a way that a third party is not aware of the secret communication.

Historically, steganographic methods date back thousands of years and include the use of invisible ink, microdots, and tattooing the scalps of slaves. Modern steganographic applications in the digital realm provide a covert communications channel by hiding some type of binary data in another file. The original file that contains the hidden information is called the ***carrier medium;*** the modified carrier file that contains the hidden information is called the ***steganographic medium.*** Steganalysis is the detection and recovery of that hidden information—and is the role of the computer forensics examiner for both law enforcement and antiterrorism investigations.

For steganography to be effective, the sender and receiver must agree on several details for its use: the stego software (both parties must use the same application), the carrier file, and, typically, a password to open the file. Most of the free stego software supports graphic files as carriers, and now many can use audio files as well.

### IN PRACTICE: Steganography Examples

To understand the power of steganography, see Gary Kessler's *Steganography Examples* at **www.garykessler.net/library/fsc_stego.html**. The simple steganography example shown below is taken from his Web site. The 11,067-byte GIF map of the Burlington, Vermont, airport (Figure 7.8) is hidden in a GIF file of the Washington Monument (Figure 7.9).

CONTINUED ON NEXT PAGE

▶▶ CONTINUED

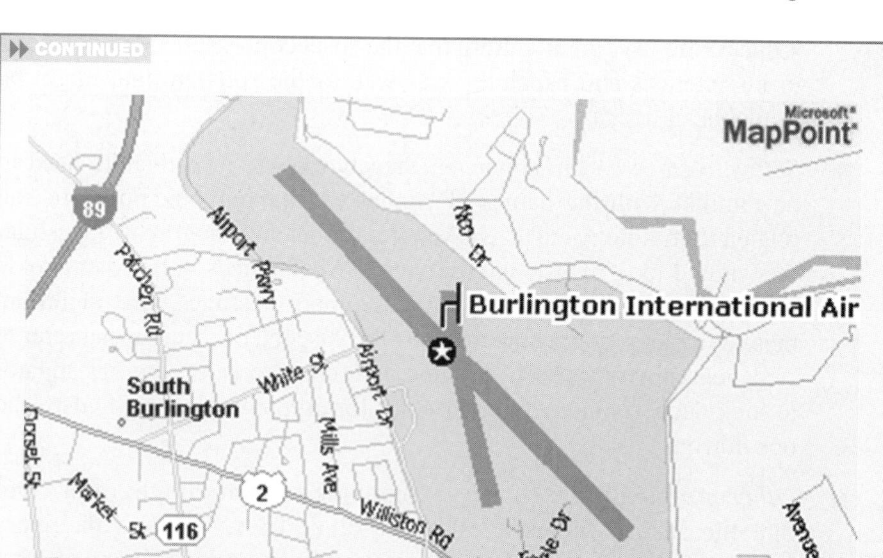


**FIGURE 7.8** The hidden message is a GIF map image.

**FIGURE 7.9** The map image is hidden in this GIF photo of the Washington Monument.

Because graphic and audio files are so prevalent in today's culture, it is difficult and time consuming to determine which ones may be holding steganographic data. Here are some clues that might indicate stego use:

- *The technical capabilities or sophistication of the computer's owner.* Look at the books, articles, magazines, and software manuals in the suspect's library; the literature that the suspect possesses gives clues as to his interests and capabilities as well as the software that might be available.

- *Software clues on the computer.* Steganographic investigators need to be familiar with the names of common steganographic software and related terminology and even Web sites about steganography. Investigators should look for file names, Web site references in browser cookie or history files, registry key entries, e-mail messages, chat or instant messaging logs, comments made by the suspect, or receipts that refer to steganography. These will provide hard clues to cause the investigator to look deeper. Finding similar clues for cryptography might also lead one down this path.
- *Other program files.* Nonsteganographic software might offer clues that the suspect hides files inside other files. Users with binary (hex) editors, disk-wiping software, or specialized chat software might demonstrate an inclination to alter files and keep information secret.
- *Multimedia files.* Look for the presence of a large volume of suitable carrier files. While a standard Windows computer will contain thousands of graphics and audio files, for example, most of these files are very small and are an integral part of the graphical user interface. A computer system with an especially large number of files that could be steganographic carriers is potentially suspect; this is particularly true if there are a significant number of seemingly duplicate carrier files.
- *Type of crime being investigated.* Some types of crime may also make an investigator think more about steganography than other types of crime. Child pornographers, for example, might use steganography to hide their wares when posting seemingly innocent pictures on a Web site or sending them through e-mail. Crimes that involve business-type records are also good steganography candidates because the perpetrator can hide the files but still maintain easy access to them; consider accounting fraud, identity theft (lists of stolen credit cards), drugs, gambling, hacking, smuggling, terrorism, and more.

As can be seen, there is still much to learn about steganography in a forensic environment. Even when a file is suspected, retrieving the hidden data can present quite a challenge. With the easy access of USB flash drives, an intruder can store the stego software and run it from the removable media without leaving a footprint on the hard drive. For more information on steganography, tools, and downloads, visit **www.garykessler.net/library/steganography.html** and **www.stegoarchive.com**.

## IN PRACTICE: Child Pornography

Another exploitation of stego is child pornography. By hiding the existence of criminal content in "innocent" files, a perpetrator can distribute or exchange material with customers using public forums and Web sites. Consider a hypothetical but plausible scenario:

"By pre-agreement, the leader of a child pornography distribution ring puts items for sale on eBay every Monday and posts photographs of the items. The items for sale are legitimate; bids are accepted, money is collected and products are dutifully shipped. But at some pre-arranged time during the week, versions of the photos are posted that contain hidden pictures. The ring members know when that time is and download the new photos. Unless the individuals are under active investigation, it is unclear that anyone will notice this activity. Furthermore, the sheer volume of people downloading the pictures will make it difficult to distinguish between the legitimate buyer and the conspirator" (Kessler, 2004).

In July 2002, investigators broke up the Shadowz Brotherhood, a child pornography ring that operated like a terrorist cell using encryption and stego to hide their activities (BBC News, 2002).

7

## Summary

You have learned that evidence search times can be reduced by looking in predictable areas, such as default folders and operating systems artifacts, during the beginning of the investigation before initiating intense and detailed probes. The skill level of the user will more than likely determine whether this is effective for your case. A savvy user can hide data by using nonstandard file folders to place information, renaming file types, using layered graphics, and masquerading data with steganographic techniques.

## Test Your Skills

### MULTIPLE CHOICE QUESTIONS

1. What are the two types of data files to review?
   A. User/system data and artifacts.
   B. Documents and spreadsheets.
   C. E-mail and Internet history.
   D. User data and hidden files.

2. Computer memory files written to the hard drive are called
   A. metadata.
   B. spool files.
   C. swap files.
   D. user profiles.

3. Why is the inability to secure files with the FAT system important in forensics?
   A. They are too big to process.
   B. You cannot find any pertinent information.
   C. The userid must always be used to access the files.
   D. There is no way to associate a file with a particular user, so the data could have been created or updated by anyone.

4. How does NTFS provide the ability to implement separation of duties?
   A. It allows for one generic user account.
   B. It does not require a password to authenticate a user.
   C. It provides a way to attach access permissions to individual files and folders by user account.
   D. It allows some users to clean up files while others must take notes.

5. Which of the following is *not* used to identify an operating system when viewing the file directory?
   A. The folder for the Recycle Bin.
   B. The base operating system folder name.
   C. The number of partitions on the hard drive.
   D. The construction of the Documents and Settings folder and user profile storage.

6. What is the cornerstone location where all folders and files that are specifically created for each particular user account are kept?
   A. My Special Files.
   B. The user root folder.
   C. Documents and Spreadsheets.
   D. Silhouettes.

7. What can be determined from examining the last modified date of the user registry file?
   A. The last time the user accessed the machine.
   B. The first time the user logged on.
   C. The last time the user name was changed.
   D. The current date and time of the operating system.

8. If the Internet History file has been deleted, _______ may still provide information about what Web sites the user has visited.
   A. photos
   B. spreadsheets
   C. cookies
   D. e-mail

9. What folders can provide possible leads that the user implemented removable media?
   A. Recent folder.
   B. Removable Media folder.
   C. SendTo folder.
   D. A or B.

10. In which of these folders might you find the actual graphic, text, and HTML files from Web sites visited by the user?
    A. C:\Documents and Settings\userid\Application Data.
    B. C:\WINNT\Documents and Settings\userid\Temporary Internet Files.
    C. C:\Documents and Settings\userid\Local Settings\Temporary Internet Files.
    D. C:\Profiles\userid\Application Data.

11. The _______ folder is the default location for storing files created or downloaded by the user when the PC is used in a stand-alone mode.
    A. C:\WINNT\Profiles\userid\My Documents
    B. C:\Documents and Settings\userid\Application Data
    C. C:\Documents and Settings\userid\Local Settings
    D. C:\Profiles\userid\Personal data

12. Why is descriptive metadata important to a forensic investigator?
    A. It describes the process the suspect used to create data.
    B. It provides a brief description of the user's forensic skill set.
    C. It describes the fonts used in the document.
    D. It can provide information that identifies the file, what it contains, and who authored it.
13. What information helps manage a resource, such as what time it was created, modified, or accessed?
    A. Superdata.
    B. Administrative metadata.
    C. Structured metadata.
    D. File info data.
14. You can find all configuration information needed by the Windows operating systems in the
    A. Config.ini file.
    B. Windows auto-configuration file.
    C. system registry.
    D. Win.ini file.
15. What Windows log file may be helpful in identifying the users that have logged onto the computer?
    A. Application log.
    B. Security log.
    C. Services log.
    D. System log.
16. The Recycle Bin is a potential source of evidence because
    A. someone may have thrown away a perfectly good newspaper.
    B. data can be recycled for money.
    C. it contains all of the user's personal information.
    D. the user may have deleted incriminating files thinking that would keep them from being found.
17. A _______ is the data structure as well as the processes that manage the files in a partition.
    A. super system
    B. business plan
    C. file system
    D. strategic incident management plan

18. In Linux, the home directory of a user can be found by looking in the
    A. /etc/passwd file.
    B. mailbox.
    C. /etc/shadow file.
    D. initial configuration file.
19. You can use ______, a powerful search tool, to perform keyword searches in Linux and in EnCase software.
    A. grep
    B. grub
    C. grab
    D. grunt
20. ______ is the science of "covered writing" and is one of the newer tools in the arsenal of the cybercriminal and cyberterrorist.
    A. Camouflagery
    B. Hide-and-Seek
    C. Crytoptography
    D. Steganography

7

## EXERCISES

### Exercise 7.1: Identifying Windows Operating Systems

Identifying the operating system of the suspect computer will assist in quickly locating obvious evidence, or "low-hanging fruit." The operating system typically identifies itself on start-up, but you should not be performing analysis on a live system. Most often all you have is the hard drive from the suspect machine or a previously gathered evidence file.

1. Make a chart of identifying characteristics for Windows 98, Windows NT, Windows 2000, and Windows XP that specifies where the system root, user profile, and My Documents folders can be found.
2. Go to My Computer on your own Windows machine.
3. Click the **Tools** menu and then click **Folder Options**.
4. Click the View tab.
5. In the Advanced settings window, under the Files and Folders section, go to the Hidden files and folders options. Click the radio button to select **Show hidden files and folders**.

6. Look down several lines and uncheck **Hide protected operating system files**. Click **Yes** in the resulting Warning banner.
7. Click **OK** to return to My Computer.
8. Double-click the partition where your operating system root resides (typically the C: drive). You will now see the previously hidden operating system files; they appear grayish.
9. Find the **boot.ini** file (if you are still hiding extensions, you will see just **boot**, not **boot.ini**) and double-click the file to open it.
10. Write what you have found in this file.
11. Close the file without updating it.
12. Return to the Folder Options dialog box and hide protected operating system files but do not change the setting for *Show hidden files and folders.* Close My Computer.

## Exercise 7.2: Exploring User Root Files

Many users do not know how to change their operating system defaults. This includes the place where personal documents and application customizations for their userid are kept, the user root. This exercise will enable you to determine where your user files are kept on your Windows machine.

1. Open Notepad on your Windows machine and enter the text **This is a test file for Chapter 7** in the file input area. (You can find Notepad by clicking Start > Programs (or All Programs) > Accessories > Notepad.)
2. Click the **File** menu and then click **Save As**. Make a note of the fully qualified address (the folder) that Notepad uses for the default location. Typically, this is where a user will save his data files. Type the file name **test.txt** and click **Save**. Close Notepad.
3. Use My Computer to navigate to the location where you saved your file. Explore your user root folder for other user data and note what you find.
4. Specifically look for your Internet temporary data files—can you determine the Web sites you have visited from this information? (You may need to open the Local Settings folder to find these files.)
5. Look at your History folder—now can you easily determine the Web sites you have visited? (You may need to open the Local Settings folder to find the History folder.)
6. Close My Computer.

### Exercise 7.3: Understanding Administrative Metadata

You have been asked by your manager to look at a particular file on a suspect's PC. She wants to do this quickly, while the suspect is at lunch, so there is no time to remove the hard drive. You are in luck—the suspect has left his PC logged on.

1. If you open the file, what will change?
2. After you access the file, can it still be submitted as evidence?
3. On your own PC, go to My Computer and find a file under any folder. Right-click on the file and select **Properties**. The Properties dialog box opens with the General tab displayed. Make a note of the created, modified, and accessed times.
4. Did you change the metadata when you simply looked at the file properties without actually opening the file?

### Exercise 7.4: Linux User Files

The key user management file in Linux is the /etc/passwd file. It contains an entry for every user account available on the system—including those used for operating system services. While user passwords themselves may not be found here if shadow passwords are used, there is still valuable information to be obtained, such as the default location for user data files. For this exercise, you need root access to a Linux machine.

7

1. Log on to the Linux system as a typical user (not root).
2. Open a terminal session (there are different ways to do this depending on the type of Linux system you are using).
3. Enter the command **su root** to access the root account, for which you will need to enter the associated password.
4. Enter the command **cd /etc** to navigate to the /etc folder.
5. Enter the command **cat passwd** to display the contents of the /etc/passwd file.
6. Find the account that you used to originally log on and note the home directory. This is the default location where your data files will be placed.

### Exercise 7.5: Understanding File Extensions

Windows uses the file extension to display an appropriate icon for a file and to determine the initial program to run to open the file. That means, for example, that a file that has an extension of .xls will have an icon that resembles a spreadsheet with a large X on it, and that Excel will be the initial program used to open the file. Windows does not look at the contents of the file to make this determination, simply the file extension. A user could hide graphic files from unsuspecting eyes on his computer by simply changing the file extension. This is an easy way to misrepresent files and takes very little computer knowledge.

1. Open Notepad, create a simple text document, and save it as **Ch7Ex5.txt** in the My Documents folder. Close Notepad.
2. Use My Computer to display the files in your My Documents folder. Record the icon that is displayed for the file you just created.
3. Double-click the icon to see what program opens to display the file. Close the program.
4. Rename the file **Ch7Ex5.jpg**. Click **Yes** when asked if you want to change the file extension.
5. Record the icon that is now associated with this file. Did the icon change?
6. Double-click the icon to see what program opens to display the file. Close the program and My Computer.

## PROJECTS

### Project 7.1 Alternate Data Streams

A lot of information can be hidden using the alternate data stream (ADS) feature of NTFS. To understand how this data is seen by the operating system, you will hide a picture as an alternate data stream. Then, you will use a free tool, LADS, to reveal its presence. This project requires a Windows system that uses NTFS.

1. Create the folder **4ensics** on your system's C: drive.
2. Open Notepad and type **This is simply a small test file used for an alternate data stream project** in the text input area.
3. Click the **File** menu and then click **Save As**. Save the file in the 4ensics folder as **simple.txt**. Close Notepad.

4. Download the **SampleImage1.jpg** file from the Companion Website at **www.prenhall.com/security** and save it in the 4ensics folder as **SampleImage1.jpg**.
5. Go to My Computer and locate the file you just saved, C:\4ensics\SampleImage1.jpg, and double-click on it to open it in Windows Viewer or Picture Manager (or whatever program is set to open JPEG files by default). Note the picture that is displayed.

6. Download the LADS program found at **www.heysoft.de/nt/ep-lads.htm** and choose to save it as **lads.zip** in the 4ensics folder. (You can also go to this site using the link on the Companion Website.)
7. Unzip the LADS program, storing the files in the same folder, 4ensics. You should then have the **lads.exe** program in the 4ensics folder.
8. Click **Start** and then click **Run**. Type **cmd** in the Open box and click **OK** to display the command prompt.
9. In the command prompt screen, type **cd c:\4ensics** and press **Enter** to change to the 4ensics directory.
10. List the directory contents by typing **dir** and pressing **Enter**. Note the size of the file you previously created, **simple.txt**.
11. Now enter this command to add the image file as an alternate data stream to the text file:
    **type SampleImage1.jpg > simple.txt:StreamExample.jpg**.
    Press **Enter** to complete the command.
12. Again type the **dir** command. Are there any changes? Do you see an entry for **StreamExample.jpg**?
13. Does the ADS really exist? Let's see. Type
    **mspaint simple.txt:StreamExample.jpg**
    at the command prompt and press **Enter**. Note your results and close the Paint window.
14. Now type **lads** to display the alternate data streams in this directory. Do you see an entry for **StreamExample.jpg**?
15. Write a summary of how this feature could affect a forensic investigation.
16. Type **exit** to close the command prompt window.

## Project 7.2 File Types

### Part 1—Live System

In this exercise, you will be able to see the hexadecimal representation of the file signature of several typical files. Being able to identify file signatures is necessary if you are looking for a particular type of file in a location, such as file slack or unallocated clusters, or when a person has changed the file type on purpose to mislead a common viewer. You will need to download and install hex editing software.

1. Download and install the trial version of WinHex (hex editing software) found at **www.x-ways.net/winhex/index-m.html**. (You can also go to this site using the link on the Companion Website at **www.prenhall.com/security**.) Save the zipped file in your 4ensics folder and then extract the files and store them in the same folder.

2. Download from the Companion Website the sample graphic files **SampleImage1.jpg** (if you did not already download it in Project 7.1), **SampleImage2.bmp**, **SampleImage3.gif**, and **SampleImage4.unk** for Chapter 7 and place them in the 4ensics folder.
3. Start WinHex by double-clicking the **WinHex.exe** file. (You may need to give permission to run the file and select an interface.)
4. Click the **File** menu and then click **Open**. Navigate to the C:\4ensics folder if necessary and select the **SampleImage1.jpg** file.
5. Compare the initial hexadecimal characters to the ones listed in Table 7.5. Do they match the file signature for a JPEG file?
6. Repeat steps 4 and 5 for **SampleImage2.bmp** and **SampleImage3.gif**.
7. Now open **SampleImage4.unk** in WinHex. Match the file signature to one that is listed in Table 7.5.
8. When you have found the correct file type, rename **SampleImage.unk** and change the file extension to the one you have determined to be correct.
9. Close all open programs.

### Part 2—Using Forensic Software

Most forensic software has an option to resolve files to their correct file type—regardless of how they are named. The software does this by essentially performing the same type of comparison you did in Part 1, but their list of file signatures is much broader. Go to the Companion Website at **www. prenhall.com/security** to find projects for EnCase software.

## Project 7.3 Working with Layered Graphic Files

Graphics editing software performs updates on files through layering the changes. In some programs, you have the option to save the file as a proprietary file type that preserves these layers. In this format, a person can hide pictures within the layers. Using this technique, we will see how a picture can be hidden within a graphic, using simple graphics software. It is important to recognize these layered graphics if you are searching for graphic files and do not see any indication of steganography software.

1. Download and install the graphic imaging software, GIMP, found at **gimp-win.sourceforge.net/stable.html**. (You can also go to this site using the link on the Companion Website at **www.prenhall.com/security**.) Select the correct GTK +2 run environment for your Windows OS and download it, as well as The Gimp for Windows. Note that you must install the GTK +2 first and then install The Gimp.

2. If you have not already downloaded the sample graphic files from the Companion Website, do so now by creating the folder **4ensics** on the C: drive and downloading **SampleImage1.jpg** and **SampleImage2.bmp** to this folder.

3. Run GIMP and allow all the defaults.
4. Click the **File** menu and then click **New**, which will open a Create a New Image dialog box.
5. In the Create a New Image box, make sure the image size is being measured in pixels (click the drop-down arrow beside the Height area to change the measurement system if necessary). Accept the defaults and click **OK**. This will create a new window called Untitled-1.0 (RGB, 1 Layer) 420×300.
6. In this Untitled box, bring in the **SampleImage2.bmp** file as follows:
   a. Click the **File** menu and then click **Open as Layer**.
   b. Navigate to the **C:\4ensics\SampleImage2.bmp** file and select it.
   c. Click **Open**. The title bar should now indicate *Untitled-1.0 (RGB, 2 layers) 420×300 and the SampleImage2 picture should be showing.
7. Again on the menu bar of the Untitled box, click the **File** menu and then click **Open as Layer**. Now navigate to **C:\4ensics\SampleImage1.jpg**, select it, and click **Open**. The title bar should now indicate *Untitled-1.0 (RGB, 3 layers) 420×300 and the SampleImage1 picture should be showing on top of the first picture.
8. Click the **Layer** menu, click **Stack**, and then click **Lower Layer**. Record what happens.
9. Click the **Layer** menu, click **Stack**, and then click **Raise Layer**. Record what happens, and then repeat step 8 to lower the topmost layer again.
10. Still in this window, click the **File** menu and then click **Save As**. The Save Image dialog box opens with Untitled in the Name input area. Change the file name to **LayeredImage1**. If necessary, click **Browse for other folders** and browse to change the folder to **4ensics**. Now click **Select File Type (By Extension)**, scroll down to the Photoshop image file type, select it (this will automatically change the file extension to .psd), and click **Save**.

7

11. Repeat step 10. This time, however, save the file as a JPEG image instead of a Photoshop image (when selected, the file extension will change automatically to .jpg).
12. When you click **Save**, a message appears that lets you know JPEG files can't handle transparency—in other words, it does not support layered graphics and will "flatten" the file. Click **Export**, and then click **OK** to save the file as a JPEG.
13. Close the image window.
14. Back in the original The GIMP window, click the **File** menu, click **Open**, and select **LayeredImage1.psd**. A new window should open with the title LayeredImage1.psd (RGB, 3 layers) 420×300 and showing the picture that was seen in **SampleImage2.bmp**.
    a. In this window, click the **Layer** menu, click **Stack**, and then click **Select Next Layer**.
    b. Click the **Layer** menu, click **Stack**, and then click **Raise Layer**. Record what happened.
    c. Close the file without saving it.
15. Again, back at The GIMP box, click the **File** menu, click **Open**, and select **LayeredImage1.jpg**. Repeat step 14, if possible. Explain what has happened.
16. Close all open windows and programs.

## Project 7.4 Steganography

As you learned in this chapter, steganography is the art of hiding data, such as a picture or document, within a cover file, typically a graphic file such as a JPG file. In this project, you will hide a file within a JPG and then reveal it with a steganography program called Camouflage.

1. Go to **camouflage.unfiction.com/Download.html** to get the free Camouflage steganography program, which is delivered as a self-extracting EXE file. (You can also go to this site using the link on the Companion Website at **www.prenhall.com/security**.)

2. If you have not already created a **4ensics** folder on the C: drive, do so now. Then go to the Companion Website, download **SampleImage1.jpg**, and place it in this folder if you have not already done so.
3. Go to My Computer and navigate to any file that you want to hide and right-click on it. An option to use Camouflage should now appear on the resulting menu. Select **Camouflage,** and the Camouflage program opens with the message "This file will be hidden within your camouflaged

file." The file you just selected is highlighted in the input area. Click **Next>** to continue.

4. On the next screen, you can either type in the file name of a JPEG file to act as a "cover" file, or you can use the . . . button to browse My Computer for a file. For this project, type **C:\4ensics\SampleImage1.jpg** in the Camouflage Using area and click **Next>**.
5. Now that you have chosen a cover file, you need to provide the name of the transit file (the file that will integrate the hidden file into the cover file). Override the current file and type **C:\4ensics\CamoFile.jpg**, keep the Read-only box checked, and click **Next>**.
6. Camouflage now asks you for a password for security—in this way, even if the steganography were discovered, the hidden file could not be extracted successfully. You may enter a password and its confirmation if you like. Click **Finish**.
7. Go to **C:\4ensics\CamoFile.jpg** and double-click it to open it in a viewer. Can you tell any difference between it and your **SampleImage1.jpg** file?
8. In My Computer, right-click on the 4ensics folder and create a new subfolder called **Restored**.
9. Go back to **C:\4ensics\CamoFile.jpg** and right-click on it, this time selecting **Uncamouflage** from the menu. If you used a password in step 6, enter it here, and click **Next>**.
10. The cover file and the hidden file are provided as files to extract. Let the program default to extract them both, and just click **Next>**.
11. Enter **C:\4ensics\Restored** for the folder where the files are to be extracted and click **Finish**.
12. Review the C:\4ensics\Restored folder—were both of the files recovered successfully?

7

## Project 7.5 Using EnCase® Forensic Software

For this project, you will need to order the EnCase demo software from Guidance Software at **www.guidancesoftware.com/corporate/demodiskrequest.asp**. (You can also go to this site using the link on the Companion Website at **www.prenhall.com/security**.)

1. Place the EnCase demo CD in the CD or DVD drive on your computer and let it autorun—this may take a couple of minutes, so be patient.
2. Click **Run EnCase® Demo**, and then click **Launch the V5 EnCase® DEMO**.

3. Agree to the EnCase Software Demonstration CD License Agreement by clicking **OK**.
4. The Demo will now load and will bring in the demo evidence files automatically. Note that in using a nondemo version of EnCase software, you would need to create a case file, or open an existing case file. In some versions of the EnCase V5 demo, the option to create a case file is not available and is grayed out.
5. The evidence file used for this demo should now appear in the left column and display one or more icons that look like platters from a hard drive. This symbol is used to represent a physical hard drive. The + symbol beside it indicates that this directory can be expanded to show subdirectories. Click on the +, and the partitions for this hard drive should appear using an icon like this C with the associated partition letter or volume name beside it (such as C).
6. A + beside the partition again indicates that there are subdirectories, so now click on the + beside a partition. Review the resulting folder displays and try to determine the operating system by the folders that are shown. Record your observation.
7. Using this information, navigate to where you might find user documents. Once you find an interesting My Documents folder, click on the little area that resembles a home plate beside it. This will display all of the files and folders associated with that directory. Record what you find.
8. Now, go back to the left pane and click the home plate for the entire partition. Above the right pane, click the **Gallery** option. This will display all typical graphic files that can be shown with the default image viewer. Record how many files are found.
9. On the left pane, click on the box (which is different from the home plate option) beside the partition you are currently viewing in Gallery mode. A checkmark will appear in the box (and in other boxes on the directory tree as well).
10. Click the **Search** option above the right pane—it has a magnifying glass symbol on it. The Search dialog box opens. Check **Selected Files Only** and **Verify file signatures**. Uncheck the other options, and click **Start**. The status of the operation will be displayed in the bottom right corner.
11. After the operation is complete, deselect the home plate and then reselect it. (This will refresh the display.) Note the number of graphics files now showing in the Gallery view. Did the number change? Discuss why the number of items might have changed.

### Project 7.6 Using FTK™ Forensic Software to Perform Data Carving

You can find this project on the Companion Website at **www.prenhall.com/security**. You will need to download the trial version of FTK at **www.accessdata.com/products/ftk** to perform the project and additional projects in the next chapter. (You can also go to this site using the link on the Companion Website.)

## Case Study

Several recent cases have used computer forensic evidence—especially metadata. Research these cases to determine how the evidence was discovered:

- In 2005, one file sent by the BTK killer to a Wichita television station led police to investigate Dennis Rader, a church president, and ended the 30-year murder spree of this serial killer. What evidence was pivotal in this case?
- A dossier on Iraq's security and intelligence organizations was released to the public by Prime Minister Tony Blair as a Word document on the 10 Downing Street Web site **(www.number-10.gov.uk)** in February 2003. An analysis of the document by Dr. Glen Rangwala, a Newnham College, Cambridge University, lecturer in modern politics, found that much of the material in the dossier was plagiarized from a postgraduate research student, Ibrahim al-Marashi. Mr. Marashi was based at the Monterey Institute of International Studies in California at the time. What information was used to prove that the UK government was not the original writer of this document?

# Chapter 8

# E-Mail and Webmail Forensics

## Chapter Objectives

**After reading this chapter and completing the exercises, you will be able to do the following:**

- Understand the flow of electronic mail across a network.
- Explain the difference between resident e-mail client programs and webmail.
- Understand the difference between typical desktop data storage and server data storage.
- Identify the components of e-mail headers.
- Understand the flow of instant messaging across the network.

## Introduction

According to Internet World Stats (**www.internetworldstats.com**), there were 957,783,222 Internet users in the world as of September 27, 2005. This is a 107 percent increase in the number of users since 2000. You can be sure that at least 75 percent of them use e-mail, and that is a conservative estimate.

E-mail, or electronic mail, has transcended social boundaries and moved from a convenient way to communicate to a corporate requirement in many businesses. Even so, users are typically more relaxed and unguarded using e-mail than they are when creating more formal written communications such as memos or letters sent by "snail mail" (i.e., the postal service). This psychological attribute has provided some interesting and, in many cases, incriminating unintentional documentation of people's activities or attitudes that can be found through computer forensics.

### IN PRACTICE: E-Mail in Senate Investigations of Finance Companies

Weeks before Enron filed for bankruptcy, it became apparent that several major financial institutions had helped Enron manipulate its numbers and mislead investors with secret loans. The banks disavowed any responsibility for the fact that their transactions ultimately helped bankrupt the energy company. But e-mail refuted their claims of innocence.

According to the testimony of Chief Investigator Robert Roach at the Senate hearing, the transactions with Enron totaled over $8 billion and included 12 transactions with JPMorgan Chase worth $3.7 billion and 14 transactions with Citigroup worth $4.8 billion. Barclays, Credit Suisse, First Boston, FleetBoston, Royal Bank of Scotland, and Toronto Dominion were involved in another $1 billion in transactions.

During investigations, one piece of evidence that received broad attention was an internal e-mail at JPMorgan Chase that described one of these disguised loans as a "prepay." The e-mail chain of evidence also included, "Enron loves these deals as they are able to hide funded debt from their equity analysts because they (at the very least) book it as deferred [revenue] or (better yet) bury it in their trading liabilities."

Damage to the reputation of JPMorgan Chase and Citigroup was significant, as were their multibillion dollar financial losses. Because of their active participation in Enron's fraud, the banks were the target of a Senate investigation, criminal investigations, and several lawsuits, including a class action lawsuit against Enron in which the banks are named as defendants (Brown, 2003).

8

## Importance of E-Mail as Evidence

In many cases, e-mail data can be pivotal evidence. Because of its informal nature, it does not always represent an "official" posture of an organization; however, in litigation matters such as sexual harassment cases, it does carry the onus of corporate policy.

In *Knox v. State of Indiana*, e-mail messages in which a supervisor repeatedly asked an employee for personal favors served as key evidence in a sexual-harassment suit. In *Harley v. McCoach*, an employee used e-mail received from her supervisor in a sex and race discrimination case. And in *Nardinelli et al. v. Chevron*, four employees filed suit against the firm claiming that they were sexually harassed. To show that Chevron's management allowed a hostile work environment, e-mails containing jokes such as "twenty-five reasons beer is better than women" were introduced into evidence. Chevron settled for $2.2 million plus legal fees and court costs.

As e-mail becomes the norm rather than the exception, this data can be a heavy fist—for both the good and the bad. Perhaps an employee angrily writes an inflammatory e-mail to his boss to let off steam and then decides not to send it but to file it as a draft. If this data is found later, it could be used against the employee even though he did not send it.

An estimated 26 percent of firms said they have fired workers for misusing the Internet, and an additional 25 percent have terminated employees for e-mail abuse, according to a 2005 survey by the ePolicy Institute and the American Management Association **(www.amanet.org/press/amanews/ems05.htm).** Content of those e-mail messages and logs of Internet usage are increasingly used as evidence in legal actions.

In *Adelyn Lee v. Oracle Corporation*, the plaintiff reached an out-of-court settlement of $100,000 with Oracle for wrongful termination. Lee was fired after having an affair with the CEO. Lee's suit relied on an e-mail message that was allegedly sent by her boss to the CEO, which contained the sentence, "I have terminated Adelyn per your request." Her boss insisted he had not sent the e-mail. Further investigation revealed that Lee herself had sent the e-mail. She was prosecuted, found guilty, and sentenced to one year in prison. This case shows that e-mail messages may not be reliable and may, in fact, be fraudulent in nature.

Consider another instance of discovering highly sensitive draft negotiation documents sent to supervisors that do not have management approval but are found in a corporate executive's e-mail. As an investigator, you must learn not to make unfounded assertions about the evidence you uncover.

---

## Working with E-Mail

The forensic extraction and analysis of e-mail continues to play a critical role in civil or criminal cases—and may be used by either the prosecution or the defense. E-mail evidence is typically used to corroborate or refute other testimony or evidence—or to help guide an investigation. An example of the use of e-mail forensics to support other evidence occurred in the 2005 case of Robert Petrick, who was on trial in North Carolina for killing his wife Janine Sutphin. Petrick left a trail of e-evidence including e-mail messages and a visit to the Web site bloodfest666. E-evidence included e-mails Petrick sent to women he was having affairs with and the downloaded document "22 ways to kill a man with your bare hands" from his hard drive. Investigators also retrieved e-mails that Petrick's wife had sent before her death. According to prosecutors, Robert Petrick did a Google search for the topics "neck snap break" and "hold" before she was killed (Jones, 2005). Authorities claimed that before reporting his wife missing Petrick looked up the depth and topography of a lake where her body was found.

In 2006 in San Diego, a defense lawyer whose client was on trial for murder retained an expert to conduct e-mail and IM forensics of his own client's PC and cell phone for evidence to exonerate him.

In general, e-mail is used by either side to influence alimony payments in divorce cases and to prove harassment or discrimination in employment cases. E-mail that is sent or received on computers and servers in any personal or work environment, from sole proprietors to big corporations or government offices, is subject to use as e-evidence.

## E-Mail Data Flow

A user can implement either of two standard methods to send and receive e-mail: client/server applications and webmail. You learn about the first method in this section and about webmail later in the chapter. Traditionally, many businesses have set up the client/server scenario for their corporate environment. This type of e-mail processing is characterized by the following features.

- The user has an e-mail program, such as Outlook, Outlook Express, Lotus Notes, Groupwise Client, Eudora, or Pine, installed on his PC. This software is a ***client*** program that works in concert with a ***server.*** A client accesses remote services from a server, which is typically more robust. Examples of mail server programs include Microsoft Exchange, Lotus Domino, Sendmail, Groupwise Server, Eudora Internet Mail Server, and Qmail.
- The client program is configured to communicate with one or more servers because it cannot send or receive e-mails using its software alone.
- The e-mails that are sent and received by the client program reside on the PC itself. Typically they can be found on the server machine as well, but this is not always true.
- A larger machine, usually located in a corporate data center, runs the server program that communicates with the Internet, where it exchanges data with other e-mail servers.

In the standard client/server e-mail method, the data flow for sending an e-mail follows these steps:

1. The user opens the client program on her machine, logs on to her mail account, and composes an e-mail.
2. The user then issues the send command by clicking on/selecting a button/option in the client program.

8

3. The client program moves the e-mail to the Outbox (a folder on the user's PC) and initiates a session with the associated server that has been configured for that e-mail account using the Simple Mail Transfer Protocol (SMTP). According to standards for port numbers, the TCP port number for SMTP is 25.

**FYI** *Internet Assigned Numbers Authority*

The Internet Assigned Numbers Authority (IANA) controls and assigns well-known ports and numbers, such as those used for e-mail. TCP port 25 is assigned to SMTP, which is e-mail. See **www.sockets.com/services.htm** for a list of all well-known ports and their numbers.

4. The server acknowledges the client and authenticates the user e-mail account.
5. The client then sends a copy of the e-mail to the server (which places it into a mailbox for that account) and moves the original e-mail from the Outbox to the Sent Items folder on the client PC.
6. The server sends the e-mail to the destination e-mail server, still using SMTP as a protocol, on behalf of the client.
7. If the client cannot establish a session with the server, it keeps the e-mails being sent in the client Outbox folder and continues to try to reconnect every so often (similar to when a fax machine continues to redial intermittently after getting a busy signal).

The data flow of this method for a user to receive an e-mail follows the steps below. Data flow for sending and receiving is shown in Figure 8.1.

1. The user opens the client program on his machine and logs on to his e-mail account.
2. In some cases, the client has been configured to initiate the receive action on startup. If not, the user issues the receive command by clicking on/selecting a button/option in the client program.
3. The client program initiates a session with the associated server that has been configured for that e-mail account using Post Office Protocol version 3 (POP3) or Internet Message Access Protocol (IMAP). POP3 is assigned TCP port 110, and IMAP is assigned TCP port 143.
4. The server first acknowledges the client, next authenticates the user e-mail account, and then allows the client to access the mailbox for that account. POP usually downloads all messages to the user's local

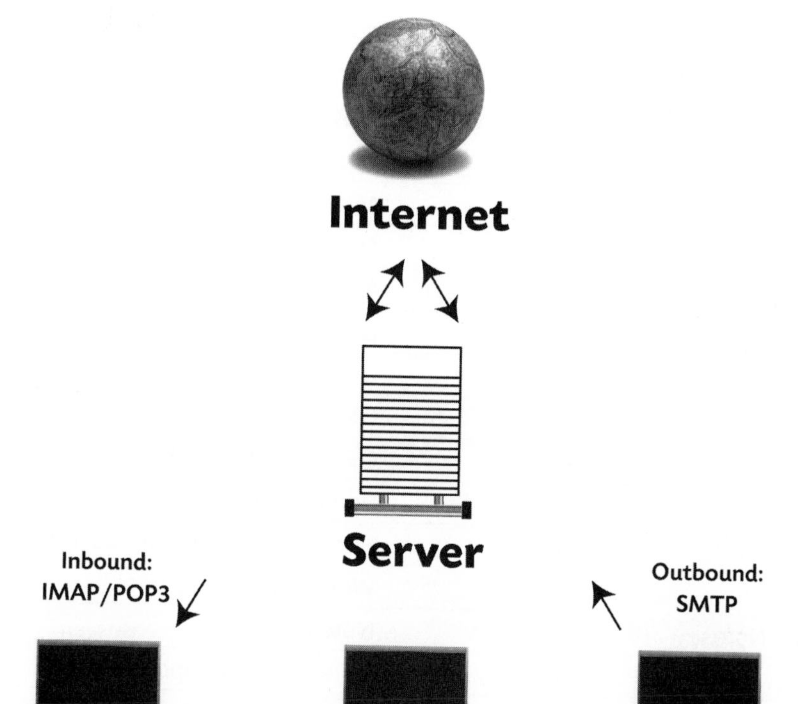


**FIGURE 8.1** E-mail data flow.



computer, placing them in the Inbox of the client and automatically deleting them from the e-mail server. With IMAP, the e-mails are also downloaded from the server mailbox and placed in the client Inbox, but they are not deleted from the server. Thus, with IMAP, a copy is kept on the server, and remote accounts can access all of their e-mail from any machine. With POP3, it is still possible that the messages are on a server if a backup was taken when the e-mail was on the server.

## Working with Resident E-Mail Files

The client/server method allows the user to review and work with e-mails offline because they are stored on the PC. This is of great benefit for the forensic investigator, because the e-mails are easily accessed when the hard drive is acquired. That is, the files are there, but the investigator often has to install an e-mail viewer to actually look at the data because it can be stored in compressed or proprietary form.

Begin your work by identifying any e-mail clients that might be installed on the system. You can look in the C:\Program Files folder to find clients such

> **Caution**
>
> **Get Authorization First!**
>
> Investigating the contents of someone's e-mail is a serious matter and requires authority to do so.

**TABLE 8.1** Common e-mail file extensions.

| E-Mail Client | Extension | Type of File |
|---|---|---|
| AOL | .abi | AOL6 organizer file |
| | .aim | AOL Instant Message launch |
| | .arl | AOL organizer file |
| | .bag | AOL Instant Messenger file |
| Outlook Express | .dbx | OE mail database (compressed file) |
| | .dgr | OE fax page |
| | .email | OE mail message |
| | .eml | OE electronic mail |
| Outlook | .pab | Personal address book |
| | .pst | Personal folder (compressed file) |
| | .wab | Windows address book |
| Lotus Notes | .box | Notes mailbox |
| | .ncf | Notes internal clipboard |
| | .nsf | Notes database (compressed file) |
| Novell Groupwise | .mlm | Saved e-mail (using WP5.1 format) |
| Eudora | .mbx | Eudora message base |

as Qualcomm Eudora or Lotus Notes. Outlook Express is installed by default on Windows, but that does not necessarily mean it is being used.

You can also search directly for e-mail stored on the PC by searching for common file extensions associated with the e-mail programs found in Table 8.1. These are but a few of the more common files—your case research should also direct you to the correct e-mail client.

Finding e-mails stored on the hard drive is a gift to the forensic investigator because they are stored in a complete form that gives the investigator access to considerable information. The e-mail headers may provide network information about the e-mail senders and the servers involved. In addition, the associated attachments may be reviewed.

The following sections discuss several popular e-mail programs. Most of these programs store e-mails in compressed files. A good basic tool to review these compressed files is Mailbox Reader, which can be downloaded free at **http://mailnavigator.com/mailbox_reader.html.**

**America Online (AOL)** In its very early years, when storage was a costly item, the AOL e-mail client always downloaded e-mails from its server to the client hard drive, then deleted them off the server. However, with the advent of new technology in storage devices and capacities, AOL moved into the webmail arena, giving users almost a month to do something with their e-mail data. If a user chooses not to download e-mails to the PC or save them to an AOL space-restricted service, then they will be deleted from the server and unavailable for use.

When saved to a PC (Windows 2000 or XP) using the AOL Personal Filing Cabinet feature, the following general folders and file types are used, where *X* is the version:

- **AOL up to 7.0:** C:\America Online *X*\Organize*AOLuserscreenname*. Look for the files that do not have a file extension. Also look for .arl files.
- **AOL 8.0:** C:\Documents and Settings*Windowsusername*\Application Data\AOL\America Online X\Organize*AOLuserscreenname*.abi. You may also look for .pfc files.
- **AOL 9.0:** C:\Documents and Settings\All Users\Application Data\AOL\America Online X\Organize*AOLuserscreenname*.abi. You may also look for .pfc files

**Outlook Express** As mentioned previously, this e-mail client is installed by default on Windows machines. It can be customized to send and receive e-mail from many different types of e-mail servers. It is designed to store e-mails and e-mail folders on the user's hard drive. With this software, a user can configure several e-mail accounts that connect to different servers. Each e-mail account is given a Microsoft "Identity," which is a unique hexadecimal representation for that account. The folders used for Outlook Express are found in the user profiles. In Windows 2000 and XP they are:

- C:\Documents and Settings*Windowsuserid*\Local Settings\Application Data\Identities\{*hex identity*}\Microsoft\ Outlook Express

There is a unique folder for each e-mail account created by this Windows user.

Within each Outlook Express folder are databases with the file type .dbx that contain all of the e-mails for the Folders, Inbox, Outbox, Sent Items, and so on. The .dbx files are similar to .zip files in that they compress all of the individual e-mail files for a service (Inbox, Outbox, Sent Items) into a single logical file for that service. Consequently, it takes a special viewer to see these files legibly. Both EnCase® software and FTK™ have these viewers built in, so no additional tools are required if you are using one of these popular forensic toolkits.

**Outlook** This e-mail client comes with the Microsoft Office product suite and is a personal information manager in addition to being e-mail communication software. It is a fairly feature-rich program that provides calendar, task, and contact management functions, as well as note taking and journaling abilities. With this product, you can set up different e-mail accounts, but they all feed into one main database, so you do not have to switch identities.

8

To find all of this tasty data, navigate to C:\Documents and Settings\ *Windowsuserid*\Local Settings\Application Data\Microsoft\Outlook and look for the .pst files. Typically the main file to review is the Outlook.pst compressed file. As with Outlook Express, this file cannot be simply viewed in a hex editor; it requires a viewer. Both FTK and Encase software can view the .pst files.

**Eudora** Eudora is a popular free e-mail client that can be downloaded at **www.eudora.com/download.** Many Macintosh OS X users like this program. The default location for Eudora files on Mac OS X is Users/Documents and in Windows 2000/XP it is C:\Documents and Settings\ *Windowsuserid*\Application Data\Qualcomm\Eudora. Look for .mbx files to find e-mails, which also require a special reader (such as Mail Navigator).

**Lotus Notes** IBM Lotus Notes is an integrated client option for the Lotus Domino server that provides e-mail delivery, calendar and scheduling capabilities, integrated instant messaging (proprietary through an IBM Lotus Sametime server), and many other workplace tools along with a powerful desktop platform for collaborative applications. Because of its many features, a lot of different evidence opportunities exist. This information is stored in a Notes database, which, somewhat like a compressed file, is a single file that contains multiple e-mails. The database is located by default at C:\Program Files\Lotus\Notes\Data and has an .nsf file extension. A special program is required to read this database. One such program, besides Notes itself, is LotusNotesRecovery by Recoveronix, Ltd. It is not free, but a demo version is available for download at **www.officerecovery.com/downloads.htm.**

**FYI** *You Are Invited to Bankruptcy Court*

E-mail evidence has emerged in bankruptcy-court proceedings, allowing plaintiffs to proceed against defendants who may have left the country or cannot be found. In one of the first rulings of its kind in the United States, a judge held that a summons could be served on the defendant by e-mail.

## Working with Webmail

An alternate method to send/receive e-mails is through a Web browser using ***webmail*** to access online e-mail servers, such as Yahoo!, Hotmail, gmail, or perhaps the e-mail server at an ISP. Behind the scenes, it is still a client/server operation, but the user does not have to run the special e-mail client on her PC.

This is particularly popular with people who may use a number of computers in a day because they can access their e-mail from any computer using the Web browser.

## Webmail Data Flow

In the webmail scenario, the data flow is as follows:

- The user opens her browser, goes to the URL of the webmail interface, and logs in.
- She does not have to take any action to receive mail—it is already placed in her Inbox by the webmail server behind the scenes using the same protocols discussed for regular e-mail.
- To send an e-mail, she uses the compose or new message function on the webmail client program, writes the message, and then initiates the send function.
- The web client communicates behind the scenes to the webmail server to send the message using the SMTP protocol as outlined for e-mail.
- Using this method, there are no e-mails stored on her PC—they are all resident on the machine owned by the webmail provider.

Often, these webmail providers offer the user the ability to use an e-mail program, such as Outlook or Outlook Express, to connect to their webmail servers and function as a true client/server. This means that if the user wants to be able to work with his webmail offline, he can download e-mails from Yahoo!, Hotmail, gmail, and so on to his PC and use his e-mail client to process them. So, as can be seen, there is no one particular way that a person works with his e-mail. Table 8.2 compares the characteristics of POP3, IMAP, and webmail.

8

## Working with Webmail Files

Because the e-mail is not being saved to the local machine, finding evidence of webmail takes a bit more effort . . . and some luck. However, here are some strategies that can be applied.

When a user implements webmail using her browser, temporary files are created that contain snapshots of the process. Thus, the best place to look for this type of data is in C:\Documents and Settings*Windowsuserid*\Local Settings\Temporary Internet Files. If you do not know a specific e-mail address, you may want to use grep-oriented generic keyword searches for all e-mail addresses in unallocated clusters, such as this grep search string: [a-z#~_\.!\#$%\^&*\(\)\-]+@[a-z#_\-]+\.[a-z#_\-\.]+. This process may result in *many* false-positives; that is, you will get search hits for e-mail addresses from

**TABLE 8.2** Comparison of POP3, IMAP, and webmail.

| Type of E-Mail Protocol | POP3 | IMAP | Webmail |
|---|---|---|---|
| E-mail accessible from anywhere | No | Yes | Yes |
| Remains stored on server | No (unless it was included in a backup of the server) | Yes | Yes, unless POP3 was used too |
| Dependence on Internet | Moderate | Very strong | Strong |
| Special software required | Yes | Yes | No |

miscellaneous Web pages for that site's support or contact address and not an address that is meaningful to the case.

Some keywords for various webmail programs are:

- **Yahoo! mail:** ShowLetter, ShowFolder Compose, "Yahoo! Mail"
- **Hotmail:** HoTMaiL, hmhome, getmsg, doattach, compose
- **Gmail:** mail[#]

Note that gmail typically uses javascript, so you may not be able to find any data for this webmail program in Temporary Internet Files.

### FYI Evidence of Reckless Indifference to Human Life

American Home Products (AHP), which manufactured and distributed the diet drug Fen-Phen, publicly denied knowing of its serious health risks. Plaintiffs were not convinced and demanded AHP e-mail related to the diet drug. After searching through over 33 million e-mails, plaintiffs' counsel discovered an e-mail from someone in accounting who complained: "Do I have to look forward to spending my waning years writing checks to fat people worried about a silly lung problem?" After that evidence was revealed, AHP agreed to settle the case for a record $3.75 billion.

# Working with Mail Servers

To actually communicate via the Internet to send and receive e-mails, an e-mail server program is necessary. As with e-mail clients, there are many different servers to utilize, each with its own mailbox and messaging structure. Because the server is used as an intermediate storage place for e-mails, you may have to use the strategy of retrieving e-mails from the server if you have been unable to find evidence on a local machine.

Working with these e-mail servers takes more specific product knowledge than can be covered in this book, but there are some general similarities among servers. The important thing to note is that these programs service many e-mail accounts, possibly hundreds or thousands—not just one or two as we looked at for e-mail clients. Also, because the server does interface with so many e-mail users in a production environment, trying to get data from a server for investigative purposes may not be an easy task. In many cases, it simply may not be possible to get forensic access to these servers, and the investigator may have to rely on extracted files (such as a particular user's mailbox for a certain time period) provided by the owner of the e-mail server. However, in small to medium companies, servers may not be quite so inaccessible.

It is also advisable to check the corporate retention policy to determine if the e-mails are even available. Since the days of the Enron scandal when over a million e-mails were entered as discoverable evidence, many companies have started to review their policies covering how long electronic data is to be kept and how backups are to be used. Securing a warrant in a criminal case to access an Internet service provider's e-mail server may also be difficult, and as an added challenge, the retention period on these servers is usually quite short.

Storage for servers is another matter. For most investigative work, we have looked at individual PCs, with one or perhaps two hard drives. However, because of the scenario of providing services to many users and the need for redundancy for availability, servers typically utilize a data structure that implements multiple physical hard drives to look like one logical drive called a redundant array of independent (formerly "inexpensive") disks (RAID).

## Redundant Array of Independent Disks (RAID)

RAID utilizes two or more hard drives accessed in parallel to create a pool of storage that provides the user better performance and fault tolerance. This technology can be implemented via software or hardware and at several different levels. The RAID levels determine how the data is written to the disks to provide this advanced functionality. A forensic investigator needs to understand the basic concepts of RAID levels to determine how he may collect the data necessary for his case.

The different RAID levels utilize varying combinations of writing to disks through techniques known as ***mirroring, striping,*** and ***parity.*** Mirroring, from a simplistic perspective, is writing the same data in two places (a mirror image). Striping divides the data into blocks and writes these units across several drives (as opposed to keeping the data together on one drive). Parity, also known as *error-corrective coding* (ECC), is an additional measure used to check the validity of data that is striped to determine if the correct orientation (odd or even) of bits were written to the hard drive. There are a number (more than 9) of implementations, or levels, of RAID, of which RAID 1, 3, and 5 are the most popular. Windows machines recognize only RAID 0, 1, and 5.

- **RAID 0: Basic disk striping.** This implementation provides robust performance by spreading out the data blocks of a file across two or more disks. No redundancy or ECC is provided with this RAID level.
- **RAID 1: Disk mirroring.** As defined above, disk mirroring writes data simultaneously to two different drives, providing redundancy. Thus if one drive fails, the other still has all the data. The two drives may be connected to one physical disk controller, mirroring, as shown in Figure 8.2.
- **RAID 3: Striping with parity.** RAID 3 uses a minimum of three disks—two or more disks are used for byte-level striping, and one disk is used to store the parity information. See Figure 8.3.
- **RAID 5: Striping with distributed parity.** This is the most popular implementation of RAID because it provides the most performance with block level striping of data and good fault tolerance by distributing the parity information across a minimum of three drives.
- **RAID 0+1 and 10 (1+0): Mirror of stripes and striped mirroring.** Confusing but interesting combinations of RAID 0 with RAID 1. RAID 0+1 stripes the data over two disks and then mirrors the striped

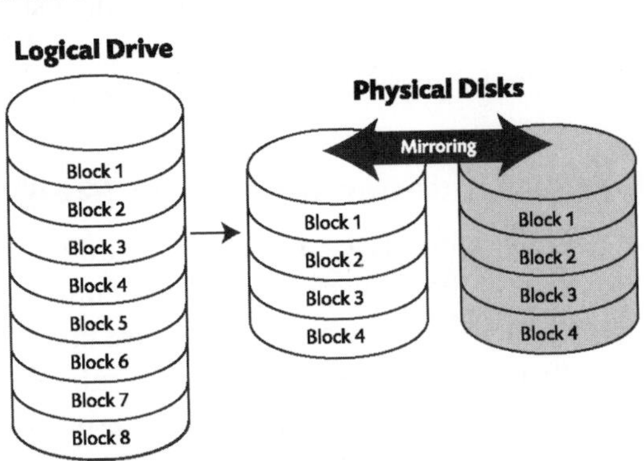


**FIGURE 8.2** RAID 1.

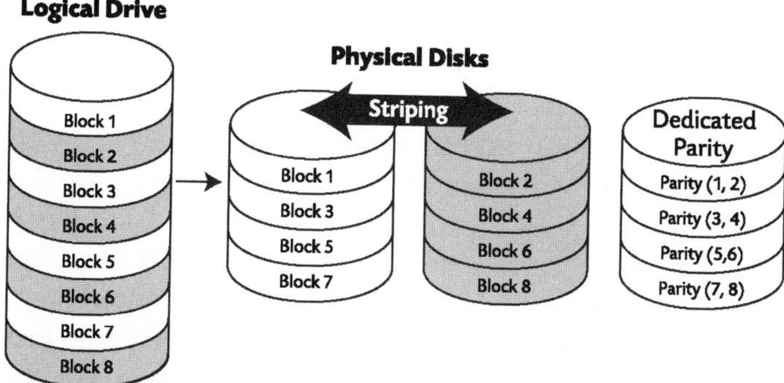


**FIGURE 8.3** RAID 3.

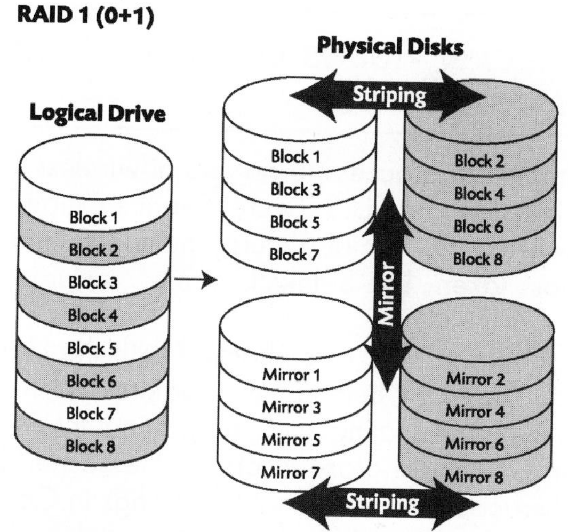


**FIGURE 8.4** RAID 1+0+1.

8

data to two disks. RAID 1+0 mirrors data on two disks and stripes it across two disks. The difference is subtle but worth noting. See Figure 8.4.

## Harvesting Data from Servers

As can be seen from the descriptions above, RAID is a complicated technology from which to harvest physical drives. If the investigator images each hard drive, she must have the same RAID controller as the original configuration and understand the order and size of any striping. The easiest way to get this data, then, is to acquire it across a network connection using the logical view of the array presented by the original RAID controller. Two main considerations of

**Caution**

**They're Everywhere!**

On any given day, 3 to 3.5 million bots are active around the world getting into hundreds of thousands of computing and communications devices.

performing the acquisition of a RAID array are the size (typically servers have extremely large storage pools) and the transmission speed of the medium used to transfer the data to an evidence file. A review of these issues may impose a critical time factor to your case.

In addition to the physical technological complications that you may encounter when trying to harvest data from a server, there are productivity and authorization factors to consider as well. Because you have moved from a single-user system to a multiuser environment, quarantining the server may not be tolerated in a production setting because the server will need to be offline while the data is gathered. Often, a higher authority, typically an executive, will need to give permission for the server downtime. Make sure that you have the appropriate authorization before taking any steps toward bringing down a production server.

**FYI** *Hacker Reads U.S. Secret Service E-Mail*

A computer hacker had access to servers at wireless T-Mobile for at least a year. He monitored U.S. Secret Service e-mail, obtained customers' passwords and Social Security numbers, and downloaded candid photos taken by Sidekick users, including Hollywood celebrities.

Nicolas Jacobsen, 29, was charged with the intrusions after a Secret Service informant helped investigators link him to sensitive agency documents circulating in underground Internet Relay Chat (IRC) chatrooms. The case arose as part of the Secret Service's Operation Firewall crackdown on Internet fraud rings in October 2004, in which 19 men were indicted for trafficking in stolen identity information and documents and stolen credit and debit card numbers (Poulsen, 2005).

## Examining E-Mails for Evidence

Obviously the text, or body, of an e-mail contains readable information that may be used for evidence. However, there is more to e-mail than meets the eye—the unseen portion called the e-mail header. This part of the e-mail can provide interesting information about who created it, what software was used to create it, what IP address was used to send it, and the path through the Internet across intermediate e-mail servers. Attachments to e-mails can also supply important information.

## Understanding E-Mail Headers

Within every e-mail is a ***header*** that records information about the sender, receiver, and the servers that it passes along its journey. If you think of the e-mail as a letter, consider the e-mail header as the envelope containing the e-mail body. It is from the header that the from, to, subject, and date items on the e-mail are populated. In most e-mail clients, the header is shown in short form, so all of the technical details, such as the IP addresses, are not revealed. Figure 8.5 shows a typical e-mail header. However, in some programs, the option to show the long form can be selected, resulting in the information shown in Figure 8.6.

| | |
|---|---|
| **From:** | "Sleazy Spammr " <slzyspmmr@yipea.com > |
| **To:** | recipientxyz @yahoo.com |
| **Subject:** | Re: zyvec news |
| **Date:** | Wed, 26 Apr 2006 02:22:11 -0700 |

Dear Home Owner ,

Your credit doesn't matter to us ! If you OWN real estate

**FIGURE 8.5** Typical displayed e-mail header.

| | |
|---|---|
| **X-Apparently-To:** | recipientxyz@yahoo.com via 10.142.207.117; Wed, 26 Apr 2006 02:21:53 -0700 |
| **X-Originating-IP:** | [192.168.5.17 ] |
| **Return-Path:** | <slzyspmmr@yipea.com> |
| **Authentication-Results:** | mta212.mail.re4.yahoo.com from=aha.com.au; domainkeys=neutral (no sig) |
| **Received:** | from 192.168.5.17 (HELO abx12.com) (192.168.5.17:) by mtmlr116.mailer4.yahoo.com with SMTP; Wed, 26 Apr 2006 02:21:53 -0700 |
| **Message-ID:** | <000001c66912$e60653e0$55dda8c0@zdt9> |
| **Reply-to:** | " Sleazy Spammr " <slzyspmmr@yipea.com> |
| **From:** | " Sleazy Spammr " <slzyspmmr@yipea.com> Add to Address Book Add Mobile Alert |
| **To:** | recipientxyz@yahoo.com |
| **Subject:** | Re: zyvec news |
| **Date:** | Wed, 26 Apr 2006 02:22:11 -0700 |
| **MIME-Version:** | 1.0 |
| **Content-Type:** | multipart/alternative; boundary="----=_NextPart_000_0001_01C668D8.39A77BE0" |
| **X-Priority:** | 3 |
| **X-MSMail-Priority:** | Normal |
| **X-Mailer:** | Microsoft Outlook Express 6.00.2800.1106 |
| **X-MimeOLE:** | Produced By Microsoft MimeOLE V6.00.2800.1106 |
| **Content-Length:** | 1424 |

Dear Home Owner ,

Your credit doesn't matter to us ! If you OWN real estate

**FIGURE 8.6** Expanded e-mail header.

If you are working on a live system, you can use the following options to display the full header for common e-mail clients:

- **Yahoo! Mail:** Select Options > Management > General Preferences > Messages > Show all headers on incoming messages. Use the Save button to save the new setting.
- **Hotmail:** Access the Mail tab and select Options > Mail Display Settings > Message Headers > Advanced. Use the OK button to save the new setting.
- **Gmail:** Open the desired e-mail and then click More options > Show original.
- **Outlook:** Right-click the desired e-mail (don't open it) and select Options. The e-mail header will be displayed in the Internet Headers box.
- **Outlook Express:** Select (highlight) an e-mail. On the Outlook Express menu bar (under the title bar), select File > Properties > Details.
- **OWA (Outlook Web Access):** As of the writing of this book, there is no option provided by this program to view full e-mail headers.

Because the full header is actually part of the e-mail, it is visible in the file itself when using forensic software to analyze this data.

The most common parts of the e-mail header are the logical addresses of the sender and receiver, such as slzyscammr@yipea.com. The logical address is composed of two parts, the ***mailbox,*** which comes before the @ sign, and the ***domain*** or ***hostname,*** which follows the @ sign. For this example, slzyscammr is the mailbox. In almost every case, the mailbox is the same as the userid used to log in to the e-mail server.

The domain, also referred to as the hostname, is the Internet location of the server used to do the actual e-mail transmission. Although the user sees the domain name as letters, such as yipea.com in the example above, the Internet actually sees it as an IP address. A network server typically provided by the Internet service provider, called a domain name server (DNS), resolves the domain name to the actual IP address.

Reviewing the full e-mail headers can offer some clues as to the true origin of the e-mail, the program used to send the message, and other interesting details. Here are some common e-mail header fields and their descriptions:

- **Apparently-To:** This is a nonstandard header and is used by some e-mail programs when encountering a mailing list or a long list of recipients.
- **Bcc:** Bcc (blind carbon copy) is found only on the header of the e-mail that would be associated with the sender. It is not seen on the e-mail that the To recipient receives, and for the Bcc recipient, it changes to X-Apparently-To.

- **Cc:** Cc (carbon copy) is used to indirectly involve other e-mail destinations in addition to the main recipient(s) specified in the To field. Cc requires a different action from the recipient(s) when replying to the message. The reply option will ignore the Cc header, while the reply to all option will include those addresses in the Cc header.
- **Content-Type:** This header deals with nontext items, such as HTML or pictures, that are included in the e-mail content. It identifies what type of content to expect in the message with terms such as "text/plain" or "multipart/mixed." If this is a multipart message (contains possibly text and attachments), the boundary label between the parts is designated.
- **Date:** No surprise here—this contains the data pertaining to when the e-mail was sent. However, be careful in trusting this data as an accurate time source, because the clock on the sending PC may not be set to the correct time.
- **From:** While this appears to be the sender's e-mail address, and often is, it is one of the key e-mail header fields that can be spoofed by a spammer or malicious user.
- **Message-ID:** This is a critical field if your investigation takes you to a server environment. It is a unique identifier assigned to each message by the first e-mail server it encounters, usually the sender's local e-mail server or the ISP's e-mail server if webmail is used. Its form generally consists of a long string of what appear to be random printable characters followed by the @ sign, then either the user PC's computer name or the e-mail server name. This can be forged, so beware of relying solely on this data.
- **In-Reply-To:** This field appears, somewhat obviously, when a user replies to an e-mail and typically contains the Message-ID of the original e-mail.
- **MIME-version:** MIME, discussed later in the chapter, is the way nontext data is handled within an e-mail. This header specifies what version of MIME was used by the sender.
- **Received:** This can be a very important field when trying to trace the path of an e-mail. Each server that relays the message puts its IP address and the date and time the e-mail was processed in a received header, so you may see multiple occurrences of this header.
- **References:** The message ID of a previous message that has been replied to.
- **Subject:** The subject text shown for the e-mail.
- **To:** The intended recipient e-mail address(es), which can be easily spoofed. If, however, you were carbon copied, your e-mail address would not appear in this field but in the Cc header field. If you were blind carbon copied, you would not see your e-mail address in the header at all.

- **X-Confirm-Reading-To:** A field that appears if the sender has requested an automated confirmation from the recipient when the e-mail is acknowledged, or read, by the recipient.
- **X-Mailer:** This field is typically generated by e-mail clients, not webmail programs, and can be a tasty bit of evidence that shows the software the sender used to compose the e-mail.
- **X-Originating-IP:** The local IP address of the sender if an e-mail client was used; otherwise it is the Internet address seen by the webmail program for the sender.
- **X-Priority:** The X-Priority field appears if a priority other than normal was set on the e-mail by the sender. A value of 1 typically means a high priority. It is unusual for webmail programs to supply this option; generally it is found on e-mail client software.

There are many more header fields that can be generated by different combinations of sending, replying, and forwarding options, but this list provides a quick look at the most common ones.

The information supplied by these header values may help in tracing the path of an e-mail. To begin a trace, you must work from the bottom of the header up. Figure 8.7 is an example of an e-mail that has passed through several e-mail servers. Starting at the bottom, it came from nefarious@sndmailer.com; then it went to its local e-mail server at IP address 10.48.233.18; next to another internal server at 10.48.214.2; then it was sent to a final internal SMTP server that communicates with the Internet using the hostname of smtp.sndmailer.com

```
      From :    Roqueroo Stealthitos <nefarious@sndmailer.com>
      Sent :    Friday, May 5, 2006 5:15 AM
      To :      bl4cksh33p <bl4cksh33p@rcvmailer.com>
      Subject : Get tha kgz!

     MIME-Version: 1.0
5 ──►Received: from smtp.sndmailer.com ([192.168.182.259]) by mc5-f15.rcvmailer.com with Microsoft SMTPSV
4 ──►Received: by smtp.sndmailer.com with SMTP id a27so89717nfc for <bl4cksh33p@rcvmailer.com>; Fri, 05 M
3 ──►Received: by 10.48.214.2 with SMTP id m2mr1332971nfg; Fri, 05 May 2006 02:15:34 -0700 (PDT)
2 ──►Received: by 10.48.233.18 with HTTP; Fri, 5 May 2006 02:15:34 -0700 (PDT)
     X-Message-Info: LsUYwwHHNt0iBRCA8Qq9o1mBkmeRWBjew0EHmS3i4Ok=
1 ──►Return-Path: nefarious@sndmailer.com
     X-OriginalArrivalTime: 05 May 2006 09:15:35.0045 (UTC) FILETIME=[775E7350:01C67024]

     View E-mail Message Source

      Content-Type: multipart/alternative; boundary="----=_Part_4328_13566644.1146820

       Content-Type: text/html; charset=ISO-8859-1
       Content-Transfer-Encoding: quoted-printable
       Content-Disposition: inline

        I got the animlz - need to keep em at ur place.
```

**FIGURE 8.7** E-mail path.

(192.168.182.259); and last it was received by the e-mail server mc5-f15.rdvmailer.com, where it was put into the mailbox of bl4cksh33p on that server. Note that because a webmail program was used, there is little or no information on the actual address of the sender. More information is recorded from an e-mail client that might assist in tracking down the location of the sender.

The previous example used fictitious IP addresses and server names, but real public (Internet) IP addresses must be registered with an international registration authority. Because of the number of addresses available, there are five international Regional Internet Registries to search:

- African Network Information (AfriNIC), **www.afrinic.net/cgibin/whois,** for Africa
- Asia Pacific Network Information Centre (APNIC), **www.apnic.net/apnic-bin/whois.pl** for Asian-Pacific countries, including Australia, Taiwan, Japan, the People's Republic of China, and Korea
- American Registry for Internet Numbers (ARIN), **www.arin.net/whois/** for North America, which includes the United States, U.S. Islands, and Canada
- Latin American and Caribbean Internet Addresses Registry (LACNIC), **www.lacnic.net/cgi-bin/lacnic/whois** for Mexico, Central America, and South America
- Réseaux IP Européens Network Coordination Centre (RIPE NCC), **www.ripe.net/perl/whois** for Europe, the Middle East, and parts of Central Asia

The governing authority over IP addressing, the Internet Assigned Numbers Authority (IANA), has allocated several blocks of IP addresses for private (local) use only. This means that these addresses are not recognized on the Internet as valid but are good to use in private networks. Table 8.3 shows the IP address classifications and allotments.

Sometimes a large ISP, such as AT&T, may hold a vast number of IP addresses that it uses to resell to other smaller ISPs. In this case, you must contact that company to get a more focused view of the IP address in question.

## Understanding E-Mail Attachments

When electronic mail was first introduced, it could handle only simple text messages based on 7-bit ASCII coding. There was no mechanism to include attachments such as pictures or documents. A new standard called ***multipurpose Internet mail extensions (MIME)*** was implemented to correct this shortcoming. Practically all e-mail transmitted today uses the MIME standard, which allows for inclusion of HTML and multimedia images. Attachments can typically be handled by using Base64, which is a binary-to-text encoding scheme

**TABLE 8.3** IP address classifications.

| IP Address Range | Classification | Use |
|---|---|---|
| 0.0.0.0 to 0.255.255.255 | Class A: Default Network | Special IP used for the default network. It is not recognized as a valid public address. |
| 1.0.0.0 to 9.255.255.255 | Class A: Public | Public addresses on the Internet. |
| 10.0.0.0 to 10.255.255.255 | Class A: Private | Local network use—not recognized on the Internet. |
| 11.0.0.0 to 126.255.255.255 | Class A: Public | Public addresses on the Internet. |
| 127.0.0.0 to 127.255.255.255 | Loopback | Used by local network. The 127.0.0.1 is the loopback address used by a local machine to test its NIC. |
| 128.0.0.0 to 172.15.255.255 | Class B: Public | Public addresses on the Internet. |
| 172.16.0.0 to 172.31.255.255 | Class B: Private | Local network use—not recognized on the Internet. |
| 172.32.0.0 to 191.255.255.255 | Class B: Public | Public addresses on the Internet. |
| 192.0.0.0 to 192.167.255.255 | Class C: Public | Public addresses on the Internet. |
| 192.168.0.0 to 192.168.255.255 | Class C: Private | Local network use—not recognized on the Internet. |
| 192.169.0.0 to 223.255.255.255 | Class C: Public | Public addresses on the Internet. |
| 224.0.0.0 to 239.255.255.255 | Class D | Multicast. |
| 240.0.0.0 to 248.255.255.255 | Class E | Experimental. |
| 249.0.0.0 to 255.255.255.254 | Reserved | Reserved by IANA. |
| 255.255.255.255 | Broadcast | Broadcast. |

that takes an arbitrary sequence of bytes and converts them to a sequence of printable ASCII characters. The sequences of characters examined without a viewer will simply look like gibberish. However, many forensic analysis tools are able to show the attachment in its converted form so that it is readable.

When using the forensic analysis software, you may not even realize that you are looking at a Base64-encoded attachment, so why talk about it? The reason is that you may be able to find these e-mail attachments in unallocated clusters or file slack by searching for the keyword *base64*. Once you have found the evidence, you need to use data carving techniques to pull the significant data from the unallocated space. See Chapter 7 for more information on data carving.

### IN PRACTICE: Attempted Attack by Chinese Hackers

In December 2005, the British Parliament was under attack. Targeted e-mails were being sent to 70 members in an attempt to take control of their computers. Those e-mails never reached their target destinations.

MessageLabs, the e-mail filtering provider, identified that the attacks had come from China because they logged the IP addresses. The messages played on people's natural curiosity by claiming to come from a government security organization. A Trojan was hidden as an attachment called map.wmf.

The body text of one of the e-mails read:

```
    Attached is the digital map for you. You should
meet that man at those points separately. Delete
the map thereafter. Good luck. Tommy
```

Clicking on the map installed a Trojan on the computer (Espiner, 2006).

## Anonymous Remailers

As discussed previously in the chapter, e-mail headers contain a lot of information that can lead an investigator to a suspect. While this is very useful in a criminal setting, there are many people out there who felt that the right to speak their thoughts in e-mail form without repercussion (citing the First Amendment) was an inherent American freedom, and that e-mail headers violated that privacy aspect. Thus the original anonymous remailers were created to enable people to remove their identifying IP tracks in order to post e-mails that they wanted to keep private. The types of people who used this service spanned from those who wanted to express religious ideas that might not be welcome in their community to whistleblowers who were afraid of losing their jobs.

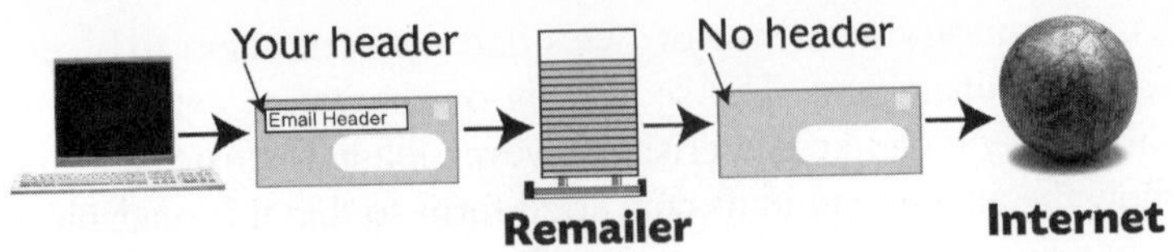


**FIGURE 8.8** How remailing works.

However, like everything else today, the bad comes with the good. Now spammers and phishers use these remailers so you cannot respond to their evil eruptions of annoying and dangerous e-mails. Thus, in your investigation, you may not always be able to track down the e-mail sender simply by using the e-mail header because the address has either been removed or changed to an erroneous one (spoofed). Figure 8.8 shows how the process of remailing works.

**FYI** *E-Mail Authentication*

Sender ID and DomainKeys technologies enable e-mail recipients to positively identify the sender of an e-mail message. These technologies use IPS tools to identify those who launch spam and phishing attacks. E-mail authentication does not solve the spam problem, but it is a tool to stop the spoofing of a sender's e-mail address, which would reveal the actual e-mail source of spammers (Lemos, 2006).

## Working with Instant Messaging

In today's world, ***instant messaging (IM)*** is an often-used tool that enables people to communicate quickly without the overhead of composing and sending lengthy e-mails. While users may believe they are "talking" directly to the other party when they use IM, this is really another client/server application that sends the message from the client to a server from which it is routed to the client of the other party.

Because there is no one standard for IM, both IM participants typically have to communicate using the same chat software. A user has to set up his account on a particular service utilizing a screen name and password, and he identifies other users who can chat with him. Regardless of the software, the users involved in instant messaging have to be logged into the same server environment. This provides the centralized sensing of who is available and who is not, so the appropriate icon can let others know who on their "buddy" list is available to send/receive messages.

The most widely used IM applications include:

- **Windows Messenger.** This program is installed by default on some Windows systems, including Windows XP, and starts up automatically when you open your Windows session. It communicates via the .NET Passport Microsoft network infrastructure. By default, files received using this forum are saved in C:\Documents and Settings*Windowsuserid*\My Documents\My Received Files.
- **Google Talk.** A proprietary free download IM program that uses an open protocol for IM chatting. It is Web-based, so it does not save files to the user's PC. Instead, if requested, the chat logs and files exchanged in this forum are saved on the user's gmail account.
- **AIM (AOL Instant Messenger).** This is the AOL offering. Chat logs and downloads are saved to the same directories as the AOL e-mail Personal Filing Cabinet.
- **ICQ ("I Seek You") Instant Messenger.** This is a Web-based instant messaging service that also provides e-mail access. ICQ logs conversations by default in a .dat file located in the ICQ directory. This information can be recovered and read using third-party applications in conjunction with forensic software. Other ICQ conversations may be recovered in hidden areas of the hard drive, such as unallocated clusters or the system's virtual memory.

8

Whether or not forensic analysis of computers using IM programs can recover those conversations depends on the software that was used. IM logging is available on most IM services, but the user may decide not to log this information and the default setting may not create logs automatically, making it virtually impossible to capture evidence of these events. An IM session comes very close to an interactive phone conversation to which the investigator is not privy. The chat messages are ephemeral, and their fleeting presence may only by chance be captured in RAM slack or a memory dump. Most of the servers do not log the conversation content either, but they may log the event of a conversation, which could at least provide a timeline.

### FYI Vermont Supreme Court Affirms Conviction Based on IM Evidence

In Vermont, the appellate court agreed with the trial court's decision that IM conversations were sufficient evidence to support the defendant's conviction for promoting a lewd performance by a child and inciting another

CONTINUED ON NEXT PAGE

▶▶ CONTINUED

to commit a felony. The prosecutor introduced evidence recovered from a computer forensics examination of the computer and floppy disks taken from the child's home. The computer forensics expert recovered text from IM conversations in which the defendant discussed with the child's mother a plan to have a lewd photo shoot. The court concluded:

> The evidence was sufficient to support the convictions where IM texts found on the victim's mother's computer indicated that the defendant had requested that she pose her child and take photos for his viewing, and suggested his own lewd photo session, and where he was later found alone in the house with the victim, rubbing her back and flattering her, and a digital camera was found in the room. The issue of whether the IM texts had been doctored was one of credibility, and for the jury to determine.

At trial, the expert noted that IMs are not usually saved on a computer, so saving them to floppy disks required deliberate effort. Based on the IM evidence, the jury found the defendant guilty. The defendant argued that the IM text was "meager evidence" of guilt because the text had allegedly been altered and edited. The court rejected this claim, finding that the retrieved electronic conversations, together with witness testimony, offered sufficient evidence to support the jury's findings.

*Source: State v. Voorheis* (Vermont, Feb. 13, 2004, http://dol.state.vt.us/gopher_root3/supct/176/2002–478.op).

Though IM is typically handled the same as e-mail in litigation, forensic discovery of IM evidence can be more incriminating than e-mail. The smug comfort of believing that chat messages are not readily discoverable gives many users an even more relaxed and unguarded attitude that leads them to say more informal and candid things in chat messages that they would never include in regular communications. Because of this, and the ability to circumvent the controlled corporate e-mail, more companies are turning to internal messaging servers and blocking public chat mechanisms. In the same context as e-mail servers, internal IM servers may be configured to intermediately hold messages and log activity.

## Summary

Electronic mail and instant messages can be important evidence to find. They provide a more realistic view of the candor of a person because of their ubiquitous use and informality. For both of these technologies, a client program and a server are required. The client program may be resident on a user's PC and store data on the hard drive, or the client may be Web-based. Web-based clients often do not leave a complete data trail on the PC itself and may require an investigator to harvest this data from the server or servers involved in the transmission of the message. When trying to recover data from a server, you must determine the data storage structure being used and the size of the composite data storage pool, plus you need to ensure that you have appropriate authorization to work on the server. You must compose a good plan with realistic values for time and storage requirements before beginning a forensic review of a server.

Using e-mail headers and IM logs can provide additional sources of possible data locations, such as recipient/sender PCs and intermediate servers. Tracing the IP addresses may involve the use of regional Internet registries, such as ARIN, to determine the registered owner of an IP address range and a contact address for that owner.

IM has become a mechanism that users believe to be inherent in daily life. Like e-mail, it is a client/server–based technology; however, with today's clients, the messages may not be saved to any hard drive. Because of the volume of IM, public servers such as AOL and Google typically do not keep logs of message content and may not even keep transaction logs. IM may be as intangible as a phone conversation. However, if IM messages can be found, they often contain very powerful evidence because most people use them with unguarded attitudes.



# Test Your Skills

## MULTIPLE CHOICE QUESTIONS

1. What type of software is used to actually send and receive e-mail across the Internet?
   A. Electronic message conveyance program.
   B. E-mail server.
   C. E-mail client.
   D. Instant Mail program.

2. Which of the following programs stores e-mail files on the PC itself?
   A. Outlook.
   B. Yahoo! Mail.
   C. Gmail.
   D. Hotmail.

3. What is the file extension of a typical Outlook Express mailbox?
   A. .dbx.
   B. Outlook Express does not place files on the hard drive.
   C. .arl.
   D. .oem.

4. ________ uses a browser to perform e-mail activity.
   A. Java
   B. Webmail
   C. ActiveX
   D. Perl

5. If a suspect used a program such as Yahoo! Mail, it may be possible to find e-mail evidence in
   A. the Yahoo! archives.
   B. the .yem files.
   C. Internet History.
   D. Temporary Internet Files.

6. What type of corporate policy may affect the availability of electronic data on a server?
   A. The corporate employee termination policy.
   B. The Paperless Shredding Act of 2005.
   C. The corporate accountability policy.
   D. The corporate electronic data retention policy.

7. A robust storage structure called ________ is used by most servers.
   A. robust storage media
   B. redundant array of independent disks
   C. real awesome intelligent digitization
   D. robust and recoverable data disks

8. What are some considerations to take into account when attempting to acquire hard drive images of servers?
   A. Amount of data to be recovered, time for the data transfer, and proper authorization.
   B. Location of the server, time and date of the latest board meeting, and proper environmental conditions.
   C. Proximity of the closest electrical outlet, number of servers in the room, and type of cables to be used.
   D. Authorization from the help desk, number and types of cables needed, proximity of power source.

9. In which of the following e-mail clients can you *not* view the complete e-mail header?
   A. Outlook.
   B. Gmail.
   C. Outlook Web Access.
   D. Hotmail.
10. In which e-mail header field can you find the sender's IP address (if it has not been spoofed)?
   A. From.
   B. References.
   C. X-Originating-IP.
   D. In-Reply-To.
11. What information does the References e-mail header field provide?
   A. The sender's IP address.
   B. The receiver's IP address.
   C. The IP address of an intermediate e-mail server.
   D. The home phone number of the sender.
12. A(n) _________ provides privacy for an e-mail sender and can use several intermediate servers to further cloak the path.
   A. fake name
   B. anonymous remailer
   C. first amendment e-mail server
   D. independent mail carrier
13. What encoding is used for e-mail attachments?
   A. Base64.
   B. MIMOSA.
   C. GLUE.
   D. Base16.
14. Which of the following is most like typical instant messaging chat conversations?
   A. Whispering in the White House.
   B. An interactive private phone call.
   C. Shouting in a public gathering.
   D. Talking in a meeting.

15. What can make IM evidence somewhat more incriminating than e-mail or memos?
    A. IM is a new technology.
    B. IM is a paperless media that may be easily erased.
    C. IM encourages a more relaxed and casual attitude for unguarded expression.
    D. IM is only used by malicious people.

## EXERCISES

### Exercise 8.1: Identifying E-Mail Clients and Servers

If you have ever sent an e-mail, you have used an e-mail client. Perhaps you use different e-mail accounts for different purposes, as many people do, such as one for your general public contacts, one for private e-mail, one for business electronic correspondence, and so on.

1. Make a list of the e-mail programs you use and classify them as either resident or webmail.
2. Research the e-mail servers that are used for each of the clients on your list.
3. On your Windows system, look for the Outlook Express files. Note the default files and folders. If you have not used Outlook Express, note the default size of these objects as well. You may be able to refer to this later in an investigation to quickly determine if a suspect has used this e-mail client.

### Exercise 8.2: Exploring E-Mail Headers

Because of its technical nature, most e-mail programs do not show the e-mail header by default. Refer back to your list from the previous exercise and change the settings in your e-mail programs to show the entire e-mail header.

1. Determine the sender's IP addresses from ten e-mails across several e-mail programs.
2. Document the intermediate e-mail servers you see in the e-mail headers.
3. Some e-mail programs identify the software used to create the e-mail. How many of your ten e-mail headers include the software used by the sender? Do you notice a pattern?

### Exercise 8.3: Ownership of IP Addresses

All addresses on the Internet, called public addresses, have a unique IP address. When you connect to an ISP, the ISP provides you with a public IP address. Because all addresses must be registered with a Regional Internet Registry, you can identify in what area of the world a particular IP address originates.

1. Find your current public IP address by going to one of these sites: **www.ecsi.net/cgi-bin/bcgi.exe?showip**, **www.whatismyip.com/**, or **www.grc.com/x/ne.dll?bh0bkyd2** (you may have to scroll down and locate the address in a paragraph of text) and record it.
2. Now go to **www.arin.net/whois/** and enter the IP address you found in step 1.
3. What entity owns this IP address? Can you find a contact point you could use if you needed to get more information about this IP address for an investigation?

### Exercise 8.4: Finding Public Server Information

Given the IP address of a public server, you can take steps to try to find a bit more information about that server, such as the operating system that is being used and its domain name.

1. Log on to the Internet, go to **www.grc.com/id/idserve.htm,** and click on the IDSERVE screen shot, which will prompt you to either run or save the file **IDServe.exe**. With your instructor's permission, you may run this application directly, or you can download it and then execute it.
2. Click the Server Query tab and enter one of the IP addresses of the intermediate servers that you documented in Exercise 8.2.
3. Note the details that can be found about this server. Repeat this for four other server IP addresses.
4. Now go to **www.samspade.org/** and repeat the same process. Did you get the same information?



## PROJECTS

### Project 8.1: Using EnCase® Forensic Software to Investigate E-Mail

For this project, you will need to order the EnCase demo software from Guidance Software at **www.guidancesoftware.com/corporate/demodiskrequest.asp.**

(You can also go to this site using the link on the Companion Website at **www.prenhall.com/security.**)

1. Place the EnCase demo CD in the player on your computer and let it autorun—this may take a couple of minutes, so be patient.
2. Select **Run EnCase® Demo**, and click on **Launch the V5 EnCase® DEMO**.
3. Agree to the EnCase Software Demonstration CD License Agreement by clicking **OK**.
4. The Demo will now load and will bring in the demo evidence files automatically. Note that in using a nondemo version of EnCase software, you would need to create a case file or open an existing case file. In some versions of the EnCase V5 demo, the option to create a case file is not available and is grayed out.
5. The evidence file used for this demo should now appear in the left viewing pane and display one or more icons that look like platters from a hard drive. This symbol is used to represent a physical hard drive. The + symbol beside it indicates that this directory can be expanded to show subdirectories. Click on the +, and the partitions for this hard drive should appear using an icon C like this with the associated partition letter or volume name beside it (such as C).
6. A + beside the partition again indicates that there are subdirectories, so now click on the + beside a partition. Keep navigating in this fashion to locate a user directory for a user name such as Bob Hunter to view Outlook Express e-mail files (for example, try C:\Documents and Settings\userid\Local Settings\Application Data\Identities\{SID hex characters}\Outlook Express).
7. Click on the little area that resembles a home plate beside the Outlook Express folder. This will display all of the files and folders associated with that directory. Record what you find. Click the home plate again to go back to your regular display.
8. Now, go back to the right viewing pane, right-click on an interesting .dbx folder, and select **View File Structure** from the shortcut menu. A decision box appears. For this exercise, leave *Calculate unallocated space* unselected and click **OK**. A new folder called DBX Volume appears in the left viewing pane under the .dbx folder you selected. If you home plate this folder, you will see all of the e-mails and associated attachments that are contained in it.
9. Do this for each of the .dbx folders. Document all of your findings. Note that some folders may not contain any e-mails.

## Project 8.2 Using FTK™ Forensic Software to Investigate E-Mail

You will need to download the trial version of FTK at **www.accessdata.com/products/ftk** to perform this project, if you have not already done so. (You can also go to this site using the link on the Companion Website at **www.prenhall.com/security**.)

A woman named Sneekie Badinuf filed a complaint with the police on May 14, 2006, stating that her cat and two dogs had been abducted. She had received an e-mail from a correspondent named NFarious that demanded $5,000 in ransom, or the animals would be harmed. She claimed her pets had been gone for an entire week, and she was worried that the abductor may already have injured the animals.

In a subsequent interview with Ms. Badinuf, it was revealed that she took out a $20,000 insurance policy on her pets in September 2005 that would not be active for 6 months.

Because e-mail was involved, the police got permission from Ms. Badinuf to inspect her PC for any leads and have provided you with the evidence stored in a file.

1. Download from the Companion Website at **www.prenhall.com/security** the **CHAPTER8.E01** file and save it in the **C:\4ensics** folder you created in Chapter 7. (If you did not do the projects in Chapter 7, create the **4ensics** folder on the C: drive now.)

2. Download and install the FTK software.
3. Run FTK. If prompted about the absence of the KFF Hash library, click **OK**. If prompted about the absence of a dongle (a USB license key), click **OK**, and FTK will continue in Demo mode. Click **OK** at the demo mode prompt.
4. In the AccessData FTK Startup dialog box, click the **Start a new case** option button if necessary and then click **OK**.
   a. On the resulting New Case screen, enter your name as the Investigator.
   b. Use the current date as the case number. Insert the date in YYYYMMDD order (i.e., for a date of May 13, 2006, the case number would be 20060513).
   c. Type **Badinuf Animal Abduction** as the Case Name.
   d. Update the Case Path to **C:\4ensics**, and enter a brief description of the case in the Case Description area.
   e. Click **Next** to continue.
5. The Case Information page appears. Fill in as much detail as needed as if this were a real case. (Note: You do not need to use real information,

such as your address or phone number for this project). Click **Next** to continue.

6. Leave all defaults on the Case Log Options page and click **Next** to continue.
7. Leave all defaults on the Processes to Perform page and click **Next** to continue.
8. Click the **Include All Items** button on the Refine Case – Default page, and click **Next** to continue. Then accept all defaults on the Refine Index – Default page by clicking **Next** to continue.
9. On the Add Evidence to Case page, click the **Add Evidence** button. In the resulting dialog box, keep the default of Acquired Image of Drive, and click **Continue**. In the resulting Open dialog box, navigate to C:\4ensics and select **CHAPTER8.E01**. Click **Open**.
10. Using the drop-down arrow for Local Evidence Time Zone, select Eastern Time with Daylight Savings, and click **OK**. Click **Next** to continue. Then click **Finish**. FTK will begin opening the evidence file.
11. As you work through the remaining steps, create a running log on paper of all the work you perform in this part of the investigation.
12. Click the E-Mail tab. On the left view pane of this display, click on the + symbols to expand the Outlookx.pst folder until the Top of Personal Folders shows all of the user e-mail folders, such as Calendar, Deleted Items, Inbox, and so on.
13. In the left pane, select the Deleted Items folder. Four messages should appear in the right viewing pane.
14. In the right viewing pane, select the top message by clicking on the file name (do not put a check in the box beside it)—it will appear in easy-to-view format in the bottom viewing pane. Use your down arrow key (in the right viewing pane) to traverse through the other messages. Note your results.
15. Now, go back to the left viewing pane and select the Inbox folder. Repeat the viewing instructions, and record your results. What do you notice about the "From" address? Look at the details of the e-mail header by going to the bottom viewing pane and scrolling down. Note your findings.
16. What is Sneekie's e-mail address? What other e-mail addresses did you discover?
17. Now click the Search tab. Type **Badinuf** in the Search Term input area and click **Add**. How many hits are reported for this search?

18. Select *Badinuf* in the Search Items pane and click the **View Item Results** button. Leave the default as All fFiles in the Filter Search Hits dialog box and click **OK**. The results will appear in the right viewing pane.
19. In the right viewing pane, review your results by expanding each item (clicking the +) and viewing the information in the bottom viewing panel. Be sure to note your findings.
20. With just this brief canvas of the evidence, what can you ascertain about this case? How has the e-mail data affected this case?

## Project 8.3 Using an Anonymous Remailer

With free e-mail accounts widely available these days, you can set up a fake e-mail address and send e-mails from it and stay fairly anonymous. However, these accounts are regularly mined and checked by ISPs and are not very private. Anonymous remailers can provide the same type of masquerade, but they also have the ability, for a fee, to transmit encrypted e-mails undercover. Most remailers use webmail clients.

1. Log on to your browser and go to **www.hushmail.com**. Click the **Sign up for free email** button. Select the Hushmail Free! Service, but do look over the paid services and record the differences. After you have done your comparison, click the **Sign up now** button.
2. Complete the steps needed to create your account. Once an account has been attained, create an e-mail and send it to yourself at one of your regular e-mail accounts.
3. Now go to that regular e-mail account and review the headers of the hushmail e-mail. Record your findings.
4. Next, go to **www.mytrashmail.com/send_fake_email_new.aspx**, which is another anonymous remailer.
5. Once again, you will have to create an account to use the free service.
6. After setting up the account, send yourself an anonymous email from this site.
7. Go back to your regular e-mail account and review the header on the mytrashmail e-mail you just received. Record your findings.
8. How did the two anonymous remailers compare? How could this impact your case?

## Case Study

Several recent cases and incidents have included e-mail as evidence. Two examples are:

- In 2005, a high-profile deal between media owner Ronald Hale and Quantum Communications went sour. Quantum had executed a preliminary deal with Hale to purchase two radio stations. However, before the deal was complete, Hale sold one of the stations to a competitive media company, Cumulus Media, Inc. Quantum took Hale to court and won an injunction to stop the sale of the radio station primarily because of e-mail evidence.
- In February 2006, the Abramoff scandal investigation reached into the electronic communications of the White House. New e-mail evidence found while investigating Jack Abramoff indicated that the relationship between Abramoff and President George W. Bush may have been closer than previously alleged. The e-mails prompted a request to the White House for all records of meetings and correspondence with Abramoff and the appointment of a special counsel to oversee the investigation.

1. In each of these situations, consider how e-mail made an impact on the case and write a paragraph or two on your observations.
2. How might the criminals have attempted to cover up the trails of e-mails?
3. Draft a plan as to where and how you might get e-mail evidence for a trial in one of these cases.

# Part Four

## Detecting Intrusions, Malware, and Fraud

Identity theft, botnet attacks, fraud, phishing, extortion, malware infections, threats to critical infrastructures, Internet-based hostilities, and cyberterrorism have an element in common relevant to forensics—they generate network traffic. The complexity of computing environments has made network perimeters essentially borderless meshes of connectivity to customers, criminals, and those with the intent to do harm on a large scale. These chapters provide a framework for understanding and investigating large-scale attacks and insidious fraud activities that typically require the collaborative effort of national or international agencies.

Part

# Detecting Intrusions, Malware, and Fraud

# Chapter 9

# Internet and Network Forensics and Intrusion Detection

## Chapter Objectives

**After reading this chapter you will be able to do the following:**

- Explain the operation of intrusion detection systems (IDSs).
- Discuss the value of using a network forensic analysis toolkit (NFAT).
- Identify the components of an NFAT.
- List the different areas from which data can be extracted.
- Understand how to use an NFAT to capture physical and logical network data.
- Identify the most common NFAT systems.

## Introduction

This chapter introduces you to another aspect of the study of computer forensics: the field of network forensics. This field is in some ways a new field in that the computer forensics concepts generally applied to single static computers are now being applied across enterprise networks. Network forensic analysis has actually been around as long as there have been networks; tcpdump and to a lesser extent windump have been used for years to analyze network traffic. In the past few years, however, network forensic software has become as sophisticated as applications designed for host-based forensics. The FBI's notorious Carnivore was one of the first widely deployed network forensics tools.

At this point, the topic of network forensic analysis toolkit (NFAT) systems cannot be thoroughly explored without an understanding of intrusion detection systems (IDSs). The most recently developed NFAT systems are being used and/or bundled with IDS software. As you will read in this chapter, NFAT systems use the output of the IDS to analyze or troubleshoot incidents on the network. You will also discover the many limitations both technical and legal when an NFAT system is used throughout an enterprise system or the Internet.

---

## An Introduction to Network Forensics and Intrusion Detection

**Caution**

**Network Forensic Investigations Needed for Compliance**

Network forensics investigations help organizations comply with regulations, such as the HIPAA and Sarbanes-Oxley Act, both of which require employers to account for end-user activity on their network.

As mentioned in the introduction, ***network forensic analysis toolkits (NFATs)*** are a recent addition to the world of computer forensics. An NFAT product records network traffic related to an intrusion and provides the tools to perform forensic analysis of the event.

The computer forensics field has traditionally been concerned with the collection of evidence from a host such as a personal computer. There has been relatively little concern with the network aspect of the investigation. The general consensus was that very little information was saved on a network, so it was not worth the effort or time to recreate the event.

From a historic perspective, networks were designed to be very efficient at delivering data. They were never designed to actually store data because storage was very limited in the early days of networking. The assumption was that host machines would store data as needed. Consequently, network security was not concerned with attacks on the networks themselves. That situation has changed with the advent of determined attacks and other network intrusions.

### Intrusion Detection Systems (IDSs)

The first attempt to address the increasing number of attacks on networks was the development of ***intrusion detection systems (IDSs).*** An IDS looks for ***anomalies,*** or out-of-the-ordinary activity, on the network. To detect anomalies on a network, the IDS registers activity that differs from an established baseline. A ***baseline*** is nothing more than the standard operating procedures of the network when it is running normally. For example, if a new port is opened up on a border router, the IDS senses the change and produces some form of output to alert the network administrator to this change.

IDSs have historically been categorized into two distinct types: signature-based and anomaly-based. Signature-based detection systems work like antivirus software in that they store known "signatures" of threats in a database. Whenever a threat matches one of those signatures, the IDS is triggered. A limitation with this approach is that new threats generally do not match any signatures currently in the IDS database, and thus an attack can proceed undetected for a time until a signature is created to identify the attack.

The anomaly approach looks for any change in the network and "reacts accordingly," as these systems put it. "Reacting accordingly" can result in widely varying numbers and types of alerts. If the security threshold is set too high, the IDS may generate so many alerts that a network administrator stops paying close attention—the "cry wolf" syndrome.

The newest IDSs use a hybrid approach that combines the best of both approaches (or if you're really unlucky, the worst of both worlds). The following is a list of common IDS solutions available today:

- Cisco Secure IDS
- Enterasys™ Dragon®
- Elm 3.0
- GFI LANguard S.E.L.M.
- Intrust Event Admin
- Snort®
- Tripwire
- *e*Trust®

## From Reactive to Active Sensing Systems

An IDS is considered by most system administrators to be a reactive security system that attempts to detect intruders after they have penetrated the first layers of security. An IDS is like a burglar alarm—it tells you someone has broken in and basically where the break-in occurred, but it does not recreate or record how the burglary is taking place. Nor is an IDS able to gather forensic e-evidence that is admissible in a court of law for prosecution at a later date.

For more active sensing, NFAT systems are needed. These tools enable an investigator to replay, isolate, and scrutinize an intrusion.

System administrators have long recognized the need to recreate a security incident to study and understand how an incident occurred—and learn how to defend against its happening again. This need led to the development of NFAT systems.

Developers of network forensics tools faced a number of challenges:

- Lack of infrastructure for forensic data collection, storage, and dissemination
- Rapid growth in network traffic, making prolonged storage, processing, and sharing of raw network data infeasible
- Labor-intensive forensics processes that span multiple administrative domains, resulting in long response times
- Current logging mechanisms that prevented forensic analysts from exploring networks incrementally

As you will learn in this chapter, these challenges have been largely overcome by the most recently released NFATs.

## Real-Time Analysis Using NFAT Systems

You have been introduced throughout this book to the concept of collecting forensic evidence after the security breach, crime, or event of interest has taken place. With an NFAT system in place, an event or security breach can be detected, monitored, and traced in real time as it is happening. The implications of real-time monitoring for system security and forensics are profound. Electronic leads grow cold very quickly in a network forensic investigation. The more quickly you can be alerted to an attack, breach, or policy violation, the more promptly you can collect evidence forensically and follow up on any cyberleads.

> **Caution**
>
> **Inside Threats**
>
> A company's worst enemy could very well be inside the network. Whether insiders are malicious or inadvertently making mistakes, a company has a network full of proprietary information it cannot afford to have compromised.

The important forensics functions that an NFAT system should perform are to

- Forensically capture complete and correct e-evidence
- Keep up with ever increasing network speeds
- Store captured e-evidence for long periods of time for extended investigations
- Keep the e-evidence secure to preserve the integrity of collected e-evidence

The newest NFAT systems show your entire network in a GUI format and correlate information so rapidly you can literally view the event taking place. This can be important because humans tend to understand data much better when it is presented in graphic format than as simple text and numbers. Issues such as diversionary attacks versus denial of service (DoS) attacks can be seen more clearly on a graphical interface than on a text printout.

Another factor to consider in a real-time detection system is the ability to counter the attacker before he can do devastating damage or steal confidential information the company has a fiduciary duty to protect.

This has historically been the area the military refers to as cyberwarfare: the ability to outmaneuver your cyberfoe using real-time analysis of the attack. The corporate world has since caught up with this mindset because they are essentially under attack by hackers and other criminal elements using what amounts to cyberwarfare to infiltrate or compromise corporate systems.

As with many other technology advances, the U.S. Government was the main catalyst for the development of this class of software. Government intelligence services are renowned for being able to collect and store vast amounts of electronic information. But there still remained the problem of sifting through the data, making sense of what was collected, developing profiles of persons of interest—and being able to do so in real time as needed. Some of the original software designed for this purpose was used to analyze, replay, and even isolate network traffic that was of interest to the federal government. The highly criticized Carnivore was used at the ISP level to catch data of interest—as most people know. But few know that NFAT systems such as the *e*Trust Network Forensics program from Computer Associates (CA™) (**www.ca.com**) can trace their origins to the federal government intelligence services. This software has the ability to sort large amounts of network data to recreate how an intruder broke in, identify who is communicating with whom on a network, determine what the contents of those communications are, and store network data streams as they occur for replay later.

**Caution**

**Network Forensics Abuse**

With a network forensics tool, anyone can spy on users' e-mail, capture passwords, know what Web pages were viewed—even covertly see the contents of a customer's shopping cart. With this much power, these tools are obviously subject to abuse.

**FYI** *FBI's Carnivore—a Network Forensics Tool*

Carnivore was an Internet packet sniffer used with other FBI tools to capture e-mail messages and reconstruct Web pages exactly as the target saw them while surfing the Web. Carnivore became a controversial topic among civil libertarians in 2000 when an ISP's legal challenge brought the surveillance tool's existence to light. One controversy revolved around the legality of the FBI's use of the device to obtain e-mail headers and other information without a wiretap warrant. Congress legalized the practice in the 2001 USA PATRIOT Act.

Under Section 216 of the Act, the FBI can conduct a limited form of Internet surveillance without first meeting with a judge and establishing probable cause that the target has committed a crime. The FBI is authorized to capture routing information such as e-mail addresses or IP addresses but not the contents of the communications. Cases investigated under section 216 involved alleged mail fraud, controlled substance sales, providing material support to terrorism, and making obscene or harassing telephone calls within the District of Columbia.

The newest generation of NFAT systems takes this capability one step further and allows the user of the NFAT to forensically gather data not only from the network but also from host machines connected to this network. In other words, the current generation of NFAT systems can make a forensic image of your machine remotely and generally without your knowledge. This technology not only works within a corporate network, it also works on any machine that is connected to a network. A computer attached to the Internet could conceivably be imaged remotely without the user's being aware of the process. The newest forms of malware are using the same techniques used by NFATs to extract data from unsuspecting users on the Internet.

With the capabilities to image data remotely and immediately, organizations no longer have to wait hours or days to do an investigation. This delay often resulted in the loss of important data and increased costs in terms of lost productivity and forensic labor costs. For example, suppose you have an incident in Sweden involving a single computer on a network. The original method of forensic examination was to either transport the computer to the technician or transport the technician to the computer. Both methods involved downtime when the computer was taken out of production, as well as travel expenses. With an NFAT system, you can image the computer remotely in less time than it would take to get to the airport for your flight to Sweden.

As they become more sophisticated, NFAT systems are also becoming much easier to use. The original versions of both IDS and NFAT systems were essentially command-line driven. The latest versions are GUI and offer a detailed graphical view of a network. The view is so advanced that you can literally watch packets flow across a network via the NFAT interface. From a network administrator's point of view, that means you can view bottlenecks in your system as well as monitor the content of e-mail messages. The type of traffic that cannot be viewed easily at this time is encrypted traffic. NFAT systems can view the encrypted data flowing in the network but cannot read the contents of the packets to do any analysis.

## Components of an NFAT System

The common components of an NFAT system are:

- **Agents.** Software modules installed on hosts or network components used to monitor, retrieve, or intercept data on a network.
- **Server.** Centralized computer or computers that hold the data collected from the network. Usually the server is a large database array such as the one shown in Figure 9.1.
- **Examiner computer.** Computer where the forensic/security examiner does the analysis of data. This computer is usually not the same machine where the network data is stored.

## Using an NFAT to Capture Data

NFAT software can use one of two methods to capture data: "catch it as you can" and "stop, look, and listen." Both methods require relatively large amounts of storage space to hold the data captured. They differ in how they extract data for future analysis.

**Catch It As You Can** The "catch it as you can" method attempts to capture every single piece of information that comes across the network by writing the data flow into a file. This generally requires large amounts of storage space,

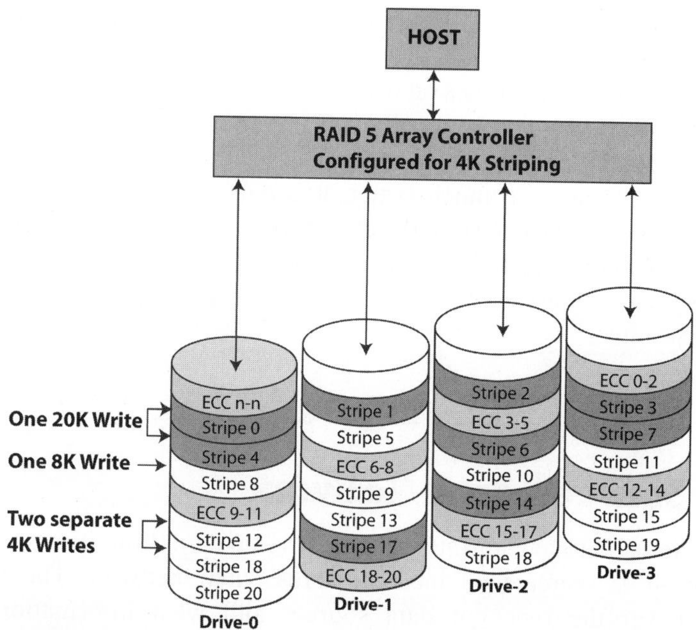


**FIGURE 9.1** A server is a large database array such as this RAID 5 array.

such as a RAID system, and if the network is fast enough, a large memory buffer to handle peak network loads that may occur. Because this data is saved in bulk, the data analysis is broken down into large segments or batches and the analysis is usually done in response to an incident rather than as a proactive measure. The large data sets are essentially there as an insurance policy in case an attack is detected. When an attack is detected, you have to retrieve and analyze the data to determine what occurred.

Because this system catches everything, privacy and legal issues are a significant concern for the organization capturing the data. From a corporate standpoint, the issue of employee privacy is usually a low concern. U.S. courts have consistently ruled that employees have no expectation of privacy on corporate networks if they have been notified and have given their consent. From a law enforcement perspective, the issue of search warrants and privacy is significant because most law enforcement activities are narrow in scope. Using this method, all data is captured, not just data of interest to the investigation.

**Stop, Look, and Listen** The “stop, look, and listen” method uses a filtering system approach. The data going across the network is analyzed on the fly using basic methods such as keywords. Packets of interest are filtered out and then written to a storage device for further analysis later. The FBI Carnivore system is a prime example of a tool that uses this method. The FBI system uses keyword matches to flag data for further analysis and essentially ignores the rest of the data stream.

Because this system relies on real-time analysis, the amount of processing speed and buffer memory are much more important than the "catch it as you can" method. Additionally, certain operating systems such as FreeBSD or other UNIX-based systems are much better at capturing these data packets than Windows-based systems because the control of the I/O of the network interface cards is handled differently. The general rule is that the faster the network, the more likely it is you are going to need a UNIX or Linux platform for efficient NFAT data capture.

---

## Data Sources on a Network

Organizations that have an internal network have multiple data sources that can be used to recreate an incident across their network. The following sections cover the types of data sources and what information can be retrieved from them. The relevance of the data in recreating an incident or event may not be obvious or intuitive to investigators, particularly new network investigators.

### Host Computers

A major source of forensic data both in the stand-alone computer field and in the network forensic field is the host computer. NFAT software now has the ability to access running systems remotely without changing any data. An entire hard drive can be imaged without making any changes. In addition, the software can image other storage devices attached to the computer. With a live system (as opposed to a static forensic investigation), you can remotely image volatile areas such as RAM or open applications *without* changing their contents.

### Firewalls

***Firewalls*** are usually the first line of defense in the networks of most organizations when the internal network is connected to an external network such as the Internet. There are a wide range of firewalls, but many of them provide limited information of how and when an attack started. In a secure network environment, firewalls have basic logging enabled to document any failed or denied connections. Firewalls with more robust logging capabilities can be set to log every single packet that passes through. Middle-of-the-road firewalls usually log IP source and destination addresses, date/time, protocol type, and port number used. This information in isolation will usually not be a smoking gun, but it is a good starting point for reconstructing what happened and how.

## FYI The First Firewall

Marcus Ranum, who developed the first commercial firewall in 1990, founded Network Flight Recorder Security, which produced one of the first network forensics tools. He warned that if nobody is ever going to look at log files, then companies should not bother keeping any logs at all.

Firewalls also have the capability to map internal IP addresses (addresses that are used inside your network that are not accessible directly from the Internet) in such a way that they appear to be part of another network. An external IP or public IP is an IP that is accessible on the Internet and is used by firewalls or routers directly connected to the Internet. This capability is called network address translation (NAT) and is used primarily as a way to connect computers on an internal private network to a public network without using public IP addresses internally. The type of information that can be gleaned from a NAT firewall is the mapping done (via port numbers) between the external and internal networks. In other words, you can see the IP traffic from internal to external sources via a NAT log.

A special type of firewall is called a ***proxy.*** A proxy essentially acts like a mediator between the internal and external network. A proxy operates much the same way a NAT firewall works but takes the process one step further. A proxy literally intercepts the request from the internal computer and reads the contents of the packet to determine if the packet breaks any security rules that have been assigned, such as packets destined for pornographic sites. If no security rules are violated, the proxy then forwards the packet to its destination with the proxy's IP address listed as the originating IP address. For traffic from the external network (Internet), the process is reversed and any logging is done as well. Proxies also log standard information such as IP source and destination addresses, date/time, protocol type, and port numbers.

Firewalls are usually categorized according to which of the above functions they perform. The following list summarizes the firewall categories:

- **Network layer.** This type of firewall acts like an IP filter (working at OSI layers 3 and 4; see Chapter 6). Packets are compared via tables to determine if they have been listed in the table as not permitted or denied.
- **Application layer.** This type of firewall works at the application layer (OSI layer 7) to permit or deny packets based on application utilities such as FTP or HTTP.
- **Proxy firewall.** This type of firewall acts as a mediator between internal hosts/applications and external connections such as the Internet.

9

### DHCP Servers

Dynamic host configuration protocol (DHCP) servers are used to dynamically assign IP addresses to computers on a network when the computers connect to the network or their "leases" expire and a new IP is assigned. The data or information logged within a DHCP server contains the IP address assigned, the MAC address of the computer, the date/time when this IP was assigned, and when the lease expires. This information by itself is insignificant, but it adds another piece to the puzzle to reconstruct what happened during an event.

**FYI** Check Your IP

If you want to check the IP currently assigned to your computer and all the lease information just for fun, type **ipconfig /all** at the command prompt.

### NFAT/IDS Agents

Current IDS and NFAT systems rely on software clients called ***agents*** that are installed on host machines throughout the network. These agents are designed to collect any and all information from the host in response to the NFAT/IDS server request. In addition to collecting information, agents can be used to determine a baseline when first installed to provide a comparison set of parameters for later use. The role of agents will be further explored later in this chapter, but for the purposes of this section, they are a data source for information found on the host, network segment, or node part of the network.

**IN PRACTICE:** Collect Evidence from Secondary Sources

During analysis, strive to collect every piece of evidence related to the incident, which can be obtained from secondary sources in addition to the primary system under investigation. For example, if documents were illegally transferred over the network through e-mail or alternative means, logs of network traffic or connections can be invaluable in identifying the parties involved, as well as the relevant dates and times.

The company's information security policy should mandate logging and archiving transactions throughout the network, including IDS and proxy logs, firewall logs, and SMTP or mail server logs.

## IDS/Network Monitoring Software

The traditional monitoring of network system performance has become an integral part of most IDS packages. Baseline information is created as the metric for comparing real-time network traffic to determine, for example, if a surge in network traffic is within normal operating parameters. Depending on a software's capability and price, information such as protocols, IP addressing, traffic patterns, and logs can be used to gather information.

## Packet Sniffers

***Packet sniffers*** are designed to collect data straight from the network media and thus are capable of collecting vast quantities of information. This is a boon for data collection but creates a problem when you have to sift through huge volumes of collected data in the future.

Most packet analyzers also function as protocol analyzers. A protocol analyzer is handy when you have to recreate data streams. In other words, protocol analyzers can piece together network conversations into a format humans or NFAT systems can read. Because most NFAT systems are also protocol analyzers, this feature of packet sniffers is usually not used unless you are doing an analysis independent of the NFAT.

### IN PRACTICE: Detecting Credit Card Fraud

In mid-2003, several credit card associations and major credit card issuers noticed a jump in fraud. By reviewing the fraud patterns, they identified one company (Company A) as the probable source of the fraud. Company A provided electronic payment software to retail outlets, including restaurants, retail stores, and Internet companies. The associations and credit card issuers collaborated and contacted Ubizen to help conduct the cybercrime investigation. Company A cooperated with Ubizen's forensic examiners, who would investigate the possibility that a security breach had occurred within Company A's production network environment.

The team found that the fraud resulted from duplicated credit cards used in "card-present transactions." Legitimate account numbers were fraudulently reproduced on unauthorized duplicate cards and used by criminals to purchase goods or services in person. To accurately duplicate a credit card with account information, the criminal must have gained access to the data contained in the magnetic stripe. A credit card magnetic stripe contains two separate tracks of information. Track 1 data contains information printed on the card, such as

CONTINUED ON NEXT PAGE

9

CONTINUED

the cardholder's name. Track 2 contains more sensitive information, including the CVV (card verification value) code.

The fraud pattern made it likely that data had been stolen in large batches and that full mag-stripe information had been taken from Company A's network. Investigators needed to locate where on the network this information resided. The forensic experts studied the layout of Company A's computer network to determine where it was vulnerable. The most common targets are Internet-visible systems, such as Web servers and FTP servers, or weakly configured wireless network access points. The team found that Company A's network was not sufficiently hardened against an attack.

The FBI was notified to help collect evidence. The team first collected mirror images of Company A's payment gateway. Because Track 2 information had been compromised, they needed to understand where data resided in the network in order to find what systems had been touched by the attacker.

The team found files on the network that had been installed by a hacker, including keystroke loggers and a backdoor program called HackerDefender. FBI agents and the Ubizen team reviewed files and audit logs to find the hacker's footprint and attack signature; that is, how the hacker broke in and what the hacker did once he had access. The intruder had installed hacking tools and utilities within the systems. When tracing the hacker's steps, the investigators looked at dates and time stamps to determine when the hacker last penetrated the company's network. They found files created by the hacker the day before the investigation began, proving an ongoing breach and the ability to catch the attacker in the act.

After repairing the breach to lock out the hacker, information collected onsite was preserved, including hard drives from the compromised systems and logs from the IDS, firewall, and routers. The information was shipped to Ubizen's labs for in-depth analysis and preservation for evidentiary purposes. Tools that had been tested extensively in court were used to ensure that e-evidence would be admissible.

Investigators were ready to catch the hacker in the act by setting a trap with three parts. The first part was a packet sniffer, a laptop with EtherPeek software that would watch traffic in and out of the servers. EtherPeek allowed investigators to monitor any data the hacker was sending, such as keystrokes, and the machines the intruder was attempting to access. Also, the sniffer would capture firsthand

CONTINUED ON NEXT PAGE

▶▶ CONTINUED

evidence of files removed from the network. Next, the files on those servers were loaded with dummy credit card information to prevent additional fraud from occurring and to keep the hacker unaware that he or she had been noticed. The third part of the trap was the use of Tripwire to monitor the integrity of files. Tripwire was configured to set off an alarm the moment any of the date and time stamps of the files were changed. That would allow the investigators to know exactly when the attacker hit so that they could catch the intruder in the act.

When the hacker began copying the fake credit card information, he was identified and the FBI began the hunt for the suspect. They contacted a law enforcement computer-crime liaison group in the Eastern European country where the hacker was located. The college-age male hacker was arrested and extradited (Sartin, 2004).

## Physical Aspects of Capturing Data

Up to this point, we have covered the areas or devices where information can be collected from a network. The next section deals with the physical aspects of collecting data from a network. In covering the areas where data can be collected in the previous section, we also covered some of the basic equipment used to harvest this data. However, those devices are not designed for the data storage or retrieval requirements of an NFAT system. The devices that follow are specifically designed for this purpose. They are also designed to minimize any adverse effects on the network traffic itself. The following list summarizes the devices used by IDS and NFAT tools to collect information:

- **Switch port analyzer (SPAN).** This feature of modern switches is also known as ***port mirroring.*** This feature duplicates the information going into one or any port to the SPAN port for the IDS/NFAT tool to analyze.
- **Test access port (TAP).** This tool is used much like a cable splice. TAPs have an input side and an output side where the IDS/NFAT monitoring software or monitor is attached. This type of tool does not degrade network performance because it is a passive data collection device.
- **Host inline device.** A variant of the TAP, a host inline device is a computer with two network interface cards to act as the input and output. In this design, the host inline device acts essentially like a repeater but with the added benefit that it records all data passing through it.

- **Hubs.** The most basic method of collecting information is the hub. A hub repeats all data received on any port to the remaining ports, including the port where the IDS/NFAT system is located. Because hubs introduce extra traffic and collisions to a network, they are slowly being replaced by switches and SPAN systems.
- **Wireless access points (WAPs).** WAPs transmit and receive data via radio frequency (RF) in the open. NFAT systems essentially set up a wireless receiver to record and analyze the traffic coming off the AP for any anomalies.

---

## Logical Aspects of Capturing Data

The NFAT software used to capture data packets is much more than simply a network forensics tool. One of the main functions of the NFAT is to acquire forensic images remotely. However, the newest NFAT systems are actually a combination of IDS and forensic software. The true power of modern NFAT systems is in their ability to gather data from different sources such as agents, router logs, or TAPs and sift through all this to get a clear picture of what has occurred on the network. After this is done, then the forensic technician can use the remote forensic capabilities to start gathering evidence from a host device.

### Agents

Agents are one of the main tools used by NFAT systems. Agents are nothing more than small programs located on a network host that allow the NFAT server to view, copy, or even modify a host remotely. Today's software agents are so small and can be hidden so well that most users will not know when one is installed on their system. For those users who do know, it is virtually impossible to see which process is the agent or to see when an image is being done on the host computer. Guidance Software has refined the agent software to a degree that the packets sent by the agent are encrypted and appear random to everyone except the NFAT server. To make things more interesting, the agent file is usually less than 200KB in size and is disguised so as not to be found easily.

Agent software can be installed normally during the course of an upgrade by the IT department with everyone knowing. The agent software can also be installed covertly for an investigation in a variety of ways. Taking a ploy from the hacker playbook, agent software can be disguised in an e-mail or even a pop-up. In the case of the pop-up or Web site, the agent is downloaded in what is commonly called a *drive-by*. The software is downloaded in the background. This latter method is seldom used simply because Microsoft has patched this Windows flaw, but it can still be done if the browser settings allow for downloading in a certain way.

### Logs

In addition to agents, NFAT software can be configured to accept input from almost any device that generates a log file. This may seem simple on the surface, but keep in mind that an enterprise network has the ability to generate millions of log entries in a short period of time. The ability of an automated NFAT system to sift through all this data (using algorithms) and piece together disparate data (more algorithms) from different logs makes them an invaluable resource in both sheer time savings and analysis.

Remember the example of the NFAT system developed by the U.S. Government for intelligence purposes? The need to sift through millions of bits of information to extract that one needed nugget of information has been simplified with the use of NFAT tools.

### Network Data

Data collected via sniffers is usually stored on large database servers for analysis at a later date. Depending on the manner of collection, the data may be in raw format or organized in fields that can be queried. The NFAT software usually contains a query language such as SQL that is used to extract the information. With immense processing power plus large storage capacities, the NFAT software can drill through vast quantities of information in a relatively short period of time.

---



## Examining Data

Because most modern NFAT systems are two products in one—IDS and forensic tools—the following section covers both areas as one approach. With the evolution into GUI tools, the report generation of NFATs is no longer a monitor with IP addresses whizzing by on the screen. Current NFAT systems have the ability to show the user real-time data flow analysis over the entire network. Or it can show the exact screen view the remote user is viewing depending on what function you are using on that NFAT.

### Verifying the Integrity of the Data

The primary problem associated with enterprise-level IDS tools is the sheer amount of data that is collected, as you have seen in the previous sections. The solution to this avalanche of data is twofold.

1. Larger storage solutions have become the standard practice.
2. Faster processors allow the software to process data that much more quickly.

The examination of refined data (essentially data that has been filtered) is where the NFAT tool comes into play. It is *before* and *after* this part of the sequence that the manual job of analysis comes into play. The before part occurs when an NFAT system accepts any input you have told it (using rules) to accept. Computers are marvelous in that they do exactly what you tell them to do. The disadvantage is that the NFAT will analyze data that has been compromised or incorrect. The old phrase "garbage in equals garbage out" applies in these situations.

There are several areas you must be extremely clear on when doing a forensic examination of network data. Unlike disk forensic examinations, where the data is static and can be hashed to prove integrity, network data such as logs and data streams are dynamic. The field of disk forensics is relatively mature in that courts of law have ruled in one form or another on what types of evidence are admissible and what types are not. The field of data forensics has a very high bar for evidence admissibility for which network forensics is still formulating an approach. As an example, time and date stamps on a single personal computer are easy to prove using BIOS time information and file system time stamping. On a network system, correlating time stamps from not merely one device but possibly dozens is problematic. Add to that evidentiary challenge the ability of hackers to change the time and date on compromised devices to hide their tracks and you have a formidable problem to solve.

One of the primary areas where an analyst should be concerned in a network forensic investigation is the integrity of original data sources. The following guidelines can help you ensure data integrity.

- **Logs.** The generation of logs on devices such as routers, proxies, and firewalls should always be set to the maximum setting at which your network can operate. The setting will depend on network bandwidth and storage capacity. The integrity of logs should always be assumed invalid until you can prove the log has not been compromised. This can be done by correlating log data with other data or establishing that the device has not been compromised. The secondary issue with logs is in the transmission of log data across the network infrastructure. Generally speaking, this point is where the NFAT software has direct control of the data and can hash the data *before* transmission to the central database. The same forensic principle used to compare before and after hashes for disk forensics then applies to before and after hashes for data transmitted across the network. Another factor that can increase the integrity of the transmitted data is the ability to hide the data from prying eyes. Applying the military principle of being able to gather intelligence on your foes by knowing more than they know, it is always important to deny your enemy intelligence by making it difficult to intercept your data. Data can be both compressed and encrypted to protect it while it is being transmitted across the network.

- **Time/date stamps.** As briefly mentioned in a prior section, the issue of collecting data from multiple devices across the network can be problematic when it comes to dates and times. To build an effective timeline of events, the devices must have their time stamps synchronized across your network. In an ideal world this might happen, but in the computer forensics world this is rare. Most devices have a clock function that tends to drift slightly, and there is always the possibility an attacker changed the time settings. Because the devices you are collecting evidence from will usually be out of sync with regard to time stamps, use the NFAT system as your third-party system to create a trusted time stamp that essentially becomes your baseline when comparing time/date stamps of device data.
- **IDS alerts.** Alerts from an IDS are generally a good indication that something has happened or is happening in your network. The NFAT system will use the incoming data from the IDS to try to determine what is happening. A problem that may occur with IDS alerts is "false positives." A false positive is when an IDS mistakenly flags an innocent file as being suspicious. Because IDSs work on a trigger basis (some signature or event triggers an alert), they sometimes are triggered by normal processes. You must find a fine balance between setting your threshold too high or too low to minimize your rate of false IDS alerts, or your NFAT system will analyze for threats that do not exist.
- **Database integrity.** Once the data has been collected from the various sources across your network, it is usually deposited in a storage medium of some type or a large database. To maintain the integrity of the data, the data must be protected even at this point. If an attacker can gain access to your network, she can gain access to the data that will help you track her down. Safeguard your NFAT database by using encrypted remote access, hardened operating systems where the database management system is residing, and enabling encryption on the database.



## Analyzing the Data for Attacks

Once you have verified the integrity of your data, the process of analyzing the data for attacks begins. Whether you are doing real-time analysis or querying a database to recreate an attack, the objective is the same. You are trying to determine what has occurred and how it has occurred. Let's take a brief example of how the NFAT system will work in both the IDS function and the forensic function. The following example is simplified, but it demonstrates the latest advances in network forensics.

Assume you have a network that spans several continents with all the associated hardware to go with it. A worm has infected your enterprise network, and you need to find the entry point. Assume also that the NFAT system is doing real-time analysis and you can watch the worm travel across the network in real time.

The first step in this analysis is to find how this worm is traveling across your network. Using the query function, you can find where there has been increased activity either in network ports or e-mail servers. With this information, you can then begin to backtrack these increases in activity until you find the point of entry. Usually, you will use time stamps to backtrack in time until you get to the original host or point of entry. At this point, your NFAT has been working as an IDS but has also been collecting data forensically (hashing and encrypting data) from the network.

In this example, assume the point of entry is a computer in your Hong Kong office. To preserve the evidence on this host for possible future court presentation, you now use the forensic side of the NFAT tool. Using the agent already installed on the host, you can extract a forensic image of the entire computer including hard drive, RAM, and any other storage area volatile or otherwise. This information is then stored on your database management system for further analysis. While you are doing this forensic image, you casually do a minimal search for obvious clues such as e-mail and Internet history logs.

The analysis in this example from start to finish can be done in literally minutes with the latest versions of NFAT systems. The only real bottleneck in the forensic imaging of the host may be the network's bandwidth limits on transferring the image.

### IN PRACTICE: Protect Logs from Malicious Attack

Although most log entries are accurate, not all of them are. If you are going to use a log as evidence in a case, you cannot assume that the log is accurate. If a crime has taken place, it is possible that the intruder intentionally corrupted the logs.

To minimize the chance of log files' being maliciously modified—and increase the chance that logs will hold up in court—store them on a special log server to which access is restricted.

## Pattern Analysis

Pattern analysis applies the concept of baselines to determine what is normal for your network. In the preceding example, you read how looking for a spike in network traffic can be used to track down a worm or virus. Patterns in data traffic such as late-night spikes or increases of traffic between computers are also signals something has changed on the network. See examples of traffic spikes due to the Slammer worm on Arbor Networks' Web site at **www.arbornetworks.com/worm.php.**

## Content Analysis

Content analysis, also known as deep packet inspection, is usually used on NFAT systems for real-time analysis of content on the network to analyze such things as e-mail or text documents. The heart of this analysis relies on using sophisticated algorithms to identify similarities in traffic going across the network to establish a possible link between sender and receiver. For example, assume there is evidence your company's R&D information is being leaked to a competitor. Using content analysis, you can either see this information in real time going over the network or do an analysis of the archived network traffic for this information to determine if it was sent on the network. The FBI Carnivore system is a simple version of this system that uses keywords to flag data for future analysis.

### Processes to Analyze Internal Crimes Are Lacking

Consider a case of intellectual property theft where an employee leaked confidential documents to a competitor. In a 2004 survey conducted by *Network Computing*, half of the respondents answered no to the question: "Do you have processes in place to analyze what occurred and then prosecute those involved?"

## Timeline Sequencing Analysis

Determining the sequence of events is essential in constructing a timeline to show a link from event to event. An NFAT system extracts data from disparate network devices, creating an overview picture of what is happening on your network. The NFAT system can thus correlate time events and then order them even if the threat vectors are from different sources or entries. The importance of timeline analysis is important to show a progression of the events and document the analysis for court purposes.

## Playback Analysis

NFAT systems have the ability to play back specific network communication "conversations" based on a variety of parameters such as protocols, hosts, applications, and even users. Refer to the example of R&D intellectual property theft again. You can play back all traffic between computers you know contain sensitive information and essentially drill down to examine this traffic while ignoring the rest to determine how the information is being leaked. From a forensic point of view, this information has been archived forensically and can be replayed without fear of changing any data or tainting any e-evidence.

9

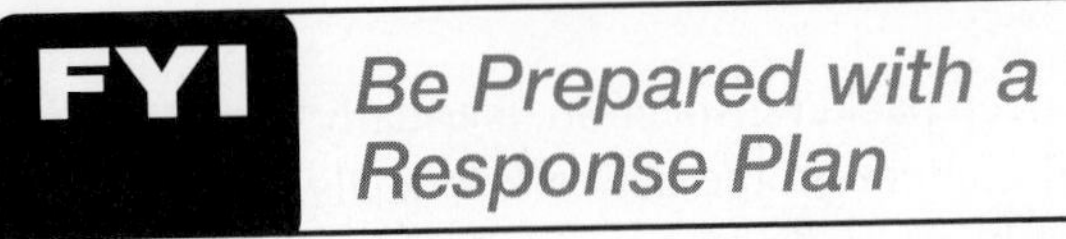


All organizations should have a response plan and capabilities to investigate internally and produce evidence that will stand up in court.

## NFAT Software Tools

The current generation of NFAT tools are used on large enterprise networks to handle IDS functions and provide forensic capabilities to handle incidents that arise during the normal course of business. Since 2001, NFAT software vendors have dramatically improved the functionality of their software to the point where real-time analysis and real-time responses are within its capabilities.

In the following section, you are introduced to the major vendors and the capabilities of their software. While capabilities vary by product, all of the applications discussed below offer these features:

- Real-time network data capture
- Content analysis
- Forensic knowledge base
- Reporting

### Computer Associates

Computer Associates' *e*Trust Network Forensics has a pedigree dating back to government service in the intelligence field. Computer Associates has developed and refined the product even further to make the GUI interface and functionality much easier to work with.

In addition to the standard capabilities listed above, *e*Trust has several very robust capabilities:

- GUI visualization
- Pattern analysis
- Incident playback
- Communication sequencing

Computer Associates has taken a network analysis tool and tweaked it to perform at the level of a forensic tool. *e*Trust's network analysis capabilities rank at the top of the list for both real-time analysis and graphical display of events in real time. The second area where Computer Associates has excelled is in the ability of its software to parse and isolate network conversations across a network to monitor only data relevant to an investigation. As a side note, you can license certain algorithms from the NSA to further enhance the power of *e*Trust.

## Guidance Software

Guidance Software has extended the capabilities of their highly rated EnCase® software to include IDS and network forensic capabilities. The cost of the software makes it practical for large corporations only, but the software does perform well for its intended purpose.

Guidance Software has also expanded its software to be able to perform enterprise-wide keyword searches. That is, you can forensically search for data on your *entire* network using nothing more than keywords or phrases. The search capabilities of this software are such that you can also find deleted or hidden files across your network that fit specific search criteria. The enterprise edition also creates an audit trail for anyone using this software to ensure a proper chain of custody and also to audit any abuses that may occur from its use. All data sent between the agents and the secure server (called SAFE) are encrypted for added security.

The examiner usually sits at her workstation and logs into the SAFE server to get authenticated. Once the examiner is authenticated, the data is extracted from the computers of interest via the network in an encrypted form. In this manner, chain of custody, security, and data integrity are all taken care of. Once the data is collected and analyzed, it is usually stored in a database for future use. An example of a SAFE architecture is represented in Figure 9.2.

As a final safeguard to prevent abuse, only a forensic technician authorized to use the software is allowed to interact with the agent via a PKI key system. In other words, if your login credentials do not allow you to image the CEO's computer, you can image every other computer except that one. From a forensic standpoint, Guidance Software has expanded their gold standard product into the network world.

## Paraben Software

Paraben® software has expanded from the world of stand-alone computers to network forensics. Paraben is a relatively new entry into the world of network forensics with P2® Enterprise, but the software uses the same basic concepts of agents, servers, and examination workstation.

Paraben has taken steps to preserve the integrity of the data collected from the agents via encryption both from agent to server and from the examiner's station to server. The naming of the different modules is unique among enterprise NFAT systems. Taking off on the name of the system, Enterprise, Paraben uses

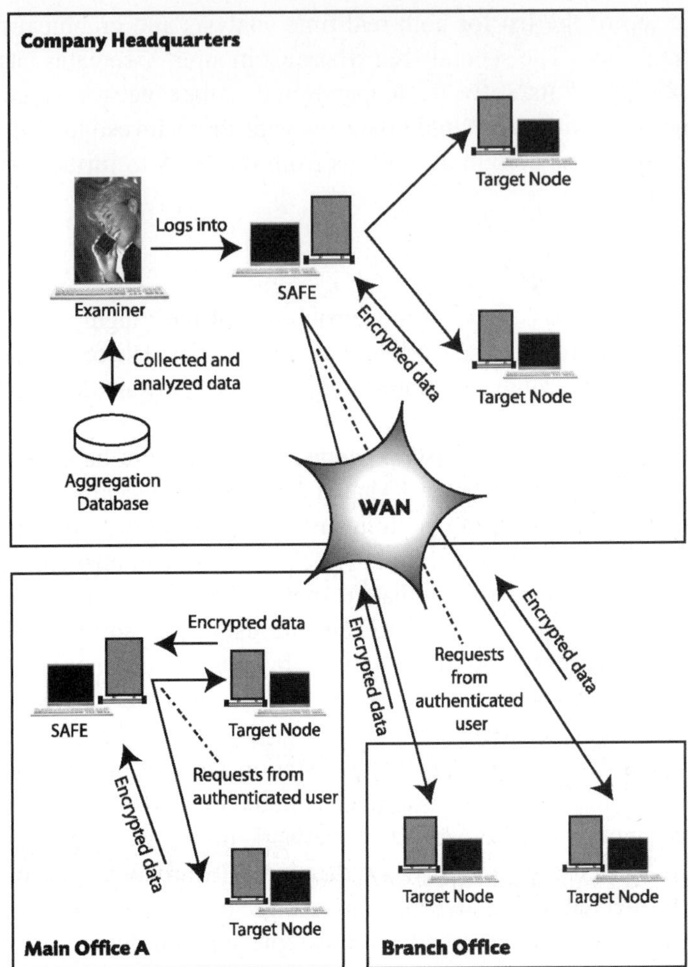


**FIGURE 9.2** Example of SAFE architecture.

the *Star Trek* theme in naming the various components. The examination computer is called the Captain Module and the agents are Crew Agents; the proxy server is simply called proxy, however.

Paraben's system relies heavily on the power of what it calls the Central Authentication Server (CAS). Paraben recommends a dual processor enterprise-level server running at least Microsoft Server 2000 with Microsoft SQL 2000 or 2005 Enterprise. The areas Paraben stresses for performance are RAM and storage space. The standard specifications for this are 2GB of RAM and 146GB of storage space to make sure the software has enough room to work.

Figure 9.3 illustrates the architecture Paraben uses for its NFAT system:

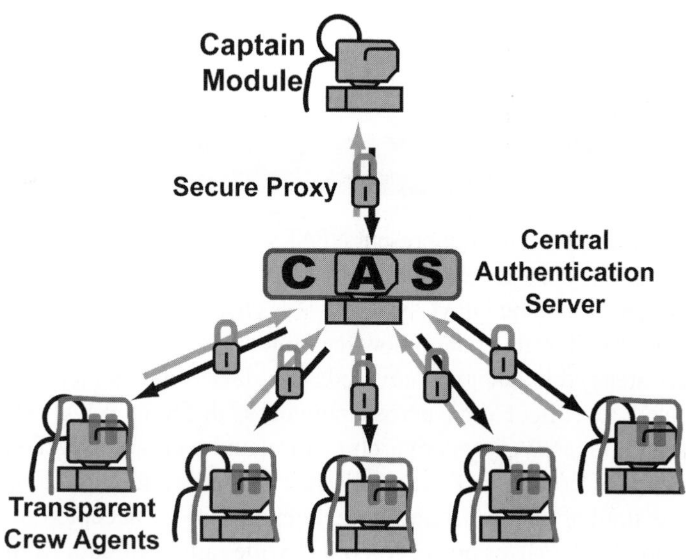

*Source:* Paraben's P2 Enterprise Edition Software, Paraben Corporation.

**FIGURE 9.3** Paraben's P2 Enterprise Edition architecture.

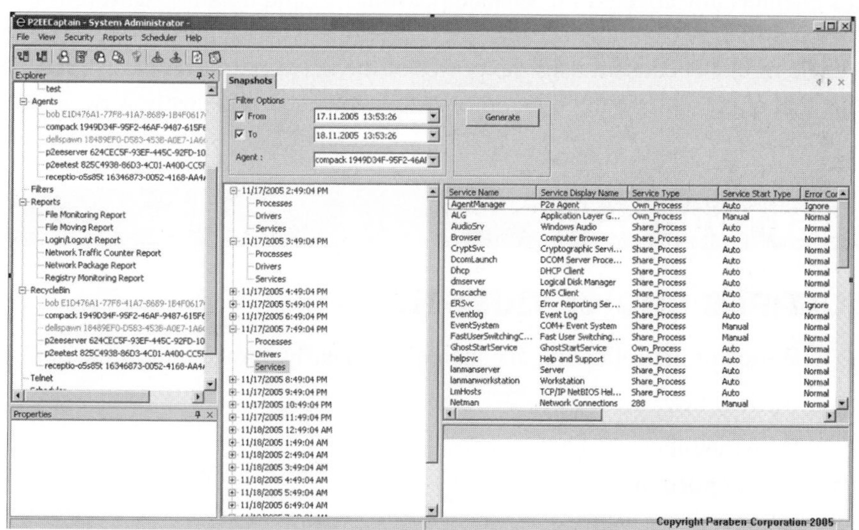


**FIGURE 9.4** Paraben P2 Enterprise lets you take a snapshot of a host machine.

Paraben's software has the same capabilities of other NFAT software packages to constantly record information coming across your network for real-time analysis or to review at a later date. Paraben also has the ability to take "snapshots" of host machines and archive the results as shown in Figure 9.4.

With the addition of network forensic software, Paraben has added to their impressive collection of forensic tools.

## Summary

This chapter takes a brief look at present NFAT software capabilities. It covered the basic history of NFAT systems and how the IDSs of the past are now being used as the input systems for some NFAT systems. This chapter also explored the forensic capabilities of NFAT software and how data integrity issues have been overcome.

Other areas this chapter covered are data sources across networks, methods used to collect data across networks, different NFAT system data collection methods, NFAT system architecture, and common NFAT systems.

This area of computer forensics is just beginning to expand to the point where the technology is robust and reliable enough to be accepted in a court of law. Additionally, the sheer power to collect wide ranges of data from networks is now well within the computational and storage power of most organizations. This factor, coupled with the fact that NFAT systems can enable an organization to deal in real time with internal and external network threats and to recreate what happened for future use, make this type of software extremely versatile. This chapter only covered the surface possibilities and uses for the forensic use of such software. More and more organizations will eventually move to this forensic model because it uses the power of the network to accomplish forensic tasks that at present are done in a more labor intensive and costly way.

## Test Your Skills

### MULTIPLE CHOICE QUESTIONS

1. Which of the following is considered an early network analysis tool?
   A. Tripwire.
   B. tcpdump.
   C. SilentRunner.
   D. *e*Trust.

2. Standard operating procedures or parameters on a network are used to establish
   A. baselines.
   B. standards.
   C. inputs.
   D. medians.

3. Intrusion detection systems fall into two categories:
   A. reactive and proactive.
   B. character-based or GUI-based.
   C. signature-based and anomaly-based.
   D. host-based or network-based.

4. The major advantage of modern NFAT systems is the ability to conduct
   A. real time analysis.
   B. host forensic analysis.
   C. intrusion detection.
   D. e-mail forensics.

5. The Internet packet sniffer used by the FBI in the past is called
   A. Predator.
   B. Scanner.
   C. Carnivore.
   D. Reaper.

6. The software module installed on a host computer in an NFAT configuration is called a(n)
   A. agent.
   B. server.
   C. terminal.
   D. program.

7. Attempting to catch everything that comes across a network is called the
   A. stop, look, and listen method.
   B. catch it as you can method.
   C. butterfly net method.
   D. fish net method.

8. Attempting to filter the data for later analysis is called the
   A. stop, look, and listen method.
   B. catch it as you can method.
   C. butterfly net method.
   D. fish net method.

9. The type of firewall that acts as the mediator between internal and external connections is a
   A. DNS server.
   B. proxy server.
   C. file server.
   D. DHCP server.

10. A server that automatically assigns an IP to a computer is called a
    A. DNS server.
    B. proxy server.
    C. file server.
    D. DHCP server.

11. Collecting data straight from the network and generating large data files is the job of a
    A. packet sniffer.
    B. network analyzer.
    C. traffic analyzer.
    D. frame sequencer.

12. Port mirroring on a switch can be accomplished with a
    A. SPAM.
    B. POMA.
    C. SPAN.
    D. PAM.

13. The concept of baselines to determine what is normal for your network is called
    A. packet analysis.
    B. pattern analysis.
    C. e-mail analysis.
    D. network analysis.

14. Determining the sequence of events is called
    A. timeline analysis.
    B. sequential analysis.
    C. data analysis.
    D. packet analysis.

15. The NFAT software that uses a Captain Module is
    A. *e*Trust.
    B. SilentRunner.
    C. P2 Enterprise.
    D. None of the above.

## EXERCISES

### Exercise 9.1: Snort

1. Using the Internet, do a search for information on an intrusion detection system called Snort.
2. Snort is considered the de facto standard for open-source intrusion detection. Write a two-page paper documenting why this is.

### Exercise 9.2: Ethereal

1. Go to **www.ethereal.com** and download a version of Ethereal for your computer with the permission of your instructor. (You can also go to this site using the link on the Companion Website, at **www.prenhall.com/security.**)

2. Install Ethereal on your computer.
3. Use Ethereal to sniff your local network for all traffic.
4. Write a two-page paper on what traffic you find and explain the significance of what types of traffic you find.



### Exercise 9.3: ZoneAlarm® Firewall

1. Go to **www.zonelabs.com** and download a version of ZoneAlarm with the permission of your instructor. (You can also go to this site using the link on the Companion Website, at **www.prenhall.com/security.**)

2. Install ZoneAlarm on your computer.
3. Use ZoneAlarm to monitor the traffic in and out of your computer.
4. Use the log feature of ZoneAlarm to see what traffic has been denied or allowed.
5. Write a one-page report on how the logs could be used with an IDS.

### Exercise 9.4: Wireless Sniffing

1. Using the Internet, research the different software packages used to sniff wireless access points.

2. With input from your instructor, determine which wireless sniffer is acceptable for use with your local wireless network.
3. Using the wireless sniffer, determine which protocols are being transmitted in the immediate area.
4. Document your findings and explain how an IDS would use this information.

### Exercise 9.5: Visual Network Analysis

1. Using the Internet, look for tools that graphically trace a packet's route on the Internet.
2. Once you find a tool, visually trace a packet from your computer to any computer in the United States.
3. Trace the route again to see if the packets take a different route.
4. Document how this can be used to graphically view network traffic.

## PROJECTS

### Project 9.1: Analysis of Network Data

1. Using Ethereal, record the network traffic on your network for one hour.
2. During this one hour, have two students log in to e-mail and, using a messenger service, start a chat session.
3. Use Ethereal to discover which protocols are being used by which service.
4. Attempt to recreate "conversations" using Ethereal and see if you can find the chat session.
5. Use Ethereal to recreate the e-mail data stream created when the students logged in and created their e-mails.

### Project 9.2: View Host Log Files

Using a Windows XP computer, adjust and view the log settings.

1. To access the logs in an XP system, click Start > Control Panel > Performance and Maintenance > Administrative Tools, and finally select the Event Viewer.
2. Select one of the three logs (Application, Security, or System).
3. Click the **Action** menu and then click **Properties** to view the settings for the highlighted log. Change the settings and see what effects those changes have on the logs.
4. Click the **Action** menu again and then click **Clear all Events**.

5. Reboot the computer and return to the Event Viewer. What changes occur to the logs once the computer is rebooted?
6. Document your changes and their effect in a one-page report.

### Project 9.3: Using Snort

Snort is the de facto IDS standard on the Internet today. For this project, you are going to install Snort as a passive network tap.

1. Go to **www.snort.org** and download a version of Snort with the permission of your instructor. (You can also go to this site using the link on the Companion Website, at **www.prenhall.com/security.**)
2. Place the computer where Snort is installed on the network segment you wish to monitor.
3. Download a rule set from **www.snort.org.** Use a precanned version.
4. Review the logs generated by Snort as it monitors the traffic on the network segment.
5. Sift through the logs. Search the Internet for tools used to make this process easier.
6. Document and write a two-page report on the use of Snort in your lab.

Companion Website

9

## Case Study

You are the head of the IT department for a Fortune 100 company. Up until now you have been unaware of any serious break-ins to your company, but you have the sneaky suspicion you may not know because you do not have the tools to see the attacks. You have been approached by the CIO to look into an enterprise-wide IDS system. Your network spans several continents and has multiple entry points onto the Internet. Your research so far has pointed to using an NFAT system instead of using an IDS, but you are debating on how to implement NFAT across your enterprise network without straining your budget and network.

Research the different types of NFAT systems and how they are deployed. Design a topology using agents, servers, and forensic technician computers that will cover a network of this size efficiently. Explain the role of firewalls, hosts, and any network devices you have on the network within the framework of the NFAT system. Remember to account for large amounts of data and how the NFAT system will analyze these data streams.

# Chapter 10

# Tracking Down Those Who Intend to Do Harm on a Large Scale

## Chapter Objectives

**After reading this chapter and completing the exercises, you will be able to do the following:**

- Identify tactics and digital media used in the preparation and planning of devastating crimes or large-scale attacks and the cybertrails they leave.
- Understand how the Internet is used as a tool for terrorism or virtual warfare.
- Explain the objectives of hackers and those involved in criminal commerce.
- Explain the process of collecting e-evidence in computer hacking cases.

## Introduction

This chapter applies your legal, technical, and investigative knowledge to the investigation of large-scale criminal activities, ones that are geographically widespread or highly destructive. You will understand the complexities involved in such cases and the demanding verification requirements, although their detailed investigative techniques are beyond the scope of this book. E-evidence of the preparation and planning of devastating crimes may provide crucial intelligence to avert attacks or supply circumstantial evidence linking the perpetrators (perps) to the crime. In many cases, e-evidence provided leads to wider areas of investigative interest and helped narrow the scope of possible perps. E-evidence showed that Timothy McVeigh used the Internet to find plans for making a truck bomb like the one used to blow apart the Oklahoma City federal building in April 1995, killing

168 people. Clearly, it is important to know how criminals use the Internet and digital resources to prepare for, plan, and execute their crimes.

The financial damages and disruption caused by hackers, phishers, spammers, identity thieves, and malware worldwide are tremendous. Computer Economics (**www.computereconomics.com**), an independent research firm, estimated that in 2001 the Code Red worm and its variants had a worldwide economic impact of $2.62 billion, Sircam cost $1.15 billion, and Nimda cost $635 million. Despite strong efforts to defend against malware, during 2003 the worldwide impact caused by only four new viruses—Slammer, Blaster, Nachi, and SoBig.F—was $3.2 billion. Driven by egotistic or profit motives, these criminals use the Internet to hijack large numbers of PCs to spy on users, spam them, shake down businesses, and steal identities.

Those driven by ideological or political motives and the intent to do harm use the Internet to plan and coordinate their activities, as was done to plan operations for September 11, 2001. Terrorists use every tactic and technology to carry out their destructive plans—hacking, spamming, phishing, identity theft, Web site propaganda and recruitment, and DoS attacks. Computers seized in Afghanistan reportedly revealed that al Qaeda was collecting intelligence on targets and sending encrypted messages via the Internet. In this chapter, we begin by examining cyberplanning, terrorist, and virtual warfare activities. We then explore the characteristics of hacker attacks.

---

## Large-Scale Investigations

Computer forensics experts may be called upon to assist in a large-scale investigation on behalf of a corporation, an industry, or national security agency. They might be part of a team of investigators who need to verify that Web servers are not being used directly or indirectly to carry out a crime of mass disruption or destruction. Or they might be called when a breach of security is suspected, such as discovering an intrusion into a company's computer system and restricted files, if that intrusion is part of a massive attack. These are just a few examples of large-scale investigations. At the outset, large-scale attacks are not easily distinguishable from smaller ones.

Regardless of scale, a first step is to find out as much about the intruder's identity as possible, including motives and any group affiliation. In massive attacks carried out by those with criminal intent, it is very likely that the attacker used software that routes Internet communications through untraceable IP addresses or some other identity-concealing method. Another challenge is that ISPs participated in the criminal operations without knowing it. It's important for investigators to know what could possibly have happened. Consider two actual situations.

- **Hosting the al Qaeda Web site.** During 2002, the al Qaeda Web site **www.alneda.com** was located in Malaysia until May 13, then in Texas at **http://66.34.191.223/** until June 13. On June 21, it reappeared at **www.drasat.com** in Michigan until it was shut down on June 25. The ISPs hosting the site claimed that they knew nothing about the content of the site or even the fact that it was housed on their servers.
- **Hijacking computers and launching a DoS attack.** Aaron Caffrey, a 19-year-old from Dorset, England, was accused of launching a denial of service (DoS) attack on September 20, 2001, against the Port of Houston, one of the biggest U.S. ports (BBC News, 2003). There was undisputed evidence that the port's Web servers had been crashed by a program coming from Caffrey's computer. Investigators found on his hard drive a list of over 11,000 IP addresses of vulnerable (infected) computers that Caffrey could control to launch attacks. Caffrey admitted to being a member of a group called Allied Haxor Elite and hacking into computers for friends to test their security. But he insisted he was not responsible for the attack on the Port of Houston. He claimed that the program and files had been put there by malicious hackers and that he was an innocent victim.

## Isolated or Large-Scale Crime?

In these cases, the identities that were "found" were three ISPs and a teenage hacker who all claimed they know nothing and were unwitting victims. Some of the many questions raised about these cases are whether or not the ISPs and the hacker were accomplices or victims; what other evidence existed to corroborate or refute their claims; and what was the ultimate goal of the real guilty parties?

In the first case, there is evidence that a terrorist group or sympathizers were involved in the Web hosting and that a large-scale investigation might be warranted. More important, what was the function of the Web site? Did it contain stego hiding details of an impending attack? Was it being used to recruit extremists or solicit funding for training camps?

What about the DoS attack from England against one of the largest ports in the United States? Police believed it to be the first electronic attack to disable a critical part of a country's infrastructure. The attack stopped the port's Web service that contained vital data for shipping and mooring companies responsible for helping ships navigate in and out of the port. In effect, this attack crippled part of the national transportation infrastructure.

The outcome of Aaron Caffrey's trial was disappointing to prosecutors. The case hinged on whether the jury believed the defendant's argument that his computer had been taken over by a hacker using a Trojan-horse program. Computer forensics experts found no evidence to support his claim that his PC was hacked or used as a zombie. However, the jury believed Caffrey and acquitted him of all charges under the Computer Misuse Act in October 2003. Laws and court cases will be covered in Chapter 12.

### Digging Deeper to Find the Facts

Some other evidence suggested the possibility that the intended target was not the Port of Houston, but rather Bokkie, a 17-year-old South African girl. Bokkie had upset Caffrey by making derogatory remarks about Americans during a late night Internet chat session. Caffrey logged on to the chat session under the name Aaron X shortly after midnight on September 20, 2001. Aaron X performed a "who is" command to discover Bokkie's IP address and then inserted that IP address into a denial of service program (ComputerWeekly.com, 2003). Whether Caffrey intended an attack against Bokkie or if such an attack somehow turned into an attack against the Port of Houston was not verified.

> **Caution**
>
> **Remain Objective**
>
> It is tough not to jump to conclusions about who is telling the truth and who is lying. Stay objective, or you put the entire investigation at risk.

Based on verified e-evidence, it could be concluded that Caffrey was responsible for launching the DoS attack against the Port, which indicates that the infrastructure attack was isolated and not part of a large-scale debilitating attack on a critical infrastructure.

The cases above highlight a few of the challenges of dealing with large-scale crimes. First responders need to consider the possibility that they are seeing only the tip of the iceberg. With limited resources, not every case can be fully investigated. A reasonable judgment about whether the attack is isolated or an instance of a large-scale plot has to be made. That decision may need to be referred to a team of experts.

It might not be possible to determine with confidence what actually happened or to identify who was responsible. However, it remains necessary to use computer forensics investigative techniques and tools to identify cybercriminal activities in the global effort to mitigate their impacts.

Studying examples of attacks and malicious applications may help forensics investigators better understand hacker and terrorist methodologies, and enable them to recognize where and what to look for on the Internet and telecommunication devices. The huge resources under the control of, or available to, those with the intent to do harm make them a formidable opponent.



---

## Terrorism, Virtual Warfare, and Other Types of Internet-Based Hostilities

Anonymity, command-and-control resources, and many other features make the Internet the criminals' conduit for coordinating and carrying out an agenda. E-mail, VoIP (voice over Internet Protocol), chat rooms, and Web sites with stego continue to be used as ***cyberplanning*** tools to coordinate and

**TABLE 10.1** Cyberplanning Web sites.

| Web Site | Beliefs about the Web Site's Alleged Use or Function |
|---|---|
| **alneda.com** | Contained encrypted information to direct al Qaeda members to more secure sites, featured international news on al Qaeda, and published articles, fatwas (decisions on applying Muslim law), and books. Al Qaeda ran two Web sites, **alneda.com** and **drasat.com,** to discuss the legality of the September 11 attacks. |
| **drasat.com** | Run by the Islamic Studies and Research Center, which some allege is a fake center. Contains posts of al Qaeda news. |
| **assam.com** | Used by jihad in Afghanistan, Chechnya, and Palestine. |
| **jihadunspun.net** | Contained a 36-minute video of Osama bin Laden. |
| **7hj.7hj.com** | Aimed to teach visitors how to conduct computer attacks. |
| **aloswa.org** | Contained quotes from bin Laden tapes, religious legal rulings that "justified" the terrorist attacks, and support for the al Qaeda cause. |
| **mwhoob.net**<br>**aljehad.online** | Alleged to have flashed political-religious songs, with pictures of persecuted Muslims, to denounce U.S. policy and Arab leaders, notably Saudi. |

*Adapted from Thomas, 2003.*

integrate attacks. Cyberplanning refers to the digital coordination of an integrated plan stretching across geographical boundaries that may or may not result in bloodshed (Thomas, 2003). Because of the scope and nature of these crimes, they require a team approach and involve the FBI, other national and local investigative agencies, the private sector, and the cooperation of foreign governments.

Since September 11, U.S. sources have monitored several Web sites linked to al Qaeda that show how they use the Internet for cyberplanning. Those Web sites are listed in Table 10.1.

## Terrorism and the Internet

Terrorist or organized crime groups have used the Internet in more ways than most people realize. The following list gives examples of their activities, including many that leave digital trails.

- Terrorist groups and extremists use the Internet for intelligence collection and propaganda purposes. They perform text searches of online media to find vulnerabilities in computer systems or airport security systems (Thomas, 2003).
- After the September 11 attacks, al Qaeda operatives used the Internet to fight for the "hearts and minds" of the Islamic faithful worldwide, mostly those who had condemned their deadly tactics (Eedle, 2002).
- A captured al Qaeda computer contained engineering and structural architecture features of a dam that engineers could use to plan catastrophic failures (Gellman, 2002).
- An al Qaeda laptop found in Afghanistan had been used to link to the French Anonymous Society Web site containing an online *Sabotage Handbook* (Thomas, 2003).
- Web servers are hijacked and configured to control or redirect unsuspecting users to scam or phishing sites. Terrorist as well as other criminal organizations and crime networks exploit the global information, financial, and transportation networks (Hearing of the Senate Armed Services Committee, 2006).
- Jean-Francois Ricard, one of France's top antiterrorism investigators, noted that many Islamist terror plots in Europe and North America were financed from funds acquired through credit card fraud (Thomas, 2003).

The implication is that the Internet and Web technologies will continue to be used by these groups, so prevention and early detection of their activities depend on computer forensics and intelligence efforts. Some military experts suggest that war between major nations is becoming obsolete and that our future defense will rely far more on intelligence officers with databases than upon battle tanks and artillery (Hastings, 2005). A key lesson of September 11 is that America's intelligence agencies must work together as a single unified intelligence enterprise (Hearing of the Senate Armed Services Committee, 2006).



### FYI Definition of Cyberterrorism

The Naval Postgraduate School has defined cyberterrorism as the unlawful destruction or disruption of digital property to intimidate or coerce people.

## Spoofed Sites Used for International Identity Theft

In March 2006, it was learned that a Chinese bank's server was hosting spoofed Web sites that phishers were using to steal the identities of customers of American banks and Web-based businesses. Criminals had hacked the China Construction Bank (CCB) Shanghai branch's Web server. They then used the hijacked server to host phishing sites that were used to carry out identity theft attacks. One identity theft attack consisting of fake e-mails designed to make Chase Bank customers give out financial information was launched on March 11, 2006. Figure 10.1 shows an example of the e-mail. Those e-mails had been linked to an IP address assigned to the CCB Shanghai branch.

The phishing pages were located in hidden directories with the server's main page displaying a configuration error. This is the first instance of one bank's infrastructure being used to attack another institution.

Netcraft (**www.netcraft.com**) and other security firms pointed out that the attack on Chase offered recipients the chance to earn a $20 reward by filling out a user survey. When a user clicked the link, he was taken to a phished site where he was asked for a user ID and password so the "reward" could be deposited to the proper account. The form also requested the victim's

**Date:** Thu 16 Mar 01:32:29 EST 2006
**From:** "Chase Manhattan Bank" <service@chase.com>
**Subject:** $20 Reward Survey
**To:**

Dear Chase Bank Customer,
**CONGRATULATIONS!** You have been chosen by the Chase Manhattan Bank online department to take part in our quick and easy 5 question survey.
In return we will credit $20 to your account - Just for your time!
Helping us better understand how our customers feel benefits everyone.
With the information collected we can decide to direct a number of changes to improve and expand our online service.

We kindly ask you to spare two minutes of your time
in taking part with this unique offer!

SERVICE: **Chase Online� $20 Reward Survey**
EXPIRATION: **March - 17 - 2006**
Confirm Now your **$20 Reward Survey** with **Chase Online� Reward** services.

The information you provide us is all non-sensitive and anonymous
No part of it is handed down to any third party groups.
It will be stored in our secure database for maximum of 3 days while we process the results of this nationwide survey.

Please do not reply to this message. For any inquiries, contact Customer Service.

Document Reference: (87051203).

Copyright 1996 - 2006 Chase Bank, N.A. Member FDIC Copyright � 2006

**FIGURE 10.1** Phishing message used in widespread international identity theft scam.

bankcard number, personal identification number (PIN), card verification number, mother's maiden name, and social security number. The entered data was then sent to a form processing service on a server in India. The same IP address at CCB Shanghai was used to host a fake eBay login screen in a similar fraud attempt.

SurfControl (**www.surfcontrol.com**), an Internet content protection company, tracked the new ***phishing kit*** that was distributed to phish for these Chase account numbers. Spam probes used by SurfControl Global Threat Experts have received several different variants of the message, each using a different server, but the source code for each survey page is very similar. At the time, SurfControl had detected a 30 percent increase in phishing kit attacks.

Referring to the March 2006 attack, Susan Larson, vice president of SurfControl's Adaptive Threat Intelligence Service, stated: "Today's threat is like no other we have seen in that the first reported instance of this Chase bank phishing scam was being hosted on a compromised server owned by a bank in China. Even more interesting is that many of the web pages involved in this scam contain nearly identical source code leading us to believe this phishing attack is using a phishing kit and could become more widely distributed" (PR Newswire, 2006).

## Virtual Warfare and Internet-Based Hostilities

Over several months in 2005, a series of attacks believed to have originated in China and South Korea hit dozens of key public and private Web sites hosted in Japan. Authorities described it as the heaviest assault ever perpetrated on the nation's computer systems from overseas (Faiola, 2005).

At an Internet security firm, a team of experts tracked overseas hackers through billions of lines of data on computer screens indicating cyberwarfare aimed at Tokyo.

Occurring about the same time were violent anti-Japanese street protests in Beijing and Shanghai. The angry demonstrations were motivated by strategic rivalry as China's economic power grows and Japan looks to redefine its regional military role. China was opposing Japan's bid to become a permanent member of the U.N. Security Council, saying it is unfit for such leadership until it faces up to its past aggressions in the region. Chinese were also outraged by new textbooks from Japan's education ministry that critics say whitewashed Japan's imperialist history.

A coordinated attack was staged May 1, 2005, against the Web site of the Japanese embassy in Beijing. The attacks caused financial loss and disrupted work at government agencies, businesses, and religious centers. Attacks brought down or defaced the Web sites of the National Police Agency, the Defense and Foreign Ministries, Japanese universities, and companies such as Sony Corporation's subsidiary in China.

**FYI** *Sino–U.S. Cyberwar*

Analysts compared the anti-Japanese campaign to the "Sino–U.S. cyberwar" of 2001. In April 2001, a Chinese fighter jet collided with a U.S. spy plane conducting surveillance off the coast of China. The Chinese jet crashed into the South China Sea, triggering a diplomatic confrontation. In retaliation, hackers in China claimed to have launched attacks on a thousand U.S.-based Web sites.

Itsuro Nishimoto, executive director of the security firm SecureNet, said the Chinese and Korean hackers "used to just have fun with us, but now they have become more vicious and have a clear intent to do damage. These attacks have given us a taste of what role computer systems might play in a real war, in Japan or anywhere" (Faiola, 2005). His company has had to dispatch more emergency response teams to clients and government agencies to cope with the attacks.

In March 2005, tensions between Japan and South Korea grew after Japan reclaimed a group of small islands occupied by South Korea. Anti-Japanese feelings soared in South Korea, where almost half the population accesses the Internet via broadband cable networks.

Internet security companies traced the attacks to locations in both China and South Korea. But the authorities knew that hackers disguise attacks by routing them through other nations, which made it difficult to issue official protests. "We could provide them with the evidence, and they could easily throw it back at us and say, 'You have no proof someone in another country didn't route their attack through us,'" said one Japanese official (Faiola, 2005). In cases dealing with crimes committed outside national borders, and by nations unwilling to cooperate, bringing cybercriminals to justice might be impossible.

Wan Tao, one of China's best-known hackers, suggested that the cyberwar was at least partly precipitated by Japanese hacker attacks on Chinese Web sites. On his Web server, blog postings against Japan were prevalent; and other Web sites in China were soliciting and organizing attacks against Japanese Web sites at specific dates and times.

## Military Espionage

The Pentagon relies on numerous communication systems such as data encryption and GPS-guided missiles. The ever-present military risk is that an adversary will learn about and then disable those systems. FBI officials in an espionage investigation are trying to verify whether communist Chinese spies are hacking into U.S. government computer systems. There is evidence that they are. Finding out who is actually behind the spying is very difficult because officials cannot just jump on a plane and go to China and start questioning people.

In 2002, 40,000 attacks were launched against the Pentagon's computer networks from Chinese Web sites. Two years later, the number doubled to 79,000. The Department of Defense (DOD) won't say if the intruders are operating from China or using the country as a hop.

Michael Wessel, a member of the U.S.–China Economic and Security Review Commission, is confident the Chinese military is behind the cyberattacks. Adversaries unable to counter the U.S. military on the battlefield instead exploit military networks.

With businesses and government agencies relying more heavily on computers and the Internet, opportunities increase for cybercriminals. Governments need to take strong investigative measures to detect and identify intruders who damage computer systems.

**Caution**

**Definition of Botnet**

Botnets are large groupings of hacked, remote-controlled computers or bots used to distribute and install their software. A single botnet can consist of thousands of computers of innocent users who have no idea that a virus infection is allowing a hacker to use their PCs for illegal purposes.

## FYI Botnet Industry

J. James Ancheta, 20, was arrested on charges of spreading viruses to 400,000 military and other computers to gain control over them and turn them into robots, or bots. Among the computers infected were machines operated by the Naval Air Warfare Center in China Lake and the DOD's Defense Information Systems Agency. Ancheta used the botnet together with adware programs so he could profit from spam e-mail attacks. In addition, he charged other hackers and spammers for access to his botnet. He was indicted in November 2005 on 17 federal charges that he used malicious software to seize control of thousands of computers and then sold command of his drone army to spammers and hackers (Menn, 2005).

He came to the attention of investigators after advertising on an Internet chat channel, called botz4sale, the sale of access to the infected computers to spammers and others who said they wanted to launch denial-of-service attacks on corporate Web sites. His ad included a price list. The underground industry is so competitive that the sale of access to 2,000 compromised PCs brings in as little as $400, or 20 cents per machine.

There are an estimated 50 million compromised systems with their computing power for sale to the highest bidder.

## Botnets and Criminal Commerce

The original motives of most hackers were stealing bandwidth or bragging rights. Profit-motivated hackers are much more common today. These hackers, like others discussed in this chapter, have the intent to do harm in pursuit of money and use increasingly stealthy and resilient techniques. In this section, you learn about the latest hacker criminal techniques. These techniques are capable of causing widespread disruption or destruction. Detecting and investigating these cases require investigators to:

- Understand the vocabulary
- Learn how the attacks are orchestrated and executed
- Know the signs and symptoms of an attack
- Understand the motives and tactics of attackers
- Monitor chat rooms where hackers advertise or recruit

These are the topics discussed next.

### Crime Waves of Botmasters

***Bots*** and ***botnets*** are the sources of a significant portion of criminal commerce on the Internet. ***Botmasters,*** the equivalent of Web gangsters or extortionists, who control these computer networks are often the source of DoS attacks. Their extortion demands are for tens of thousands of dollars in protection money from businesses for not attacking them. If the businesses refuse to pay, the criminals order their botnets to flood the Web sites with meaningless traffic, crippling the businesses and costing them thousands or hundreds of thousands of dollars in lost revenue. Figure 10.2 illustrates how a botmaster might configure a botnet using an IRC to launch a large-scale attack.

The typical steps involved in launching a large-scale attack using a botnet and IRC are:

1. A botmaster sends out viruses to infect computers.
2. Infected PCs follow instructions to log in to an IRC server.
3. A spammer (or criminal) buys access to the botnet from the botmaster.
4. The botmaster or spammer sends instructions to the infected PCs using the IRC server, which triggers them to send out spam messages to other servers.

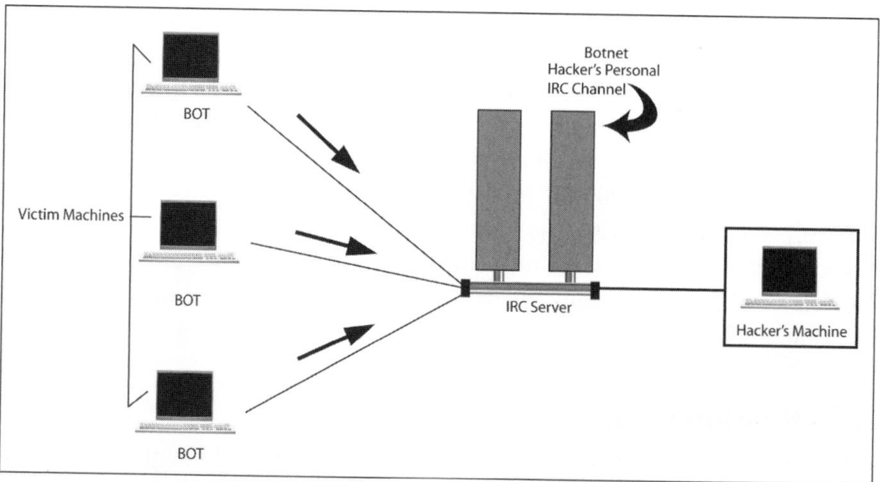


**FIGURE 10.2** Components of an IRC botnet.

### IN PRACTICE: Creating a Botnet—Computer Sleeper Cells

Creating a botnet is a relatively simple process that is very similar to launching a virus attack. In a virus attack, a virus is released that exploits software vulnerabilities to infect one computer, which then transmits the infection to other computers. To create a botnet, hackers exploit the same vulnerabilities, then take one more step by instructing the infected computers to wait for further commands. The computers become computer sleeper cells. A bot-herder can command thousands of bots simultaneously by secretly taking control of a server.

## Botnet Takes Down a Hospital

During 2005, Seattle's Northwest Hospital and Medical Center experienced operational crises. Key cards would not open operating-room doors, computers in the intensive-care unit had shut down, and doctors' pagers would not work. Hospital officials called the FBI immediately, and an agent went to the scene while the attack was in progress. Federal investigators found that the hospital's computers, along with up to 50,000 others across the country, had been turned into a botnet by Christopher Maxwell, 20, of California.

A botnet repeatedly sends out messages looking for computers to attack. The repeated messages tie up computer networks and sometimes shut them down, as they did at Northwest Hospital. No patients were harmed, but First Assistant U.S. Attorney Mark Bartlett said this kind of attack could easily endanger lives.

Maxwell joined an affiliate program with several mainstream adware companies, which pay a commission each time their adware is installed on a computer—regardless of user consent. Maxwell created a program instructing his bots to download the adware. The bots then "phoned home" to the adware company, which credited the hacker's account. Maxwell, along with two juveniles, earned about $100,000 in the process, according to court documents. Maxwell was charged with one count of conspiracy to intentionally damage a protected computer and with one count of intentional computer damage that interferes with medical treatment. The crimes carry a sentence of up to 10 years in prison, a $250,000 fine, and restitution.

### Investigation Challenges

Bot-herders try to hide their activities and cover their tracks with sites such as **www.anonymizer.com** before the computer owner realizes what has happened. What FBI agents described as a "twisted and difficult" trail eventually led them to Maxwell. Investigators found he had hacked into servers at the University of Michigan; California State University, Northridge; and the University of California, Los Angeles, to carry out his plan.

### IN PRACTICE: Criminal Infrastructure Driven by Commercial Interests

In 2004, venture capitalists invested $40 million in a company called 180 solutions to support its growth. The company claimed revenues of more than $50 million delivering online ads for America's corporations, including JPMorgan Chase, Cingular, T-Mobile, Monster.com, and Expedia.com.

By 180's own count, its adware is installed on 20 million computers. The people who use those computers receive pop-up ads based on what they are searching for online. If the user searches for the term "travel," 180's software looks through its database of clients in the travel business and presents an ad from the company that bid the most on that search term. The next time the user searches using the same term, 180 serves the ad of the next-highest bidder for that word, and so on. 180 then gets paid from 1.5 to 2.5 cents for each ad it delivers to the user. The more computers with 180's adware, the more revenue each ad generates.

According to a survey by the National Cyber Security Alliance and America Online, 61 percent of home PCs were infected with spyware and adware in 2005, but this was a decrease from the 80 percent infected rate in 2004 (Kawamoto, 2005).

### Bot-Herder 0x80

Bot-herder 0x80 (pronounced X80) controlled over 13,000 computers in more than 20 countries. He staggers the installation of spyware on his commandeered PCs at the rate of a few hundred at a time to avoid detection. After typing the command "pstore" (short for password store), he sees on his computer screen a listing of every user name and password that the owner of each infected computer has stored in the Microsoft Internet Explorer Web browser on her computer.

---

## Tracking Criminals' Trails

Hackers, terrorists, and others with the intent to do harm are criminals. For simplicity, the term *criminals* will be used here to refer to all those who are involved in large-scale criminal activity. The investigative objectives are familiar to you.

1. Identify the perpetrator.
2. Identify the method or vulnerability of the network that allowed the perpetrator to gain access into the system.
3. Conduct a damage assessment.
4. Preserve the evidence for trial or legal action.

### Tracking the Creator of the Melissa Virus

The Melissa virus was first released on March 26, 1999, and distributed via e-mail. Damages were estimated at $1.2 billion. Melissa's creator, David L. Smith, was arrested within two weeks of its release. E-evidence that led to his identity consisted of the following. As with almost all cases, the significance of the e-evidence may not be apparent until later evidence links it to the perp.

- **Hardware ID:** Instrumental in tracing Melissa's origins were unique hardware numbers, known as GUIDs, that were stored in Microsoft Office 97 document files. This meant that the Melissa file contained a digital print traceable to the computer on which it was created.
- **AOL return address:** The virus's original post contained an AOL address.
- **AOL's log files:** AOL had a record of the phone line used to make the posting. It belonged to David Smith.

Having learned that David L. Smith was a person of interest, the investigation continued, focused on him. The FBI investigated Smith's:

- Bulletin board postings and all e-mail addresses.
- Online names, including VicodinES, and his characteristic signatures, which are any traits that characterize the virus creator. (The significance of this e-evidence would be learned later.)

Investigators discovered that:

- Smith's e-mail indicated his interest in viruses.
- VicodinES's e-mail referred to DLSmith and was sent from an e-mail account that included the name Smith.
- Both Smith and VicodinES signed off with "peace," which was a key signature.

Smith tried to hide incriminating evidence by deleting files related to Melissa from his PC. He even tried to destroy the computer and disposed of his PC in his apartment complex's trash bin. Those attempts were not clever enough to throw off the FBI. David L. Smith became the first person prosecuted for spreading a computer virus.

From this case, you learn that the process of collecting electronic evidence in computer hacking cases generally divides into three steps.

1. It begins with the collection of stored evidence from third-party servers.
2. It turns next to prospective surveillance.
3. It ends with the forensic investigation of the suspect's computer.

These three steps encompass the basic mechanisms of digital evidence collection:

1. Collecting digital evidence while in transit.
2. Collecting digital evidence stored with friendly third parties.
3. Collecting digital evidence stored with hostile parties such as the target.

Each mechanism presents unique facts and requires special considerations.

The first investigative step is obtaining stored records from the system administrators of the various computer servers used in the attack. If a hacker connected to five computers, for example, to commit the attack, each server should have retained records of the connection. Those records need to be assembled to trace back the attack through the intermediary computers to the ISP in a step-by-step manner. This tedious procedure is required because the packets contain only their immediate origin and destination points. The ISP should be able and willing to reveal the identity of the user based on IP address and exact time of the transmission. But even with a full audit trail showing that a user came from a particular account on a particular ISP, only billing information for the account is available. Sometimes this is sufficient. Other times, the identity cannot be determined because the account may have been stolen, set up with false billing information, or shared with others.

## Hackers Won't Claim Prize Money

Mac enthusiast Colin Nederkoorn kicked off a competition to see if it was possible for two operating systems, Apple's OS X and Microsoft's Windows XP, to run independently on an Apple computer. The winners would receive $13,854 in prize money.

However, the prize money is unlikely to be collected by the verified winners. The winners of the contest are hackers who want to maintain their anonymity and are known only by the handles "narf" and "blanka."

### Tracking Criminals in IRC

Another way to track criminals is in chat rooms. Criminals meet in IRCs to advertise, learn, or teach their skills. They may also discuss their personal lives. To be a truly effective investigator, you must become familiar with the social culture of these criminals.

System logs help track down criminals because they hold evidence that a crime has been committed and where the intrusion occurred. System logs cannot identify the intruder; that is, who was physically using the keyboard. However, in an IRC, that identity might be found.

Hackers often do not connect to IRC directly. By using a variety of hosts, a hacker can subvert a ban or trick others into thinking he is someone else. Usually a hacker's goal is to hide his real IP address so no one can monitor him.

A ***bounce program*** reads from one port and writes to another; that is, it is a proxy. The most famous bounce programs are BNC (which is the word *bounce* without the vowels) and WinGate. Both accept a TCP connection, connect to a destination, and then relay anything from the original connection to the destination. If a hacker has access to a WinGate, he can bounce through the WinGate server to hide his tracks.

Even if a complete audit trail shows that an intruder came from a specific account on a specific ISP, the only evidence will be billing information for the account, which does not prove identity. The account might have been stolen, set up with fake billing information, or shared. It is possible for the IRC administrator to "listen" to the hacker on IRC using sniffer software and review configuration information on IRC tools left behind. Just as the content of e-mail messages may help reveal identity, as with David L. Smith, a hacker might brag about compromising a company's network, which may constitute a full confession if she is logged in. IRC tools may be configured to permit particular ISP connections, which may help in tracking down their location. From a set of data from logs and sniffed content, deductive reasoning can be applied to track down a hacker, including name, location, and characteristic signatures.

When hackers use IRC, administrators can monitor their actions and learn about their methodologies and habits. This knowledge helps investigators track criminals more effectively.

## Summary

In this chapter, you learned about methods used by those intent on causing harm on a large scale. The same challenges that face investigators of small cases involving one or a few individuals apply to large-scale cases. Each type of forensics, namely e-mail, network, data, cell phone, and IRC forensics, come into play when investigating terrorists, cyberextortionists, hackers, and botmasters. It is critical to understand their motives and methods, intelligence activities, and concealment tactics.

Investigations of these criminals require the resources and cooperation of the FBI, other federal agencies, and foreign governments. Computer forensics experts may be called upon to support these agencies and defend against crimes aimed at destroying human life, critical infrastructures, or private property.

## Test Your Skills

### MULTIPLE CHOICE QUESTIONS

1. Finding out as much as possible about the intruder's identity
   A. is impossible, so the focus needs to be on identifying the damage.
   B. is the first step in large-scale investigations.
   C. includes learning about the intruder's motives and affiliations.
   D. Both B and C.

2. The DoS attack originating from Aaron Caffrey's computer against the Texas Port of Houston that crashed the port's Web servers was *unique* in that
   A. officials believed it to be the first electronic attack to disable a critical part of a country's infrastructure.
   B. Caffrey claimed he was an innocent victim because a Trojan-horse program had been installed on his PC by malicious hackers.
   C. he was convicted under the Computer Misuse Act by the jury.
   D. because he was a citizen of England, he could not be tried in an American court of law.

3. Which of the following is *not* true when dealing with a large-scale crime?
   A. At the outset, investigators may observe only a small segment of a larger crime or attack.
   B. A reasonable judgment has to be made about whether the attack is isolated or an instance of a large-scale plot.
   C. The case must be fully investigated.
   D. Decisions regarding the case may need to be made by a team of experts.

4. What features make the Internet a good conduit for coordinating and carrying out a criminal agenda?
   A. Anonymity.
   B. Command and control resources.
   C. Global reach.
   D. All of the above.

5. __________ refers to the digital coordination of an integrated plan stretching across geographical boundaries that may or may not result in bloodshed.
   A. Cyberterrorism
   B. Cyberplanning
   C. Criminal intent
   D. Cybersynchronization

6. Why do terrorist groups perform word searches of online media to find vulnerabilities in computer systems?
   A. For intelligence purposes.
   B. To get sympathy for their cause.
   C. For recruiting purposes.
   D. For extortion purposes.

7. Jean-Francois Ricard, an antiterrorism investigator, pointed out that many Islamist terror plots in Europe and North America were financed from funds acquired through
   A. donations from supporters received via al Qaeda Web sites.
   B. electronic fund transfers.
   C. credit card fraud.
   D. hacks into large commercial banks.

8. Some military experts suggest that
   A. war between major nations is becoming obsolete.
   B. future defense will rely more heavily on intelligence officers with databases than upon tanks and artillery.
   C. increasing animosities between Japan and China pose a serious threat.
   D. A and B

9. The March 2006 phishing scam where the Shanghai branch of China Construction Bank's server hosted spoofed Web sites was used
   A. for identity theft of customers of American banks and Web-based businesses.
   B. to launch DoS attacks against Japan's Department of the Ministry.
   C. to distribute propaganda against South Korea's imperialism.
   D. for cyberextortion against major U.S. banks.

10. Which statement is true about military espionage?
    A. The Pentagon has decreased its reliance on vulnerable communication systems, such as data encryption and GPS-guided missiles.
    B. Adversaries who are unable to counter the U.S. military on the battlefield try to exploit military networks to reduce their disadvantage.
    C. Between 2002 and 2004, there was a 10 percent increase in the number of attacks against the Pentagon's computer networks launched from Chinese Web sites.
    D. The DOD releases all information about intruders to keep citizens and other nations aware of current dangers.

11. How did J. James Ancheta come to the attention of investigators?
    A. From e-evidence found on Naval Air Warfare Center computers that he had infected.
    B. From adware programs he remotely installed on thousands of computers.
    C. From advertising in the IRC channel botz4sale.
    D. From e-evidence obtained from DoS attacks on corporate Web sites.

12. What are botnets?
    A. A large number of virus-infected PCs.
    B. Numerous remote-controlled computers used to distribute and install software.
    C. A network of adware-infected PCs shared by marketing agencies.
    D. Tools used to conceal the identity of spammers.

13. What e-evidence helped investigators quickly identify the identity of the Melissa creator?
    A. Hardware GUID.
    B. AOL log files.
    C. AOL return e-mail address.
    D. All of the above.

14. Which is *not* one of the three basic mechanisms for collecting evidence of hacking activity?
    A. Collecting digital evidence from chat rooms and instant messages.
    B. Collecting digital evidence while in transit.
    C. Collecting digital evidence stored with friendly third parties.
    D. Collecting digital evidence stored with hostile parties such as the target.

15. What do hackers use to conceal the identity of their IP addresses?
    A. Bots.
    B. Phishing sites.
    C. Bounce programs.
    D. Encryption.

## EXERCISES

### Exercise 10.1: Using the Internet for Intelligence Purposes



It is important to consider how terrorists use the Internet and digital resources for intelligence purposes. *Intelligence* refers to information that provides insight and context for developing alternative courses of action and then deciding among them. Intelligence is used to assess the effectiveness (outcome) of pursuing a course of action.

1. Make a list of five different types of Internet sites (e.g., banks or nuclear energy) that might be used by a terrorist or extremist group to gather intelligence information.
2. Explain what intelligence might be gained from each of these types of Internet sites.

### Exercise 10.2: U.S. National Intelligence Strategy

Download and read the National Intelligence Strategy of the United States of America (dated October 2005) from the Web site of the U.S. Department of National Intelligence at **www.dni.gov** or directly from **www.dni.gov/publications/NISOctober2005.pdf.**

1. Make a list of three objectives of U.S. national intelligence.
2. Explain the "new approach" to national intelligence proposed by John D. Negroponte, Director of National Intelligence.

### Exercise 10.3: Factors Affecting Hacker Threat Level

Consider the model: Intent + Capability = Threat.

According to this model, the two factors that determine the threat level are intent and capability. The greater the intent and capability, the greater the threat.

1. Identify four digital resources that provide or enhance the capability to carry out a hacker attack.
2. Explain the type or location of e-evidence left by these resources.
3. State whether that e-evidence could be used to prevent an attack. Explain why or why not.

### Exercise 10.4: Botnets

1. Refer to the description of the activities of J. James Ancheta that led to the federal charges against him.
2. Identify each of the tools and techniques he used to conduct his bot business. Classify each tool or technique as either relatively new or old (e.g., viruses). Are most of them old or new?
3. In your opinion, are botnets a new technology or a new application of older existing technology? Explain your opinion.

### Exercise 10.5: Hacker and Criminal Commerce Cases

Detecting and investigating hacker and criminal commerce cases require understanding the vocabulary, hackers' motives and tactics, chat rooms, how attacks are orchestrated and executed, and the signs and symptoms of an attack.

1. You have been tasked with helping investigators understand and keep current about those issues and methods. Create a list of at least five online resources that would help investigators get up-to-date or stay current.
2. Briefly explain each resource.

## PROJECTS

### Project 10.1: Distinguishing a Large-Scale Attack from an Accidental Crisis

Consider the massive power blackout in New York City on August 14, 2003. When the power grid crashed just days after the outbreak of the destructive Blaster worm, many people feared that the blackout represented a digital Pearl Harbor or another act of terrorism. Within hours of the blackout, CNN reported from the paralyzed streets of Manhattan that U.S. officials were investigating the possibility that Blaster had caused the outage.

In the 10 months after the blackout, no evidence linking Blaster to the outage was found. An exhaustive report written by a joint U.S.–Canadian committee formed to study the blackout's effects determined there was no connection to any deliberate malicious attack on the power companies' computers.

1. Explain why the initial fears were that the blackout was caused by a large-scale computer worm or cyberterrorist attack.
2. Explain why the investigation into a connection between a malicious attack and the blackout might have taken 10 months to verify.
3. List the types of e-evidence the investigators may have examined.

### Project 10.2: Assessing the Threat of Criminal Acts

In the months following the terrorist attacks of September 11, 2001, counterterrorism became the highest priority for the FBI and Secret Service, the two federal agencies responsible for most of the government's cybercrime investigations. That shift took its toll on the computer crime units at both agencies, and nearly 20 Secret Service agents who were working on cybercrime at the time of the attacks were transferred to terrorism investigations.

You have been tasked with assessing the threat of cyberterrorism and threat of cybercrime and determining whether one poses a greater threat than the other.

1. Research an online database or the Internet for articles discussing the threat of each of these criminal acts. You might visit EWeek.com at **www.eweek.com** or Forbes at **www.forbes.com.**
2. Review cases of cybercrime and cyberterrorism.
3. Research how likely it is that cybercrime and cyberterrorism will occur. Should resources be reallocated back to cybercrime investigations?
4. Write a report of your assessment.

## Project 10.3: Terrorism or Espionage?

Even using advanced computer forensic methods, law enforcement officials sometimes cannot identify or verify the identity of the individual hackers behind virus and hacker attacks. These hacks may be the product of industrial espionage rather than terrorism. For example, Hong Kong, a key financial center, is a hotbed for cyberattacks on its financial services industry.

Several experts believe that some of the hacker attacks may be a kind of training exercise for terrorists. A number of terrorist organizations have developed rudimentary technical skills. For example, in 1997, the Tamil Tigers, a Sri Lankan rebel army known for terrorist bombings and assassinations, hacked into and shut down the servers of Sri Lanka's embassies in Seoul and Washington. Why haven't they done more of it? Bruce Hoffman, a terrorism expert with the Rand Corporation, hypothesizes that they didn't need to because their conventional weapons, guns and bombs, were sufficient.

But the new war on terrorism has hindered terrorists' ability to operate elaborate base camps and has dramatically tightened security for physical infrastructure at airports, power plants, and government buildings. If that is the case, then cyberwarfare may represent a safer, more effective alternative. According to Hoffman, "You don't need training camps or a robust logistical and intelligence support structure. . . just a modem and a safe house. . . This is the ultimate anonymous attack."

1. Identify at least two difficulties when investigating the identity of the individual hackers behind virus and hacker attacks.
2. In your opinion, is the difference between a hacker attack and a terrorist attack primarily the intent of the attacking group?
3. Consider Hoffman's assessment of the shift toward cyberwarfare due to hardened security efforts. Research whether his assessment is valid.
4. Write a report explaining the extent to which you believe that Hoffman's assessment is valid.

The Kosovo crisis was the first known major use of information warfare. In 1999, during the Kosovo crisis and NATO bombing campaign, Yugoslav hackers reportedly launched a DoS attack against a NATO Web site with viruses and thousands of e-mails daily. Serbian supporters clogged nonmilitary Internet sites in the United States. In the "first cyberwar," Serbian supporters also used e-mail to warn of NATO strikes and to send messages of support.

After NATO mistakenly bombed the Peoples' Republic of China (PRC) embassy in Belgrade, PRC-based sources brought down the U.S. White House Web page and defaced the U.S. embassy Web site in Beijing.

The U.S. military has acknowledged that NATO's air war against Serbia included "limited" computer warfare. The United States used computer attacks on Yugoslav President Milosevic's and other Serbian leaders' foreign bank accounts in 1999.

Earlier, during the 1990–1991 Gulf War, hackers in the Netherlands reportedly offered to help Iraq by penetrating and attacking coalition information networks, but Iraq rejected the offer.

Adapted from George K. Walker. *Conflicts and Computer-Based Attacks: Information Warfare and Neutrality.* **law.vanderbilt.edu/journal/33-05/33-5-1.html** (accessed March 20, 2006).

1. Create a list of each use of the Internet in the conflicts described in the Case Study. Classify each use as either a criminal or noncriminal use. Explain the reason for each classification.
2. Search online databases or the Internet for information about examples of Internet resources or Internet-based attacks that have been used in the war with Iraq. Draft a report describing those resources or attacks and where e-evidence of their existence might be found.
3. In your opinion, how does an investigation of cyberwarfare activities differ from an investigation of profit-motivated hacker attacks?

# Chapter 11

# Fraud and Forensic Accounting Investigation

## Chapter Objectives

**After reading this chapter and completing the exercises, you will be able to do the following:**

- Understand the challenges of fraud investigations.
- Describe the common types of fraud committed against and on behalf of companies and organizations.
- Explain the characteristics and symptoms of fraud.
- Identify the role of computer forensics in fraud detection and deterrence.
- Understand the purposes of forensic accounting investigations and how to participate in them.

## Introduction

Fraud is a crime that is carried out using deceit instead of a weapon. The fraudster may deceive others by lying, concealing facts, or somehow misrepresenting the truth to cause them to act to their disadvantage. It can be a trick or a dishonest act to deprive others of their money or property. An essential element of fraud is ***intent,*** or the conscious desire and will to deceive. Under the law, there is no such thing as an "accidental" or "negligent" fraud. Finding someone guilty of fraud requires showing intent, or *mens rea* (mental state, "guilty mind"). Often evidence of intent is found in e-mail or other electronic correspondence. As evidence that Merrill Lynch's stock analyst Henry Blodget intended to deceive investors, prosecutors produced several e-mails in which Blodget disparaged stocks at the same time that he was recommending them. In one e-mail, Blodget referred to InfoSpace as a "powder keg" and their stock as a "piece of junk," yet he published a "buy" recommendation stating, "InfoSpace continues to be one of the best ways to play the wireless Internet." Blodget was convicted of fraud and other securities violations.

Frauds involving dishonesty in business, such as cheating customers or insider trading on the stock market, are also referred to as *white collar crimes.* When managers commit fraud that impacts a company's financial statements, those frauds are investigated by the offices of district attorneys, attorneys general, or the SEC. In cases involving fraudulent financial reporting issues, such as listing phony assets or concealing debts, a forensic accounting investigation is conducted. Forensic accounting investigations are a specific type of fraud investigation used, for example, to distinguish between cases of illegal criminal fraud and legal "creative accounting." Fraud investigators of all types typically include the search for e-evidence of concealing, altering, or destroying documents or financial transactions.

This chapter helps you understand fraud and forensic accounting cases so that you understand and effectively participate as a computer forensics investigator in such cases. Computer forensics and electronic discovery tools to discover and compile electronic evidence have proven necessary to prosecute acts of fraud. This method leads to the most incriminating evidence because people are candid and careless with e-mail and instant messaging—and they like to gloat or confess this way.

---

## Challenges of Fraud Investigations

As you learned in Chapter 1, it is critical to ask the right questions at the outset of an investigation. When fraud is suspected, some of those questions are:

- Has fraud been committed? Is the fraud still going on? Who might have done it? Who might have been involved?
- Did someone break into the network? Did an employee gain access to a system, such as payroll or payments systems, beyond the level of their authority? How?
- Has someone overridden the controls in a financial system? How?
- How do we prevent what has happened from happening again?

If fraud is detected, it is always advisable to do a thorough forensic investigation of all computers and other devices where documentation might have originated or be stored. A complete and thorough probe is conducted to determine the nature, scope, and duration of the fraudulent transactions in question. The investigator retrieves user-access log-on reports, time and date stamp reports, and other system log reports that establish what events occurred, whose user identification was associated with each event, and which application systems were involved. As with any forensics investigation, fraud and accounting cases involve creating a complete reconstruction of the incident in question. Forensics rules must be strictly followed or evidence will not be admissible.

## Scope of Fraud

Fraud is on the rise in both scope and scale—and no organization is immune. The number of business and financial transactions being conducted online has opened new ways to commit fraud as well as new types of fraud. The problem is so extensive that the FBI has labeled fraud the fastest growing crime and committed approximately 24 percent of its resources to fighting fraud (Albrecht and Albrecht, 2004).

Given that every organization suffers from fraud, computer forensics experts can expect to be involved in investigations of suspected corporate and ***occupational fraud.*** In its *2004 Report to the Nation on Occupational Fraud and Abuse* (**www.cfenet.com/pdfs/2004RttN.pdf**), the Association of Certified Fraud Examiners (ACFE) defined occupational fraud as "The use of one's occupation for personal enrichment through the deliberate misuse or misapplication of the employing organization's resources or assets."

Examples of occupational fraud help illustrate how challenging they are to investigate and the huge losses that can result.

- A multinational fraud case involved 90 computers in 18 countries and required searching 2.6 million e-mail messages (Tait, 2005). The investigation was in response to allegations that revenues of a manufacturer had been manipulated deliberately to show high profitability. This resulted in inflated bonuses to senior staff. After the six-month investigation, incriminating e-mail messages revealed that senior staff members were behind the accounting fraud. Some were dismissed and asked to repay their bonuses.
- In 2001, two former accountants at Cisco Systems, Inc., received 34-month jail terms for using their access privileges to Cisco's computer systems to credit themselves with nearly $8 million in company stock (Leibs, 2002).
- A former database administrator at Prudential Insurance Co. was charged with money laundering, credit card fraud, and identity theft. He was alleged to have copied personal information on 60,000 employees and attempted to sell the data over the Internet (Leibs, 2002).
- As part of a series of internal probes into possible fraud and corruption among San Diego city employees, federal investigators searched the computer databases of employees' e-mail and other documents, which private computer forensics consultants had compiled for the government

in late 2005 (Hall, 2005). A 240GB database was needed to hold that e-evidence. In addition, an independent investigation team from Kroll, Inc., a New York risk-management firm, was hired by the city council to conduct an investigation related to failures to disclose the depth of a $1.4 billion pension deficit. In order for the audit committee to perform their work, a database had to be created to store and organize the data. The city council paid an independent company, Electronic Evidence Discovery, Inc., a Washington firm, $727,500 in September 2005 to create the database for the auditors.

The frauds at Cisco and Prudential show how employees with computer access and technical proficiency can easily exploit weaknesses in internal controls to electronically steal millions of dollars. As the City of San Diego's fraud investigation illustrates, independent forensics companies may be needed to support government agencies. The use of independent computer forensics investigators is not uncommon. Not only does using an independent firm help avoid perceptions of a coverup by providing an assurance of objectivity, it may also be needed if the government agencies cannot investigate quickly because of their workload.

## Fraud to Trial Process

Most investigations carried out to find fraud originate from one of six sources:

1. Internal audits
2. Outside or external audits
3. Regulatory inquiries, primarily by the SEC
4. Shareholder actions, such as class action lawsuits
5. Complaints from customers or vendors
6. Anonymous tips

Regardless of the source, there are general steps in the process from the time a fraud is committed until the case goes to trial, which are shown in Figure 11.1. The work of fraudsters can be detected only after enough damage has been done to arouse suspicion. It is important to act quickly and efficiently to find sufficient preliminary evidence of a fraud, if it exists, to warrant investing in a full-scale investigation. Expediency is important because the person may still be defrauding the company, its trading partners, or its stakeholders.



**FYI** Corporate Fraud

See *Significant Criminal Cases and Charging Documents* of the President's Corporate Fraud Task Force at **www.usdoj.gov/dag/cftf/cases.htm.**

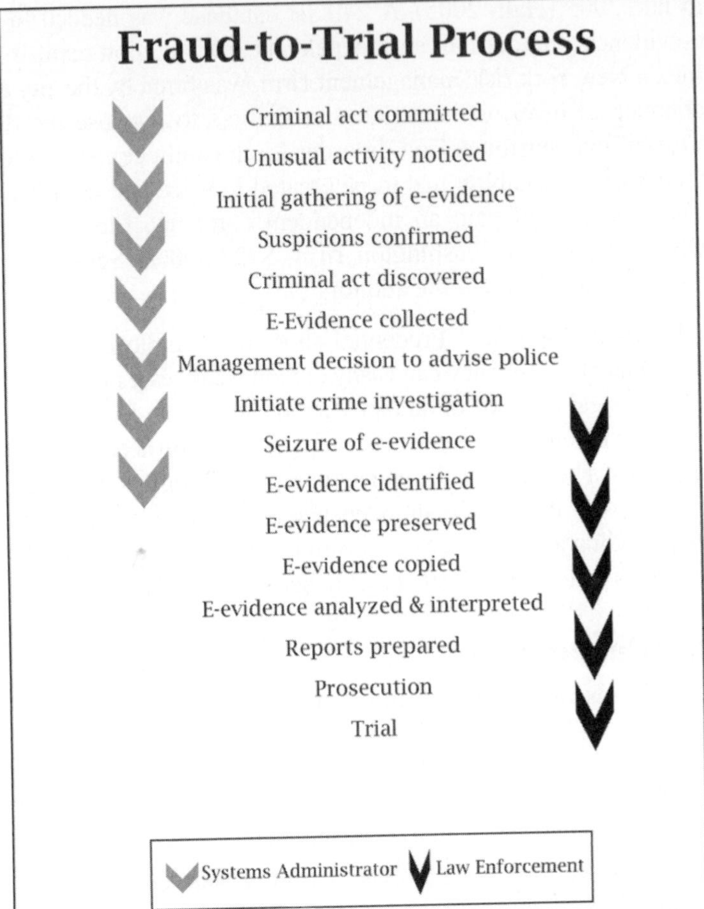


**FIGURE 11.1** Steps in the fraud-to-trial process.

## Special Protection Considerations

In suspected occupational (or employment) fraud cases, investigations pose special challenges. They often need to be done covertly at night when suspects are away from their offices. The investigators may need to respond quickly and make a forensic copy of the hard drive and other media without disturbing anything that might alert the employee—or anyone else. The investigation must be kept secret to avoid the risk of harming someone's reputation. A cautious approach is also necessary to protect companies from exposure to lawsuits.

In addition, the ways that documents are collected, organized, and used need careful consideration at the outset of every fraud investigation. In particular, the investigation team must have a good understanding of the ***law of***

***privilege*** and how it relates to both contemporaneous documents and the ***work product*** of the investigation. Privileged information is protected by law from being released. Work product consists of notes, reports about conversations with a client or witness, or other confidential materials that an attorney has created while representing a client. A work product may not be released, even through a subpoena, because it contains the confidential tactics or theories to be used by the attorney.

Once the search is conducted, electronic documents need to be reviewed to verify whether they are relevant and, if so, whether any are considered privileged and therefore protected. The review process is labor-intensive and requires significant human intervention.

An additional complication occurs when one component of a document is privileged and another is not, such as an e-mail that has an attachment. Special protection requirements make it necessary for computer forensics investigators to team with legal experts to avoid compromising the case or violating a person's rights.

Other legal elements of fraud that impact the investigation are discussed in the following section.

**Caution**

**Investigator Independence**

Forensics experts are needed in fraud investigations because of their specialized experience and objectivity. Their reports carry an impartiality that might not be true of reports from a company's auditors.

## Legal Elements of Fraud

In order for an act to be considered a fraud, the law requires that certain conditions be met. Fraud—both criminal and civil fraud—depends on intentional (willful) acts of ***misrepresentation.*** Misrepresentation is a false statement. Under common law, specific elements are required to prove fraud:

1. A material false statement
2. An intent to deceive (i.e., ***scienter,*** the person had knowledge that the statement was wrong)
3. A victim's reliance on the statement
4. Damages to the victim

Something is ***material*** if it is relevant and significant to the situation. These elements are more fully outlined in Table 11.1.

Note that in all fraud cases, the prosecution or plaintiff must prove that the deceit, concealment, or false statement was intentional and part of a deliberate scheme to defraud.

**Proving Intent** What separates error from fraud is *intent*. Assume a company's financial statements contain material false statements: Were they caused by error or fraud? The ability to provide convincing evidence of error or intent is critical. The problem with proving intent is that it requires determining a person's state of mind. As a result, intent usually is proven circumstantially.

**TABLE 11.1** Legal elements of fraud.

| Legal Elements of Fraud | Instances of a Fraud | Evidentiary Issues | Types of Cases the Element Applies To |
|---|---|---|---|
| A material false statement (misrepresentation) or concealment of a material fact . . . | An individual (perp) deceives another (victim) by making a false or deceitful representation. | Demonstrating *materiality* means showing that statements made by the suspected fraudster were not only false but furthered the act of fraud.<br>Proof that the concealed fact was material is an important factor. There is no liability, or fraud, if the withheld or concealed information had no effect on the other party. | Applies to civil cases and criminal cases. |
| . . . made with knowledge of its falsity . . . | The perp knew the representation was false. | Only deliberate misrepresentations are actionable as fraud. Accidental misrepresentations do not qualify as an element of fraud. | Applies to civil cases and criminal cases. |
| . . . which is relied upon by the victim . . . | The representation was intended to provoke or lead to an action by the victim. | In civil suits, plaintiffs (victims) must show they relied upon the information. | Applies only to civil cases.<br>The government is not required to show that anyone ever actually fell for the fraudulent representation, just that a misrepresentation was made with fraudulent intent. |

CONTINUED ON NEXT PAGE

▶▶ CONTINUED

| Legal Elements of Fraud | Instances of a Fraud | Evidentiary Issues | Types of Cases the Element Applies To |
|---|---|---|---|
| . . . who suffers damages as a result. | The victim suffered some damage or loss because he reasonably assumed the representation was true. | In civil suits, plaintiffs must show they actually suffered damages as a result of a fraudulent act. In some criminal prosecutions, prosecutors do not have this burden of proof. | Applies only to civil cases. In a criminal trial, prosecutors do not have to show that the fraud caused damage to another party; only that it was intended to defraud someone. |

Some of the ways to help prove intent by circumstantial evidence include:

- **Motive.** The motive for fraud is a strong circumstantial element.
- **Opportunity.** In addition to motive, it helps to show that the fraudster had opportunity to commit the fraud.
- **Repetitive acts.** A majority of frauds continue and even escalate. If the investigator can find multiple examples of the same "error," it is much more difficult for the fraudster to claim the fraud was unintentional.
- **Concealment.** Destruction of documents prior to an audit or investigation could be powerful circumstantial evidence of intent.

Sometimes intent is uncovered simply by reading an employee's e-mail, which can provide evidence in the form of thank-you notes to business partners whose lavish gifts have clearly been provided in return for special treatment.

### Showing the Victim Relied on the False Statement and Was Harmed

In civil suits, even when there is a material false statement and the intent to deceive can be proved, the case does not meet the legal test for fraud unless a victim relied on the false statement and suffered harm as a result.

The final legal element of fraud concerns damages—usually in terms of money. In some federal criminal cases—for example, bank frauds—an actual loss is not required. But normally even when there is a material false statement, intent, and victim reliance, there is no fraud if the victim is not damaged. For example, if shareholders suffered no damage because the fraud had no effect on the stock price, there would not be a lawsuit.

**Caution**

**High-Dollar Crimes**

Federal law is often used to prosecute high-dollar or unusually serious crimes, primarily because of the extensive resources of federal law enforcement agencies and their nationwide jurisdiction.

### Tough Fraud Requirements

A plaintiff in a traditional negligence case can file a claim by simply making the accusation—for example, that the defendant's lack of attention while driving caused an accident—without including any details or supporting evidence. Under the Federal Rules of Civil Procedure, fraud claims have to meet tougher requirements than many other civil actions. Rule 9(b) says that the plaintiff's grievance must be stated with "particularity." That is, a fraud plaintiff has to make the plea in detail:

- What misrepresentations were made
- To whom the misrepresentations were made
- How they were false
- Why the plaintiff relied on them

**Caution**

**Finding Fraud**

Companies will not find fraud unless they search for it.

Assume an unscrupulous individual (debtor) has filed for bankruptcy. The trustee responsible for investigating the debtor in an attempt to recover assets for creditors needs to conduct a digital forensic accounting investigation. Trustees have the duty to investigate the financial affairs of the debtor and to ensure that financial records are properly turned over to them. Computer forensics experts would be retained by the trustee to properly investigate financial data and business assets stored in computer databases. You'll learn more about digital forensic accounting later in this chapter.

**IN PRACTICE: Bank Fraud and Conspiracy**

In October 2005, Kenneth J. Flury, 41, was sentenced to 32 months in prison and three years of supervised release for bank fraud and conspiracy (DOJ Computer Crime Case, Feb. 28, 2006). From April 15, 2004, to May 4, 2004, Flury obtained stolen CitiBank debit card account numbers, PINs, and personal identifier information of the true account holders, which he then fraudulently encoded onto blank ATM cards. After encoding blank cards with the stolen account information, Flury used the counterfeit ATM over the 3-week period to withdraw cash and obtain cash advances totaling over $384,000 from ATM machines located in the Greater Cleveland area.

CONTINUED ON NEXT PAGE

▶▶ CONTINUED

After Flury fraudulently obtained the funds, he transferred approximately $167,000 of the fraud proceeds via Western Union money transfers to the individuals supplying the stolen CitiBank account information located in Europe and Asia. Law enforcement officers seized approximately $157,080 in cash from Flury on May 5, 2004, and also intercepted an additional $32,345 Flury had attempted to transfer via Western Union to Russia in May 2004.

In addition, Flury was one of 19 defendants indicted by a federal grand jury in New Jersey in October 2004, as a result of the ***Shadowcrew investigation,*** a long-term online undercover investigation. The Shadowcrew investigation was conducted by the U.S. Secret Service targeting domestic and international subjects engaged in identity theft, credit card fraud, and production of false identification documents. Flury consented to the transfer of his New Jersey case to the Northern District of Ohio in 2005 and pleaded guilty to one count of conspiracy in connection with his activities as a moderator and administrator on the Shadowcrew Web site.

## Handling a Fraud Suspect

When investigating a fraud suspect, it is important to recognize that the investigation is part of a legal process. Suspicious documents and electronic documents (e-documents) should be treated as evidence and electronic evidence (e-evidence). Two important factors are the admissibility of evidence and privacy invasion.

To avoid charges of privacy invasion, employees should have agreed to the terms of an acceptable use policy (AUP) which specifies that they have no expectation of privacy regarding their use of company computer equipment.

Follow standard industry practices for evidence handling. Under the "best evidence" rule accepted by courts, if the original documents are lost or destroyed, a copy can substitute for the original. *The following guidelines are not legal advice. They are good advice.*

- Make copies of all suspicious paper documents secretly and keep the copies in a secured location. The copies should be made by an unbiased person.
- Don't tell the suspect that she is going to be interviewed to avoid destruction of evidence.
- Do not interview the suspect in his office or other familiar "comfortable" location. Interview the suspect in a location unfamiliar to him when seeking an admission of guilt. There is a higher probability of obtaining a confession if you create *stress* in the person, who might admit the fraud to reduce the stress.

- Don't show the suspect the evidence, unless necessary for a confession. Let the person assume that you found all incriminating evidence and that the best course of action is to confess.
- Have a verbal confession converted into a written statement and then signed.

### IN PRACTICE: Fifth Amendment Right Against Self-Incrimination

The Fifth Amendment to the U.S. Constitution guarantees that one cannot "be compelled in any criminal case to be a witness against himself." The Fourteenth Amendment applies that guarantee to state cases. Witnesses who are afraid that they could be charged with a crime in the future if they testify may invoke their Fifth Amendment right against self-incrimination. Invoking the right against self-incrimination does not imply that they think they are guilty or have committed a crime. Refusing to testify in court on the basis that the testimony may be self-incriminating is referred to as ***"taking the Fifth."***

This right does not apply in all situations. For example, a person who invoked this right, but could no longer be charged because she had left the company over five years ago (the number of years it typically takes to prepare and prosecute complex white-collar cases), could be forced to testify. It is easy to understand why it takes five years to prosecute a fraud case by considering the complexities of the City of San Diego fraud case.

## Types of Fraud

There are various ways to categorize fraud based on who committed the fraud and who was victimized. ***Internal fraud*** is committed by someone within the organization, such as an executive, manager, or employee. ***External fraud*** is committed by an external party, such as a vendor, supplier, or customer. When fraud is committed against a company, the company is the victim of the fraud. In contrast, when fraud is committed on behalf of a company, the victims may be shareholders, customers, suppliers, or employees. Frauds often are a mixture of both external and internal characteristics. Another very common type of fraud is healthcare fraud, which you will read about later in this section. In the case of healthcare fraud, healthcare providers, patients, and fraudsters may all be involved in submitting false claims to insurance providers or federal organizations such as Medicare.

**TABLE 11.2** Types of fraud and examples.

| Fraud Category | Examples |
|---|---|
| Computer crime | Hacking |
| | Phishing |
| Insider fraud (e.g., employees and managers) | Theft of intellectual property |
| | Payroll fraud |
| | Extortion |
| | Expense account abuse |
| | Misappropriation of assets |
| External fraud (e.g., vendors or customers) | Bribery |
| | Kickbacks |
| | Conflicts of interest |
| | Bid rigging |
| | Price fixing |
| | Duplicate billings |
| | Extortion |
| | False invoices |
| | Bogus vendors |
| | Inventory theft |
| | Theft of intellectual property |
| Misconduct | Conflict of interest |
| | Corruption |
| | Insider trading |
| Customer fraud | Check fraud |
| | Credit card fraud |
| | Fraudulent merchandise returns |
| | Identity theft |



A summary of the types of fraud and examples are listed in Table 11.2. Common healthcare frauds are covered later in this section.

## Fraud Committed Against a Company

Frauds committed against a company tend to take advantage of weaknesses in internal controls. An example of an internal control is accounting software that verifies products have actually been ordered and received by the company before issuing payment for those products.

Types of fraud committed against a company include:

- **Operating-management corruption.** This is also called nonfinancial statement fraud. Typically, this type of fraud occurs *off the books*. The median loss due to corruption is $530,000, which is over six times greater than the $80,000 median loss resulting from misappropriation.
- **Misappropriation of assets.** This fraud is also called ***embezzlement.*** Embezzlement is the theft of money or property by a person to whom it has been lawfully entrusted. It is a type of fraud that involves breaching one's ***fiduciary responsibility.*** A person who was given responsibility over assets, such as money, abuses her position to the detriment of the company. One of the most common instances of embezzlement is employee theft. Employees may have access to company property, creating the opportunity for embezzlement.
- **Conflict of interest.** Often, this type of fraud is a breach of confidentiality. For example, a company that wants to win a bid for a job may convince an employee to reveal bids from competitors. Typically, conflicts of interest involve bribery.
- **Bribery.** This is the use of the power of one's position or money to influence others to support or carry out criminal acts. ***Commercial bribery*** refers to the corruption of a private individual to gain a commercial or business advantage. Courts have held that actions such as lavish gifts and entertainment, payment of travel and lodging expenses, payment of credit card bills, "loans," promises of future employment, and interests in businesses can be bribes if they were given or received with the intent to influence or be influenced.
- **Extortion.** This is often the flip side of a bribery case. ***Extortion*** is defined as the obtaining of property from another when the other party's "consent" has been induced by wrongful use of actual or threatened force or fear. Fear might include the apprehension of possible economic damage or loss. A demand for a bribe or kickback is also extortion. In most states and the federal system, extortion is not a defense to bribery. That is, a person who makes a bribe payment upon demand of the recipient still is culpable for bribery. In New York State, however, extortion may be a defense in certain circumstances.
- **Kickbacks.** An employee, usually in the purchasing department, may receive money for buying from a particular vendor. The kickback may be offered by the vendor or demanded by the employee.

- **Theft of trade secrets.** These thefts include secret formulas, proprietary information such as customer lists, business plans, or other confidential information that has a value to the business and would cause a loss if stolen or disclosed. In order to file a claim against this fraud, the company may need to prove that it exercised due diligence to protect those secrets.

## IN PRACTICE: Kickback and Embezzlement Red Flags

Red flags indicating possible kickback fraud call for a closer look at the activities of the suspects. Behavior that might indicate embezzlement could also be the zealous actions of an honest and loyal company employee, making fraud detection difficult and requiring secrecy in the investigative process.

Red flags of kickbacks include:

- Suspect doesn't take time off.
- Suspect has personal financial problems.
- Suspect's lifestyle is too extravagant for his income.
- Suspect and vendor have a close personal relationship.
- Suspect shows favoritism toward one vendor.
- Suspect makes excessive purchases from one vendor.
- Prices charged are higher than market average.
- Expenditures come in just under the review limit.
- Multiple purchases are made from same vendor over too short a time period.
- Products or services are poor quality.

There are a number of warning signs of embezzlement. Some red flags include:

- Missing documents
- Delayed bank deposits
- Holes in accounting records
- A large drop in profits
- A jump in business with one customer
- Customers complaining about being double billed
- Repeated duplicate payments
- Disproportion between accounts payable and receivable

## Fraud Committed for a Company

Frauds may be committed on behalf of a company for the purpose of improving its profitability. These financial frauds typically involve overvaluing assets, improperly recognizing revenues, or hiding expenses. Often they also involve financial benefit for the perpetrators and ultimately lead to fraud against the company. Forensics accounting investigations are conducted in these types of cases.

There are three main types of frauds committed for a company:

- **Senior management financial reporting fraud.** These frauds typically involve a massive breach of trust and leveraging of power to force others to falsify financial information.
- **Accounting cycle fraud.** These frauds are violations of generally accepted accounting principles (GAAP).
- **Bribery.** These frauds use positional-power or money to influence others.

## Healthcare Fraud

Healthcare fraud has been defined as "the intentional misrepresentation of a material fact submitted on, or in support of, a claim for payment of a healthcare insurance claim, or the theft of money or property belonging to a health plan or health insurance company" (Carozza, 2006). The Health Insurance Portability and Accountability Act (HIPAA) was passed in 1996 to deter healthcare frauds such as those listed in Table 11.3 and impose stiffer penalties for violations.

**TABLE 11.3** Common types of healthcare fraud.

| Fraud | Description | Perpetrated By |
| --- | --- | --- |
| Phantom billing | Charging for services not performed or fabricating claims | Billing or healthcare provider |
| Upcoding | Charging for a more expensive service, such as a visit to a specialist, when the patient was actually treated by a nurse | Billing or healthcare provider |
| Doctor shopping | Visiting multiple doctors to get multiple prescriptions for controlled substances | Patient |

CONTINUED ON NEXT PAGE

| Fraud | Description | Perpetrated By |
|---|---|---|
| Unnecessary care | Giving unnecessary surgeries, tests, or other procedures | Healthcare provider |
| Misrepresenting services | Performing uncovered services but billing insurance companies for different services than are covered | Billing or healthcare provider |
| Unbundling | Charging separately for procedures that are actually part of a single procedure | Billing or healthcare provider |
| Masquerading as health-care professionals | Delivering health-care services without proper license | Fraudster |
| Identity theft | Using another person's health insurance card or identification to obtain health care or to impersonate that individual | Patient |

*Source:* **www.bcbsa.com**.

## Relationship of Job Level and Type of Fraud Committed

Based on the frauds listed in the sections above, it is clear that the type of fraud committed depends on opportunity, which differs based on the person's position in an organization. Of course, that position also determines the person's power to influence or force others to participate in the fraud. An employee who is against participating in a fraud may still do so out of fear of losing her job. Conversely, an employee may willingly participate if given a good enough financial incentive. The following list shows the relationship between a job level and type of fraud.

- Senior Management—financial statement fraud
- Operating Management—bribery and corruption; "off the books"
- Administrative Management—asset misappropriation; "on the books"
- Employees—embezzlement, doctor shopping, identity theft
- Nonemployees, e.g., contractors, suppliers, customers—conflict of interest
- Medical doctors or healthcare providers—phantom billing, upcoding, unnecessary care

11

## IN PRACTICE: Fraudulent Dossier about Saddam's Regime

The British government of Prime Minister Tony Blair maintained that trusted intelligence sources produced a report, or dossier, on Iraq and Saddam Hussein's regime. In reality, the report had been compiled by the Foreign Office and Downing Street staffers and, therefore, did not represent trusted intelligence. It represented whatever slant the Cabinet and Prime Minister wanted to place on Iraq. The following is a description of how that fraud was detected.

The dossier was published as a Microsoft Word file on the Number 10 Downing Street Web site at **www.number-10.gov.uk/.** An interested reader, Richard M. Smith, downloaded the file and examined its metadata. (Smith's article is at **www.computerbytesman.com/privacy/blair.htm.**) Smith extracted the file's revision log, which recorded the previous ten iterations of the document. As shown below, the revision log listed the last ten edits of a document, the names of the people who worked on the document, and the various filenames of the document.

```
Rev. #1: "cic22" edited file "C:\DOCUME~1\phamill\
   LOCALS~1\Temp\AutoRecovery save of Iraq -
   security.asd"
Rev. #2: "cic22" edited file "C:\DOCUME~1\phamill\
   LOCALS~1\Temp\AutoRecovery save of Iraq -
   security.asd"
Rev. #3: "cic22" edited file "C:\DOCUME~1\phamill\
   LOCALS~1\Temp\AutoRecovery save of Iraq -
   security.asd"
Rev. #4: "JPratt" edited file "C:\TEMP\Iraq -
   security.doc"
Rev. #5: "JPratt" edited file "A:\Iraq -
   security.doc"
Rev. #6: "ablackshaw" edited file "C:\ABlackshaw\
   Iraq - security.doc"
Rev. #7: "ablackshaw" edited file "C:\ABlackshaw\
   A;Iraq - security.doc"
Rev. #8: "ablackshaw" edited file "A:\Iraq -
   security.doc"
```

CONTINUED ON NEXT PAGE

▶▶ CONTINUED

```
Rev. #9: "MKhan" edited file "C:\TEMP\Iraq -
   security.doc"
Rev. #10: "MKhan" edited file "C:\WINNT\Profiles\
   mkhan\Desktop\Iraq.doc"
```

Revision logs are hidden and cannot be viewed in Microsoft Word. Smith had written a program to extract and display revision logs and other hidden information in Word .doc files.

The "cic22" in the first three entries of the revision log stands for "Communications Information Centre," a unit of the British Government. The names in the log file were

- Paul Hamill: Foreign Office official
- John Pratt: Downing Street official
- Alison Blackshaw: Personal assistant of the Prime Minister's press secretary
- Murtaza Khan: Junior press officer for the Prime Minister

This evidence indicated that the dossier had not originated from the intelligence agencies, as claimed. The government officials were unaware that entire paragraphs could be recovered from documents that were deleted during the editing process, as well as prior versions of reports and documents using forensic tools.

## Why Fraud Is Not Reported

In the past, many companies have decided not to report fraud or their fraud losses. The most common reasons are:

- Insufficient police resources to investigate it
- Concern that a lengthy investigation will be expensive and not worth the cost
- Concern that the news will harm the brand image or business reputation and scare away customers

However, Section 302 of the Sarbanes-Oxley Act compels companies to report all occupational fraud regardless of the amount of the loss. That is, information on any fraud that involves employees who are involved with internal activities must be reported to auditors—and investigated to learn how to prevent the fraud from happening again.

## Characteristics and Symptoms of Fraud

Consider the following true case. A bookkeeper changed the payee of checks prior to the checks' being issued, then changed them back again to the correct payee. The checks were made payable to the bookkeeper's mortgage company. This went on for several years as she diverted $330,000 in company funds to mortgage payments. She was caught when she was unexpectedly sick for a week. During that time, a temporary bookkeeper found preaddressed checks in her drawer and began an audit.

Fraud is more likely to occur when someone:

1. Feels *pressure* to commit fraud
2. Has the *opportunity* to commit fraud as a result of weak controls or lack of oversight provided
3. Can *rationalize* the fraud

The three factors—pressure, opportunity, and rationalization—are common to every fraud (Albrecht and Albrecht, 2004). Whether the fraud is one that benefits the perpetrators directly, such as employee fraud, or one that benefits the perpetrator's organization, such as management fraud, the three elements are always present. Here is an example of how these factors might lead to management fraud:

- **Pressure.** The need to make earnings look better to meet expectations
- **Opportunity.** A weak audit committee or useless internal controls
- **Rationalization.** Belief that it is necessary to "cook the books" in this quarter to get through a temporary slump and to make up for it in the next quarter

In addition to investigating computer logs and transactions to detect fraud, an investigation of the pressures and opportunities of a suspect can produce a lot of incriminating circumstantial evidence. Understanding what pressures may have motivated the fraud can help direct the investigator to valuable sources of evidence.

### Pressures to Commit Fraud

The pressures that most commonly drive people to commit fraud are financial. Financial pressures can build up over a long period of time or occur suddenly. Examples of financial pressures include:

- Greed
- Living beyond one's means
- High bills or personal debt
- Poor credit
- Personal financial losses

- Unexpected financial needs
- Vices or addictions, such as gambling, drugs, and alcohol
- Expensive extramarital relationships

These pressures are often interrelated, and multiple pressures may exist. For example, poor credit may lead to personal debt. Putting pressure on executives or employees to make target profits may be a good motivator, but when the pressure becomes too intense, people may resort to fraud to *make the numbers.* Vices tend to be the worst or most powerful kind of pressure—and lead to other types of financial pressures.

## Opportunities to Commit Fraud

Weaknesses in an organization that create opportunity for fraud include:

- Lack of controls that prevent or detect fraud
- Overriding of internal controls
- Failure to search out and discipline fraud perpetrators
- Lack of access to information
- Lack of an audit trail, of which the perp is aware

## Rationalizations for Fraud

The fraud factor that is the most difficult to investigate is rationalization, or attitude, because it cannot be seen. Fraudsters might make reference to their pressures or opportunities in e-mail or text messages.

Possibly the greatest danger companies face in financial reporting is that top managers and other employees can rationalize certain questionable behaviors that eventually escalate into massive fraud (Albrecht and Albrecht, 2004).



### IN PRACTICE: Jack Abramoff—E-Records Reveal Fraud Driven by Greed

In February 2006, Jack Abramoff, a formerly powerful Republican lobbyist, agreed to give evidence against top politicians whom he allegedly bribed, in what may be the biggest congressional scandal in U.S. history. Abramoff pleaded guilty to engaging in a conspiracy involving "corruption of public officials," fraud, and tax evasion after agreeing to a deal with federal prosecutors (Glaister, 2006).

CONTINUED ON NEXT PAGE

▸▸ CONTINUED

His e-mails show that he blatantly deceived Indian tribes and did business with people linked to the underworld.

Padding of bills was openly discussed, according to Abramoff's e-mails. In April 2000, Abramoff had lobbyist Shawn Vasell working on a monthly invoice to the Choctaw Indians, telling him to "be sure we hit the $150k minimum. If you need to add time for me, let me know."

Vasell e-mailed back: "You only had 2 hours. We are not even close to this number . . . " Abramoff's reply was: "Add 60 hours for me," and "pump up" the hours for three or four other lobbyists (Schmidt and Grimaldi, 2005).

The Choctaws gave more than $80 million to Abramoff between 2000 and 2003. Not only were tribes paying Abramoff's lobbying firm, they were also paying Abramoff's secret outside partner, Michael Scanlon. Scanlon charged the Indians millions of dollars for public relations work and kicked half the money back to Abramoff. Abramoff and Scanlon referred to their scheme in e-mail as "Gimme Five." E-mail evidence also showed that Abramoff put his money into various political and personal projects.

---

## Fraud Investigation and Deterrence

Red flags indicating fraud might be detected by analyzing data, as shown in the following case. In 2002, a Medicare examiner noticed a significant increase in claims for powered wheelchairs around Dallas, Texas. His review of health insurance payouts for the chairs revealed a 300 percent increase in the region, as well as huge payouts in parts of California and Florida. By the time the inspectors filtered through all the national data for wheelchair payouts, Medicare learned that paid claims had tripled across 21 states in four years. Fraudsters had obtained taxpayer-ID numbers and other data, submitted false claims for $5,000 wheelchairs, and left the country with millions of dollars after evading investigators for four years. Until the data was compiled and analyzed, the fraud could not be detected. Once fraud had been confirmed, the perps were gone, so the government could not recover its losses.

In addition to detecting fraud, computer forensics can actually help prevent fraud by acting as a deterrent. Figure 11.2 illustrates how this is possible. Someone who knows that a computer forensics investigation will detect the fraud and the identity of the fraudster and that the evidence can be used to prosecute is much less likely to commit the fraud in the first place.

Perception of detection is an effective deterrent to fraud. If the company shows its employees that a computer forensics investigator can find out

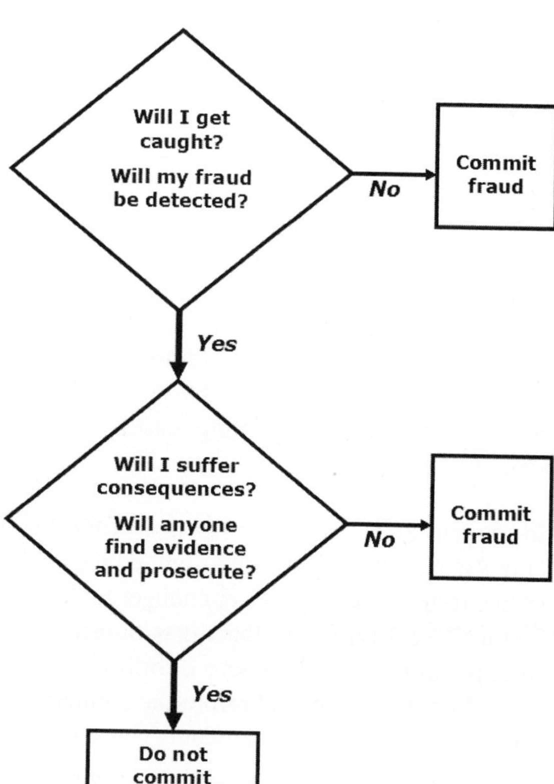


**FIGURE 11.2** Fraud risk assessments.

everything that every employee does and use that evidence to prosecute the person to the fullest extent, then the feeling that "I can get away with it" drops drastically.

11

**FYI** *Healthcare Fraud Escalating Despite HIPAA*

In an effort to deter and control healthcare fraud, HIPAA, an antifraud and privacy law, was passed in 1996. However, as you have already read in this chapter, healthcare fraud is alive and well. Estimates of the amount of U.S. healthcare fraud range from 3 to 5 percent of filed claims. That translated into an estimated $57 billion to $94 billion in losses in 2004. According to Tim Delaney, chief of the FBI's health-care fraud unit, the problem is growing at a 7 to 10 percent annual increase; by 2010, $154 billion in claims a year could be bogus (Babcock and McGee, 2004).

## Digital Forensic Accounting

Forensic accounting involves identifying, collecting, analyzing, and interpreting financial and accounting data with methodologies that produce independent reports and expert individual opinions that will stand up in legal action. Forensic accounting is also referred to as forensic financial investigations. The key distinction between accounting (or financial) audits and forensic accounting (or forensic financial investigations) is the use of proper evidentiary methods to ensure the admissibility of the evidence in legal action.

Three high-profile forensic accounting cases were Adelphia, Global Crossing, and Tyco.

- **Adelphia.** A year after the public learned of the $600 million Enron scandal, the Rigases, the family who founded the cable giant Adelphia, made Enron's fraud look like pocket change. In 2002, Adelphia admitted to "loaning" $2.3 billion to the Rigas family. The SEC uncovered the misappropriation and theft of tens of billions of dollars. In addition to the $2.3 billion the family stole from the company for their personal use, the DOJ claimed that the defendants caused losses to investors of more than $60 billion.
- **Global Crossing.** Corporate insiders knowingly sold more than $1.5 billion of artificially inflated company stock. In April 2005, the SEC filed a settled action for civil penalties against Global Crossing's former CEO, CFO, and VP of finance for aiding and abetting the fraud. Each executive agreed to pay a $100,000 civil penalty.
- **Tyco.** In 2003, the SEC charged former CEO Dennis Kozlowski, CFO Mark Swartz, and Chief Corporate Counsel Mark Belnick with many counts of fraud. Kozlowski and Swartz had swindled over $170 million in corporate loans and pocketed $430 million by manipulating the company's stock price. Belnick was indicted for falsifying business records to hide $17 million in loans given to him by Tyco.

The objective of accounting fraud is to accomplish a desired result by deception, trickery, concealment, or dishonesty. Fraud always involves deception, confidence, and trickery. It is difficult to con anyone out of anything unless the deceived person or company has trust and confidence in the deceiver. Also, fraud depends on trust. Fraud perpetrators are often the least suspected and the most trusted of all the people with whom victims associate.

### FYI: SEC Relaxes Policy on Routine E-Mail Inspection

As of mid-2005, blanket requests for all e-mails are no longer the norm in routine inspections of public companies, according to Gene Gohlke, associate director of the SEC's Commission's Office of Compliance Inspections and Examinations. Public companies are those that file forms with the SEC and raise money from the public, typically through selling stock on a stock exchange.

Blanket requests for e-mail were used extensively after trading scandals that were revealed in 2003. But during 2004 and 2005, that approach turned up less and less information, which led to a change in the SEC e-mails policy. Companies still have a duty to retain all material e-mail and IM messages.

Gohlke also explained that suspects' tactics had changed. The sweeps and requests for e-mail as evidence became so well known that fraudsters switched to the telephone or other methods of communication to further their schemes.

**Caution**

**Change in Perspective**

Accounting maneuvers that were once praised in the financial press as "earnings management" are now attacked in the courtroom as fraud.

Forensic accounting combines three core skills:

1. Forensic and investigative accounting: uncovering the facts
2. Economic loss calculation: establishing the correct numbers
3. Financial valuation: determining business value

When a forensic accounting investigation is needed, an investigative team is created consisting of outside experts with expertise in accounting, fraud, Sarbanes-Oxley compliance issues, e-evidence discovery procedures, and computer forensics techniques. The investigative team can work collaboratively with the company or auditors to unscramble complex transactions, reconstruct events from incomplete or corrupt data, uncover relevant evidence, trace funds and assets, prepare reports, and testify regarding their findings.

### IN PRACTICE: Government and Nonprofit Organizations

Accounting fraud is easy to commit and hard to detect, even in government agencies. There are countless ways to hide fiscal malfeasance. The problem may be worse in government and nonprofit entities that rarely have adequate accounting and internal control systems.

CONTINUED ON NEXT PAGE

CONTINUED

The problem is so bad at the federal government level that auditors are unable to express an opinion on the fairness of the consolidated financial statements of the United States. For example, NASA was unable to explain $565 billion in year-end adjustments to its books (Hines, 2004). The adjustments might have been needed as a result of bad accounting, fraud, waste, or abuse. Without adequate records, no one really knows what the cause is. The $565 billion amount is astounding, especially when compared to frauds at Enron and WorldCom, which combined cost less than $100 billion in shareholder equity.

## General Purposes of Forensic Accounting Investigations

There are three general purposes for a forensic accounting investigation:

1. Fraud investigation
2. Dispute analysis or litigation
3. Data recovery

In a standard accounting audit, there is a presumption of honesty within the company. With a forensic accounting investigation, there is a presumption of dishonesty. Table 11.4 lists the main reasons for a forensic financial investigation.

**TABLE 11.4** Reasons for forensic accounting investigations.

| Reasons for a Forensic Accounting Investigation | Forensics Investigator Hired By |
|---|---|
| To investigate suspicions that fraud has occurred | Management |
| To provide expert witnesses in court to help quantify damages from a contract that has gone bad or some other business dispute | Lawyer |
| To investigate a company before entering into a contract | Investors, venture capitalists, potential business partners |
| To investigate a company before contemplating a merger | Investors, venture capitalists, potential business partners |
| To investigate a company before investing in their stock | Financial services |
| To determine whether a company problem was due to error or fraud | Lawyers, prosecutors |

**TABLE 11.5** Comparison of forensic accounting fraud and investigation.

| Forensic Accounting | Fraud Examination |
|---|---|
| A broad discipline applying accounting skills to legal matters in a wide range of issues | A focused discipline relating entirely to the issue of fraud |
| Addresses a past event | Addresses past, present, and future events |
| Uses financial information | Uses financial and nonfinancial information |
| Produces information about finances | Produces information about finances, people, and their actions |
| For use in judicial proceedings | For use in business and government internal proceedings and private and judicial proceedings |

Table 11.5 summarizes the overlapping features of forensic accounting and fraud examination.

The essential components of forensic accounting include an attempt to piece together or reconstruct a past event or events using financial information where that reconstruction is likely to be used in some judicial proceeding—criminal court, civil court, deposition, mediation, arbitration, settlement negotiation, or plea bargaining.

**FYI** *Case Wrap Up*

After an investigation is concluded, the investigative team needs to report the findings to those who hired them or need to know what happened. Wrap up each case with a formal findings meeting.

## Summary

In this chapter, you have learned that in this Internet era, more and more frauds will be perpetrated using computers and networks. Whether the potential fraudster is a disgruntled employee, greedy executive, or unethical business partner, there are many opportunities to defraud a company or organization.

Pressure, opportunity, and rationalization are the three elements of every fraud. Investigators should look for evidence of each of these factors—and not focus solely on opportunity. In order to prove fraud, the prosecutor must show intent and deceit. E-mail and other electronic communication media often contain evidence of deceit and intent as well as pressures or rationalization for stealing from a company.

The purpose of a fraud or forensic accounting investigation is to detect ongoing fraud or to investigate it after it has occurred. The word *forensic* in financial investigations implies that the information that is uncovered is capable of being used in court. Forensic accounting is the investigation and analysis of financial evidence that, like other forensic investigations, requires proper procedures and detailed evidence to ensure its admissibility.

## Test Your Skills

### MULTIPLE CHOICE QUESTIONS

1. Fraud is a crime carried out
   A. using a weapon.
   B. using deceit.
   C. to steal trade secrets.
   D. to steal money.

2. Which method is *not* used by fraudsters to deceive others to cause them to act to their disadvantage?
   A. Lying.
   B. Concealing facts.
   C. Physical force.
   D. Misrepresenting the truth.

3. Finding someone guilty of fraud always requires showing
   A. intent, or *mens rea*.
   B. that money was stolen.
   C. that the victim suffered a loss.
   D. that the person caused a loss.

4. Which of the following statements is false?
   A. Fraud is on the rise in both scope and scale.
   B. Fraud is the fastest growing crime.
   C. The FBI has committed approximately 10 percent of its resources to fighting fraud.
   D. Fraud committed by managers is called white collar crime.

5. Most investigations carried out to find fraud originate from which of the following sources?
    A. Internal or external audits or regulatory inquiries.
    B. Complaints from customers or vendors.
    C. Anonymous tips.
    D. All of the above.

6. Which cases pose special challenges and require a cautious approach because of the risk of lawsuits?
    A. Occupational fraud.
    B. Industrial espionage.
    C. Defamation.
    D. Illegal gambling.

7. Why does the law of privilege require a labor-intensive review process of the collected documents?
    A. Privileged information is protected by law from being released.
    B. Investigators must verify that the electronic documents are relevant.
    C. Privileged documents must be material to be released.
    D. Only law enforcement officials can view privileged documents.

8. Which elements are required to prove fraud in a civil case?
    A. A material false statement; intent to deceive; victim's reliance on the statement; and damage to the victim.
    B. A material false statement; intent to deceive; and damage to the victim.
    C. A material false statement; intent to deceive; and victim's reliance on the statement.
    D. A material false statement; and intent to deceive.

9. Which elements are required to prove fraud in a criminal case?
    A. A material false statement; intent to deceive; victim's reliance on the statement; and damage to the victim.
    B. A material false statement; intent to deceive; and damage to the victim.
    C. A material false statement; intent to deceive; and victim's reliance on the statement.
    D. A material false statement; and intent to deceive.

10. Which is an important principle to follow when handling a fraud suspect?
    A. Inform the suspect that he is going to be interviewed to avoid lawsuits.
    B. Show the suspect all of the evidence that has been recovered to get a confession.
    C. Interview the suspect in a familiar or comfortable location.
    D. Have a verbal confession converted into a written statement and then signed.

11. What are examples of fraud committed against a company?
    A. Corruption and asset misappropriation.
    B. Extortion and conflict of interest.
    C. Bribery, accounting fraud, financial statement fraud.
    D. A and B

12. What are the three factors common to every fraud?
    A. Pressure, rationalization, and opportunity.
    B. Deceit, trickery, and theft of money.
    C. Motive, intent, and deceit.
    D. Corruption, bribery, and kickbacks.

13. Why is computer forensics an important fraud tool?
    A. Computer forensics is used to detect fraud.
    B. Computer forensics is used to detect and deter fraud.
    C. Computer forensics is used to deter fraud.
    D. Computer forensics is used to find red flags of fraud.

14. What is the key distinction between accounting audits and forensic accounting investigations?
    A. Forensic accounting investigations involve the use of proper evidentiary methods to ensure the admissibility of the evidence in legal action.
    B. Accounting audits involve the use of computer forensics investigators.
    C. Accounting audits involve the use of proper evidentiary methods to ensure the admissibility of the evidence in legal action.
    D. Forensic accounting investigations involve the use of computer forensics investigators.

15. Which of the following is not a core skill of forensic accounting?
    A. Uncovering the facts.
    B. Establishing the correct numbers.
    C. Recognizing revenues.
    D. Determining business value.

## EXERCISES

### Exercise 11.1: Changes in the Incidence of Telecom and Financial Frauds

1. Use the Internet to download the CSI/FBI Computer Crime and Security Survey at **www.cybercrime.gov/FBI2005.pdf.**
2. Review the survey results to determine the trend in telecom fraud and financial fraud. Is it increasing, decreasing, or remaining steady?
3. Write a brief report describing the general trend in telecom and financial frauds. What are some possible reasons for the trend?

### Exercise 11.2: Behavioral Red Flags

1. Access **www.isaca.org/** and search for the article "Fighting Internal Crime Before It Happens" by Allen Lux and Sandra Fitiani. (The direct link is **www.isaca.org/Content/ContentGroups/Journal1/20023/Fighting_Internal_Crime_Before_It_Happens.htm).**
2. Read about the behavioral characteristics of job candidates that might be red flags of future fraud.
3. Create a table that lists four red flags. For each red flag, identify a future potential financial pressure that could lead to fraud.

### Exercise 11.3: Legal Elements of Fraud

1. Review Table 11.1 on the legal elements of fraud.
2. Explain how a computer forensics investigator could help support a federal prosecutor in a criminal case.
3. Explain how a computer forensics investigator could help support a defense lawyer in a civil case.

### Exercise 11.4: Deterring Fraud

Massive fraud by senior executives at WorldCom, Enron, and HealthSouth Corporations led to bankruptcy or stock plunges after they were revealed. The ultimate goal of the federal government in seeking convictions of top executives was deterrence. Executives found guilty face penalties in the tens of millions of dollars and ten or more years in jail. That is, the convictions signal to top executives that even though chances of detection are low, the consequences of being caught are so severe that committing fraud would be irrational.

1. Review the risk assessment decision flowchart in Figure 11.2.
2. Develop a risk assessment flowchart that shows the decisions that senior executives might make given that the chances of detection are low and consequences of being caught are severe.
3. Develop another risk assessment flowchart that shows the decisions that senior executives might make given that the chances of detection are high and consequences of being caught are severe.
4. Briefly describe how increasing the chances of detection could change a person's decision about committing fraud.

### Exercise 11.5: Traces of E-Evidence Left by Fraudsters

1. Review the FYI "SEC Relaxes Policy on Routine E-Mail Inspection" near the end of this chapter.
2. Based on what was covered in this chapter, do you think that the change to no longer request all e-mails in routine inspections of public companies will have an impact on incidence of fraud in public companies? Explain your answer.
3. What other methods of communication might fraudsters use instead of e-mail to further their schemes?

## PROJECTS

### Project 11.1: Distinguishing Between Error and Fraud

Computer forensics investigators often are tasked with finding evidence of intent in a suspected fraud case.

1. Explain why it is difficult to prove intent.
2. Identify three types of circumstantial evidence that could help prove intent.

3. Explain where each type of circumstantial evidence might be found.
4. Write a list of two other challenges that you would be facing as a fraud investigator.

### Project 11.2: Bringing Fraudsters to Justice

1. Visit the Web site of the Association of Certified Fraud Examiners (ACFE) at **www.acfe.org.**
2. Review the cases listed under *Recent News.*
3. Select one of the cases and describe the fraud, how it was committed, and who was involved.
   a. Was the fraudster(s) brought to justice? Why or why not?
   b. If e-evidence was used in the case, how or where was that evidence recovered? If no e-evidence was used, suggest two types of e-evidence that could have helped to find the truth.

### Project 11.3: Fraud and Ethics

1. Go to the antifraud Web site of the American Institute of Certified Public Accountants (AICPA) at **http://aicpa.org/antifraud/homepage.htm.**
2. Click on the link *Fraud and Ethics Case Studies and Commentaries for Business and Industry* and review several cases.
3. Select one case that involved the use of computers or networks to commit the fraud. Write a brief report on the role of computers or networks in the fraud and any e-evidence that was discovered.
4. Write how the outcome of the case might have been different if e-evidence had not been found.

## Case Study

An ongoing scam was discovered when John Kothanek, PayPal's lead fraud investigator, noticed too many Hudsens and Stivensons opening accounts with PayPal, Inc., an online payment processing company in Palo Alto, California. Ten names opening batches of 40 or more accounts were being used to buy high-value computer goods in auctions on eBay.com (Radcliff, 2005).

One of PayPal's merchants reported being redirected to a mock PayPal site. Sniffer software, which catches packet traffic, was set up at the mock site. The software showed that operators of the mock site were using it to capture PayPal user log-ins and passwords.

Investigators also used the sniffer to log the perpetrators' own IP address, which they then used to search against PayPal's database. It turned out that all of the accounts in question were opened by the same IP address. Using two freeware network-discovery tools, Trace-Route and Sam Spade, PayPal found a connection between the fake PayPal server address and the shipping address in Russia to which the accounts were trying to send goods.

Using the EnCase® forensic toolkit, Kothanek's team helped the FBI tie its case to PayPal by using keyword and pattern searches familiar to the PayPal investigators to analyze the slack and ambient space, on a mirror-image backup of the suspects' hard drives. Links were established between their machine's IP address, credit cards, and the Perl scripts they were using to open accounts.

You have been asked to write a report that identifies and explains the types of e-evidence that could be used at trial. Organize your report according to the Figure 11.1 fraud-to-trial process and the legal elements of fraud outlined in Table 11.1.

# Part Five

## Legal, Ethical, and Testimony Topics

Part Five focuses on the Federal Rules of Evidence and rules of procedure that govern the admissibility of e-evidence and the testimony of expert witnesses. It covers laws governing privacy protection, national security, and privacy versus security challenges. It discusses how laws are changing or are expected to change in response to new crimes, global terrorism, and threats to critical infrastructures.

In addition to technical skills, computer forensics investigators need a working knowledge of the legal system and excellent communication skills to carry out expert testimony in court. The integrity of the investigator—and the legal system itself—depends on uncompromising ethical conduct. Opinions cannot and should not be bought or used as a means to justify an end. The last chapter covers ethical and professional issues and challenges.

- **Chapter 12:** Federal Rules and Criminal Codes
- **Chapter 13:** Ethical and Professional Responsibility in Testimony

Chapter 12

# Federal Rules and Criminal Codes

## Chapter Objectives

**After reading this chapter and completing the exercises, you will be able to do the following:**

- Identify federal rules of evidence and other principles of due process of the law.
- Explain the legal foundation and reasons for pretrial motions regarding evidence.
- Identify the limitations on expectations of privacy.
- Explain the major anticrime laws and amendments impacting discovery and use of e-evidence.

## Introduction

Federal rules and laws are changed to bring them up to date with new technology, crimes, threats, and evidence. Rules are regulations that govern legal conduct, procedures, and practices. Laws are regulations that govern the conduct of the people of a society or nation. These rules and laws directly impact investigative procedures and the admissibility of evidence. Investigators who do not understand them run the risk of compromising cases, convicting innocent people, or letting guilty people go free. You need to know what constitutes a legal search, what laws govern obtaining e-evidence and securing it so that the chain of evidence is not compromised, what telecommunications may lawfully be intercepted or examined after they have been received, and what privacy rights employees and other individuals have. Consider the need to understand rules and laws in these cases. Before seizing a computer or other hardware, one needs to consider whether the Fourth Amendment requires a search warrant.

Before accessing stored electronic communications, one needs to consider the requirements of the Electronic Communication Privacy Act. To conduct real-time electronic surveillance, a wiretap order may be needed from a judge.

In this chapter, you learn about due process of the law, federal rules of evidence and procedure, and anticrime laws. These laws are important to know because even cases that center on physical evidence and eyewitness testimony may require collecting e-evidence to guide or corroborate the physical evidence. You will learn about the authority granted to investigators under privacy laws and the limitations those laws impose to protect civil rights. Many of these laws are highly controversial and subject to heated debates. At the same time, crimes are increasingly computer-technology–dependent. These forces will drive changes in privacy laws as the privacy versus security battles play out. This chapter also provides the framework for understanding the ethical challenges and demands of giving testimony in court that are covered in the next chapter.

## Due Process of the Law

***Due process of the law*** is a fundamental principle to ensure that all civil and criminal cases follow federal or state rules to prevent any ***prejudicial,*** or unequal, treatment. This chapter focuses on federal rules and cases for two reasons. First, cases that involve the Internet or telecommunications typically are federal cases because they cut across state boundaries. Second, states' rules are patterned after federal rules and are sufficiently similar for the level of this chapter.

Due process is guaranteed in the Fifth Amendment to the U.S. Constitution, which states: "No person shall . . . be deprived of life, liberty, or property, without due process of law."

Federal Rules of Civil Procedure, Federal Rules of Criminal Procedure, and Federal Rules of Evidence, which were introduced in Chapter 1, are the primary rules ensuring due process. In federal courts, evidentiary rules are governed by the Federal Rules of Evidence. State courts follow their own state rules of evidence. This chapter discusses the rules in greater detail now that you have a solid understanding of the technology and criminal components of e-evidence.

### FYI Links to Federal Rules of Procedure

The Law School of Cornell University maintains up-to-date Federal Rules of Criminal Procedure at **www.law.cornell.edu/rules/frcrmp/.**

Federal Rules of Civil Procedure are at **www.law.cornell.edu/rules/frcp/.**

## Federal Rules of Procedure Regulate Production of Evidence

The Federal Rules of Civil Procedure were adopted in 1938. Until 1970, rules had developed to deal only with physical or tangible evidence. Specifically, the law of criminal procedure has evolved to regulate the mechanisms common to the investigation of physical crimes, namely the collection of physical evidence and eyewitness testimony—and not e-evidence (Kerr, 2005). So the rules you learn about are expected to change.

Rules 26 and 34 regulate the production of evidence. Then an amendment in Rule 34(a) took effect that made electronic data subject to discovery, while also providing protections (in the form of exceptions to the rule) for the party whose electronic data was being searched. For decades, this amendment had no striking impact because only computer hard-copy printouts were routine in legal matters. A far-reaching impact did not begin until the late-1990s when the discovery of "electronically stored information" contained on the computer itself became routine. This change raised issues about e-evidence—how it could be authenticated, proved to be reliable, and determined to be admissible in criminal or civil proceedings. This section reviews the current and evolving status of laws pertaining to the processes of authentication, reliability, and admissibility. It also discusses the requirements for laying a proper foundation for e-evidence and serving as an expert witness.

### IN PRACTICE: Supreme Court Approves E-Discovery Changes

On April 12, 2006, the U.S. Supreme Court approved the proposed amendments to the Federal Rules of Civil Procedure. These rules concern the discovery of "electronically stored information" (ESI). These rule changes affect Rules 16, 26, 33, 34, 37, 45, and Form 35.

The rules have been sent to Congress and will become effective on December 1, 2006, unless Congress acts to change or defer the amendments. The amendments are available on the U.S. Courts' Web site at: **www.uscourts.gov/rules/newrules6.html#cv0804.**

Proposed amendments will impose greater precision and further change the way lawyers and courts approach e-discovery. In particular, Rule 16(b)(5) requires the disclosure of e-discovery during the initial pretrial conference. Discovery requests would have to be more specifically tailored because of the huge volume of

CONTINUED ON NEXT PAGE

12

CONTINUED

e-evidence. This discussion should be specific regarding the subject matter, time periods, and identification of persons or groups from whom discovery may be sought. And the parties need to negotiate how the documents will be produced very early in the case. It could take lawyers months to negotiate the format in which documents would be produced—images, TIFF, PDF, or native format—and what metadata would be included (Hsieh, 2006). For example, in *Lauren Corp. v. Century Geophysical Corp.*, the plaintiff sought to inspect the defendant's computers for evidence to support its claim that the defendant had unlawfully used the plaintiff's licensed software. It took the parties and the court over a year to resolve various discovery disputes. The court finally compelled inspection of the computers.

Proposed amended Rule 34(b) would allow the requesting party to "specify the form in which electronically stored information is to be produced." Specific information on these pending rules and the status of other amendments can be found by selecting the "Pending Rules Amendments Awaiting Final Action" hyperlink in the upper left corner of the Web page **www.uscourts.gov/rules/#judicial0905.** Also see **www.uscourts.gov/rules/comment2005/CVAug04.pdf.**

Another proposed change to Rule 26(b)(2)(B) would require a court order for e-evidence that is "not reasonably accessible because of undue burden or cost." This rule may lead to lengthy discussions about what is or is not reasonably accessible because it shifts the cost burden to the requesting party.

## Laying a Proper Foundation for E-Evidence

In 1975, the Federal Rules of Evidence were adopted. They govern the admissibility of evidence, including electronic records or data. Some of these rules are referred to as ***exclusionary rules*** because they specify the types of evidence that are excluded—and thus cannot be presented at trial. In establishing admissibility, many rules of evidence concentrate first on the evidence's relevancy. After evidence is found to be relevant, then it must survive several tests based on the rules of evidence in order to be admissible. Figure 12.1 shows that relevant evidence which has not been excluded is admissible evidence.

**Exclusionary Rules** Exclusionary rules are specific Federal Rules of Evidence that test whether evidence will be admissible. Some of these rules test whether there is a specific rule that bars the admissibility of

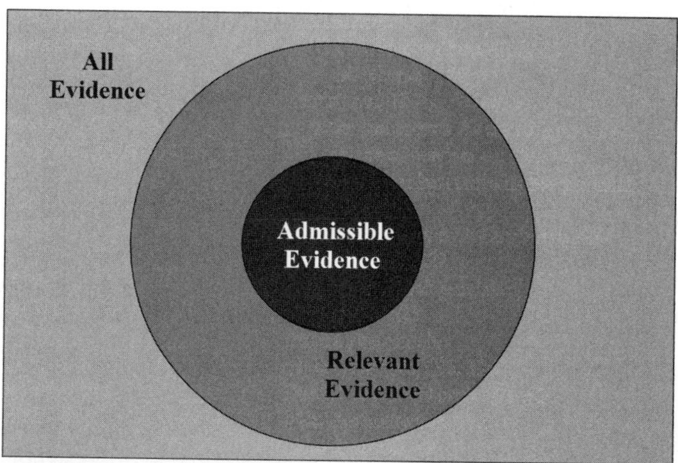


**FIGURE 12.1** Relevant evidence that has not been excluded is admissible evidence.

evidence, such as hearsay or privilege. Even if there is a specific rule that bars its admissibility, there may be exceptions to the rule, such as the business rule exception to the hearsay rule. Exclusionary rules pertain to the following:

- **Relevancy.** The evidence has a logical and valuable connection to an issue of the case.
- **Privilege.** Protects attorney-client communications and keeps those communications confidential.
- **Opinion of expert.** Qualified experts may testify under certain conditions even though they were not eyewitnesses.
- **Hearsay.** Rule against using "out of court" statement offered to prove truth.
- **Authentication.** The evidence is what it purports (claims) to be.

These rules as they apply to e-evidence are described in Table 12.1. The Legal Information Institute (LII) of Cornell University publishes the eleven articles of the Federal Rules of Evidence at **www.law.cornell.edu/rules/fre/.** This is a free service provided by the LII.

As the Rules listed in Table 12.1 describe, evidence may be inadmissible if it falls into a category that makes it inadmissible, such as hearsay or privilege; or it is irrelevant, prejudicial, misleading, or causes delays that substantially outweigh its ***probative value.*** Evidence has probative value if it is sufficiently useful to prove something important.

**TABLE 12.1** Federal Rules of Evidence pertaining to e-evidence.

| Federal Rules of Evidence | Description |
|---|---|
| Rule 104(a). Preliminary Questions of Admissibility Generally | Preliminary questions concerning the qualification of an expert witness or the admissibility of evidence are decided by the court. |
| Rule 401. Definition of Relevant Evidence | Relevant evidence means evidence that can make some fact or issue more probable or less probable than it would be without the evidence. |
| Rule 402. Relevant Evidence Generally Admissible; Irrelevant Evidence Inadmissible | All relevant evidence is admissible, except as otherwise provided by the Constitution of the United States, by Act of Congress, by these rules, or by other rules of the Supreme Court. Evidence that is not relevant is not admissible. |
| Rule 403. Exclusion of Relevant Evidence on Grounds of Prejudice, Confusion, or Waste of Time | Even if it is relevant, evidence may be excluded if its probative value is substantially outweighed by the danger of unfair prejudice, confusion of the issues, misleading the jury, unnecessary delay, or waste of time. |
| Rule 702. Testimony by Experts | This rule broadly governs the admissibility of expert testimony. It outlines what is necessary to be qualified as an expert. A witness is qualified as an expert by knowledge, skill, experience, training, or education. Under Rule 702, the test is: If scientific, technical, or other specialized knowledge will help the ***trier of fact*** (jury or judge) understand the evidence, a *qualified expert* may testify if (1) the testimony is based upon sufficient facts or data, (2) the testimony is the product of reliable principles and methods, and (3) the witness has applied the principles and methods reliably to the facts of the case. |
| Rule 704. Opinion on Ultimate Issue | Testimony in the form of an opinion—that is not inadmissible for some other reason—is allowed because the opinion is an issue for the trier of fact to decide. |

CONTINUED ON NEXT PAGE

CONTINUED

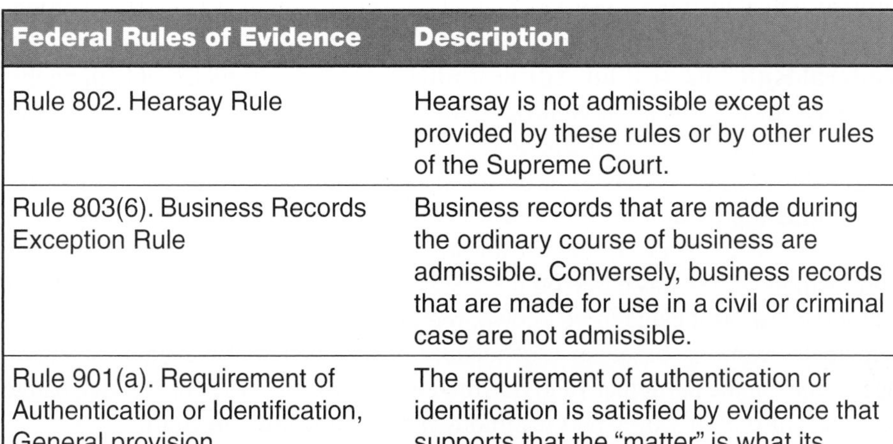

| Federal Rules of Evidence | Description |
|---|---|
| Rule 802. Hearsay Rule | Hearsay is not admissible except as provided by these rules or by other rules of the Supreme Court. |
| Rule 803(6). Business Records Exception Rule | Business records that are made during the ordinary course of business are admissible. Conversely, business records that are made for use in a civil or criminal case are not admissible. |
| Rule 901(a). Requirement of Authentication or Identification, General provision | The requirement of authentication or identification is satisfied by evidence that supports that the "matter" is what its proponent claims it is. |

### Cybrary—The World's Criminal Justice Directory

Visit Prentice-Hall's Cybrary at **www.talkjustice.com/cybrary.asp** for a comprehensive directory of Web sites related to laws, evidence, forensics, and other criminal justice topics.

**Hearsay Evidence** Hearsay Rule 802 can block admissibility unless some exception applies to the evidence. For example, if the author of an electronic record is not available to verify the truth of the matter, the electronic record would be hearsay. As such, it would be inadmissible unless it fit into one of the exceptions to the hearsay rule. Electronic records that are business records made during the ordinary course of business are admissible under the *business records exception rule* in Rule 803(6). Therefore, business records, which are hearsay, can be admitted as evidence because they are an exception to hearsay. The reason for their exception is that their regular use in the business of a company ensures a high degree of accuracy so additional verification is not needed.

**Motions to Suppress Evidence** Questions of admissibility and motions to suppress evidence are handled before trial. A judge may hold a hearing to determine whether or not evidence is admissible. In those cases, the jury never hears of the evidence. A motion by a lawyer for such a hearing before trial is called a ***motion in limine*** (pronounced *lim-in-nay*). Courts prefer this approach because it limits the jury's exposure to inadmissible evidence, which might influence jury members regardless of attempts to ignore it (Eichhorn, 1989).

**Federal Rule 702 Test for Admissibility** Evidence is not the only thing that is subject to tests of admissibility. A forensic examiner's qualifications can be challenged or the tools or methodologies used in a forensic investigation can be objected to. These challenges or objections are heard outside the presence of the jury during a pretrial hearing under Federal Rule 702 (as defined in Table 12.1).

From 1923 to 1993, the test for admissibility of expert witness testimony and methodologies was based on the 1923 ruling in *Frye v. United States* (1923). The Frye test, as it came to be known, requires that the scientific principle upon which the work is based is "sufficiently established to have gained general acceptance in the particular field in which it belongs." Using *Frye*, a judge had to test the admissibility of expert testimony before allowing it in court.

In part because of the problems caused by the "general acceptance" criteria, the Frye test that Rule 702 had been relying on was replaced (superceded) by the Daubert test in 1993. In 1993, the Supreme Court issued an opinion in the case of *Daubert v. Merrell Dow Pharmaceuticals* that abandoned the earlier Frye standard in federal cases and set a new standard. A judge must take into account the following:

1. Whether the theory or technique can be and has been tested
2. Whether it has been subjected to peer review and publication
3. The known or potential error
4. The general acceptance of the theory in the scientific community
5. Whether the proffered testimony is based upon the expert's special skill

The Daubert test is primarily a question of relevance, or "fit," of the evidence. The Supreme Court holds that in order for testimony to be used it must be sufficiently tied to the facts of the case to help understand an issue being disputed (Norberg, 2006). For the full text of the Daubert test, visit the Supreme Court Collection of the Legal Information Institute at **supct.law.cornell.edu/supct/html/92–102.ZS.html.**

## Authenticating E-Mail Messages and Other E-Evidence

A physical document can be authenticated by either direct evidence or circumstantial evidence. Examples of circumstantial evidence would be the paper document's appearance, content, or substance. The same circumstantial evidence the courts use to authenticate physical documents applies to e-mail messages.

In order to authenticate an e-mail message, Rule 901 requires that the person (proponent) who introduces the message provide "evidence sufficient to support a finding that the [e-mail message] is what its proponent claims."

The reliability of e-evidence itself and the reliability of the methods and procedures used must be established, too. Rule 901 generally can be satisfied by proof that:

1. The computer equipment is accepted in the field as standard and competent and was in good working order.
2. Qualified computer operators were employed.
3. Proper procedures were followed in connection with the input and output of information.
4. A reliable software program and hardware were used.
5. The equipment was programmed and operated correctly.
6. The exhibit is properly identified as the output in question.

Proof must be provided for all six of these issues or for all issues that apply to the handling of the evidence. It is not a surprise that opposing counsel will challenge the authentication of the e-evidence. In fact, evidence should be challenged to ensure that it accurately and fully represents the truth.

**Circumstantial E-Mail Evidence Authenticates Other E-Mail** A good of example of how e-mail messages can be authenticated to meet Rule 901 is in *United States v. Siddiqui* (Robins, 2003). In *Siddiqui,* the defendant was convicted of fraud, making false statements, and obstructing a federal investigation in connection with an award he had applied for from the National Science Foundation (NSF). The issue of the case was that the defendant, Siddiqui, had falsified documents (letters recommending him for the NSF award) in the names of two other individuals; and the defendant had then urged those two individuals to support the falsified documents. E-mail messages between Siddiqui and the two individuals containing incriminating information were recovered and used as e-evidence.

Siddiqui appealed. He challenged the district court's decision to admit into evidence several e-mail messages between himself and the two individuals. The court held that the appearance, contents, substance, internal patterns, and other circumstances of these e-mail messages authenticated them. The Eleventh Circuit pointed to the following facts:

12

1. The e-mail messages reflected an e-mail address that included a variation of the defendant's name and a uniform resource locator (URL) for the defendant's employer.
2. The e-mail address in these messages was consistent with one in another e-mail message that was introduced into evidence by the defendant as an e-mail message from the defendant to one of the two other individuals.
3. The contents of the messages indicated that the author knew the details of the defendant's conduct in connection with the NSF award.

4. One of the e-mail messages referred to a visit the defendant had made to a particular event attended by the defendant and by the recipient of the message.
5. The e-mail messages referred to the author by a nickname recognized by the recipients.
6. The e-mail messages occurred during the same time period in which the recipients spoke to the defendant by telephone and had conversations consistent in content with the e-mail messages.

This case presents several important lessons for computer forensics investigators. It illustrates the larger and more comprehensive role of e-mail evidence in a case. E-mail messages not directly on point may be relevant to the case as the proof needed to authenticate other e-mail. The content of e-mail messages may relate to other documents of the author, or have a style that is consistent with other communication patterns.

The issue of style is equally critical when e-mail has been planted or forged. E-mail forgers may not be aware of distinctive writing styles or rules of evidence and, out of habit, use their own writing style.

### IN PRACTICE: The Importance of Style

In a sexual harassment case brought by an accountant against her manager, the manager produced an e-mail message allegedly sent to him by the accountant, which she denied having sent. The company at which both employees worked required personnel to share computers. Employees were also required to reveal their e-mail passwords, so that if an employee was out of the office, colleagues could have access to e-mail messages on that employee's computer. The computer forensics investigator concluded that, based on these policies, it was not possible to verify whether or not the accountant had sent e-mail. The accountant produced e-mail she had sent to the manager and that he had sent to her over a year's time. The grammar, sentence structure, punctuation, and other style features in the disputed e-mail message clearly differed from other e-mail sent by the accountant and supported her claim that she had not sent the disputed e-mail. The contradictory evidence triggered a wider search of e-mail of the manager and information technology staff.

**Circumstantial Evidence Authenticates Chat Room Session** Circumstantial evidence was used to authenticate e-evidence in the *United States v. Simpson* case. The case involved a hard-copy printout of an online chat room session that Simpson had participated in. The government was able to authenticate a printout of a chat room session between a detective and the defendant Simpson. Even though Simpson did not use his full name in the chat room when communicating with the detective, he provided his first initial and last name. The initial and last name were the same as the defendant's, and the e-mail address belonged to the defendant. Pages found near a computer in Simpson's home contained the name, street address, e-mail address, and telephone number that the detective had given to the individual in the chat room session.

When considered all together, the circumstantial evidence was sufficient to authenticate the communication as one that occurred in a chat room session between Simpson and the detective.

This case illustrates how different types of evidence can be used for authentication. It also reaffirms the importance of detailed documentation of materials found near a computer, as was discussed in prior chapters. Next, we will examine the anticrime and privacy laws.

**Caution**

**Risk**

An employee who uses his employer's computer for personal communications assumes the risk that these communications may be accessed by the employer or by others.

## Anticrime Laws

Congress responds to changing technology and high-tech crimes by amending existing laws if possible or by issuing new laws (statutes). The most authoritative federal statutes affecting computer forensics are the Electronic Communications Privacy Act (ECPA), the Federal Wiretap Statute, the Pen/Trap Statute, the CFAA, and the USA PATRIOT Act. The ECPA extended the Wiretap Statute to include authority over digital transmissions over computer networks.

A highly contentious response by President George W. Bush as part of his war against terrorism was the use of warrantless electronic surveillance. The order was issued without the consent of Congress and violates the Fourth Amendment.

### Electronic Communications Privacy Act of 1986

In certain situations, the Electronic Communications Privacy Act (ECPA) of 1986 takes precedence over the right to privacy guaranteed by the Fourth Amendment. The ECPA applies to stored computer files that had been transmitted over a network. This law applies only to stored computer information and not to real-time interception of communications. Real-time interception of computer information in transit falls under the Federal Wiretap Statute of 1968.

The ECPA permits an ISP to look through all stored messages, including e-mail waiting in an inbox, or recently sent and received mail. Some ISPs temporarily store all messages that pass through the system. The ECPA normally prevents the ISP from disclosing the messages to others, but there are exceptions. Law enforcement with proper warrants or administrative subpoenas can collect basic information about users from ISPs, including their names. They might also be allowed access to the content of stored messages.

**Caution**

**Supreme Court Defers to Congress**

The courts usually defer to Congress's judgment when confronted with Fourth Amendment challenges to electronic surveillance.

Congress made the ECPA the primary law by which to address claims of privacy violations in the communications field. This law's goal is to balance privacy rights with law enforcement needs—while protecting Fourth Amendment rights against unreasonable search and seizure whenever possible.

The authority given to law enforcement by the ECPA has sparked fierce opposition by privacy advocates. The full text of the ECPA is available at **www.usiia.org/legis/ecpa.html.**

**Limitations of Privacy Laws** The belief that a person has a reasonable expectation of privacy under all circumstances is wrong. People try to hide their crimes by claiming that they expected privacy. By law, privacy expectations depend on several factors. For example, if circumstances show that a computer user had no reasonable expectation of privacy, then police do not need a search warrant to obtain information (Nimsger, 2003). Users of computer equipment owned by an employer, company, or government agency fall into this category. Companies and government agencies can specify explicitly in their acceptable use policies (AUP) that employees have no right to privacy or privacy expectations when they use company equipment for e-mail or the Internet.

In the case of *U.S. v. Simons* (2000), a government employee working for the Central Intelligence Agency (CIA) was suspected of using his office computer to download pornography. Without getting a warrant, the CIA remotely accessed Simons' computer and found files containing photos of child pornography, which is a federal crime. Simons tried to suppress the photos by claiming a Fourth Amendment violation of his expectation of privacy. However, the CIA had an AUP that allowed it to "periodically audit, inspect, and/or monitor . . . users' Internet access." The Court determined that because of this AUP, Simons had no reasonable expectation of privacy and that no warrant was required for the search—making his files admissible.

**IN PRACTICE:** Constitutional Rights Are Not Unlimited

Alan Scott had shredded documents into strips 5/32 of an inch wide to destroy the evidence they contained of his income tax evasion. Government agents retrieved those strips from the trash in front of Scott's home and then reassembled them into documentary evidence that helped prove Scott's crime. After he was charged with a crime, Scott argued that he had created a reasonable expectation of privacy in the documents by shredding them, so that reconstructing them without a warrant violated his Fourth Amendment rights (Kerr, 2001).

CONTINUED ON NEXT PAGE

▶▶ CONTINUED

According to the First Circuit Court, Scott's case revealed "a failed attempt at secrecy by reason of underestimation of police resourcefulness, not invasion of constitutionally protected privacy."

The use of technology—the shredder—to destroy the paper does not provide constitutional protection. As a result, agents did not need a warrant to reconstruct Scott's shredded documents and return them to a readable form. The government's reconstruction of Scott's communications did not violate his reasonable expectation of privacy because he had no foundation for that expectation.

In terms of e-evidence, a person who encrypts incriminating electronic documents and then deletes them, assuming they won't be deciphered by authorities, cannot make a valid claim that he had an expectation of privacy.

**Courts' Interpretation of Fourth Amendment Protection** In the 1980s, a series of court cases were triggered by defendants' claiming that their right to Fourth Amendment protection had been violated. For example, in *United States v. Jacobsen,* the Supreme Court considered whether the Fourth Amendment required the government to obtain a search warrant before conducting a field test on white powder that agents had seized from the defendant. The purpose of the field test was to determine whether the powder contained cocaine. The defendant argued that the chemical field test violated his reasonable expectation that the contents of the white powder would remain a secret (private), and thus violated his Fourth Amendment "reasonable expectation of privacy." In an opinion by Justice Stevens, the Supreme Court disagreed with that logic by stating:

> *The concept of an interest in privacy that society is prepared to recognize as reasonable is, by its very nature, critically different from the mere expectation, however well justified, that certain facts will not come to the attention of the authorities. . . . A chemical test that merely discloses whether or not a particular substance is cocaine does not compromise any legitimate interest in privacy.*

Because cocaine was illegal contraband, the defendant had no right to possess it and no extraconstitutional right to stop the government from conducting the test to identify it. The defendant's expectation that the identity of the illegal powder would remain a secret did not establish a constitutionally recognizable reasonable expectation of privacy.

## Federal Wiretap Statute of 1968

The ECPA amended the Federal Wiretap Statute of 1968 to include the interception of electronic communications, including e-mail. The USA PATRIOT

Act also expanded the list of criminal activities for which wiretaps can be ordered. Wiretaps are ordered when terrorist bombings, hijackings, or other violent crimes are suspected.

The Federal Wiretap Statute provides,

> *"Immediately upon the expiration of the period [covered by the wiretap order] . . . recordings shall be made available to the judge issuing such order and sealed under his directions. . . . The presence of the seal . . . or a satisfactory explanation for the absence thereof, shall be a prerequisite for the use or disclosure of the contents" of the intercept. [18 U.S.C. 2518(8)(a)]*

This provision of the statute requires that the recordings captured during the time of the wiretap be given to the judge within a reasonable amount of time—or the contents of those recordings are inadmissible. The judge must, in effect, "seal the evidence" to prevent tampering as part of the chain of custody. This period of time is not specified in the statute. Defense attorneys had tried to get wiretaps thrown out by claiming that there was a delay getting the recordings to the judge.

In some cases, courts have used the "service provider exemption" to find that any company furnishing computer hardware and software may access its employees' e-mail files. For example, in *Bohach v. City of Reno* (1996), a federal court rejected privacy claims under the ECPA raised by two police officers in Reno, Nevada. Officer John Bohach had sent messages to other members of the department over the department's Alphapage messaging system. Several months later, an internal affairs investigation was being conducted based on the contents of those messages. Bohach and another officer filed a lawsuit against the City of Reno claiming that the department's accessing and retrieving the old messages violated the federal wiretap statutes. The court disagreed. The court reasoned that because the nature of the Alphapage messages were essentially e-mail, the officers could not have reasonably believed them to be private. Also, the court cited a department order informing employees that their messages would be "logged on the network" and that sending certain types of messages was prohibited. The court found that the city was a "service provider" as defined under the ECPA and was "free to access the stored message as it pleased." Therefore, the court found that the city had not violated the ECPA.

## Pen/Trap Statute, Section 216

"Trap and trace" information is so called because collecting the information originally required the telephone company to trace the phone line using a tool known as a *terminating trap*. The ***pen register*** is a mechanical device that can be attached to a specific telephone line at a telephone office.

A pulsation of the dial on a line to which the pen register is attached records on a paper tape dashes equal to the number dialed. The paper tape then becomes a permanent and complete record of outgoing calls and the numbers called on the particular line. Immediately after the number is dialed, but before the call is answered, the pen register mechanically and automatically disconnects. There is no recording or monitoring of the conversation.

The pen register and trap and trace statute, or the ***Pen/Trap Statute,*** governs the collection of noncontent traffic information associated with communications, such as the phone numbers dialed by a particular telephone. Rather than the strict probable cause necessary for wiretaps, ***pen register orders*** require only certification from a law enforcement officer that "the information likely to be obtained is relevant to an ongoing criminal investigation." If the application for installation of a pen/trap device contains these elements, the court will authorize it.

This statute was enacted as part of ECPA. Section 216 updates the Pen/Trap Statute in three ways:

1. The amendments clarify that law enforcement may use pen/trap orders to trace communications on the Internet and other computer networks.
2. Pen/trap orders issued by federal courts now have nationwide effect.
3. Law enforcement authorities must file a special report with the court whenever they use a pen/trap order to install their own monitoring device on computers belonging to a public provider.

## Counterfeit Access Device and Computer Fraud and Abuse Act

Congress's first battle against computer crime was the passage of the Counterfeit Access Device and Computer Fraud and Abuse Act in 1986. This legislation primarily covered illegal access or use of protected government computer systems. It was aimed at individuals who broke into or stole data from government computers. This law was too narrow, so Congress amended it twice, once through the CFAA in 1994 and then through the National Information Infrastructure Protection Act (NII) in 1996. The CFAA is also referred to as Title 18 USC §1030.

Title 18 of the CFAA deals with "Crimes and Criminal Procedure." Section 1030 of Title 18 deals with "Fraud and related activity in connection with computers." Under 18 USC §1030, the government does not have to prove that an individual who accessed a federal interest computer network unauthorized had intended to damage it, *only that he intended to access it.*

12

## IN PRACTICE: Federal Wiretap Authority

There are two sources of authority for federal wiretaps within the United States.

The first authority is the Federal Wiretap Act, or Title III, of 1968. It was expanded in 1986 by the ECPA. It sets procedures for court authorization of real-time surveillance of electronic communications, including voice, e-mail, fax, and Internet, in criminal investigations. Before using a wiretap, an affidavit must be submitted to a judge that there is probable cause to believe that a crime has been, is being, or is about to be committed. Based on the affidavit, the judge then issues the wiretap or denies it. Under extreme circumstances, a judge's order may not be necessary.

The second authority is the Foreign Intelligence Surveillance Act (FISA) of 1978. FISA allows wiretapping in the United States based on probable cause that the person is a member of a foreign terrorist group or an agent of a foreign power. For U.S. citizens and permanent resident aliens, probable cause that the person is engaged in criminal activities is needed. For others, suspicion of criminal activity is not required for the wiretap. The USA PATRIOT Act allows prosecutors to use FISA for the purpose of gathering evidence in criminal investigations of national security crimes.

**Caution**

**Section 225 Immunity**

Section 225 of the act is relevant to computer forensics investigators. It gives immunity from civil lawsuits to any person who provides technical assistance in obtaining electronic information pursuant to a court order or valid request for emergency assistance.

### USA PATRIOT Act

Even before the USA PATRIOT Act, federal agencies had broad legal powers to monitor telephone conversations, e-mail, pagers, wireless phones, computers, and all other electronic communications and communications devices. The USA PATRIOT Act greatly broadened the FBI's authority to gather this information. The USA PATRIOT Act made it lawful for an officer to intercept a computer trespasser's wire or electronic communication transmitted to or through a protected computer. The act included new guidance relating to computer crime and e-evidence. The *Field Guidance on New Authorities that Relate to Computer Crime and Electronic Evidence Enacted in the USA Patriot Act of 2001* provides the authority to do several things. Authorizations include:

1. Intercepting voice communications in computer hacking investigations
2. Allowing law enforcement to trace communications on the Internet and other computer networks within the pen and trap statute (pen/trap statute)
3. Intercepting communications of computer trespassers
4. Writing nationwide search warrants for e-mail
5. Deterring and preventing cyberterrorism

The law raised the maximum penalty for hackers who damaged protected computers. See the *Field Guidance on New Authorities That Relate to Computer Crime and Electronic Evidence Enacted in the USA Patriot Act of 2001* at **www.usdoj.gov/criminal/cybercrime/PatriotAct.htm.** The guide develops and supports cybersecurity forensic capabilities. Visit **www.cybercrime.gov/PatriotAct.htm** for the latest provisions of the law.

### FYI Digital Millennium Copyright Act

The 1998 Digital Millennium Copyright Act permits music companies to force ISPs to turn over the names of suspected music pirates upon subpoena from any U.S. District Court clerk's office and without a judge's signature.

### IN PRACTICE: Defendant's Attempt to Exclude E-Evidence Rejected

In *United States v. Forest and Garner*, the U.S. Court of Appeals for the Sixth Circuit (January 27, 2004) rejected a defendant's efforts to exclude evidence that had been obtained by federal agents who used ***cell-site data.*** Agents used data from the defendant's cellular telephone service provider to track his movements after the agents lost visual contact. The court rejected his arguments, which he had based on Title III of the Omnibus Crime Control and Safe Streets Act of 1968 and Fourth Amendment. Drug Enforcement Agency (DEA) agents secured court orders giving them authority to intercept the defendant's cellular phone calls. It also required the cellular service provider to disclose all subscriber information relevant to the investigation.

While conducting surveillance of the defendant and a codefendant, the agents lost track of them. The agents then dialed the defendant's cell phone several times and used the provider's computer data to determine which cell transmission towers were being "hit" by that phone. The cell-site data revealed the defendant's general location and helped catch him.

On appeal of his conviction, the defendant argued that the cell-site data and resulting evidence should have been suppressed because they turned his phone into a tracking device—and that violated his rights under both Title III and the Fourth Amendment.

CONTINUED ON NEXT PAGE

▶▶ CONTINUED

In an opinion by Judge Ronald Lee Gilman, the court found that the cell-site data clearly does not fall within Title III's definitions of oral communication or wire communication, and that the only other statutory category that the data might fit into is electronic communication. The court pointed out, however, that even assuming that cell-site data does meet the definition of electronic communication, Title III provides suppression as a remedy only for the illegal interceptions of oral or wire communications and not for the illegal interception of electronic communications.

The court reached the same conclusion with regard to the defendant's argument that the authorities turned his cell phone into a tracking device within the meaning of 18 U.S.C. §3117. The court ruled that §3117 does not provide suppression as a remedy—regardless of whether or not a phone fits the definition of a tracking device under that statute.

The defendant also claimed that the cell-site data and resulting evidence should be suppressed under the exclusionary rule of the Fourth Amendment. But the court ruled that the defendant had no legitimate expectation of privacy in his movements along a public highway.

**Sneak and Peek Provision** The primary stated purposes of the USA PATRIOT Act are to "deter and punish terrorist acts in the United States and around the world [and] to enhance law enforcement investigatory tools." The Act changed the point at which individuals being searched—the targets—are to be notified of that search. Prior to this Act, the target was notified when the physical search was being made. The PATRIOT Act permits an investigator to delay notification (Wegman, 2004).

This notification delay has been described as a ***sneak and peek*** provision, mostly by critics of the act (Shulman, 2003). Law enforcement can delay notifying the target for up to 90 days and then get another delay by showing some good cause. To obtain authority for delayed notification, an investigator must show a need for the delay, such as danger to the life or safety of an individual, risk of flight from prosecution, witness or evidence tampering, or that immediate notice would "seriously jeopardize" an investigation (Wegman, 2004).

**Expanded Power for Surveillance** Three examples of expanded powers for surveillance and search of e-evidence provided by the act are:

1. Judicial supervision of telephone and Internet surveillance by law enforcement is limited.
2. Law enforcement and intelligence agencies have broad access to sensitive medical, mental health, financial, and educational records with limited judicial oversight.

3. The government has the power to conduct secret searches of individuals' homes and businesses, including monitoring books bought from bookstores or borrowed from libraries.

The USA PATRIOT Act requires that an agency that sets up surveillance using its own pen/trap device on a packet-switched public data network identify:

1. Any officers who installed or accessed the device to obtain information from the network
2. The date and time the device was installed and uninstalled, and the duration of each time the device was accessed
3. The configuration of the device at the time of installation, plus any later modification
4. Any information that the device has collected

**Caution**

**Internet Interests Are Revealing**

Evidence of Web surfing reveals much more about an individual than the telephone numbers she has dialed.

## Electronic Surveillance Issues

The issue of electronic surveillance became a grave matter in the United States in late 2005 and early 2006—and the resolution may impact the use of wiretapping and collection of electronic evidence.

On December 16, 2005, James Risen and Eric Lichtblau of the *New York Times* reported that President George W. Bush authorized the National Security Agency (NSA) to spy on Americans without warrants. (Their article is reprinted at **www.commondreams.org/headlines05/1216-01.htm.**) This order ignored procedures of the Foreign Intelligence Surveillance Act (FISA).

The *New York Times* article reported that in 2002 Bush issued an executive order authorizing the NSA to track and intercept international telephone and e-mail traffic into or out of the United States when one party was believed to have ties with al Qaeda. Initially, neither Bush nor the White House confirmed nor denied that the president had ignored the law. In his radio broadcast on December 17, 2005, Bush admitted that the *New York Times* was correct.

Many legal scholars have argued that by issuing the warrantless wiretapping in violation of FISA and bypassing Congress, the president committed an impeachable offense. Only Congress can decide whether to allow such wiretaps (Dean, 2005).

First reports indicated that the NSA limited monitoring to foreign calls originating in the United States or abroad and that fewer than 500 calls were being monitored at a time. But later reports indicated that the NSA was "data mining" millions of calls by using access to telecommunications companies' switching stations through which foreign communications traffic flows.

On January 6, 2006, Morton H. Halperin, the executive director of the Open Society Policy Center at **www.opensocietypolicycenter.org,** released the memo addressing the legal issues in "A Legal Analysis of the NSA Warrantless Surveillance Program." In response, on February 6, 2006, the Hon. Alberto R. Gonzales, attorney general of the United States, released a prepared statement available at **www.usdoj.gov/ag/speeches/2006/ag_speech_060206.html** in which he defended the surveillance program. His defense was "Congress and the American people are interested in two fundamental questions: is this program necessary and is it lawful. The answer to both questions is yes." Gonzales also attacked critics by stating that "These press accounts are in almost every case, in one way or another, misinformed, confused, or wrong."

For articles on the current state of this issue, visit the *National Security Agency (NSA)* section of Findlaw news archives at **news.findlaw.com/legalnews/documents/archive_n.html.**

## Computer Fraud and Abuse Act

The CFAA was the first law to address computer crime in which the computer is the subject of the crime. That is, it applies to crimes that do not have an analogy in traditional crime. Such crimes include the use of viruses or other malware, sniffers, logic bombs, and bots. The CFAA has been used to prosecute virus creators, hackers, information and identity thieves, and people who use computers to commit fraud.

Table 12.2 lists key terms used in the Computer Fraud and Abuse Act.

**TABLE 12.2** Definitions of the key terms in the *Computer Fraud and Abuse Act* (Federal Statute 18 U.S.C. §1030).

| Key Terms | This Term Means . . . |
|---|---|
| Protected Computer | A protected computer means a computer that:<br>■ Is used by a financial institution (broadly defined)<br>■ Is used by the U.S. government<br>■ Affects domestic, interstate commerce or communications of the United States<br>■ Affects foreign commerce or communications of the United States<br>In effect, every computer connected to the Internet is a protected computer. Protected computers include computers located outside the United States. This allows U.S. prosecution of hackers who attack foreign computers. |
| Authorized Access | There are two references regarding authorized access specified in the statute:<br>■ Without Authorization—"Access without authority"applies to any outsider who breaks in and uses a computer for any purpose. (Because this applies only to outsiders, it does not apply to employees.) |

CONTINUED ON NEXT PAGE

▶▶ CONTINUED

| Key Terms | This Term Means . . . |
|---|---|
| | ■ Exceeding Authorized Access—"Access in excess of authority" applies to anyone who has authorized access to a computer and uses that access to obtain or alter information that he is not allowed to obtain or alter. |
| Damage | Damage is defined as any impairment to the integrity or availability of data, a program, a system, or information. That impairment must cause:<br>■ A loss to one or more persons (or companies) during any 1-year period totaling at least \$5,000 in value<br>■ The modification or impairment of medical records<br>■ Physical injury to any person<br>■ A threat to public health or safety<br>■ Damage to a government computer system used for administering justice, national defense, or national security |
| Loss | Loss is defined as any reasonable cost to any victim, including the cost of:<br>■ Responding to an offense<br>■ Conducting a damage assessment<br>■ Restoring the data, program, system, or information to its condition prior to the offense<br>■ Lost revenue or other damages because of interruption of service |
| Conduct | If there has been damage to a protected computer that has caused damage, the next issue is whether the conduct was intentional, reckless, or negligent.<br>■ "Intentional conduct" means conduct by anyone who knowingly transmits a "program, information, code, or command" that causes damage to a protected computer. This applies to both insiders and outsiders.<br>■ "Reckless conduct" means intentional access to a protected computer without authority that unintentionally but recklessly causes damage. This applies only to outsiders. |

12

## IN PRACTICE: Applying Crime Laws

A trail of electronic data from U.S. Web sites led to the convictions of more than 22 British customers who had bought psychedelic drugs online. Customers were identified from e-evidence collected during a U.S. DEA sting operation—Operation Web Tryp. The evidence led police to addresses across the UK.

For several years, psychedelic drugs known as "research chemicals" had been sold openly from U.S. Web sites. Since many of the research drugs are too powerful psychedelically to catch on with users or dealers, they are available only from e-commerce sites.

The online drug trade came to the attention of U.S. law enforcers in March 2004 after James Downs, 22, died from an accidental overdose of 2-CT-21 he ordered online. Investigators traced his purchases to a Las Vegas research chemicals Web site, which imported chemicals from labs in China and India. That year, the DEA shut down the Web sites and arrested the site operators.

Each e-commerce Web site had thousands of customers in the United States and Europe. Customers could order their drugs with one-click systems of payment via credit card or PayPal, and their purchases were delivered the next day by FedEx and other carriers. Customer records and credit card details were gathered from seized computers. After investigators had verified the intelligence, details were sent to UK police forces.

Research chemicals are not officially listed as controlled substances under U.S. drug laws. Therefore, the Web site operators were prosecuted under a law that prohibits the possession and supply of chemicals "substantially similar" to controlled drugs. All the operators face life sentences, and several have been charged with causing death or serious injury. In May 2005, operator David Linder was found guilty on 27 charges, including drug conspiracy and money laundering. He was sentenced to a total of 410 years in prison and ordered to pay back $700,000 in profits from the Web site. The severity of his sentence was related to the death of an 18-year-old New York man who overdosed on the drug alpha-methyltryptamine (AMT) purchased from Linder's site (McCandless, 2005).

## Summary

In this chapter, you have learned about the Federal Rules of Evidence and Procedure that directly impact investigative procedures and the admissibility of evidence. Actual federal cases and court decisions were presented to illustrate the tough challenges to an investigator's experience, evidence handling, hardware, and procedures. Clearly, investigators need a working knowledge of what constitutes a legal search so as not to compromise cases, convict innocent people, or let guilty people go free. Before seizing computers, Fourth Amendment search warrant requirements need to be met. Before accessing stored data, the requirements of the Electronic Communication Privacy Act must be considered. Conducting real-time electronic surveillance may require a wiretap order from a judge. In the next chapter, you will learn how to present testimony about evidence and methods in court or legal action.

Amendments to anticrime legislation, particularly the USA PATRIOT Act, have given greater search and seizure authority to law officials and investigators—at the expense of privacy. The next chapter also examines ethical issues and dilemmas.

## Test Your Skills

### MULTIPLE CHOICE QUESTIONS

1. What is the fundamental principle guaranteed by the Fifth Amendment to ensure that civil and criminal cases follow federal or state rules fairly?
   A. Due process of the case.
   B. Due process of the law.
   C. Rules of criminal evidence.
   D. Due protection under the law.

2. What is meant by prejudicial treatment?
   A. Deprived protection.
   B. Discrimination against minorities.
   C. Equal treatment.
   D. Unequal treatment.

3. When the 1970 amendment to Rule 34(a) made electronic data subject to discovery, what type of evidence was used soon afterward in legal actions?
   A. Computer printouts.
   B. Internet history records.
   C. E-mail.
   D. Cellular phone records.

4. Which sequence represents the progression of evidence from outset of the case to trial?
   A. All evidence, relevant evidence, admissible evidence.
   B. All evidence, admissible evidence, relevant evidence.
   C. All evidence, authenticated evidence, relevant evidence.
   D. All evidence, privileged evidence, admissible evidence.

5. What governs the admissibility of evidence, including electronic records and data?
   A. Business Records exceptions to hearsay.
   B. Privacy Rules.
   C. Federal Rules of Evidence.
   D. Fourth Amendment.

6. What does the term *relevant evidence* mean?
   A. Evidence that cannot be excluded.
   B. Evidence provided by expert witnesses or eyewitnesses.
   C. Evidence that can make some fact or issue more probable or less probable than it would be without the evidence.
   D. Direct evidence that is not prejudicial.

7. Which rule of evidence holds that testimony in the form of an opinion is allowed unless it is inadmissible for some other reason?
   A. Rule 702.
   B. Rule 704.
   C. Rule 802.
   D. Rule 803.

8. Which of the following is not a condition that must be met in order for a qualified expert to testify?
   A. The testimony is based upon sufficient facts or data.
   B. The testimony is the product of reliable principles and methods.
   C. The witness has not been paid to testify.
   D. The witness has applied the principles and methods reliably to the facts of the case.

9. Which of the following statements is *not true* about a motion by a lawyer for a hearing before trial to determine whether or not evidence is admissible?
   A. Courts prefer this approach.
   B. It can protect the accused because the jury does not hear inadmissible evidence.
   C. It is called a *motion in limine*.
   D. It is a motion to express evidence.

10. What test is primarily a question of relevance or fit of the evidence?
    A. Daubert test.
    B. Hearsay test.
    C. *In limine* test.
    D. Prejudicial test.

11. A physical or electronic document's appearance, content, or substance can be authenticated using
    A. eyewitness testimony.
    B. hearsay evidence.
    C. circumstantial evidence.
    D. probative testimony.

12. Which law allows law enforcement with proper warrants or subpoenas to collect basic information and the content of stored messages about users from ISPs?
    A. Electronic Communications Privacy Act.
    B. Federal Wiretap Statute.
    C. Pen/Trap Statute.
    D. Counterfeit Access Device and Computer Fraud and Abuse Act.



13. Which act expanded the list of criminal activities for which wiretaps can be ordered?
    A. Federal Wiretap Statute.
    B. USA PATRIOT Act.
    C. Pen/Trap Statute.
    D. ECPA.

14. Which is true about the Digital Millennium Copyright Act of 1998?
    A. The act was amended by the USA PATRIOT Act of 2001.
    B. It requires that ISPs notify their customers before releasing private information about them.
    C. It requires that subpoenas be signed by a judge before an ISP can turn over names of suspected music pirates.
    D. It allows music companies to force ISPs to turn over the names of suspected music pirates by submitting a subpoena from any U.S. District Court clerk's office.

15. The PATRIOT Act permits an investigator to delay notifying an individual of a search. This delay is referred to as the ______ provision.
    A. sneak and peek
    B. serious jeopardy
    C. target
    D. 90 day

## EXERCISES

### Exercise 12.1: Interpretation of Federal Rules of Criminal Procedure

1. Access the Federal Rules of Criminal Procedure at the Legal Information Institute at **www.law.cornell.edu/rules/frcrmp/.**
2. Notice the 60 rules of procedure. Select Rule 2, *Interpretation,* and read it.
3. Based on what you have learned in this chapter, explain why the Federal Rules of Criminal Procedure are to be interpreted as described in Rule 2.

### Exercise 12.2: Purpose of Legal Procedures

1. Access the *Overview of Civil Procedure* at **www.law.cornell.edu/wex/index.php/Civil_procedure.**
2. Read "Civil Procedure: An Overview."
3. In your own words, explain the purpose of a procedural system.
4. Explain how a majority of suits filed in the United States are settled. Explain why.

### Exercise 12.3: Daubert Test

1. Go to Wikipedia, the free encyclopedia, at **http://en.wikipedia.org/.**
2. Do a search on the Daubert Standard.

3. Identify the two prongs of Daubert's two-pronged test of admissibility that is applied to expert witness testimony. Explain each of them and give an example of each.

### Exercise 12.4: Identifying Distinctive Features of E-Mail

Refer to the *United States v. Siddiqui,* discussed in this chapter. The case showed that distinctive e-mail writing styles could be used to authenticate e-mail.

1. Review five of your e-mail messages that you have recently sent to one person.
2. Identify at least three elements of your distinctive style.
3. Review five e-mail messages that you have received from a classmate, faculty, or family member.
4. Identify at least three distinctive elements of that person's style.
5. Explain whether or not you could authenticate e-mail from that person based on the features you identified.

### Exercise 12.5: Service Provider Provisions of the ECPA

1. Review the DEA sting operation, *Operation Web Tryp,* near the end of the chapter.
2. Identify at least two sources of e-evidence used by the DEA.
3. Explain how the DEA might have collected that e-evidence.
4. If the DEA collected e-evidence from a service provider as defined under the ECPA, would a subpoena or search warrant be needed? Explain why or why not.

## PROJECTS

### Project 12.1: United States Court System

1. Visit the U.S. Courts Web site at **www.uscourts.gov/.**
2. Click the *Court Links* button. Based on the map, identify which of the eleven circuits your state is in.
3. Get a listing of the types of courts in that circuit by using the "Search by" feature. Select one of the district courts by clicking it. Then click the court's Internet Web site link. Explore the features and content of the district court's Web site.

4. Write a brief report on three types of useful features or content you find at this Web site.
5. Return to the U.S. Courts Web site at **www.uscourts.gov/.** Click the *Library* button and select *Commonly Used Terms* to access the glossary. Or go directly to the glossary using **www.uscourts.gov/library/glossary.html.**
6. In your own words, explain the following terms: *due process, hearsay, motion in limine,* and *pretrial conference.*

## Project 12.2: Sections 201–220 of the USA PATRIOT Act

1. Visit the FACT SHEET: USA PATRIOT ACT PROVISIONS SET FOR REAUTHORIZATION on the Department of Justice Web site at **www.usdoj.gov/opa/pr/2005/April/05_opa_163.htm.**
2. Review the discussion of Sections 201 through 220 that apply to this chapter.
3. Select three sections and explain the impact of the provision in a criminal or civil case.

## Project 12.3: Limits to Expectations of Privacy

*Smyth v. Pillsbury Co.* (1996) was the first reported case relating to privacy of an employee's e-mail on a company's computer system. The Pillsbury Company "repeatedly assured its employees, including plaintiff, that all e-mail communications would remain confidential and privileged." Smyth sent e-mail to his supervisor that, among other things, "concerned sales management and contained threats to 'kill the backstabbing bastards' . . . " Smyth was terminated from his job for "inappropriate and unprofessional comments over defendant's e-mail system." The court dismissed Smyth's complaint. The court said

> *[W]e do not find a reasonable expectation of privacy in e-mail communications voluntarily made by an employee to his supervisor over the company e-mail system notwithstanding any assurances that such communications would not be intercepted by management. . . . [P]laintiff voluntarily communicated the alleged unprofessional comments over the company e-mail system. We find no privacy interests in such communications. . . . Moreover, the company's interest in preventing inappropriate and unprofessional comments or even illegal activity over its e-mail system outweighs any privacy interest the employee may have in those comments.*

1. In your opinion, did Smyth have a reasonable expectation of privacy when he sent the e-mail? Explain your answer.
2. Use an online search engine to find more information about the *Smyth v. Pillsbury Co.* (1996) case.

3. Identify additional information about the case. Which Federal Rule of Civil Procedure did Pillsbury use in its defense?
4. Based on the additional information, has your original opinion changed? Explain why or why not.

### Project 12.4: Junk Science and Identification Evidence

Prior to trial, courts may exclude an expert witness from testifying if the witness does not have relevant expertise or his methods are "junk science" that cannot be relied upon to produce accurate and reliable results. Sometimes the junk science argument is referred to as the Daubert-Frye argument.

1. Go to the Web site of Forensic-evidence at **www.forensic-evidence.com/site/ID/Cole_junksci.html** and read "Court Excludes Fingerprint Critic's Testimony as 'Junk Science.'"
2. Search the Internet for more information about the Daubert-Frye argument.
3. Identify and explain the reasons that the Court barred Dr. Cole from testifying as an expert in this case.
4. Based on what you have learned, do you agree with the Court's junk science argument decision against Dr. Cole? Justify your answer.

## Case Study

The majority opinion in *Daubert v. Merrell Dow Pharmaceuticals, Inc.*, 509 U.S. 579 (1993), was authored by Justice Blackmun. According to the opinion, "general acceptance" is not a necessary condition for the admissibility of scientific evidence under the Federal Rules of Evidence. But according to the Rules of Evidence, trial judges need to ensure that an expert's testimony both rests on a reliable foundation and is relevant to the task at hand.

1. Read "Daubert in a Nutshell" at **www.daubertontheweb.com/Chapter_2.htm.**
2. What was the Frye test? What rule replaced (supplanted) Frye?
3. How does Daubert help prevent "absurd and irrational pseudoscientific assertions" by expert witnesses?
4. What was the response to the fear that Daubert's new evidentiary standards would sometimes stifle courtroom debate?

12

# Chapter 13

# Ethical and Professional Responsibility in Testimony

## Chapter Objectives

**After reading this chapter and completing the exercises, you will be able to do the following:**

- Understand the importance of adhering to ethical duties in court.
- Identify the responsibilities of an expert witness to the legal system of justice.
- Explain courtroom procedures and the requirements and challenges of testifying.
- Explain how to offer effective testimony.
- Identify academic and professional degree and certificate programs.

## Introduction

Every investigative step from acquisition through to analysis of the e-evidence may someday need to be explained in court on direct examination—and then defended on cross-examination. Cross-examination is when the other side's (opposing) lawyer attempts to ***impeach,*** or discredit, your testimony. To impeach, the opposing lawyer may attack your credentials, integrity, forensics methods, or written and verbal statements. Computer forensics investigators whose methods and chain of custody cannot withstand cross will lose the jurors' trust. Jurors' trust of expert witnesses' skills and credibility impacts the outcome of trials.

Therefore, in prior chapters, you learned defensible approaches to data collection and preservation, investigative procedures to verify the chain of custody, computer and networking infrastructure, forensics tools, rules of evidence, and relevant laws. You learned how to secure devices and their contents, discover and recover files, and analyze contents so that the e-evidence would be admissible in court or legal action.

Working in the legal system carries a huge responsibility to perform your work with diligence, competence, and good judgment. There may not have been any eyewitnesses to a crime. Without the benefit of direct testimony, juries rely on experts to "connect the dots" of the circumstantial evidence. To help juries understand the e-evidence and what it reveals, computer forensics professionals are called on to give testimony about the investigation they performed or to serve as expert witnesses to critically review and then validate or refute the testimony of other investigators. Witnesses need to be prepared for scrutiny from a judge, the jury, and attorneys who often know very little about e-evidence.

This chapter prepares you to perform a significant role in the justice system—to provide testimony as an expert witness. Given what is at stake, witnesses have ethical responsibilities that cannot be compromised. You learn about the common challenges of giving testimony in open court and the stages of a trial.

## The Importance of Forensic Expert Witnesses and Expert Reports

You are well aware of the necessity of maintaining the integrity of e-evidence. But evidence alone does not always win a court case. Investigative efforts may turn out to be valuable only if forensics experts testify with integrity and credibility. In order for evidence to lead to a conviction or acquittal of someone on trial for a crime or to decide a civil case, juries or judges need to understand and be convinced of what the evidence means. That is the role of the expert witness. Witness integrity is thus as essential as evidence integrity. And the witness's credibility and court presentation skills have a strong influence on what the triers of fact believe.

Eyewitnesses are able to give direct testimony because they have observed events through their senses—usually they either saw or heard what happened. In contrast, expert witnesses have technical, scientific, or other specialized knowledge to reconstruct or explain what happened without having observed it directly (Waltz and Park, 2005). An expert witness is the *only* witness who may give an opinion about what happened without having been there.

**Caution**

**Conflict of Interest**

Before accepting a case, an expert must verify that there is no ***conflict of interest,*** a situation in which an expert cannot be unbiased for any reason. The penalty for acting as an expert in a conflict of interest includes being disqualified from testifying, which could destroy the case.

### Qualified Expert Witnesses

As you learned in Chapter 12, Rule 702 defines the qualifications needed for someone to testify as an expert witness. Qualifications are skill or knowledge from education or experience. Qualified computer forensics investigators can serve as expert witnesses and give opinions or make inferences about what happened even though they were not eyewitnesses because they help judges or juries (triers of fact) understand e-evidence. Inarguably, those opinions and inferences must be based on critical evaluations of the evidence. Weaknesses in the evidence or investigation need to be revealed.

Depending on the situation, the expert witness may either raise doubt in or remove doubt from the minds of the jury. With such power comes the responsibility to ensure that the testimony is truthful and complete. The objective of giving testimony should never be based solely on winning the case.

Scientific testimony such as an expert witness can supply is not automatically presented or considered in trials; the court is not obliged to seek the services of an expert witness. Only on rare occasions does a court select its own expert to inform itself or the jury. Instead, scientific testimony is typically presented in the context of our adversary system wherein each party is entitled to present its position on an issue in the best light possible. In an adversary system, each of the opposing parties has an opportunity to state his viewpoint before the court. The plaintiff argues for the defendant's guilt (criminal) or liability (civil). The defense argues for the defendant's innocence (criminal) or against liability (civil).

The jury makes the ultimate determination about the facts or issues in dispute. Each side of a controversy selects the witnesses, experts, and scientific testimony that make its own position the most compelling to the jury. The logical premise for this system is that each adversary's own self-interest will result in vigorous and effective cross-examination. The benefit to the system of justice is that the jury will be able to consider all opinions and possibilities before reaching its verdict.

**Caution**

**Compensation**

Compensation must be disclosed according to federal rules. Unreasonably high compensation gives the impression that one's opinion has been bought.

Before serving as a ***testimonial witness*** (an expert witness who will give testimony in trial), an expert must submit a vita and disclose:

- Qualifications, including all publications
- Compensation being paid
- List of cases in which the witness testified as an expert during the past four years

For this chapter, all discussion pertains to testimonial expert witnesses. Nontestimonial witnesses are those who serve as consultants but will not be called at trial.

After officially being designated as an expert, all of your materials or *work product*—analysis, notes, reports, correspondence, opinions, research, and so on are subject to discovery. Be very careful with your work product practices to avoid creating misleading materials.

## Expert Reports

Federal Rule 26 requires specific disclosures from the expert before trial. Under Rule 26(a)(2)(B), the expert must write and sign an ***expert report*** containing "a complete statement of all opinions to be expressed and the basis and reasons therefore." Figure 13.1 contains a template that shows other requirements of an

*<Name of Legal Case or Lawsuit>* **CASE**

**Name of Forensics Expert, Credentials**

**EXPERT'S REPORT** **Date**

**A. INTRODUCTION**

Describe the incident or case in broad and general terms. Say right up front what is alleged to have happened, caused the incident, or led to the case.

Describe your scope of work. For example: The purpose of my investigation was to determine if . . . .

**B. MATERIALS AVAILABLE FOR REVIEW**

List the information you were given that related to this incident or case. Include your inspection of digital devices, media, and photos at the incident or case site, if any. List material that is case-specific. Doing this will be very convenient for you at later stages of the case.

1. Investigation materials (as appropriate)
   a. Electronic evidence, log files, hard copies
   b. Report of another expert
   c. Digital images of the computers, devices, scene or other items

**C. BACKGROUND**

Describe the background of the case and the investigation that was performed. For example, a bit-stream image of the 80GB hard drive of the Dell Latitude D800 laptop (serial number ###) was made using <forensics toolkit> to preserve the integrity of the media on the laptop as of <date>. Then I used <forensics software> to identify files <created, deleted, modified, etc.> between <beginning date> and <ending date>.

Include what the lawyer(s) have explained to you and what is alleged to have happened.

**D. DESCRIPTION OF THE FACTS OF THE INVESTIGATION AND CASE**

Limit this to relevant facts. Everything you say should have some meaning to you in your analysis and findings or at least be there to set the scene for the reader. Use references to software tools, hardware devices, and digital images to help your description, and include them at the end of the report.

If you have different items you would like to list separately, create a subheading using an underline. This would be appropriate when listing related but separate items. For example:

Internet Links

Text would be typed here.

Network Drawings

Text would be typed here.

*Source:* Adapted from template provided courtesy of Robson Forensic, Inc., **www.robsonforensic.com**

**FIGURE 13.1** Computer forensics expert report template.

**Caution**

**Expert Must Write the Expert Report**

While a lawyer may help the expert in preparing the report, the lawyer cannot write the report because the expert may need to testify under oath that she actually wrote it.

13

CONTINUED ON NEXT PAGE

**E. CAUSES OF THE INCIDENT OR CASE**

Through analysis (reconstruction of what happened) relate how the incident or events occurred and what conditions were (or were alleged to be) causes of the incident or case. Use this section to set up the flow for the technical sections that follow. Refer to your chain of custody documentation. Generally, basic computer or network technology principles are useful in identifying causes and related conditions.

**F. ANALYSIS**

Use as many sections as necessary to explain what happened, how it happened, when, and by whom it was done. Use references from the technical community to develop support for your opinions. Show examples of other similar conditions, if appropriate. The more of a historical development that you can build into your reports, through repeated cases and secondary references, the better. Include your experiences from prior investigations related to the same issue. If there are negative aspects to your case, consider listing them here. When referencing materials, state the author, title, journal or manual, publisher, date, and what it is. Then state how the materials pertain to your findings.

**G. FINDINGS**

Within the bounds of reasonable (professional) certainty and subject to change if additional information becomes available, it is my professional opinion that: (list)

Within the bounds of reasonable (professional) certainty, and subject to change if additional information becomes available, it is my professional opinion that:

1. Statement 1.
2. Statement 2.
3. Statement 3.

Go back to your description of scope of work and make the scope match with the findings.

**REFERENCES**

Include references.

**FIGURES, PHOTOS, APPENDICES, OR ATTACHMENTS**

Include things to show the basis for your opinion. Diagrams and images may be needed for the lawyer and jurors to understand computer or Internet technologies. Include extracts from documents to show the standard of care that you think should have applied. Give opinions, and the factors you used in determining the opinion, and reference any important papers. Label and order these as figures, photos, or attachments. Do not use other terms, such as the term *exhibit*.

________________________________________

Name, Title

effective expert report. This template is also available in Appendix C in a slightly expanded form.

Ultimately, this expert report must be provided to the opposing lawyer, who will use it during cross-examination or have another expert attempt to find fault with it. This report is critical and must be complete because it defines what you will and can testify to in court under oath. The term *complete* is difficult to define. For the report, a good rule of thumb is that it should explain what you did with enough detail that another computer forensics expert could replicate your work.

## IN PRACTICE: Judges' View of Expert Testimony after Daubert

In 1991 and again in 1998, the Federal Judicial Center conducted a survey of federal judges about their experiences with expert testimony in civil cases (Johnson et al., 2001). Of interest in the 1998 survey was whether the Daubert decision (*Daubert v. Merrell Dow Pharmaceuticals,* 1993) had an impact on the use of expert witness testimony.

Judges answered specific questions about their most recent relevant civil trial and their overall experience with expert testimony in civil cases. Comparing the survey results, the center found that judges were more likely to scrutinize expert testimony before trial and that lawyers were filing *motions in limine* challenging the admissibility of expert testimony more frequently after *Daubert.*

## Increasing Reliance on Forensic Experts

E-evidence will increasingly be used in court trials as a natural outcome of increasing use of digital communication—e-mail, IM, chat rooms, and smart phones. IDC, a market research firm in Framingham, Massachusetts, projects that the market for computer forensics will increase from $310 million in 2005 to $634 million by 2009 (Zimmerman, 2006). Many criminals keep detailed spreadsheets of their finances or attempt to fabricate e-mails to create an alibi or defense. Combined with the introduction and amendments to laws discussed in Chapter 12, this is generating criminal offenses that demand e-evidence in order for successful prosecution. Uncovering e-evidence and data trails can be a deciding factor in criminal cases. When data has been deleted or moved to disguise the trails, only a computer forensics expert can recover those electronic trails and evidence—and then testify in court.

Explaining forensically sound recovery and authentication of e-evidence and responding to cross-examination challenges in court to nontechnical jurors is hard work. The investigation, interpretation, and presentation of e-evidence are complex and filled with technical terms and concepts that are not easy to translate into terms jurors can understand and remember when they get to deliberate all of the testimony (Best, 2004).

### Caution

**People May Attempt to Falsify E-Evidence**

People have falsified evidence, altered it, or claimed that it was something other than what it really was. Because of these risks, lawyers have a right and obligation to question the validity of e-evidence.

## IN PRACTICE: Expert Opinion Is Subject to Challenge

Determining which issues should be decided by the jury is a complex issue. In *State v. Summers*, 176 N.J. 306 (2003), Justice Peter G. Verniero decided that the testimony of the New Jersey State's narcotics expert did not infringe on the right of the defendant to have a jury decide his guilt. The court found or noted that:

- The expert's opinion was highly probative of the distribution offenses and was necessary to assist members of the jury, who presumably were unschooled in the drug trade.
- The expert's testimony helped jurors understand how drugs were packaged, priced, concealed, and sold, consistent with distribution in high-crime areas.
- Although the expert's testimony was declarative in nature and covered issues that the jury had to decide, the testimony was permissible under N.J. R. Evid. 704.
- The jury had been properly informed that it (the jury) was the ultimate finder of fact and that it had to determine the appropriate weight to give the expert testimony.
- Expert opinion testimony (that is admissible) cannot be objected to because that testimony is an issue to be decided by the jury. However, such testimony is subject to exclusion if the risk of undue prejudice substantially outweighs its probative value.

Courts widely agree that expert testimony about drug-trade practices is admissible. The relevant case in New Jersey is *State v. Odom* (1989). In *Odom*, the prosecutor asked the state's expert to assume a set of facts consistent with those of trial. Based on those facts, the prosecutor asked the expert witness to express a view on whether the defendant possessed the drugs for his own use or with the intent to distribute them. The defense lawyer objected but was overruled. The expert testified that in his opinion the drugs were possessed with the intent to distribute them. Odom was convicted. The Supreme Court agreed with the defendant's conviction, setting forth guidelines for the appropriate use of a hypothetical question in a drug case.

CONTINUED ON NEXT PAGE

CONTINUED

The Supreme Court ruled that:

- The testimony must be limited to the facts adduced at trial.
- The prosecutor may ask the expert's opinion, based on those facts, whether the drugs were possessed for distribution or personal consumption. The expert should inform jurors of the information on which the opinion is based and must avoid parroting statutory terminology whenever possible. Trial courts, in such cases, should instruct the jury about the proper weight to be given to the expert's opinion and should remind jurors that the ultimate decision concerning a defendant's guilt or innocence rests solely with them.

## The Trial Process

A number of tasks take place before a case actually goes to trial. As you learned in Chapter 1, the process of discovery ensures that all parties have access to the materials that will be used as evidence in the case. The judge also hears any pretrial motions and rules on them before the trial gets under way.

Another part of the process that takes place before the parties actually enter the courtroom is depositions. A *deposition* is a statement taken under oath. Depositions are done out of court but under the same oath as in court. A court reporter has the witness raise her right hand and swear to tell the truth and then records everything that is said. The court reporter takes down words spoken aloud and does not record nonverbal motions, such as nodding. The opposing attorney asks questions. The other attorney is present in order to object to any improper questions.

As an expert witness, you may have to be deposed as a part of your participation in a case. The attorney may ask you to disclose any information of a personal nature that may diminish your effectiveness as a witness.

Typically, after a civil case has proceeded through discovery and survived any pretrial motions, the case can be dropped by the plaintiff, settled, or proceed to trial. In criminal cases, the case can be dropped by the prosecutor; the defendant can accept a plea bargain; or the case can proceed to trial.

During the trial, lawyers publicly present their evidence and legal theories to the judge and jury. One of the judge's duties is to ensure that only proper evidence and theories are considered by the jury to reach a verdict of guilty or not guilty. When a lawyer objects to evidence that has been presented, the trial judge can sustain the objection or overrule it. If an objection is sustained, the evidence is excluded and cannot be considered by the jury.

### FYI Jurors Are Not Einsteins

In the first five years of pretrial discovery in *United States v. IBM* (S.D.N.Y. 1975), the parties produced over 64 million pages of documents. During the discovery phase of another federal suit, Washington Public Power Supply System Securities Litigation, 19 F.3d 1291 (9th Cir. 1994), the parties exchanged more than 200 million pages of documents. Even if the jury consists of 12 Einsteins, the jurors cannot digest that much information (Imwinkelried and Schlueter, 2004).

In the early 1990s, the American Bar Association (ABA) Special Committee on Jury Comprehension released the results of surveys of jurors who had participated in complex federal and state cases (Spec. Comm. on Jury Comprehension, ABA Litigation Section, Jury Comprehension in Complex Cases, 1990). The researchers asked the jurors what complaints they had against the attorneys who had tried the cases. By a wide margin, the primary complaint was that the litigators went overboard and swamped the jury with information, particularly an excessive number of exhibits. In the infamous McMartin child abuse prosecution in California, prosecutors called 124 witnesses and introduced 974 exhibits, requiring more than 33 months of trial and consuming nearly 64,000 pages of transcript (Benedictis, 1990).

It is the jury members who ultimately decide the weight and credibility of evidence they are allowed to consider (Waltz and Park, 2005). Given the jury's dependence on evidence provided by expert witnesses, the role of witnesses is to give opinions or inferences truthfully and without exaggeration.

Lawyers have duties to the court and professional rules of ethics, which are beyond the scope of this book but can be found at **www.abanet.org/cpr/rules/allrules.html** and **www.abanet.org/cpr/mrpc/preamble.html.** Lawyers are obliged to try to impeach a witness; that is, to attempt to discredit a witness by proving that the witness lied or that his testimony was inconsistent or by producing contrary evidence. This adversarial approach helps to ensure the validity of evidence being presented at trial.

There will be conflict with respect to what each side claims are the facts. These factual disputes are resolved by the jury during their deliberation after hearing all of the testimony. Juries base their decision on clear and convincing evidence.

**FYI** *Clear and Convincing Evidence*

In civil cases, evidence must prove a matter by the "preponderance of evidence." In a criminal case, the standards are tougher, requiring evidence "beyond a reasonable doubt" to convict. See **www.nycourts.gov/cji/1-General/CJI2d.Presumption.Burden.Reasonable_Doubt.pdf** for jury instructions related to reasonable doubt.

## An Expert Witness's Ethical Duty to the Court

Everyone involved in the courts has an ethical duty to protect the legal system and Constitution. People are presumed innocent until proven guilty. Those who testify do so under the oath "to tell the truth, the whole truth, and nothing but the truth." Except for cases where you are hired by the court, you will have been hired by the prosecutor, plaintiff lawyer, or defense lawyer. As a professional, your duty is to the truth and not to the person who hired you. Performing that duty can be extremely difficult.

To fulfill their ethical duties to the court and judicial system, investigators need a basic understanding of the stages of a trial, the testimony process, and dynamics of court testimony. To illustrate, if a lawyer objects to a question and the judge sustains the objection, the witness cannot answer the question. Also, a jury may perceive witnesses who "try too hard" as being biased.

**Caution**

**Weak Testimony**

Preparing to testify requires a lot of time and effort to be sure that all arguments are based on sound practices and strong logic. In court, weak arguments weaken strong cases.

## Voir Dire

In cases that rely on information provided by an expert witness, such as most computer forensics cases, the jury will have to consider the credibility of the expert witness's testimony, but the expert will have had to survive voir dire to be able to testify.

***Voir dire*** (pronounced "vwar deer") is a preliminary examination of prospective witnesses under oath to determine their competence or suitability. An expert witness is examined to establish her credibility before the witness is allowed to testify in court. The witness's credibility is examined to prevent damaging evidence from a witness who may not be credible. Voir dire prevents wasting court time on testimony that cannot be used by the jury.

**Caution**

**Voir Dire**

Voir dire means "to speak the truth." It is often used as a tool to cast doubt on the expert witness's opinion testimony.

Regardless of how many times an expert has testified, the process of voir dire can be extremely intimidating or unnerving. You are questioned not only about your credentials, experience, and methodology, but also in many cases about your personal life, associations, whether you have given proper credit to others, and when you last updated your technical skills.

Voir dire also applies to jurors. The purpose is to find out if the potential jurors have experiences, associations, or knowledge that will make them biased. As with experts, the goal of the voir dire examination is to produce fair and impartial jurors.

## Testimony During a Trial

The Sixth Amendmentof the U.S. Constitution guarantees the right of an accused in a criminal prosecution to be confronted with the witnesses against him. The right to confrontation is fundamental to a fair trial under both the federal and state constitutions. Testimony is the means by which the prosecution presents evidence against the accused.

**Testimony Process** There is a process for presenting testimony in court that is specifically designed to keep improper evidence from being considered by the jury. The general steps in the testimony process are listed in Table 13.1. Notice

**TABLE 13.1** Testimony process in court.

| Steps in the Testimony Process | Definitions, Purposes, and Examples |
|---|---|
| 1. Opening statements | Brief statements made by the prosecutor* and the defense lawyer to tell their account of the events. These statements do not involve witnesses or evidence. Prosecutors make the first opening statement because they have the burden of proving that the defendant committed the crime.<br>The purpose of the opening statement is to outline the general nature of the case and the types of evidence that will be presented. |
| 2. Prosecutor's direct examination (also called *direct*) | The first questioning of a witness after the opening statements. Because of the burden of proof, the prosecutor introduces evidence to support the allegations. |
| 3. Defense lawyer's cross-examination (also called *cross*) | The questioning of a witness by the opposing lawyer after direct. The questions on cross-examination are limited to the subjects introduced in the direct examination of the witness. However, the attorney is allowed to ask ***leading questions*** (but not misleading ones). A leading question is one that suggests its answer.<br>An example of a leading question is: "Is it true that you put the suspect's laptop computer in the trunk of your car?" An example of a direct question is: "What did you do, if anything, with the suspect's laptop computer?" |

CONTINUED ON NEXT PAGE

CONTINUED

| Steps in the Testimony Process | Definitions, Purposes, and Examples |
|---|---|
| | The purpose of cross-examination is to create doubt in or impeach the testimony of the witness. Despite the lawyer's purpose, cross-examination might result in the witness's effectively defending prior testimony, which strengthens the witness's credibility. |
| 4. Prosecutor's redirect examination (also called *redirect*) | Follows cross-examination. Questioning of a witness about issues that were uncovered during the cross-examination. |
| 5. Defense lawyer's recross examination | Follows redirect examination. This recross examination gives both sides equal opportunity to ask questions. |
| Steps 2–5 repeated for each prosecution witness | Steps 2 through 5 are repeated until all of the prosecutor's witnesses have testified. |
| 6. Prosecution rests | Prosecution testimony ends. After direct examination, cross-examination, redirect, and recross of all the witnesses is complete, the prosecutor rests her case. After the prosecutor rests, no more witnesses can be called to the stand or evidence introduced by the prosecutor or plaintiff attorney. |
| 7. Directed verdict of acquittal (possible) | If the prosecution has not proved its case, the defense lawyer may make a motion for a *directed verdict.* If the judge agrees, the trial does not proceed. This verdict saves time because there is no reason to complete a trial if the case has already been lost. If the judge does not agree, the trial continues. |
| 8. Defense presents evidence and witnesses (like steps 2–5, but with roles reversed) | After the prosecutor rests her case, the defense attorney begins the same direct examination of his own witnesses and using his evidence, with the roles reversed, until all defense's witnesses have testified. |
| 9. Defense rests | Defense testimony ends. |
| 10. Closing or final arguments | After all evidence is presented, lawyers for each side make final or *closing arguments*. |

CONTINUED ON NEXT PAGE

▶▶ CONTINUED

| Steps in the Testimony Process | Definitions, Purposes, and Examples |
|---|---|
| 11. Instructions and charges to the jury | Following the closing arguments, the judge informs the jury of appropriate law and what they must do to reach a verdict. |
| 12. Deliberation by the jury and verdict | Jurors consider the evidence and reach a verdict of guilty or not guilty. In some cases, the jury is unable to reach a verdict. |
| 13. Posttrial appeal | Either party may appeal the verdict. |

**Prosecutor* refers to the prosecuting or plaintiff lawyer.

that a witness is subject to rigorous or aggressive questioning multiple times by both sides and needs to be prepared to appear credible to the jury. A full explanation of expert witness preparation and testimony is far beyond the scope of this chapter. It is a duty of lawyers to prepare their witnesses for trial.

## IN PRACTICE: Importance of Instructions to the Jury

In April 2003, investment banker Frank P. Quattrone was indicted for obstruction-of-justice, obstructing an agency proceeding, and witness tampering. His case was one of many corporate misconduct cases that followed the collapse of Enron. Mr. Quattrone's case was seen by some lawyers as among the weakest of the white-collar cases because the obstruction charge hinged on a one-line e-mail message. That message was to his staff endorsing a colleague's direction to "clean up those files." He sent the e-mail on the eve of government and grand jury investigations into his activities. The jury concluded that his e-mail obstructed justice (Raider and Williams, 2005).

Quattrone appealed the verdict.

In March 2006, an appeals court ruled that Judge Richard W. Owen had given flawed instructions to the jury at Quattrone's trial. Judge Richard C. Wesley overturned (reversed) the guilty verdicts and granted him a new trial. Judge Wesley said Judge Owen's instructions to jurors were faulty because they did not require jurors to determine that Mr. Quattrone knew that the documents he was asking associates to destroy were the ones being sought by investigators (Sorkin, 2006).

### Caution

**Expert Witness Jury Instructions**

For an example of instructions to a jury regarding expert witness testimony, download www.nycourts.gov/cji/1-General/ CJI2d.Expert.pdf.

**Dynamics of Court Testimony** Members of the jury probably will not have the technical, financial, or specialized knowledge to understand evidence presented to them without the help of an expert witness. Jurors begin a case in a state of ignorance. Jurors need to rely on expert witnesses to understand e-evidence and computer technology matters of the case. There has been extensive research on juries, including how to persuasively communicate with jurors. It is well established in the literature on persuasive communication that jurors do not respond only to what is said in determining the credibility of a witness. Verbal and nonverbal behaviors are both taken into account when assessing the credibility of others.

Research in New Zealand gave some insight into jury dynamics (Carruthers, 2001). Some of the findings were:

> *In 11 of the 48 trials at least one juror, and sometimes up to half of those interviewed for a particular trial, volunteered that they or other jurors had difficulty concentrating. These difficulties were exacerbated when the oral evidence was boring or presented in a boring fashion, was confusing or repetitive, or involved lengthy technical evidence.*

In the courtroom, an expert witness's verbal and nonverbal behaviors affect what the jurors believe about his competence and trustworthiness. Competence measures whether the witness knows and understands the issues and is qualified to speak about them. Subjective impressions of trustworthiness determine whether a witness is credible. Given human dynamics of the jury, witnesses need to prepare content to present to the jury and prepare their presentation style. For example, witnesses who keep calm and convey concise, clearly stated information can have a key impact on the outcome.

### IN PRACTICE: Evidence Not Admitted During Trial Is Not Allowed

On April 25, 2006, the jurors in the trial of Zacarias Moussaoui asked for a dictionary for use during their deliberations on whether the September 11, 2001, conspirator should receive a death sentence or life in prison. That request to have a dictionary in the jury room was denied by Judge Leonie Brinkema because sending a dictionary in would be like adding additional evidence in the case. The judge invited them to come back if they had questions about specific definitions. She warned them against doing their own research, including looking up definitions (Barakat, 2006).

In the next section, you learn in greater detail how to effectively testify as an expert witness in court or deposition.

> **Caution**
>
> **Perjury Is a Crime**
>
> Perjury is intentionally making a false statement under oath. It is a criminal offense punishable by imprisonment or fine.

> **Caution**
>
> **Work Product Subject to Scrutiny**
>
> If you are retained as an expert witness, your work product is subject to discovery, which means opposing counsel has the right to review it and attempt to refute your findings. Work product is the set of notes, conclusions, or opinions developed for an attorney for trial.

## Guidelines for Testifying

Testifying in court requires telling the truth under oath. The effectiveness of your testimony requires doing so clearly, precisely, concisely, and completely. Plus you need to explain your findings in a manner that the jurors find credible. Do not underestimate how tough and demanding giving expert testimony can be. There are several powerful forces at work—those with an opposing view will fight fiercely to prevent the jury from believing you.

Never forget that you are being paid for your time and expertise, but you are not getting paid for your opinion. If a prosecutor or defense attorney asks you to skew the information presented instead of just presenting the facts, explain that your opinion is not for sale.

You need to know how to respond to questions, when to respond, and when not to respond. Above all, you must be careful, precise, and truthful in your deposition and on the stand. Opposing lawyers or their expert witnesses will point out extremely small mistakes or omissions to get your testimony excluded. For some, cross-examination can be frustrating and demeaning. For others, it can be the most interesting part of the job as they get to defend their skills and match wits with lawyers during a critical time in the trial. Juries tend to pay close attention during cross-examination, so points made under cross fire leave strong impressions.

Regardless of your attitude about being cross-examined, you must remain unaffected by it. Witnesses who keep calm and convey concise, clearly stated information—in depositions or under an opposing attorney's attempts to discredit their testimonies—can have a key impact on the case's outcome.

### Preparing for Testimony

One of the most important parts of your work as an expert witness is preparation. There should be no inconsistencies in your testimony. Prepare by reviewing documentation made during the investigation, methods and tools used, and results of the analysis. Make sure your dates about what happened are correct.

Part of your preparation includes working closely with the attorney to review the details of your testimony and anticipate questions that you will need to answer—without panic. The time and effort spent preparing for testimony range from a short telephone call to a full day of personal training. The length of the preparation depends on the complexity of the case, the role of the expert, and the issues and money at stake.

Remember that even though pretrial Daubert hearings filter out flawed expert testimony, the jury may still reject what it cannot understand or believe. Not only do you need to be able to answer questions, you will also have to justify them when asked: "What did you rely on in formulating your opinion?"

When giving direct testimony, the expert can give opinions or make inferences. During cross-examination on an expert's opinion or inference, that opinion or inference may be impeached because of

- Bias or partiality
- Interest, or amount of pay
- Prior inconsistency
- Insufficient qualifications
- Insufficient basis

Adequate preparation can help you eliminate such weaknesses in your testimony. Keep in mind that it is the opposing counsel's duty to challenge testimony to ensure that you or your testimony is not biased or deficient. Stay composed and objective.

### IN PRACTICE: The Risk of Forensic Fraud

Forensic fraud can be a major problem. According to a judicial report, analyst Fred Zain committed fraud at a West Virginia crime laboratory. His misconduct included (1) overstating the strength of results, (2) overstating the frequency of genetic matches on multiple pieces of evidence, (3) misreporting the frequency of genetic matches on multiple pieces of evidence, (4) reporting that multiple items had been tested, when only a single item had been tested, (5) reporting inconclusive results as conclusive, (6) repeatedly altering laboratory records, (7) grouping results to create the erroneous impression that genetic markers had been obtained from all samples tested, (8) failing to report conflicting results, (9) failing to conduct or to report conducting additional testing to resolve conflicting results, (10) implying a match with a suspect when testing supported only a match with the victim, and (11) reporting scientifically impossible or improbable results. (In *re Investigation of the W. Va. State Police Crime Lab, Serology Div.*, 438 S.E.2d 501, 503 [1993].)

Zain's misconduct was not an isolated case. Similar cases of forensic fraud were discovered in Oklahoma, Texas, Montana, Florida, and Colorado, potentially affecting the validity of thousands of criminal convictions (Taslitz, 2005).

## Presenting Your Evidence

As mentioned earlier, juries pay as much attention to *how* you present your testimony as they do to what you actually say. You can ensure the best reception of your evidence by maintaining a professional demeanor at all times and responding appropriately to the questions you are asked by counsel. Given the numerous laws, rules, and credibility factors to consider, a conservative approach to testimony is generally best.

**Presenting a Professional Appearance and Demeanor** Your appearance and demeanor in court have a great impact on how your message is received. Consider the points below as guidelines for your actions in court.

- Always act like a professional.
- Speak slowly and distinctly. Do not get excited, and focus on speaking slowly.
- Do not use inappropriate nonverbal communication. Do not detract from what you are saying by what you are doing with your arms, face, or body. Nonverbal messages to avoid include fidgeting, not facing the jury, failing to maintain good eye contact with the jury, or getting rattled by questions.
- Be truthful, careful, and precise. You are under oath, so you are swearing to everything you say.
- Be patient.
- Dress like an expert.
- Never argue, shout, or refuse to answer questions. Don't become argumentative or defensive. Avoid displays of negative behavior.
- Try to be relaxed and look at the jury when answering. Confidently explain, clarify, and simplify and maintain eye contact with the jury.

**Responding to Counsel** Your testimony on the stand will consist of interactions with counsel for both prosecution or plaintiff and defendant. How you respond to the questions of attorneys on both sides of the case can have considerable impact on how the jury receives your testimony.

- Wait for each question to be presented to you. Never start to speak until the other person has stopped talking. Do not speak at the same time as anyone else. This is important because the court reporter must record all testimony and cannot record more than one person at a time. Do not interrupt or speak over other people.
- Learn to speak for the record. That means avoiding vague words such as *this* or *that* or other inexact words without clarifying what the *this* is referring to.
- Make sure you understand the question before beginning to answer. Wait until the entire question is asked. Then pause for a second or two

before answering. The pause gives you time to prepare your answer and a lawyer time to object, if needed. If an attorney objects, do not speak until you are told to continue.

- Answer the question specifically. State only what you know, directly responding to each specific question. Answer concisely, completely, and then stop. If you can answer a question with a simple *yes* or *no*, then that is all you need to say. If you do not know the answer, admit that you do not know. Your credibility depends on your telling the truth even with regard to what you know and do not know.
- Do not try to avoid answering a question. You will not be able to change your story later without losing some credibility, plus you are under oath.
- Do not answer an ambiguous question. If you are unable to respond to a question, say so and request clarification—never attempt to answer a question that you don't really understand.
- Do not try to educate the questioner on the topic by providing a fuller explanation than is needed to answer the question.
- Stay composed and take time to answer so that you do not get, or appear to get, confused. Do not allow anyone to rush you.
- Do not try to argue your point, bluff, or hide harmful facts. Never guess at an answer to a question.
- When being cross-examined, do not volunteer information that was not asked or an explanation to your answer. By trying to explain your testimony on cross-examination, you will look very defensive on the witness stand and harm your own credibility.
- Do not forget who is deciding the case. Direct your replies to the judge and jury. You are speaking to people who will base their understanding and acceptance of your testimony on your professionalism. If the testimony's full positive benefit is to have an impact on the court's decisions, they must trust you.

You will be asked questions that you do not understand or that could be interpreted in more than one way. Do not answer such questions. Instead, ask for clarification of any question. For example, ask, "Would you please rephrase the question?" You are given an opportunity to review and correct your testimony later, but it is better to avoid testimony that needs to be corrected.

Be alert for a common trap used by lawyers. They will ask you to offer opinions outside your area of expertise. Do not even attempt to give such opinions. Federal rules do not permit expert witnesses to give opinions outside their area of expertise. But there are no rules against lawyers trying to trick experts into giving such opinions. If you give opinions about anything outside your specific area of expertise, you may discredit yourself or your testimony. The lawyer can point out that you gave testimony outside your area—and that you may have given other testimony outside your area that no one had caught yet.

Your interactions with counsel may resemble the following exchanges (Wall and Paroff, 2005):

1. *What is the evidence, or what does it purport to be?*
   Forensics Expert: "This is a printout of data that I recovered on 6/15/2006 from the hard disk drive primarily used by John Doe of the Big Ace Corporation.";
2. *From where did the evidence allegedly come?*
   Forensics Expert: "The hard drive was taken from the office of John Doe on 5/15/2006. It was contained within a Generic PC bearing model XXXX and S/N YYYY."
3. *Who created, discovered, or recovered the evidence?*
   Forensics Expert: "The data appears to have been created by John Doe. I discovered and recovered it from his hard disk drive using computer forensic techniques."
4. *How was it created, discovered, or recovered?*
   Forensics Expert: "I made an image of the hard disk drive using a forensic imaging device. This device is designed to make a perfect copy of a disk and does not alter the data on the disk being copied."
5. *Were there any material changes, alterations, or modifications during the recovery of the evidence such that it may no longer be what it once was?*
   Forensics Expert: "No. Our processes as well as the tools that we use are designed to ensure that no changes whatsoever occur to the original media and data we work on. We use write-blocking devices as an extra precaution in this regard. We test our tools, both software and hardware, in order to validate that no changes are made to the original media, and to ensure that a perfect image is made of that media."
6. *What has happened to it since the time it was created, discovered, or recovered? Is there any chance that the evidence was changed, altered, or modified between the time you imaged the drive and today?*
   Forensics Expert: "Here is our chain-of-custody documentation that indicates where the media has been, in whose possession it has been, and the reason for that possession. There is no chance that during that time any of the evidence was changed/altered/modified from the form in which it existed on the drive that we imaged on 6/15/2006."

**Handling Painful Testimony** Widespread use of computers, PDAs, wireless Internet technology, and e-mail means that computer forensics investigators may need to testify in a full range of crimes from harassment to homicide and from human or drug trafficking to securities fraud. Regardless of how reprehensible a crime, testimony must not be influenced by the witness's emotional reaction to the case because emotions may impair one's judgment. No matter the circumstances of the case in which you are testifying, even if you personally find them abhorrent, you must be prepared to discuss the evidence directly and professionally.

## Witness Immunity Doctrine

It is important to the functioning of the legal system that an expert witness be free from liability because the party who retained the expert is dissatisfied with the substance of the opinions. An expert witness must be able to explain the basis for her opinion without fear that a verdict unfavorable to the client will result in a lawsuit. This immunity does not extend to perjury or negligence in formulating an opinion. Negligence can expose an expert to litigation because the judicial process requires that an expert witness provide services with professional care, skill, and proficiency.

The witness immunity doctrine was designed to encourage witnesses to testify freely and honestly without fear of lawsuits arising from their testimony. In general, a lawsuit may not be filed against an expert witness on the basis that the substance of an expert witness's testimony was unacceptable. However, an expert witness may be sued on the basis that the expert was negligent in formulating the opinion given at trial.

**Caution**

**Attack Strategy**

Lawyers know that attacking the opposing expert's theory or conclusions is much more difficult than attacking his qualifications.

### IN PRACTICE: By Any True Accounting, the Deed Was Fraud (Excerpts)

Jim Wanserski, FEI Atlanta Chapter member and former financial services manager at MCI, recounts what happened in a well-publicized case and offers his firsthand account of the discovery of fraud and his testimony.

One line of MCI's business was carriers, who were wholesale customers that bought telecommunication capacity from MCI and resold it to their own customers. In April 1996, I took over the management of carrier billing and collections and was tasked to clean up this portfolio. From April 1996 until his separation, senior manager Walter Pavlo reported to me.

My primary emphasis was enforcing MCI's customer contracts, including carrier contracts. Ultimately, I uncovered carrier fraud being committed by Pavlo and others, dealt

CONTINUED ON NEXT PAGE

CONTINUED

with it internally, and worked actively with white-collar crime resources. We communicated regularly with law enforcement. I also prepared for and testified in subsequent litigation, totaling 40 hours under oath.

### Internal Fraud Discovered

"Proof-positive" of the fraud was uncovered in February 1997. I confronted the internal perpetrators with their inappropriate transactions. However, finding the hard evidence was only the "smoking gun." Pavlo resigned—the first time. I was convinced of fraud, but needed to get him back into the office to collect more evidence. I convinced Pavlo to return under the pretense that he was needed in a "transition period to make organizational changes." More fraudulent transactions were discovered and with this hard evidence in hand, I confronted the fraudsters. In a phone conversation with Pavlo, he asked, "Well, Jim, so how much do you know?" He quickly resigned a second time and hired legal counsel, first civil, then criminal.

Both internal and external perpetrators manipulated accounting records to hide illicit activities. I uncovered illegal dealings with outsiders during the internal investigation. Two things I did not anticipate: the reactions of certain executives and the unsubstantiated accounts of this fraud that appeared in the press.

### Speak from Fact during Testimony

A key reflection on testifying: speak from fact. Presenting the truth is the best offense, and the only defense. To insure that others understood the facts, I explained them in detail, but in simplest terms.

Defense attorneys continually tried to "put words in my mouth" from their clients. Developing a working knowledge of the facts required much time, study and attention. You must develop a mastery of the data by wading painstakingly through the details.

Overall, testifying skills are similar to those developed for negotiating, except you're on the receiving end.

- You wait for each question to be presented, state what you know, directly responding to each specific question.
- You must also admit when you don't know, and that is sometimes difficult.

CONTINUED ON NEXT PAGE

CONTINUED

- Your inclination is to educate the questioner on the topic, which is not your role.
- Wait for the question to be asked and then answer it specifically; fuller explanation can be given during cross-examination
- Get prepared by learning all of the facts, a requirement for success.
- Document as if you are going to court. Early on in detection efforts, document everything; you will likely need all that material.

**Q&A about Testimony**

Q: Describe some comical events.
A: You've heard that rule, "never ask a question you don't know the answer to?" One attorney interrogated me on a topic where he believed he had all the answers. When I replied far differently than he expected, he torturously skipped over five pages of further questions! By reputation, he was a tough guy. I enjoyed that one very much.

I recall testifying on a particular event where my account totally conflicted with a defendant's. His attorney quizzed me about how I could so confidently know the defendant was wrong. I simply said, "Because I asked the person the defendant said he had gotten approval from, and that person told me neither had he given [the perpetrator] approval, nor had he ever seen the document in question." I liked that one, too—that's called a "gotcha" in legal terminology.

Q: Was testifying intimidating?
A: Anticipation was the worst part. I had been deposed in prior civil proceedings; this was much different. At times, I felt my own integrity was being questioned. Counsel's recommendation was simply to "own the facts." I would rate my performances on the stand as a bit stiff to very good. The ultimate compliment, however, was the "high fives" I received from FBI and Treasury agents.

## Professional and Educational Resources

In response to the growing demand, a wide range of academic and professional computer forensics programs are being offered. Degree programs may be affiliated with computer science, criminal justice, or information systems departments.

### Graduate Degree or Certificate Programs

- National Center for Forensics Science (NCFS), University of Central Florida, Graduate Certificate in Computer Forensics (GCCF) **(ncfs.ucf.edu/home.html),** Orlando, Florida.
- The George Washington University, Master of Forensic Sciences with a Concentration in High Technology Crime Investigation, Graduate Education Center **(nearyou.gwu.edu/htc/),** Arlington, Virginia.
- Florida Atlantic University, Master of Accounting in Forensic Accounting **(www.masters-in-forensic-accounting.com).** On campus and online. Boca Raton, Florida.
- Utica College, Bachelor's and Master's degree programs in Economic Crime **(www.economiccrimedegrees.com),** Utica, New York.

### Undergraduate Bachelor and Associate Degrees

- Champlain College Degree in Computer and Digital Forensics. Bachelor and Associate degree programs. Champlain College **(www.champlain.edu/majors/digitalforensics),** Burlington, Vermont.
- Metropolitan State University, Bachelor of Applied Science in Computer Forensics, **(www.metrostate.edu/cas/csci/forensic.html),** Minneapolis–St. Paul, Minnesota.
- Pittsburgh Technical Institute, Information Technology Network Security and Computer Forensics. Associate degree program **(www.pti.edu/programs/computer-network-systems.html),** Pittsburgh, Pennsylvania.
- Tompkins Courtland Community College, Computer Forensics A.A.S. Degree **(www.sunytccc.edu)** Dryden, New York.

### Academic Certificate Programs

- California State University, Computer Forensics Certificate **(www.fullerton.edu),** Fullerton, California.
- Medaille College, Professional Studies Certificate in Computer Crimes and Investigation **(www.medaille.edu),** Buffalo, New York.

### Professional Training

- CompuForensics, in association with universities and colleges in Georgia, Illinois, Ohio, Texas, and Tennessee, offers computer forensics training **(www.compuforensics.com/home.htm).**
- NTI Computer Forensics Training Course. Computer forensics theory and evidence processing procedures **(www.forensics-intl.com/forensic.html).**
- NTI Expert Witness Course, Computer Evidence in the Courtroom. For individuals who have expertise in computer forensics **(www.forensics-intl.com/expert.html).**
- Defense Computer Investigations Training Program (DCITP). Computer investigation training for DoD organizations, Defense Criminal Investigative organizations, Military Counterintelligence agencies, and law enforcement organizations **(www.ncjrs.gov/spotlight/forensic/training.html).**
- SEARCH High-tech Crime Training. Trains investigators for the U.S. Secret Service, U.S. Customs, FBI, U.S. Postal Service Inspection, Office of Juvenile Justice and Delinquency Prevention Internet Crimes Against Children Program, state and local investigators **(www.search.org/programs/hightech/).**

## Summary

In this chapter, you have learned that working in the legal system imposes a huge responsibility on you to perform your work with diligence, competence, and good judgment. Computer crimes do not have eyewitnesses, so juries rely on forensics experts to help them understand the meaning of the e-evidence. Jurors are not required to hold any professional qualifications, and there are no technical jury qualification guidelines for cases involving complex computer data. Working as an expert witness can be as challenging as the investigation and perhaps more demanding. You may need to critically review and then validate or refute the testimony of other investigators—or be the subject of another expert's critique of your methods and opinions. Witnesses need to be prepared to be able to withstand scrutiny from judges, jurors, and attorneys who may know very little about e-evidence.

This chapter prepares you to perform a significant role in the justice system—to provide testimony as an expert witness. Given what is at stake, witnesses have ethical responsibilities that cannot be compromised. In addition to understanding the technologies that may be at issue in a given case, to be an effective expert witness you must understand the legal system, specific courtroom communication skills, skills for enduring cross-examination, and how to prepare for legal testimony.

## Test Your Skills

### MULTIPLE CHOICE QUESTIONS

1. What is the legal term that means to *discredit a witness*?
   A. Disgrace.
   B. Degrade.
   C. Impeach.
   D. Indict.

2. In order for evidence to lead to a conviction or acquittal of someone on trial for a crime, judges and jurors
   A. need to understand evidence and be convinced of what it means.
   B. need eyewitness testimony.
   C. rely solely on direct evidence.
   D. rely solely on circumstantial evidence.

3. The integrity of a witness
   A. has a relatively minor influence on jurors.
   B. is as essential as the integrity of the evidence.
   C. is more important for direct evidence than for circumstantial evidence.
   D. is more important for indirect evidence than for circumstantial evidence.

4. A situation in which an expert has a bias that excludes her ability to testify is called
   A. conflict of interest.
   B. witness perjury.
   C. acquittal.
   D. nontestifying witness.

5. Can qualified computer forensics investigators serve as expert witnesses and give opinions about what happened?
   A. No, because they were not eyewitnesses.
   B. No, because that would be hearsay.
   C. Yes, because the court selects its own expert to inform itself or the jury.
   D. Yes, because they help judges or juries understand the e-evidence.

6. What must an expert disclose before serving as a testimonial witness?
   A. Qualifications, compensation, and cases in which the witness testified as an expert during the past four years.
   B. Education, compensation, and cases in which the witness testified as an expert during the past ten years.
   C. Qualifications and compensation paid on past four cases.
   D. Education, publications, and certifications.

7. What is an expert report?
   A. A partial statement of key opinions to be expressed and the basis and reasons therefore.
   B. A complete statement of all opinions to be expressed and the basis and reasons therefore.
   C. A preliminary statement of key opinions of the expert.
   D. A complete statement of all facts to be expressed and the basis of the facts.

8. Which of the following about an expert report is false?
   A. The expert report must be provided to the lawyer who retained the expert and to the opposing lawyer before the trial begins.
   B. The lawyer who retained the expert should write the report with the help of the expert.
   C. Opinions in the report can be used during cross-examination by opposing counsel to try to impeach the witness.
   D. A good rule of thumb for the report is that it should explain what an expert did with enough detail that another computer forensics expert could replicate the work.

9. What is an out-of-court testimony made under oath?
   A. Affidavit.
   B. Perjury.
   C. Opinion.
   D. Deposition.

10. What is the effect of an adversarial approach in court trials?
   A. It guarantees a fair trial and correct verdict.
   B. It requires the defendant to testify in court.
   C. It helps to ensure the validity of evidence being presented at trial.
   D. It ensures that only clear and convincing evidence is presented to the jury.

11. What is a preliminary examination of prospective witnesses under oath to determine their competence or suitability?
    A. Expert review.
    B. Voir dire.
    C. Credibility validation.
    D. Testimonial witness inspection.

12. During ____________, an opposing lawyer may attempt to discredit a witness
    A. direct examination
    B. cross-examination
    C. legal examination
    D. deposition

13. Why do opposing lawyers ask expert witnesses to offer opinions outside of the expert's area of expertise?
    A. To get clarification of the expert's testimony.
    B. To ask questions that the expert does not understand.
    C. To trick the expert.
    D. To confuse the jury.

14. Which of the following is *not* a guideline for expert witnesses?
    A. When being cross-examined, do not volunteer information that was not asked or an explanation to your answer.
    B. Do not try to educate the questioner on the topic by providing a fuller explanation than is needed to answer the question.
    C. Do not pause before answering any question.
    D. Try to be relaxed and look at the jury when answering.

15. What was the witness immunity doctrine designed to accomplish?
    A. To encourage witnesses to testify honestly without fear of lawsuits from those dissatisfied with the substance of their opinions.
    B. To encourage witnesses to testify honestly without fear of lawsuits for any reason.
    C. To protect witnesses from being attacked by other expert witnesses.
    D. To protect witnesses from negligence lawsuits.

## EXERCISES

### Exercise 13.1: Direct Examination in Court

Assume that Owen is the owner of an equipment rental business, Rent-from-Us. Bud had been a bookkeeper at Rent-from-Us for over five years. Bud was fired for violating the company's acceptable use policy by allegedly using the company's network and desktop computer to send offensive e-mail to several other employees. A computer forensics expert confirmed that the offensive e-mail messages had been sent over one week's time during working hours from Bud's e-mail account to fellow employees. Bud (plaintiff) filed a lawsuit against Owen (defendant) for wrongful termination claiming that he had not sent the e-mail and, therefore, should not have been fired.

You have been retained as the expert witness by Bud's lawyer. Bud explains that at Rent-from-Us, it was customary for all employees in his office to tape their passwords under their keyboards so that e-mail could be accessed, if needed, when any employee was not at work. The case went to trial.

1. During direct examination, Bud's lawyer (who retained you) asks you, "Could anyone other than Bud have sent the offensive e-mail messages?" How would you reply to this question?
2. That lawyer also asks you, "Why would anyone send offensive e-mail from Bud's account?" Could you answer that question? Why or why not?
3. Consider your demeanor. What would you do to portray a positive demeanor in court? List three things you would do.

### Exercise 13.2: Cross-Examination in Court

Assume the same situation as in Exercise 13.1.

1. During cross-examination, the defendant's lawyer asks you the following leading question: "Are you saying that it was *someone other than Bud* who sent those offensive e-mail messages during that week?" What would be an appropriate response? Why?
2. During cross-examination, the lawyer continues to hammer away at you by asking leading questions to confuse you. What would you do or not do to ensure your integrity with the jury? List three actions you would take or not take.

### Exercise 13.3: Two of the Required Disclosures of an Expert Witness

Before serving as a testimonial witness, an expert must disclose his qualifications, including all publications and compensation being paid.

1. Explain how a lawyer during cross-examination might use the content of an expert's publications to impeach his testimony.
2. During cross-examination, how could a lawyer use the amount of the compensation to cast doubt about the expert's testimony? Explain.

### Exercise 13.4: Testimony Process in Court

Computer forensics cases depend largely on the testimony of experts. You have one duty as an expert witness, which is to tell the truth.

1. Review the chapter, thinking about some ways to make telling the truth easier.
2. Do you think an exaggeration is an untruth?
3. Do you think an omission (failing to mention a material fact) is an untruth?
4. Write a list of three guidelines a witness should follow that would help guard against telling an untruth.

### Exercise 13.5: Ethical Responsibility

Consider the following statement: Lawyers know that attacking the opposing expert's theory or conclusions is much more difficult than attacking her qualifications.

1. Why would that be true? Explain your reasoning.
2. As an expert witness, what would be your ethical responsibilities during cross-examination when your theory or conclusions were undergoing attack?
3. Referring to your answer above, do those responsibilities change if attacks are against your qualifications? Explain your answer.

## PROJECTS

### Project 13.1: Legal Actions Brought Against Expert Witnesses

1. Visit **www.forensic-evidence.com/site/EXP/MAL_PR.html** and read the article discussing legal actions brought against expert witnesses.

2. Use a legal dictionary to find definitions of defamation and negligence. In your own words, explain those terms.
3. Select three key issues pertaining to the witness immunity doctrine. Explain those issues.
4. Describe what you have learned from this article.

### Project 13.2: Testimony Process in Court

1. Review Table 13.1 outlining the testimony process in court.
2. Search an online dictionary for an explanation of *burden of proof.* In your own words, explain burden of proof. In a criminal case, who has the burden of proof?
3. Do you think that being an expert witness for the side with the burden of proof is different from working for the side that does not have that burden? Explain your opinion.
4. In your own words, explain the four types of examination—direct, cross, redirect, and recross.
5. Explain why there are four types of examination.

### Project 13.3: Ethical Role Playing

Assume a criminal case in which the defendant Ditto has been charged with downloading and possessing illegal images of child pornography (contraband). The prosecution has e-evidence of the images from Ditto's laptop computer, which Ditto confirmed had not been used by anyone else. The prosecution also has log files spanning several months that show the details (file names with extensions, dates, file size, and date and time) of hundreds of files that had been downloaded to Ditto's laptop from the F drive of a suspected child-porn distributor. The file names and other details of the downloaded contraband match the contraband on Ditto's laptop. Ditto's lawyer contends that spyware or a virus caused the contraband content to appear on the hard drive of Ditto's laptop. That is, that malware exists and can be deployed in such a way as to unwittingly download illegal images.

Divide the class into three groups—one group for the prosecution side, one group for the defense side, and one group to act as the triers of fact. Select one person from the prosecution side to act as the expert witness for the prosecution and another to act as the prosecutor. Select one person from the defense side to act as the expert witness for the defendant and another to act as Ditto's defense lawyer. Select one person from the triers of fact group to act as judge; the others serve as the jury.

1. Each group should prepare opening statements and questions for the direct, cross, redirect, and recross examination of the expert witness, as appropriate.
2. Conduct a mock trial starting with opening statements. Lawyers may object to questions. The judge must decide whether to sustain or overrule any objections.
3. When both sides have rested their cases, the jury determines which side has provided the more convincing arguments and renders a verdict.
4. The triers of fact comment on how the expert witnesses performed their ethical duties.

## Case Study

USA PATRIOT Act, Section 225 gives immunity to one who complies with a court order or valid request for emergency assistance. If the government has a court order, there is no problem. Without a court order, however, immunity is not automatic because a court might later determine that the "emergency" was not valid.

Imagine, for example, that you are a network administrator. A federal officer comes to your office and says that he believes that a terror attack is planned in an hour. He needs confidential customer information in your custody. He does not have a court order, warrant, or any other formal authority. If you turn over the information, you may save lives, but you are also exposing yourself and your firm to potential civil liability if a court later determines that no valid emergency existed.

1. What ethical dilemmas do you face in this situation?
2. Discuss what you should do. How much evidence should you demand before you turn over the information?
3. In your opinion, does the heavy-handed use of techniques such as sneak-and-peek searches violate ethical rules or legal obligations under the Constitution? Explain your opinion.

# Appendix A

# Online Resources

Resources listed in this appendix are correct at the time of writing (last accessed May 2006). As with any resource resident on the Internet, links and page content may change without warning. If you do not find the information you expect when you use these links, a search will easily locate these resources.

---

## Technology Tools and Toolkits

### File Viewers:

Quick View Plus **www.avantstar.com**

### Image Viewers:

ThumbsPlus **www.cerious.com**

### Password Crackers:

John the Ripper **www.openwall.com/john**
Passware **www.passware.net/**

### Format-Independent Text Search:

dtSearch® **www.dtsearch.com**

### Drive Imaging:

Norton Utilities Ghost™ **www.symantec.com**

### Computer Forensics Toolkits and Systems:

Forensic Toolkit™ **www.foundstone.com**
The Coroner's Toolkit **www.porcupine.org/forensics/tct.html**
Forensic Computers **www.forensic-computers.com**
ForensiX **www.all.net/ForensiX/index.html**

Computer Incident Response Suite **www.forensics-intl.com/tools.html**
EnCase® Forensic Software **www.encase.com**
NetWitness® **www.netwitness.com**

---

## Spyware and Scanners

### Active@ UNDELETE, Data Recovery Tool

**www.active-undelete.com**

Data recovery software that helps to recover lost, deleted, and formatted data on local, network, and removable drives; and digital media.

### PC Monitoring Software (Spyware)

**www.acespy.com**

Discreetly monitors a PC's activity, including chats, e-mails, and other Internet activity. Runs in complete stealth mode.

### NetScanTools

**www.netscantools.com**

### SpyBuddy, Monitors PC Activity

**www.exploreanywhere.com/sb-features.php**

Records and logs Yahoo Messenger instant messages and AOL/MSN/ICQ/AIM chats and instant messages. Tracks Web sites visited, programs used, windows opened, every keystroke, text/images sent to the clipboard, and printed documents. An optional stealth mode provides more monitoring features. Can secretly take snapshots of a desktop to visually track any activity.

### Spytech SpyAgent for Local and Remote PC Monitoring

**www.spytech-web.com/spyagent.shtml**

### TCPDump Programs

**www.tcpdump.org**

### WinDump: tcpdump for Windows

**www.winpcap.org/windump**

WinDump is free and is released under a BSD-style license

### Network Forensics Analysis Tool: NetIntercept®

**www.sandstorm.net/products/netintercept**

**Network Security Toolkit (NST)**
**www.networksecuritytoolkit.org/nst/index.html**
**nst.sourceforge.net/nst (mirror site)**

**Meta-Website of Numerous Online Tools**
**www.networksecuritytoolkit.org/nst/index.html**

**Snort® intrusion detection system, open source**
**www.snort.org**

**Wardialer Detector, Sandtrap®**
**www.sandstorm.net/products/sandtrap**

---

## Hard Drive Duplicator

**Logicube**
**www.logicube.com**

Hard drive duplication, backup, and data recovery.

---

## Standards

**Forensic Examination Procedures**
**www.iacis.info/iacisv2/pages/forensicprocedures.php**

Procedures established as the IACIS® Forensic Examination standards to ensure that competent, professional forensic examinations are conducted by IACIS® members.

---

## Freeware and Shareware

**Ad-Aware**
**www.lavasoftusa.com**

Free multi-spyware removal utility that scans memory, registry, and hard drives for known spyware components.

**NeoTrace Express 3.25**
**www.networkingfiles.com/PingFinger/Neotraceexpress.htm**

Traces Web sites and IP addresses.

**Ping and Trace Software**
**www.networkingfiles.com/PingFinger/pingfinger.htm**

**Remote Access Software**
**www.networkingfiles.com/RAS/RAS.htm**

**Freeware and Shareware Downloads**
**www.webattack.com**

**LADS Alternate Data Stream (ADS) Revealer**
**www.heysoft.de/nt/ep-lads.htm**

**WinHex Hexadecimal Viewer**
**www.x-ways.net/winhex/index-m.html**

**The GIMP Graphics Editing Software**
**http://gimp-win.sourceforge.net/stable.html**

---

## Wireless Sniffers

**AirTouch Network War-Driving Kit**
**www.airtouchnetworks.com**

Commercial war-driving kit, with sniffing software, 802.11b adapter, antenna.

**MacStumbler**
**www.macstumbler.com**

Freeware AP discovery software for Mac OS X and Apple Airport adapters.

**NetStumbler**
**www.netstumbler.com**

Freeware AP discovery tool for Win32 systems.

**WaveStumbler**
**www.cqure.net/wp**

Freeware WLAN mapper for Linux.

## To Look up MAC Address

**Vendor/Ethernet MAC Address Lookup and Search**
**www.coffer.com/mac_find**

For looking up the MAC address itself.

## Cables for Cell Phone Forensics

**DataPilot®**
**www.datapilot.com/phones_universal.htm**

Needed: one USB computer connector and one phone connector for DataPilot to transfer data to and from computer and mobile phone.

## Software for Steganography

**Steganography Application Fingerprint Database (SAFDB)**
**www.sarc-wv.com**

Can be used to detect the use of information-hiding applications to conceal evidence of various types of criminal activity.

Contains four different hash values for every file (artifact) associated with 250 steganography applications obtained as freeware, shareware, or purchased as a commercially licensed product.

A free license to SAFDB is available for qualifying law enforcement, government, and intelligence agencies (**www.sarc-wv.com**). Licenses to SAFDB are also available for the private sector.

**Camouflage Steganography Application**
**http://camouflage.unfiction.com/Download.html**

No longer sold or supported, but can still be downloaded from the Web site above.

# Appendix B

# Government and Legal References

## Government and Organization References

**Federal Guidelines for Searching and Seizing Computers, U.S. DOJ**
**www.usdoj.gov/criminal/cybercrime/searching.html**

**Federal Rules of Civil Procedure**
**www.law.cornell.edu/rules/frcp**

**Federal Rules of Evidence**
**www.law.cornell.edu/rules/fre/overview.html**

**Legal Information Institute**
**www.law.cornell.edu**

**U.S. Constitution**
**http://www.law.cornell.edu/constitution/constitution.overview.html**

**Utica College, Computer Forensics Research and Development Center**
**www.e-evidence.info/index.html**

**Public Affairs Office, District of New Jersey**
**www.usdoj.gov/usao/nj/publicaffairs/NJ_Press/break.html**

**Alameda County (California) District Attorney's Office**
**www.acgov.org/da/pov/documents/web.htm**

**Searching and Seizing Computers and Obtaining Electronic Evidence in Criminal Investigations, Computer Crime and Intellectual Property Section Criminal Division, July 2002**
**www.usdoj.gov/criminal/cybercrime/s&smanual2002.htm**

---

## Legal and Commercial References

**Computer Forensics, Cybercrime, and Steganography Resources**
**www.forensics.nl**

**Court Rules: Summary of State Codes and Federal Local Rules**
**www.lexisnexis.com/applieddiscovery/lawlibrary/courtRules.asp**

Discovery rules apply to electronic documents as they do to paper, but some jurisdictions have additional electronic discovery provisions.

**Discovery Documents (Sample Documents)**
**www.forensics.com/html/resource_sampledocs.html**

**Filesystem Hierarchy Standard**
**www.pathname.com/fhs**

A reference on how to manage a UNIX filesystem or directory hierarchy.

**Practical Guide for Avoiding Metropolitan Opera Mishaps**
**www.lexisnexis.com/applieddiscovery/NewsEvents/PDFs/PracticalGuideAvoidingMishaps.pdf**

---

## White Papers

**Document Retention and Destruction Policies for Digital Data**
**www.lexisnexis.com/applieddiscovery/lawlibrary/whitePapers/ADI_DocumentRetention.pdf**

The risks of ignorance about document retention.

**Electronic Discovery Best Practices: The Secret to Success**
**www.lexisnexis.com/applieddiscovery/lawlibrary/whitePapers/ADI_ImplementEDiscBestPractices.pdf**

Overview of electronic discovery case law and ten tips for implementing electronic discovery best practices.

**Embedded Information in Electronic Documents**
**www.lexisnexis.com/applieddiscovery/lawlibrary/whitePapers/ADI_MetaData.pdf**

Why metadata matters.

**File Formats for Electronic Discovery Review**
**www.lexisnexis.com/applieddiscovery/lawlibrary/whitePapers/ADI_PDFTrumpsTIFF.pdf**

Why PDF is a better file format than TIFF.

---

## Articles

**Avoiding the Pitfalls of Electronic Discovery**
**www.lexisnexis.com/applieddiscovery/lawlibrary/whitePapers/ADI_Mealeys_AvoidingPitfallsOfEDisc.pdf**

Matthew M. Neumeier and Brian D. Hansen, Mealey's Litigation Report, Nov. 2003.

**Electronic Discovery Best Practices**
**www.lexisnexis.com/applieddiscovery/NewsEvents/PDFs/200404_RichmondJournalLawTech.pdf**

Virginia Llewellyn, Richmond Journal of Law and Technology, University of Richmond School of Law, April 2004.

**E-Discovery: A Common Term That Is Little Understood**
**www.lexisnexis.com/applieddiscovery/NewsEvents/PDFs/E-DiscoveryACommonTerm.pdf**

Greg McPolin, Applied Discovery, New York Law Journal, Jan. 2003.

**Network Forensics**
**www.sandstorm.net/downloads/netintercept/ni-2–0-datasheet.pdf**

**Paper or Plastic?—The Hunt for Electronic Treasure During Discovery**
**www.lexisnexis.com/applieddiscovery/lawlibrary/whitePapers/ADI_Mealeys_PaperPlastic.pdf**

Matthew M. Neumeier, Brian D. Hansen, and Irina Y. Dmitrieva, Jenner and Block. *Mealey's Litigation Report,* Dec. 2003.

**Scope of Electronic Discovery Turns on Accessibility of Data**
**www.lexisnexis.com/applieddiscovery/NewsEvents/PDFs/200306LADailyJournal_zubulake.pdf**

Julie Locke, Applied Discovery, LA Daily Journal, June 20, 2003.

**Sniffing the Air for Trouble, April 2003**
**infosecuritymag.techtarget.com/2003/apr/sniffingair.shtml**

**The Next Discovery Frontier: Preparing for Backup Data Requests**
**www.lexisnexis.com/applieddiscovery/NewsEvents/PDFs/200310_ACC Docket.pdf**

Virginia Llewellyn and Richard Corbett, Applied Discovery, ACC Docket, Oct. 2003.

**Zubulake IV: New Guidelines for Duty to Preserve Backup Data**
**www.lexisnexis.com/applieddiscovery/NewsEvents/PDFs/200311_nyljZubulakeIV.pdf**

Greg McPolin, Applied Discovery, New York Law Journal, Nov. 18, 2003.

---

## Videos

**Special Report: Wardriving Computer Hackers**
**www.airtouchnetworks.com/WarDrivingReport.avi**

What is wardriving?

---

## Case Summaries

### Cost Allocation Cases

**www.lexisnexis.com/applieddiscovery/lawlibrary/CaseSummaries_BTCAF.asp**

***Zubulake v. UBS Warburg LLC,* 2003 U.S. Dist. LEXIS 12643 (S.D.N.Y. July 24, 2003).**

Court's analysis of discovery cost-shifting in cases involving information from backup tapes or other inaccessible data.

***Zubulake v. UBS Warburg LLC,* 2003 U.S. Dist. LEXIS 7939, 91 Fair Empl. Prac. Cas. (BNA) 1574 (S.D.N.Y. May 13, 2003).**

Court considers the extent to which inaccessible electronic data is discoverable and who should pay for its production.

***Rowe Entm't, Inc. v. William Morris Agency, Inc.,* 205 F.R.D. 421, 2002 U.S. Dist. LEXIS 488, 51 Fed. R. Serv. 3d (Callaghan) 1106, 2002–1 Trade Cas. (CCH) P73567 (S.D.N.Y. Jan. 16, 2002).**

Judge upholds earlier Rowe order shifting costs of tape restoration.

***Murphy Oil USA, Inc. v. Fluor Daniel, Inc.*, 2002 U.S. Dist LEXIS 3196 (E.D. La. 2002).**

Court considers factors determining whether to shift discovery costs of backup tape restoration to requesting party.

***Rowe Entertainment, Inc. v. William Morris Agency, Inc.*, 2002 U.S. Dist. LEXIS 488 (S.D.N.Y.), motion denied, 2002 U.S. Dist. LEXIS 8308 (S.D.N.Y.).**

Court considers factors determining whether to shift costs of backup tape restoration to requesting party.

***McPeek v. Ashcroft*, 202 F.R.D. 31, 2001 U.S. Dist. LEXIS 12061, 50 Fed. R. Serv. 3d (Callaghan) 528 (D.D.C. Aug. 1, 2001).**

Court applies marginal utility analysis to decide whether to order restoration of backup tapes.

## Document Retention and Destruction Cases

**www.lexisnexis.com/applieddiscovery/lawlibrary/CaseSummaries_BTDRP.asp** If you cannot access these cases directly using the links on the By Topic page, choose to view cases by alphabetical order, select the appropriate letter of the alphabet, and then locate the desired case.

***Rambus, Inc. v. Infineon Technologies*, 2004 U.S. Dist. LEXIS 4577 (E.D. Va. Mar. 17, 2004).**

Court assesses the validity of a plaintiff's document retention/destruction plan. Plaintiff claims its plan was instituted to avoid production costs of keeping too much data for too long.

***Kier v. UnumProvident Corp.*, 2003 U.S. Dist. LEXIS 14522 (S.D.N.Y. Aug. 22, 2003).**

Court describes insufficient steps taken by defendant to preserve e-mail and other computer data.

***Cobell v. Norton*, 2003 U.S. Dist. LEXIS 12833 (D. D.C. July 28, 2003).**

Court orders disconnection of systems from Internet to prohibit destruction of computer data.

***Landmark Legal Foundation v. EPA*, 2003 U.S. Dist. LEXIS 12684 (D. D.C. July 24, 2003).**

Environmental Protection Agency held in civil contempt of preliminary injunction ordered to prevent destruction of responsive computer materials, including materials on hard drives and backup tapes.

***Positive Software Solutions, Inc. v. New Century Mortg. Corp.*, 2003 U.S. Dist. LEXIS 7659 (N.D. Tex. May 2, 2003).**

Existing backups and images of servers must be preserved and party must refrain from deleting computer files while discovery is stayed pending arbitration of underlying claims.

## Spoliation Cases

**www.lexisnexis.com/applieddiscovery/lawlibrary/CaseSummaries_BTSS.asp**

## General Rulings Regarding the Duty to Produce Electronic Materials

### Disclosure

**www.lexisnexis.com/applieddiscovery/lawlibrary/CaseSummaries_BTDREED.asp**

### Production

**www.lexisnexis.com/applieddiscovery/lawlibrary/CaseSummaries_BTDREEPG.asp**

### Production of Backup Tapes

**www.lexisnexis.com/applieddiscovery/lawlibrary/CaseSummaries_BTDREEPBT.asp**

# Appendix C

## Sample Legal Forms, Letters, and Motions

### Chain of Custody Form

| e-fense Case #: | Page: of |
|---|---|

**HARD DRIVE/COMPUTER DETAILS**

| Item #: | Description: | |
|---|---|---|
| Manufacturer: | Model #: | Serial #: |

**CHAIN OF CUSTODY**

| Tracking No: | Date/Time | FROM: | TO: | Reason |
|---|---|---|---|---|
| | Date | Name/Organization | Name/Organization | |
| | Time | Signature | Signature | |
| | Date | Name/Organization | Name/Organization | |
| | Time | Signature | Signature | |
| | Date | Name/Organization | Name/Organization | |
| | Time | Signature | Signature | |
| | Date | Name/Organization | Name/Organization | |
| | Time | Signature | Signature | |
| | Date | Name/Organization | Name/Organization | |
| | Time | Signature | Signature | |
| | Date | Name/Organization | Name/Organization | |
| | Time | Signature | Signature | |
| | Date | Name/Organization | Name/Organization | |
| | Time | Signature | Signature | |
| | Date | Name/Organization | Name/Organization | |
| | Time | Signature | Signature | |

**FIGURE C.1** Sample chain of custody form.

# Chain of Custody Form for Forensic Images

## EVIDENCE CHAIN OF CUSTODY FORM – FOR FORENSIC IMAGES ONLY

e-fense Case #: Page: of

### HARD DRIVE/COMPUTER DETAILS

| Item #: | Description: | |
|---|---|---|
| Manufacturer: | Model #: | Serial #: |

### IMAGE DETAILS

| Date/Time Image Created: | Created By: | Method Used: | Image Name: | HASH: | Drive Used To Store Image: |
|---|---|---|---|---|---|
| | | | | | |

### CHAIN OF CUSTODY

| Tracking No: | Date/Time | FROM: | TO: | Reason |
|---|---|---|---|---|
| | Date | Name/Organization | Name/Organization | |
| | Time | Signature | Signature | |
| | Date | Name/Organization | Name/Organization | |
| | Time | Signature | Signature | |
| | Date | Name/Organization | Name/Organization | |
| | Time | Signature | Signature | |
| | Date | Name/Organization | Name/Organization | |
| | Time | Signature | Signature | |
| | Date | Name/Organization | Name/Organization | |
| | Time | Signature | Signature | |

**FIGURE C.2** Sample chain of custody form for forensic images.

## General Case Intake Form

**CASE INTAKE FORM**

**INQUIRY DATE** ____________

**SUBMITTED BY** ____________

**CASE #** ______ ______

**CLIENT DATA**

Name ____________ Phone: ( ) ____________

*Contact if other than client ____________ Fax: ( ) ____________

Firm Name ____________

Address ____________

Address ____________

City ____________ State ______ Zip ____________

**REFERRAL:** Name ____________ Firm/Location ____________

Plaintiff Name(s) ____________

Defendant Name(s) ____________

Other Parties ____________

Client Type: Plaintiff ______ Defense ______ Insurance ______ Criminal ______

Case Type ______ ______ ______ Claim/Policy/Client File # ____________

Site Location ____________ Date of Incident ____________

Details:

**FIGURE C.3** Sample general case intake form, page 1.

**WHAT HAPPENED?**

Description:

**ACTION TO BE TAKEN**

Travel From ______________ Send White Book ________ Send One Pagers ________

Lead Experts ______________ Other Experts ______________

Other:

**FIGURE C.3, CONTINUED** Sample general case intake form, page 2.

# Computer Forensics Expert Report Template

Computer Forensics Expert's Report

of the

***<Name of Legal Case or Lawsuit>* CASE**

By:

*Xxxxxxxxx X. Xxxxxxxx, Credentials*

Month 00, 200#

***<Name of Legal Case or Lawsuit>* CASE**

**COMPUTER FORENSICS EXPERT'S REPORT** **Month 00, 200#**

## A. INTRODUCTION

Describe the incident or case in broad and general terms. Say right up front what is alleged to have happened, caused the incident, or led to the case.

Describe your scope of work. For example: The purpose of my investigation was to determine if . . . .

## B. MATERIALS AVAILABLE FOR REVIEW

List the information you were given that related to this incident or case. Include your inspection of digital devices, media, and photos at the incident or case site, if any. List material that is case specific; do not list reference standards that you researched.

Doing this will be very convenient for you at later stages of the case.

1. Investigation materials (as appropriate)
   a. Electronic evidence, log files, hard copies
   b. Report of another expert
   c. Digital images of the computers, devices, scene, or other items

## C. BACKGROUND

Describe the background of the case and the investigation that was performed. For example, a bit-stream image of the 80GB hard drive of the Dell Latitude D800 laptop (serial number ###) was made using <forensics toolkit> to preserve the integrity of the media on the laptop as of <date>. Then I used <forensics software> to identify files <created, deleted, modified, etc.> between <beginning date> and <ending date>.

Include what the lawyer(s) have explained to you and what is alleged to have happened.

## D. DESCRIPTION OF THE FACTS OF THE INVESTIGATION AND CASE

Limit this to relevant facts. Everything you say should have some meaning to you in your analysis and findings or at least be there to set the scene for the reader. Use references to software tools, hardware devices, and digital images to help your description, and include them at the end of the report.

If you have different items you would like to list separately, create a subheading using an underline. This would be appropriate when listing related but separate items. See the example given later.

<u>Internet Links</u>

Text would be typed here.

<u>Network Drawings</u>

Text would be typed here.

CONTINUED ON NEXT PAGE

CONTINUED

## E. CAUSES OF THE INCIDENT OR CASE

Through analysis (reconstruction of what happened), relate how the incident or events occurred and what conditions were (or were alleged to be) causes of the incident or case.

Use this section to set up the flow for the technical sections that follow. Refer to your chain of custody documentation.

Generally, basic computer or network technology principles are useful in identifying causes and related conditions.

## F. ANALYSIS

Use as many sections as necessary to explain what happened, how it happened, when, and by whom it was done. Use references from the technical community to develop support for your opinions. Show examples of other similar conditions if appropriate.

The more of a historical development that you can build into your reports, through repeated cases and secondary references, the better. Include your experiences from prior investigations related to the same issue. If there are negative aspects to your case, consider listing them here.

When referencing materials, state the author, title, journal or manual, publisher, date, and what it is. Then state how the materials pertain to your findings.

If this information is a direct quote and greater than 3 lines, place this information in the same format as mentioned above for excerpts, indented at both ends as its own section. When citing a book with 1 author, use this style footnote.[1] When citing a book with 2 to 3 authors, cite as shown.[2] When citing a book with more than 3 authors, you will use only the first and middle initials and last names for all authors.[3] For additional quotation styles, please continue to follow a Style Citation Guide.

## G. FINDINGS

Within the bounds of reasonable (professional) certainty, and subject to change if additional information becomes available, it is my professional opinion that: (list)

Within the bounds of reasonable (professional) certainty, and subject to change if additional information becomes available, it is my professional opinion that:

1. Statement 1.
2. Statement 2.
3. Statement 3.

---

[1]Author Last Name, First. Year. *Title*. City: Publishing Company.

[2]Author1 Last Name, First, and Author2 First and Last Name. Year. *Title*. City: Publishing Company.

[3]Author1, F.M., F.M. Author2, F.M. Author3, and F.M. Author4. Year. *Title*. City: Publishing Company.

CONTINUED ON NEXT PAGE

▶▶ CONTINUED

Go back to your description of scope of work and make the scope match with the findings.

**REFERENCES**

Include via footnotes or table after findings.

**FIGURES, PHOTOS, APPENDICES OR ATTACHMENTS**

Include things that you would want to show to your client or to the jury to show the basis for your opinion. Diagrams and images may be needed for the lawyer and jurors to understand computer or Internet technologies.

Include extracts from documents to show the standard of care that you think should have applied. Give opinions, and the factors you used in determining the opinion, and reference any important papers.

Label and order these as Figures, Photos, or Attachments. Do not use other terms, such as the term *Exhibit*.

________________________________________

Name, Title

## Proposed Request for Production of Documents and Things (Sample)

Sample forms such as those shown in this appendix are available from *Kroll OnTrack*™ **www.krollontrack.com**.

United States District Court
District of [jurisdiction]

Court File No.:

________________________,
Plaintiff,

v. DOCUMENT REQUEST

________________________,
Defendant.

**PLAINTIFFS' REQUEST FOR PRODUCTION OF DOCUMENTS AND THINGS**

Pursuant to Rules 26 and 34 of the Federal Rules of Civil Procedure ("FRCP") Plaintiffs, by counsel, hereby request Defendants to produce the documents specified below, within thirty (30) days of service, to **[counsel name and address],** or at such other time and place, or in such other manner, as may be mutually agreed upon by the parties. Defendants' production of documents shall be in accordance with the Instructions and Definitions set forth below and Rule 34 of the FRCP.

**INSTRUCTIONS AND DEFINITIONS**

(a) Whenever reference is made to a person, it includes any and all of such person's principals, employees, agents, attorneys, consultants and other representatives.

(b) When production of any document in Plaintiffs' possession is requested, such request includes documents subject to the Plaintiffs' possession, custody, or control. In the event that Defendant is able to provide only part of the document(s) called for in any particular Request for Production, provide all document(s) that Defendants are able to provide and state the reason, if any, for the inability to provide the remainder.

(c) "Document(s)" means all materials within the full scope of Rule 34 of the FRCP including but not limited to: all writings and recordings, including the originals and all nonidentical copies, whether different from the original by reason of any notation made on such copies or otherwise (including, but without limitation to, e-mail and attachments, correspondence, memoranda, notes, diaries, minutes, statistics, letters, telegrams, contracts, reports, studies, checks, statements, tags, labels, invoices, brochures, periodicals, telegrams, receipts, returns, summaries, pamphlets, books, interoffice and intraoffice communications, offers, notations of any sort of conversations, working papers, applications, permits, file wrappers, indices, telephone calls, meetings or printouts, teletypes, telefax, invoices, worksheets, and all drafts, alterations, modifications, changes, and amendments of any

CONTINUED ON NEXT PAGE

CONTINUED

of the foregoing), graphic or aural representations of any kind (including, without limitation, photographs, charts, microfiche, microfilm, videotape, recordings, motion pictures, plans, drawings, surveys), and electronic, mechanical, magnetic, optical, or electric records or representations of any kind (including, without limitation, computer files and programs, tapes, cassettes, discs, recordings), including metadata.

(d) If any document is withheld from production under a claim of privilege or other exemption from discovery, state the title and nature of the document, and furnish a list signed by the attorney of record giving the following information with respect to each document withheld:

  (i) the name and title of the author and/or sender and the name and title of the recipient;
  (ii) the date of the document's origination;
  (iii) the name of each person or persons (other than stenographic or clerical assistants) participating in the preparation of the document;
  (iv) the name and position, if any, of each person to whom the contents of the documents have heretofore been communicated by copy, exhibition, reading, or substantial summarization;
  (v) a statement of the specific basis on which privilege is claimed and whether or not the subject matter or the contents of the document is limited to legal advice or information provided for the purpose of securing legal advice; and
  (vi) the identity and position, if any, of the person or persons supplying the attorney signing the list with the information requested in subparagraphs above.

(e) "Relate(s) to," "related to" or "relating to" means to refer to, reflect, concern, pertain to or in any manner be connected with the matter discussed.

(f) Every Request for Production herein shall be deemed a continuing Request for Production and Defendant is to supplement its answers promptly if and when Defendant obtains responsive documents which add to or are in any way inconsistent with Defendant's initial production.

(g) These discovery requests are not intended to be duplicative. All requests should be responded to fully and to the extent not covered by other requests. If there are documents that are responsive to more than one request, then please so note and produce each such document first in response to the request that is more specifically directed to the subject matter of the particular document.

(h) Any word written in the singular herein shall be construed as plural or vice versa when necessary to facilitate the response to any request.

CONTINUED ON NEXT PAGE

▶▶ CONTINUED

(i) "And" as well as "or" shall be construed disjunctively or conjunctively as necessary in order to bring within the scope of the request all responses which otherwise might be construed to be outside its scope.

## DOCUMENT REQUESTS

1. All documents with reference to or written policies, procedures, and guidelines related to Defendant's computers, computer systems, electronic data, and electronic media including, but not limited to, the following:
    a. Backup tape rotation schedules;
    b. Electronic data retention, preservation, and destruction schedules;
    c. Employee use policies of company computers, data, and other technology;
    d. File naming conventions and standards;
    e. Password, encryption, and other security protocols;
    f. Diskette, CD, DVD, and other removable media labeling standards;
    g. E-mail storage conventions (e.g., limitations on mailbox sizes/ storage locations; schedule and logs for storage);
    h. Electronic media deployment, allocation, and maintenance procedures for new employees, current employees, or departed employees;
    i. Software and hardware upgrades (including patches) for [relevant time period] (who and what organization conducted such upgrades); and
    j. Personal or home computer usage for work-related activities.
2. Organization charts for all Information Technology or Information Services departments or divisions from [relevant time period].
3. Backup tapes containing e-mail and other electronic data related to this action from [relevant time period].
4. Exact copies (i.e., bit-by-bit copies) of all hard drives on the desktop computers, laptop computers, notebook computers, personal digital assistant computers, servers, and other electronic media related to this action from [relevant time period].
5. Exact copies of all relevant disks, CDs, DVDs, and other removable media related to this action from [relevant time period].
6. For each interrogatory set forth in Plaintiffs' First Interrogatories, produce all documents which Defendant referred to, relied upon, consulted or used in any way in answering such interrogatory.
7. All documents that contain or otherwise relate to the facts or information that Defendants contend refute, in any way, the allegations contained in the Complaint in this action.
8. All reports, including drafts, submitted by any expert witness or potential expert witness retained or consulted by any Defendant with respect to the issues raised in this case.

Date: Respectfully submitted,

____________________

# Preservation Letter to a Client (Sample)

[DATE]

________________________

________________________

________________________

________________________

RE: [Case Name]—Data Preservation

Dear ______________:

Please be advised that the Office of General Counsel requires your assistance with respect to preserving corporate information in the above-referenced matter.

Electronically stored data is an important and irreplaceable source of discovery and / or evidence in this matter.

The lawsuit requires preservation of all information from [Corporation's] computer systems, removable electronic media, and other locations relating to [description of event, transaction, business unit, product, etc.]. This includes, but is not limited to, e-mail and other electronic communication, word processing documents, spreadsheets, databases, calendars, telephone logs, contact manager information, Internet usage files, and network access information.

Employees must take every reasonable step to preserve this information until further notice from the Office of General Counsel. *Failure to do so could result in extreme penalties against [Corporation].*

If this correspondence is in any respect unclear, please contact [designated coordinator] at [phone number].

Sincerely,

# Preservation Letter to an Opponent or Third Party (Sample)

[DATE]

______________________________

______________________________

______________________________

______________________________

RE: [Case Name]—Data Preservation

Dear _______________:

Please be advised that [Plaintiffs / Defendants / Third Party] believe electronically stored information to be an important and irreplaceable source of discovery and / or evidence in the above-referenced matter.

The discovery requests served in this matter seek information from [Plaintiffs' / Defendants'] computer systems, removable electronic media, and other locations. This includes, but is not limited to, e-mail and other electronic communication, word processing documents, spreadsheets, databases, calendars, telephone logs, contact manager information, Internet usage files, and network access information.

The laws and rules prohibiting destruction of evidence apply to electronically stored information in the same manner that they apply to other evidence. Due to its format, electronic information is easily deleted, modified, or corrupted. Accordingly, [Plaintiffs / Defendants / Third Party] must take every reasonable step to preserve this information until the final resolution of this matter. This includes, but is not limited to, an obligation to discontinue all data destruction and backup tape recycling policies.

If this correspondence is in any respect unclear, please do not hesitate to call me.

Sincerely,

# Federal Rules of Civil Procedure 30(b)(6) Deposition Notice (Sample)

UNITED STATES DISTRICT COURT
DISTRICT OF [jurisdiction]

Court File No.:

__________________,
Plaintiff,

v.

NOTICE OF TAKING DEPOSITION PURSUANT TO FED. R. CIV. P. 30(b)(6)

__________________,
Defendant.

PLEASE TAKE NOTICE that, [Plaintiff / Defendant Corporation] take the deposition, before a qualified notary public by oral examination, of [Plaintiff / Defendant Corporation] on [date] commencing at [time], at [location]. The deposition will continue thereafter until adjournment.

Pursuant to Federal Rule of Civil Procedure 30(b)(6), [Plaintiff / Defendant] corporate designee(s) shall be prepared to testify regarding the following subjects, all with respect to [Plaintiff's / Defendant's] information technology systems:

1. Number, types, and locations of computers (including desktops, laptops, PDAs, cell phones, etc.) currently in use and no longer in use;
2. Past and present operating system and application software, including dates of use and number of users;
3. Name and version of network operating system currently in use and no longer in use but relevant to the subject matter of the action, including size in terms of storage capacity, number of users supported, and dates/descriptions of system upgrades;
4. File-naming and location-saving conventions;
5. Disk and/or tape labeling conventions;
6. Backup and archival disk or tape inventories/schedules/logs;
7. Most likely locations of electronic records relevant to the subject matter of the action;
8. Backup rotation schedules and archiving procedures, including any automatic data recycling programs in use at any relevant time;
9. Electronic records management policies and procedures;
10. Corporate policies regarding employee use of company computers, data, and other technology;

CONTINUED ON NEXT PAGE

CONTINUED

11. Identities of all current and former personnel who have or had access to network administration, backup, archiving, or other system operations during any relevant time period.

Date:_______________

ABC LAW FIRM
BY:_______________
[Address]
Attorneys for [Plaintiff / Defendant]

## Interrogatories (Sample)

United States District Court
District of [jurisdiction]

Court File No.:

_______________,
Plaintiff,

v.

_______________,
Defendant.

INTERROGATORIES TO [party name]

1. Identify all e-mail systems in use, including but not limited to the following:
   a. List all e-mail software and versions presently and previously used by you and the dates of use;
   b. Identify all hardware that has been used or is currently in use as a server for the e-mail system including its name;
   c. Identify the specific type of hardware that was used as terminals into the e-mail system (including home PCs, laptops, desktops, cell phones, personal digital assistants ["PDAs"], etc.) and its current location;
   d. State how many users there have been on each e-mail system (delineate between past and current users);
   e. State whether the e-mail is encrypted in any way and list passwords for all users;
   f. Identify all users known to you who have generated e-mail related to the subject matter of this litigation;

CONTINUED ON NEXT PAGE

   g. Identify all e-mail known to you (including creation date, recipient(s) and sender) that relate to, reference, or are relevant to the subject matter of this litigation.

2. Identify and describe each computer that has been, or is currently, in use by you or your employees (including desktop computers, PDAs, portable, laptop and notebook computers, cell phones, etc.), including but not limited to the following:

   a. Computer type, brand, and model number;
   b. Computers that have been reformatted, had the operating system reinstalled or been overwritten and identify the date of each event;
   c. The current location of each computer identified in your response to this interrogatory;
   d. The brand and version of all software, including operating system, private and custom-developed applications, commercial applications, and shareware for each computer identified;
   e. The communications and connectivity for each computer, including but not limited to terminal-to-mainframe emulation, data download and/or upload capability to mainframe, and computer-to-computer connections via network, modem and/or direct connection;
   f. All computers that have been used to store, receive, or generate data related to the subject matter of this litigation.

3. As to each computer network, identify the following:

   a. Brand and version number of the network operating system currently or previously in use (include dates of all upgrades);
   b. Quantity and configuration of all network servers and workstations;
   c. Person(s) (past and present including dates) responsible for the ongoing operations, maintenance, expansion, archiving, and upkeep of the network;
   d. Brand name and version number of all applications and other software residing on each network in use, including but not limited to electronic mail and applications.

4. Describe in detail all interconnectivity between the computer system at [opposing party] in [office location] and the computer system at [opposing party # 2] in [office location # 2] including a description of the following:

   a. All possible ways in which electronic data is shared between locations;
   b. The method of transmission;
   c. The type(s) of data transferred;
   d. The names of all individuals possessing the capability for such transfer, including list and names of authorized outside users of [opposing party's] electronic mail system;
   e. The individual responsible for supervising interconnectivity.

CONTINUED ON NEXT PAGE

CONTINUED

5. As to data backups performed on all computer systems currently or previously in use, identify the following:
   a. All procedures and devices used to back up the software and the data, including but not limited to name(s) of backup software used, the frequency of the backup process, and type of tape backup drives, including name and version number, type of media (i.e., DLT, 4 mm, 8 mm, AIT). State the capacity (bytes) and total amount of information (gigabytes) stored on each tape;
   b. Describe the tape or backup rotation and explain how backup data is maintained and state whether the backups are full or incremental (attach a copy of all rotation schedules);
   c. State whether backup storage media is kept off-site or on-site. Include the location of such backup and a description of the process for archiving and retrieving on-site media;
   d. The individual(s) who conducts the backup and the individual who supervises this process;
   e. Provide a detailed list of all backup sets, regardless of the magnetic media on which they reside, showing current location, custodian, date of backup, a description of backup content, and a full inventory of all archives.
6. Identify all extra-routine backups applicable for any servers identified in response to these interrogatories, such as quarterly archival backup, yearly backup, etc., and identify the current location of any such backups.
7. For any server, workstation, laptop, or home PC that has been "wiped clean" or reformatted such that you claim that the information on the hard drive is permanently destroyed, identify the following:
   a. The date on which each drive was wiped;
   b. The method or program used (e.g., WipeDisk, WipeFile, BurnIt, Data Eraser, etc.)
8. Identify and attach any and all versions of document/data retention policies used by **[opposing party]** and identify documents or classes of documents that were subject to scheduled destruction. Attach copies of document destruction inventories/logs/schedules containing documents relevant to this action. Attach a copy of any disaster recovery plan. Also state:
   a. The date, if any, of the suspension of this policy *in toto* or any aspect of said policy in response to this litigation;
   b. A description by topic, creation date, user, or bytes of any and all data that has been deleted or in any way destroyed after the commencement of this litigation. State whether the deletion or destruction of any data pursuant to said data retention policy occurred through automation or by user action;

CONTINUED ON NEXT PAGE

▶▶ CONTINUED

   c. Whether any company-wide instruction regarding the suspension of said data retention/destruction policy occurred after or related to the commencement of this litigation and if so, identify the individual responsible for enforcing said suspension.

9. Identify any users who had backup systems in their PCs and describe the nature of the backup.
10. Identify the person(s) responsible for maintaining any schedule of redeployment or circulation of existing equipment and describe the system or process for redeployment.
11. Identify any data that has been deleted, physically destroyed, discarded, damaged (physically or logically), or overwritten, whether pursuant to a document retention policy or otherwise, since the commencement of this litigation. Specifically identify those documents that relate to or reference the subject matter of the above referenced litigation.
12. Identify any user who has downloaded any files in excess of ten (10) megabytes on any computer identified above since the commencement of this litigation.
13. Identify and describe all backup tapes in your possession including:

   a. Types and number of tapes in your possession (such as DLT, AIT, Mammoth, 4 mm, 8 mm);
   b. Capacity (bytes) and total amount of information (gigabytes) stored on each tape;
   c. All tapes that have been reinitialized or overwritten since commencement of this litigation and state the date of said occurrence.

---

# Language and Citations to Support a Motion to Compel Discovery of Electronic Evidence (Sample)

## Discoverability

It is well settled that relevant electronic documents and e-mails are discoverable according to the same principles as paper documents. *In re Bristol-Myers Squibb Securities Litigation,* 2002 WL 169201 (D.N.J. Feb. 4, 2002); *McPeek v. Ashcroft,* 202 F.R.D. 31 (D.D.C. August 1, 2001); *Pierce v. Wal-Mart, Inc.,* 2001 WL 793023 (Ala. July 13, 2001); *Demelash v. Ross Stores, Inc.,* 20 P.3d 447 (Wash. Ct. App. 2001); *Kleiner v. Burns,* 2000 WL 1909470 (D. Kan. Dec. 15, 2000); *Superior Consultant Co. v. Bailey,* 2000 WL 1279161 (E.D. Mich. Aug. 22, 2000); *Simon Property Group v. mySimon, Inc.,* 194 F.R.D. 639 (S.D. Ind. 2000); *Linnen v. A.H. Robins Co.,* 1999 WL 462015 (Mass. Super. June 16, 1999); *Playboy Enters., Inc. v. Welles,*

60 F.Supp.2d 1050 (S.D. Cal. 1999); *Storch v. IPCO Safety Prods. Co.,* 1997 WL 401589 (E.D. Pa. July 16, 1997); *Anti-Monopoly, Inc. v. Hasbro, Inc.,* 1995 WL 649934 (S.D.N.Y. Nov. 3, 1995); *Crown Life Ins. Co. v. Craig,* 995 F.2d 1376 (7th Cir. 1993); *Santiago v. Miles,* 121 F.R.D. 636 (W.D.N.Y. 1988); *Bills v. Kennecott Corp.,* 108 F.R.D. 459 (C.D. Utah 1985).

## Costs

The producing party must normally obtain, translate, and bear the costs associated with the production of electronic evidence. *Hayes v. Compass Group USA, Inc.,* 202 F.R.D. 363 (D. Conn. 2001); *Toledo Fair Hous. Ctr. v. Nationwide Mut. Ins. Co.,* 703 N.E.2d 340 (Ohio C.P. 1996); *Anti-Monopoly, Inc. v. Hasbro, Inc.,* 1995 WL 649934 (S.D.N.Y. Nov. 3, 1995); *In re Brand Name Prescription Drugs Antitrust Litig.,* 1995 WL 360526 (N.D. Ill. June 15, 1995); *Delozier v. First Nat'l Bank of Gatlinburg,* 109 F.R.D. 161 (E.D. Tenn. 1986).

According to a new trend, courts can use an eight-factor balancing test to allocate costs. *Rowe Entertainment, Inc. v. The William Morris Agency,* 2002 WL 975713 (S.D.N.Y. May 9, 2002); *Murphy Oil USA, Inc. v. Fluor Daniel, Inc.,* 2002 WL 246439 (E.D. La. Feb. 19, 2002).

## Spoliation

Failure to preserve e-mail and electronic documents (whether intentional or inadvertent) is sanctionable as spoliation of evidence. *Lombardo v. Broadway Stores, Inc.,* 2002 WL 86810 (Cal. Ct. App. Jan. 22, 2002); *Trigon Ins. Co. v. United States,* 2001 WL 1456388 (E.D.Va. Nov. 9, 2001); *Pennar Software Corp. v. Fortune 500 Sys. Ltd.,* 2001 WL 1319162 (N.D.Cal. Oct. 25, 2001); *Danis v. USN Communications,* 2000 WL 1694325 (N.D. Ill. Oct. 23, 2000); *Illinois Tool Works, Inc. v. Metro Mark Prod., Ltd.,* 43 F.Supp.2d. 951 (N.D. Ill. 1999); *Telecom Int'l Amer., Ltd. v. AT & T Corp.,* 189 F.R.D. 76 (S.D.N.Y. 1999); *Lauren Corp. v. Century Geophysical Corp.,* 953 P.2d 200 (Colo. Ct. App. 1998); *ABC Home Health Servs. v. IBM Corp.,* 158 F.R.D. 180 (S.D. Ga. 1994).

Courts have routinely awarded sanctions for spoliation of electronic evidence. Reasonable sanctions include:

- **Default Judgment:** *Cabinetware Inc., v. Sullivan,* 1991 WL 327959 (E.D. Cal. July 15, 1991); *Computer Assocs. Int'l, Inc. v. American Fundware, Inc.,* 133 F.R.D. 166 (D. Colo. 1990); *William T. Thompson Co. v. General Nutrition Corp.,* 593 F. Supp. 1443 (C.D. Cal. 1984).
- **Adverse Inferences:** *Trigon Ins. Co. v. United States,* 2001 WL 1456388 (E.D.Va. Nov. 9, 2001); *Minnesota Mining & Mfg. v. Pribyl,* 259 F.3d 587, (7th Cir. 2001); *Linnen v. A.H. Robins Co.,* 1999 WL 462015 (Mass. Super. June 16, 1999).
- **Attorney's Fees:** *Trigon Ins. Co. v. United States,* 2001 WL 1456388 (E.D.Va. Nov. 9, 2001); *Pennar Software Corp. v. Fortune 500 Sys.*

*Ltd.*, 2001 WL 1319162 (N.D.Cal. Oct. 25, 2001); *Lauren Corp. v. Century Geophysical Corp.*, 953 P.2d 200 (Colo. Ct. App. 1998); *In re Cheyenne Software, Inc. v. Securities Litig.*, 1997 WL 714891 (E.D.N.Y. Aug. 18, 1997).

- **Costs/Fines:** *RKI, Inc. v. Grimes,* 177 F.Supp.2d 859 (N.D. Ill. 2001); *Mathias v. Jacobs,* 197 F.R.D. 29 (S.D.N.Y. 2000), *vacated* 2001 WL 1149017—F.Supp.2d—(S.D.N.Y. Sept. 27, 2001); *Danis v. USN Communications,* 2000 WL 1694325 (N.D. Ill. Oct. 23, 2000); *Illinois Tool Works, Inc. v. Metro Mark Prod., Ltd.*, 43 F.Supp.2d. 951 (N.D. Ill. 1999); *Lauren Corp. v. Century Geophysical Corp.*, 953 P.2d 200 (Colo. Ct. App. 1998); *Gates Rubber Co. v. Bando Chem. Ind.*, 167 F.R.D. 90 (D. Colo. 1996); *Capellupo v. FMC Corp.*, 126 F.R.D. 545 (D. Minn. 1989).
- **Punitive Damages:** *RKI, Inc. v. Grimes,* 177 F.Supp.2d 859 (N.D. Ill. 2001).

### Sanctions for Failure to Produce

Sanctions, under Fed. R. Civ. P. 37, are readily available for failure to produce electronic evidence. *Cobell v. Norton,* 2002 WL 481132 (D.D.C. Mar. 29, 2002); *Lexis-Nexis v. Beer,* 41 F.Supp.2d 950 (D. Minn. 1999); *Crown Life Ins. Co. v. Craig,* 995 F.2d 1376, 1382–83 (7th Cir. 1993).

### Neutral Expert

It is proper protocol in a case involving electronic evidence to appoint a neutral expert to manage the electronic discovery process. *Munshani v. Signal Lake Venture Fund II,* 2001 WL 1526954 (Mass.Super. Oct. 9, 2001); *Simon Property Group v. mySimon, Inc.*, 194 F.R.D. 639 (S.D. Ind. 2000); *Playboy Enters., Inc. v. Welles,* 60 F.Supp.2d 1050 (S.D. Cal. 1999); *Gates Rubber Co. v. Bando Chem. Ind.*, 167 F.R.D. 90 (D. Colo. 1996); *National Assoc. of Radiation Survivors v. Turnage,* 115 F.R.D. 543 (N.D. Cal. 1987); *United States v. IBM,* 76 F.R.D. 97 (S.D.N.Y. 1977).

---

## Language and Citations to Oppose a Motion to Compel Discovery of Electronic Evidence (Sample)

### Proportionality

A party producing electronic evidence must be protected against undue burden and expense associated with the production. *Stallings-Daniel v. Northern Trust Co.*, 2002 WL 385566 (N.D. Ill. Mar. 12, 2002); *McPeek v.*

*Ashcroft,* 202 F.R.D. 31 (D.D.C. August 1, 2001); *Simon Property Group v. mySimon, Inc.,* 194 F.R.D. 639 (S.D. Ind. 2000); *Playboy Enters., Inc. v. Welles,* 60 F.Supp.2d 1050 (S.D. Cal. 1999); *Van Westrienen v. Americontinental Collection Corp.,* 189 F.R.D. 440 (D. Or. 1999); *Symantec Corp. v. McAfee Assoc., Inc.,* 1998 WL 740807 (N.D. Cal. Aug. 14, 1998); *Strasser v. Yalamanchi,* 669 So.2d 1142 (Fla. Dist. Ct. App. 1996); *Fennell v. First Step Designs, Ltd.,* 83 F.3d 526 (1st Cir. 1996); *Murlas Living Trust v. Mobil Oil Corp.,* 1995 WL 124186 (N.D. Ill. Mar. 20, 1995); *Lawyers Title Ins. Co. v. United States Fidelity & Guar. Co.,* 122 F.R.D. 567 (N.D. Cal. 1988).

Courts may limit the scope of the electronic discovery in order to reduce the burden on the producing party where appropriate.

*Ex Parte Wal-mart, Inc.,* 809 So.2d 818 (Ala. 2001); *Demelash v. Ross Stores, Inc.,* 20 P.3d 447 (Wash. Ct. App. 2001); *Van Westrienen v. Americontinental Collection Corp.,* 189 F.R.D. 440 (D. Or. 1999); *Symantec Corp. v. McAfee Assoc., Inc.,* 1998 WL 740807 (N.D. Cal. Aug. 14, 1998). *Alexander v. FBI,* 188 F.R.D. 111 (D.C. Cir. 1998).

## Privilege

Parties should be protected from discovery of their privileged electronic materials. *Rowe Entertainment, Inc. v. The William Morris Agency,* 2002 WL 63190 (S.D.N.Y. Jan. 16, 2002); *United States v. Sungard Data Systems,* 2001 WL 1335090 (D.D.C. Oct. 30, 2001); *Unnamed Physician v. Board of Trustees of St. Agnes Medical Center,* 2001 WL 1340580 (Cal. Ct. App. Nov. 1, 2001); *IBM v. Comdisco, Inc.,* 1992 WL 52143 (Del. Super. Ct. Mar. 11, 1992). *Burroughs v. Barr Lab., Inc.,* 143 F.R.D. 611 (E.D.N.C. 1992), *vacated in part on other grounds* 40 F.3d 1223 (Fed. Cir. 1994).

When the requesting party's need for the privileged information is so great that undue hardship would result if not produced, courts have ordered the producing party to deliver the data after removing any portions that contain privileged information. *Scovish v. Upjohn Co.,* 1995 WL 731755 (Conn. Super. Ct. Nov. 22, 1995).

## Production

Courts have been inconsistent in determining whether the data must be produced in a paper or electronic format. Often, the technical facts of the particular case, including the age of the data, the amount of the data, the expense of printing, the expense of restoring the data to an electronic format, or the need for electronic searchability, dictate the terms of the court's production order. *Timken Co. v. United States,* 659 F. Supp 239 (Ct. Int'l Trade 1987); *Williams v. Owens-Illinois, Inc.,* 665 F.2d 918 (9th Cir. 1982); *Adams v. Dan River Mills, Inc.,* 54 F.R.D. 220 (W.D. Va. 1972).

# A Rule 16(c) Pretrial Conference Agenda for Computer-Based Discovery (Checklist)

Computer Based Discovery in Federal Civil Litigation

Federal Courts Law Review
October 200x
Kenneth J. Withers

The following checklist represents a maximalist approach. It should be scaled to fit the needs of the particular case, the resources of the parties, and the litigating styles of the attorneys involved.

## I. When is a Detailed Rule 16 Notice Most Appropriate?

- When the substantive allegations involve computer-generated records, e.g., software development, e-commerce, unlawful Internet trafficking, etc.
- When the authenticity or completeness of computer records is likely to be contested
- When a substantial amount of disclosure or discovery will involve information or records in electronic form, e.g., e-mail, word processing, spreadsheets, and databases
- When one or both parties is an organization that routinely used computers in its day-to-day business operations during the period relevant to the facts of the case
- When one or both parties has converted substantial numbers of potentially relevant records to digital form for management or archival purposes
- When expert witnesses will develop testimony based in large part on computer data and/or modeling or when either party plans to present a substantial amount of evidence in digital form at trial
- In any potential "big document" case in which cost associated with managing paper discovery could be avoided by encouraging exchange of digital or imaged documents (especially if multiple parties are involved)

The purpose of a detailed Rule 16 notice is to save the parties time and expense by anticipating the most common issues of computer-based discovery, developing a reasonable discovery plan, and avoiding unnecessary conflict. A detailed Rule 16 notice would not be appropriate if, in the opinion of the judge, the notice might serve to alarm the parties needlessly, raise unreasonable expectations or demands, or encourage the parties to engage in wasteful discovery.

CONTINUED ON NEXT PAGE

CONTINUED

## II. Preservation of Evidence

A. What steps have counsel taken to ensure that likely discovery material in their clients' possession (or in the possession of third parties) will be preserved until the discovery process is complete? If counsel have not yet identified all material that should be disclosed or may be discoverable, what steps have been taken to ensure that material will not be destroyed or changed before counsels' investigations are complete?

If more specific direction is needed:

B. Have counsel identified computer records relevant to the subject matter of the action, e.g.,

- Word processing documents, including drafts or versions not necessarily in paper form
- Databases or spreadsheets containing relevant information
- E-mail, voice-mail, or other computer-mediated communications
- Relevant system records, such as logs, Internet use history files, and access records

C. Have counsel located the following computer records:

- Active computer files on network servers
- Computer files on desktop or local hard drives
- Backup tapes or disks, wherever located
- Archival tapes or disks, wherever located
- Laptop computers, home computers, and other satellite locations
- Media or hardware on which relevant records may have been "deleted" but are recoverable using reasonable efforts

D. Have counsel made sure all relevant computer records at all relevant locations are secure, e.g.,

- Suspended all routine electronic document deletion and media recycling
- Segregated and secured backup and archival media
- Created "mirror" copies of all active network servers, desktop hard drives, laptops, and similar hardware

E. Have counsel considered entering into an agreement to preserve evidence?

F. Does either party plan to seek a preservation order from the court?

## III. Disclosure and Preliminary Discovery

A. Have counsel designated technical point-persons who know about their clients' computer systems to assist in managing computer records and answering discovery requests?

CONTINUED ON NEXT PAGE

CONTINUED

B. Have counsel prepared a description of their respective parties' computer systems for exchange? Does either party need to know more before discovery can proceed? If, after considering whether the hints in the following list may do more harm than good, the judge determines that the parties are unclear as to what they need to know at this stage and should get further guidance, the judge may suggest that they exchange information on the following points:

- Number, types, and locations of computers currently in use
- Number, types, and locations of computers no longer in use but relevant to the facts of the case
- Operating system and application software currently in use
- Operating system and application software no longer in use but relevant to the facts of the case
- Name and version of network operating system currently in use
- Names and versions of network operating systems no longer in use but relevant to the facts of the case
- File-naming and location-saving conventions
- Disk or tape labeling conventions
- Backup and archival disk or tape inventories or schedules
- Most likely locations of records relevant to the subject matter of the action
- Backup rotation schedules and archiving procedures, including any backup programs in use at any relevant time
- Electronic records management policies and procedures
- Corporate policies regarding employee use of company computers and data
- Identities of all current and former personnel who had access to network administration, backup, archiving, or other system operations during any relevant time

C. Do counsel anticipate the need to notice any depositions or propound any interrogatories to obtain further information about the opposing party's computer systems or electronic records management procedures?

D. Have counsel explored with their clients (in appropriate situations) the procedures and costs involved to:

- Locate and isolate relevant files from e-mail, word processing, and other collections
- Recover relevant files generated on outdated or dormant computer systems (so-called "legacy data")
- Recover deleted relevant files from hard drives, backup media, and other sources

CONTINUED ON NEXT PAGE

CONTINUED

E. Do counsel anticipate the need to conduct an on-site inspection of the opposing party's computer system?

- Consideration of an agreed-upon protocol
- Permission to use outside experts
- Agreement on neutral expert

**IV. Electronic Document Production**

a. Will counsel use computerized litigation support databases to organize and store documents and other discovery material?
b. Have counsel considered common formats for all electronic document exchange, e.g., TIFF images with OCR-generated text, e-mail in ASCII format, etc.?
c. Have counsel (particularly in multiparty cases) considered a central electronic document repository?
d. Have counsel considered an attorney-client privilege nonwaiver agreement to avoid the costs associated with intensive privilege screening before production?
e. Do counsel anticipate requesting data in nonroutine format, e.g.,

- Printing by respondent of electronic documents not normally in print form
- Creation by respondent of customized database reports
- Performance by respondent of customized searches or data mining

f. Have counsel agreed upon cost allocation outside the usual rule that parties absorb their own disclosure costs, e.g.,

- Requesting parties will pay nonroutine data retrieval and production costs
- Parties will negotiate data recovery and legacy data restoration costs

g. Does either party anticipate objecting to the production of computer records or software necessary to manipulate the records based on:

- Trade secret
- Licensing restrictions
- Copyright restrictions
- Statutory or regulatory privacy restrictions

**V. Testifying Experts**

a. Will any testifying expert(s) rely on computer data provided by either party or rely on his or her own data?
b. Will any testifying expert(s) use custom, proprietary, or publicly available software to process data, generate a report, or make a presentation?
c. Do counsel anticipate requesting discovery of either the underlying data or the software used by any testifying expert?

CONTINUED ON NEXT PAGE

CONTINUED

## VI. Anticipating Evidentiary Disputes

Have counsel considered discovery procedures designed to reduce or eliminate questions of authenticity, e.g.,

- Computer discovery supervised by neutral party
- Neutral, secure electronic document repository
- Exchange of read-only disks or CD-ROMs
- Chain-of-custody certifications

# Appendix D

# Summaries of Court Cases

You can read more detailed accounts of these court cases at: **www.forensics.com/html/resource_case_must_read.html** or **www.forensics.com/html/resource_case_by_topic.html**

---

## Cases Involving Electronic Evidence

***United States v. Microsoft Corporation*, 1999 (D.C.,)** E-mail evidence helped prove that Microsoft had abused its monopoly power to restrain trade.

***GTFM, Inc. v. Wal-Mart Stores, Inc.*, 2000 (S.D.N.Y.)** In a trademark infringement case, GTFM asked for transaction documents from Wal-Mart. Wal-Mart's legal counsel responded that the company's computer systems were not capable of tracking the purchase and sale of goods for a particular period of time. A year later, in a deposition, Wal-Mart's vice president admitted that Wal-Mart's computers did in fact have the capability to track the purchase and sale of goods. The court ordered Wal-Mart to pay all plaintiffs' attorneys' fees and costs related to failing to give accurate information.

***Linnen v. A.H. Robins Co.*, 1999 (Mass. Super. Ct.)** In a pharmaceutical products liability case, Linnen acquired a document preservation order from the court and served it on the defendants, Robins. Robins did not stop recycling their backup tapes as required by the order to preserve documents. The court ordered Robins to restore the backup tapes and search for the documents, and ordered a "spoliation inference." That is, the jury was instructed that they could infer that Robins destroyed documents because they contained incriminating evidence.

***Kucala Enterprises, Ltd. v. Auto Wax Co., Inc.*, 2003 (N.D.Ill.)** In a patent infringement case, in response to a discovery request by the defendant, the district court ordered that a plaintiff's computer be inspected. The defendant's forensic investigator analyzed the computer, which revealed that the plaintiff had used Evidence Eliminator on the computer to delete and overwrite over 12,000 files. The court stated, "Any reasonable person can deduce, if not from the name of the product itself, then by reading the website, that Evidence Eliminator is a product used to circumvent discovery." The court found the plaintiff at fault for not preserving evidence that it had a duty to maintain.

***In re Bristol-Myers Squibb,* 2002 (D.N.J.)** The court emphasized the importance of the Federal Rules Civil Procedure 26 meeting and the Rule 16 pretrial conference to prevent e-discovery problems.

***In re DoubleClick Inc. Privacy Litigation,* 2001 (S.D.N.Y.)** A class action lawsuit was brought against DoubleClick for using personal information it gathered without the knowledge of the Internet users in violation of the Electronic Communications Privacy Act, Federal Wiretap Act, and the Computer Fraud and Abuse Act. The court held that class members did not have a cause of action under any of these federal acts.

***Rowe Entertainment, Inc. v. Wm. Morris Agency, Inc.,* 2002 (S.D.N.Y.)** The court identified eight factors to consider when allocating costs of e-discovery. Those eight factors are specificity of the discovery requests; likelihood of discovering critical information; availability of such information from other sources; purposes for which the responding party maintains the requested data; relative benefit of the information to the requesting party; total cost associated with production; relative ability of each party to control cost; and resources available to each party.

---

## Scope of Discovery Cases

***Byers v. Illinois State Police,* 2002 (N.D. Ill.)** In a discrimination lawsuit against the Illinois State Police, the plaintiff requested the production of archived e-mails authored by one of the defendants that related to her or her coplaintiff. Defendants argued that it would be too burdensome to search for archived e-mail and would cost $20,000 to $30,000. The court noted that e-mail has replaced informal chat around water coolers and in break rooms but that e-mail is difficult to search. Plaintiffs argued there was a high probability they would find inflammatory e-mail but could not prove that this e-mail existed. The court decided that the plaintiffs would be required to pay the cost of recovery of e-mails if they decided those e-mails were important enough.

***Stallings-Daniel v. The Northern Trust Co.*, 2002 (N.D. Ill.)** The plaintiff in an employment discrimination case wanted to do extensive e-discovery. The court refused because she had too little evidence that anything would be found.

***U.S. v. Tucker*, 2001 (D. Utah)** In a possession of child pornography case, the court considered the fact that the defendant had taken time to delete image links from his computer cache file, which showed that he had knowledge that the links were there and what they were and that he, therefore, had control over them. The evidence showed that the images were not on his computer due to ignorance, mistake, or accident because he had paid a user fee and acquired a password to access the contraband Web sites.

***In re Verizon Internet Services, Inc. v. Verizon Internet Services*, 2003 (D.C.)** Verizon argued that a subpoena for the identity of users of Verizon's services who allegedly downloaded music from the Internet was not valid because information was not stored on its systems—but rather only transmitted over it. Therefore, it was outside the power of the subpoena. The court analyzed the Digital Millennium Copyright Act and concluded that Verizon had to comply with the subpoena.

## Costs and Allocation Case

***Zubulake v. UBS Warburg LLC*, 2003 (S.D.N.Y.)** This New York court described the five different types of data available for discovery. Regarding who pays for discovery, the court determined that the proper question is how accessible is the data rather than the media it may be stored on or the reason for its creation.

## Criminal Cases

***New Jersey v. Evers*, 2003 (N.J.)** Evers, charged with a criminal offense, challenged the validity of a search warrant because information used to get the search warrant violated his reasonable expectation of privacy, among other laws. The New Jersey court concluded that the search warrant was valid and the conviction could stand.

***South Dakota v. Guthrie*, 2002 (S.D.)** The defendant was charged with murdering his wife. The defendant waited until after the prosecution had rested

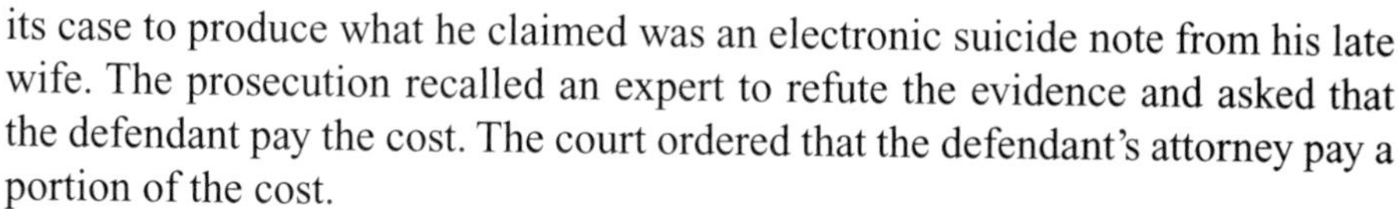

its case to produce what he claimed was an electronic suicide note from his late wife. The prosecution recalled an expert to refute the evidence and asked that the defendant pay the cost. The court ordered that the defendant's attorney pay a portion of the cost.

***Thompson v. Thompson*, 2002 (D.N.H.)** A divorce case turned into federal litigation because the plaintiff husband brought a claim under the Electronic Communications Privacy Act and the Wiretap Act against the defendant for copying his stored e-mail. The court dismissed the case because copying stored e-mail is not an interception of electronic communication.

---

## Reliability of Electronic Evidence Case

***Premier Homes and Land Corp. v. Cheswell, Inc.*, 2002 (D. Mass.)** After the mirror imaging of the defendant's computer system, the plaintiff's counsel disclosed that one of its employees had manufactured evidence. The court discussed how forged electronic documents can be created and identified.

# Glossary

## A

**active data** Data readily available and accessible to users.

**admissible evidence** Any type of proof legally presented at trial and allowed by the judge.

**admission of evidence** A judge's acceptance of evidence in a trial.

**agent** A type of software used to gather information about a network or host for NFAT systems.

**alternate data streams (ADS)** A feature of Windows implementation of metadata that allows information to be attached to a file without being part of the file.

**anomaly** An irregularity or nonstandard event.

**artifact evidence** Any change in crime scene evidence or addition to crime scene evidence that could potentially cause an investigator to infer incorrectly that the "evidence" is related to the crime.

**authenticate** To have sufficient proof that something is what it claims to be.

## B

**bad sector** A portion of a disk that is flawed and unusable.

**baseline** A standard used to establish what is considered normal for a network.

**"best evidence rule"** The federal rule stating that the original evidence is required. For computer data, any printout or other readable output that reflects the data accurately is considered an original.

**BIOS** Basic Input Output Systems, or BIOS, is used to store information a computer uses such as hard drive specifications, floppy drives, time/date, and other hardware.

**bit-stream image** An advanced drive image that starts at the very beginning of the drive and makes a copy of every bit (0 or 1) to the end of the drive without in any way deleting or modifying the contents or characteristics of the evidence. Also called a *sector-by-sector image.*

**boot sequence** The sequence in which a computer searches for a bootable operating system.

**bot** Compromised computer, or robot, that is controlled by those who infected the computer.

**botmasters** Originators and controllers of botnets. The equivalent of Web gangsters or extortionists, who use botnets for their personal gain.

**botnets** Groups of bots used to distribute and install software or carry out attacks.

**bounce program** A proxy program that reads from one port and writes to another.

**buffer** A storage area where transient data is kept until used, such as print data.

## C

**carrier medium** The file in stegonography used to cover the hidden data.

**carve** The action of extracting specific data from a large assortment of mixed data.

**cell site data** Data from a cellular telephone service provider that can be used to track the cellular phone user's movements.

**chain of custody** The process by which computer forensics specialists or other investigators preserve the crime scene and evidence throughout the life cycle of a case.

**chain of custody log** Documentation that evidence was handled and preserved properly and that it was never at risk of being compromised.

**circumstantial evidence** Evidence that is not directly from an eyewitness or participant but, rather, shows surrounding circumstances that logically lead to a conclusion of fact. E-mail is an example.

**client** A program that typically runs on a personal computer that works in tandem with a complementary piece of software running on a server.

**cluster** A fixed block of data that consists of an even number of sectors, such as 1,024 bytes or 4,096 bytes.

**commercial bribery** The corruption of a private individual to gain a commercial or business advantage.

**compromise** An intrusion or malicious access of a computer or network.

**computer forensics science** The forensic discipline of acquiring, preserving, retrieving, and presenting electronic data.

**computer fraud** Computer crime involving money. Also called *e-fraud.*

**Computer Fraud and Abuse Act (CFAA)** Law that makes unauthorized access to a federal computer a crime.

**conflict of interest** A situation in which an expert cannot be unbiased for any reason.

**content files** Temporary storage files that hold the text and graphic images of a Web site that has been visited.

**crime** An offensive act against society that violates a law and is punishable by the government.

**criminal law** A law that protects the public, human life, and private property.

**cryptographic hash verification** An encryption method to fingerprint a drive image and verify the accuracy of the image.

**cyberplanning** The digital coordination of an integrated plan stretching across geographical boundaries that may or may not result in bloodshed.

**cybertrails** Digital indicators left by Internet and e-mail usage and digital devices.

**cyclic redundancy check (CRC)** Mathematical computations to validate that the copy is exactly the same as the original.

**cylinders** A division of data on a hard drive, usually consisting of a circular or concentric slice through various platters.

## D

**data carving** A technique whereby specific data types, such as HTML pages or JPEG pictures, are located by their file signature in a large composite of data, such as unallocated clusters, and extracted from the composite.

**data header** The initial hexadecimal characters in a file that reflect information about the file and are not part of the useable file data.

**data salvaging** Another term for *data carving.*

**dead analysis** An examination of a suspect's computer or device performed when it is not running. Also referred to as a *postmortem analysis* because the crime or incident has already happened.

**defendant** The person or parties being charged in a criminal or civil case.

**defensible approach** An objective and unbiased approach performed in accordance with best forensic principles and investigative practices.

**demonstrative evidence** Items that are not actual evidence, such as pictures, models, videos, or other visual aids, that clarify facts for a judge or jury.

**denial of service (DoS)** An attack on a network or Web site server causing it to receive more hits (requests for service) than it can respond to—resulting in "denied service."

**deposition** Testimony under oath before a trial.

**device driver** A type of software used to manage or interpret communications between an operating system and hardware.

**directory** An area in a file system used to keep files organized in a logical manner. Also known as a *folder* in some operating systems.

**directory tree structure** The hierarchical representation of the way folders and files are structured in a file system, showing the parent-child relationships.

**discovery** The process of gathering information in preparation for trial, legal investigation, or administrative action.

**discovery request** An official request for access to information that may be used as evidence.

**documentary evidence** Physical evidence or electronic evidence. Unlike testimony of a witness, which is direct evidence, documentary evidence is circumstantial evidence.

**domain** The name given to a network of IP addresses associated with a particular entity.

**dongle** With regard to security, it is a hardware device to restrict access to specific software applications.

**drive geometry** The specifications used to determine the size of a hard drive. Usually determined by cylinders, heads, and sectors.

**drive imaging** A means of evidence preservation that captures a "snapshot" of everything on the drive.

**drive slack** Slack space that is created to fill the area from the end of a sector (EOS) to the end of a cluster (EOC).

**due process of the law** A fundamental principle to ensure that all civil and criminal cases follow federal or state rules to prevent any unequal treatment.

# E

**electronic evidence** Evidence in digital or electronic form, such as e-mail, computer files, and instant messages.

**electronic fraud (e-fraud)** Computer crime involving money. Also called *computer fraud.*

**embezzlement** Theft of money or property by a person to whom it has been lawfully entrusted.

**encapsulation** The layering of protocol information within the OSI model framework from the top going down. Essentially it is the manner in which each layer adds a header and possibly a footer to an existing block of data as it passes through that particular OSI layer.

**events** Any significant occurrences in a system or a program, such as logging on.

**evidence** Proof of a fact about what did or did not happen. Used to support or refute the allegations of a crime or civil wrong.

**evidence-mail** E-mail used as evidence.

**exchange principle** A theory stating that whenever a criminal comes into contact with a victim, an object, or a crime scene, she leaves behind some evidence of her presence and also takes away some evidence.

**exclusionary rules** Those Federal Rules of Evidence that specify the types of evidence that cannot be presented at trial. Exclusionary rules protect civil liberties by requiring that any evidence obtained by law enforcement using a method that violates a person's constitutional rights is inadmissible in a criminal prosecution against that person.

**exculpatory evidence** Evidence that contradicts or helps rebut a given theory.

**expert report** A complete statement of all opinions that an expert will express at trial and the basis and reasons for those opinions.

**expert testimony** The opinions of an expert witness that are stated during a trial or deposition.

**expert witness** A person who is a qualified specialist in a subject.

**external fraud** Fraud committed against a company by someone outside the organization.

**extortion** Obtaining property from another when the other party has been forced to give "consent" out of fear.

# F

**Faraday bag** Also known as a Faraday cage, a container in which electromagnetic fields are effectively eliminated from reaching a device inside the bag or cage. Used in forensics to keep radio frequency signals from reaching mobile phones or PDAs and changing any data.

**Federal Rules of Civil Procedure (Fed. R. Civ. P.)** The rules by which the Federal Court of the United States determines proper procedure for civil cases, including what information is subject to discovery.

**Federal Rules of Evidence (Fed. R. Evid.)** The rules by which the Federal Court of the United States determines what evidence is admissible at trial.

**fiduciary responsibility** The legal duty or responsibility to protect the assets of a company or other party with honesty and integrity.

**file** A collection of data that is grouped together, such as a word processing document or spreadsheet.

**file allocation table (FAT) system** A file system used by Microsoft to organize data across a hard drive or storage device. Used primarily on MS-DOS computers up to Windows Me.

**file header** The area of a file that contains the file creation date, date of last update, and file size. The file header is accessible only by the operating system or by specialized program. It reveals the true identity of the file.

**file signatures** The first several hexadecimal bytes of a file that identify the file type.

**file system (filesystem)** The data structure as well as the processes that manage the files on a partition.

**file-wiping software** Software that is used to delete and overwrite data.

**firewall** A software or hardware device on a network that limits or eliminates communication that is unauthorized or harmful to a network.

**folder** An area in a file system used to keep files organized in a logical manner. Also known as a *directory* in some operating systems.

**forensic accounting** The integration of accounting, auditing, and investigative skills to discover and investigate financial crimes.

**forensic copy** The technical term for the end-product of a forensics acquisition of a computer's hard drive or other storage device.

**forensically wiped** All areas of the disk are written with a single character, usually "0," thus overwriting every file ever stored on the drive.

## G

**general case intake form** A form used by organizations to begin the documentation process in a computer forensics investigation. Used primarily to document the equipment and peripherals seized or investigated.

## H

**hash** A file's identifying fingerprint. A value generated by a file and used to identify the file or confirm that it has not been altered. Also called a *message digest.*

**header** The first part of a file that includes information about the file, but is not part of the actual data contained by the file.

**hearsay evidence (hearsay)** Secondhand evidence because the witness does not tell what he heard, saw, or knew personally, or firsthand, but only what others have said to him secondhand.

**hearsay rule** Rule stating that testimony that quotes a person who is not in court is inadmissible because the reliability of the evidence cannot be confirmed. There are many exceptions to the hearsay rule.

**hostname** The name of a server in the domain, or network, of a particular entity.

## I

**Identities** The Global User Identifiers used by Windows to hold personalized information such as e-mail account data.

**immaterial evidence** Evidence that is not relevant and significant to a case or lawsuit.

**impeach** To discredit.

**inadmissible evidence** Evidence that is not allowed.

**inculpatory evidence** Evidence that supports or helps confirm a given theory.

**indictment** A grand jury charge that the defendant should stand trial.

**instant messaging (IM)** A type of private interactive (chat) client/server environment that allows real-time communication across a network

**intent** Conscious desire or will to do something.

**internal fraud** Fraud committed by someone within the organization.

**Internet Protocol (IP) address** The address assigned to a user for a specific online or network session.

**intrusion detection system (IDS)** Software used across a network to detect activity on a network that is considered out of the ordinary.

## J

**just cause** A legitimate reason.

## K

**kernel** The core piece of an operating system.

## L

**law of privilege** A law that defines what types of information are protected from being released.

**leading question** A question that suggests its answer.

**legacy data** Older data on a disk, which may indicate prior uses of the computer.

**live analysis** Analysis of a computer or network in its own onsite environment while it is running.

## M

**mailbox** A storage area on an e-mail server assigned to a user that holds the e-mails for that user.

**material** Something that is relevant and significant to a situation or case.

**material evidence** Evidence that is relevant and significant to a case or lawsuit.

**message digest (MD)** A unique digital signature for the data generated by hashing.

**metadata** Data describing a file or its properties, such as creation date, author, or last access date. Or invisible information that programs such as Microsoft Word, Excel, and Outlook attach to each file or e-mail.

**mirror image** One method of capturing or copying all data on a drive, or drive imaging.

**mirroring** A technique used to store a data file simultaneously on two different hard drives.

**misrepresentation** A false statement.

**motion in limine** A motion by a lawyer for a hearing to determine whether or not evidence is admissible before trial.

**multipurpose Internet mail extensions (MIME)** A specification for formatting nontext (non-ASCII) attachments to e-mails so they traverse the network.

## N

**network forensic analysis toolkit (NFAT)** The newest generation of software used to collect information across a network to analyze data for intrusion or investigative purposes.

**New Technology File System (NTFS)** A file system used by Microsoft that addressed shortcomings in the FAT system. Used in all newer Microsoft operating systems.

**nonvolatile data** Data that still exists after the computer is turned off or the power is removed.

## O

**occupational fraud** Using one's occupation for personal gain through the deliberate misuse or misapplication of the employing organization's resources or assets.

**Open System Interconnection (OSI) model** A network protocol standard used to show the sequence and breakdown of network communication.

**operating system** The software that manages the hardware and software resources of a computer.

## P

**packet sniffers** Software used to monitor and record network traffic.

**page file** A file located on a hard drive that is used by the operating system to temporarily hold memory data that is not being currently accessed.

**parity** The orientation of the number of data bits in a packet as being either even or odd. It is used for integrity/validity checking to ensure no data bits were lost during data transfer.

**partition** Logically separate sections into which a hard drive may be divided. The use of partitions allows a drive to use more than one operating system.

**pen register** A mechanical device that can be attached to a specific telephone line at a telephone office.

**pen register orders** Orders allowing for the collection of information associated with communications. These orders require only certification from law enforcement that the information is likely to be relevant to an ongoing criminal investigation.

**Pen/Trap Statute** Law that governs the collection of noncontent traffic information associated with communications, such as the phone numbers dialed by a particular telephone.

**persistent data** Nonvolatile data.

**personal information management (PIM)** An application commonly found in personal digital assistants (PDAs) that is used to record or manage information such as e-mail, address books, calendars, and other personal information.

**phishing** Sending an e-mail to a user falsely claiming to be a legitimate enterprise in an attempt to scam the user.

**phishing kit** A collection of tools that makes it easier for unskilled people to conduct phishing attacks.

**plain view doctrine** A legal doctrine that allows law enforcement to "search and seize" objects in plain view after determining probable cause. This is customarily used as a basis for "search and seizure" without a warrant.

**platter** A circular component of hard drives composed of aluminum or other material that is magnetically coated. Hard drives store data on the drive using positive and negative magnetic charges.

**port mirroring** Used by NFAT systems to copy information from one or more ports on a switch to a port that is monitored by the NFAT.

**postmortem analysis** An analysis conducted after the crime or incident has already happened.

**prejudicial** Unequal or biased.

**probable cause** A legal standard which states that there must be proof beyond just the possibility that a crime has been committed.

**probative value** Evidence that is sufficiently useful to prove something important.

**proxy** A type of server that acts as the mediator between client and server computers.

# R

**RAM slack** The area from the end of the file to the end of a sector, except for the last sector.

**read-write heads** Devices that read and write data from hard drives based on the polarity or magnetic charges stored on the platter.

**Regional Computer Forensic Laboratory (RCFL)** A government lab that provides computer forensic expertise to any law enforcement agency in their specific service area in support of federal, state, and local criminal investigations and prosecutions.

**residual data** Data that has been deleted but not erased.

**root** The administrative account on a Linux system that controls all of the processes and services.

**root access** The same privileges as the system's administrator. Root access gives the intruder full access to the computer system.

**Rule 26 of the Federal Rules of Discovery** The rules stating that each company has the duty to preserve documents that may be relevant in a case.

**Rule 34** The Federal Rule of Civil Procedure that made e-records and communications subject to subpoena and discovery for use in legal proceedings.

**rules of evidence** The rules by which a court determines what evidence is admissible at trial.

# S

**scienter** In a fraud case, a person who knows that a statement is a misrepresentation.

**search warrant** A written order issued by a judge allowing law enforcement to conduct a search of specified premises for specified things or persons and to seize those items or people.

**sector** The smallest unit that can be accessed on a disk. A sector is 512 bytes. Computer hard drives can "grab" data only in sector-size chunks.

**sector-by-sector image** See *bit-stream image.*

**security key** A hardware device to control access to data or files to authorized users.

**server** In the context of a client/server environment, an application that runs on a machine (also known as a server) that provides services for multiple users through interface software running on each user's machine (known as a client).

**Shadowcrew investigation** The long-term online undercover investigation conducted by the U.S. Secret Service targeting domestic and international subjects engaged in identity theft, credit card fraud, and production of false identification documents.

**shell** The interface used by an operating system such as a command-line interface or graphical user interface.

**slack space** Unused space in a cluster, which is found at the end of a file.

**sneak and peek** The term used by critics of the PATRIOT Act referring to the notification delay that allows law enforcement to conduct a search without notifying the individual for up to 90 days.

**sniffer software** A software program that monitors data traveling over a network or records keystrokes.

**spoliation** Destruction of evidence, which is a crime because it is an obstruction of justice.

**spoofing** To trick, disguise, or deceive. A spoofed Web site is a phony site that replaces a legitimate Web site address.

**statute** Statutes define crimes in terms of required acts and a required state of mind, or intent. Criminal laws are defined in rules called statutes.

**steganographic medium** The modified carrier file that contains the hidden data.

**steganography** The science of "covered writing" typically characterized in the computer field by hiding encrypted data in media files, particularly pictures.

**stream identifier** The syntactical portion of a command that references an alternate data stream.

**striping** A technique used in redundant arrays of independent disks (RAID) that writes pieces of a file across several disks, rather than just on one.

**subscriber identity module (SIM)** The device in a mobile phone that stores the information identifying a subscriber to the mobile phone network. Information such as text messages, phone numbers, and call information can also be stored on a SIM.

**super user** A user who has root access.

**suppression hearing** A hearing before a criminal trial during which the judge determines whether the Fourth Amendment has been followed correctly by the police in the search and seizure of evidence.

**system data and artifacts** Data/files produced by the operating system itself rather than the user.

# T

**tainted evidence** Evidence that has been altered or obtained from an illegal search or seizure and therefore is inadmissible.

**"taking the Fifth"** Refusing to testify in court on the basis that the testimony may be self-incriminating.

**TCP/IP model** The de facto protocol standard used on the Internet to communicate.

**techno-trespass** The technological equivalent of criminal trespass. In these crimes, the intruder uses the computer to steal information or damage/disrupt computer operations.

**techno-vandalism** Unauthorized access to a computer that damages files or programs for the challenge or sport rather than for profit.

**testimonial witness** An expert witness who gives testimony in trial.

**three Cs of evidence** Care, control, and chain of custody. These are legal guidelines to ensure that the evidence presented is the same as that which was seized. It requires documentation of the maintenance of evidence in its original state and preparation for civil or criminal proceedings.

**time bomb** A malicious computer program that is programmed to trigger on a specific date or time-related event.

**Trash** The Macintosh and Linux equivalent to the Windows Recycle Bin. Files go to an individual's Trash folder before being completely deleted, so a user could easily recover the file if needed. The file is no longer easily recovered after the Trash folder has been emptied.

**trier of fact** Judge or jury.

**trophy hunting** Refers to the cybercriminals' motive, which is to brag about their exploits.

**trusted environment** Computing environment or lab with dedicated systems set up for the sole purpose of conducting computer forensics investigations.

# U

**unallocated space** Space on a disk that is not currently used to store an active file.

**untrusted environments** Onsite locations used to conduct computer forensics investigations.

**USA PATRIOT Act of 2002** This law expanded the list of records that law enforcement authorities may obtain with a subpoena. It gave law enforcement agencies greater authority to gather e-evidence. Subsection 2703(c)(2) of the act states that authorities can gain access to "records of session times and durations" and "any temporarily assigned network address."

**user data** Data/files created by the user, not by the operating system.

**user root folder** The primary default location for files created by or for a particular user. User configuration preferences are also kept in this folder.

**userid** The computer account name created to access (log on to) a computer or other resource.

## V

**virtual private network (VPN)** A network communications scheme used to encode or encrypt private data on a public network. Can also be used inside a network to achieve a level of privacy different from other users.

**voir dire** A preliminary examination of prospective witnesses under oath to determine their competence or suitability.

**volatile** Electronic content that can be intentionally or unintentionally altered, deleted, lost, corrupted, or overwritten.

## W

**wardriving** Driving around with a laptop computer and antenna looking for unprotected wireless Internet connections to tap into.

**webmail** An e-mail server that sends and receives e-mail by interfacing with a user's browser rather than a client program running on the user's machine.

**white collar crime** Nonviolent crimes, such as fraud and extortion.

**work product** Any notes, reports about conversations with a client or witness, or other confidential materials that an attorney or investigator has created during a case.

**write-blocking** Devices that prevent any writing or overwriting to the drives attached.

# References

## Chapter 1

Arent, L. M., R. D. Brownstone, and W. A. Fenwick. 2002. E-discovery: Preserving, requesting and producing electronic information. *Santa Clara Computer and High Technology Law Journal,* December, 19(131).

Bridis, T. 2003. Al-Jazeera Web site is sabotaged by hackers. *Associated Press,* March 28.

Conry-Murray, A. 2002. Deciphering the cost of a computer crime. *Network Magazine,* April 1.

Eoannou, C. L. 2003a. Briefs filed in high-profile Fifth Circuit "Case about document destruction." *Digital Discovery and e-Evidence*, July.

Eoannou, C. L. 2003b. "Explosive" e-mails allowed into evidence in Enron loan trial. *Digital Discovery and e-Evidence,* January.

Gleim, I. N. and J. B. Ray, with E. P. O'Connor. 1992. *Business Law/Legal Studies,* Gainesville, FL: Gleim Publications, Inc.

Harrington, M. 2002. Computer experts to root out missing files. *Newsday,* February 5.

Iwata, E. 2002. Enron case could be largest corporate investigation. *USA Today,* February 18. **www.usatoday.com/life/cyber/tech/2002/02/19/detectives.htm** (accessed May 2006).

Jones, A. 2002. Discovery becomes electric. *New York Law Journal,* March 11.

Melnitzer, J. 2003. Keeping track of the invisible paper trail: What legal departments can learn from Boeing's experience. *Corporate Legal Times*, February.

*Newsday.* 2003. Protesters for and against war target Web sites. March 29.

Nimsger, K. M. and M. C. S. Lange. 2002. Computer forensics experts play crucial role. *The Lawyers Weekly,* 22(2).

Raysman, R. and P. Brown. 1999. Viruses, worms, and other destructive forces. *New York Law Journal,* July 13.

Reason, T. 2002. Reporting: See-through finance? *CFO Magazine,* October.

Rowan, D. 2003. Tech salvos. *The Times* (London), March 25.

Scheindlin, S. A. and J. Rabkin. 2000a. Electronic discovery in federal civil litigation: Is Rule 34 up to the task? *Boston College Law Review* 41(327).

Scheindlin, S. A. and J. Rabkin. 2000b. Outside counsel retaining, destroying and producing e-data: Part 1. *New York Law Journal* 227, May 8.

Scheindlin, S. A. and J. Rabkin. 2002. Outside counsel retaining, destroying and producing e-data: Part 2. *New York Law Journal* 227, May 8.

Sleek, S. 2000. Good e-recordkeeping saves you money, protects you from liability. *Digital Discovery and e-Evidence*, February.

Varchaver, Nicholas. 2003. The perils of e-mail. *Fortune,* February 3.

Zaslow, J. 2003. To fight e-mail sharing, firms try new rules, software. *Wall Street Journal,* May 28. **online.wsj.com/article/0, SB1054058502622724000,00.html** (accessed May 2006).

## Chapter 2

Brenner, S. W. and B. A. Frederiksen. 2001/2002. Computer searches and seizures: Some unresolved issues. *Michigan Telecommunications and Technology Law Review* 8(39).

Burke, Francis J. 2003. The discoverability of computerized information. **d2d.ali-aba.org/_files/thumbs/course_materials/SK063-CH12_thumb.pdf** (accessed May 2006).

Burke, P. J. 2002. Learning from Wall Street's e-mail nightmare: Discovery and admissibility of e-mail. *The Metropolitan Corporate Counsel,* September.

Dershowitz, A. M. 2002. *Why terrorism works*. New Haven, CT: Yale University Press.

EDP Weekly's IT Monitor. 2005. One third of all software in use still pirated, major study finds. May 23. 20(46).

Etzioni, Amitai. 2002. Implications of select new technologies for individual rights and public safety. *Harvard Journal of Law and Technology* 15(257).

Federal Trade Commission. 2004. FTC releases top 10 consumer complaint categories in 2003. Report of January 22, **www.ftc.gov/opa/2004/01/top10.htm** (accessed May 2006).

Gleim, I. N. and J. B. Ray, with E. P. O'Connor. 1992. *Business Law/Legal Studies.* Gainesville, FL: Gleim Publications, Inc.

Jackman, Tom. 2002. Lack of e-mail trail irks Moussaoui judge: FBI ordered to hand over Internet file. *The Washington Post,* August 29.

McConnell, Bruce. 2000. Cyber crime . . . and punishment? Archaic laws threaten global information. McConnell International. December. **www.mcconnellinternational.com/services/cybercrime.htm** (accessed May 2006).

McGreevy, Patrick, Noam N. Levey, and Jessica Garrison. 2004. Emails to, from Hahn's office sought. *Los Angeles Times*, April 16.

Nimsger, Kristin M. and Alan E. Brill. 2002. Computers are not the only source of important e-evidence. *Legal Times*, October 28.

Wegman, Jerry. 2004. Computer forensics: Admissibility of evidence in criminal cases. Working paper. University of Idaho.

## Chapter 3

Harris, Shon. 2005. To catch a thief. *Information Security.* December.

## Chapter 5

Donnelly, Derrick. 2005. iPods sing for investigators. *Security Management.* March 1, 49(3).

Lewis, Peter. 2006. The shape of rings to come. *CNN Money,* April 11. **money.cnn.com/2006/04/10/technology/CTIAwireless_fortune/index.htm** (accessed May 2006).

## Chapter 6

Hayes, Stephen F. 2006. Saddam's terror training camps: What the documents captured from the former Iraqi regime reveal—and why they should all be made public. *The Weekly Standard*, January 16. 11(17).

Lemos, Robert. 2006. Man charged with accessing USC student data. *News Brief,* April 20, 2006. **www.securityfocus.com/brief/191** (accessed May 2006).

Texas sues Sony BMG for spyware. *The Computer & Internet Lawyer.* February, 2006, 23(2).

## Chapter 7

BBC News. 2002. Accessing the secrets of the brotherhood, July 2, **news.bbc.co.uk/1/hi/sci/tech/2082657.stm** (accessed May 2006).

Kessler, Gary. 2004. Steganography: Implications for the prosecutor and computer forensics examiner. April, **www.garykessler.net/library/ndaa_stego.html** (accessed May 2006).

## Chapter 8

American Management Association. 2005. Electronic monitoring and surveillance survey: Many companies monitoring, recording, videotaping—

and firing—employees, **www.amanet.org/press/amanews/ems05.htm** (accessed May 10, 2006).

Brown, Gary M. 2003. Senate investigator to Enron's lawyers: It's not over. *Corporate Board Magazine*, Special Legal Issue.

Espiner, Tom. 2006. Hackers attacked Parliament using WMF exploit. January 23. **news.zdnet.co.uk/internet/security/0,39020375,39248387,00.htm** (accessed May 2006).

Jones, K. C. 2005. Murder suspect's Google searches spotlighted in trial. *InformationWeek,* Nov. 11. **www.informationweek.com/story/showArticle.jhtml?articleID=173602206** (accessed May 10, 2006).

Lemos, Robert. 2006. E-mail authentication gaining steam. *SecurityFocus,* April 20. **www.securityfocus.com/news/11388** (accessed May 2006).

Poulsen, Kevin. 2005. Hacker breaches T-Mobile systems, reads US Secret Service email. *SecurityFocus*, January 12. **www.theregister.co.uk/2005/01/12/hacker_penetrates_t-mobile** (accessed May 2006).

*State v. Voorheis* (Vermont, Feb. 13, 2004, http://dol.state.vt.us/gopher_root3/supct/176/2002–478.op).

## Chapter 9

Sartin, Bryan. 2004. Tracking the cybercrime trail. *Security Management*, September 1, 4899.

## Chapter 10

BBC News. 2003. Questions cloud cyber crime cases. October 17. **news.bbc.co.uk/go/pr/fr/-/1/hi/technology/3202116.stm** (accessed May 2006).

ComputerWeekly.com. 2003. Denial of service attack meant for chatroom user. October 13. **www.computerweekly.com/SiteMapArticle/Articles/2003/10/13/c2128/197877/Denialofserviceattackmeantforchatroomuser.htm** (accessed May 2006).

Eedle, Paul. 2002. Al-Qaeda takes fight for "hearts and minds" to the Web. *Jane's Intelligence Review,* August. **www.freerepublic.com/focus/news/729748/posts** (accessed May 2006).

Faiola, Anthony. 2005. Anti-Japanese hostilities move to the Internet. *Washington Post*, May 10.

Gellman, Barton. 2002. FBI fears al-Qaeda cyber attacks. *San Francisco Chronicle,* June 28. **www.sfgate.com/cgi-bin/article.cgi?file=/c/a/2002/06/28/MN93329.DTL** (accessed May 2006).

Hastings, Max. 2005. New weapons, old wars. *Sunday Telegraph,* July 31.

Hearing of the Senate Armed Services Committee on Worldwide Threats to U.S. National Security. 2006. Washington, D.C. *Federal News Service.* February 28.

Kawamoto, Dawn. 2005. Survey: Most home PC users lack security. *CNET News.com*, Dec. 7. **news.com.com/Survey+Most+home+PC+users+lack+security/2100–1029_3–5986344.html** (accessed May 2006).

Menn, Joseph. 2005. Man is accused of dealing in "bots." *Los Angeles Times,* Nov. 4.

PR Newswire, 2006. Attacks becoming more sophisticated with increased use of phishing kits. March 13. sev.prnewswire.com/computer-electronics/20060313/SFM10164032006–1.html (accessed May 2006).

Thomas, Timothy L. 2003. Al Qaeda and the Internet: The danger of "cyberplanning." *Parameters.* March 22, (33)1.

## Chapter 11

Albrecht, W. Stephen and Chad Albrecht. 2004. *Fraud examination and prevention.* Mason, OH: South-Western.

Babcock, Charles and Marianne K. McGee. 2004. Filter out the frauds. *Insurance and Technology,* September 1.

Carozza, Dick. 2006. Healthcare fraud drains lifeblood from patients, system. *Fraud Magazine,* March/April. **www.fraud-magazine.com** (accessed May 2006).

*DOJ Press Release.* 2006. Cleveland, Ohio, Man sentenced to prison for bank fraud and conspiracy. February 28, **www.cybercrime.gov/flurySent.htm** (accessed May 2006).

Glaister, Dan. 2006. First picture of Bush with disgraced lobbyist. *The Guardian,* Feb. 13.

Hall, Matthew T. 2005. Investigators search through e-mail data. *San Diego Union-Tribune,* December 28.

Hines, Cragg. 2004. Loose change and no change at NASA. *The Houston Chronicle,* June 2.

Leibs, Scott. 2002. First, who's on? *CFO Magazine,* August.

Radcliff, Deborah. 2002. Cybersleuthing solves the case. *Computerworld,* Jan. 14. **www.computerworld.com/securitytopics/security/story/0,10801,67299,00.html** (accessed May 2006).

Schmidt, Susan and James V. Grimaldi. 2005. The fast rise and steep fall of Jack Abramoff: How a well-connected lobbyist became the center of a far-reaching corruption scandal. *Washington Post*, Dec. 29.

Tait, Nikki. 2005. Computer records provide 80% of fraud case evidence. *Financial Times,* Oct. 18.

## Chapter 12


Dean, John W. 2005. George W. Bush as the new Richard M. Nixon: Both wiretapped illegally, and impeachably. *Findlaw.com,* Dec. 30, **writ.news.findlaw.com/dean/20051230.html** (accessed May 2006).

Eichhorn, Lisa. 1989. Social science findings and the jury's ability to disregard evidence under the Federal Rules of Evidence. *Law and Contemporary Problems*, Autumn 52(4).

Hsieh, Sylvia. 2006. E-discovery: Business is booming and lawyers are getting in. *Kansas City Daily Record (*originally in *Missouri Lawyers Weekly*), March 9.

Kerr, Orin S. 2001. The Fourth Amendment in cyberspace: Can encryption create a "reasonable expectation of privacy"? 33 *Connecticut Law Review* 503, Winter.

Kerr, Orin S. 2005. Essay: Digital evidence and the new criminal procedure. 105. *Columbia Law Review* 279, January.

McCandless, David. 2005. Dawn raids mark crash of online designer drugs trade. *The Guardian*, May 26.

Nimsger, Kristin M. 2003. Digging for e-data. *Trial,* January.

Norberg, Peter. 2006. Daubert in a nutshell. Chapter 2, *Daubert on the Web.* **www.daubertontheweb.com/Chapter_2.htm/** (accessed May 2006).

Robins, Mark. 2003. Evidence at the electronic frontier: Introducing e-mail at trial in commercial litigation, 29. *Rutgers Computer and Technology Law Journal,* 219.

Shulman, R. 2003. U.S.A. Patriot Act: Granting the U.S. Government the unprecedented power to circumvent American civil liberties in the name of national security. *University of Detroit Mercy Law Review,* 80(3), Spring.

Wegman, Jerry. 2004. Computer forensics: Admissibility of evidence in criminal cases. Working paper. University of Idaho.


## Chapter 13


Barakat, Matthew. 2006. Moussaoui's fate in jury's hands: Judge denies panel's request for dictionary. *Associated Press,* April 25.

Benedictis, Don L. 1990. Preschool lessons: Abuse case plagued by botched investigation, too many counts. *A.B.A. Journal.* April.

Best, Arthur. 2004. *Evidence*. 5th edition. New York: Aspen Publishers.

Carruthers, John. 2001. Influencing the jury. *The Journal,* 46(7) July. **www.journalonline.co.uk/article/1000969.aspx** (accessed May 2006).

Imwinkelried, Edward J. and David A. Schlueter. 2004. Evidentiary tactics: Selecting the "best" evidence to simplify the case, 19. *Criminal Justice* 20, Spring.

Johnson, Molly T., Carol Krafka, and Joe S. Cecil. 2001. Scientific, technical, and other specialized knowledge evidence in federal and state courts. *Federal Judicial Center,* April.

Raider, Ron and Danielle Williams. 2005. Taking on a modern hydra. *National Law Journal,* July 25, 27(45).

Sorkin, Andrew Ross. 2006. Banker granted retrial in a case from the 90's boom, *New York Times*, March 21.

Taslitz, Andrew E. 2005. Convicting the guilty, acquitting the innocent: The ABA takes a stand. 19 *Criminal Justice* 18, Winter.

Wall, Christopher and Jason Paroff. 2005. Cracking the computer forensics mystery. *The Computer and Internet Lawyer,* April 22(4).

Waltz, Jon R. and Roger C. Park. 2005. *Evidence*. 18th ed. Gilbert Law Summaries. Chicago, IL: Thompson.

Zimmerman, Eilene. 2006. Cyberthreats? Call a digital Sherlock Holmes. *CNN Money,* March 9. **money.cnn.com/2006/03/09/magazines/fsb/8370334/** (accessed May 2006).

# Index

## A



## B

# D

## J



## K



## L

# T



# U

# V